A Theory of Punishable Participation in Universal Crimes

Terje Einarsen and Joseph Rikhof

2018
Torkel Opsahl Academic EPublisher
Brussels

This and other publications in TOAEP's *Publication Series* may be openly accessed and downloaded through the web site www.toaep.org, which uses Persistent URLs for all publications it makes available (such PURLs will not be changed). This publication was first published on 7 December 2018.

ISBNs: 978-82-8348-127-3 (print) and 978-82-8348-128-0 (e-book).

To Aria and Torstein.

For the sake of present and future generations who will strive to prevent universal crimes and provide justice for "children, women and men [who] have been victims of unimaginable atrocities that deeply shock the conscience of humanity" (Preamble, Rome Statute)

The basic assumption must be that in international law as much as in national systems, the foundation of criminal responsibility is the principle of personal culpability: nobody may be held criminally responsible for acts or transactions in which he has not personally engaged or in some other way participated (*nulla poena sine culpa*).

International Criminal Tribunal for the former Yugoslavia, Appeals Chamber, in the Tadić case (1999)

If it be thought for even a moment that the part played by Rudolf Brandt was relatively unimportant when compared with the enormity of the charges proved by the evidence, let it be said that every Himmler must have his Brandt else the plans of a master criminal would never be put into execution.

Nuernberg Military Tribunals in the Medical case (1947)

PREFACE

Despite the ambiguities of international law in general and international criminal law ('ICL') in particular, serious crimes committed, organised, or tolerated by representatives of different kinds of power structures are now of concern to the world community. These crimes may occur in the context of war or form part of a larger pattern of aggressive behaviour by powerful actors within a society. They are often directly linked to abuse of political or military systems or to an absence of effective state institutions. Such 'international crimes', which might also be referred to as 'universal crimes' because of their inherent gravity and violation of universal values and interests, are also attacks on the rule of law.

We are still living in an age of uncertainty regarding which specific types of crimes are punishable directly under international law and might also be prosecuted on a regular basis before international courts. In addition, the scope of personal criminal liability for alleged punishable participation in recognised universal crimes has been contested in ICL theory and practice on a number of points. This situation has even prompted calls for a comprehensive theory of personal criminal liability applicable to this particular field of law. In response, this book is an attempt to establish and test a general theory of personal liability that would strengthen our ability to understand, explain, and predict the outcomes of the legal issues involved in ICL and universal crimes cases.

The book is the second in a four-part series on universal crimes entitled "Rethinking the Essentials of International Criminal Law and Transitional Justice". While the first book in the series concentrated on the concept of universal crimes and the general issues involved in classifying certain offences, this second volume discusses personal liability for different kinds of participation in universal crimes. The forthcoming third and fourth volumes will shift attention to the legal consequences of alleged participation in universal crimes: book three focuses on alternative forms of accountability and jurisdiction as important aspects of universal crimes, while the fourth and final book in the series is about fair trial in universal crimes cases. The basic research idea underlying the universal crimes project was developed by Terje Einarsen, author of the first book in the series, *The Concept of Universal Crimes in International Law* (TOAEP, Oslo, 2012). The particular ideas and research design of the present volume have been further developed in close co-operation with Joseph Rikhof. This book is the result of an extensive joint enterprise between the two co-authors, in which the workload was shared equally and collaboration on the development of concepts and analysis of data was fully reciprocal. Thus, both authors are jointly responsible for any mistake or unwarranted omission in the analysis and empirical surveys undertaken. Finally, as the title of this volume suggests, the emphasis of the book is on punishable participation only, not on possible defences like justifications or excuses for involvement in criminal activities. That aspect of accountability will be covered by the next volume.

This work, which is current as of 17 July 2018, is addressed to all with an interest in ICL and related disciplines like human rights, humanitarian law, transitional justice, and transnational criminal law. We hope it will contribute to a more coherent and practical understanding of criminalisation and attribution of personal liability within the field of ICL. Due to the character of the general theory presented and tested in this book through empirical surveys including both international and domestic criminal law, the scientific value of a theory of punishable participation in universal crimes could well reach beyond its core international law features.

ACKNOWLEDGEMENTS

This book, the second of four planned volumes, is the product of a research project that was initially intended to address certain issues of complicity in international criminal law ('ICL'). It originated from a postdoctoral research project started by Terje Einarsen in 2008, which brought the author to Arusha, Tanzania, to visit the Rwanda tribunal the same year. In Arusha he met for the first time with Joseph Rikhof, who was already an established figure within ICL and related fields. Their professional collaboration continued, and Rikhof, among others, provided most helpful comments on the draft of the first book in the series, *The Concept of Universal Crimes in International Law* (2012). The focus of that book project had shifted meanwhile towards the concept of international crimes and universal crimes, while issues of complicity – by then framed more broadly as punishable participation in universal crimes – were reserved for a later book. This second book was contemplated as a joint venture between the two authors.

It was perhaps an overly optimistic plan, given that in 2012 Einarsen was still a judge at the Gulating High Court (Court of Appeals) for Western Norway, while Rikhof was busy as senior counsel at the War Crimes and Crimes against Humanity Section of the Canadian Department of Justice and adjunct professor of international criminal law at the University of Ottawa. In addition, there was as yet no particular funding for the joint research project or the new book. That year, however, Einarsen received a generous grant from the Norwegian association of professional authors and translators (*Norsk faglitterær forfatter- og oversetterforening*) for the purpose of starting work on the book in his spare time while still serving as a judge, and this turned out to be an important first step. A next step came in 2013 when Einarsen moved from the court to become a professor of law at the University of Bergen, where he established a course in international criminal law for Norwegian and foreign law students. Einarsen would like to thank the dean at the time, Asbjørn Strandbakken, and the Faculty of Law more generally for welcoming him and for providing immediate opportunities to teach ICL while also undertaking research for the book.

In 2014, the authors met twice in Bergen and Amsterdam and discussed the way forward, based on a draft introductory chapter and a table of contents. It was difficult, however, to find common space for substantially increased efforts due to other responsibilities, and during 2015–16 the work moved ahead slowly. In 2017 Einarsen was granted a six-month leave from administrative and teaching obligations at the faculty based on three years of service, and he was able to devote full time to the book. In addition, the association of professional authors and translators again came to the rescue by providing a travel grant that enabled Einarsen to renew the writing process. Rikhof meanwhile retired from his government position and was able to work more or less full time on the book project. The common space finally materialised; maybe we should thank our good fortune for that.

This project has benefited from the aiding and abetting of five assistants. At the Faculty of Law in Bergen, Agnieszka Barbara Bulat helped collect and prepare sources, especially for Chapter 6, the literature survey. Espen Haugsvær Verling checked sources and provided an initial draft of Chapter 6, as well as drafts of parts of Chapter 9 on domestic universal crimes cases based on territorial jurisdiction. He also helped to refine tables and figures for Chapter 3. Later, Marius Mikkel Kjølstad carefully compiled the bibliography and table of cases from the footnotes. From India, Dan Meester provided assistance with source collection and also drafted parts of Chapter 9, while in Ottawa Rozmin Mediratta provided the research document that became the basis for Chapter 3. We thank them all for their valuable contributions. We also wish to recognise the administrative and scholarly leadership of the Faculty of Law in Bergen, including Berte-Elen Konow, Anne Marie Frøseth, and Henning Simonsen, who provided strong support for the completion of this book.

We would like to warmly thank Cathy Sunshine, who also copyedited the book published in 2012, for her editorial expertise, sense of humour, intelligence, and professional care for the book. Without Cathy, it would not have been possible to proceed as fast as we did for the last six months of this exhausting, but still fun and rewarding, process. At an earlier stage, she also advised us to reconsider the structure of the book, which led to a better organisation of the chapters and, possibly, to material for a future publication.

Morten Bergsmo, Editor-in-Chief of Torkel Opsahl Academic EPublisher ('TOAEP'), believed in the project and brought it into being; without his commitment there would be no book. Many thanks also to the other professionals at TOAEP for providing competent support in the final stages of the publication process, especially Devasheesh Bais and CHAN Ho Shing Icarus. Finally, we are grateful to our partners, Ruth Walden in Ottawa and Elin Skaar in Bergen, for their essential support, inspiration, and encouragement throughout this long project.

Terje Einarsen and Joseph Rikhof
Bergen and Ottawa, 6 November 2018

TABLE OF CONTENTS

ABBREVIATIONS

ABiH	Army of the Republic of Bosnia and Herzegovina
AC	Appeals Chamber
AFRC	Armed Forces Revolutionary Council (Sierra Leone)
BiH	Bosnia and Herzegovina
CAH	crime(s) against humanity
CAVR	Commission for Reception, Truth and Reconciliation (East Timor)
CC10	Control Council Law No. 10
CIL	customary international law
DINA	Chilean secret police
DRC	Democratic Republic of Congo
EAC	Extraordinary African Chambers
ECCC	Extraordinary Chambers in the Courts of Cambodia
ECHR	European Court of Human Rights
ECJ	European Court of Justice
FDLR	Forces Démocratiques de Libération du Rwanda
FOCA	Abacunguzi Fighting Forces (Rwanda)
HRL	human rights law
HVO	Croatian Defence Council
IACHR	Inter-American Court of Human Rights
ICC	International Criminal Court
ICJ	International Court of Justice
ICL	international criminal law
ICTR	International Criminal Tribunal for Rwanda

ICTY	International Criminal Tribunal for the former Yugoslavia
IHL	international humanitarian law
ILC	International Law Commission
IMT	International Military Tribunal
IMTFE	International Military Tribunal for the Far East
JCE	joint criminal enterprise
KhAD	Afghan state security and intelligence agency
KLA	Kosovo Liberation Army
LRA	Lord's Resistance Army (Uganda)
LTTE	Liberation Tigers of Tamil Eelam (Sri Lanka)
MICT	Mechanism for International Criminal Tribunals
MRND	National Republican Movement for Democracy and Development (Rwanda)
NMT	Nuernberg Military Tribunals
OSP	Office of the Special Prosecutor (Ethiopia)
PCIJ	Permanent Court of International Justice
PTC	Pre-Trial Chamber (ICC)
R2P	responsibility to protect
RTLM	Radio Télévision Libre des Mille Collines (Rwanda)
RUF	Revolutionary United Front (Sierra Leone)
SA	Sturmabteilung
SC	Security Council (UN)
SCSL	Special Court for Sierra Leone
SCU	Serious Crimes Unit (East Timor)
SD	Sicherheitsdienst
SDS	Serb Democratic Party
SFRY	Socialist Federal Republic of Yugoslavia
SPSC	Special Panel for Serious Crimes (East Timor)

SS	Schutzstaffel
STL	Special Tribunal for Lebanon
TC	Trial Chamber
TCL	transnational criminal law
TRCP	Transitional Rules of Criminal Procedure
UK	United Kingdom
UN	United Nations
UNAMET	United Nations Mission to East Timor
UNHCR	United Nations High Commissioner for Refugees
UNTAET	United Nations Transitional Administration in East Timor
UNWCC	United Nations War Crimes Commission
VCLT	Vienna Convention on the Law of Treaties
VRS	Bosnian Serb Army
WCC	War Crimes Chamber (Bosnia and Herzegovina)
WWI	World War I
WWII	World War II

1

———

Introduction:
Defining the Problem

1.1. Justification for the Book

This book confronts several well-known issues of international criminal law ('ICL'): How does ICL distinguish punishable acts of typical mass participation in grave international crimes from other acts that may also have contributed to such crimes? How are different kinds of participation in mass crimes labelled or classified in international judicial practice, and what are the legal repercussions of a particular classification? What are the best theoretical and judicial approaches to answering these and other related questions concerned with personal liability in ICL? Is there a need for a general theory of personal criminal law liability that would strengthen our ability to understand, explain, and predict the outcomes of the legal issues involved? This book is premised on the view that the answer to the last question is yes, and that now is the time to develop such a theory.

These issues underlying important parts of current ICL are especially important when prosecutors and judges ultimately determine individual criminal responsibility in cases before international criminal courts. They are also significant because the norms of ICL are reproduced in national jurisdictions and applied in trials concerned with international crimes in domestic courts. Several aspects of this subject matter have been controversial in legal theory and practice in recent decades and have thus received significant attention in the literature, as we shall see. Determining the forms of participation may also affect prosecutorial decisions during investigation, the relationship between indictment and lawful judgment, and the sentencing when a person has been found guilty.

Much has already been written on the topic of individual criminal responsibility for participation in mass crimes.[1] However, the internation-

---

[1] For comprehensive studies published by well-known authors within a brief period of time (2012–13), see Elies van Sliedregt, *Criminal Responsibility in International Law*, Oxford University Press, Oxford, 2012; Kai Ambos, *Treatise on International Criminal Law*, vol.

al debate on the scope of individual liability is as vibrant as ever, on many different points.[2] This book responds to the continuing need for well-founded analysis and critique of the legal developments that have taken place so far, a rationale detailed further in Section 1.3. of this chapter. It is also an issue whether established concepts and distinctions ought to be consolidated or revised, and whether current ICL should be supplemented with additional concepts on personal liability. Last but not least, there is a more basic scientific question at stake: Is ICL with respect to personal criminal law liability actually premised on a sufficiently clear and transparent general scientific theory? And if not, is it possible at least to identify the components of such a theory, which would also be useful for the further development of this field of law?

This book is addressed to all with an interest in international criminal law and related disciplines like domestic criminal law, human rights, humanitarian law, and transitional justice. In addition, there is increasing awareness of the often intertwined, triangular relationship between ICL, domestic criminal law, and the new autonomous field of 'transnational criminal law'.[3] This means that a general theory on punishable participation, although developed in particular with a view to ICL, may have wider application or provide inspiration to other fields as well. First and fore-

---

1, *Foundations and General Part*, Oxford University Press, Oxford, 2013; M. Cherif Bassiouni, *Introduction to International Criminal Law: Second Revised Edition*, Martinus Nijhoff, Leiden, 2012; and Antonio Cassese, *Cassese's International Criminal Law*, 3rd ed., rev. by Antonio Cassese, Paola Gaeta, Laure Baig, Mary Fan, Christopher Gosnell, and Alex Whiting, Oxford University Press, Oxford, 2013. A number of other authors have also contributed to this particular field of ICL with specialised monographs, anthologies, and journal articles, covering a wide range of theoretical and practical issues. Quite a few authors have treated the subject matter as part of more general books on international criminal law, as illustrated by the works of Ambos, Bassiouni, and Cassese mentioned above. An overview and discussion of relevant literature is presented in Chapter 6.

2   One example is the eight articles originating from a symposium devoted to macro-criminal conduct and printed in the *Journal of International Criminal Justice*, 2014, vol. 12, no. 2. Again, the debate since then has just continued to broaden, in a number of different forums and publications.

3   In short, transnational criminal law concerns crimes that have trans-boundary effects and are of substantial international concern, but that *stricto sensu* do not constitute international crimes under ICL. On the triangular relationship mentioned, see, for example, Robert J. Currie and Joseph Rikhof, *International & Transnational Criminal Law*, 2nd ed., Irwin Law, Toronto, 2013.

---

most, however, the present work provides an opportunity to contribute to a more coherent and practical understanding of international criminal law.

As explained in the preface, this book is concerned with theoretical and empirical research and analysis relating to personal criminal law liability, including historical and sociological perspectives. In the following sections of this introductory chapter, we seek to define the problem of punishable participation in universal crimes in more detail.

1.2. The Subject Matter: Punishable Participation in Universal Crimes

1.2.1. Participation in Universal Crimes

In ordinary language, participation is the action of participating in something. To participate is to "take part or become involved in an activity".[4] The notion of taking part in something or becoming involved in an activity implies that more than one person is involved. The activity could be anything, but it could also be criminal by nature. In this book, the activity we are interested in concerns inherently grave crimes: typically, serious criminal acts constituting breaches of human rights or humanitarian law on a large scale, justifying characterisations such as mass atrocity[5] or system criminality.[6]

This is the second volume in a planned four-volume series entitled "Rethinking the Essentials of International Criminal Law and Transitional Justice".[7] The first book in the series concerned the concepts of international crimes and universal crimes in international law.[8] The series is an integral part of the Universal Crimes Project, which seeks to explore and

---

[4] *Oxford Advanced Learner's Dictionary: Encyclopedic Edition*, Oxford University Press, Oxford, 1992, p. 653.

[5] See, for example, Mark Osiel, *Making Sense of Mass Atrocity*, Cambridge University Press, Cambridge, 2009.

[6] See, for example, André Nollkamper and Harmen van der Wilt, *System Criminality in International Law*, Cambridge University Press, Cambridge, 2009.

[7] See also the preface to this book.

[8] Terje Einarsen, *The Concept of Universal Crimes in International Law*, Torkel Opsahl Academic EPublisher, Oslo, 2012 (www.legal-tools.org/doc/bfda36/). See also Terje Einarsen, "New Frontiers of International Criminal Law: Towards a Concept of Universal Crimes", in *Bergen Journal of Criminal Law and Criminal Justice*, 2013, vol. 1, no. 1, pp. 1–23.

advance the concept of universal crimes in international criminal law.[9] As has been explained in more detail elsewhere, the term 'universal crimes' covers the same ground *lex lata* as the more familiar concept of 'international crimes', but it also includes universal crimes *lex ferenda*, that is, crime types that have the potential to become international crimes or universal crimes in future law because they fulfil certain key criteria, notably with respect to gravity and universal character.[10] The terms 'international crimes' and 'universal crimes' are sometimes used interchangeably in this book, but in general 'universal crimes' is the preferred term.

Definitions may be of different types, and the first book in the series established important distinctions between a 'theoretical definition' of universal crimes, a 'conceptual legal definition' of universal crimes, and an 'enumerative legal definition' of universal crimes, with the distinction between ICL *lex lata* and *lex ferenda* cutting through the latter two definitions. The current conceptual legal definition of universal crimes *lex lata* was formulated on the basis of five cumulative criteria:

> The term 'universal crimes' applies to conduct which (1) manifestly violates a fundamental universal value or interest, provided that the offence is (2) universally regarded as punishable due to its inherent gravity, (3) recognised as a matter of serious concern to the international community as a whole, and (4) proscribed by binding rules of international law, and provided that (5) criminal liability and prosecution is not dependent upon the consent of a concerned state (the territorial state where the crime was committed or the national state of an alleged perpetrator or victim).[11]

---

[9]   A profile of the Universal Crimes Project is available on the University of Bergen web site.

[10] Understanding the twin concepts of *lex lata* and *lex ferenda* is also important to the particular subject matter of this book. As explained in more detail in Chapter 4, Section 4.5., the rule of law depends on the principle that it is possible to determine the correct interpretation of any rule (*lex lata*) within a legal order on the basis of the relevant legal sources. The point is that the content of a current rule is valid and applicable even when it is not the preferred (*lex ferenda*) legal solution to the problem (a different solution may be preferred on some important moral or political grounds, or because it is more compatible with an overarching legal theory). However, views *lex ferenda* today may have the potential to be transformed to *lex lata* tomorrow, since the law is a dynamic social construct and its development is influenced by reasoning *lex ferenda*.

[11] Einarsen, 2012, p. 297, see *supra* note 8.

An elaborate enumerative definition was also provided in the same book.[12] Without complicating the subject of universal crimes more than necessary for the present purpose, this book deals basically with participation in the universal crime categories of genocide, crimes against humanity, crime of aggression, and war crimes.[13] Some other crime categories and crime types sometimes enter the discussion as well, for instance, serious discrete crimes such as torture connected to a power structure in society,[14] and terrorist crimes.[15]

---

[12] For a consolidated list of universal crimes (although preliminary and incomplete), see *ibid.*, pp. 319–28. The list encompasses three 'classes of universal crimes', 10 'universal crime categories', and 150 'universal crime types'; see further explanation at *ibid.*, pp. 319–20.

[13] Of these crime categories in ICL, only the crime of aggression may still have a somewhat disputed legal status under international law. This is the case even though it was heavily prosecuted at Nuremberg and Tokyo after World War II and was included in the Rome Statute of the International Criminal Court ('ICC') in Article 5 and eventually defined in Article 8*bis*. In line with the first book in the series, we consider the crime of aggression to be a core universal/international crime (Einarsen, 2012, p. 278, see *supra* note 8). At the Assembly of States Parties of the ICC in December 2017, the court's formal jurisdiction with respect to this crime was finally activated, although jurisdiction to convict a person for the crime of aggression is still more limited as compared to the other core crimes.

[14] The term 'power structure' is used in this book in the same way as in Einarsen, 2012, pp. 13, 68–72, 81, 202, see *supra* note 8. It denotes an entity or organisation with actual power within a society that provides its key members with opportunities to take, facilitate, or enforce decisions that may have a substantial impact on society and on the lives and well-being of individuals. A power structure is often large, like the governmental or military structures of a state, but it also can be small or form part of a larger entity or organisation; some power structures are non-state entities. It may function basically to the benefit of society or some parts of it, but may also be abused for criminal purposes and, notably, used to commit universal crimes.

[15] The status of even serious terrorist crimes is still not entirely clarified for the purpose of ICL. Terrorism is clearly a type of crime of international concern, but it is often classified as a 'transnational crime' rather than as an international/universal crime. See, for example, Currie and Rikhof, 2013, pp. 317–23, *supra* note 3. In practice, the underlying acts of terrorist crimes may in some cases be quite similar to (other) universal crimes. For example, terrorist crimes committed in war-torn Syria are sometimes prosecuted under active nationality jurisdiction or universal jurisdiction in Western states, where the facts of the cases may indicate that the acts also constitute war crimes or even crimes against humanity ('CAH') and thus could just as well have been prosecuted as such. War crimes, or CAH, may thus also be prosecuted in concurrence with terrorism. See further Chapter 4, Section 4.6.2., of this volume. In addition, membership in a terrorist organisation is currently also being prosecuted as a distinct crime under national legislation of several states. The latter development is interesting with respect to the idea of prosecuting membership in criminal

The linkage of the relevant crimes to power structures or especially powerful actors is generally a defining feature of international crimes. That is certainly true in a descriptive or sociological sense, while it might be disputable whether such a connection is absolutely necessary in legal terms, that is, whether it is a requirement for criminal liability under international law. It should, however, usefully be considered part of a *theoretical* definition of universal crimes, which in turn might also be a tool for identifying possible new universal crimes *lex ferenda*. In the first book in the series the following theoretical definition was offered:

> The term 'universal crimes' shall apply to any conduct which manifestly violates a fundamental universal value or interest, is universally regarded as punishable due to its gravity, and is usually committed, organised, or tolerated by powerful actors, and which therefore may require prosecution before international courts.[16]

This definition points out the typical causal nexus between the acts of individual persons and powerful organisations or entities in society with respect to universal crimes. That is also relevant to both *lex lata* and *lex ferenda* discussion regarding the scope of personal criminal law liability for different modes of participation in these complex crimes, which often pose great danger not just to victims but to societies as well.

1.2.2. Why Participation in Universal Crimes Is Different

Universal crimes may occur in the context of armed conflict, but they may also form part of a pattern of aggressive behaviour by states or by powerful non-state actors within a society that is not at war. They are often directly linked to abuse of political or military systems or to an absence of effective state institutions able and willing to protect civilians against serious harm or the risk of harm. Mass participation in such multifaceted crimes raises a number of difficult questions of fact and law with respect to determining individual liability.

For example, the prosecutorial challenges relating to mass atrocity are often very different from the investigation and prosecution of most common crimes. In the latter case – to simplify the matter a bit – the ques-

---

organisations committing universal crimes as a distinct crime, as was already the case at Nuremberg. See further discussions of 'membership' liability later in this book.

[16] Einarsen, 2012, p. 298, see *supra* note 8.

tions are fairly straightforward: Has a crime been committed? And if so, who did it and who might have assisted in the crime? In comparison, universal crimes such as genocide, crimes against humanity, and most war crimes "are possible only when the state or other powerful organizations mobilize and coordinate the efforts of many people".[17] Responsibility for mass atrocity is thus typically widely shared, often by thousands; yet international criminal law prefers – or has no other option than – to blame particular individuals, although they might be part of a pervasive social and criminal pattern existing at the time. When many people get involved in grave crimes and cause great danger to potential victims and to society at large, a paradox appears – namely, that in the aftermath of the actual crimes, and during transitional justice trials, each person may have considered himself "nothing but a cog in the machine and reasoned that it was the machine, not he, that was responsible".[18] Robert Conot coined this description with reference to the euthanasia program in Nazi Germany, which served as a "prototype for the extermination of millions that was to follow".[19]

The euthanasia program was part of the effort to "Aryanise" Germany and get rid of everybody who did not fit into the scheme. It originated from ideas expressed earlier in Hitler's *Mein Kampf*. The program demonstrated how, through fragmentation of authority and tasks, it was possible to fashion an administrative murder machine with implied impunity for participation and excesses – and with wilful lack of exact knowledge at the highest political level. It came into being at Hitler's initiative, but the system was then operated through different levels of already existing power structures:

> Hitler had enunciated an offhand, extralegal decree, and had not wanted to be bothered about it again. Brandt had ordered the 'scientific' implementation of the program and, like Hitler, wished to hear no complaints. [Dr. Karl Brandt was the Reich Commissioner for Health and Sanitation, and Hitler's personal physician.] The directors and personnel of institutions rationalized that matters were out of their hands and that they were just filling out questionnaires for the 'experts'

---

[17]   Osiel, 2009, unnumbered first page, see *supra* note 5.

[18]   Robert Conot, *Justice at Nuremberg*, Basic Books, New York, 2009, p. 211.

[19]   *Ibid.*, p. 210.

in Berlin, though in reality each form was the equivalent of a death warrant. The specious 'experts' perused the questionnaires only to cull out prominent persons that might have been accidentally included, then passed them on to Himmler's myrmidons, who transported the afflicted to the annihilation installations. The personnel at the end of the line excused themselves on the basis that they were under compulsion, had no power of decision, and were merely performing a function. Thousands of people were involved [...].[20]

Although perhaps not always defensible at the end of the day (see, for example, the Nuremberg Medical Case[21]), this perception of the individual being just a cog in the machinery may contain some truth from a legal standpoint as well. Responsibility under current ICL *is* often hard to establish with sufficient precision and fairness for most participants in situations of mass crimes. While international tribunals have typically focused on the allegedly most responsible persons at the top, or at least at the intermediate levels, of power structures, national institutions have more often prosecuted direct perpetrators of the underlying crimes and low-level leaders at the crime scenes.[22] In the most serious crimes, however, most participants are never held responsible.

In one of the subsequent Nuremberg trials known as the Pohl case (*United States v. Oswald Pohl, et al.*),[23] the (US) Nuremberg Military Tribunal confronted this paradox. The case concerned Pohl and 17 other offi-

---

[20] *Ibid.*, pp. 210–11. A Czech commission estimated after the war that 275,000 people were killed or starved to death in the euthanasia program (p. 211).

[21] For highly positioned leaders, the 'cog in the machinery' argument is not always a reliable, let alone justifiable, defence. With regard to the euthanasia program, Karl Brandt and six of his colleagues were sentenced after the war to death by hanging; five others were sentenced to life imprisonment, and four others to prison terms ranging from 10 to 20 years. See Nuernberg Military Tribunals ('NMT'), "The Medical Case", Judgment, 20 August 1947, in *Trials of War Criminals before the Nuernberg Military Tribunals under Control Council Law No. 10: Nuernberg, October 1946–April 1949*, vol. II, US Government Printing Office, Washington, DC, 1950, pp. 298–300 (www.legal-tools.org/doc/c18557/).

[22] See Chapters 3 and 7 (cases before international tribunals) and Chapters 8 and 9 (domestic cases).

[23] NMT, "The Pohl Case", Judgment, 3 November 1947, in *Trials of War Criminals before the Nuernberg Military Tribunals under Control Council Law No. 10: Nuernberg, October 1946–April 1949*, vol. V, US Government Printing Office, Washington, DC, 1950 (www.legal-tools.org/doc/84ae05/).

cials of the SS (Schutzstaffel)[24] Economic and Administrative Main Office (Wirtschafts und Verwaltungshauptamt) and the administration of concentration camps and labour camps in the Third Reich. According to the prosecution, approximately 10 million people had been imprisoned in these camps. Specific charges included imprisonment of civilians, nationals of foreign countries, and prisoners of war; exploitation of inmates as laborers; medical experiments conducted on prisoners; extermination of Jews; sterilisation; mistreatment of prisoners of war; euthanasia; and deportation of foreign nationals and plundering of their property. These charges involved two different forces in the SS system, which sometimes overlapped and sometimes competed against each other: those engaged in generating revenue for the SS by exploiting captive labour for profit, and those engaged in punishing and exterminating people considered enemies of the Nazi state. The power structure that facilitated the mass crimes was thus both well organised and quite complex.

Against this backdrop the tribunal made the following observation with regard to the inherently difficult issue of identifying possible individual responsibility for different kinds of participation in these grave mass crimes:

> An elaborate and complex operation, such as the deportation and the extermination of the Jews and appropriation of all their Property, is obviously a task for more than one man. Launching or promulgating such a programme may originate in the mind of one man or a group of men. Working out the details of the plan may fall to another. Procurement of personnel and the issuing of actual operational orders may fall to others. The actual execution of the plan in the field involves the operation of another, or it may be several other persons or groups. Marshalling and distributing the loot, or allocating the victims, is another phase of the operations which may be entrusted to an individual or a group far removed from the original planners.[25]

---

[24] The SS (Schutzstaffel, or 'protection squadron') was an elite paramilitary organisation under Hitler and the Nazi party in Nazi Germany from 1933 to 1945. It also operated throughout German-occupied Europe during World War II.

[25] See *ibid.*, Supplementary Judgment, p. 1173.

These remarks go to the heart of the subject matter of punishable participation in universal crimes more generally. They highlight the gravity and quantity of the crimes as well as the complexity of large criminal enterprises, and thus they also point indirectly to the enormous difficulty of identifying, proving, and assessing fairly the acts of various individual participants.

A particular aspect of the evidentiary problem is the attempt by suspects to shift responsibility to other participants, referred to in the Pohl case as the "shuttlecock" problem:

> As may be expected, we find the various participants in the program tossing the shuttlecock of responsibility from one to the other.[26]

Although this phenomenon is common to all kinds of criminal cases with several suspects, the chances of success in shifting blame are much better in cases of mass participation. Such behaviour may be most common at the intermediate and lower levels of the power structure involved, but it can be pervasive at all levels. This seems to have frustrated the judges in the Pohl case, who described the attitude of defendant Pohl and the other participants in the liquidation program as follows:

> The originator says: "It is true that I thought of the program, but I did not carry it out." The next in line says: "It is true I laid the plan out on paper and designated the modus operandi, but it was not my plan, and I did not actually carry it out." The third in line says: "It is true I shot people, but I was merely carrying out orders from above." The next in line says: "It is true that I received the loot from this program and inventoried it and disposed of it, but I did not steal it nor kill the owners of it. I was only carrying out orders from a higher level."[27]

Interestingly, in the Pohl judgment three of the defendants were fully acquitted, while some other defendants were partially acquitted. Four of those convicted received the death penalty, and the others received prison sentences ranging from 10 years to life imprisonment. Needless to say,

---

[26] "The Pohl Case", p. 1173, see *supra* note 23. A shuttlecock is the feathered projectile used in badminton. It is also a traditional Native American sport in which a shuttlecock made of cornhusks and feathers is thrown from one player to another.

[27] *Ibid.*

many other persons had participated in the crimes committed in the camps, yet were not even indicted. Hence the Pohl case may also illustrate the limits of international criminal trials.

Some acquittals in the Pohl case were due to lack of sufficient evidence, but the acquittal of Joseph Vogt is interesting because it concerned a person positioned at a certain level of the power structure. His particular office, however, had no authority to "either start or stop a criminal act".[28] He had knowledge of crimes, but according to the tribunal, in his position this was not enough to constitute consent to the crimes,[29] under the doctrine and legal basis of taking "a consenting part" in the crimes, as set out in Control Council Law No. 10, Article II(2)(c).[30] It is also interesting that Vogt was found not guilty on the separate count of membership in a criminal organisation, despite serving as an auditor and attaining the rank of colonel in the SS, an organisation deemed to be criminal by the International Military Tribunal ('IMT') and by Article II(2)(d) of Control Council Law No. 10.[31] The tribunal seems to have been influenced by the personal acts of Vogt when he reported crimes he had discovered to his superiors and sought to distance himself from the whole criminal enterprise:

> Again, the Tribunal is impelled to ask, what should he have done? Unless we are willing to resort to the principle of group responsibility and to charge the whole German nation with these war crimes and crimes against humanity, there is a line somewhere at which indictable criminality must stop. In the opinion of the Tribunal, Vogt stands beyond that line.[32]

This illustrates that not all kinds of contributing activity, even within a criminal organisation, was considered by the tribunal to constitute personal 'membership' in a substantive, criminal law sense, even though Vogt had voluntarily joined the National Socialist Party and the SS before the war.[33]

---

[28] *Ibid.*, p. 1002.

[29] *Ibid.*, pp. 1001–4.

[30] For a discussion of this form of liability, see Kevin Jon Heller, "'Taking a Consenting Part': The Lost Mode of Participation", in *Loyola of Los Angeles International & Comparative Law Review*, 2017, vol. 39, no. 1, pp. 247–58.

[31] "The Pohl Case", p. 1004, see *supra* note 23.

[32] *Ibid.*

[33] *Ibid.*, p. 1001.

On the other hand, Leo Volk, who was a bit higher up in the hierarchy and was head of the legal section of another division, was convicted of the mistreatment of concentration camp inmates even though he did not have the power to prevent it. The tribunal stressed among other points that he used his knowledge and professional capabilities to promote the continuance and furtherance of those crimes. In other words, he was in a better position to object to the criminal activity than was Joseph Vogt; by not objecting he was thus 'taking a consenting part' in the crimes.[34]

Although the crimes before the tribunal in the Pohl case were extreme in gravity and scale, and although the problem of mass participation presents itself in a number of variations, the essence of the legal and evidentiary problems seems to be much the same in relation to universal crimes on a lesser scale.

Participation in universal crimes, therefore, poses some unique challenges that are different from participation in common crimes. At the same time, there are also important common aspects of criminal law concepts in general, which need to be taken into account in our analysis as well.[35] Criminal organisations represent a particularly interesting crossover.[36]

1.2.3. Why the Notion of the 'Principal Perpetrator' Is Not So Useful

When several people take part in universal crimes, they usually take on different roles or have different functions in the early planning, preparation, and execution of the acts, as well as in connected acts undertaken after the execution phase of the concrete crimes. Those who finally execute the crimes directly might be referred to as the 'principal perpetrators', typically those who physically kill or ill-treat the victims.

---

[34] The special forms of liability expressed through the concepts of taking a consenting part and membership are discussed at various places later in the book.

[35] Consider the many useful works on comparative criminal law and transnational criminal law. For a theoretical analysis of a proposed overarching criminal law structure, see, for example, George P. Fletcher, *The Grammar of Criminal Law: American, Comparative, and International*, vol. 1, *Foundations*, Oxford University Press, Oxford, 2007.

[36] See, for example, the comparative discussions at different levels in Almin Maljevic, *'Participation in a Criminal Organisation' and 'Conspiracy': Different Legal Models Against Criminal Collectives*, Duncker & Humblot, Berlin, 2011.

However, these *executors*, as we prefer to call the direct or principal perpetrators, may only 'take part' in the criminal activity seen as a whole. The typical executor of mass crimes is just one among many participants in universal crimes and works in tandem with others who may not merit the label of principal perpetrator. The reason for this insight has to do with the character of universal crimes, where it is never the concrete 'underlying crimes' alone, for example, murder, rape, or torture, that define the nature of the universal crime types. Rather, it is only when the relevant underlying crimes are committed within a certain socio-political context, expressed in legal terms through contextual 'gravity clauses',[37] that the universal crimes are constituted as such. Hence it is the existence and applicability of a particular gravity clause that turns murder into possible criminal liability for genocide, crimes against humanity, or war crimes.

It seems to follow logically from these special features of universal crimes that a clear-cut distinction between 'principals' as executors and others who may take part as 'accomplices' is too imprecise and simplistic for meaningful determination of responsibility under ICL. The reason is that the executor is usually not criminally liable for *universal crimes* independent of other participants. An executor might be liable for more ordinary, *domestic* crimes, such as murder or rape, independent of others who take part in the planning or preparation. The executor may thus usefully be considered the principal perpetrator for the purpose of common crimes. However, if an applicable contextual component in the form of a specific universal gravity clause is lacking, or lacks applicability for the executor because he or she was not aware of the broader context, the person committing the underlying crime is not criminally responsible *under ICL*, for instance, for crimes against humanity.[38] In essence, this means

---

[37] The particular term and notion of 'gravity clauses' for all universal crimes proper was developed in Einarsen, 2012, pp. 253–54 and pp. 301–13, see *supra* note 8. Other terms have often been used to express much the same reality with respect to particular international crime categories, for instance, the 'contextual element' of 'crimes against humanity'. See, for example, Cassese, 2013, p. 92, *supra* note 1.

[38] While we use 'he or she' here for inclusivity, in the rest of this book we will, for the sake of readability, generally use male pronouns to denote the natural person involved in the crime. In choosing between male and female pronouns, we have opted for male because men account for nearly all participants in universal crimes cases to date at both the international and domestic levels. In the few cases where offenders are female, we have noted that in the text. We have not assessed gender with respect to the victims of such crimes (a much more difficult and uncertain exercise), but we assume those numbers are split more evenly.

that an executor usually depends on other participants for planning and preparation, as well as on others who maintain or support the power structure that makes the crimes possible on a large scale, and on still others who may participate at the execution stage. Hence the term 'principal perpetrator' employed with reference to the executors of universal crimes is not accurate enough. In addition, even when a low-level executor of the underlying crime is aware of the context, the label 'principal' may not be appropriate as compared to those persons at the leadership level who organised and maybe directly ordered the crimes. It might, however, be appropriate to use in cases of a notorious executing offender and in some cases where a person or a small group of persons commit certain war crimes jointly. But in these cases, other and better terms are available, as we shall see.

Furthermore, from an empirical as well as a philosophical and moral point of view, persons other than the executors on the ground might bear just as much responsibility for the crimes. Some of those higher up in the hierarchy, despite not being present at the crime scenes, are often 'the most responsible persons'.[39] This latter term may apply to the leaders and senior officials of the relevant organisations or power structures, that is, persons with a certain authority who planned, organised, ordered, and/or incited the preparation and execution of the crimes. But even other contributors or facilitators, the aiders and abettors, may share much of the same responsibility in collective crimes when one takes into account the extreme social danger posed by certain criminal enterprises.

Intuitively one may assume that persons who merely assist the perpetrators of universal crimes would have to be located at low levels of the power structure through which the crimes are executed, or even outside any relevant power structure. But this is not always the case, because powerful leaders may also use their power to assist perpetrators outside their own organisation or government. In other cases, they may themselves be assisted by 'support structures' or members of organisations with some kind of affiliation to the main power structures in society;[40] they may even support or be supported by power structures outside their

---

[39] This term is closely linked to the (sociological) notion of high-level participants in crimes committed within power structures. For further elaboration, see Chapter 3.

[40] See Chapter 3, Sections 3.1. and 3.6., on international prosecution of members of power support structures.

own country. A case in point, illustrating the latter scenario, is the Taylor case before the Special Court for Sierra Leone ('SCSL') Trial Chamber and Appeals Chamber.[41] The Appeals Chamber in 2013 upheld the Trial Chamber's conviction of the former president of Liberia, Charles Taylor, for aiding and abetting the rebels of the Revolutionary United Front and the Armed Forces Revolutionary Council in the commission of war crimes and crimes against humanity in Sierra Leone, and for participating in planning rebel attacks. The Trial Chamber sentenced Taylor to a 50-year prison term. Although the Appeals Chamber affirmed the sentence, it concluded that the Trial Chamber had "erred in law in finding that aiding and abetting liability generally warrants a lesser sentence than other forms of criminal participation".[42]

Extended social danger is a feature of group crimes in society, and especially so with respect to participation in universal crimes. The International Criminal Tribunal for the former Yugoslavia ('ICTY') Appeals Chamber made a similar point in the Tadić case, when it underlined the moral gravity of participation in such crimes through contributions that facilitate the commission of the crimes:

> Most of the time these crimes do not result from the criminal propensity of single individuals but constitute manifestations of collective criminality: the crimes are often carried out by groups of individuals acting in pursuance of a common criminal design. Although only some members of the group may physically perpetrate the criminal act (murder, extermination, wanton destruction of cities, towns or villages, etc.), the participation and contribution of the other members of the group is often vital in facilitating the commission of the offence in question. It follows that the moral gravity of such participation is often no less – or indeed no different – from that of those actually carrying out the acts in question.[43]

---

[41] SCSL, *Prosecutor against Charles G. Taylor*, Judgment, SCSL-03-01-A, 26 September 2013 (www.legal-tools.org/doc/3e7be5/).

[42] *Ibid.*, p. 305.

[43] ICTY, Appeals Chamber, *Prosecutor v. Tadić*, Judgment, IT-94-1-A, 15 July 1999, para. 191 (www.legal-tools.org/doc/8efc3a/).

Also from the perspective of international prosecutors, and in ICL legal theory, it often makes more sense to label the allegedly most responsible political and military leaders as the 'principal perpetrators'.[44]

Analytically, and in strict legal terminology, it might be better to avoid or downplay this particular, quite ambiguous characterisation. However, this also means that there is a need for a comprehensive terminology that distinguishes more clearly between different kinds of participants with their different roles, positions, and responsibility, and this book aims to develop such a terminology or classification.

1.2.4. The Rome Statute Does Not Resolve the Interpretative Issues

If broad and ambiguous characterisations of participatory conduct should be avoided in international criminal law, it seems to follow that legal determination of individual responsibility must instead be facts-based and assessed concretely. This may allow judges a great deal of discretion in determining personal guilt. Alternatively, the legal thought process could be facts-based *in conjunction* with the possible application of certain predetermined categories and more precisely defined subcategories or modes of participation – each with its particular legal conditions to be met. Under the latter approach the scope for judicial discretion is reduced, but not eliminated.

Most international lawyers would probably intuitively opt for the latter choice, influenced by the legality principle.[45] The prevailing perception is that law, especially criminal law, needs foreseeable 'rules'. Vague principles leave too much discretion to prosecutors and judges in the particular case – at least before a sizable tower of jurisprudence has been gradually built by the judicial engineers at international criminal courts. The question is where ICL stands now, and where it should be heading on important aspects of participation liability.

A natural starting point for further appraisal is the Rome Statute, Article 25(3), which prescribes individual liability for punishable conduct that falls under at least one of the enumerated categories of participation:

---

[44] See, for example, Héctor Olásolo, *The Criminal Responsibility of Senior Political and Military Leaders as Principals to International Crimes*, Hart, Oxford, 2009.

[45] On the legality principle in general, see, for example, Kenneth S. Gallant, *The Principle of Legality in International and Comparative Criminal Law*, Cambridge University Press, Cambridge, 2009.

3. In accordance with this Statute, a person shall be criminally responsible and liable for punishment for a crime within the jurisdiction of the Court if that person:

(a) Commits such a crime, whether as an individual, jointly with another or through another person, regardless of whether that other person is criminally responsible;

(b) Orders, solicits or induces the commission of such a crime which in fact occurs or is attempted;

(c) For the purpose of facilitating the commission of such a crime, aids, abets or otherwise assists in its commission or its attempted commission, including providing the means for its commission;

(d) In any other way contributes to the commission or attempted commission of such a crime by a group of persons acting with a common purpose. Such contribution shall be intentional and shall either:

(i) Be made with the aim of furthering the criminal activity or criminal purpose of the group, where such activity or purpose involves the commission of a crime within the jurisdiction of the Court; or (ii) Be made in the knowledge of the intention of the group to commit the crime;

(e) In respect of the crime of genocide, directly and publicly incites others to commit genocide;

(f) Attempts to commit such a crime by taking action that commences its execution by means of a substantial step, but the crime does not occur because of circumstances independent of the person's intentions. However, a person who abandons the effort to commit the crime or otherwise prevents the completion of the crime shall not be liable for punishment under this Statute for the attempt to commit that crime if that person completely and voluntarily gave up the criminal purpose.

This fairly detailed provision, which must be supplemented by Article 28 on command responsibility and by Article 30 on mental elements,[46]

---

[46] The mental element is theoretically part of the fundamental 'principle of culpability', which also includes defences; see Chapter 2, Section 2.2.2.3. In the Rome Statute, defences, in the form of either excuses or justifications, are set forth mainly in Articles 31–33. Defences are not a principal subject matter of this book; instead they are part of the planned third work in this series because, in our view, they concern 'accountability' for

sets forth *prima facie* binding rules on personal criminal liability for crimes under the jurisdiction of the International Criminal Court ('ICC'),[47] in particular for the prosecution of genocide crimes, crimes against humanity, and war crimes.[48] However, these provisions were the result of compromises during the drafting between legal traditions stemming from different national jurisdictions, and they were partly also inspired by transnational law treaties, as noted by, among others, Hans Vest. He also points out that different parts of Article 25(3) may have different origins and might not necessarily be clearly distinguishable concepts:

> Already a short look at Article 25(3) ICC Statute clearly shows that the provision is the result of a *doctrinal compromise* reached by proponents and experts from different legal systems who based their proposals on their own national laws; these experts found it, in the words of an insider, 'hard to understand that another legal system might approach the issue in another way'. A lawyer familiar with German criminal law may find subparagraph (a) to be influenced by Article 25 of the German Penal Code. Subparagraph (b) with its multiplied forms evidently refers to the common law tradition, since in civil law instigation usually is defined in more abstract terms. Subparagraph (c) was at least partially taken from the US Model Penal Code. Subparagraph (d) was modelled on Article 2(3) of the 1997 International Convention for the Suppression of Terrorist Bombings.[49]

---

crimes being committed (see also the preface to this book). Likewise, some issues concerning 'jurisdiction' of international tribunals that are closely tied to accountability are also deferred to the third book. See, for example, the Rome Statute, Article 26, on exclusion of jurisdiction over persons under 18; Article 27, on the irrelevance of official capacity; and Article 29, on non-applicability of statute of limitations.

[47] See the Rome Statute, Article 5(1).

[48] With respect to the crime of aggression, the very crime description limits liability to persons involved in the planning, preparation, initiation, or execution, "by a person in a position effectively to exercise control over or to direct the political or military action of a State"; see Rome Statute, Article 8*bis* (1). This is followed up in Article 25(3*bis*) with seemingly even more limited language, on the one hand providing for the applicability of general Article 25(3), while on the other hand stating that "the provisions of this article shall apply only to persons in a position effectively to exercise control over or to direct the political or military action of a State".

[49] Hans Vest, "Problems of Participation: Unitarian, Differentiated Approach, or Something Else?", in *Journal of International Criminal Justice*, 2014, vol. 12, no. 2, p. 300.

Consequently, it cannot be expected that Article 25(3) of the Rome Statute necessarily constitutes a precise and sufficient expression of the content or limits of international criminal law on participation in universal crimes.[50] Furthermore, the relevant modes of liability in the statutes of other international criminal tribunals may sometimes have been quite pragmatically drawn.[51]

The law on punishable participation has so far been one of the most contested legal subject matters at the international criminal institutions, and notably also at the ICC. The ICC rendered its first judgments in 2012, in the cases of Lubanga Dyilo and Ngudjolo Chui.[52] Both judgments came with sharply dissenting opinions on the understanding of certain forms of participation, which involved disagreement on the structure and normative character of Article 25(3). Also, in the 2014 ICC Katanga judgment,[53] the judges were sharply divided on several issues relevant to the subject matter of this book. In particular, the controversy regarding the notion of 'indirect co-perpetration' has continued, although it appears to have abated somewhat – maybe temporarily, depending on changes among the current pool of judges, or because a certain understanding is about to be settled.[54]

Clearly, these and other more recent judgments are not the end of what must be seen as a natural and necessary legal discourse. They are thus important decisions that need to be examined at some length in this book. The point at this stage is that the Rome Statute does not provide easy answers to the broad questions posed at the outset of this chapter.

1.2.5. The 'Differential' and 'Unitary' Models and Their Limits

The statutes and jurisprudence of international criminal courts seem to have proven that the real choice is not between two clear, comprehensive

---

[50] On the methodological challenges relating to the legal bases of universal crimes norms and personal liability, see Chapter 4.

[51] See the overview in Currie and Rikhof, 2013, pp. 642–43, *supra* note 3.

[52] ICC, Trial Chamber, *Prosecutor v. Lubanga*, Judgment, ICC-01/04-01/06, 14 March 2012 (www.legal-tools.org/doc/677866/); and ICC, Trial Chamber, *Prosecutor v. Chui*, Judgment, ICC-01/04-02/12, 18 December 2012 (www.legal-tools.org/doc/2c2cde/).

[53] ICC, Trial Chamber, *Prosecutor v. Katanga*, Judgment, ICC-01/04-01/07, 7 March 2014 (www.legal-tools.org/doc/f74b4f/).

[54] See further documentation and discussion at various points in Chapters 6–9 and conclusions in Chapter 10, Section 10.5.2.3.

models: on the one hand, a so-called 'differential model' that typically includes defined subcategories of punishable participation, and on the other hand, a simpler 'unitary model' that may distinguish only between perpetrators and accomplices, or may not even distinguish between perpetrators and other participants in a crime. Such theoretical or analytical models, while too limited, may nevertheless help to clarify our thinking and could potentially assist in solving interpretative issues. A separate problem in this regard, though, is that the 'model' terminology is not clear, and an accurate distinction between the two models has not been generally agreed upon.[55]

One way of explaining the distinction is to identify two different versions of each model, resulting in four model types:[56]

1) Unitary model, strong version

2) Unitary model, light/modified version

3) Differentiated model, light/modified version

4) Differentiated model, strong version

In the first alternative, all sufficiently blameworthy/socially dangerous participants are considered perpetrators. Their different roles and degrees of participation are, however, defined and taken into account for sentencing purposes. This provides for a flexible, cost-effective, no-empty-pockets system of liability attribution, but at the same time it allows for a great deal of legal uncertainty and possibly also abuse with respect to which acts of contribution are punishable and prosecuted. It does not in itself resolve issues concerned with 'inchoate liability', that is, possible liability when the crime is not completed (for example, liability for conspiracy, planning, or attempt).

In the second alternative, all punishable participants are considered to be either perpetrators or accomplices. Whether a person is one or the other may be decided at conviction, but there is no legal requirement to so decide. The participants' different roles and degrees of participation are,

---

[55] See also Chapter 6, Section 6.2.2.2., on unitary and differentiated approaches to classifying personal criminal law liability.

[56] The following explanation is adapted from lectures by one of the authors (Einarsen) in courses on ICL at the University of Bergen, Norway.

however, defined and taken into account for sentencing purposes. The pluses and minuses are much the same as for the first model type.

In the third alternative, all punishable participants are again considered to be either perpetrators or accomplices, but under this model each person's status in that respect *must* be decided at conviction. Under this version accomplices typically get lighter sentences, all else equal.

In the last alternative, all punishable participants or contributors to the criminal enterprise must fulfil the material and mental elements of particular legal subcategories or 'modes' of participation/liability as requirements before conviction. This option also offers clear solutions to different forms of inchoate liability. As a strong version of the differentiated model, it provides the advantage of more foreseeability (legal certainty) and, in principle, fair labelling, but it has the disadvantage of being less flexible and more complex, and thus also less cost-effective to apply properly without well-trained prosecutors, lawyers, and judges. Under this version, participants being attributed some form of accomplice (or inchoate) liability typically also get lighter sentences than participants attributed some form of commission liability. But here the different modes of liability may, in combination with the guilty person's placement within the relevant power structure, provide somewhat more precise guidance to the sentencing – although the gravity assessment central to sentencing cannot be done meaningfully without also taking the actual crimes at the relevant crime scenes into account.[57]

However, other descriptions of the different models are also possible. For example, Stewart maintains a blog on forms of attribution in ICL in which he highlights three different versions of what he terms 'the unitary theory'.[58] He explains that the first one, a 'pure unitary theory', "treats a causal contribution to a crime coupled with the requisite blameworthy moral choice announced in the criminal offence charges as neces-

---

[57] In Chapter 10, Section 10.7.3., the relationship between personal liability and proportionate sentencing in universal crimes cases is illustrated through two closely related graphs, showing the 'gravity function model' and the 'responsibility function model'.

[58] James G. Stewart, "An Open Invitation to Further Debate (Instead of an Amicus Brief)", blog of James G. Stewart, 18 October 2017 (www.legal-tools.org/doc/bdfc1d/). Thus, according to Stewart, "the various forms of participation that exist in current ICL (aiding and abetting, JCE, co-perpetration etc.) are stripped of their autonomous existence and folded into a more capacious single notion of attribution".

sary and sufficient elements of responsibility (excuses and justifications aside)".[59] This resembles the 'strong version' (alternative 1) of the unitary model outlined above. Stewart's second version provides more detail without compromising the unitary core, through "different forms of causal connections that might apply within a unitary framework". This has a different emphasis than the light version (alternative 2) of the unitary model. The third version of the unitary theory within Stewart's framework is only concerned with sentencing: "subjecting accomplices to the same range of punishment as perpetrators also constitutes a weak type of unitary theory". Although Stewart himself is a well-known proponent of the unitary theory, preferably the pure unitary theory as we understand him, blog posts by other authors on Stewart's site express different views.[60]

A unitary model may typically define the *executors* of the underlying crimes as perpetrators, whereas all other participants who have contributed to the commission of the crime are considered *accomplices*, even though the punishment may be the same. These other participants may alternatively fall under different forms of 'extended' liability, as compared to the 'principal' (core) liability of the executor. If these are recognised as separate categories of criminal liability, the system would change character to a 'differential' model. According to a more limited version of the unitary concept set forth by Vest, however – or, conversely, a broad definition of the differentiated model – "every system that distinguishes – by statute – between perpetrators and accessories" ought to be classified as following a differentiated model.[61] The same point of view is shared by Stewart[62] and by Finnin:

> In contrast to the unitary perpetrator model, under the differential participation model it is possible to distinguish at least

---

[59] *Ibid.* The other quotations in this paragraph are also from the same blog post by Stewart.

[60] For example, Albin Eser, "Questions from the Unconvinced", 14 October 2017 (www.legal-tools.org/doc/e559fc/), expresses serious doubts in general on a number of points, while Jørn Jacobsen, "Norway: Three Codes, Three (Somewhat) Different Solutions", 8 October 2017 (www.legal-tools.org/doc/4d020e/), argues from a domestic perspective that "the history of Norwegian criminal law at least is not a particularly strong argument for the potential of a unitary theory internationally".

[61] Vest, 2014, p. 306, see *supra* note 49.

[62] James G. Stewart, "The End of 'Modes of Liability' for International Crimes", in *Leiden Journal of International Law*, 2012, vol. 25, no. 1, pp. 165–219. He assumes that under a unitary model, complicity disintegrates into a broader notion of perpetration.

---

two types of parties to a crime, being principal perpetrators and accessories.[63]

A fully unitary system may have some advantages, especially with respect to sentencing for crime types with a simpler structure, while it is arguable whether it will facilitate fair prosecution of more complex crimes. But it should also be noted that a more differentiated system, especially when applied to complex universal crimes, may run the risk of leaving (partially) 'empty pockets' of space for blameworthy or socially dangerous conduct in cases where conduct is not easily covered by any of the enumerated and 'differentiated' categories of punishable participation. This may put judges in a difficult situation, caught between expectations of the legality principle or broader notions of the rule of law, on one hand,[64] and the object of minimising impunity as well as not being forced to understate the degree of responsibility, on the other.

One famous example is the ICTY Tadić case mentioned earlier. In this case the judges solved the dilemma by establishing a new subcategory of participation, called 'joint criminal enterprise' ('JCE'), notably without a clear legal basis in the wording ("committed [...] a crime") of Article 7(1) of the ICTY Statute. Despite being contested, especially the further subcategory of JCE referred to as JCE III, JCE has been much applied in the jurisprudence of the ICTY and other international criminal tribunals, notably the International Criminal Tribunal for Rwanda ('ICTR'). The underlying issue is illustrated more generally, especially in Chapters 2 and 7. In Chapter 2, we shall provide a theoretical explanation, and thus implicitly also a possible legal justification, for this judicial creation, which might be compatible with our proposed general theory on personal criminal law liability.

The Rome Statute, Article 25(3), clearly falls under a differentiated model of participation. Other international court statutes and transitional

---

[63] Sarah Finnin, *Elements of Accessorial Modes of Liability: Article 25(3)(b) and (c) of the Rome Statute of the International Criminal Court*, Martinus Nijhoff, Leiden, 2012, pp. 12–13, at p. 13.

[64] A recurrent theme in this book concerns a possible theoretical and/or normative distinction between expectations of the international legality principle and somewhat 'softer' expectations of the broader notion of rule of law, precisely with regard to attribution of criminal law liability. See Chapter 2, Section 2.2.2.1., Chapter 4, Section 4.3.7., Chapter 6, Section 6.2.2.4., and Chapter 10, Section 10.8.

justice models seem more difficult to classify properly. For example, Vest has argued that the Statutes of the Nuremberg and Tokyo Military Tribunals "are typical examples of the unitary approach since even they do not distinguish between different forms of perpetration or participation at all".[65] The International Law Commission ('ILC'), on the other hand, when extracting the Nuremberg Principles from the very same statutes and trials, clearly distinguished between one who commits a crime under international law and complicity in the commission of such a crime:

> Principle I: Any person who commits an act which constitutes a crime under international law is responsible therefor and liable to punishment.

> Principle VII: Complicity in the commission of a crime [...] is a crime under international law.[66]

Consequently, under a strict definition of the unitary model, the Nuremberg Principles contain a differentiated model, while they express a unitary model according to a somewhat broader definition of that model. Moreover, it is not always made clear in the literature whether the models are applied to the expression of guilt or to the sentencing, or to both. Under a differentiated model, the point would be that the classification of punishable participation typically has some direct consequences for the level of punishment, while under a unitary model there would not be differentiated starting points on that basis.

Strangely enough, perhaps, the differentiated model of Rome Statute Article 25(3) with respect to personal liability is combined with a unitary approach to sentencing, since the range of punishment is the same regardless of the particular mode of participation. But even this proposition must be further qualified, because Rule 145(1) of the Rules on Procedure and Evidence of the Rome Statute holds that the judge when determining the sentence "shall" give consideration to the "degree of participation" of the convicted person. While the "degree" of participation is not *per se* equal to the mode or form of participation, and while the degree of participation might rather be considered a function of the mode and a

---

[65] Vest, 2014, p. 306, see *supra* note 49.

[66] International Law Commission ('ILC'), *Principles of International Law Recognized in the Charter of the Nürnberg Tribunal and in the Judgment of the Tribunal*, reprinted in *Yearbook of the International Law Commission, 1950*, vol. II, para. 97 (www.legal-tools.org/doc/0d1ffe/).

more specific assessment of the individual contribution to the crime as well as placement within the relevant power structure, the particular mode of participation may have an impact on the sentencing.[67] That seems to underpin the viewpoint that classification of participation is to some extent compulsory under the Rome Statute, presumably in compliance with the structure set out in Article 25(3).[68] In fact this latter observation touches on a much larger discussion of the need for these and similar classification exercises in the theory and practice of ICL, spurred in particular by Stewart.[69] We will revisit this discussion of principles later in this book.

In conclusion, one has to be quite careful when employing the language of 'unitary' and 'differentiated' models or approaches in ICL discourse.[70] It might be useful to keep in mind that ICL recognises a perpetrator-accomplice distinction in labelling guilt, while sentencing is predominantly unitary.[71] The main point at this stage, however, is simply that the models cannot by themselves solve the interpretative issues posed at the outset of this book. Furthermore, and importantly from a theoretical perspective, a general theory of personal criminal law liability should not be established on the basis of a more or less well-argued *policy choice* between the unitary and differentiated models (or their variations), at least not on such a basis alone. In order to seek a general theory, it might be necessary to start elsewhere.

1.3. The Need for a General Theory of Participation

In contemporary ICL, both legal theory and practices may at first glance appear to be amazingly unsettled on many issues of punishable participa-

---

[67] See, for example, Vest, 2014, pp. 308–9, *supra* note 49. Vest has proposed a somewhat different approach, namely a "two-step model" for sentencing determination that "must consider first, the mode and second, the degree of participation". The difference is arguably concerned only with best labelling, not with substance. The relationship between participation and sentencing is also discussed in Chapter 10, Section 10.7.3., of this book.

[68] See *ibid.*, pp. 307–8 (with further references to other authors).

[69] See, for example, Stewart, 2012, *supra* note 62.

[70] This seems also to be the conclusion of Van Sliedregt, 2012, p. 73, see *supra* note 1: "What appears from the overview of criminal participation is that the distinction between the two 'meta-models', between differentiated systems and unitary systems, [...] is fading. [...] On paper, differentiated and unitary models are distinct but in practice, by borrowing elements from one another, the line between them is difficult to draw".

[71] Along the same lines, see *ibid.*, p. 37.

tion. The problem concerns not only overall content and the formulations of relevant categories and subcategories of participation, but also how many categories and possible combinations of categories are lawful or useful in order to determine and classify punishable participation – and, consequently, how one exempts other kinds of participation from criminal liability.

Several authors have noted that substantive international criminal law is under-theorised and lacks a common general part, and that uniformity rather than pluralism should be the norm at the level of *international* criminal law. This argument is made by, among others, Van Sliedregt:

> By looking beyond labels and concepts differences may be minimized to allow for developing a true international theory of criminal responsibility. Such an approach may have added value in that it stays the current trend of fragmentation in international law. [...] Pluralism at the international level should be accepted only to the extent that international statutory law compels to do so.[72]

A general theory of punishable participation in universal crimes may thus serve to meet some of the pressing need for synthesising seemingly isolated bits and pieces of ICL, also seeking in the long run to harmonise conflicting rules and inconsistent jurisprudence of international criminal law. This project to advance the concept of universal crimes as well as a principled theory of punishable participation should therefore also be seen in light of the reasoning of the International Law Commission, which has claimed that international law is a legal system and that its rules and principles "should be interpreted against the background of other rules and principles".[73]

Fletcher has furthermore argued that "we should actively encourage the writing of theoretical works that lay out the foundational principles of international criminal law", including "debates among scholars about the correct interpretation of special offences as well as the general principles

---

[72] *Ibid.*, p. 12.

[73] ILC, *Conclusions of the Work of the Study Group on the Fragmentation of International Law: Difficulties Arising from the Diversification and Expansion of International Law*, 2006, conclusion no. 1, reprinted in *Yearbook of the International Law Commission*, 2006, vol. II, part II (www.legal-tools.org/doc/6f7968/).

of liability".[74] He contrasts such works to the descriptive texts that are "necessary to disseminate practical knowledge about the way the court works and the role of the various parties to the proceedings",[75] but which are not sufficient for improvements of the law.

This research understanding seems now to be common across many parts of ICL, either intuitively applied or consciously implied in many scholarly works. The same trend is also expressed indirectly, as evidenced by the many "journal pages and abstract services [that] brim with rigorous, sophisticated, inter-disciplinary and theoretical works scrutinizing ICL from a multiplicity of perspectives".[76] But Ambos has argued that more needs to be done with respect to liability for 'macrocriminality':

> However, the growing practical importance of decentralized and supranational prosecutions of international atrocity crimes has not been accompanied by the development of a sufficiently theorized and principled system of liability for macrocriminal conduct drawing on sufficiently sophisticated rules of imputation (or attribution).[77]

The term 'macrocriminal conduct', as used by Ambos, was first developed by German criminologist Herbert Jäger "to capture the massive and systematic crimes of the Nazi dictatorship".[78] This concept is thus similar to other descriptive concepts such as 'mass atrocity' ('atrocity crimes') or 'system criminality', which characterise certain essential features typical of universal crimes (see Section 1.2.1. above).

Ambos has underlined another point that is relevant to our project, namely that ICL "must ultimately develop into an autonomous *sui generis* system duly taking into account the particularities of macrocriminal (as

---

[74] George P. Fletcher, "The Theory of Criminal Liability and International Criminal Law", in *Journal of International Criminal Justice*, 2012, vol. 10, no. 5, pp. 1029–44 (at pp. 1030–31).

[75] *Ibid.*, p. 1031.

[76] Darryl Robinson, "International Criminal Law as Justice", in *Journal of International Criminal Justice*, 2013, vol. 11, no. 3, pp. 699–711 (at p. 699).

[77] Kai Ambos, "Individual Liability for Macrocriminality: A Workshop, A Symposium and the Katanga Trial Judgment of 7 March 2014", in *Journal of International Criminal Justice*, 2014, vol. 12, no. 2, p. 219.

[78] *Ibid.* See Herbert Jäger, *Makrokriminalität: Studien zur Kriminologie kollektiver Gewalt*, Suhrkamp, Frankfurt am Main, 1989.

compared to ordinary) criminal conduct".[79] The words to be highlighted here are "autonomous" law and "the particularities" of such crimes. With respect to the latter, we have already pointed out briefly why participation in universal crimes is different from participation in most common crimes.[80] This theme will necessarily resurface throughout this book, because an understanding of both differences and similarities is important to the project.

Regarding the need for autonomous law, it would almost be a contradiction in terms if ICL as a field of 'international law' were *not* to be considered autonomous in the sense of being legally separate and to some extent also clearly independent from both national criminal law and international politics. Ambos's observations and advice are still very much to the point, though, because as he notes, ICL continues to "borrow its main elements and structures from domestic criminal law".[81] Consequently, prosecutors, defence lawyers, and judges at international tribunals might be inclined to rely more heavily on comparative criminal law studies and prevailing domestic doctrines or known traditions for interpretative purposes *lex lata* than would be justifiable under a developed system of autonomous international criminal law.[82]

The notion of a 'Dogmatik', as highlighted by Fletcher, might be helpful in this regard. He argues that "the absence of a Dogmatik may prevent the formation of an authentic system of international criminal law", while there is in actuality "room to build a proper theory of criminal liability in international criminal law".[83] Fletcher refers to the assertion of Günther Jakobs that a system of international criminal law requires an already existing and actually supreme Dogmatik,[84] and to a statement by Ernst von Caemmerer that the law is not "what the cases say, but the way in which the scholars read the cases".[85] In other words, a theory securing a place for an autonomous ('authentic') theory of criminal liability in ICL

---

[79] Ambos, 2014, p. 219, see *supra* note 77.

[80] See Section 1.2.2. in this chapter.

[81] Ambos, 2014, p. 219, see *supra* note 77.

[82] On the sources and methodology of ICL and the concept of *lex lata* as contrasted to *lex ferenda*, see Chapter 4.

[83] Fletcher, 2012, p. 1029, see *supra* note 74.

[84] *Ibid.*

[85] *Ibid.*, p. 1044.

should be built by scholars first and then applied by judges, instead of ICL being developed by judges and then just communicated by scholars as 'legal journalists'.

Although we agree with Fletcher and others that there is now a need for a proper theory of criminal liability in ICL to be worked out by scholars, it should be pointed out that the notion of Dogmatik is also ambiguous. It may denote *authoritative legal theory and legal writing independent from prevailing jurisprudence* (law in books, different from legal practice as law in action), as suggested by Fletcher. But we assume – perhaps more in accordance with mainstream Nordic legal theory – that it could also be taken to mean simply *autonomous law (lex lata)*, that is, the best legal end product (rule/interpretation) based on a proper legal methodology and the current legal sources and the closely linked considerations that are inherent in the relevant part of the legal system. The latter understanding would then include, among other sources, both 'judicial decisions' *and* 'the teachings of the most highly qualified publicists of the various nations' as important subsidiary sources of interpretation, in compliance with Article 38 of the Statute of the International Court of Justice ('ICJ').[86]

Hence there is not necessarily a choice to be made *between* a theory of criminal liability in ICL and the international sources of law (the legal bases, the interpretative sources, and the priority principles).[87] Rather, such a general theory should ideally be built analytically on the basis of all relevant texts and empirical sources, taking into account guidance and valuable viewpoints in the literature as well as in court cases and other legal materials, and it should recognise the distinction between *lex lata* and *lex ferenda* required to uphold the rule of law. A general theory should not necessarily be in opposition to current law at the operational levels, because the nature of the relationship between theory and practice depends on both factors. On the other hand, a certain practice may deviate on certain points from the theory and even from general international law. Thus, it does not make sense to develop a general theory applicable to the

---

[86] Fletcher himself notes that the "history of international documents is not entirely friendly to the German idea", and that while Article 38 of the ICJ Statute stipulates "the most highly qualified publicists" as a subsidiary source of law, the Rome Statute of the ICC seems to have "left out" the scholars (*ibid.*, p. 1030).

[87] See Chapter 4.

field of universal crimes that is unable to work within certain overarching legal parameters, including, but not limited to, the basic requirements of rule of law and fundamental human rights. If it does not take such a more general legal and values-based perspective into account, the theory is doomed to be useless within any criminal law subsystem aspiring and seeking to comply with those requirements, as is certainly the case of ICL. This means, conversely, that the theory may well aim to contribute to a better law in the future by keeping international law and practice in line with the theory and by bringing it into line where it is not, and may slowly influence domestic practice as well, also with regard to its *lex ferenda* parts; but the theory itself should not claim status as 'the law'.

This principled position echoes the standpoint taken in the first book in the series: the conception of 'universal crimes' includes both universal crimes *lex lata* (international crimes) and potential universal crimes *lex ferenda*.[88] In the same way, a general theory of punishable participation should accept that there might be certain parts or potential parts of the theory that are not necessarily clearly reflected in current law (*lex lata*), because the theory might be open to different solutions. For example, under a general theory it could be that some types of contributions to universal crimes through participation in the relevant power structures should be considered distinct crimes *lex ferenda* under certain conditions, and thus may in the future be constituted as crimes *lex lata*. If so, this assertion might fall within the predictions and functioning of such a general theory.

What is meant, then, by a general theory of participation in international crimes or universal crimes? The main points are that it needs to be 'general' and 'a theory'. A 'theory' is a rational type of abstract thinking or generalising, or the results of such thinking. Today theories are viewed as scientific models, and this also applies to law. A model is a logical framework intended to represent reality, in our case normative legal reality. This means that the model must relate to descriptive and normative facts represented by the relevant sources of law, just as a map is a graphic model that represents the physical territory of a city or country. Note, however, that it is also meaningful to make a map that shows, for example, how a city should be reconstructed or extended by new buildings and streets. In the same way, it is possible to provide a model of law that takes

---

[88] See generally Einarsen, 2012, and Einarsen, 2013, *supra* note 8.

into account both current law and how the law should be revised in order to fulfil the necessary criteria for a 'good law' according to certain standards or agreed principles of criminal law. That the theory in our case should be 'general' means that the theory should apply with the same content across all parts of international criminal law, including when ICL is applied in domestic proceedings. However, even if the *theory* is general, the theory may be open to different models such as the unitary and differentiated models, and, even more important, open to the formulation and application of personal criminal law liability within different operational criminal law subsystems. In Chapters 5–9 we shall survey the use of different ICL liability concepts in different sources at both the international and domestic levels, while Chapter 10 considers the possibility of an autonomous ICL matrix consistent with the general theory.

Consequently, it would seem logical to characterise the possible *result* of such a scientific enterprise as a 'universal theory of punishable participation in atrocity', to borrow a bit from a similar expression used by Stewart.[89] He argues on 10 different but interconnected grounds for a *universal concept of participation*,[90] which would apply whenever an international crime is charged, regardless of the jurisdiction hearing the case, while at the same time he attempts to remain agnostic about the *content* of this universal notion of participation that he advocates.[91] Since the universal crimes project is based on similar reasoning, we shall take his conclusion at face value for this book. Such a concept – if possible and desirable to establish – may perhaps apply most intuitively to the *horizontal* (international) level of ICL. It would then serve the purpose of achieving greater unity at the international level. It might also be applicable to the *vertical* level of ICL, that is, to domestic universal crimes cases based on or inspired by international law. To be applicable and useful at one or both levels, however, a *universal* concept of participation must have a sound liability theory behind it. Any theory claiming such status must be built on both theory and practice, as well as on the broader legal frameworks of ICL such as fundamental human rights. Furthermore, it is of utmost im-

---

[89] James G. Stewart, "Ten Reasons for Adopting a Universal Concept of Participation in Atrocity", in Elies van Sliedregt and Sergey Vasiliev (eds.), *Pluralism in International Criminal Law*, Oxford University Press, Oxford, 2014, pp. 320–41.

[90] *Ibid.*, p. 321.

[91] *Ibid.*, p. 322.

portance to our project that we, probably in contrast to Stewart, make a distinction between, on one hand, *the theoretical/analytical levels*, where we seek a general theory of personal criminal law liability – indeed with a view to global or 'universal application' within ICL – and, on the other hand, application of this theory as presumably useful ramifications and guidance for fair attribution of liability at *the operational level* of the various subsystems of criminal law. This book is thus primarily concerned with the search for and the components and content of such a theory, and with its empirical foundation and operational legal context.

When exploring the preconditions for establishing a general theory, one may ask whether other theoretical works seem to be particularly useful for the analytical part of this book. What we have been looking for in that regard is works that transcend the domestic/international criminal law division and specific national criminal law traditions. The theoretical and analytical 'matrix' developed by Hallevy on derivative criminal liability represents such a work.[92] This matrix has not been developed with a view to international criminal law or universal crimes in particular, but is meant to provide a theory of derivative criminal liability in general. We shall make substantial use of his work in Chapter 2, where the meaning of 'derivative' liability is explained and discussed.[93]

Before proposing any potential general legal theory, it might also be useful to undertake a sociological survey on the participants in universal crimes that have been prosecuted before international courts.[94] Criminology ideally should be consulted, especially with a view to understanding the *causal* factors of mass atrocity,[95] which might be useful when seeking,

---

[92] Gabriel Hallevy, *The Matrix of Derivative Criminal Liability*, Springer, Heidelberg, 2012.

[93] In brief, 'derivative' criminal liability has usually been taken to mean that the liability of one person is dependent upon the commission of the crime by another person; see Finnin, 2012, p. 94, *supra* note 63. Thus, it is the execution that 'constitutes the crime' in question, so to speak, and the liability of others is therefore made dependent upon the acts of the executor. However, in this book we critique such a conceptual understanding; see in particular Chapter 2, Section 2.2.2.4., on the principle of fair attribution of personal liability.

[94] One such study is undertaken in Chapter 3, with regard to the positions of the various participants within the power structures and support structures employed to commit universal crimes in society.

[95] For an interesting account, differentiating between situational aspects and the characteristics of the individual perpetrators, see Stefan Harrendorf, "How Can Criminology Contribute to an Explanation of International Crimes?", in *Journal of International Criminal Justice*, 2014, vol. 12, no. 2, pp. 231–52.

for instance, to measure the preventive effect of criminalisation of different forms of participation. In addition, before recommending the general theory for analysis within ICL, it also seems necessary to undertake more empirical surveys of liability concepts that have so far been used internationally as well as domestically in universal crimes cases,[96] before finally drawing conclusions on the usefulness of the theory.[97]

The main point thus far, however, has been to demonstrate that there is now some important scholarly support for the need to develop and discuss a general theory of personal ICL liability relating to punishable participation in universal crimes. Practitioners at international criminal institutions may also support such a move, since progress towards harmonisation of liability guided by a general theory might be considered more beneficial to the future of ICL than pluralism or fragmentation by those actors who are ultimately responsible for judging the criminal responsibilities of particular persons.[98] Hence we agree with Van Sliedregt and Vasiliev that theorists of pluralism "ought to be aware of how pluralism is experienced on the ground in refining their normative arguments".[99]

However, this last point can be generalised beyond pluralism; in fact it applies to all kinds of theoretical legal works, we believe. In this book we have at least attempted to let that wisdom guide our own work on this most challenging subject matter. Whether the project turns out to be successful or not in that regard remains to be seen.

1.4. Chapter Previews

Chapter 2, entitled "Establishing the General Theory of Personal Liability", attempts to establish a general theory of personal criminal law liability that applies to punishable participation in universal crimes. It is in many ways the key chapter of the book. The chapter first sets forth the

---

[96] See Chapters 5–9.

[97] See Chapter 10.

[98] See Elies van Sliedregt and Sergey Vasiliev, "Pluralism: A New Framework for International Criminal Justice", in Elies van Sliedregt and Sergey Vasiliev (eds.), *Pluralism in International Criminal Law*, Oxford University Press, Oxford, 2014, p. 38: "By the same token, certain chapters – especially those written by the practitioners – evince deep suspicion about pluralism and make a case for a greater consolidation of ICL; however, other contributions, typically written by scholars, show more benevolence toward the phenomenon at issue. This in itself is a revealing finding".

[99] *Ibid.*

theoretical preconditions and requirements for a sound scientific theory of personal criminal law liability. It then presents a comprehensive theory consisting of a four-level normative structure: (1) the *supra*-principle of free choice; (2) four fundamental principles of personal criminal law liability; (3) four secondary principles of fair attribution of liability, with further derivative principles that are key to understanding how the general theory provides a framework for predicting and organising criminal liability, not only theoretically but also practically; and (4) the specific provisions of the operational criminal law systems. The fourth level is where the modes of liability (or modes of participation) form part of the general theory. The different components of the general theory, their relationship, and the important implications of a basic type of criminal liability are set forth in detail. However, the theory also needs to be tested against the backdrop of empirical surveys of personal liability concepts in ICL sources (see below).

Chapter 2 also identifies three classes of personal liability – inchoate liability, commission liability, and accomplice liability – and 12 liability categories, as well as further derivative forms of personal liability. This analytical tool is later employed explicitly or implicitly when organising the empirical studies and assessing the findings, although with some flexibility. The chapter concludes by making the case for the possibility of developing an ICL matrix on formation and modes of liability.

Chapter 3, "Universal Crimes Participation in Historical and Sociological Context", provides broader perspectives on the legal liability analysis undertaken in other parts of this book. Notably, this chapter identifies 20 sociological *categories* of participants and groups them into four overarching classes: (1) high-level participants, that is, individuals in the upper ranks of main power structures; (2) mid-level participants, those in the intermediate ranks of main power structures; (3) low-level participants, those at the lower ranks of main power structures or, in some cases, within lesser power structures; and (4) participants in power support structures. The chapter also attempts to couple the sociological analysis with an extensive survey of the different modes of liability employed in the cases prosecuted at international tribunals. This leads to some interesting findings that are useful for the further work on the general theory as well.

Chapter 4, "Legal Bases of Universal Crimes Norms and Personal Liability", provides additional context to the general theory. It confronts methodological issues and notes the fragmented character of current international criminal law. It suggests that a concept of universal crimes that also includes a general theory of personal ICL liability may contribute to a more coherent understanding of the existing legal framework. In this regard, the application of different liability concepts in ICL – which may sometimes lack a clear basis in the statutes of international tribunals – is discussed under the heading of the legality principle and attribution of personal criminal law liability. The chapter explains the need to distinguish the law-creating sources from other interpretative sources of international law and to keep in mind a clear, principled distinction between the law as it is (*lex lata*) and the law as it should be (*lex ferenda*).

Chapters 5 through 9 examine the concepts or categories that have been used in various parts of international criminal law and related fields to express punishable participation. Chapter 5, "Personal Liability Concepts in Treaties, Statutes, and Works of the ILC", surveys the early treaties and statutes of international institutions in both international criminal law and transnational criminal law, preparatory works, and statements of the International Law Commission. It notes shortcomings in the ILC's recent work on attribution of personal criminal liability and concludes that the commission's aspiration to reflect both progressive development and codification of international law has thus far not been accomplished in the area of criminal participation in universal crimes – not in the codification aspect and even less so in the progressive development of international law. This critique undoubtedly reflects the general difficulty of the subject matter, but it may also be that the work of the ILC in this area suffers from the lack of a general theory of ICL personal liability.

Chapter 6, "Personal Liability Concepts in the Literature", considers the main viewpoints in the scholarly literature on personal ICL liability. It includes the works of authors who discuss punishable participation at large – issues like comparative law versus autonomous ICL approaches, and unitary versus differentiated approaches – as well as authors who treat specific concepts of participation. The attribution of personal criminal liability for participation in universal crimes has been a highly controversial topic, causing a number of disagreements and at times confusion within the scholarly literature. The chapter asserts an urgent need to situate the smaller but often important subtopics within a larger theory of attribution that would be capable of addressing all issues simultaneously.

Chapter 7, "Personal Liability Concepts in the International Jurisprudence", surveys the jurisprudence of six international criminal tribunals since 1993 with respect to attribution of personal liability and the concepts employed. The chapter organises the modes of liability in three classes –inchoate liability, commission and omission liability, and accomplice liability – with a total of 15 derivative forms across the three classes. A general trend has been to use all three liability classes, although inchoate liability only to a limited degree. Most of the 12 liability categories have also been used during this period, as well as several further derivative forms of personal liability. Through these legal formations, participants in different parts of large criminal enterprises closely connected to power structures in society have been held responsible for universal crimes at the international level. This has served to develop the contours of ICL as an autonomous legal field, one that reflect a common jurisprudence despite the various ICL subsystems it originates from. This does not mean, however, that there have not been disagreements or controversies between judges or between the different institutions.

Chapters 8 and 9 shift the focus of the empirical survey to what has been happening in domestic universal crimes cases, when personal liability concepts have been interpreted and applied under the possible influence of ICL at the international level. Chapter 8, "Personal Liability Concepts in Domestic Universal Crimes Cases Based on Nationality and Universal Jurisdiction", surveys and discusses the law and jurisprudence of 15 Western countries that have used extra-territorial jurisdiction to prosecute participants in universal crimes for acts committed elsewhere in the world. Chapter 9, "Personal Liability Concepts in Domestic Universal Crimes Cases Based on Territorial Jurisdiction", likewise examines prosecution of participants in crimes committed and prosecuted under territorial jurisdiction in 12 countries on four continents. The two chapters find that despite some notable differences, the parameters of concepts often used at international courts, such as co-perpetration and aiding and abetting, were remarkably consistent in Asia, Africa, Europe, and Latin and North America, and also consistent with the general trends of application at the international courts, even when no explicit reliance was placed on international precedents or jurisprudence. Hence this part of the empirical survey underpins the view that reasonably consistent application of key liability concepts within all levels and subsystems of ICL is possible and within practical reach.

Chapter 10, "Towards an Autonomous ICL Matrix of Personal Liability", summarises and discusses the results of the preceding analysis. It seeks to answer the question of whether there is a theoretical as well as an empirical basis for identifying an autonomous ICL matrix of personal criminal liability, in compliance with our proposed general theory of punishable participation in universal crimes. After a review of essential findings of the earlier chapters, Chapter 10 concludes that the general theory as a scientific model, now tested by means of empirical studies, in effect provides us with such a matrix. This means that any possible form of personal liability for universal crimes – whether a mode of liability is currently in existence or foreseeable in the future – can be described and classified theoretically and evaluated for (further) implementation. Because the ICL matrix has been especially developed to apply to universal crimes and is not limited to a particular international or national subsystem, the matrix has an autonomous character in the sense of not being tied to the law as it currently stands in time and space. Appendix I also explains the matrix of personal criminal liability as developed in this book, and contains a list of the basic and derivative forms of liability as well as the recommendable parameters (criteria) of each derivative form listed.

From a future-oriented, practical perspective, the ICL matrix is differentiated and flexible in nature and thus easily applicable to different purposes. More importantly, it provides for foreseeable criminalisation and attribution of liability. This means that fair labelling and fair attribution of liability based on differentiated forms of liability are very much possible now, whereas backtracking to a new choice between a unitary and differentiated approach at the international level likely would have led to a great deal of legal uncertainty in future universal crimes cases. The book concludes by asserting that the main principles inherent in the general theory of punishable participation in universal crimes are actually part of general international law, and as such, are essential to aspirations of an international rule of law seeking a secure substantial basis for holding responsible persons to account.

2

Establishing the General Theory
of Personal Liability

2.1. Searching for a Theory of Personal Criminal Law Liability

2.1.1. Introductory Remarks and Delimitations

This chapter provides theoretical, historical, and sociological perspectives on participation in universal crimes. The purpose of the chapter is to search for and consider a basis for a general theory of personal criminal law liability, one that has general application and can be further developed as a model for assessing punishable participation. The next section (2.2.) is concerned with the theoretical preconditions, requirements, and potential components of such a theory. It should be noted from the outset that the theory we seek is not intended to constitute a complete theory of criminal law or criminal law liability. Thus this chapter, in accordance with the book as a whole, focuses upon aspects relevant to the identification, assessment, and, ultimately, application of personal criminal law liability for punishable participation in criminal enterprises and collective crimes relevant to universal crimes, which is of great theoretical and practical interest to the field of ICL. The key concepts will be further explained as this chapter proceeds.

In the remainder of this first section, we start our analysis with a basic issue: What is the 'legitimate aim' of criminal law liability under the 'rule of law'? From this simple but important point of departure we shall move to the prerequisites of a sound scientific theory of personal criminal law liability.

2.1.2. The Legitimate Aim of Criminal Law

A classic dictionary definition of 'crime' is "an offence for which one may be punished by law".[1] Criminal law usually refers to a body of substantive legal rules prescribing some kind of punishment for acts considered un-

---

[1] *Oxford Advanced Learner's Dictionary of Current English, Encyclopedic Edition*, Oxford University Press, Oxford, 1992, s.v. 'crime'.

lawful. This definition and explanation is socially and politically neutral and might be useful for several analytical purposes. However, if the purpose is to search for a general theory of 'criminal law', complete neutrality is not desirable or scientifically sustainable. The reason is that criminal law is part of human society, and human societies are never 'neutral' with respect to the infliction of criminal liability and punishment.

A distinction needs to be drawn between societies that have implemented social structures that seek to adhere to the rule of law, on one hand, and societies under the rule of man, on the other. A general theory of criminal law liability only makes sense in societies of the first type, because in the second type people would be punished arbitrarily and with no respect for the meaning of 'law'. For the purpose of this book, the distinction does not create any particular problem, however. International criminal law has been developed within the United Nations ('UN') paradigm of international law, which includes respect for human dignity and international human rights law, as well as respect for international humanitarian law. By implication, human rights norms in particular provide limitations with respect to the types of social harm and endangerment that may legitimately be criminalised. At the same time, human rights norms express fundamental social values and interests of a society governed by rule of law and thus might usefully be upheld and reinforced through attribution of criminal law liability as well.

Typically, the law criminalises culpable commission of offences because of the social and human harm caused by their commission and because of the social need to (1) facilitate justice for victims, (2) uphold social values in compliance with fundamental human rights and the rule of law, (3) influence behaviour in society, and (4) prevent similar offences in the future. Sometimes prevention is emphasised more than victim justice and other reasons for punishment, and sometimes it is the other way around. Modern societies also accept social endangerment or risk of harm, in addition to actual social and human harm, as a basis for criminalisation. To prevent harm and to prevent endangerment are both recognised legitimate aims of criminal law.[2] In the preamble to the Rome Statute, the States Parties express the aim "to put an end to impunity" for the perpetra-

---

[2] At the domestic level, across national jurisdictions, there is a vast amount of literature on the purpose of criminal law and the aims of criminalisation that cannot be referenced here.

tors of the relevant crimes "and thus to contribute to the prevention of such crimes". The purpose of ending impunity in effect comprises all four social goals mentioned above with respect to the crimes that are punishable under the Rome Statute.

The more sophisticated justifications for criminal law liability and punishment fall outside the scope of this book. Although this may sound surprising, since the book addresses a general theory of criminal liability, the reason is simple. This work is concerned with the construction and viability of a theory of punishable participation that takes the foregoing legitimate aims of criminal law liability for granted, in line with mainstream social and legal science within a rule of law context. This does not imply that our analysis cannot provide new insights on the subject matter of concern.

An important underlying proposition is the following: when several people choose to participate in a criminal enterprise, the social endangerment or risk of harm may be increased several times over because offences committed by a group are more likely to succeed. This is so because each member may contribute special skills and assist the others, and – closely connected – because the social endangerment is larger than the actual harm committed at a given crime scene.[3] While there is usually a limit to how many times a single offender can repeat the same criminal conduct without being caught, especially if the crime is serious, a criminal organisation can replace individual members, more easily change the *modus operandi*, and survive criminal prosecution of low-level participants identified as being involved in a particular crime or caught at a particular crime scene.

In consequence, this logic requires criminalisation by legislation or judicial attribution (through case law) of other forms of liability in addition to singular 'perpetration', that is, the physical completion of the crime committed by one person. Examples of such other forms are 'joint

---

[3]   See Gabriel Hallevy, *The Matrix of Derivative Criminal Liability*, Springer, Heidelberg, 2012, p. 33: "Because offenses committed by complicity [in a broad sense] are more likely to succeed, their prevention by the authorities is more difficult. As a result, complicity is considered socially more dangerous than the actual perpetration of the offense. Coordination between members of the offending group enables the group to commit more sophisticated and efficient offenses, many more times". It should be noted that Hallevy uses the concept of 'complicity' here in a broad sense.

perpetration', 'conspiracy', 'complicity', and 'incitement'. Certain forms of participation might be criminalised as distinct crimes when related to specific conduct, for instance, 'conspiracy' to terrorist crimes or 'incitement' to violent acts or 'public incitement' to genocide.[4] In some cases it might be uncertain whether the relevant conduct is criminalised as a distinct (inchoate) crime or only through the modes of liability.[5] The point for now is that harmful or dangerous contribution to a criminal enterprise is often made punishable, either expressly, through distinct criminalisation of the relevant conduct in statutes, or implicitly, through judicial attribution of criminal liability for the participation in completed crimes. This is necessary in order to more effectively influence or direct how people should act, and to uphold, transform, and develop the values and social behaviour considered important by society. The most serious crimes typically constitute substantial social harm, but they tend also to be socially very dangerous and clearly blameworthy acts – although a justification or an excuse for the individual actor who engages in the proscribed conduct could be available in law and applicable, or at least arguable, as a defence in some cases.[6]

Universal crimes obviously differ from serious common crimes in several ways, but the rationales of social harm, social endangerment, and blameworthiness all apply. To begin with, universal crimes are serious crimes that are usually of greater magnitude and graveness than common crimes. In the preamble to the Rome Statute of the International Criminal Court, they are considered able to "shock the conscience of humanity" and even "threaten the peace, security and well-being of the world".[7] Such

---

[4] This is an issue to which we shall return later in this chapter, and at several other points in this book.

[5] This is also an issue to which we shall return later in this chapter.

[6] Issues of justifications and excuses receive only cursory attention in this book, which focuses on the material and mental elements of universal crimes participation. Instead those issues will be analysed in a planned later book in this series, on accountability for universal crimes participation. See the preface to this book and as well as the preface to the first book in the series: Terje Einarsen, *The Concept of Universal Crimes in International Law*, Torkel Opsahl Academic EPublisher, Oslo, 2012 (www.legal-tools.org/doc/bfda36/).

[7] See Rome Statute of the International Criminal Court (hereafter cited as Rome Statute), 17 July 1998, Preamble, paras. 3 and 4 (www.legal-tools.org/doc/7b9af9/). The Rome Statute is a living instrument, as the ICC's Assembly of States Parties can periodically amend it according to a certain procedure. References to the Rome Statute in this book are to the current version, which for all practical purposes is identical to the 2010 amended version.

crimes usually occur when collective entities – powerful organisations – are used to order or encourage atrocities to be committed, or when they permit or tolerate the commission of grave crimes. Taken together they constitute what has been termed collective criminality, or 'system criminality'.[8]

The nature of universal crimes also affects the nature of *universal crimes participation*. Any meaningful criminalisation of contributions in some form to such criminal enterprises must take into account not only the more or less blameworthy acts of each individual who participates to some degree and in some form, but also the increased social endangerment of collective criminal enterprises.

In this regard, criminalisation of universal crimes participation has something in common with criminalisation of organised crime more generally, for example, as part of a domestic or transnational fight against mafia-like organisations and syndicates that thrive on trafficking in persons or goods and that often benefit from weak or corrupt state institutions. To the extent that some terrorist acts are considered domestic crimes or 'transnational crimes' but not 'international crimes', the criminalisation of terrorism and participation in terrorist organisations also has similarities with the criminalisation of participation in universal crimes. Especially as the distinction between international crimes (universal crimes *lex lata*) and transnational crimes might be difficult to draw with respect to certain transnational crimes that may emerge as international crimes in the foreseeable future,[9] it makes sense to appreciate parallel ICL issues within transnational criminal law.[10]

The situation of 'system criminality' is often much more dangerous, however, because the scale may be significantly larger and the criminality more pervasive. Much of the social fabric may be infested – including the organs and entities that are supposed to protect citizens from external and internal threats, such as the military (which may abuse its power and turn

---

[8] On the concept of system criminality, see André Nollkaemper and Harmen van der Wilt, eds., *System Criminality in International Law*, Cambridge University Press, Cambridge, 2009.

[9] On distinguishing, comparing, and discussing the two fields of international and transnational criminal law, see, for example, Robert J. Currie and Joseph Rikhof, *International & Transnational Criminal Law*, 2nd ed., Irwin Law, Toronto, 2013.

[10] See *ibid.*, pp. 325–434, on transnational crimes of international concern.

against its own citizens), the police, and the courts. Indeed, experience has shown that universal crimes may be organised at the highest levels of society.[11] Hence, "participation in international crimes often stems from obedience rather than deviance".[12] Political violence often creates circumstances whereby authority is exercised to induce crimes on the part of subordinates and create a culture of impunity.[13] Experiences from the international criminal tribunals and from 'transitional justice' mechanisms employed at the national level indicate that the human capacity to resist perceived authority is limited, a finding also affirmed by scientific experiments.[14] When ordinary citizens and civil servants join or assist the most responsible perpetrators and their organisations, something that happens frequently in times of turmoil, how can individual guilt and personal criminal law liability be fairly and effectively assessed and allocated in hindsight?

As pointed out in Chapter 1 of this book, criminalisation and prosecution of universal crimes participation raises many difficult issues; but international legal history since 1945 has also shown that it is indeed possible to successfully prosecute such conduct in a principled, and sometimes effective, manner.

---

[11] See the historical and sociological overview in Chapter 3, Section 3.3., on state leaders, ministers, and other high-level personnel who have been prosecuted and convicted for universal crimes.

[12] Marina Aksenova, *Complicity in International Criminal Law*, Hart, Oxford, 2016, p. 3.

[13] *Ibid.*

[14] The most famous are the Milgram experiments undertaken by Yale University psychologist Stanley Milgram in 1963; see, for example, Saul McLeod, "The Milgram Experiment", 2007. Milgram examined the 'obedience' defence for genocide offered by the accused at Nuremberg, that is, that they were just following orders. In his experiments with volunteers, Milgram found that most ordinary people (65 per cent) were extremely willing to follow orders given by an authority figure even when the order was to inflict pain on an innocent human being, provided they were able to believe that the authority would accept responsibility for what happened. The perceived status and the physical presence of the authority figure greatly influenced the result: the obedience level dropped to 20 percent if the order came from a person without status as an authority, and to the same level if an authority figure gave the order but was not present at the scene. If other participants were seen to disobey the order, the obedience level fell to 10 per cent. On the other hand, if participants could instruct an assistant to inflict the pain instead of doing it themselves, the obedience level rose to 92 per cent. The experiment thus points to the social endangerment that results from erasing the individual's sense of personal liability when acting within a power structure.

It follows from the vast experience underlying the aforementioned assertions in the Rome Statute preamble that universal crimes, and punishable participation in them, may constitute a serious danger to an entire society. Such crimes may also affect other countries and international peace and security, regionally and even globally.[15] Large-scale atrocities often have serious repercussions for the prospects of stable and well-functioning state structures, development projects, environmental protection, and food security, and they may destroy the long-term capacity of different political, social, and ethnic groups to co-exist and co-operate for the common good.[16] In addition, as part of war and violent conflict, such crimes force people to move internally or flee their countries, thus adding to the world population of refugees and displaced persons that is now at a record high.[17]

Although it is often leaders of states and non-state organisations that are alleged to be most responsible for the crimes – persons who should not be difficult to identify for possible investigation and prosecution – impunity more often than not still prevails. This is a painful point, considering that the Rome Statute laid the foundation 20 years ago for a general international criminal court, the ICC. Nonetheless, we would argue that the shortcomings of the ICC are not the principal problem. The persistence of impunity is, rather, a clear warning that the most important powers lie elsewhere. Quite likely, a significant percentage of top political

---

[15] Transnational crimes, which include organised crime offences, trafficking in persons, illicit manufacturing of and trading in firearms, and corruption, among others, may possibly also have such effects. It is partly for this reason that states have adopted a number of so-called 'suppression treaties'; see Currie and Rikhof, 2013, pp. 327–36, *supra* note 9.

[16] Such possible effects seem to be quite unique to ICL crimes and are closely related to the gravity of universal crimes. Gravity is central to the concept and definition of universal crimes; see Einarsen, 2012, pp. 231–87, *supra* note 6. Hence the most serious crimes are the universal 'core crimes' comprising genocide, crimes against humanity, war crimes, and the crime of aggression; see Rome Statute, Article 5.

[17] At the end of 2016, the global population of individuals forcibly displaced by persecution, conflict, violence, or human rights violations stood at 65.6 million. See United Nations High Commissioner for Refugees ('UNHCR'), "Global Trends: Forced Displacement in 2016" (www.legal-tools.org/doc/dfae39/). Of these, 22.5 million were international refugees, with 17.2 million under the mandate of UNHCR and 5.3 million under the mandate of United Nations Relief and Works Agency for Palestine Refugees. While children below 18 years of age make up an estimated 31 per cent of the world population, they constituted about half of the refugee population in 2016. Developing countries hosted 84 per cent of the world's refugees under UNHCR's mandate.

and state leaders, as well as many heads of large corporations and powerful non-state organisations around the world, are large-scale violators of human rights, even war criminals. Many are corrupt – kleptomaniacs who siphon off national resources and economic benefits through self-dealing commercial contracts entered on behalf of the state. Or they are willing to conceal or tolerate serious crimes by others, in their own interests or for so-called state interests, which in many cases they perceive as one and the same. Unfortunately, one does not have to move very far down in the country rankings on the World Justice Project Rule of Law Index to find such leaders; indeed, they are probably more the norm than the exception at the intermediate and lower ranks.[18]

The first book in this series linked the goals of ICL to the rule of law, which includes *accountability* and eventually punishment for leaders and others who take part in grave crimes.[19] It demonstrated that the rule of law concept applies to international law and its legal regimes, and that there are important connections between the rule of law and the legal frameworks for prosecution of universal crimes.[20]

In essence, the norms and institutions of the international community must be able to protect human beings and societies. Peaceful means, such as fair criminal prosecution of the most serious crimes, are indispensable in this regard. Unfortunately, it seems much easier (and more lucrative) for many world leaders to spend disproportionate resources on arms and security systems while criminal law and unequal prosecutions become part of a repressive judicial system aimed at keeping the ruling circles in power.

Within the UN paradigm of international law there is also a 're-sponsibility to protect' (R2P),[21] which includes an obligation to facilitate

---

[18] See World Justice Project, *Rule of Law Index 2016*, Washington, DC, 2016. In this report, 113 countries were assessed, with emphasis on criminal law and procedures.

[19] See Einarsen, 2012, pp. 28–38, *supra* note 6.

[20] *Ibid.*, p. 38.

[21] On the origin and content of the R2P doctrine as first set out, see, for example, Gareth Evans, *The Responsibility to Protect: Ending Mass Atrocity Crimes Once and for All*, Brookings Institution Press, Washington, DC, 2008; and Nicholas J. Wheeler, *Saving Strangers: Humanitarian Intervention in International Society*, Oxford University Press, Oxford, 2000. There are also several United Nations documents on this topic, for example, UN General Assembly, *Implementing the Responsibility to Protect: Report of the Secretary-General*, A/63/677, 12 January 2009 (www.legal-tools.org/doc/0d8171/).

prevention and suppression of genocide and other serious crimes, through international criminal prosecution if necessary.[22] Territorial states and their leaders have the primary obligation to protect against such crimes in accordance with the rule of law.[23] This includes fighting impunity for those who organise or incite universal crimes.[24] When state leaders fundamentally fail their duty to protect, international criminal proceedings often become necessary, according to a proportionality assessment, in order to employ the least forceful but still effective means. International prosecutions may offer a constructive compromise solution to the often-proclaimed dilemma of the international community, which must decide, when faced with an emergency situation, between doing practically nothing to protect civilians against violent conduct (for example, war crimes and crimes against humanity in Syria and Yemen, genocide and crimes against humanity against the Rohingya people in Myanmar) and taking action that risks excessive or misguided use of force that may worsen the situation (for instance, in Libya). The referral of the situation in Libya to the ICC by the Security Council in 15 February 2011[25] might be perceived as a case of 'too little too late', insufficient to set the legal record straight and provide necessary protection to victims. However, while the mechanism of international criminal prosecutions is an inherent part of the R2P concept, such prosecutions can be justified on other grounds as well, in particular with respect to the international law purpose of "justice and respect for the obligations arising from treaties and other sources of international law".[26]

Consequently, while crimes committed, organised, and tolerated by powerful persons fall within the core field of ICL, universal crimes require at least a minimum of consistent use of retributive justice in order to

---

[22] See Evans, 2008, pp. 99–100 and 166–68, *supra* note 21.

[23] See UN General Assembly, *Implementing the Responsibility to Protect*, 2009, para. 47, *supra* note 21.

[24] *Ibid.*, para. 54: "It is now well established in international law and practice that sovereignty does not bestow impunity on those who organize, incite or commit crimes relating to the responsibility to protect".

[25] See UN Security Council, Resolution 1970 (2011), 26 February 2011 (www.legal-tools.org/doc/00a45e/).

[26] See Charter of the United Nations, Preamble, San Francisco, 1945 (www.legal-tools.org/doc/6b3cd5/).

prevent leaders and others from causing even more damage to entire societies as well as to individual victims in the future.[27]

Furthermore, compared to common crimes, universal crimes have a different legal basis: they must have a foundation not only in law, but also in *international law*. Hence *criminalisation* at the level of international law typically requires a legal basis in customary international law or in the general principles of international law, or both, and in treaties as well.[28] When this is the case, criminal responsibility can be lawfully enforced through agreements,[29] UN Security Council resolutions,[30] or multilateral treaties,[31] all of which may establish international criminal tribunals for the prosecution of such crimes. It can also be lawfully enforced at the domestic level, even under the doctrine of (permissible) universal jurisdiction when the crime has been committed in another state by non-nationals against non-nationals.[32] Universal jurisdiction, of course, is different from substantial universal crimes, and the legal relationship between the two concepts under international law is complex.[33]

Thus, a characteristic feature of universal crimes is that individual criminal liability arises directly under international law, implying that consent of the national state for the prosecution of these crimes is in principle not required. For example, the UN Security Council – despite lack of consent by the authorities in Belgrade – in 1993 lawfully established the ICTY for the purpose of prosecuting serious crimes committed within the

---

[27] See Einarsen, 2012, pp. 68–72 and 83–86, *supra* note 6.

[28] On the possibility of combined or multiple legal bases, see Chapter 4, Section 4.3.6.

[29] See, for example, the agreement of the Allied nations enacting the Charter of the International Military Tribunal (the London Agreement) at Nuremberg (www.legal-tools.org/doc/844f64/).

[30] See the Security Council resolutions establishing the ICTY and the ICTR.

[31] The Rome Statute of the ICC is today the most important example of an additional treaty basis for the prosecution of four crime categories, each containing several crime types: the crime of aggression, war crimes, genocide, and crimes against humanity. On the distinction between crime categories and crime types, see Einarsen, 2012, pp. 221–30, *supra* note 6.

[32] See the empirical studies in Chapter 8 and the normative discussion in Chapter 4, Section 4.1.

[33] Universal jurisdiction is not necessarily limited to universal crimes, while on the other hand domestic exercise of universal jurisdiction may require fulfilment of additional conditions. The purpose and underlying rationale of the two concepts of 'universality' are different and only partly overlapping.

territory of the former Yugoslavia. This means that universal crimes lend themselves particularly well to investigative and prosecutorial efforts and inter-state co-operation at the international level, provided that sufficient political will is present.

The dominant position among scholars of ICL has similarly been that it is lawful to hold persons taking part in universal crimes directly responsible under international law for having committed or otherwise participated in such crimes.[34] It does not matter under general international criminal law *where* the crimes were committed, or which *formal position* or *nationality* the participant held.[35] And this fundamental principle of ICL liability for participation in universal crimes does not only apply to the executors at the crime scene and those 'most responsible'. Rather, it may apply to (all)

> participants who with mental awareness and intent have made an actual contribution to or towards the completion of the relevant crime.

At least, this seems to be a reasonable working definition for punishable participation in universal crimes at this stage of the book.

The general scheme of individual liability for crimes under international law has often been historically grounded in the Nuremberg Judgment, in which the International Military Tribunal ('IMT') famously stated:

---

[34] See Kevin Jon Heller, "What Is an International Crime? (A Revisionist History)", in *Harvard International Law Journal*, 2017, vol. 58, no. 2, pp. 353–420. Heller argues, however, that the prevailing principle or dominant legal perception, which he refers to as the 'direct criminalisation thesis', ought to be replaced with a more limited 'national criminalisation thesis', which he claims is more in line with legal positivism. However, why a philosophical notion of 'legal positivism' should decide the matter is not clear to us, especially since the prevailing principle is deeply rooted in the Nuremberg legacy of ICL, human rights, and the still-existing UN paradigm of current international law.

[35] With a great deal of foresight and sensitivity towards the newly enacted Charter of the United Nations, Justice Jackson (US), chief prosecutor at Nuremberg, proclaimed in 1945: "The definition of a crime cannot, however, be made to depend on which nation commits the act. I am not willing to charge as a crime against a German official acts which would not be crimes if committed by officials of the United States". See Robert H. Jackson (United States Representative to the International Conference on Military Trials, London, 31 July 1945), "Notes on Proposed Definition of 'Crimes'", 1945 (www.legal-tools.org/doc/a6ad44/).

> Crimes against international law are committed by men, not by abstract entities, and only by punishing individuals who commit such crimes can the provisions of international law be enforced [...] individuals have international duties which transcend the national obligations of obedience imposed by the individual state.[36]

It is clear from the judgment as well as the whole context that the word "committed" was not meant to exclude participants who had not themselves executed the crimes at the crime scenes. Indeed, the case concerned only the 'major war criminals', who typically had not personally murdered or ill-treated their victims but had instead acted as the most responsible masterminds and facilitators of the large criminal enterprises designed at the leadership levels of the principal Nazi power structures.

The exact state of legal affairs at Nuremberg in 1945–46 might perhaps still be hard to understand from a purely positivistic legal point of view, especially without taking into account as informative legal context the full events of World War II and the United Nations paradigm of international law that had by then emerged.[37] Although the IMT also provided a positive legal justification for its application of crimes such as aggression, crimes against humanity, and war crimes – by drawing on legal developments before the war, including treaties, international custom, and general principles of law – the tribunal could not avoid factoring in the consequences of impunity for the horrendous attacks on humanity and human dignity and balancing these against the lack of clear international criminalisation at the time when the offences were planned, organised, and executed.[38]

---

[36] International Military Tribunal ('IMT'), *Trial of the Major War Criminals before the International Military Tribunal: Nuremberg, 14 November 1945–1 October 1946* (hereafter cited as *Trial of the Major War Criminals*), vol. I, Nuremberg, 1947, p. 223 (www.legal-tools.org/doc/f21343/).

[37] See further Einarsen, 2012, pp. 38–51, *supra* note 6.

[38] On the question of retroactive application of the provisions of the London Charter at Nuremberg, see IMT, *Trial of the Major War Criminals*, vol. I, p. 219, *supra* note 36. The IMT argued that there were two conflicting principles of justice at stake: the *legality principle* and the *principle of substantive justice* (just retribution, also, from a victim's point of view). As judges, they would have to prioritise and make a decision in an exceptional case. They opted for substantive justice, and rightly so from an international law and human rights point of view. See further Einarsen, 2012, pp. 114–19, *supra* note 6.

In other words, there was an element of law making, or underlying judicial will to develop the law on universal crimes, in order to establish a better foundation of international criminal law norms, in compliance with the newly stated principles of the UN Charter that included respect for and protection of universal human rights. The flip side of the coin must have been the assumption that individuals also had real duties to respect the rights of others, and that individuals consequently may also incur criminal liability and punishment for serious violations constituting 'crimes against international law', to use the words of the IMT in the quotation above.[39] The question of which crimes have such particular status under current international law, and the criteria employed when distinguishing international or universal crimes from other crimes, are another matter.[40] For the purpose of this book, we presume that at least genocide, crimes against humanity, war crimes, and aggression are crimes relevant to ICL and to our subject matter of punishable participation in universal crimes. Hence, we shall not engage in further debate on the concept of universal (international) crimes here.[41]

The issue in the following thus concerns only the criminalisation of acts or forms of punishable *participation* in the crimes. The concept of participation is only meaningful when more than one person with poten-

---

[39] IMT, *Trial of the Major War Criminals*, vol. I, *supra* note 36. Interestingly, the conception of *crimes against international law* is currently used in Swedish legislation and jurisprudence as a distinct crime category (in Swedish, *folkrättsbrott*), comprising, for example, violations of Common Article 3, Geneva Conventions. See the Swedish cases mentioned in Chapter 8, Section 8.5., of this volume.

[40] See Kai Ambos, *Treatise on International Criminal Law*, vol. 1, *Foundations and General Part*, Oxford University Press, Oxford, 2013 (with further references); and Heller, 2017, *supra* note 34.

[41] It is worth noting, however, that even Heller, in his interesting 'revisionist' article, ultimately *does not reject* the principle of individual criminal responsibility under international law. Rather, he concludes on the basis of a positivist theory that some crimes usually considered universal crimes might not fall into this category (for example, crimes against humanity), while some other crimes usually not considered (distinct) universal crimes might have such status (for example, financing terrorism). This suggests, however, that the real issue is not the notion of direct criminalisation under international law, but is rather under which descriptive and normative criteria such individual responsibility arises under international law. See, for example, Einarsen 2012, *supra* note 6, proposing five cumulative criteria that need to be fulfilled before a crime should be considered a universal crime – in effect reconciling the two theoretical positions Heller invites us to choose between (see Heller, 2017, *supra* note 34).

tial personal criminal law liability is involved in the crime, and within the field of ICL a number of persons are typically involved. In this book, we shall to some extent use the term 'joint criminal enterprise' or just 'criminal enterprise' as a broad descriptive concept denoting relevant group crimes. However, 'joint criminal enterprise' has also become a term of art within ICL and may thus take on a more specific meaning as a mode of liability as well, depending on context.

It should be noted, furthermore, that the concept of 'participation' is a bit complicated by the criminalisation of 'inchoate crimes', which is a legislative technique employed pro-actively in order to increase the preventive effect of criminalisation. The method, which is being used in modern criminal law generally, is to criminalise certain preparatory steps *towards* completion of a crime (say, crime A) as *distinct* crimes (say crimes B, C, and D). The classic example is criminalisation of attempt to crime A (or a class of crimes, for example, attempt to crimes A1–A10), which then becomes accessorial crime B (or crimes B1–B10). Other inchoate crimes might include conspiracy, incitement, and even the further planning and preparation of crime A. This makes it possible to prosecute preparatory acts causing social endangerment, whether or not the main crime (A) is eventually completed successfully. A closely related technique is to criminalise as distinct crimes certain indirect forms of participation in a criminal enterprise. Such contributions may consist of encouragement or assistance before or at the execution stage, or assistance after the fact. For instance, some domestic jurisdictions have increasingly criminalised certain forms of complicity to certain crimes as distinct crimes as well, so the conduct can be prosecuted whether or not the main crime is completed or can be prosecuted against a principal offender.[42]

These techniques are not *per se* contradictory to the legitimate aims of criminalisation, but they extend the reach of criminal law, and this may in turn raise new issues. The point we will make for now is just that such criminalisation of distinct 'accessorial crimes' needs to be taken into account when considering a theory of criminal law liability applicable to

---

[42] With respect to the more recent developments in general United Kingdom ('UK') criminal law and criminal law statutes, see, for example, Jeremy Horder, *Ashworth's Principles of Criminal Law*, 8th ed., Oxford University Press, Oxford, 2016, pp. 469–508 (with critical comments and conclusions on the new, distinct offences of 'encouragement' and 'assisting' at pp. 500–1).

universal crimes. The relationship between the main universal crimes in the sense above – the A crimes – and the 'inchoate' B crimes will be clarified later in this book, including legal consequences pertaining to criminalisation of distinct crimes as compared to forms of liability for completed crimes.[43]

In our opinion, the criminal law reach of liability for punishable participation in substantive universal crimes must currently (still) be understood within the particular legal, political, and broad community framework of the UN paradigm of international law. This means that the issue cannot be viewed merely as a technical one, that is, how best to phrase liability for such participation in legal terms. Broader principles come into play, both with respect to fair and effective criminalisation in compliance with the nature of universal crimes participation, and with respect to the inherent limitations on aggressive criminalisation according to fundamental principles of criminal law and additional human rights norms. The nature of such participation is often that the relevant act 'scores' high on both dangerousness and blameworthiness, and thus on inherent gravity. On the other hand, persons who have actually contributed to such crimes also need legal security. Their acts are not always – and should not always be considered – punishable. In this regard, it is especially necessary to identify the fundamental principles of criminal law, which may come to the rescue of a suspected participant or accused person, including within the field of ICL. However, there is also a need for an overarching theory of personal criminal law liability.

2.1.3. Complying with Scientific Requirements for a General Theory

At one level, criminal law is a tool that society can use to direct and shape conduct and values. From a realistic, political point of view, people in direct or indirect charge of the most powerful institutions of a society – like the legislative bodies and the courts, but in particular the executive branch, including the police – can use the criminal law system for good or abuse it for bad. Elections and formal democracy do not provide sufficient guarantee against severe violations of human rights. From a scientific point of

---

[43] The most important issue here concerns the legality principle in international law and its reach with respect to personal criminal law liability for universal crimes. See Section 2.2.2.1. in this chapter and Chapter 4, Section 4.3.7.

view, however, criminal law is a scientific field.[44] Law as science does not develop from legislation and court decisions, but through legal research, studying this field and its development using the relevant research methodologies. This is also the reason for situating legal studies in criminal law within academia.[45]

Ideally, a single scientific theory should govern criminal law and be applicable to ICL as well, despite its particular features. Scientific theory must describe accurately all relevant events, without resorting to random elements, and also must predict accurately all relevant future events. This is, however, a bit more than can realistically be expected. According to Stephen Hawking, some modification of the two requirements is warranted, and the result still qualifies as a good scientific theory:

> A theory is a good theory if it satisfies two requirements. It must accurately describe a large class of observations on the basis of a model that contains only a few arbitrary elements, and it must make definite predictions about the results of future observations.[46]

Without going into the extensive discussions on law as science and on how the purpose of legal science and academic legal works might or should be defined, whether more or less in line with – or independent from – science generally, we find it interesting to note that the requirements of a 'good legal theory' actually fit quite well with the modified definition provided by Hawking.

The first requirement – to describe a large class of (legal) observations (typically relating to the sources of law and legal practice) on the basis of a model with as few arbitrary elements as possible – suggests that a theoretical model for understanding the causes or reasons behind the observations must be developed. For instance, criminal law and ICL must develop a model with helpful components that can explain the observations within the field, for instance, why judges making decisions at an international criminal tribunal reach a *certain result* on ICL liability and provide *certain legal reasons* for their results in a concrete case and in a number of other similar cases (while reasons relating to establishment of

---

44   See, for example, with further references, Hallevy, 2012, p. 13, *supra* note 3.
45   *Ibid.*
46   Stephen Hawking, *A Brief History of Time*, Bantam Books, New York, 1988.

the facts are basically a different matter). The components must consist of certain fundamental principles that are (nearly) always complied with by criminal law judges, and possibly a set of more specific rules as well, which are required for understanding of the law and how it should be applied in order to be in compliance with the model.

The second requirement, that of accurate prediction, is more difficult to fulfil in law than in natural science. The classes of judgments and other decisions often observed by legal scientists consist of acts by human beings. Judges, like other lawyers, make errors of law; sometimes they may bend the law in order to reach a just result in a special case. Judges may even deliberately deviate from the law in certain cases in order to achieve results that they would prefer for extrajudicial reasons. This may happen regularly in systems with little respect for rule of law, but it can also happen in systems that are generally fair and based on the rule of law. Through the reasons provided and the relative openness of legal methodology, it may be possible to mask irregular motives on the part of a judge. In such a case the result either would be difficult to explain under the scientific 'model' applied or would cast doubt for the wrong reasons on the model itself.[47] Therefore, a straightforward, inductive scientific approach of the type suited to the natural sciences, whereby a single contrary observation can falsify a theory and render it useless, cannot be applied to legal science. If it were so applied, a perfectly valid and useful legal theory might have to be discarded simply as a result of human error or even manipulation of the law by a judge in a single criminal law case. From a common-sense point of view, that would just pay extra tribute to faults and abuse of power, contrary to the purpose of law.

Conversely, the concept of law is inherently based on the notion that it is *in principle* possible to explain the 'one best interpretation' of the relevant legal rule and the correct application of the law and thus the result in a specific case. Without such a basic principle, the whole notion of rule of law becomes meaningless, because one would be substituting human whims for law. This does not mean that legal scientists and lawyers in general do not accept that more than one interpretation and result can

---

[47] The study of extrajudicial factors that may motivate a judge is almost a separate field of political or social science. Although we recognise the phenomenon, and we accept that it might be important for understanding some cases generally, the matter falls outside our project, which is concerned with understanding the law on punishable participation as such.

be arguable and thus difficult to choose between. To the contrary, this is how lawyers and legal scientists make their living. But essential distinctions must be drawn between what *is* current law and what *is not* current law (for example, a misunderstanding of the law or an unlawful exercise of power), and, furthermore, between the law as it is (*lex lata*) and the law as it should be (*lex ferenda*).

In light of these distinctions, and given the difficulties that sometimes arise in ascertaining the law (*lex lata*), legal science will typically seek to identify and clarify the law under the second scientific requirement. It will thus seek to predict the results of future observations either *explicitly* (under unchanged conditions)[48] or *implicitly*, by writing the text so that it can also be read as making predictions. Legal theory and textbooks often silently rely on the assumption that judges normally adhere strictly to the law, and such legal texts are therefore taken to be able to explain and predict future case law if the analysis itself is sound. This concept of legal science as making predictions by implication seems to us to be the most realistic description of traditional legal science.

Legal scholars are diverse and take an interest in many different matters concerned with the law and how it operates. Nonetheless, it cannot be denied that many legal scholars first and foremost try to explain the law as best they can to their readers based on the most important legal sources available, and thus at least implicitly also make predictions of results and reasoning in future cases. Often it will be quite reasonable to read a legal text that way. This is also why textbooks on criminal law are considered very useful by practitioners and fellow legal scientists in the field, when they have to seek scholarly assistance to figure out the state of the law and maybe try to refine the legal arguments and further clarify the law on specific points for different practical purposes.

---

[48] Some legal philosophers have discussed at length the possibility of predicting future judgments and the question of whether this should be the (only) task of legal science. If it is, a verification and falsification process that resembles natural science testing might be a logical consequence. See, for example, the classic work by Danish law professor Alf Ross, a proponent of such a streamlined view of legal science, who argues that 'the law' ultimately is to be found in the minds of Supreme Court judges within a national jurisdiction like Denmark. Alf Ross, *Om Ret og Rætferdighed: en indførelse i den analytiske retsfilosofi* [On Law and Justice], Nyt Nordisk Forlag, Copenhagen, 1953.

Some textbooks on criminal law may to some extent just take a certain 'model' of criminal law for granted. There is nothing wrong with that, from a scientific point of view. No scientific theory requires that a single researcher fulfil both requirements. To the contrary, science is based on a co-operative model within the scientific community in the sense that scientists are free – and in fact are encouraged – to build on the works of other scientists. Other books and articles on criminal law may, however, be concerned with the model as such, or with particular components of it. They pay attention to the first scientific requirement, thus complementing more traditional textbooks that are mainly concerned with the second requirement. Books that both propose a 'model' and test how the allegedly improved model would work to explain the law and predict future observations of legal practice may be less common, except with respect to carefully delimited subject matters.

In this book, we will seek to comply with the requirements of legal science as explained, and our ambition is to do so with regard to both requirements. Through a combined theoretical/analytical and historical/ sociological approach (Chapters 2–3), followed by methodological explanations and preconditions (Chapter 4) and broad empirical studies (Chapters 5–9), we have developed and tested a new model for understanding punishable participation, at least within ICL, which is our main subject matter.

In the next section, we shall seek to provide a theory of punishable participation. In particular, we aim to clarify an important but often not fully explained part of criminal law, namely the theoretical construction of personal criminal law liability in cases involving several participants. Here we are concerned in principle with the first requirement of scientific theory, the 'model' itself. This model will be referred to in this book as the general theory of personal criminal law liability, or just 'the general theory'.

2.2. The Four-Level General Theory

2.2.1. First Level: Supra-principle of Free Choice

In what Hallevy refers to as the 'general theory of criminal law' in his book *The Matrix of Derivative Criminal Liability*, there are different levels of theoretical application for the principles of personal criminal law liability.[49] He distinguishes four hierarchical levels:

Formation of the Four-Level General Theory

1) *Supra*-principle of free choice
2) Fundamental principles
3) Secondary principles
4) Specific legal rules

We basically agree with Hallevy on these overarching points, and we believe that a substantial part of the general theory he proposes may be an interesting and scientifically sound model that is also applicable to ICL. However, this does not mean that the theory cannot be improved on other points. It also needs to be specified or clarified with particular reference to ICL, as Hallevy, in his book, is not concerned with ICL. Although our work does not treat criminal law in general or focus on Hallevy's model as such, we think his theory provides a good framework and starting point for the more specific theory of punishable participation in universal crimes that we seek to develop in this book.

For this reason, we shall present the core content of Hallevy's general theory and relate it in this section to the law and principles under the Rome Statute, currently the most important subsystem of ICL.

One observation from the outset is warranted, though. When Hallevy speaks of 'criminal law' in his book, he is concerned only with its core aspect, namely, substantive criminal law liability. His theory might thus have been termed a 'general theory of criminal law liability'. Our point here is that there are other substantive aspects of criminal law, such as those related to criminal law sanctions, that is, forms of punishment and sentencing. In relation to this latter part of criminal law, other fundamental principles might exist as well. One is the principle of proportionality, referring to the relationship between the gravity of the crime – including circumstances and the concrete acts as well as culpability (mental state and blameworthiness) of the accused – and the sanction to be imposed within the relevant criminal law subsystem. Hence the punishment,

---

[49] Hallevy, 2012, pp. 12–23, especially figure 1.2, see *supra* note 3.

and the sentence, should basically reflect the gravity of the crime.[50] In addition, there are procedural principles of fairness and equality (fair trial) that are indirectly relevant to but fall outside the scope of the present inquiry.

Furthermore, there are also important, and some would say just as fundamental, human rights principles relevant to the 'positive' aspects of criminal law justice. These include, in particular, the duty of the territorial state to investigate and prosecute the most serious crimes (for example, murder and torture), especially when such crimes are related to abuse of state powers, in order to combat impunity and provide equal justice for all under the rule of law.[51]

And, finally, there are also fundamental human rights principles relevant to the 'negative' aspects of criminal law justice, concerned with substantive limits on criminalisation of conduct. On this point, we find it necessary to supplement Hallevy's account of the general theory of criminal law, because certain human rights norms interfere and interact with some of the fundamental principles of criminal law liability. For example, conduct in full compliance with the freedom of expression, freedom of belief, freedom of peaceful assembly, right to form associations, and right to respect for privacy and human dignity cannot in our view be criminalised without also conflicting with the legitimate aim of criminal law and our conception of a general theory of criminal law liability.[52]

---

[50] Within the field of ICL, on crimes satisfying the concept of 'international crimes' (universal crimes), gravity assessment might be described as a function of the 'crime level' and the 'responsibility level'. See discussion in Einarsen, 2012, pp. 73–82 and Figure 1 ("Gravity as a Function of Crime Level and Responsibility Level") at p. 81, *supra* note 6. See also Chapter 10, Section 10.7.

[51] The duty of the territorial state to investigate and prosecute universal crimes, as well as a number of other legal consequences under international law of the commission of universal crimes, is outlined and briefly discussed in Einarsen, 2012, pp. 231–35, *supra* note 6. The regional human rights courts of Europe and the Americas have ruled in a series of cases on the alleged lack of effective investigation and prosecution of serious crimes in violation of the human rights to respect for life and freedom from torture. The duty of the territorial state to investigate, prosecute, and punish persons responsible for genocide is inherent in the Genocide Convention (see Articles IV, V, and VI, read in conjunction), with the exception that an international criminal tribunal may have jurisdiction instead (Article VI) (www.legal-tools.org/doc/498c38/).

[52] See Section 2.1.2.

In the following, however, we will concentrate on the more specific scientific model or general theory of criminal law *liability*. Human rights provide a normative framework and delimitations of legitimate criminal law liability. However, there is at the same time a normative linkage between the (internal) fundamental principles of criminal law liability and (external) human rights norms, as we shall see, for example through the legality principle that is part of both set of norms.

At the first level of the theory, the *supra*-principle of free choice is the core of criminal law liability: all other levels are subordinated to it.[53] No criminal liability can be imposed on an individual unless he or she has chosen to commit, or chosen to participate in, the criminal enterprise or offence.[54] Criminal liability presupposes freedom to act lawfully. That condition does not hold when the person was coerced to act without any real conduct alternative. Thus free choice could also have been termed freedom of choice.

The principal social concept behind the *supra*-principle is the autonomy of the human being,[55] meaning that each individual has the capacity to choose and act independently of the will of others. Criminal law liability is thus ultimately premised on the view that individuals are rational persons who are morally responsible for their own acts.[56] To function as the *supra*-principle of the general theory of criminal law, sufficient freedom of choice as opposed to coerced acts must be well defined.[57]

Coercion is not an entirely clear concept, however. Some acts would be viewed as coerced according to the ordinary meaning of the word, while not being the kind of coercion that negates free choice under criminal law. In particular, the existence of constraints on the range of possible choices available to the individual is not the same as coercion in legal terms. Under the Rome Statute, the concepts of duress and superior orders imply situations that may constitute coercion and therefore do not

---

[53]   See Hallevy, 2012, p. 14, *supra* note 3.

[54]   *Ibid.*

[55]   *Ibid.* See also, for example, H.L.A. Hart, *Punishment and Responsibility: Essays in the Philosophy of Law*, Clarendon Press, Oxford, 1968.

[56]   See similarly Aksenova, 2016, p. 1, *supra* note 12, with further reference to Andrew Ashworth, *Principles of Criminal Law*, 2nd ed., Oxford University Press, Oxford, 1995, p. 83.

[57]   See Hallevy, 2012, p. 14, *supra* note 3.

justify criminal liability.[58] Hence they might be invoked as defences in criminal proceedings before the ICC, but they would presumably only be successful in exceptional cases.[59] To impose strict conditions for the defences of duress and superior orders is neither contrary to nor an exception to the principle of free choice.

Exception to the principle of free choice requires that the entire general theory of criminal law be replaced.[60] Criminal law in enlightened societies is preconditioned on free choice.[61] If it were not, the model would be unable to predict future events in criminal law with any certainty. If the precondition turned out to be scientifically not sustainable, the model would have to be replaced, or at least fully reconsidered. If we decide that human beings do not enjoy free choice, but instead only act on predetermined impulses, like robots, then we must reconsider whether any human being can be held criminally responsible in a meaningful way.[62]

---

[58] See Rome Statute, Article 31(1)(d) on duress and Article 33 on superior orders, both under strict conditions. Duress is essentially defined as a threat of imminent death or bodily harm, while an order might come from a military or civilian authority.

[59] For discussion of the case law on duress and superior orders within ICL more generally, see, for example, Ambos, 2013, pp. 348–56 and 377–79, *supra* note 40; Elies van Sliedregt, *Individual Criminal Responsibility in International Law*, Oxford University Press, Oxford, 2012, pp. 249–60 and 296–99; M. Cherif Bassiouni, *Introduction to International Criminal Law: Second Revised Edition*, Martinus Nijhoff, Leiden, 2012, pp. 416–37 and 438–52; and Antonio Cassese, *Cassese's International Criminal Law*, 3rd ed., rev. by Antonio Cassese, Paola Gaeta, Laure Baig, Mary Fan, Christopher Gosnell, and Alex Whiting, Oxford University Press, Oxford, 2013, pp. 228–40. A number of authors discuss the defence of duress specifically in relation to the Erdemović case at the ICTY. See, for example, Rosa Ehrenreich Brooks, "Law in the Heart of Darkness: Atrocity and Duress", in *Virginia Journal of International Law*, 2003, vol. 43, no. 3, pp. 861–88; Illan Rua Wall, "Duress, International Criminal Law and Literature", in *Journal of International Criminal Justice*, 2006, vol. 4, no. 4, pp. 724–44; and Valerie Epps, "The Soldier's Obligation to Die When Ordered to Shoot Civilians or Face Death Himself", in *New England Law Review*, 2003, vol. 37, no. 4, pp. 987–1013.

[60] Hallevy, 2012, p. 14, *supra* note 3.

[61] Consider Hallevy (*ibid.*, p. 15): "Certain [dictatorial] regimes that rejected the concept of free choice were deemed illegitimate".

[62] Discussions between proponents and opponents of behavioural determinism have been going on for many years from a philosophical point of view, while medical scientists have made progress in better understanding the functioning of nerves and the human brain. There is no substantial scientific support so far, however, for the view that human beings act socially without exercising free choice – although the range of available choices might often be more or less severely limited under some conditions and in some specific situations.

Conversely, if we assume that robots of the future will act like 'human machines' based on advanced algorithms and computer programs, we may ask whether it will be socially meaningful to charge robots for criminal acts when they solve their problems in ways that cause social harm or endangerment. The answer, presumably, is no, precisely because robots will not exercise free choice even if they become very advanced in other respects. More appropriate sanctions would be to order modification or destruction of the robot's programs and to consider prosecuting the individuals (and corporations) who manufactured the 'criminal' robot or controlled its acts through programs or surveillance.[63]

From the *supra*-principle of free choice derive four fundamental principles of criminal law liability:[64]

Formation of Second-Level Fundamental Principles

Principle of legality

Principle of conduct

Principle of culpability

Principle of fair attribution of personal liability

The next section briefly discusses each of these principles and relates them to the Rome Statute. However, these principles will be with us later in the book as well.

2.2.2. Second Level: Fundamental Principles

2.2.2.1. Principle of Legality

Hallevy succinctly explains the major position of the legality principle in criminal law theory:

---

[63] The issue of 'killing drones' is a case in point. Although they may help in identifying targets and assessing information, they do not execute a decision to kill independent from their owners, at least not so far. Even if they were to start taking and executing decisions as well, artificial data programs would predetermine their 'choices'. It would not change anything in this respect if the data programs were to be made and installed by other robots. That could in theory create a situation out of control, but criminal law liability for the robots would not be part of the solution.

[64] In this we again generally agree with Hallevy; see further Hallevy, 2012, pp. 14–19, *supra* note 3. However, we have changed his 'principle of personal liability' to 'principle of fair attribution of personal liability' because that is more informative and precise.

> The rules of formation of what is permitted and prohibited
> are embodied in the first fundamental principle of the gen-
> eral theory of criminal law, the principle of legality.[65]

This principle, we would add, also constitutes a necessary component of the model of criminal law liability.[66] To enable a person to choose to act lawfully, and thus to have free choice in practical legal terms, society needs to draw a precise borderline between what is permitted (lawful) and what is legally prohibited conduct.[67] The principle of legality requires the law (the prohibited or mandatory act) to have been known or foreseeable to the individual when the choice to act contrary to the law was made. Retroactive criminalisation is prohibited under the general theory of criminal law liability.

The legality principle is today also well recognised in international human rights law. It is explicitly or implicitly part of domestic criminal law, and has been made part of constitutional law in many countries. It has generally also achieved an increasingly prominent place within ICL discourse.[68] It is explicitly recognised as a fundamental 'general principle of criminal law' and is specified in some detail in the Rome Statute.[69]

The principle of legality, strictly speaking, is concerned with formal requirements, including foreseeability and a certain minimum of specificity, and not with the substantive content of the criminal law provisions. However, formal does not necessarily denote written law only. With respect to ICL, the criminalisation of acts rising to the level of international crimes (universal crimes) is set forth in the law-creating sources of international law, which include customary international law and general principles of law, as possible legal bases for the proscribed acts. In addition,

---

[65] *Ibid.*, p. 16.

[66] See Section 2.1.3. in this chapter on the first requirement of a scientific theory.

[67] See also Hallevy, 2012, p. 16, *supra* note 3.

[68] See, for example, Kenneth S. Gallant, *The Principle of Legality in International and Comparative Criminal Law*, Cambridge University Press, Cambridge, 2009; Thomas Rauter, *Judicial Practice, Customary International Criminal Law and Nullum Crimen Sine Lege*, Springer International, Cham, Switzerland, 2017.

[69] See Rome Statute, Part 3 (General Principles of Criminal Law), specifically Article 22 (*Nullum crimen sine lege*), Article 23 (*Nulla poena sine lege*), and Article 24 (Non-retroactivity *ratione personae*).

according to the requirement of double legality in ICL,[70] the material jurisdiction consisting of the applicable universal crimes of an international criminal court must always be laid down in written rules in the charter or statute of the specific court. Importantly, this also applies to inchoate crimes, that is, distinct criminalisation of conduct that prepares or facilitates the completion of universal crimes and that is punishable whether or not the crime is actually completed.

Furthermore, the legality principle with respect to criminal law cannot be seen in isolation from a broader and even more fundamental 'rule of law' principle comprising not only formal requirements, but substantive law requirements as well.[71] The law must, in other words, conform to certain standards of justice, both substantial and procedural.[72] As a result, the legality principle is part of the rule of law concept, while it does not make additional, substantive requirements superfluous. As already pointed out, in our opinion any general theory of criminal law liability must take fundamental human rights principles into account both as limits on the scope of criminalisation and with respect to the obligation to criminalise and prosecute grave violations. This is particularly relevant to the principle of conduct.

---

[70] See also Terje Einarsen, "New Frontiers of International Criminal Law: Towards a Concept of Universal Crimes", in *Bergen Journal of Criminal Law and Criminal Justice*, 2013, vol. 1, no. 1, pp. 1–21, at p. 16: "First, the relevant crimes must fall within the jurisdiction of an international tribunal established for the purpose of such prosecution, as explicitly stated in its statutes. Secondly, the crimes included in the statutes must also be crimes according to general international law. Prosecution of other crimes types at an international tribunal, for example, of crimes according to the national criminal laws of the territorial states where the crimes were committed, will require special provisions in the statutes and the consent of the concerned state(s) to apply domestic law before the tribunal". By 'concerned state(s)' is here meant either the territorial state where the crimes were committed, or another state with criminal law jurisdiction over the matter in compliance with international law (including also applicable treaty law).

[71] See discussion in the first book of the series, Einarsen, 2012, pp. 28–38, *supra* note 6.

[72] With respect to international law, see Ian Brownlie, *The Rule of Law in International Affairs: International Law at the Fiftieth Anniversary of the United Nations*, Kluwer Law International, Alphen aan den Rijn, Netherlands, 1998, pp. 213–14.

2.2.2.2. Principle of Conduct (Material Element)

The second fundamental principle of scientifically based criminal law is the principle of conduct.[73] It concerns what is frequently referred to in ICL as the material element of crimes.

When an individual chooses to commit a prohibited (unlawful) act, the act must – at a minimum – be carried out in the physical world to justify the imposition of criminal liability. There must be an objective expression of free choice that manifests itself through a physical act of some kind. Otherwise mere thoughts or feelings could be criminalised, if revealed. Thoughts and emotions arise in the minds of individuals and are impossible to completely suppress and control; this includes thoughts and emotions constituting a preliminary mental plan to commit a prohibited act. Such thoughts and emotions do not constitute free choice, which is exercised by committing acts that are possible in the physical world and sometimes by resisting, or suppressing, acts that were required in a particular situation. Acts may in principle include both physical acts and speech,[74] including expressions through symbols and art. If a person forms a mental plan to commit a crime but takes no kind of action, however, no crime has occurred. Hence a person cannot be held responsible under criminal law for a thought or even for a detailed mental plan without any additional conduct. A material element of any 'crime' is thus mandatory.

An act in criminal law might therefore usefully be defined as a "material performance through factual-external presentation".[75] The factual-

---

[73] See Hallevy, 2012, p. 16, *supra* note 3.

[74] While freedom of speech (expression) is a human right, and is protected under international law, hate speech and aggressive expressions may constitute crimes and violations of the human rights of others in breach of international law. With particular reference to ICL, the term 'atrocity speech' has recently been coined to refer collectively to speech (expressions) that in different forms and different ways may constitute universal crimes or punishable contributions to such crimes. See Gregory S. Gordon, *Atrocity Speech Law: Foundation, Fragmentation, Fruition*, Oxford University Press, Oxford, 2017. See also Richard Ashby Wilson and Matthew Gillett, *The Hartford Guidelines on Speech Crimes in International Criminal Law*, Peace and Justice Initiative, The Hague, 2018, pp. 29–82 (www.legal-tools. org/doc/104910/), distinguishing speech charged as a crime (direct and public incitement to commit genocide, hate speech as persecution, other inhumane acts) and speech charged as a contribution to a crime (ordering, instigating, aiding and abetting, other forms of complicity, superior responsibility, co-perpetration, joint criminal enterprise, attempt).

[75] Hallevy, 2012, p. 171, see *supra* note 3.

external presentation of an act in the physical world distinguishes action from culpability, which includes the mental element in criminal law. But when a person starts acting with the required intent, the principle of conduct may not protect against criminal law liability. Hence the criminalisation of, for instance, attempt is possible for an act that does not result in completion of the crime, as long as the necessary mental element is fulfilled as well. Conversely, criminalisation without any factual-external presentation of conduct is not possible under the general theory of criminal law liability.

The requirement of conduct, however, is not limited to positive acts, or positive performance (the word 'positive' as used here does not, of course, denote any positive moral assessment of the acts as good, constructive, or helpful). Conduct may also involve negative performance, constituted by omission or qualified inaction. Such cases are clearly distinguishable from mere thoughts and mental planning. They concern instead qualified instances of inadequate conduct or criminally relevant inactivity when specific acts would instead be expected; see further below.

In our conception of the general theory of criminal law liability, the principle of conduct must also include a negative aspect, that is, limits on criminalisation grounded in respect for human dignity. Hence inherent in the fundamental principle of conduct is respect for human rights that are necessary to preserve sufficient scope of freedom and autonomy of the human person in societies under the rule of law. Such principles are stated in the Universal Declaration of Human Rights and have been reinforced in a number of human rights treaties. Human rights norms set absolute limits on how far criminalisation is lawful, although the distinction between, for example, freedom of expression and lawful proscription of illegal expressions can sometimes be difficult to draw and may develop within a human rights perspective. This absolute limitation on lawfully prohibited conduct also applies to the field of ICL.

Under the Rome Statute of the ICC, the principle of conduct is implied in the material elements of the crime of genocide, crimes against humanity, war crimes, and the crime of aggression, enumerated in Article 5 and specified in Articles 6–8*bis*. None of these provisions raise an issue with respect to the substantive human rights limit on criminalisation. To the contrary, the provisions are important as a precondition for long-term, more effective implementation of the duty to investigate and prosecute serious transgressions of international human rights law and international humanitarian law worldwide.

Any proscribed and prosecuted act must be sufficiently related in the physical world to the relevant crime description *lex lata*, although the crime as such does not need to have been fully completed, or perpetrated singularly by the accused in order to be punishable. In accordance with the legality principle, however, a proscribed criminal act must have been committed or prepared in a way that satisfies or would have satisfied the material elements and specific mental elements of the (substantive) crime description upon its completion (execution).[76] If an inchoate offence is criminalised as a distinct accessorial crime, the same applies in principle to its crime description. For example, criminal law liability for participation in a genocidal enterprise requires that the material and mental elements of the crime of genocide be expressed in the statutes of an international criminal tribunal. If, for example, incitement to genocide is criminalised (in some form) as an inchoate crime,[77] the specific elements of punishable incitement to genocide must be expressed in the statute as well before the conviction of any person for incitement to genocide when the crime of genocide was not completed. If the crime of genocide was completed, one question might be whether it is possible to charge and convict a person for incitement to genocide as a distinct crime *in addition to* instigation of the completed crime, or whether the incitement in such cases is assimilated by the more serious charge of instigation to genocide.[78]

With respect to the material elements of a criminal act, it is common to distinguish between elements of performance (or conduct in strict meaning), circumstance, and consequence (result). How these elements appear and are specified in the crime descriptions depends on the crime type. Legal traditions may also in part determine whether the term 'consequence' is taken to relate only to actual harm, or also to the creation of

---

[76] Thus, the term 'crime description' refers to the substance of the criminal conduct, without excluding crimes and crime descriptions developed in common law or jurisprudence, or – with particular respect to universal crimes – developed in or compatible with customary international law or general principles of law.

[77] See Rome Statute, Article 25(3)(e).

[78] For a comprehensive discussion of the concepts of 'incitement' and 'instigation' in ICL, see Gordon, 2017, *supra* note 74, especially pp. 242–47 on the tendency to conflate instigation with incitement.

danger or a substantially increased risk of harm. Concepts such as risk or danger might be viewed as separate material elements in crime descriptions where the creation of undesirable risks is criminalised. They may also form an inherent part of the normative process of attribution of personal criminal liability through modes of liability.

All crime descriptions and modes of liability within a criminal law system compatible with rule of law make use of one or more of the three mentioned components as criminal law 'building blocks'. Within ICL, most of the types of conduct that have so far been criminalised through *lex lata* crime descriptions, among others, the universal core crimes of aggression, war crimes, genocide, and crimes against humanity, include a certain consequence (result) in the underlying crimes/offences, but not always. Consequences are typically linked to an individual perpetrator through causation, meaning that his or her act caused the undesired result (harm or danger/increased risk of harm), or that the act was a causal factor contributing to it.

With respect to, for instance, omissions, speech, and psychological pressure and influence that might be exerted through the silence of a person with authority, it should be noted that causation is an (important) element in legal assessments of liability, but not a separate fundamental principle under the general theory of criminal law liability. One reason for this is that not all crimes and crime descriptions require a consequence. Another reason is that not every form of liability requires that a responsible person have (directly) caused the unlawful consequence, for example, the death of a person as the consequence of a successful attempt of killing. This is especially clear with regard to inchoate forms of liability for incomplete offences, but it may also be the case with more remote forms of participation in criminal enterprises committing a number of crimes at different places and with different executors on the ground. The latter example illustrates that the concept of causation is complex and cannot easily be reserved for direct causation of physical harm. It may include mental effects on the beliefs and attitudes of others and causal factors in the creation of a dangerous social environment and thus a substantially increased risk of serious harm. Partly cross-cutting liability norms of causation thus seem to belong to the secondary principles at a lower level of the general theory; see Sections 2.2.3.2. and 2.2.3.3. below.

With respect to core universal crimes, it is noteworthy that a certain social gravity context – the circumstances – is decisive for constituting core crimes of genocide, crimes against humanity, and war crimes.[79] For instance, a conviction for crimes against humanity is considered to require a particular social and abusive context, defined in the Rome Statute as "a widespread or systematic attack directed against any civilian population, with knowledge of the attack", which must therefore exist in addition to the relevant underlying crimes such as murder, extermination, enslavement, torture, persecution, and others.[80]

Furthermore, a 'circumstance' component may also be a necessary or optional requirement of the underlying crime description. For instance, the crime of rape first includes an account of the relevant sexual acts in abstract or enumerated terms, or both (performance). It has furthermore been common, as a general rule, to set a threshold of qualified lack of consent by requiring use of force or threats against the victim, thus causing fear of violence or creating an environment of coercion, as additional elements of performance and circumstance. This is the case for the concept of rape under the Rome Statute, although it is also considered rape if the bodily invasion was committed against a person who was incapable of giving genuine consent and thus unable to exercise free choice.[81] There is no required consequence element of harm in addition to performance and circumstance for the crime of rape. Hence, proving physical or mental harm is superfluous in rape cases from a legal point of view, although the presence of harm may be used as evidence of lack of consent. However, the causing of fear and an oppressive context for the sexual acts may also be considered a consequence element of an initial use of force against the victim. Modern criminal law in domestic jurisdictions seems, however, to

---

[79] For a discussion of the 'inherent gravity clauses' in universal crimes, see Einarsen, 2012, pp. 302–5, *supra* note 6.

[80] See Rome Statute, Article 7, para. 1.

[81] See Rome Statute, Article 9 (Elements of Crimes), and Elements of Crimes, Crime against humanity of rape, p. 8, as amended by the 2010 Review Conference (www.legal-tools.org/doc/3c0e2d/). In paragraph 1 the relevant sexual acts are enumerated and linked to the concept of "invasion" of a person's body, thus making clear that the victim did not consent to the conduct of the perpetrator. In addition, however, paragraph 2 requires that the invasion "was committed by force, or by threat of force or coercion, such as that caused by fear of violence, duress, detention, psychological oppression or abuse of power, against such person or another person, or by taking advantage of a coercive environment, or the invasion was committed against a person incapable of giving genuine consent".

be moving towards requiring only lack of consent as circumstance for the performed sexual acts.[82]

Hence the crime of rape may also illustrate the sometimes intricate relationship between the elements of performance, circumstance, and consequence as building blocks of crimes. However, this is not always the case: with respect to the crime of murder it does not make sense to speak of murder unless the consequence (result) of the act was that somebody died. A straightforward consequence element always implies causation, that is, a causal link between the act and the result.[83] Another question, to which we shall return later, is whether a causation link is required for personal criminal law liability for participation in or contribution to a criminal enterprise involved in murder when the accused was not the direct perpetrator (executor).

Negative performance concerns omission and qualified inaction, as mentioned above. Omission might usefully be defined as "inaction that contradicts a legitimate duty to act".[84] The duty to act is external to the concrete situation, in the sense that the duty is based on norms related to the profession, status, or role of the person with respect to protecting another person or overseeing acts that potentially or actually may cause harm to a victim, typically within an organisation or structure. A special legal relationship may also be relevant in this regard, for instance between

---

[82] The crime description of rape, then, focuses more on the factual opinion, awareness, and intent of the victim and less on additional elements of 'performance' by the accused or any 'consequence' element. This shifts the attention more to culpability, including the mental element of the perpetrator, in law and in fact. It does not solve all problems in rape cases and may create new ones, but it is considered a step towards generally better human rights protection of rape victims. Important legal issues, then, concern the definition of (lack of) 'consent' and the required culpability of the accused with respect to 'lack of consent' when the accused has not used force or threats: for instance, should knowledge of the lack of consent be required, or is some kind of negligence standard sufficient? For an illustrative and thorough discussion of the difficult legal and evidentiary problems, including the intricate system of legal presumptions relating to non-consent in modern UK rape law, see, for example, Horder, 2016, pp. 354–68, *supra* note 42.

[83] See Rome Statute, Article 9 (Elements of Crimes), and Elements of Crimes, Crime against humanity of murder, p. 5, as amended by the 2010 Review Conference. Paragraph 1 states as a requirement that the perpetrator "killed one or more persons", while footnote 7 to the concept "killed" in paragraph 1 explains that "the term 'killed' is interchangeable with the term 'caused death'".

[84] See Hallevy, 2012, p. 175, *supra* note 3.

a child and its legal guardian (usually parents). Qualified inaction concerns the inactivity of a person in a situation where only the factual situation itself may give rise to an expectation to act in a certain way or where the person has created a situation where further inaction might be criminal.

For example, because person A had a professional duty to act on an imminent threat, but instead chose to do something else – say, continue reading a book while being called to action as a firefighter – the performance of A is not mere inaction, but inaction that contradicts a legitimate duty to act. The concept of conduct and potential criminal law liability is thus fulfilled by omission, and modern criminal law, according to Hallevy, "acknowledges no substantive or functional differences between acts and omissions, and therefore any offence may be committed both by act and by omission".[85] The condition is, however, that omission liability requires a legitimate duty to act. However, such a rule does not by implication or *a contrario* necessarily mean that qualified inaction without an external duty to act cannot be criminalised as well, as discussed further below.

Another example may illustrate the difference between omission and mere inaction. Inside a prison, one inmate (A) gets hold of a knife and stabs another inmate (B) to death through repeated stabs over a two-minute period. A will be liable for murder. A third inmate (C) happens to be present in the room and watches the incident without interfering because he is afraid for his own life. C cannot be liable for murder because he did not have a legitimate duty to interfere. If C should be held criminally responsible in some way, that would require a particular legal basis for responsibility on the part of bystanders, which either explicitly or in effect establishes a general duty to rescue in criminal law. A prison guard (D) is also present, and armed, but chooses not to interfere although he could have done several things to seek to prevent B's death. Because of his role as a prison guard, he had a legitimate duty to protect inmates from violence and protect their right to respect for their life. D is thus liable for commission of murder by omission.

It is important to note that persons at the crime scene are not the only ones who can be held responsible for crimes by omission.[86] ICL has

---

[85] *Ibid.*

[86] This issue has been discussed, for instance, in the jurisprudence of the ICTR, especially in the context of aiding and abetting genocidal acts during the genocide in Rwanda in 1994; see Chapter 7, Section 7.2.3.3.

also developed particular liability categories of omission liability for military and civil leaders and senior figures within a power structure. The basic condition is that they have been entrusted with superior authority and a legitimate duty to act in order to prevent serious crimes by their subordinates and to hold individuals responsible for criminal excesses. Culpability and liability may thus arise when they have failed a reasonable expectation to act with awareness of a real risk of serious crimes being committed or being committed with impunity by their subordinates. Such leaders are often distant from the crime scene, although not always. The key point with respect to possible liability is, however, not the physical presence or remoteness of the commander or civilian leader, but whether the person in relation to his position undertook meaningful action at a meaningful time to prevent the planning and execution of crimes by his subordinates, or had put in place meaningful mechanisms for preventing foreseeable crimes and for the punishment of subordinate planners and perpetrators before or after the fact. This in essence is the criminal law liability category of 'command and superior responsibility'.[87]

On the other hand, inaction without a legitimate duty to act is seemingly the complete opposite of acting, and is also different from omission because there is no external duty to act flowing from status, position, or role within an organisation. Criminalisation of mere inaction fundamentally contradicts the principle of conduct.

Only acts and omissions thus seem to be punishable. However, if a person's inaction is in line with a criminal plan, the inaction may need to be considered not in isolation but in conjunction with earlier conduct, the plan and its purpose, and mental elements. It is thus also possible to criminalise instances of what we have termed qualified inaction without violating the principle of conduct. In some cases, such criminalisation would be in full compliance with the legitimate aim of criminal law of preventing and suppressing conduct that causes or increases social endangerment or risk of harm.

For example, A hires B through an oral agreement to murder C. B shall receive payment when C is dead; A shall in the meantime do nothing. The criminal plan is executed. Following the initial agreement, the further conduct of A with regard to the murder was seemingly just inaction, but

---

[87] See, for example, Rome Statute, Article 28.

he could still be held liable for joint perpetration, whether he pays B or not, since his subsequent inaction was indeed part of the plan and the murder was completed. In this case the required conduct element consists of the oral agreement and its inclusion of A's further inactivity as part of the plan until the murder has been completed. Hence the planned inaction in this case is clearly distinguishable from mere inaction, especially since the agreement in this case was premised upon a further act, payment after the fact. Put otherwise, innocent inactivity is different from criminal inactivity. If it were not seen as different, A would only be liable for incitement (instigation) or complicity to murder, and might – because of his lack of further contribution to the murder – receive too lenient a punishment. Correct labelling and attribution of liability is generally important under the general theory of criminal law liability, and qualified inaction linked to participation in crimes is in principle relevant to all forms of participation.[88]

There might, however, exist a liability grey zone between mere inaction and qualified inaction, what might also be termed 'inaction plus'. The cases we have in mind concern a social or contextual expectation that a person will seek to prevent a crime from being committed even though the person has no independent duty do so arising from profession, status, or role. This is not about a general expectation that the innocent bystander should always act like a hero and put his or her own life or freedom at great risk for the sake of another human being. It might instead concern a reasonable human expectation that one will aid a helpless or injured person, especially if the bystander partly created the situation through his or her own acts. For example, A and B choose to solve their disagreement with a fight; A falls by accident against a stone and seriously injures his head. If B understands the need for medical assistance immediately and is able to call the emergency services but instead does nothing, B might be liable for some offence, whether A dies or not. Even C, who then arrives at the scene and finds A seriously injured, but also chooses to do nothing, might be liable for an offence. Some criminalisation of a failure to assist a person in serious need of help might be justified in order to reinforce values of human dignity and social solidarity, and does not by definition violate the fundamental principles of criminal law liability.

---

[88] See the discussion of various examples in Hallevy, 2012, pp. 178–84, *supra* note 3.

The question of responsibility for bystanders may be particularly relevant to the issue of punishable participation in universal crimes. As pointed out by Botte-Kerrison, having large numbers of victims and perpetrators inevitably also results in a large number of bystanders.[89] She defines bystanders for the purpose of her analysis not as innocent bystanders, but rather as persons "who were aware that crimes were being committed but chose not to react" and who, at the same time, "indirectly contributed to their perpetration".[90] Bystanders' roles may range from deliberately looking the other way to taking advantage of the situation.[91] She mentions as historical examples those who exploited vulnerable victims for the purpose of gaining access to low-cost labour or who occupied housing vacated by victims of genocide during World War II.[92] The point is, furthermore, that bystanders participate in creating the social conditions for successful mass crimes because their acts or lack of opposition are perceived as approval by the perpetrators. In many situations mass crimes could not have been committed on a large scale without the tacit approval and passivity of the bystanders.[93] With respect to universal crimes, one potentially interesting group of bystanders consists of the leaders of other states not directly involved in crimes committed by a foreign government, as well as leaders of international organisations and corporations, who were aware that crimes were being committed but chose not to react within their possible range of actions and statements – and thus indirectly may have encouraged, condoned, or taken advantage of the situation.

However, the role of bystanders, and the possible 'duty to rescue', have so far been "left outside the legal definition of international crimes".[94] On the other hand, a duty to rescue may in some circumstances be close to liability by omission, or 'commission by omission', as discussed below. A possible solution advocated by Botte-Kerrison, therefore,

---

[89] See Auriane Botte-Kerrison, "Responsibility for Bystanders in Mass Crimes: Towards a Duty to Rescue in International Criminal Justice", in *International Criminal Law Review*, 2017, vol. 17, no. 5, pp. 879–908, at p. 880.

[90] *Ibid.*

[91] *Ibid.*

[92] *Ibid.*

[93] See *ibid.*, p. 881, with further reference to other authors.

[94] See Laurel Fletcher, "From Indifference to Engagement: Bystanders and International Criminal Justice", in *Michigan Journal of International Law*, 2005, vol. 26, no. 4, pp. 1013–95, at p. 1016.

is to implement the duty to rescue more forcefully at the domestic level of criminal law in order to acknowledge the responsibility of the silent crowd in the commission of crimes, and instead employ traditional liability concepts such as command/superior responsibility and aiding and abetting at the international level.[95]

Even more interesting to ICL and our project, from a current legal point of view, is the issue of whether a person with a certain status and authority within a power structure might be liable for (qualified) inaction while having knowledge of the crimes, even though he or she was positioned outside the relevant direct chain of command or did not have any formal or explicit authority to act on the matter. In other words, this issue concerns situations that fall outside omission liability under the category of command and superior responsibility based upon a legitimate duty to act. Nevertheless, persons entrusted with a certain status and authority might be seen as taking a consenting part in crimes close to their own field of operation when they choose inaction while still being able to exert influence on the criminal acts. Such cases concern the possible liability category within ICL termed 'taking a consenting part' in a power structure, which to some extent was employed in the subsequent Nuremberg trials based on Control Council Law No. 10 for the Allied-occupied zones of Germany after World War II.[96] This category may also be taken to constitute a *sui generis* subcategory of accomplice liability or to form part of a broader category of complicity possibly different from (only) aiding and abetting.[97] These persons are also bystanders who fit the definition provided by Botte-Kerrison, but with an additional status and authority that increases their responsibility to the extent that their acts or omissions (in-

---

[95] See Botte-Kerrison, 2017, pp. 907–8, *supra* note 89.

[96] See Control Council Law No. 10, Article II(2)(c), "took a consenting part therein" (www.legal-tools.org/doc/ffda62/). For contrasting views on the application of this form of liability, see Kevin Jon Heller, *The Nuremberg Military Tribunals and the Origins of International Criminal Law*, Oxford University Press, Oxford, 2012, p. 260: "Unlike the *Pohl* tribunal, the *Einsatzgruppen*, *Farben*, and *Ministries* tribunals specifically viewed TCP as an omission-based mode of participation. In their view, a defendant had taken a consenting part in a crime if three conditions were satisfied: (1) he knew that a crime had been or was going to be committed; (2) because of his authority, he was in a position to object to the criminal activity; and (3) he nevertheless failed to object to it. TCP was thus broader than command responsibility".

[97] See Section 2.2.3.3. See also Chapter 10, Section 10.6., and Appendix I.

action) might constitute punishable participation under current ICL, or ought to *lex ferenda*.

We shall now move on to the last issue of this section: in addition to the material elements discussed so far, some crime descriptions may contain specific mental elements as inherent components of the crime. For instance, performing an act of negligent behaviour may not constitute 'murder' because the crime of murder requires intent within the relevant criminal jurisdiction. This means that a certain mental element is necessarily part of the crime description of 'murder' and thus falls under the principle of conduct as well as being relevant to the principle of culpability. Likewise, with respect to the crime of genocide, specific intent to destroy a particular group of human beings is a necessary component of the particular crime description of genocide. It is important to note, however, that the crime description does not by itself determine or exclude criminal law liability for participants who may not personally share the specific intent. Whether shared specific intent is a requirement or not, notably with respect to someone who aids, abets, or otherwise assists in the commission of genocide, must finally be determined by also employing other fundamental principles, as well as interpreting the specific provisions within the relevant criminal law subsystem. In ICL, with respect to genocide, this issue is more important to accomplice liability than to commission liability, since specific intent is clearly required for conviction as a perpetrator of genocide, while omission liability as command/superior responsibility does not require that the commander share the specific intent. With respect to aiding and abetting acts of genocide, the answer has generally been that the accomplice does not have to share the specific intent.[98]

In conclusion, liability for the act must essentially be attributable to one person or several persons because of their concrete participation in the crime event and the fulfilment of specific legal requirements in that regard – recalling that such events, in the context of atrocity and ICL, often involve large criminal enterprises. This relationship between forms of participation and criminal law liability, that is, conduct constituting punishable participation in universal crimes, is the main subject of this book. The relationship is specifically embodied in the fundamental principle of

---

[98] See Chapter 7, Section 7.2.3.3.

fair attribution of personal liability (see the fourth principle, Section 2.2.2.4. below). However, the principles of conduct and personal liability are also closely related to the principle of culpability, as we will now see.

2.2.2.3. Principle of Culpability (Mental Element and Defences)

The third fundamental principle is the principle of culpability. It is the subjective expression of free choice (*mens rea*).[99] The principle includes situations where a person has not exercised a fully conscious free choice, but where more careful conduct and specific other acts were possible choices in the real world and were expected from the perspective of society. The latter situations are often labelled with terms such as recklessness and negligence that express a social judgment of the acts, which are different from a subjective exercise of a fully conscious free choice. In order to recognise both main forms of culpability, the concept of *culpability* seems more appropriate than 'mental element' as the general concept within criminal law and ICL.[100] However, 'mental element' has become a term of art in ICL, and for that reason we will use it as the generic term in the empirical surveys.[101]

There are both positive aspects ('mental element') and negative aspects to the principle of culpability, the latter represented by possible defences ('excuses' and 'justifications'):

> The positive aspects are embodied in the mental elements of the offense, the negative aspects in the general defenses. Thus, for the imposition of criminal liability, an offense may require a specific intent, which is a positive aspect (mental element). When the individual is incapable of forming culpability (*doli incapax*), owing to mental disease, very young

---

[99] See Hallevy, 2012, p. 16 and also pp. 195–200, *supra* note 3.

[100] See, for example, Fletcher's critique of the "old-fashioned division of the elements of crime into physical and mental elements – plus defences", a perspective underlying even the Rome Statute, which (also) "uses the terms 'mental element' to translate *mens rea* as a required state of culpability". According to Fletcher, this is "the outmoded structure we still find in French law, the Rome Statute, and the vast majority of the criminal legislation around the world". See George P. Fletcher, "The Theory of Criminal Liability and International Criminal Law", in *Journal of International Criminal Justice*, 2012, vol. 10, no. 5, pp. 1029–44 (at p. 1037).

[101] It could also be argued that culpability without a subjective expression of free choice (*mens rea*) is equivalent to 'mental omission', and that situations of mental omission (variations of negligence) quite naturally fall under the concept of 'mental element'.

age, lack of self-control, uncontrollable intoxication, etc., the possibility of imposing criminal liability is negated because of subjective reasons related to the negative aspects.[102]

Without any kind of culpability, criminal law liability is not justified. Culpability presupposes at the very least a real possibility of an alternative choice of conduct for the individual concerned. It is noteworthy that this requirement applies to all those who make some punishable contribution to a crime, not only to the direct perpetrator. If such a real possibility does not exist in the real world, the principle of culpability prohibits criminal law liability (negative aspects). If it does exist, the principle of culpability allows for criminal liability if the individual has acted with the required level of culpability as determined by the general principles of criminal law liability and the applicable specific provision within the relevant subsystem of criminal law (positive aspects).

As pointed out by Hallevy in the quotation above, the negative aspects concern the general defences of criminal law liability (excuses and justifications). If the person is unable to make an informed choice of conduct due to serious internal circumstances beyond his control – mental incapacity – he might be excused. Mental incapacity may stem from underdeveloped or diminished mental capacity because of mental illness, brain damage, or other conditions that seriously impair normal abilities of cognition and volition, including temporary impairment such as lack of mental orientation or consciousness. The underlying causes may relate to young age, congenital mental limitations, exposure to stressful situations, brain damage caused by accidents or violence, irresponsible use of alcohol or drugs, or a combination of such conditions. (Circumstances are not considered beyond a person's control if he chooses to lose or weaken his control, typically by voluntarily using alcohol or drugs with such well-known effects.)

If the person, on the other hand, is unwilling to choose another kind of conduct due to the existence of serious external circumstances beyond his control, his action might still be justified. Such situational or mental emergency concerns an especially stressful situation for the individual, producing a state of mind that may justify his otherwise criminal act or at least justify his choice of conduct under the circumstances. Such a situa-

---

[102] See Hallevy, 2012, p. 16, *supra* note 3.

tion might entail severe coercion, or some other circumstance that seriously threatens life or health. In this scenario the alternative choice of action may, in reality, be severely limited – making it unreasonable of society to demand such alternative action by means of criminal law liability – or the stressful situation may make it difficult for the person to act with full awareness of the consequences or the alternative options available. It would therefore be unreasonable to hold the person criminally liable for his acts. The imminence of serious harm or a potential threat to survival is a case in point, including in situations where an otherwise criminal act in self-defence is necessary in order to protect oneself or another person from an unlawful attack.

Self-defence, however, has another, parallel justification as well, apart from the state of mind of the individual actor: namely, that self-defence is also recognised – at least to some extent – as constituting an element of objective law enforcement. This is so when other law enforcement mechanisms are missing or not available for the purpose of countering the initial unlawful attack, an imminent use of force against the actor or another potential victim of violence, or a threat to unlawful destruction of property or means essential to their survival. Self-defence usually requires that the defensive act be proportionate to the degree of danger to the actor or to the other person or interest protected.[103] Recognition of the possible existence of such human emergencies (and possible lack of available effective social law enforcement mechanisms) normally constitutes a humane and necessary part of a well-defined general theory of criminal law liability in accordance with experiences of human nature as well as human conditions in the real world.

Without going into detail here, there are three main forms of the positive aspect of culpability, that is, the mental element in a broad sense. These are (1) *mens rea* culpability; (2) negligence culpability (serious or simple); and (3) strict liability. *Mens rea* culpability comprises several subcategories, typically including specific intent, or *dolus directus* of the

---

[103] This requirement has not always been consented to in domestic criminal law theory and practice, because it has been argued that self-defence is a means to prevent wrongdoing in the first place, and that to require proportionate self-defence undermines its effectiveness as a law enforcement mechanism. However, current ICL recognises that acts of self-defence must be restrained as well, and thus requires acts in self-defence to be proportionate to the degree of danger; see Rome Statute, Article 31(1)(c).

first degree; intent (regular intent), or *dolus directus* of the second degree; *dolus eventualis*; recklessness (a borderline subcategory); awareness; and knowledge. For some practical criminal law purposes, several of the categories might be combined with respect to certain crimes (typically awareness/knowledge and intent). The different forms represent different levels of cognition and volition. Volition is most strongly present in *dolus directus* of the first degree, that is, when the aim and object of the act is to bring about an unlawful consequence, even if the chance of the desired result is small.

Mens rea requires that the offender be positively aware of the factual reality, including probable consequences of his conduct. Negligence, on the other hand, is cognitive omission (unawareness or insufficient awareness of factual reality) when the offender had a duty to act with care and to be aware of the possible consequences of his acts. Strict liability provides for a rebuttable legal presumption of negligence, based on the factual situation alone. For example, the speed limit is 50 km per hour and person A exceeds 80; he is thus liable for a criminal offence because of the unacceptable risk created in such situations. It may require something special to rebut such a legal presumption of negligence: for example, a combination of decreased risk (say, because traffic was light at the time) and a good cause (he was driving an injured person to hospital). Taken together, these might provide a special cause for not noticing the speed limit, as well as provide a possible justification for breaking it.

Hence the positive aspect of culpability in criminal law concerns the concrete involvement of the human mind in the commission of (and participation in) the offence. Better scientific understanding of how the human mind and body work and interact may help explain human behaviour from a biological, medical, and social point of view, and hence may also be potentially important for improved assessment of culpability and criminal law liability in general.[104] However, when the *supra*-principle of

---

[104] Criminal law experts have long recognised that more scientific knowledge on these themes is required, along with a better understanding of the social causes of criminality, in order to intervene more effectively against criminality. Those studying this problem include, among others, the International Association of Penal Law (IAPL/AIDP), founded in 1924 as the successor to the International Union on Penal Law, which was founded in 1889 by, among others, Franz von Liszt. The IAPL has devoted much of its activity to problems of international criminal law and the responsibility of authors of internationally committed crimes.

criminal law liability is determined to be free choice, and not philosophical determinism,[105] human beings are generally presumed to be able to choose their behaviour within their physical, mental, and external constraints.[106] If this foundational legal presumption were to be considered scientifically unsustainable, the general theory of criminal law liability would also have to be reconsidered. In the meantime, the rule of law, including criminal law liability, is in general and for good common-sense reasons based on the principle of free choice, and in this book we shall leave it at that.

Culpability based on free choice exhibits two different but related features: cognition and volition.[107]

Cognition is the individual's awareness, knowledge, and/or deeper understanding of the factual reality. The concept may also denote the mental process of acquiring knowledge and understanding through thought, experience, and senses, encompassing elements such as attention, memory, judgment, evaluation, reasoning, problem solving, and decision making. Awareness, knowledge, and understanding are in this respect synonymous. Although they may point to different degrees of cognition, they all concern information, data, and understanding of facts in the physical world and the common conceptual world of human beings in society, from the past to the present.[108] The performance and circumstance com-

---

See "History of the International Association of Penal Law" (available on International Association of Penal Law web site).

[105] Determinism is a philosophical position that stipulates that for every event there exist conditions that could cause no other events. It might be applied to all or more specific areas of science. When applied to the conduct of human beings, causal determinism is the opposite of freedom of choice.

[106] This does not mean that choices are easy to track scientifically, or that human choices cannot be part of complicated biological, emotional, psychological, and logical 'systems' that influence choice through inherited and developed steering mechanisms that may be different in different individuals. It might also be that such mechanisms are, or could be envisaged as, split into two different systems, one for 'fast' reasoning and decisions and the other for 'slow' reasoning and decisions; the first of these works almost automatically and hardly involves conscious choice, while the second makes it possible to consider and reconsider a range of possible factors before a choice is finally made. A well-known exposition of the two-system theory is Daniel Kahneman, *Thinking Fast and Slow*, Farrar, Straus and Giroux, New York, 2011.

[107] In the same vein, see Hallevy, 2012, p. 196, *supra* note 3.

[108] See similarly Hallevy, *ibid*.

ponents of conduct exist in the present when a person is committing a crime. As long as the person is aware of his own acts and the relevant circumstance, the precondition for criminal law liability is fulfilled. A consequence in criminal law occurs in the future, from the same perspective, but the possibility of its occurrence is closely tied to the mindset and acts of the perpetrator (and possible other participants). While prophecy skills are not required for criminal law liability,[109] this closeness makes it legitimate to punish the perpetrator for crimes that require a certain consequence.

For example: A aims a gun at B while they are walking together in the woods, and A pulls the trigger. A is aware of his performance and the circumstance in the present (that B is a human being and not some animal A is hunting), and he is aware of the possibility of B's death in the future as a result of his conduct. The causal connection between conduct and result is also clear: B dies as a consequence of the bullet fired by A. A is thus liable for murder.[110]

Volition concerns the will or willpower of a person, that is, what the individual wishes to happen and thus the purpose of his act. It is also a cognitive process, but with the focus on committing to a course of action and purposive striving, and as such it is recognised as one of the primary human psychological functions. Volition is relevant in different ways. Without any degree of volition, a person cannot be liable for participation in *mens rea* offences. The legal problem with the notion of volition is that it is not subject to objective factual reality. Cognition is to some extent subject to factual reality, because it might at least be objectively established which kind of information and sometimes knowledge a person had when acting. This raises the question as to whether will, or volition, is a helpful concept, especially since the underlying notions are impossible or difficult to observe or even explain scientifically. The phenomenon seems to derive from psychological processes in the human mind, which presumably involve interactions between emotions, interests, values, external pressures, and internalised social norms, as well as knowledge of the subject matter and some degree of reflection back and forth, leading finally to a decision to act or refrain from acting in a certain way.

---

[109] *Ibid.*
[110] The example is taken from Hallevy, *ibid.*, pp. 196–97, although a bit modified.

The problem is that all kinds of human acts are linked to volition in this sense, and this makes volition difficult to use for the purpose of distinguishing between different acts. A possible solution, as Hallevy points out, is to recognise that "volition is not binary because there are different levels of will".[111] The main categories are, however, positive will (A wants X), neutral will (A is indifferent to X), and negative will (A does not want X). And although volition is not subject to factual reality, volition might still be inferred from the conduct and common knowledge of human behaviour and the human mind, and maybe from specific knowledge about the particular person. Often cognitive and volitional aspects are combined to form the mental elements, typically with respect to crimes that require a particular purpose or specific intent.

The Rome Statute deals with both main aspects of the culpability principle. Article 30(1) sets forth the general rule on the mental element, requiring that the material elements of a crime within the jurisdiction of the ICC be committed with 'intent' and 'knowledge' – in other words, a *mens rea* standard must be met:

> Unless otherwise provided, a person shall be criminally responsible and liable for punishment for a crime within the jurisdiction of the Court only if the material elements are committed with intent and knowledge.

These concepts are further defined in Article 30(2) on intent (including both cognition and volition)[112] and Article 30(3) on knowledge/ awareness (cognition),[113] with some overlap.[114] Briefly, however, it can be pointed out that while a discussion of various types of *mens rea* in ICL

---

[111] *Ibid.*, p. 196.

[112] Rome Statute, Article 30(2), states that "a person has intent where: (a) [in] relation to conduct, that person means to engage in the conduct; (b) [in] relation to a consequence, that person means to cause that consequence or is aware that it will occur in the ordinary course of events".

[113] Rome Statute, Article 30(3), states that "'knowledge' means awareness that a circumstance exists or a consequence will occur in the ordinary course of events".

[114] 'Intent' in relation to a consequence and 'knowledge' in relation to a consequence are both (partly) defined with reference to awareness that a consequence "will occur in the ordinary course of events"; see Rome Statute, Articles 30(2)(b) and 30(3). Only 'intent' concerns will (volition), that is, that a person *means* to engage in conduct (performance) or *means* to cause a consequence, while 'knowledge' (awareness) of a circumstance is required, and sufficient.

has taken place at the ICC in several cases before the court, the ICC has essentially limited the general forms of culpability with respect to crime descriptions entailing a certain consequence to two types: (1) when the consequence of the relevant conduct was meant to occur (*dolus directus* of the first degree), and (2) when the consequences of the relevant conduct were almost certain to follow (a strict version of *dolus directus* of the second degree). Thus, *dolus eventualis* and recklessness have been ruled out as relevant general concepts.[115]

Article 32 on mistake of fact and mistake of law also concerns the mental element insofar as these concepts negate the mental element required by law. In these cases, there is a concrete, relevant cognition defect. Article 26 on exclusion of jurisdiction over persons under eighteen, Article 31(1)(1)(a) on mental disease or defect, and Article 31(1)(b) on intoxication all concern various issues of mental incapacity relating to the negative aspect of culpability.

2.2.2.4. Principle of Fair Attribution of Personal Liability

The fourth and final fundamental principle of criminal law liability is the principle of fair attribution of personal liability.[116] The principle naturally concerns individual human beings (natural persons), but may apply to juridical persons/entities as well, for example corporations; see Section 2.2.3.4. below.[117] The remainder of this section only uses language relevant to liability for natural persons.

Because the imposition of criminal liability requires freedom of choice on the part of the individual, it must be that particular individual who has exercised free choice.[118] No individual is criminally responsible solely for the free choice of another person.[119] From this point of depar-

---

[115] See the principled discussion in ICC, Pre-Trial Chamber II, *Situation in the Central African Republic, Prosecutor v. Jean-Pierre Bemba Gombo*, Decision Pursuant to Article 61(7)(a) and (b) of the Rome Statute on the Charges of the Prosecutor Against Jean-Pierre Bemba Gombo, ICC-01/05-01/08, 15 June 2009 (www.legal-tools.org/doc/07965c/).

[116] For points of departures, see Hallevy, 2012, pp. 16–23 (using the terms 'fundamental principle of personal liability' or 'principle of personal liability', *supra* note 3.

[117] Although negotiations on the Rome Statute discussed whether to include juridical entity liability for corporations, it was concluded that personal liability under the Rome Statute should be limited to natural persons; see Rome Statute, Article 25(1).

[118] Hallevy, 2012, p. 16, *supra* note 3.

[119] *Ibid.*

---

ture it can be derived that, for instance, spouses or children cannot be held responsible for the free choice of their husbands, wives, or parents to commit a crime. Nor can any other person, regardless of the potential preventive or other social effects that might be achieved by also punishing persons related to or under the care of an offender. A contrary judicial practice is sometimes referred to as guilt by association. Regimes that resort to such methods act not in accordance with the rule of law but under the arbitrary rule of man, where the aims justify the means; punishments for acts labelled crimes are then no more than a capricious abuse of power and cannot be justified as being part of criminal law as 'law'.

The principle of fair attribution of personal liability, however, permits criminal law liability not only for the physical executor of the crime (for instance, person A, who with intent stabbed B to death and thus committed murder), but also for others who exercised their freedom of choice to participate in a criminal plan or enterprise (for example, to murder person B). This makes it possible to attribute criminal liability to persons other than the principal perpetrator for the exact roles they played in carrying out the offence.[120]

The fundamental principles must apply to their respective contributions to the crime: the legality principle (to the extent it is applicable), the principle of conduct, and the principle of culpability. However, measuring the effect of a contribution in factual and legal terms might be more difficult – and may require additional secondary principles and more specific liability rules – when several persons, or a large number of people, participate in a criminal enterprise, as compared to the acts of a single person and groups of participants in common crimes. Many issues become normatively as well as factually more complex, typically those concerned with attributing responsibility to persons and different groups of actors who contribute to or facilitate criminal enterprises far removed from the crime scenes. Equally complex are certain issues of causation and particular forms of omissions (command and superior responsibility), atrocity speech (for instance, incitement to universal crimes), and psychological influence over actors within a power structure (for example, whether a person may incur accomplice liability for taking a consenting part without action or for encouragement/abetting through mere inaction or silence).

---

[120] *Ibid.*, p. 20.

While the fundamental principles must be respected even when the social context is different, the liability issues relating to large-scale universal crimes may need continuous and principled rethinking, particularly in these highly charged situations. The application of each of the three fundamental principles mentioned above has thus quite naturally caused substantial debate within ICL discourse on fair attribution of criminal liability, and some confusion as well – and probably none more than the legality principle.[121]

The principle of legality requires in general that the law – the prohibited act – be known or foreseeable to the individual when he makes the choice to act contrary to the law. If the criminal nature of an act is not foreseeable, and thus criminal law liability for its commission would contradict the legality principle, criminal law liability for any kind of participation in the act would also be ruled out. But if the criminal nature of the act is sufficiently foreseeable, then it is also foreseeable that informed participation in the completed act will be unlawful. For example, it is foreseeable that sexual intercourse without consent of the other person is prohibited and criminalised as rape, so informed participation in the rape of another person is unlawful as well. If a person exercises his freedom of choice to take part in or support a criminal enterprise with the aim of rape, and the crime is committed, he should be no more and no less protected by the legality principle than the one who physically commits the rape.

However, if the crime is not completed, perhaps because the target victim cannot be found or escapes before rape can be committed, it is not obvious that incomplete acts at the planning and preparation stages are punishable. For that to be the case, the incomplete acts must, in accordance with the legality principle, be made punishable as inchoate (incomplete) crimes, with a separate specific crime description, or through a general crime description of the particular forms of inchoate acts that are punishable for certain crimes (or classes of crimes) – for example, attempt to commit genocide, crimes against humanity, and war crimes.[122]

In other words, it is necessary and justifiable to draw a line between the 'crime' – the proscribed act that falls under the legality principle, in-

---

[121] For different positions, see Chapter 4, Section 4.3.7. and Chapter 6, Section 6.2.2.4.

[122] See, for example, Rome Statute, Article 25(3)(f), criminalising in general attempts to commit crimes within the jurisdiction of the court.

cluding 'inchoate' crimes – and 'attribution' of (derivative) liability for different forms of participation in a completed crime. Aksenova underscores the latter distinction in her recent book on complicity in ICL,[123] with particular reference to points made earlier by Fletcher. As Fletcher points out, the question of wrongdoing is dealt with under primary legal norms, prohibiting or requiring particular acts, while the question of attribution is resolved under an entirely distinct set of norms. These latter norms, notably, "are directed not to the class of potential violators, but to judges and jurors charged with the task of assessing whether individuals are liable for their wrongful acts".[124] These norms, we shall argue in different parts of this book, are constituted at the theoretical level through secondary derivative principles at the third level of the general theory, and at the practical (fourth) level through more or less well-formulated and specific written rules as well as principles developed in the jurisprudence of the various subsystems of criminal law.

It is our view that the different set of norms referred to by Fletcher belong to different fundamental principles: on one hand, the legality principle (crime description), and on the other hand the principles of conduct, culpability, and personal liability (attribution), although with the important caveat that liability for inchoate crimes requires distinct criminalisation in compliance with the legality principle. This does not imply, however, that personal liability can be attributed freely by prosecutors and courts. There are two other limitations as well. First, general human rights principles set an absolute limit on the material scope of lawful criminalisation. Second, general principles of a broader rule of law character, including due process or fairness in criminal law proceedings and trials (fair trial), require that norms of attribution be formulated and expressed in statutes or at least in the judgment attributing criminal law liability for a certain kind of contribution to the crime, with respect to both material conduct elements and mental culpability elements. This feature forms part of the general theory of criminal law liability. Hence the concept of derivative criminal liability needs to be analysed with care, as discussed further below in Section 2.2.3.5.

---

[123] Aksenova, 2016, p. 18, see *supra* note 12.

[124] George P. Fletcher, *Rethinking Criminal Law*, Little, Brown, Boston, 1978, pp. 491–92.

Finally, the fundamental principle of fair attribution of personal liability, as applicable under the rule of law and in compliance with fundamental human rights, also includes the idea and implied principle of fair labelling.[125] Both aspects of fair attribution mean essentially that liability and punishment must reflect the nature, role, and actual contribution as well as culpability of the accused, taking into account the mode and degree of participation and the gravity of the crimes committed. Thus, there is a need for secondary principles concerned with fair attribution of personal liability, which provides for more precise classifications of different forms of criminal law liability in addition to fair labelling of the criminal offence (substantive crime) itself.[126] Only then would a general theory of criminal law liability ultimately be able to guide and provide for fair attribution of liability at the operational fourth level of the general theory.

2.2.2.5. Linkage of the Fundamental Principles and the Next Levels of the General Theory

Before leaving the fundamental principles for now, we find it useful to make two additional comments.

First, we would remind readers that this book is basically concerned with personal liability within the context of criminal law liability more generally, and especially within ICL. Hence at the next levels of the general theory, our main focus will be on further principles and rules relating

---

[125] The function of the principle of fair labelling is "to ensure that the label describing criminal conduct accurately reflects its wrongfulness and its severity", according to David Nersessian. He claims that the principle of fair labelling, broadly stated, "requires offenses to fairly represent both the injury at issue and the offender's wrongdoing (what he did and what he meant to do). Although not an element of any offense, it nevertheless is a fundamental principle of criminal justice. Its premise is that 'justice not only must be done, but must be *seen* to be done'" (italics in original). David Nersessian, "Comparative Approaches to Punishing Hate: The Intersection of Genocide and Crimes against Humanity", in *Stanford Journal of International Law*, vol. 43, 2007, pp. 221–64, at p. 255.

[126] See, for example, *ibid.*, discussing what would be fair labelling of the intended destruction of political groups as a crime under international law. See also Douglas Guilfoyle, *International Criminal Law*, Oxford University Press, Oxford, 2016, p. 318: "The correct label for an offence should sum up the crime committed. Relevant considerations will include: the interests affected (for example, harm to people or harm to property), 'the gravity of the harm', and the mental state of the perpetrator". This statement is applicable to fair labelling with respect to the criminal offence itself and to labelling with respect to forms of participation. Hence Guilfoyle frequently employs the term in his chapter on modes of participation.

to (derivative) liability and attribution of liability for participation in universal crimes, as also conveyed through the title of the book and the concept of 'punishable participation'. In other words, our main point is the relationship between the particular fundamental principle of personal liability and the next levels. This means, for instance, that a more in-depth analysis of the principle of culpability is not undertaken in this book. However, the mental elements of personal liability norms fall clearly within the ambit of the book, and will be analysed and discussed.

Second, we seek to provide an initial understanding of what the next two levels of the general theory are, and how they are connected to each other and to the principle of personal liability, before we elaborate in more detail on the theoretical aspects in the following section (2.2.3.).

In addition to the *supra*-principle and the fundamental principles, the other main components of the general theory of personal criminal law liability are the secondary principles (third level) and the specific legal provisions (fourth level). The theory is meant to be without exceptions:

> From each of the four fundamental principles derive four secondary principles, which form a concrete and specific template for the application of the fundamental principles. From each of the secondary principles derive specific legal provisions, which are the applications of the secondary principles. The legal provisions represent concrete rules of imposition of criminal liability upon individuals. [...] There are no exceptions to the general theory of criminal law, not in its structure and not in its content.[127]

We have one reservation with respect to Hallevy's proposition here: in our view, the specific legal provisions (we generally prefer to use the term 'specific legal rules') at the fourth level of the general theory are not derived from the secondary principles. What *is* derived from the secondary principles is instead further theoretical and analytical categories and subcategories of liability for participation, what Hallevy later in his book terms the 'typology' of derivative criminal law. The specific legal rules – the legal rules on criminalisation and attribution of specific forms or modes of liability at the fourth level – are thus not theoretically derived from theoretical and analytical concepts; rather, they are enacted or de-

---

[127] Hallevy, 2012, p. 16, see *supra* note 3.

termined and implemented by state actors such as legislators and judges, or other authorised representatives within actually existing and operational subsystems of criminal law, preferably in full compliance with the general theory of criminal law liability, including the secondary principles. When this important correction is kept in mind, Hallevy's statement quoted above becomes, in our opinion, more consistent with other parts of his own book.

The four secondary liability principles express the applicability of the principle of personal liability for the imposition of criminal liability basically in line with a scheme presented by Hallevy,[128] but we would like to also add another ('class') perspective on the formation as well, marked by the arrows:

Formation of Secondary Liability Principles and Classes of Liability

Principle of partial participation → class of inchoate liability

Principle of direct participation → class of commission liability

Principle of indirect participation → class of accomplice liability

Principle of juridical entity participation → all three classes relevant

Each of these four principles is discussed below in Section 2.2.3., where the more specified derivative principles are also presented and discussed. The secondary principles, we assert, represent classes of possible punishable participation and personal liability at the highest level of generality. The principle of partial participation represents or implies inchoate liability, which we shall refer to as the class of inchoate liability; the principle of direct participation represents or implies the class of commission liability; while the principle of indirect participation represents or implies the class of accomplice liability. The principle of juridical entity participation is different: it cuts across the other principles and classes in the sense that all the other principles/classes might be relevant to juridical entity participation as well as to individual liability. So far, juridical entity participation has not been criminalised as such within ICL, nor has this liability class in its derivative forms been attributed *lex lata* to relevant entities within any particular ICL subsystem at the fourth level of the general lia-

---

[128] *Ibid.*, pp. 17–18. A slight difference is that we prefer to use 'principle of juridical entity participation' instead of Hallevy's 'principle of legal participation'.

bility theory – for instance, under the Rome Statute. The possible content of juridical entity participation is sketched out below in Section 2.2.3.4., while the legal status of juridical entity participation under customary international law is discussed in Chapter 4, Section 4.3.7.

The derivative principles represent and imply possible further theoretical categories and subcategories of punishable participation and personal liability, still at the theoretical third level of the theory. As mentioned, the modes are being located at the practical (operational) fourth level of the general theory, where the specific legal rules are created in legislation or in court statutes and even in case law.

For example, within ICL, 'joint perpetration' is a category within the class of direct participation (leading to possible commission liability), while joint criminal enterprise is a further theoretical subcategory and a possible mode of participation *lex lata*, for instance, within the ICL subsystems of the ICTY and the ICTR, and possibly within the Rome Statute of the ICC as well. Subcategories of JCE are also possible, both theoretically and practically, in the forms of JCE I, JCE II, and JCE III.[129] The outline below may illustrate the general scheme and how the third and fourth levels are linked together within our proposed general theory of criminal law liability, through an example, modelled on JCE liability that might be derived from commission liability – as was actually done in ICTY jurisprudence for the first time in the famous Tadić case. The main point here is not, however, whether such a linkage can be proven to have been established in legal practice, but rather how the linkage is perceived from a theoretical point of view.

Linkage of the Third and Fourth Levels of the General Theory of Personal Liability

- Third-level secondary principles:

    - Class (for example, direct participation/commission liability)
        - Derived category under the class of direct participation (for instance, joint perpetration)

---

[129] The point here is just to explain the theoretical framework, not to determine or express any particular legal opinion as to whether, for instance, JCE *is* or *is not* a current lawful mode of participation under customary international law, or should be considered so in a *lex lata* or *lex ferenda* perspective, for example, under the Rome Statute, Article 25(3)(a) or (d).

- JCE as a derivative subcategory of commission, joint perpetration, accomplice liability, or a combination thereof
  - JCE I, II, and III as further derivative forms of JCE
- Fourth-level specific legal rules:
  - Commission (example: ICTY Article 7(1) – "committed")
    - o Derived category: joint perpetration
      - JCE as a specific subcategory of commission liability
        - JCE I, II, and III as modes of liability under JCE

All four levels of the general structure presented above are relevant to our project, including the specific legal rules and how they are being applied in practice. Such specific legal rules at the fourth level of the theory of criminal law liability within ICL are represented by, for example, Rome Statute Articles 25 and 28 on personal liability and modes of participation.[130] In this book we will use the term mode of liability only for forms of liability at the fourth level, that is, forms of liability clarified or at least presumed *lex lata*, and possible modes *lex lata* in the future discussed within a perspective *lex ferenda*. It should be noted in this regard, however, that the specific written provisions included in, for example, the statutes of a particular tribunal, or some of them, may not be complete expressions of proper modes that contain or set forth all the necessary and sufficient conditions for their application in actual cases. To the contrary, mode descriptions in court statutes may have been no more than briefly enumerated in the statutes of international criminal tribunals, without the inclusion of specified material and mental conditions for their applicability. The Rome Statute of the ICC is the most complete international court statute in this regard; but even here, text on some of the modes is lacking a great deal with respect to information on the material and mental elements that are required. This means that the content of the applicable mode has had to be further defined and discussed and determined in the jurisprudence – eventually by the judges – simultaneously with its first-time application in a concrete case. The most famous example is probably

---

[130] See also Chapter 1, Section 1.2.4., presenting in particular Rome Statute, Article 25.

the discussion and application of JCE liability in the Tadić case at the IC-
TY, taking the mode and concept of commission in the ICTY Statute as a
point of departure.

It should further be noted that Hallevy's general theory of criminal
law liability is developed more through deductive reasoning than through
empirical studies and induction, although its structure and formation is
also inductive in the sense that it has taken into account current trends in
domestic criminal law in several countries.[131] As we have already pointed
out, the theory is only useful in societies that adhere to the rule of law.
With this limitation, the general theory presented by Hallevy may predict
not only future prevailing trends in jurisprudence but also future forms of
personal liability, that is, at the level of new legal provisions and more
developed determination of content. In our opinion, the core of the general theory of criminal law liability is convincing and useful for the purpose of this book on ICL personal liability. Hence our theory is indebted
to and builds upon the general theory of criminal law liability as presented
and outlined by Hallevy, with some modifications. ICL, which is a *sui
generis* field of criminal law, as well as a *sui generis* field of public international law, may, however, need some further adaptation. The most important modifications for the purpose of a general theory of punishable
participation in universal crimes concern the third and fourth levels of the
model, or, arguably, the linkages or intersection between the third and
fourth levels, represented by the derivative principles and typology of derivative criminal liability.

We would like to highlight two points at this stage. First, the hierarchical structure of the general theory invites and in fact demands an attempt to discuss different issues of criminal law liability at the appropriate
level of the structure. This is important to note with respect to criminal
law liability in ICL, which is a relatively new legal field of criminal law
jurisprudence and research, albeit one that has lately been flourishing. For
instance, it may lead to some confusion in the future framing of international court statutes, in scholarly works, and in jurisprudence if discussions of the specific legal rules within the various subsystems of ICL at
the fourth level *lex lata* are not kept sufficiently apart, theoretically and
analytically, from the secondary principles and derivative principles of

---

[131] See Hallevy 2012, p. 267, *supra* note 3.

personal liability of a *lex ferenda* and analytical nature at the third level.[132] What we have in mind, in particular, is the distinction between a typology of derivative, normative categories (for instance, attempt, joint perpetration, incitement, and complicity) and further subcategories at the level of criminal law liability principles, and the modes of participation as applicable legal rules based on the specific provision within a particular criminal law subsystem at the fourth level. For example, while we shall argue in this book that 12 relevant, derivative categories of a *lex ferenda* nature might usefully be identified within ICL, the modes *lex lata* must be more specifically identified within a particular subsystem, such as the Rome Statute of the ICC.

Second, a proper scientific theory of criminal law liability is needed also for the purpose of *lex ferenda* considerations at the intersection of the third and fourth levels, especially on the assessment of current and possible future forms of criminal law liability in the specific provisions.

Hence the scientific model we take as a starting point, and seek to apply and develop further with respect to ICL, is useful not only for making 'predictions' in a narrow results-oriented manner, but also – and especially – for assessment of current provisions, and of whether new provisions or proposals are in line with a proper general theory of ICL liability or not. Thus, if a new additional subsystem of ICL, or a national jurisdiction, in the future were to consider applying current forms of ICL liability and attribution, for example, those that can be extracted from the Rome Statute, or to consider alternative forms that would also be lawful and in compliance with the general theory of criminal law liability, the matrix to be set forth and explored in this book would stipulate the general possibilities and limitations.[133] This requires, in our opinion, a minimum of substantial empirical knowledge as well, which we will seek to provide throughout large parts of this book, starting in Chapter 3. First, however,

---

[132] Awareness of the level of generality is important when discussing other aspects of ICL as well, such as the question of which and how many 'international crimes' and universal crimes can be identified as being part of current ICL. See the first book of this series, Einarsen, 2012, pp. 221–25 ("Different Levels of Generality of Definitions of International Crimes"), *supra* note 6.

[133] Compare Hallevy, 2012, p. 268, see *supra* note 3, aimed at domestic criminal law generally.

---

we shall continue at the theoretical level, turning to the secondary principles of criminal law liability.

2.2.3. Third Level: Secondary Principles of Personal Liability

2.2.3.1. Partial Participation and the Class of Inchoate Liability

The principle of partial participation relates to the (possible) imposition of criminal liability at the various phases of the attempted commission of the offence.[134] These sequences, as a matter of principle, always include the following four phases if the crime is completed and more than one person participates, although the exact labelling might vary:

Formation of Partial Participation before Execution

1) Idea phase (initial mental plan contemplating the proscribed conduct)

2) Planning phase (planning, preparation, initiation, incitement, ordering before the attempt phase)

3) Attempt phase

The fourth phase of a criminal activity, execution, concerns the successful completion of the crime, but in this section our focus is on the earlier phases, which are also relevant to our study when the crime is not actually completed.

In some cases, the time span between the idea phase, contemplating the proscribed conduct (what Hallevy terms the early plan), and the subsequent phases including execution is very short, maybe only a split second, while in other cases the planning and preparation stage might last for several years. Attempt is the stage or phase immediately before completion of the crime, when concrete and significant steps are taken in the physical world towards execution. The attempt may result in completion, but sometimes it does not because of circumstances independent of the intention of the executor.[135] For example, murder has been contemplated and planned, a gun is pointed towards the victim and the trigger is pulled, but the bullet misses the target. Had the attempt been successful, the crime

---

[134] *Ibid.*, p. 18.

[135] Under the Rome Statute, Article 25(3)(f), criminal liability for attempt is applicable when a person attempts to commit a crime within the jurisdiction of the court, namely, "by taking action that commences its execution by means of a substantial step, but the crime does not occur because of circumstances independent of the person's intentions".

would have been completed. Perhaps, however, the trigger is pulled again and this time the bullet kills the victim. The second attempt is successful, and the crime is completed.

Only the very first of the four phases above, namely the initial idea phase, when someone contemplates committing or contributing to a criminal act, cannot possibly be criminalised under the general theory of criminal law liability – the reason being, as explained earlier, that a thought in itself is not criminal.[136] At least some minimum conduct is required as well under the fundamental principle of conduct.[137] For the same reason, even the most detailed mental planning and mental preparation of a criminal act cannot lawfully be criminalised in a state aspiring to the rule of law. If the mental planning and preparation is accompanied by conduct, that is, objective acts in the physical world, criminalisation of such partial participation might be justified because of the social endangerment posed by the particular kind of criminal acts being planned and prepared.

For instance, if a person mentally plans a terrorist act, and then takes concrete steps by collecting maps, schedules, and other information, and purchases ingredients and devices for making a bomb – actions that are not unlawful in themselves – the person has objectively expressed free choice by taking necessary although still insufficient steps towards completion of the mental plan. Similarly, if a person takes concrete steps to involve another person in the contemplated criminal enterprise, to which that person consents to contribute, or initiates the concrete steps leading towards the attempt phase and completion of the crime based on the planning and preparation that has already taken place, such initiation is also conduct and expression of free choice that might be justifiably criminalised if the acts planned are very serious. In ICL, the concept of initiation has been used with respect to crimes against peace or acts of aggression.[138] Initiation is typically tied closely to planning and preparation, or to a conspiracy (see further below), and even to incitement, or ordering at the early stages. This means that acts of initiation are often assimilated by

---

[136] It does not matter in this regard whether the idea phase is fast and intuitive, or emotional, or slower and more deliberative, or more or less logical, or more or less grounded in experience.

[137] See Section 2.2.2.2.

[138] See, for example, Rome Statute, Article 8*bis* (1).

other forms of participation, so that the need for a distinct liability category of initiation may not be so useful or required in practice.

The point here is that planning and preparing terrorist acts, and some other universal crimes, already causes extraordinary social endangerment and risk of harm. It is no doubt lawful under the general theory of criminal law liability – and might be considered desirable – to criminalise conduct that has the specific intent to cause terror even at the planning and preparation phase, which may include incitement and the establishment of a common plan (conspiracy). For example, the Genocide Convention of 1948 confirmed that genocide, whether committed in time of peace or in time of war, is a crime under international law, and that even incomplete acts of genocide, including conspiracy, incitement, and attempt to commit genocide, should be punishable.[139] Under the Rome Statute, inciting others to commit genocide and attempt to commit all crimes within the jurisdiction of the ICC are punishable.[140]

Criminalisation and attribution of criminal liability may in principle take two different forms: (1) *attribution of liability* through a punishable 'mode of participation' linked to the executed (or attempted) crime, applicable also to participants other than the executor (whether termed 'complicity' or otherwise), and (2) *direct criminalisation* of distinct forms of participation, often in the form of 'inchoate crimes' such as planning/ preparation, incitement, and attempt. However, inchoate crimes are always accessorial to other main crimes, for example, the attempt to commit genocide.

With the second form, it is not a requirement for a conviction that the crime has been completed or has even reached the attempt phase. In domestic criminal law, and within the field of transnational criminal law, the planning phase of terrorist acts is currently often criminalised. In the statutes of recent international criminal courts for the prosecution and trial of individuals accused of universal crimes, however, the planning phase has so far only been criminalised under the first form (attribution). There are two exceptions. The first exception is incitement to genocide, although it should be noted that incitement is not always an act that is part of the

---

[139] See Convention on the Prevention and Punishment of the Crime of Genocide, 9 December 1948, Articles I and III (www.legal-tools.org/doc/498c38/).

[140] See Rome Statute, Article 25(3)(e) and (f).

planning phase, since the inciter could be operating outside a common plan made by others to commit genocide. The second exception today is the crime of aggression in the Rome Statute, where planning, preparation, and initiation are criminalised under Article 8*bis* as three distinct inchoate crimes all relating to the planning phase, while execution in the same provision only relates to the execution phase (completed crime of aggression). In addition, Article 25(3)(f) criminalises the attempt phase with respect to all crimes in the Rome Statute, including aggression.

For individuals who participate at the attempt phase, their participation at the planning phase is assimilated by the attempt. For individuals who participate at the execution phase, their participation at the planning and/or the attempt phase is (usually) assimilated by the completion of the crime.[141]

In addition to the requisite four phases of a completed criminal act set forth above (of which the first phase of mental planning cannot be criminalised and thus falls outside the principle of partial participation, strictly speaking), two other sequences might be relevant for imposition of criminal liability:

- Conspiracy
- Subsequent acts following completion of the crime

Conspiracy might be defined as 'an agreement or plan by a group of people agreeing, planning, or consenting to commit a criminal act'. In other words, such a sequence is only relevant when several people participate in the crime – at the very least, two individual persons must exercise their free choice and agree to commit the criminal act.

The conspiracy agreement is an act in the real world, regardless of whether it is written, oral, or concluded by silent consent upon a proposal from one of the plotters. It must necessarily be made after the initial mental plan, usually at the planning phase, but it might also be concluded instantly by the group or joined by new group members at the attempt or execution phases. However, in legal and especially ICL terms, a conspiracy is usually equivalent to a common plan to commit certain crimes that is entered into before the attempt and execution phases.

---

[141] On assimilation, see also Section 2.2.3.6.

Conspiracy might be criminalised as a distinct crime, like attempt, or as a mode of liability that can be used to attribute liability for completed crimes. Both forms are also possible within ICL. If the crime is completed at the execution phase, conspiracy is assimilated by other categories of participation, such as joint perpetration or perpetration through another – and hence is assimilated by the underlying, applicable modes such as joint criminal enterprise, co-perpetration, and indirect co-perpetration. In other words, with respect to modes of participation for individuals who participate at the execution phase, their participation in the conspiracy at earlier phases is assimilated by the completion of the crime.

The Nuremberg Judgment illustrates the possibility of contemplating conspiracy both as a distinct crime and as a mode of liability. In the Charter of the International Military Tribunal, known as the London Charter,[142] which set out the crimes within the jurisdiction of the IMT, conspiracy was mentioned in two different places. First, it was mentioned within Article 6(a) on crimes against peace (crime of aggression):

> [...] planning, preparation, initiation or waging of a war of aggression, or a war in violation of international treaties, agreements or assurances, or *participation in a common plan* or *conspiracy* for the accomplishment of any of the foregoing.[143]

While participation in a 'common plan' and participation in a 'conspiracy' for the said purposes overlap linguistically, the latter alternative in the actual context points towards the original agreements and plans, and the later amended agreements and plans, made at the top level of the Nazi power structures. The concept of conspiracy may also have been used to denote the notion of an original and single, overarching common plan, which other plans were later derived from or at least closely connected to. However, this idea may not have been specifically contemplated in the indictment, and in any case it was not considered a necessary condition by the IMT for concluding that planning, with aggressive war as the objective, had indeed been established beyond doubt at the trial for several of the defendants.

---

[142] Charter of the International Military Tribunal: Annex to the Agreement for the Prosecution and Punishment of the Major War Criminals of the European Axis (the London Agreement), 8 August 1945 (www.legal-tools.org/doc/64ffdd/).

[143] *Ibid.*, Article 6A (italics added).

It cannot be deduced from the wording of the Charter, however, that the provision was intended to criminalise conspiracy as a distinct crime that could be applied in combination (concurrence) with a completed crime of aggression relating to the same aggression (typically directed at the same country). Thus, conspiracy had the character of an accessorial inchoate crime, like attempt, that would be assimilated if the crime was completed. The natural understanding is rather that liability for the crime of aggression extended to and was limited to those involved in the planning, preparation, initiation, or waging of a war of aggression, or, alternatively, to participation in a common plan or conspiracy to plan, prepare, initiate, or wage war. The latter alternative just seems to cast the net a little wider, including also persons who closely *assisted* persons at the top level in such acts, by aiding and abetting, and maybe also ordered some parts of the planning, preparations, and waging of wars in more detail. Conspiracy as an accessorial crime would still, however, be potentially important with regard to instances where the accused had been part of a conspiracy to attack another country but where the Nazi state leadership had changed its mind after all or had been prevented from waging a war against that country. In that sense conspiracy could have been constituted in the Charter both as a distinct although accessorial crime, and a mode of liability.

The second place where the Charter mentioned conspiracy, together with common plan, was in the last paragraph of Article 6, which followed paragraphs (a) on 'crimes against peace', (b) on 'war crimes', and (c) on 'crimes against humanity':

> Leaders, organizers, instigators and accomplices participating in the formulation or execution of a *common plan or conspiracy* to commit any of the foregoing crimes are responsible for all acts performed by any persons in execution of such plan.[144]

Thus, the common plan and conspiracy were mentioned twice in relation to crimes against peace (aggression), but only once in relation to crimes against humanity and war crimes. When we take into account that most plans by the Nazi leadership to commit crimes against peace were actually executed (completed) by waging war against another country

---

[144] *Ibid.*, Article 6 (italics added).

(victory or defeat is a separate question), it might be possible to understand the Charter as providing for conspiracy to crimes against peace as a separate crime, while conspiracy at the same time was also a mode of participation for all three main crimes.

In the Indictment, under Count One, all the defendants in this case concerning the major criminals at the top level of the Nazi power structure were separately charged by the prosecutors for participation "in the formulation or execution" of the common plan or conspiracy, namely, the plans "to commit, or which involved the commission of, Crimes against Peace, War Crimes, and Crimes against Humanity".[145] Count Two then concerned the completed – actually committed – crimes against peace. Count Three concerned completed war crimes, while Count Four concerned completed crimes against humanity.[146]

The IMT, on the other hand, construed the London Charter to mean that it did not "define as a separate [distinct] crime any conspiracy except the one to commit acts of aggressive war".[147] In the opinion of the IMT, the words of the Charter "do not add a new and separate crime to those already listed". The IMT therefore partly disregarded the charges in Count One, namely that the defendants conspired to commit war crimes and crimes against humanity. It did take into account as a separate crime, though, the common plan or conspiracy to plan, prepare, initiate, and wage aggressive war.[148]

This kind of compromise solution was not obvious, but it was perhaps the most reasonable. The relationship between the two cited provisions of the London Charter was indeed ambiguous and thus needed to be clarified by the IMT one way or another. From a practical point of view, most of the accused had participated in so many completed war crimes and crimes against humanity that there was no need for conspiracy as a separate crime in this regard.

More important to this book, the disagreement between the prosecutors and the judges at Nuremberg with respect to conspiracy illustrates the point that it can sometimes be difficult to figure out whether certain forms

---

[145] IMT, *Trial of the Major War Criminals*, vol. I, p. 29, see *supra* note 36.

[146] *Ibid.*, pp. 42–68.

[147] *Ibid.*, p. 226.

[148] *Ibid.*

of participation should be considered modes of participation (modes of liability) for the attribution of liability to a person belonging to a certain group of participants, or separate (distinct) accessorial crimes, or a combination of both forms.[149] Under the general theory of personal liability both alternatives are lawful. The solution is thus left to the operational level and for each criminal law subsystem to determine.

Subsequent acts that are undertaken after, but in connection with, the completed crime can also in principle be criminalised as distinct crimes, or they can be viewed as part of a larger criminal enterprise if the subsequent acts were agreed to before (or at) the execution stage. Alternatively, the subsequent acts might constitute accessoryship (complicity) if they were agreed to prior to the main crimes by persons who had agreed to assist after the fact, for instance by placing dead bodies on a truck and then burying them in a mass grave at another place in order to conceal the crimes committed. Which alternative applies will depend on the specific factual circumstances and the applicable specific provisions. If the physical assistance was limited to covering up the completed crime, the alternatives might be either joint perpetration (because the cover-up was part of the common plan and even the truck drivers participated in the planning), complicity (because the *ex post* participants had knowledge of the crimes to be committed and intended to assist the perpetrators when agreeing to assist), or a not punishable contribution to the crime (because subsequent participation after completion of the crime did not involve knowledge of the crimes before they were executed, and such *ex post* contributions had not been criminalised either as mode of participation or as a distinct crime within the specific provisions of the particular criminal law subsystem).

In conclusion, if several individuals participate in the crime, there are five temporal sequences or phases that are relevant to punishable participation in accordance with the general theory of criminal law liability.

---

[149] More recently, it has been discussed in the literature whether command responsibility may constitute a mode of liability or a distinct crime. See, for example, Chantal Meloni, "Command Responsibility: Mode of Liability for the Crimes of Subordinates or Separate Offence of the Superior?", in *Journal of International Criminal Justice*, 2007, vol. 5, no. 3, pp. 619–37; Elies van Sliedregt, "Article 28 of the ICC Statute: Mode of Liability and/or Separate Offence?", in *New Criminal Law Review*, 2009, vol. 12, no. 3, pp. 420–32; and Darryl Robinson, "How Command Responsibility Got So Complicated: A Culpability Contradiction, Its Obfuscation, and a Simple Solution", in *Melbourne Journal of International Law*, 2012, vol. 13, no. 1, pp. 1–58, at p. 30 ff.

Participation at one or several of these phases may incur some form of liability.

Formation of Temporal Phases of Punishable Participation

1) Conspiracy (initial common plan)
2) Planning, preparation, initiation, incitement
3) Attempt
4) Execution (completion)
5) Subsequent acts linked to the criminal enterprise

The principle of partial participation, in our view, is an important component of a general theory of criminal law liability within ICL as well. Because execution (perpetration) belongs to the class of direct participation (see below), which together with indirect participation concerns completed crimes, acts that were formerly acts of conspiracy, planning and preparation, or attempt, but that are successful in the sense that they factually led to completed crimes, are assimilated. When they did not lead to completed crimes, they may be considered part of conspiracy, planning, and attempt proper, namely as distinct categories of liability, belonging to the common class of inchoate crimes or inchoate liability.

This class of inchoate liability also includes initiation (in at least some cases, as we have seen) and incitement to commit a relevant crime, whereas the concept of instigation, in contrast, should be reserved for similar acts or speech when the crime encouraged is also actually completed. 'Ordering' may also be part of the planning phase, but ordering in ICL at this stage is assimilated by the categories of direct and indirect participation. Ordering as such has not been recognised as a separate inchoate crime in ICL. However, orders as an activity may also in some cases be part of and assimilated by (other) inchoate crime categories. For instance, an order may be provided as part of a hate speech to soldiers that also constitutes incitement to commit genocide. The order might thus be prosecuted as part of the incitement, and possibly as an attempt to commit a universal crime, when the order was not successful in the sense that no genocidal acts were actually committed as a result of the speech that included the order.

In sum, the principle of partial participation has an important linkage to the liability class of inchoate crimes and its underlying categories, as discussed further in Section 2.2.3.5. below.

2.2.3.2. Direct Participation and the Class of Commission Liability

The principle of direct participation relates to the (possible) imposition of criminal liability on participants who are direct parties to a completed criminal offence. There are three generally recognised categories of direct participation through active perpetration or commission of the relevant crimes: perpetration, joint perpetration, and perpetration through another.[150] However, in addition to commission, there is also the category of omission, that is, unlawful inaction when a person had a duty to act in order to prevent a crime from being committed.[151] Together these four categories form the class of direct participation, which might also be termed the class of commission/omission liability.

A person who executes the crime successfully as an individual would be a direct perpetrator, in this book also referred to as an executor of the (underlying) crime. He or she would be responsible for having committed the crime (commission liability) – provided that the required mental elements are met and that no adequate justification (mental emergency) or excuse (mental incapacity) for the act exists, which is a general precondition for criminal liability that is not discussed further in this book.[152] With respect to universal crimes, singular perpetration is possible, but singular perpetration without any assistance is not usual. Furthermore, inherent in system criminality is a social context of armed conflict, or turmoil and oppression, and often there will be multiple crime scenes linked together by high-level organisation and common plans. Singular perpetration of certain war crimes is conceivable, however – for example, when a person acting as a guard of war prisoners suddenly on his own initiative starts shooting at a defenceless group of prisoners, or when a low-ranking officer chooses to severely mistreat a prisoner although his

---

[150] Compare Hallevy, 2012, p. 18, *supra* note 3 (though he complicates the issue a bit by also using the term 'complicity' in this regard): "The principle of direct participation relates to complicity in which the accomplices are direct parties to the offense (perpetration, joint-perpetration, perpetration-through-another, etc.)". See also Rome Statute, Article 25(3)(a), which states that a person shall be criminally responsible and liable for punishment for a crime within the jurisdiction of the court if that person commits such a crime "whether as an individual, jointly with another or through another person, regardless of whether that other person is criminally responsible".

[151] See Section 2.2.2.2.

[152] See, however, the brief discussion in Section 2.2.2.3.

---

superior only directed him to question the prisoner in accordance with recognised international rules of war.

If person A commits the crime jointly with person B, or jointly with a group of others, A would be a joint perpetrator and responsible for having committed the crime (commission liability). Joint perpetration has two analytical subcategories: joint 'multiple' perpetration, and joint 'functional' perpetration. Joint multiple perpetration happens when several persons basically perform the same criminal conduct according to a common plan. For instance, two persons kidnap the victim, each wielding a knife, and they both torture and finally stab the victim to death, and then together dispose of the body. In this example, the joint perpetrators both participated in the criminal conduct of torture and directly caused the death of the victim. Joint functional perpetration happens when several persons perform different acts or roles in the agreed criminal enterprise: for instance, one person kidnaps the victim, another tortures and finally stabs the victim to death, and a third person disposes of the body in accordance with the initial plan. The two first persons executed different crimes, but through the common plan all three persons participated in the whole criminal enterprise and thus contributed to and caused the crimes as joint (functional) perpetrators.

Some cases of joint perpetration might arguably fall outside both subcategories and may instead be considered under another class of participation (indirect participation), and thus also another category. For instance, if person A is part of an illegitimate execution squad of 10 members who all fire simultaneously at victim X, and each hits X with a bullet that caused or contributed to his death, that would in principle be a clear instance of joint multiple perpetration. Even if only some of the execution squad members fired bullets at X while the others did not, the question is whether they should still all be considered joint perpetrators since they all agreed to the plan to take part in the execution of X, even though some were present at the crime scene without firing. Arguably, it would be a case of joint functional perpetration. However, those who did not fire at A might instead be considered indirect participants as accomplices, that is, participants in the common plan who reinforced the intention of the executors through their presence at the crime scene without protesting and thus 'abetted' the crime. Another solution is also possible: since it might be impossible to find out who fired at X and caused his death, and who did not hit X or fire at all, they might all be considered liable for complicity to murder (aiding and abetting), or complicity in a war crime if the event took place within the context of war. All three solutions are within the lawful scope of the general theory of personal criminal law liability.

Again, different solutions are possible within different criminal jurisdictions (subsystems), depending on the specific criminal liability provisions, legal traditions, and *lex ferenda* considerations that have been undertaken within the particular criminal law subsystem. Some jurisdictions have for instance developed specific modes of joint criminal enterprise or co-perpetration, or other similar concepts with distinct material and mental elements. Hence the concrete legal solutions *lex lata* must ultimately be sought at the fourth level of criminal law liability.

The third category of perpetration mentioned above, perpetration through another, refers to cases where a person uses another person or persons as a means to commit a crime. The other person might not be liable, perhaps due to young age or other shortcomings (for instance, mental incapacity) that impair his or her ability to exercise free choice. If the choice was free but the range of choices was severely limited because of external pressures (mental emergency, or duress), the other person again might not be liable. The question is whether criminal law liability for the direct perpetrator releases the indirect perpetrator from criminal law liability, or changes his position to that of an inciter or accomplice in the crime.

However, under the general theory of personal criminal law liability, it should not matter whether the direct perpetrator is liable or not for his own conduct, because in no case should a person be released from his or her responsibility merely because another person who participated in the crime, even as the executor, cannot or should not be held liable due to mental incapacity or mental emergency relevant only to the individual situation of the latter. In our view, a person who uses other persons for a criminal end in accordance with his own mental plan, or in accordance with a conspiracy of which he is part, should be considered to be an indirect perpetrator and not only an accomplice or inciter (instigator).

With respect to universal crimes committed by power structures, some participants within the structure may legally or socially be put more or less involuntarily in a position where opposition to an order may cause severe risks. A soldier may, for instance, have a structural duty to act in accordance with a command, while there are limits under the rule of law with respect to manifestly unlawful orders. Power structures make it possible for senior leaders at the top level and commanders in the chain of command to use – and abuse – the power structure for criminal purposes as well as other purposes. In many such cases, if written orders or instructions were not given, or were destroyed instead of being saved, the abuse would be difficult to prove later on. These experiences lead to the development of particular kinds of omission liability for commanders and superiors, the potentially most responsible leaders, based on duties to act on relevant information within their powers to prevent universal crimes.

From a historical and an empirical point of view, ICL contains an abundant number of illustrations of universal crimes being committed indirectly by leaders, organisers, and masterminds through power structures involving large groups of other persons. Because of the heightened criminal law liability of the architects behind the executors, labels such as high-level perpetrator, principal, or the most responsible persons (the last two covering also high-level omission liability) might be particularly well justified in many such cases.[153]

2.2.3.3.   Indirect Participation and the Class of Accomplice Liability

The principle of indirect participation relates to the (possible) imposition of criminal liability on participants who are indirect parties to a completed or an attempted criminal offence. An indirect party does not complete (execute) the crime but may indirectly cause or contribute a causal factor to the occurrence of the crime. In criminal law generally, the main categories are instigation; ordering (at a lower level in the chain of command within a power structure than acts of ordering that constitute perpetration through another); and complicity (accessoryship). The latter is often labelled aiding and abetting, although complicity might be a somewhat broader concept that includes some other subcategories (aiding and abetting could be considered a subcategory of complicity).[154] Together they form the class of accomplice liability writ large.

---

[153] See also Chapter 3, Section 3.3., and Chapter 7, Section 7.2.2.

[154] One such possible other subcategory of complicity within ICL is the mode of liability set out in Control Council Law No. 10 with a view to the subsequent Nuremberg trials, referred to as 'taking a consenting part' in war crimes and crimes against humanity. This consists of liability for a person whose position gives him authority to influence the criminal behaviour of others but who instead chooses to silently condone crimes outside the scope of his own effective control.

Another possible category of indirect participation is membership liability. This is a form of liability for a distinct crime of indirect participation in the main crimes. Historically it was first used in ICL in the Charter of the IMT and made applicable by the IMT at Nuremberg to members of selected parts of the Nazi power structure that were deemed to constitute criminal organisations. It is important to note that members convicted for this particular crime in the subsequent Nuremberg trials were not, through this conviction, made personally responsible for the main crimes against peace, war crimes, and crimes against humanity). The criminal liability encompassed only membership/participation in the criminal organisation as such. It might thus be described as a form of extended accomplice liability, based on the underlying notion that all members of the criminal organisations shared a kind of minimum and 'average' responsibility for all the crimes committed through these same organisations, but without attributing specific liability for any concrete crime committed at a particular crime scene to any member by means of membership liability. This category has not, however, been used in current ICL, and the question is whether it can be lawfully employed again in the future if considered desirable (see discussion in Chapter 10, Section 10.6., and also Appendix I).

With respect to actual harm, the criminal liability imposed on indirect participators is not equal to that imposed for commission or omission liability. It is instead adjusted to the type of contribution. Hallevy provides the following explanation for the adjustment of liability to indirect participation, illustrated by lesser responsibility for instigation – termed incitement by Hallevy[155] – as compared to perpetration (execution) of the crime:

> For example, A incites [instigates] B to commit an offense, and B agrees and becomes the perpretrator. In this case, A and B exercise different types of free choice. B's free choice relates to the actual commission of the offense, whereas A's free choice has to do with the incitement of B. Applying the principle of personal liability mediated by the secondary principles of direct participation and indirect participation

---

[155] In this book we have considered it necessary to distinguish between *incitement* to crimes that were not completed, that is, possible inchoate liability, and *instigation* (and similar forms such as encouragement or inducement) to completed crimes, that is, accomplice liability.

leads to the imposition of different criminal liability on A and B, adjusted to the part each played in the commission of the offense. B is considered a perpetrator, subject to criminal liability for perpetration, whereas A is considered an inciter, subject to criminal liability for incitement. This outcome is just, fair, and it accurately reflects the free choices exercised by the actors.[156]

We agree with this analysis and its core policy implications, at least as a general point of departure. With respect to organised group crimes, the social endangerment and risk of harm of these kinds of criminal behaviour complicates the matter. In cases of system criminality and universal crimes involving complex power structures, the matter becomes even more complicated.

First, the forms of indirect participation in the criminal enterprise become more varied and cannot necessarily be considered less dangerous or less blameworthy from empirical, analytical, and ICL points of view. It might in fact be the opposite. In other words, an indirect form of participation in a criminal enterprise may incur greater responsibility than direct participation at the execution phase. In complex crimes, perhaps involving large groups of persons, it is not always clear which forms of participation are the most dangerous and which persons are most responsible. In essence, an influential instigator of genocidal policies positioned at the top level of a power structure may well be much more responsible for the ensuing genocidal acts than an individual executor at the ground who physically kills another person.

Second, because universal crimes often entail extreme social endangerment and at the same time often require mass participation in order to be executed at the intended scale, accomplices and inciters are indispensable. Hence their free choice to participate in the criminal enterprise is indeed blameworthy and should be deterred by imposing criminal liability that reflects the gravity of the planned, foreseen, and ultimately executed (or attempted) crimes, as well as the concrete contribution of the individual participant. For this reason, one may not too easily accept that forms of indirect participation necessarily imply lesser responsibility in ICL.

---

[156] Hallevy, 2012, p. 20, *supra* note 3.

2.2.3.4. Juridical Entity Participation

The principle of juridical entity participation relates to the (possible) imposition of criminal liability on juridical entities, such as corporations and organisations.[157] It makes it lawful to impose criminal liability directly on a corporation or any other non-human, juridical entity recognised within the relevant legal system. It is also socially more effective with respect to prevention than having to rely exclusively on the prosecution of individuals representing the entity. However, this principle does not imply any distinct class of liability different from the three classes already inherent in the principles relating to individual liability (see above, Sections 2.2.3.1.–2.2.3.3.).

Within ICL, criminal law liability for juridical entities has never been implemented at the international criminal tribunals. While the concept of corporate liability was discussed during the negotiation of the Rome Statute, states ultimately rejected the proposal to include corporate criminal liability within the jurisdiction of the ICC.[158] However, by 2011 "over two dozen states in the Americas, Europe, Asia, and Australasia [had] promulgated laws permitting the prosecution of corporate entities" for responsibility applicable to universal crimes.[159]

Juridical entity liability may take different forms. The 'vicarious liability model' requires that full criminal liability of an officer or employee of the entity be proved before the entity can in any way be punished.[160] Such liability for corporations for criminal offences perpetrated by company employees, within the scope of their employment and with the intent to benefit the corporation, might be considered a soft variant of juridical entity liability. It has been applied in some countries, including Austria, South Africa, and the United States.[161] An arguably even softer model is limited to holding an entity liable for offences committed only by senior members of management who were the company's 'directing mind and

---

[157] Hallevy uses the term "legal participation" for the same phenomenon; see Hallevy, 2012, pp. 17–21, *supra* note 3.

[158] See James G. Stewart, *Corporate War Crimes: Prosecuting the Pillage of Natural Resources*, Open Society Justice Initiative, New York, 2011, p. 79 (www.legal-tools.org/doc/5dcffe/).

[159] *Ibid.*

[160] *Ibid.*, p. 81.

[161] *Ibid.*

will'. Canada and the United Kingdom have endorsed this kind of identification model.[162] However, this model does not necessarily require that a particular senior member fulfil all criteria for criminal liability through his or her own acts, as joint functional perpetration by several senior members may suffice under the identification model. The third model – which has been implemented in, for instance, Australia and Switzerland – focuses on a failed corporate culture, where liability for the corporation may be activated by a failure to create a corporate policy that could have prevented the offence, independently of the criminal liability of any of its employees.[163] This kind of corporate omission liability has some similarities to superior responsibility applicable to individual leaders of a power structure. The third model may in principle be combined with one of the other models in future ICL.

From the perspective of the general theory of criminal law liability, the *supra-* and fundamental principles of free choice, legality, conduct, and culpability must be applied but must be adapted before being applied to juridical entities. Because only human beings can exercise free choice,[164] the principle of culpability is not directly applicable to a corporation as such. Instead free choice must have existed for the relevant human beings representing or acting on behalf of the corporation. Similarly, one or several persons acting on behalf of the entity must individually or together fulfil the material (and possibly) mental elements of the relevant crime description and the relevant provision on culpability. As noted, it might also be possible with omission liability for corporate failures to prevent offences. The three models mentioned above that have been implemented at the domestic level seem to fit well within the ranges of the fundamental and secondary principles of criminal law liability. Furthermore, the three liability classes of inchoate liability, commission/omission liability, and accomplice liability, relevant to individual criminal liability, would also be relevant to juridical entity liability. Hence the establishment of some forms of juridical entity liability in future ICL does not seem to run into insurmountable theoretical or practical problems, although corporate and other strong interests may resist their inclusion.

---

[162] *Ibid.*

[163] *Ibid.*, p. 82.

[164] See Section 2.2.1.

In conclusion, responsibility for corporations and other juridical entities is generally possible (lawful) through the general principles and specific provisions that might be enacted for participation in universal crimes in future statutes of international criminal tribunals. The only issue *lex lata* in this regard is whether such liability might still be prohibited by customary international law or the general principles of international law. We shall return to this issue in Chapter 4 and finally in Chapter 10.[165]

Finally, it needs to be added that *individual* criminal law liability for, for example, corporate players is not ruled out *lex lata* within ICL. Such liability requires that the ordinary conditions for individual liability be met. In practice, it might be more difficult to prosecute individuals acting within corporations compared to those in other power structures for their punishable participation in universal crimes, but it is far from impossible.[166]

2.2.3.5. Further Derivative Principles and Derivative Liability

The secondary principles of personal liability also contain more specified secondary principles, or further derivative principles leading to more specified derivative criminal law liability.

The further derivative principles concern the more specific or underlying categories and subcategories of the liability classes of partial participation (as represented by the class of inchoate liability), direct participation (commission/omission liability), and indirect participation (accomplice liability). These derivative principles too are of a theoretical and analytical nature that may help organise criminal law liability into appropriate theoretical categories and subcategories in compliance with the general liability theory. The categories, and further derived subcategories, might however next be employed to develop or determine the modes of liability for punishable participation at the operational fourth level, within the subsystems of ICL and domestic criminal law, which are compatible with the general theory of criminal liability – including rule of law and fundamental human rights.

---

[165] See Chapter 4, Section 4.3.7, and Chapter 10, Section 10.3.

[166] Several examples are provided in Stewart, 2011, pp. 76–79, see *supra* note 158. See also the cases related to businessmen in Chapter 3, Section 3.6.5.

Derivative criminal law liability by definition "refers to types of criminal liability formations derived from other types of criminal liability".[167] Imposition of derivative criminal liability on the participants in a crime thus depends on the existence of *a basic type of criminal liability* from which the derivative criminal law liability categories are derived.[168] Thus far, we fully agree with Hallevy. The basic liability types, we contend, are always constituted *in conjunction with* a relevant crime description (the abstract crime), but they are not identical to the (abstract or concrete) crime as such. For example, in the case of criminalised 'murder', the basic form is 'criminal law liability for murder'. At this point we disagree with Hallevy when he claims that the basic type of criminal liability for murder is "the offense of murder".[169] We believe Hallevy makes a mistake here, because the 'offence' of murder is not the same as 'liability' for murder. Offence (crime) and liability belong to different concept categories. Because of this error, Hallevy does not, for example, include liability for singular perpetration or omission liability in his typology of derivative criminal liability, although he includes joint perpetration and perpetration through another.[170]

We admit, however, that our definition of derivative criminal liability differs from the (not always internally consistent) definitions employed by several other authors within ICL. The tendency is to define derivative criminal liability as liability for the criminal offences of others.[171] This has led to the wrong basic question being posed, even by some of the most knowledgeable contemporary scholars of complicity in ICL, including, for example, Aksenova:

> The book uses legal tools to tackle complicity. It must be noted, however, that the concept lies at the intersection of law, philosophy, human psychology, sociology and criminology. Under what circumstances an individual is responsible

---

[167] See Hallevy, 2012, p. 22, *supra* note 3.

[168] *Ibid.*

[169] *Ibid.* See also p. 63.

[170] *Ibid.*, pp. 84–104.

[171] See, for example, Miles Jackson, *Complicity in International Law*, Oxford University Press, Oxford, 2015, p. 11: "At root, complicity is simply a derivative form of responsibility for participation in wrongdoing committed by another actor".

for the act of another person is a serious dilemma that can be approached from different angles.[172]

We agree with the first part of this statement but take issue with the question implicitly posed. We would argue that derivative liability – including inchoate and accomplice liability – is instead about liability for each individual's own contribution to the main crime, derived from the basic form of liability for the relevant crime (for instance, liability for crimes against humanity).

On its face, Article 25(3)(a) of the Rome Statute is interestingly in line with this view. It does not put perpetration (or commission) on a different level than joint perpetration and perpetration through another. Instead the three categories are given equal treatment within the same provision; this is also theoretically correct because they are in fact all categories of liability within the class of commission/omission liability derived in the first place from the basic type of criminal law liability for the relevant crime. The same is true for the other forms of liability enumerated in Article 25(3). These include the class of accomplice liability as set out in different categories – such as (3)(b) on ordering ("orders") and instigation ("solicits or induces"), and (3)(c) on aiding and abetting ("aids, abets or otherwise assists") the commission of a crime – which *complement* liability for perpetration (commission) liability in (3)(a) but are not 'derived' from it. Instead, individual liability when several persons participate and contribute to a crime is determined by the concrete physical conduct and mental state of each individual who has participated and contributed to the crime. This is illustrated by several examples presented below, and will also be a general theme throughout the book.

First, if only one person (A) is involved in the crime (in addition to the possible individual victim) and commits a completed murder, there is no need for derivative criminal liability. A is the perpetrator and is liable for commission of murder. Other forms of liability are either irrelevant (incitement, complicity, and so on) or inherently assimilated by the completion of the crime (planning, attempt). For this reason, it may seem superfluous and perhaps odd to claim that A's liability for committing the crime in this case is in principle also derived from the basic form of liability for murder. When more than one person is involved (in addition to the

---

[172] Aksenova, 2016, pp. 3–4, *supra* note 12.

possible victim), however, derivative principles and relevant liability categories serve to identify and label the contribution of each participant in legal terms and attribute the correct form of liability. In these cases, perpetration/commission liability is not theoretically different from other forms of participation and criminal law liability. It operates on the same level as other categories and serves to identify and label the contribution of the executor who completed the crime; or in the case of an indirect perpetrator (perpetration through another), it serves to identify and label the contribution of the mastermind or leader behind the criminal enterprise.

A different point is that the concept of perpetration, or execution, or commission by definition concerns acts that complete a crime, and thus theoretically concerns the most serious degree of punishable participation as compared to other forms of participation.[173] As already pointed out, however, the potential of direct commission liability for the physical executors on the ground is often subordinate to the degree of responsibility of leaders based on more indirect forms of commission/omission liability, and might even be equalised by the responsibility of others who contributed substantially to universal crimes from a higher and more important position in the relevant power structure.

Although a clear distinction between what is theoretically right or wrong may not be easily available, the best view is that the basic type of criminal law liability is the same no matter how many participants there are, and in principle even if there is only one person involved. For example, if the crime of murder was not completed but the act constituted an attempt to commit the crime, it is perfectly logical to say that the liability for attempt is also derived from the basic type of liability, for example, normative liability for murder, and thus attempted murder is the correct form of liability. The liability for attempt cannot be derived from the acts of perpetration, which did not happen. And since perpetration of murder and attempted murder are two different forms of liability at the same level, the one cannot logically be derived from the other.

It is therefore not sustainable under the general theory of criminal law liability to assert that different kinds of inchoate liability or accom-

---

[173] For this reason, it is quite natural that the three forms of perpetration are listed in paragraph (a) in Article 25(3) of the Rome Statute, while other forms are listed in paragraphs (b) through (f). This, however, is a 'soft' hierarchy and *not* a 'hard' hierarchy in the sense that the other forms are *derived from perpetration*.

plice liability are *derived* from either commission/omission liability or the act/conduct of the physical perpetrator of the crime. Sometimes the term accessorial liability is used to describe the derivative linkage between commission liability/physical act of the one completing the crime and liability for other participants.[174] This doctrinal viewpoint is in our opinion unsustainable, which may also be illustrated through examples.

If person A publicly and directly encourages persons B, C, and D to commit genocidal acts, and the crime is completed, person A is liable for instigation of genocide. Under the Rome Statute, Article 25(3)(b), person A could be convicted for having instigated (solicited or induced) the commission of the crime. If the crime was not completed, A could still be liable for incitement to genocide, because liability for such acts – in line with the general theory of criminal law liability – should be viewed as derived from the basic type of liability, that is, normative criminal law liability for the crime of genocide. Incitement to commit genocide has actually been criminalised within this subsystem of criminal law – see the Rome Statute, Article 25(3)(e). Liability for incitement to genocide is obviously not derived from either commission/omission liability or the physical act of executing genocidal acts, because none of them existed or occurred. Furthermore, if person A, for the purpose of facilitating the commission of a war crime, aids, abets, or otherwise assists at the preparatory phase, but the crime is not completed, A may still incur accomplice liability if the crime was unsuccessfully attempted.

What this should be sufficient to prove is that the notion of derivative liability, when referring to liability derived either from commission liability or from the acts of the physical perpetrator who executed the crime, is impossible to sustain without making a number of exceptions, and that it also represents an unnecessary and theoretically confusing intermediate step in the analysis of criminal liability law.

It is noteworthy, moreover, that actual criminal acts take place in the real, physical world, while the scientific theory that explains and predicts the consequences of the acts is constituted at a theoretical and normative level. Hence liability for acts of perpetration or commission liability should instead be considered a form of liability attributed to a person at the same theoretical level as accomplice liability and inchoate liability.

---

[174] See the discussion of the scholarly literature on this topic in Chapter 4, Section 4.5.2.2.

Especially with regard to universal crimes, it is useful – and in our view indeed theoretically and legally necessary – to separate the issues of criminalisation of specific forms of participation and attribution of liability from the physical execution of the crimes. In the same vein, no type of liability for crimes against humanity should be considered to be derived from the perpetration of the underlying offences/crimes, such as acts of murder, torture, or rape.

Instead, the relevant derivations are from the basic type of criminal law liability. The basic type is always defined in conjunction with a relevant crime – for example, liability for crimes against humanity. This crime, however, like other universal crime types,[175] consists of certain underlying offences plus a contextual gravity clause that includes an extra layer of circumstance constituting the crime complex as, for example, crimes against humanity, or war crimes, or genocide. In the case of CAH, for example, executors of the underlying crimes who are not aware of the particular circumstance – namely, that the offences are part of a widespread or systematic attack on a civilian population – cannot be held liable for CAH because of their mental element deficit in that regard. However, other participants might still be held responsible for exactly those underlying crimes *and* for CAH, because they had no mental deficits despite being either indirect perpetrators or accomplices. Again, one can see that such reasoning – deriving liability from commission liability of the executors – may lead to questions that are unnecessary and to intermediate steps in the analysis that might be confusing and thus lead to the wrong results as well.

Conversely, if a single executor (A) operates on his own at a particular crime scene and chooses to kill a single civilian while being aware that his crime forms part of a larger pattern constituting CAH, the person would be liable for commission of CAH. Again, the criminal law liability for A's commission of CAH is not derived from his own offence or from murder, but – obviously – from the basic type of liability for CAH.

To take another example: according to a common criminal plan contemplated and consented to at a certain level of a power structure (a conspiracy at the time), plotters identify three different crimes scenes for attacks on civilians. Taken together, the combined crimes at the three

---

[175] See discussion of the notion of 'crime types' in Einarsen, 2012, pp. 222–23 and pp. 278–86, *supra* note 6.

crime scenes fulfil the criteria of a widespread or systematic attack on a civilian population ('CAH'). Because the planners intended to destroy a minority ethnic group at large and therefore carried out attacks at three places populated by members of that minority group, the crimes constituted genocidal acts as well. The executors (direct perpetrators) were different at each crime scene and did not know about the common plan; they knew that they were participating in concerted acts of murder and rape, but they were not aware of the broader context that constituted the crimes as CAH and genocide under international law. Hence, they cannot be considered responsible for perpetration of CAH or genocide, or for other forms of participation in CAH or genocide. This should make clear that it would be incorrect as a matter of principle – even fictional – to derive criminal liability for participants with full knowledge of the relevant context for CAH and genocide from the underlying acts (offences) or from the liability of the executors (which only extends to murder and rape). Instead the liability of all kinds of fully informed participants must be derived from the basic form of 'liability for CAH', whether they were participants in the common plan, were involved in further organisation and ordering at the high and intermediate levels, or aided and abetted the crimes with full knowledge of the plan and intentions of the leadership, and with an intention to facilitate CAH and genocide.

In the same example, the conspirators, who used the relevant power structure to have CAH completed by the executors of the underlying crimes, would be liable for their own participation in the crime complex. Since crimes of CAH and genocide were completed, the initially possible liability for the common plan as a conspiracy, at least for CAH, was assimilated by commission liability. The relevant category in this case would be perpetration through another or some further derived subcategory that would be applicable in practice, since the executors on the ground were not part of and were not even aware of the common plan to commit crimes rising to the level of CAH and genocide. Thus, the executors cannot be considered to have joined the common plan before or at the execution stage, since they were not aware of the relevant increased gravity and full social context of their crimes. Within particular subsystems of ICL, modes like joint criminal enterprise or indirect perpetration might apply in this case and might be tantamount to commission liability for CAH.

Again, we see that in cases of liability for universal crimes at least – although we believe this to be a valid general point under the general theory of criminal law liability – liability for punishable participation should always be understood as derived from the basic form of liability, not from the class of commission liability or from the concrete acts of the physical perpetrator/executor.

2.2.3.6. Formation, Combination, and Assimilation of Derivative Liability

Despite our disagreement with Hallevy with respect to the *object* of derivation – 'liability for an offence' versus the 'object offence' (Hallevy)[176] – his further analysis is still very interesting for the purpose of our further work on a general theory of ICL liability. Below we point out briefly six areas where we find his findings and ideas particularly useful.

First, we agree with his proposition that "derivative criminal liability may be described by a general formation that relates the type of criminal liability to a general variable".[177] To take his example, a person incites another person to commit a robbery. The first person is not indicted for incitement alone because there is no actual meaning to incitement without the object of incitement, in this case robbery. Therefore, incitement may be described by the general formation as follows: "incitement to commit X".[178] In this formation we can replace X with any type of crime, for instance, robbery or a universal crime.

In this particular example, a special terminological problem arises, however, because at least within the field of ICL, the concept of incitement is usually reserved for the inchoate crime of incitement to commit genocide, that is, when the particular crimes incited are not completed. Other concepts, like instigation or instigates, solicits or induces, are more frequently used for attribution of liability for similar kinds of encouragement to commit a universal crime when the crime was ultimately also completed. Be that as it may, the general, valid point is that we can replace incitement/instigation in the example with any other type of derivative liability derived from the basic form of liability for crime X, for example, all relevant categories and further derived subcategories of commission liability, inchoate liability, or accomplice liability. For this reason,

---

[176] See Hallevy, 2012, p. 63, *supra* note 3.

[177] Hallevy, *ibid.*, p. 64.

[178] *Ibid.*

we find the principal derivative formation to be more precisely expressed in these terms:

General Formation of Derivative Criminal Liability

Y liability of person A for the crime of X

In this formation, Y is the category of liability derived from the basic form of liability to commit X (for instance, joint perpetration/co-perpetration), while X is the specific object offence or the crime description of that object offence. If one of these two components is not punishable, the whole formation – and the conduct of person A – is not punishable.[179]

As explained earlier in this chapter, it might be theoretically useful to distinguish between the three main derivative classes of personal criminal liability and the 12 derivative categories of personal criminal liability, as well as further derivative subcategories. Such further derivations do not require any change in the general formation. For instance, commission liability and JCE liability might both be relevant 'Y' liability, depending on the context, despite the latter (at least within the subsystem of ICTY) being considered lawfully derived from the former.

More complicated are multiple derivations, that is, combinations of derivative liability, which are also theoretically possible. For example, A instigates B to assist C to commit murder, which is completed. A is in principle liable for instigation to complicity to murder, shortened to instigation to murder although B was an intermediate agent used by A to assist C. In this particular example, it follows from the very concept of instigation that an intermediate agent must somehow have been used to commit or facilitate the murder. Thus, some kind of linkage is required. The formation could be expressed as follows, where Y1, Y2, and Y3 are three different forms of derivative liability derived from 'liability for crime X':

Formation of Multiple Derivative Criminal Liability

Y1 liability [instigation] of person A linked to Y2 liability [aiding/ abetting] of person B linked to Y3 liability [commission] of person C for the crime of X [murder]

Although multiple derivations (combinations of derivative liability) are possible and are not *per se* unlawful under the general theory of crim-

---

[179] See similarly Hallevy, 2012, p. 65, *supra* note 3.

inal law liability, multiple derivations may raise important issues *lex ferenda* as to how far criminalisation of conduct ought to go at the fourth level of specific provisions within a particular criminal law subsystem. For instance, it might be considered undesirable to criminalise a failed attempt to complicity to commit a crime because the social endangerment on balance is considered too low when weighed against freedom of conduct in society and prudent use of prosecutorial resources; while criminalising complicity to an attempted crime might be considered justified within the same subsystem because participation at the attempt phase might be considered socially more dangerous than a failed attempt to contribute to a criminal enterprise. Or, in yet another (domestic) subsystem, both cases of multiple derivations might be criminalised, but only with respect to serious offences.

That the categories of derivative liability might be lawfully combined is important and relevant to ICL. This makes it possible – in principle – to impose and adequately allocate liability for criminal conduct within power structures that would otherwise be almost impossible to prosecute when large groups of persons participate at different levels and with different roles within the structure. For example, by combining conspiracy and joint perpetration and/or perpetration through another, it becomes possible to impose commission liability on leaders at the top who jointly planned the crimes – no matter how many intermediate levels and perpetrators on the ground (executors) are also involved. This possibility at the third level of the general theory of criminal law liability in turn makes it possible to develop or enact specific modes of participation at the fourth level of actual law that specify the material and mental elements required. For example, the said combinations have made it possible for international criminal tribunals to develop modes of liability such as joint criminal enterprise derived from commission liability, and in different versions (JCE I, II, and III), and indirect co-perpetration.

Second, continuing to build on Hallevy, we find it useful to underline that the concept of punishable participation in this book refers to derivative criminal law liability at the third theoretical level as well as to the specific legal rules *lex lata* at the fourth level.

If one of the necessary components for personal criminal law liability is lacking, the entire formation is not punishable. For example, if a certain act of piracy is not an international crime under current customary international law and ICL,[180] and thus prosecution requires consent from a state with territorial or active/passive nationality jurisdiction, or is dependent upon conditioned universal jurisdiction in accordance with the UN Convention on the Law of Sea before being punishable in a domestic setting, it does not help with respect to direct ICL liability that the relevant and chargeable derivative criminal liability form would be recognised under international law. It simply could not be prosecuted before an international tribunal based only on criminal liability under international law. And if a particular form of liability is not punishable as a distinct mode of inchoate liability at the fourth level, for example, 'planning and preparation' of CAH, it does not help the prosecutor that liability for CAH is generally punishable or that such specific derivative criminal liability is possible at the third theoretical level – or perhaps ought to be punishable *lex ferenda*. However, the problem might be resolved for the prosecutor if planning and preparation were to be included among the modes of participation because it was considered desirable within the relevant subsystem of criminal law. For example, it might in the future be included in the Rome Statute.

Third, every form of derivative criminal liability requires a mental element that reflects that the purpose (volition and cognition must both be present) of each punishable contribution to a crime complex was to commit or otherwise contribute to the completion of a relevant crime.[181] The mental element for derivative liability must be intent (or specific intent) and knowledge/awareness, even when a lower mental threshold is part of the relevant crime description. For example, if negligent homicide is criminalised in addition to negligent driving – which it might be, since such criminalisation could be considered socially desirable and does not violate the fundamental principles of criminal law liability[182] – derivative criminal liability is irrelevant to the criminal law situation of the driver when he merely acted negligently. The offender did not have the volition and cognition to kill anybody as a result of his negligent conduct, but the risk

---

[180] See, for example, the discussion in Einarsen, 2012, pp. 306–13, *supra* note 6.

[181] Hallevy, 2012, pp. 66–67, see *supra* note 3, does not seem to include cognition in his discussion of 'purposefulness', but we think it may help to include cognition as well because intent and specific intent include a high level of cognition, not only volition.

[182] See Section 2.2.2.

still materialised. The basic form is instead liability for negligent driving and negligent homicide, imposed by the object-offence described in the relevant criminal provisions. It is possible to criminalise instigation and complicity to negligent conduct through the derivative principles, but only if the purpose was in some way to contribute to unlawful conduct. For example, A encourages B to drive without regard for speed limits in order to get home early, and B commits negligent homicide when driving far above the speed limit while hitting C, who dies. A is liable for instigation or complicity (aiding/abetting) to unlawful driving, and probably also for complicity to negligent homicide, although A did not have the volition and cognition to kill anybody.

Fourth, it is useful to highlight the concept of assimilation. It is complementary and inverse to derivability.[183] The direct forms of participation typically assimilate partial (incomplete) and indirect forms of participation. In other words, commission of a completed crime tends to assimilate other forms of liability, notably for a person who has also been involved in other ways. For example, A is at some point part of a conspiracy to commit a crime, which is later completed. Commission of the crime usually assimilates the otherwise inchoate liability form of conspiracy, unless it is otherwise stated in the specific provisions of the relevant criminal law subsystem. Hence the liability concept of conspiracy becomes redundant and is replaced by other liability concepts when the crime has been completed, such as liability for common plan, joint criminal enterprise, or co-perpetration/indirect perpetration.

However, there might be other instances in which preparatory acts are not fully assimilated by commission liability. For example, if A initially participated in a conspiracy that included the detailed planning and preparation of the crime, and then chose to leave the criminal group before the attempt phase, without telling the police or the potential victims about the plan, it would in theory be possible to hold A liable for conspiracy to the crime, or for planning the crime, while the other conspirators are held liable for commission liability or some derived form of commission liability.

Fifth, in some cases a person might be held liable for more than one form of participation in the same criminal enterprise. For example, A

---

[183] See Hallevy 2012, p. 67, *supra* note 3.

chooses to instigate B to instigate C to commit murder, and later A also chooses to assist C in the execution of the crime. A is then responsible for two concurrent forms of derivative liability in relation to the same crime (murder): instigation and complicity (aiding/abetting) to murder.

Sixth, the typology of derivative criminal liability – the possible classes and categories – located at the third level of the criminal law liability structure should in principle be the same for all subsystems of criminal law liability. However, the *sui generis* character of ICL and universal crimes – their system criminality nature – may challenge the prospect of a common typology. It could also be the case, however, that precisely because of their complex nature, universal crimes are especially fruitful with respect to providing the best theoretical lens available for uncovering the general structure of personal criminal law liability, and thus for constructing a general theory of personal criminal law liability. In other words, although the general theory unveiled and developed might be more specified than required for less complicated crimes within domestic criminal law, that does not mean that the theory is incorrect, just that its full applicability is not easily seen. Furthermore, as domestic criminal law is becoming significantly more complex, for instance with respect to organised crime and different types of transnational crimes, the usefulness of a general criminal liability theory – although developed initially for universal crimes – may increase within domestic jurisdictions as well. This is an issue we shall return to in the concluding chapter.

Hallevy, drawing on inductions from historical samples and to some extent from empirical surveys of domestic criminal law, and on theoretical deductions, considers only five categories of derivative criminal liability: attempt, joint perpetration, perpetration through another, incitement, and accessoryship. We, on the other hand, have already flagged that conspiracy and (further) planning/preparation are two other possibly lawful inchoate categories under the general theory of criminal law liability, although it depends upon *lex ferenda* considerations how far and with respect to what crimes these forms of derivative liability should be made applicable *lex lata* at the fourth level of the theory.

Within ICL, initiation is a form of inchoate liability closely connected to planning and preparation with respect to the crime of aggression as defined in Article 8*bis* of the Rome Statute, which may embrace both the initiative to commit an act of aggression amounting to a crime of aggression and public incitement to commit the crime (war propaganda).

The concept may, however, also include acts of instigation as a form of accomplice liability when the crime is completed, as discussed below.

We also consider single-handed commission (direct singular perpetration) of a crime to be in principle another derivative category, one that might in fact be especially important to recognise within ICL because the legal and sociological relationship between different acts committed within different parts of a power structure is significant for a proper legal analysis. In particular, we would emphasise that it may cause unnecessary confusion, both theoretically and practically, to put the acts of the executors on the ground – the actors at the lowest levels of the power structure – in the centre, and to seek to derive responsibility for other participants from the acts typically committed by low-level perpetrators, or from their liability, when they are just small cogs in the criminal enterprise machinery.

There are also some other possible categories of commission liability, which are perhaps especially important within ICL. The most prominent is omission liability in the form of derivative command/superior responsibility for a qualified omission to prevent universal crimes or to punish subordinates for such crimes; see, for instance, Article 28 of the Rome Statute.

In addition, ordering is also a possibly distinct liability category within the broader class of accomplice liability.[184] Ordering may, however, also be assimilated by commission liability and its derived forms such as perpetration through another and JCE/indirect co-perpetration when the crime is completed and the person ordering is the mastermind behind the crime or part of a joint leadership behind the crime. Hence, where ordering fits in the scheme of classification may depend on the position and role of the person giving the order within the relevant power structure. If the person is a commander at the top level, ordering will tend to be assimilated by commission liability. Acts of ordering may also occur at the preparatory phase, and in some cases even at the attempt phase. Such acts contributing towards the crime might be punishable either when they are part of a larger criminal enterprise at the preparatory phase and the substantive crimes are completed by others, or when such acts at the preparatory (or attempt) phase are criminalised as inchoate crimes. However, as a

---

[184] See, for example, Rome Statute, Article 25(3)(b).

separate (distinct) category of derivative criminal liability, ordering belongs to the class of accomplice liability.

Another distinct class of accomplice liability is instigation, that is, encouragement to commit a crime that is subsequently completed.[185] Finally, membership in a criminal organisation is also a possibly distinct liability category within the class of accomplice liability, but it is different from ordinary complicity because membership liability is more a kind of minimum average responsibility for all crimes committed by the organisation when the person concerned was a voluntary member with knowledge of the crimes.[186]

All in all, this leaves us with 12 possible categories of derivative criminal liability at the third level of the general theory of personal criminal liability, at least within ICL:

Formation of Classes and Categories of Personal Criminal Liability

Class I: Inchoate liability

1. Incitement
2. Conspiracy
3. Initiation, planning, preparation (including ordering)
4. Attempt

Class II: Commission liability

5. Perpetration (direct and singular)
6. Joint perpetration (direct and multiple)
7. Perpetration through another (indirect perpetration)
8. Omission (command and superior responsibility)

Class III: Accomplice liability

9. Ordering
10. Instigation

---

[185] See *ibid.* The article uses the terms 'solicits or induces' (the commission of a crime that in fact occurs or is attempted).

[186] As mentioned before, this category has a historical record within ICL after World War II, but it has been inactive in more recent ICL. It has, however, re-emerged within the field of criminal law dealing with terrorism at the domestic level in many states. This is interesting because serious acts of terror may in the foreseeable future form part of operational ICL.

11. Complicity (aiding/abetting)

12. Membership in a criminal organisation

The first four categories belong to the class of inchoate liability, the next four to the class of commission liability and the last four to the class of accomplice liability. In addition to the three classes and 12 categories, we have pointed out the possibility of further derivative subcategories, for instance represented by concepts such as JCE and (indirect) co-perpetration.

In subsequent chapters, we shall make use of this formation in our empirical surveys and analysis, although with some variations depending on pragmatic considerations.

2.2.4. Fourth Level: Specific Rules of Operational Criminal Law

For the sake of progression of the text with respect to the structure of the general theory of criminal law liability, we shall at this stage only briefly recall a couple of points already made regarding the fourth level of the general liability model suggested.

First, while the 12 categories identified above at the end of Section 2.2.3. are located at the third level of the general theory, it is the specific provisions and jurisprudence at the fourth level that specify the modes of liability as applicable legal rules within the relevant criminal law subsystem. The relevant subsystem might be ICL as such, based on treaties, customary international law, the general principles of law, and other sources. It may also be a subsystem within ICL, consisting, for instance, of the Rome Statute and the ICC. It could, however, also be a domestic jurisdiction implementing ICL liability for universal crimes.

With respect to any legal discussion *lex lata*, the rules concerning criminal law liability at the fourth level are essential. However, according to the general theory of personal criminal law liability, the legal rules must be framed within the possible ranges of derivative classes and categories (including subcategories), as well as in compliance with the *supra-*principle of free choice and the fundamental principles of criminal law liability. This framework should provide an appropriate amount of discretion for legislators, treaty negotiators, and decision makers within any relevant subsystem, as well as foreseeability for persons who might be considered responsible for punishable acts. In the same vein, we argue that the general theory we advocate is principled, appropriate, and sufficiently flexible, as well as fully compatible with the legality principle, human rights, and the rule of law.

Second, we believe there is still a need to further identify, systematise, and analyse possible and applicable modes of participation within ICL.

2.3. Exploring an ICL Matrix of Personal Liability

Chapter 2 has discussed theoretical preconditions, requirements under the rule of law, and possible components of a general model for explaining and assessing punishable participation in universal crimes. The discussion so far indicates that such a model in the form of a four-level theory of criminal law liability is conceivable and might be useful in the further scientific development of ICL liability. We have explained the four levels and paid special attention to the third-level secondary principles of personal criminal law liability and to further derivative principles, leading so far to the proposed theoretical classes and categories of punishable participation.

However, the ultimate goal of this work is to figure out more about the relationship between the second and third levels of the theory, on one hand, and the fourth practical legal level, on the other. It is especially in the intersection of the third and fourth levels of the general theory that there seems to be a need for a particular ICL matrix on categories and modes of liability that would better explain the ranges of lawful possibilities and need for consistent prediction and application of personal criminal law liability for participation in universal crimes. The formation of classes and categories set forth above in Section 2.2.3.6. may assist us in this further work. At the same time, we need to remain open to analytical adjustment based on the experiences of attribution of criminal liability in ICL in theory and practice.

However, if what has happened, or is currently happening, at the fourth level within ICL proves to be incompatible with our proposed general theory, the whole model will have to be dismissed or substantially reformulated. This means that the model should ultimately be tested against empirical facts and relevant legal sources (see Chapters 5–9). In Chapters 3 and 4, we shall first provide more historical/sociological and methodological context to the analysis. This will help us to not lose track of the social dimension of the subject matter in our search for a general theory of ICL liability that is ultimately supposed to be broadly applicable to the situation of human beings in society and universal crimes trials within a rule of law context.

3

Universal Crimes Participation in Historical and Sociological Context

3.1. Introduction

This chapter will address punishable participation in universal crimes from an empirical and historical perspective. The sociological categories identified and discussed are fairly numerous – 20 in all – in order to present a clear picture of the types of persons who have been subject to criminal sanctions by international criminal institutions. By 'categories' we mean different sociological or functional groups of people defined on the basis of their formal or informal positions in society, within structures that empirically have been involved in universal crimes.

These 20 sociological categories are placed within four overarching classes, defined by their level of authority within the hierarchies of which they form part. The first three classes include persons at the higher, middle, and lower ranks of main power structures, whom we will call 'high-level', 'mid-level', and 'low-level' participants, respectively; those we denote as low-level may also be members of smaller power structures. We also identify a fourth class of persons who operate within power support structures. This chapter examines these four classes and their constituent categories in turn.

Let us clarify, first, that the term 'power structure' denotes an entity or organisation that wields actual power within a society.[1] A power structure is often large, like the governmental or military structures of a state, but it could also be much smaller or could form part of a larger entity or organisation; it could be non-state as well. It may function basically for the benefit of society, or some parts of it, but may also be abused for criminal purposes and used to commit universal crimes. Hence the concept of a power structure is broader than the concept of a criminal enterprise, although the application of the two concepts may sometimes overlap: a

---

[1]   The term 'power structure' is used in the same way in Terje Einarsen, *The Concept of Universal Crimes in International Law*, Torkel Opsahl Academic EPublisher, Oslo, 2012 (www.legal-tools.org/doc/bfda36/). See also Chapter 1, Section 1.2.1., of this book.

power structure or parts of a larger power structure might be set up or used in such a way that the structure itself becomes more or less a criminal enterprise. An example could be those organisations within the Nazi regime labelled criminal organisations by the IMT at Nuremberg.

A relevant power structure for the purpose of ICL, and for this book, is always capable of being used to commit or facilitate acts that include such crimes. Thus, whether the relevant power structure is large or small, independent or part of a larger structure, is not decisive for our use of the term. Our grouping is not based on a ranking of different, specified power structures. Rather, the distinction between high-level, mid-level, and low-level participants concerns their authority within the relevant power structure. For instance, leaders of a non-state organisation committing atrocity crimes, such as war crimes or terrorist crimes, belong to the first class, that of high-level participants, although their overall power in society might not be comparable to that of state officials. With respect to a specific crime scene, such an organisation may have assumed control over the fates of the victims and is thus certainly a power structure within the meaning of the term. Moreover, a particular person might be a member of different relevant power structures in society. A general may, for example, be part of military leadership as well as part of the government, or he may have acted as a military commander at a particular crime scene in addition to being involved in politics at a high level.

In addition, power structures can be supported by entities or persons that are not part of the relevant power structures committing or being used to commit crimes. Participants in such support structures might, for instance, contribute to a crime by exercising their religious or professional authority in society. Finally, a power structure may also have transnational features as a result of the way it has been established or operated. For example, a state leader may use a power structure to attack another state, or to support a foreign power structure committing universal crimes.[2]

This chapter also investigates empirically the use of different modes of liability – or modes of participation – in this regard. For this purpose, we have decided to take the concepts employed in the jurisprudence at face value as a point of departure. Nevertheless, to some extent we have

---

[2]   See Chapter 1, Section 1.2.3., with reference to the Taylor case. See SCSL, *Prosecutor v. Taylor*, Judgment, SCSL-03-01-A, 26 September 2013 (www.legal-tools.org/doc/3e7be5/).

also assigned the legal concepts employed to broader legal categories, such as 'joint criminal enterprise', which from a purely *theoretical* perspective is also a subcategory of commission liability.[3] For example, different expressions of JCE-like modes – such as 'acting in concert', 'was connected to', 'acted jointly in pursuance of a common intent', 'committed' (as interpreted by a tribunal), and 'common purpose' – may all refer to similar concepts, and thus it might be useful for some purposes to refer to them as being under the same umbrella (JCE). The reason is that the language in the international court statutes and jurisprudence is not always consistent even when the meaning is the same. It is, finally, also important to underline that the legal concepts we identify in this chapter belong to the operational fourth level of the general theory of criminal law liability: they are 'modes of liability'. The labels used at this level do not always correspond to the most appropriate labels for the theoretical categories at the third level of the theory, also for the reason that some 'modes' are derivative forms. The overviews presented in this chapter with respect to legal categories (the modes of liability) must be understood against this background.

The scope of this chapter is limited in several ways. First, only results at the international level will be measured, not those at the domestic level. Chapter 8, which will examine universal crimes trials in countries utilising extra-territorial jurisdiction, and Chapter 9, which will do the same for countries basing their trials on territorial jurisdiction, will provide information with respect to the level of involvement by perpetrators in those trials, albeit at a less granular level than in this chapter. The same restriction will apply to some extent to post–World War II ('WWII') trials. The trials conducted by the International Military Tribunals in Nuremberg ('IMT') and in Tokyo (called the IMT for the Far East, or 'IMTFE') will be analysed in detail, while the trials conducted in German territory by allied tribunals pursuant to Control Council Law No. 10 (CC10) will be examined in less detail, as those trials were carried out by American, French, British, and Russian military tribunals exercising extra-territorial jurisdiction in their respective zones of occupation in Germany. As a result, jurisprudence of the following eight international criminal institutions will be discussed: the IMT, the IMTFE, the International Criminal

---

[3] See Chapter 2, Section 2.2.2.5.

Tribunal for the former Yugoslavia ('ICTY'), the International Criminal Tribunal for Rwanda ('ICTR'),[4] the Special Court for Sierra Leone ('SCSL'), the Extraordinary Chambers in the Courts of Cambodia ('ECCC'), the Extraordinary African Chambers ('EAC'), and the International Criminal Court ('ICC'),[5] together with a representative selection of important post-WWII trials in occupied German territory.[6]

A second limitation is that only persons who have been convicted or acquitted by the above institutions will be included in the enumeration below, as well as persons subject to other judicial decisions discussing participation, such as those by the Pre-Trial Chamber ('PTC') at the ICC (both when issuing arrest warrants and when confirming the charges) and the co-investigative judges at the ECCC. Persons who were only charged and were not subject to further judicial proceedings are not part of this data set. We believe that this approach based on approved charges will yield the most accurate information regarding the roles played by individuals in the execution of universal crimes while still providing sufficient data for a workable analysis. The acquittal aspect is included even though only a few trials led to acquittals, as it is interesting to see whether and to what extent the mode of participation had an influence on the not-guilty outcome in each case. This chapter will also, in a limited fashion, address the issue of sentencing and, where possible, the connection to modes of liability. This issue will be addressed in more depth below.

---

[4] We also refer to the Mechanism for International Criminal Tribunals ('MICT'), now known as the International Residual Mechanism for Criminal Tribunals, which is a continuation of the ICTY and ICTR. MICT was established on 22 December 2010 and started operating on 1 July 2012 with a mandate to perform a number of essential functions previously carried out by ICTY and ICTR, in anticipation of the closure of those institutions on 31 December 2017 and 31 December 2015 respectively.

[5] For a typology of all the international(ised) criminal institutions since WWII, see Joseph Rikhof, "Analysis: A History and Typology of International Criminal Institutions", in *PKI Global Justice Journal*, 2017, vol. 1, no. 15.

[6] For a comprehensive overview of the trials in occupied German territory as well as other trials at the domestic level, and the types of participation considered in those trials, see United Nations War Crimes Commission ('UNWCC'), *Law Reports of Trials of War Criminals*, vol. XV, HMSO, London, 1949, pp. 49–79 (www.legal-tools.org/doc/315827/). For a recent analysis of the British cases, see CHEAH Wui Ling and Moritz Vormbaum, "British War Crimes Trials in Europe and Asia, 1945–1949: A Comparative Study", in *Leiden Journal of International Law*, 2018, vol. 31, no. 3, pp 669-692.

3.2. Sociological Categories and Modes of Liability: Relationship and Overview

Most authors of ICL literature are educated in law and often have advanced academic law degrees or substantial working experience as lawyers, prosecutors, or judges within the field; accordingly, punishable participation in universal/international crimes is usually analysed through juridical lenses. For practical and theoretical purposes, the main object is to identify material and mental legal criteria that have to be met in order to convict a person as charged. When charging universal crimes suspects before international tribunals, so-called modes of liability are useful and indeed are often required in indictments. For this reason, the focus in the literature has quite naturally been on the correct identification, interpretation, and application of the most appropriate mode or modes of liability in different kinds of factual situations.

However, a legalistic perspective – practical and useful as it may be – is not the only perspective on punishable participation in universal crimes that is interesting from a research point of view. For instance, we assume that historical as well as sociological perspectives may provide additional knowledge on the matter. Our historical and sociological ambitions for this book are quite limited, however, in the sense that our main objective is to shed light on the possible fruitful relationship between sociological categories of participation and legal modes of liability/ participation. As a result, our analysis could perhaps be seen as a possible first step towards later, more in-depth research in this regard. At the same time, we believe that an overview of sociological categories considered in conjunction with the legal categories provides some useful insights for the overall analysis presented in this book, despite our principal emphasis on legal analysis.

In order to provide a useful data set for sociological analysis, we examined and tabulated a total of 385 persons subject to judicial decisions. Of this group, 143 persons were in post-WWII cases (although we included only a selected number of the cases decided in occupied Germany). The number of persons adjudicated since 1993 is 242, distributed as follows: 118 at the ICTY, 71 at the ICTR, 33 at the ICC, 9 at the SCSL, 9 at the ECCC, and 1 each at the EAC and MICT.

As noted above, this chapter divides participants – based on their different positions, roles, and employment conditions – into four classes by level. Low-level participants hold positions at the bottom rung of a military or civilian hierarchy, with nobody reporting to them. Those at the intermediate level include officers in military organisations, persons in positions of civilian authority at the local or regional level, such as burgomasters or mayors (prefects in Rwanda in 1994 are a prime example), and functionaries in the middle ranks of a civilian organisation, who supervise persons at lower levels and report to persons at higher levels. Lastly, high-level perpetrators are at the apex of their organisation or carry out important functions at the national level in their country. Thus the participants overall range from low-ranking personnel such as policemen and guards all the way up to heads of state. There is an additional class of people who belong to power support structures, such as the media or business organisations; such complementary structures in society may be important in facilitating system criminality, at least when committed by governments. Within these four overarching classes, a more detailed grouping will be set out, identifying a total of 20 different functional (sociological) categories.

With respect to the legal categories, the terminology for the various modes of participation has differed over time and across the international institutions mentioned above; the legal language and parameters have not always been the same. Tables 1–3 set out all types of participation in legal terms and in a descriptive manner as used in the international institutions since World War II, followed by some clarifications.

	IMTs in Nuremberg and Tokyo	CC10	ICTY and ICTR	SCSL	ECCC	ICC	EAC
Planning	No	No	Yes	Yes	Yes	No	Yes
Preparing	Only crimes against peace	Only crimes against peace	No	No	No	Only aggres- sion	No
Conspiracy	Only crimes against peace	Only crimes against peace	Only genocide	No	Only genocide	No	No
Incitement	No	No	Only genocide	No	No	Only genocide	No
Initiation	Only crimes against peace	Only crimes against peace	No	No	No	Only genocide	No
Attempt	No	No	Only genocide	No	Only genocide	Yes	No
Membership	No/Yes	Yes	No	No	No	No	No

Table 1: Class I: Inchoate Liability.

	IMTs in Nuremberg and Tokyo	CC10	ICTY and ICTR	SCSL	ECCC	ICC	EAC
Co-perpetration	No	No	No	No	No	'Commits jointly'	No
Indirect perpetration	No	No	No	No	No	'Commits through another person'	No
Indirect co-perpetration	No	No	No	No	No	'Commits jointly through another person'	No
Joint criminal enterprise	'Acting in concert'	'Was connected with' 'Jointly and in pursuance of a common intent'	'Committed'	'Committed'	'Committed'	'Common purpose'	'Committed'
Execution	No	No	No	No	No	Only aggression	No
Command or superior responsibility	'Leaders and organisers'	'High position' Only crimes against peace	Yes	Yes	Yes	Yes	Yes

Table 2: Class II: Commission Liability.

	IMTs in Nuremberg and Tokyo	CC10	ICTY and ICTR	SCSL	ECCC	ICC	EAC
Aiding and abetting	'Accomplices'	'Accessory' or 'abetted' 'Took a consenting part' 'Concerned with'	Yes	Yes	Yes	Yes	Yes
Ordering	No	Yes	Yes	Yes	Yes	Yes	Yes
Instigation	Yes	No	Yes	Yes	Yes	No	Yes
Soliciting	No	No	No	No	No	Yes	No
Inducing	No	No	No	No	No	Yes	No
Complicity	No	No	Only genocide	No	No	No	No
Participation	Only crimes against peace	Only crimes against peace	No	No	Only genocide	No	No
Accessory after the fact	No	'Accessory'	'Committed'	'Committed'	'Committed'	Possible	'Committed'
Planning	'Common plan' Only crimes against peace	Only crimes against peace	No	No	No	Only aggression	No
Membership	No/Yes	Yes	No	No	No	No	No

Table 3: Class III: Accomplice Liability.

Some clarification of the tables is useful. The notions of planning and membership[7] are included in both inchoate offences (Table 1) and completed offences (Tables 2 and 3) and because the instruments in question categorised these means of involvement in these different manners.[8] Moreover, some of the concepts set out above overlap in meaning; for instance, it has been said that the term 'inducing' in the ICC Rome Statute is synonymous with 'incitement', while the terms 'solicit' and 'instigate' are similar to each other.[9] On the other hand, with respect to the Rome Statute,

---

[7]   Where membership was criminalised in the Statutes of the International Military Tribunals of Nuremberg ('IMT') and Tokyo ('IMTFE'), it was, like conspiracy, considered to be a distinct crime. However, while conspiracy liability was seen as an inchoate offence that was punishable based upon the acts of the individual whether the crime was completed or not, membership liability was premised on the occurrence of crimes actually committed by or through a criminal organisation, whether the member charged was individually liable for any particular crime or not. See International Military Tribunal ('IMT'), *Trial of the Major War Criminals before the International Military Tribunal: Nuremberg, 14 November 1945–1 October 1946*, vol. XXII, Nuremberg, 1947, p. 500 (www.legal-tools.org/doc/d1427b/); and Shane Darcy, *Collective Responsibility and Accountability under International Law*, Transnational Publishers, Leiden, 2007, pp. 278–79.

[8]   It is not uncommon to have one particular means of involvement in crime characterised either as participation or as an inchoate offence, depending on whether this activity resulted in a crime or not. For instance, in Canada counselling can be a mode of participation (Article 22 of the Criminal Code) or an incomplete offence (Article 464 of the Criminal Code as regards counselling offences that have not been committed). The same distinction exists in the Australian Criminal Code Act 1995, Section 11.2 versus Sections 102.1(1A) and 474.29A. Incidentally, some authors contend that the statutes of the ICTY, ICTR, and SCSL also include the inchoate offence of planning. See Robert Cryer, Hakan Friman, Darryl Robinson, and Elisabeth Wilmhurst, *An Introduction to International Criminal Law and Procedure*, 2nd ed., Cambridge University Press, Cambridge, 2010, pp. 382–83.

[9]   William A. Schabas, *The International Criminal Court: A Commentary on the Rome Statute*, Oxford University Press, Oxford, 2010, pp. 432–33. Cryer, Friman, Robinson, and Wilmhurst, 2010, p. 379, see *supra* note 7, suggest that 'instigation' is largely the same as 'soliciting' or 'inducing'. For general comment regarding the relationship between the various modes of liability in the Rome Statute, see ICC, Trial Chamber, *Prosecutor v. Lubanga*, Judgment, ICC-01/04-01/06, 14 March 2012, para. 999 (www.legal-tools.org/doc/677866/); ICC, Pre-Trial Chamber, *Prosecutor v. Gbagbo*, Decision on Confirmation of Charges, ICC-02/11-01/11, 12 June 2014, para. 243 (www.legal-tools.org/doc/5b41bc/); ICC, Pre-Trial Chamber, *Prosecutor v. Blé Goudé*, Decision on Confirmation of Charges, ICC-02/11-02/11, 11 December 2014, para. 159 (www.legal-tools.org/doc/0536d5/); and ICC, Appeals Chamber, *Prosecutor v. Lubanga Dyilo*, Judgment, ICC-01/04-01/06 A5, 1 December 2014, para. 462 (www.legal-tools.org/doc/585c75/). For the distinctions between soliciting, inducing, instigating, and ordering, see ICC, Trial Chamber, *Prosecutor v. Jean-Pierre Bemba Gombo, Aimé Kilolo Musamba, Jean-Jacques Mangenda Kabongo, Fidèle Babala Wandu and Narcisse Arido*, Judgment, ICC-01/05-01/13, 19 October 2016,

---

commentators have indicated that accessory after the fact is not part of this instrument,[10] while the lack of reference to conspiracy to commit genocide has been seen as an 'oversight'.[11] Some concepts, such as initiation and execution, have not yet been subject to judicial interpretation.

3.3. High-Level Participants in Main Power Structures

3.3.1. Heads of State, Including Prime Ministers

While this chapter deals with results at the international level, an exception is made with respect to heads of state, due to the importance of their position. Twenty-eight former heads of state have been indicted, prosecuted, or sentenced for international crimes. The 13 trials begun at the international level since 1990 will be discussed below, but there have also been 15 attempts at the domestic level to take action against former heads of state since 1992, some of which will be discussed in Chapters 8 and 9.[12]

---

paras. 73–82 (www.legal-tools.org/doc/fe0ce4/). For the notion of a hierarchy between soliciting and inducing on one hand and aiding and abetting on the other, see para. 85 of the same case.

[10] See Schabas, 2010, para. 435, *supra* note 8; and Albin Eser, "Individual Criminal Responsibility", in A. Cassese, P. Gaeta, and J.R.W.D. Jones (eds.), *The Rome Statute of the International Criminal Court: A Commentary*, vol. I, Oxford University Press, Oxford, 2002, pp. 806–7. However, in the context of common purpose, see ICC, Trial Chamber, *Prosecutor v. Chui*, Judgment, Concurring Opinion of Judge Christine Van den Wyngaert, ICC-01/04-02/12, 18 December 2012, paras. 286–87 (www.legal-tools.org/doc/7d5200/).

[11] Schabas, 2010, p. 438, see *supra* note 8.

[12] In South and Central America, Argentina has indicted three former presidents, namely Isabel Perón, Jorge Videla (who is also the subject of arrest warrants from Italy and Germany), and Reynaldo Bignone, while Chile did the same with Augusto Pinochet, Peru with Alberto Fujimori, Uruguay with Gregorio Alvarez, Bolivia with Gonzalo Sánchez de Lozada, and Guatemala with Oscar Mejía Víctores and Efraín Ríos Montt. In Mexico, former president Luis Echeverría was tried for commission of genocide, albeit in his capacity as minister of the interior at the time of the crime, but he was acquitted in 2007. In addition, former president of Guatemala Ríos Montt was indicted by Spain and convicted in Guatemala, while the former president of Uruguay, Juan Bordaberry, has been indicted by Italy. Also in Italy, former military dictator Francisco Morales Bermúdez of Peru and former dictator Luis García Meza of Bolivia were sentenced to life imprisonment in absentia. In the Middle East, the Iraqi High Tribunal completed proceedings against Saddam Hussein in 2006, resulting in his execution the same year. In Africa, Mengistu Haile Mariam of Ethiopia was sentenced to death in May 2008, but he remains at large in Zimbabwe. The case of Jean-Claude 'Baby Doc' Duvalier of Haiti is not included, as he was investigated for but not charged with crimes against humanity. For background, see Hector

---

After World War II, the IMTFE, which tried 28 persons in total,[13] put on trial and convicted four Japanese prime ministers, namely Kiichiro Hiranuma, Koki Hirota, Kuniaka Koiso, and Hideki Tojo. All had served as prime minister at different times between 1928 and 1945, and all had also occupied other high positions in the Japanese government, which resulted in charges being levelled against them with respect to those latter functions. Two of them, Tojo and Hirota, were sentenced to death, and the other two to life imprisonment.

The 13 proceedings begun at the international level since the IMTFE trial – five at the ICTY, four at the ICC, and one each at the ICTR, SCSL, ECCC, and EAC – have had mixed results. The ICC originally indicted three sitting heads of state: Omar Al-Bashir, Muammar Gaddafi, and Uhuru Kenyatta. Bashir is at large, with his case in the pre-trial phase, while Gaddafi has died, and Kenyatta's trial was vacated due to a lack of evidence. One former head of state, Laurent Gbagbo, has been indicted by the ICC and his trial is ongoing.

The ICTR sentenced Jean Kambanda, who was prime minister of Rwanda during the 1994 genocide, to life imprisonment in 1998. At the ICTY, Slobodan Milošević, president of what was then known as the Federal Republic of Yugoslavia, was indicted in 1999 and 2001 and put on trial in 2002; the trial would have been completed had he not died in 2006 while in custody during the proceedings. The ICTY also put on trial Milan Milutinović, president of the Republic of Serbia, as part of a joint trial with five others, but he was acquitted in 2009 and the prosecutor did not appeal the judgment. Lastly, the ICTY also convicted three heads of smaller entities: Radovan Karadžić, who was wartime president of the Republika Srpska in Bosnia and Herzegovina, convicted in 2016 and sentenced to 40 years' imprisonment; Jadranko Prlić, president of the Croatian Defence Council ('HVO') and prime minister of the Croatian Repub-

---

Olasolo, *Criminal Responsibility of Political and Military Leaders for Genocide, Crimes against Humanity and War Crimes, with Special Reference to the Rome Statute and the Statute and Case Law of the Ad Hoc Tribunals*, Hart, Oxford, 2008; Hector Olasolo, *The Criminal Responsibility of Senior Political and Military Leaders as Principals to International Crimes*, Hart, Oxford, 2009; and Ellen L. Lutz, *Prosecuting Heads of State*, Cambridge University Press, Cambridge, 2009.

[13] See Judgment, International Military Tribunal for the Far East: Tokyo, 1 November 1948, Part C, Chapter X, pp. 1146–1211 (www.legal-tools.org/doc/09f24c/).

lic of Herceg-Bosna, in 2013, sentenced to 25 years; and Milan Babić, president of the Serbian Krajina region in Croatia, in 2005, sentenced to 13 years (after a guilty plea). While these three leaders were not heads of state, strictly speaking, they are included in this category as they occupied the highest position in the statelets in question.

The SCSL indicted the former president of Liberia, Charles Taylor, in 2006 and his trial started in early 2008; he was convicted in 2012 and sentenced to 50 years' imprisonment. Khieu Samphan, former president of Democratic Kampuchea, was investigated by the ECCC in Cambodia. His first trial started in 2011, resulting in a conviction and life sentence in 2014, while his second trial, involving allegations of genocide, has been completed apart from the issuance of a judgment. Senegal put on trial the former president of Chad, Hissène Habré, who was indicted in 2013 and convicted in 2016; his sentence of life imprisonment was upheld on appeal a year later.

Approaches to using forms of participation of accused persons differ across these cases. This largely reflects fact that specific modes of liability are of greater interest and importance to specific institutions, both immediately after WWII and more recently.

At the IMTFE, three of the accused were convicted of all three main forms of participation charged in the indictment, namely conspiracy in aggression, participation/waging of aggression, and command responsibility (Koiso, Tojo, and Hirota), while one (Hiranuma) was convicted of conspiracy and participation.[14]

Of the four cases initiated at the ICC, Bashir was charged with two forms of perpetration, namely indirect perpetration and indirect co-perpetration, while Gaddafi was also charged with indirect co-perpetration, as was Kenyatta. While the same form of participation was included in the

---

[14] Of the original 55 charges in the indictment, the Tribunal approved only nine, namely conspiracy to wage wars of aggression (count 1); participating/waging wars of aggression (counts 27, 29, 31, 32, 33, and 36); and two counts (54 and 55) pertaining to the responsibility of persons in authority for allowing war crimes to be committed (count 54 pertains to charges of ordering, authorising, and permitting such crimes, while count 55 indicates failure to take adequate steps to secure the observance and prevent breaches of the conventions and laws with respect to prisoners of war and civilian internees). See IMTFE, *Judgment, International Military Tribunal for the Far East: Tokyo, 1 November 1948*, Part A, Chapter II, pp. 32–37 (www.legal-tools.org/doc/3a2b6b/).

charge sheet for Gbagbo, he was also accused of superior responsibility, instigation, and common purpose. This seems to reflect the more recent approach by the prosecutor to lay as many charges as possible in case the one most difficult to prove, perpetration, does not stand up to scrutiny, and at the same time to signal the very senior position of the accused by including superior responsibility.

At the ICTR, Kambanda was convicted (after a guilty plea) of instigation, aiding and abetting, complicity, incitement, and conspiracy, the latter three forms of participation unique to the crime of genocide. At the ICTY, Milošević had been charged with three separate JCEs, which were the same charges leading to the conviction in the Karadžić case, while Babić's conviction was based on a single JCE, as were the charges against Milutinović and Prlić.

While the SCSL prosecutor in the Taylor case had included charges of JCE, he was only able to prove the lesser accusation of aiding and abetting. At the ECCC Samphan was convicted of JCE and superior responsibility, while at the EAC Habré was convicted of direct participation, JCE, superior responsibility, and ordering; it would appear in the last two cases that, apart from the preference for JCE at the preparatory level, the convictions also took into account the very senior positions of the accused at the execution phase by using forms of liability eminently suited to such roles, namely ordering and superior responsibility.

3.3.2. Ministers

Thirty-nine persons at the ministerial level have been charged with international crimes by the international institutions. Along with ministers, this group includes plenipotentiaries in Nazi Germany, members of a junta or presidential council (as in Sierra Leone and Bosnia, respectively), and vice presidents. Of this group, 6 were charged by the IMT, 4 by the IMT-FE, 14 by the ICTR, 9 by the ICTY, 3 by the SCSL, 2 by the ECCC, and 1 by the ICC.

Of the 24 persons in total accused at the IMT, six held ministerial-level posts in Germany: Hermann Goering, commander-in-chief of the Luftwaffe and plenipotentiary for the Four Year Plan; Joachim von Ribbentrop, minister of foreign affairs; Alfred Rosenberg, Reich minister for the occupied eastern territories; Wilhelm Frick, Prussian minister of the interior, Reich director of elections, and general plenipotentiary for administration of the Reich; Albert Speer, plenipotentiary general for armaments and member of the Central Planning Board; and Hans Fritzsche, plenipotentiary for the political organisation of the Greater German Radio). Four of these men, Goering, von Ribbentrop, Rosenberg, and Frick, were sentenced to death, while Speer received 20 years' imprisonment and Fritzsche was acquitted.

The IMTFE sentenced Okinori Kaya, the Japanese finance minister, and Sadao Araki, the minister of war and education, to life imprisonment, while two foreign ministers, Mamoru Shigemitsu and Shigenori Togo, received 7 and 20 years' imprisonment respectively.

The ICTR put on trial most members of the cabinet of the interim government of Rwanda, which had planned and implemented the genocide in 1994. The following ministers were tried: Casimir Bizimungu, minister of health; Justin Mugenzi, minister of commerce; Jérôme-Clément Bicamumpaka, minister of foreign affairs; Prosper Mugiraneza, minister of civil service; Augustin Ngirabatware, minister of planning; Callixte Nzabonimana, minister of youth and associative movements, who had also been chairman of the National Republican Movement for Democracy and Development ('MRND') in Gitarama Prefecture; André Rwamakuba, minister of primary and secondary education; Jean de Dieu Kamuhanda, minister for culture and education; Jean Bosco Barayagwiza, minister of foreign affairs; Pauline Nyiramasuhuko, minister of family and women's development; Emmanuel Ndindabahizi, minister of finance; André Ntagerura, minister of transport; Eliezer Niyitegeka, minister of information; and Callixte Kalimanzira, acting minister of the interior. These 14 persons were tried in 11 trials, comprising seven individual trials and four joint trials: the Government II trial, with the first four persons mentioned above; the Butare trial, with six persons, of whom only Nyiramasuhuko was a minister; the media trial, with three persons, of whom only Barayagwiza was a minister; and the Cyangugu trial, with three persons, of whom only Ntagerura was a minister.

The ICTR sentences varied from life imprisonment to acquittal. Nzabonimana, Kamuhanda, Ndindabahizi, Niyitegeka, and Nyiramasuhuko were sentenced to life, with the last one's sentence reduced to 47 years on appeal. Barayagwiza was sentenced to 35 years, reduced to 32 years on appeal. Mugenzi, Mugiraneza, Ngirabatware, and Kalimanzira were sentenced to 30 years, although for the last one the sentence was reduced to 25 years on appeal, while for the first two an acquittal was entered on appeal. The remaining four (Bizimungu, Bicamumpaka, Rwamakuba, and

Ntagerura) were acquitted, the first two as part of the Government II trial; as a result, all four accused in the Government II trial were eventually found not guilty.

At the ICTY a similar picture emerges. Ljube Boškoski, minister of the interior of the former Yugoslav Republic of Macedonia, was acquitted. Of the other eight, seven received substantial prison sentences: 35 years for Milan Martić, minister of defence and minister of internal affairs of the Republic of Serbian Krajina; 32 years at trial reduced to 30 years on appeal for Radoslav Brdanin, acting vice president of the government of the Republika Srpska; 25 years for Dario Kordić, vice president and a member of the presidency of the Croatian Republic of Herceg-Bosna; 20 years for Bruno Stojić, head of the Department of Defence of the Croatian Republic of Herceg-Bosna; 16 years for Valentin Ćorić, minister of the interior of the Croatian Republic of Herceg-Bosna; 22 years at trial but reduced to 18 years on appeal for Mićo Stanišić, minister of the Serbian ministry of internal affairs in Bosnia and Herzegovina. Biljana Plavšić, Serbian representative to the collective presidency of Bosnia and Herze-govina and a member of the presidency of the Republika Srpska, received a sentence of 11 years after a guilty plea. Apart from Plavšić, the others were all part of joint trials in which they occupied the highest position in their respective governments compared to the other accused.

In Sierra Leone, the SCSL found guilty three members of the Armed Forces Revolutionary Council ('AFRC') governing body, the Supreme Council of the AFRC, and sentenced them to long prison terms: 50 years for Alex Tamba Brima and Santigie Borbor Kany, and 45 years for Brima Bazzy Kamara. In Cambodia, the ECCC had to terminate proceedings against Ieng Sary, deputy prime minister and minister for foreign affairs, due to his death, as well against Ieng Tirith, minister of social affairs, due to her unfitness to stand trial.

With respect to forms of participation, the IMT charged the 24 accused with four counts:

1. A common plan or conspiracy in the planning, preparation, initiation, or waging of a war of aggression, or a war in violation of international treaties, agreements, or assurances;

2. Planning, preparation, initiation, or waging of a war of aggression, or a war in violation of international treaties, agreements, or assurances;

3. Leaders, organisers, instigators, and accomplices participating in the commission of war crimes as well as acting in concert;

4. Leaders, organisers, instigators, and accomplices participating in the commission of crimes against humanity as well as acting in concert.

Of the four ministers sentenced to death, Goering, Von Ribbentrop, Rosenberg, and Frick, the first three had been convicted of all four charges, while the fourth one, Frick, had been convicted of three charges but acquitted of the first one. Speer had been convicted of common plan/conspiracy and participation as related to counts 1 and 2, while Fritzsche, the one acquittal in this group of ministers, had been charged with counts 1, 3, and 4, common plan/conspiracy and acting in concert. At the IMTFE, Kaya and Togo were convicted of conspiracy to wage wars of aggression as well as for participation in waging such wars, while Araki was convicted only of the latter. These charges seem to be reflected in the seriousness of their sentences, namely life imprisonment and 20 years. By contrast, Shigemitsu, who received only 7 years, was convicted of participation in waging aggressive wars and superior responsibility.

At the ICTR a spectrum of forms of participation were used. The four co-accused in the Government II trial, all of whom were eventually acquitted, had all been charged with a combination of conspiracy, incitement, and JCE – the first two of these forms, as noted earlier, only possible for the crime of genocide. On the other hand, the most serious sentence of life imprisonment was based in one instance on similar charges but without resort to JCE, such as a combination of conspiracy, incitement, and instigation (in the Nzabonimana case), while in the other four cases different dual charges led to this sentence, namely ordering together with aiding and abetting (Kamuhanda), instigation and aiding and abetting (Ndindabahizi as well as Kalimanzira), and incitement and personal participation (Niyitegeka). Nyiramasuhuko, who received 47 years, had been convicted of conspiracy and superior responsibility, while Ngirabatware's conviction and 30-year sentence was based on JCE and complicity, the latter again a form of liability specific to genocide. One other individual, Barayagwiza, received a sentence of 32 years based on instigation, planning, and superior responsibility. Lastly, the acquittals in two individual trials, those of Rwamakuba and Ntagerura, were related to direct participation and superior responsibility, respectively.

The picture at the ICTY, SCSL, and ECCC is much simpler than at the ICTR. In the 13 cases across these institutions, the charges and convictions were based on JCE with two exceptions, namely the Boškoski case at the ICTY, where the indictment was based only on superior responsibility, and the Ieng Tirith case at the ECCC, where, in addition to JCE, the charges of planning, instigating, superior responsibility, and aiding and abetting were also included in the indictment. As indicated earlier, neither of these two cases resulted in a conviction. Incidentally, ministers are the only category in which women are represented, with Nyiramasuhuko at the ICTR, Plavšić at the ICTY, and Ieng Tirith at the ECCC (plus one at the ICC in a different category, namely Simone Gbagbo).

At the ICC, Abdel Raheem Muhammad Hussein, minister of national defence and former minister of the interior in Sudan, has been charged as an indirect (co-)perpetrator but no trial has been held yet.

3.3.3. Military Leadership

The category of military leadership consists of persons at the highest level of a military structure, either at headquarters or in the field; such figures are typically either commander-in-chief or commander of a corps with a rank of at least general. This section will deal with military leadership in state organisations, while senior military leadership in non-state (rebel) organisations will be discussed in Section 3.3.7.

As a preliminary comment, when we compare the 33 proceedings against military leaders (4 at the IMT, 11 at the IMTFE, 14 at the ICTY, 2 at the ICC, and 1 each at the ICTR and ECCC) with the ones just discussed above, it is striking how differently the institutions have chosen to prioritise trials of civilian versus military leaders. Not counting heads of state, who often combine both military and civilian authority, the IMT after WWII prosecuted 6 civilian leaders and 4 military ones, while the IMTFE did the opposite, with 4 civilian ministers and 11 generals. The variation can be seen even more clearly at the international tribunals, where the ICTR initiated trials against 11 ministers and only 1 general, while the ICTY proceeded against 6 ministers and 14 military leaders. The differences at the internationalised tribunals are less pronounced, with the ECCC proceeding against 1 civilian and 2 military leaders and the SCSL only against 3 civilian leaders. The ICC has started proceedings against 1 civilian and 2 military leaders.

The four senior military functionaries convicted at the IMT were Wilhelm Keitel, chief of the Armed Forces High Command; Karl Doenitz, commander-in-chief of the German Navy; Erich Raeder, admiral inspector of the Navy; and Alfred Jodl, chief of Operations Staff of the Armed Forces High Command. Keitel and Jodl were sentenced to death, which may be connected to the fact that, as was the case with their civilian counterparts, they had been convicted of all four charges in the indictment. Raeder, who had been convicted of three charges, that is, all except crimes against humanity, was sentenced to life. Doenitz received a sentence of 10 years with convictions on two charges, namely participation in crimes against peace and acting in concert in war crimes.

As indicated, the IMTFE put a large number of military leaders on trial (11 of the 28 persons tried), with a variety of backgrounds. At the highest level were commanders-in-chief such as Shunroko Hata, commander-in-chief of the expeditionary forces in China, who also served at a different time as minister of war; Seishiro Itagaki, commander-in-chief of the Army in Korea, who also served at different times as minister of war and chief of staff of the China Expeditionary Army; Heitaro Kimura, commander-in-chief of the Burma Area Army, who also served at a different time as vice war minister; and Yoshijiro Umezu, chief of the Army General Staff. At a slightly lower level were Akira Muto, vice chief of staff of the China Expeditionary Force, and Iwane Matsui, commander of the Shanghai Expeditionary Force and Central China Area Army. Following them were high-ranking functionaries such as the generals Kenryo Sato, Teiichi Suzuki, and Hiroshi Oshima (who also served as ambassador to Germany), as well as admirals, namely Takasumi Oka and Shigetaro Shimada.

Four of these men were sentenced to death (Itagaki, Kimura, Matsui, Muto), with the remaining seven sentenced to life imprisonment. Of the four sentenced to death, two were commanders-in-chief (one in China and one in Burma) while also having other very high functions in the ministry of war; the other two were the military commander and vice chief of staff in China during some of the worst crimes against civilians by Japanese armed forces. These four plus Hata, who received life imprisonment, were the only ones to have been convicted of all counts of conspiracy and participation in waging wars of aggression as well as command responsibility, acknowledging their failure to prevent or punish their troops. As for the other six who received life imprisonment, in three cases it was based on the conspiracy and participation charges (Umezu, Suzuki, and Shimada), while three were convicted based on one charge each, namely participation in waging war (Sata), command responsibility (Matsui), and conspiracy (Oshima).

At the international tribunals, an interesting picture emerges with respect to the outcomes of the trials and the modes of participation charged. In each tribunal, the Appeals Chamber ('AC') took a critical approach with respect to command responsibility, as well as other forms of participation by high military officials. At the ICTR, in the case of Augustin Bizimungu, who had been chief of staff of the Rwandan Army, the AC upheld the conviction on this ground (as well as for conspiracy and complicity in genocide) and the sentence of 30 years' imprisonment. At the ICTY, it overturned sentences on this ground in two cases, namely those of Momcilo Perišić, chief of the General Staff of the Yugoslav Army, who had been sentenced to 27 years by the Trial Chamber ('TC') for his command responsibility as well as for aiding and abetting, and of Naser Orić, senior commander of Bosnian Muslim forces in municipalities in eastern Bosnia and Herzegovina, including Srebrenica, who had been sentenced to 2 years for only command responsibility. Meanwhile, the acquittal of Sefer Halilović, deputy commander and later chief of the Supreme Command Staff of the Army of Bosnia and Herzegovina, based on command responsibility at the trial level, was upheld.

In addition, the Appeals Chamber reduced the sentences of Radislav Krstić, chief of staff and commander of the Drina Corps of the Bosnian Serb Army, from 46 to 35 years, based on aiding and abetting; of Vladimir Lazarević, commander of the Priština Corps of the Yugoslav Army, from 15 to 14 years, also for aiding and abetting; and of Enver Hadžihasanović, commander of the Army of Bosnia and Herzegovina 3rd Corps, as well as chief of the Supreme Command Staff and member of the Joint Command of the Army of Bosnia and Herzegovina, from five to three and a half years, based on command responsibility. On the other hand, it increased the sentence of Stanislav Galić, commander of the Sarajevo Romanija Corps of the Bosnian Serb Army, from 20 years to life imprisonment for ordering the commission of war crimes and crimes against humanity. It upheld the sentences of 15 and 22 years respectively of Dragoljub Ojdanić, chief of the General Staff of the Yugoslav Army, and Nebojša Pavković, commander of the Third Army of the Yugoslav Army; Pavković had been convicted based on a JCE together with four others in the Šainović trial, in which the above-mentioned Lazarević was also an accused. The Chamber did the same with two accused in the Prlić case, namely Slobodan Praljak, commander of the HVO Main Staff, and Milivoj Petković, chief of the HVO Main Staff and deputy overall commander of the HVO forces, each of whom had received 20 years. The AC did not rule substantively on the Trial Chamber decision in the case of Rasim Delić, commander of the Main Staff of the Army of Bosnia-Herzegovina, as the accused had died while on provisional release, but only indicated that the TC decision (3 years' imprisonment for command responsibility) was final. Lastly, Ratko Mladić, commander of the Main Staff of the Army of Republika Srpska in Bosnia and Herzegovina, was sentenced to life imprisonment by the Trial Chamber, and as of July 2018 his appeal has not yet been heard.

At the ICC, one conviction was rendered against Jean-Pierre Bemba Gombo in the situation pertaining to the Central African Republic, where, as president and commander-in-chief of the Mouvement de Libération du Congo, he provided military support to the president of the country against an internal rebellion. He was sentenced to 16 years' imprisonment based on command responsibility but both the conviction and sentence were overturned on appeal, leading to an acquittal. In another case, an arrest warrant was issued against Al-Tuhamy Mohamed Khaled, lieutenant general in the Libyan army and head of the Libyan Internal Security Agency; the modes of liability in this case were perpetration, common purpose, and superior responsibility. Lastly, at the ECCC, charges based on JCE were laid by the two co-investigative judges in 2015 against Meas Muth, commander of the Democratic Kampuchea Navy; the investigation was concluded in 2017 but no trial has started yet.

3.3.4. Leaders of Other Governmental Power Structures

This section deals with persons in civilian power structures who exert less authority, power, and influence than those in the three preceding categories. These persons are typically one step removed from the centre of power, holding either a slightly lower rank than the head of state or ministers in the same centralised hierarchy, or else a very high position outside the centre of power, usually outside the country. The 24 functionaries discussed in this section fall into six subcategories: very senior administrative officials; governors of occupied territory; ambassadors; high officials in security or intelligence organisations; powerful parliamentarians; and persons whose power derives from their proximity to persons mentioned in the three preceding sections.

The first group, that of very senior administrative officials, includes four persons: at the IMT, Rudolph Hess, deputy to Hitler, and Martin Bormann, secretary to Hitler; and at the IMTFE, Naoki Hoshino, chief cabinet secretary, and Koici Kido, chief secretary to the Lord Keeper of the Privy Seal. Their functions were seen as essential to the implementation of policies in both Germany and Japan, as can be seen from their sentences and from the forms of participation they were charged with. Hess was charged with common plan/conspiracy and participation in waging aggressive war and received a life sentence, while Bormann was charged with acting in concert in war crimes and crimes against humanity and was sentenced to death. At the IMTFE, similar results were achieved with both Hoshino and Kido, who were charged with conspiracy and participation to wage wars of aggression and sentenced to life imprisonment.

The second group, six governors of occupied territory, were only prosecuted, like the group before, immediately after WWII, namely at the IMT and IMTFE, as well as by a Control Council Law No. 10 tribunal. The IMT prosecuted Baldur von Schirach, *gauleiter* of Vienna, Reich governor of Vienna, and Reich defence commissioner for that territory; Arthur Seyss-Inquart, Reich governor of Austria and the Reich commissioner for occupied Netherlands; and Konstantin von Neurath, Reich protector for Bohemia and Moravia. The IMTFE prosecuted Jiro Minami, the governor general of Korea. In addition, the Permanent Military Tribunal at Strasbourg, a CC10 court, prosecuted Robert Wagner, *gauleiter* and head of civil government of Alsace, and Hermann Gustav Philipp Rohn, ex-deputy *gauleiter* of Alsace, together with five others. As with the preceding group, their activities were considered extremely serious. Death sentences were handed down for Seyss-Inquart, for participation in crimes against peace, acting in concert in war crimes, and crimes against humanity, as well as for Wagner and Rohn, based on incitement and aiding and abetting. Minami received life imprisonment for conspiracy and participation in aggression. Von Schirach was sentenced to 20 years' imprisonment for acting in concert in the commission of crimes against humanity, and Von Neurath to 15 years on all four counts.

The third group, ambassadors, consists of Franz von Papen, German ambassador to Turkey, and Toshio Shiratori, Japanese ambassador to Italy. Von Papen was acquitted on charges of common plan/conspiracy and participation in crimes against peace by the IMT, while the IMTFE gave Shiratori life imprisonment for conspiracy.

The fourth group, high officials in security organisations, includes eight persons. The IMT proceeded against Ernst Kaltenbrunner, chief of the Security Police and the SD (Sicherheitsdienst) and head of the Reich Security Head Office, and Fritz Sauckel, *obergruppenfuehrer* in both the SS and the SA (Sturmabteilung). The ICTY prosecuted Sreten Lukić, head of the Serbian Ministry of Internal Affairs; Vlastimir Đorđević, assistant minister of the Serbian Ministry of Internal Affairs and chief of the ministry's Public Security Department; Jovica Stanišić, head of the State Security Service of the Serbian Ministry of Internal Affairs; and Berislav Pušić, president of the Service for the Exchange of Prisoners and Other Persons and head of the commission in charge of all Herceg-Bosna/HVO prisons and detention facilities (and part of the Prlić trial). The ICC heard the cases of Abdullah Al-Senussi, national head of Libyan military intelligence, and Francis Kirimi Muthaura, chairman of the Kenyan National Advisory Committee and chairman of the National Security Advisory Committee.

The IMT sentenced both Kaltenbrunner and Sauckel to death on the same charges, namely acting in concert for war crimes and crimes against humanity. The ICTY Trial Chamber gave Lukić (who was part of a joint trial with five others) 22 years' imprisonment for JCE, but this was reduced on appeal to 20 years; similarly, Đorđević was originally sentenced to 27 years for JCE but this became 18 years on appeal. Stanišić was acquitted by the Trial Chamber but this was overruled by the Appeals Chamber, which ordered a new trial, which is still ongoing, based on JCE. Lastly, the sentence of 10 years against Pušić was upheld on appeal. Both cases at the ICC have been discontinued: for Senussi, who had been charged as indirect co-perpetrator, because the case was found inadmissible in 2014 due to proceedings in Libya, and for Muthaura, because the prosecutor withdrew the charges, which were the same as for Senussi, in 2013.

The fifth group, powerful parliamentarians, contains one person: Momcilo Krajišnik, who had been on the main board of the Serb Democratic Party of Bosnia and Herzegovina and served as president of the Bosnian Serb Assembly. He was sentenced for JCE to 27 years' imprisonment, reduced on appeal to 20 years.

The last group, persons whose power is due to their close proximity to heads of state, ministers, and military leaders, includes three individuals. The ICC prosecuted Simone Gbagbo, wife of Laurent Gbagbo, president of Côte d'Ivoire until 2011 (mentioned above in the section on heads of state), as well as Charles Blé Goudé, a prominent leader of pro-Gbagbo youth movements. Blé Goudé is on trial together with Laurent Gbagbo for indirect co-perpetration; Simone Gbagbo has been charged as an indirect co-perpetrator but her trial has not started yet. At the ICTR, Arsène Shalom Ntahobali is the son of Pauline Nyiramasuhuko (mentioned above in the section on ministers). He was sentenced to life imprisonment (as part of the six-person Butare joint trial), reduced to 47 years on appeal, for direct participation, ordering, and aiding and abetting.

3.3.5. Leaders of Political Parties

There have been five proceedings against leaders of political parties. At the IMT, Hans Frank, *reichsleiter* of the Nazi Party in charge of legal affairs, was sentenced to death for acting in concert for war crimes and crimes against humanity. At the ICTY, Vojislav Šešelj, president of the Serbian Radical Party and member of the Assembly of the Republic of Serbia, was acquitted of JCE but this was overturned on appeal by the MICT, resulting in a sentence of 10 years' imprisonment. At the ECCC, Noun Chea, deputy secretary of the Communist Party of Kampuchea, member of the Standing Committee and Central Committee of the Communist Party of Kampuchea, and chairman of the Democratic Kampuchea People's Assembly, was sentenced to life imprisonment for JCE and superior responsibility, while a second case with the same modes of liability but with the addition of a genocide charge has been completed and is awaiting judgment. At the ICC, Henry Kiprono Kosgey and William Joshua Arap Sang, leader and deputy leader respectively of the Orange Democratic Movement in Kenya, were charged with indirect co-perpetration, but their cases ended with non-confirmation of the charges by the Pre-Trial Chamber and a decision by the Trial Chamber to terminate the proceedings.

3.3.6. Leaders of Financial and Economic Power Structures

There have been five cases involving such leaders, all pertaining to persons working for and during the Nazi regime in Germany. Hjalmar Schacht, president of the Reichsbank, was acquitted by the IMT of common plan/conspiracy and participation in crimes against peace. Bruno Tesch, owner of the Zyklon B firm that supplied poison gas to the German concentration camps, was sentenced to death based on aiding and abetting by the British Military Court in Hamburg in the group trial called the Zyklon B Case.

The other three individuals were convicted by the US military tribunal in Nuremberg as part of the IG Farben group trial, the Krupp group trial, and the Flick group trial. The defendants with the highest positions in these trials were Carl Krauch, a senior official in IG Farben Industries AG; Alfried Felix Alwyn Krupp von Bohlen und Halbach, a senior official in Friedrich Krupp AG; and Friedrich Flick, principal proprietor and active head of a large group of industrial enterprises, including coal and iron ore mines and steel producing and manufacturing plants, and a member of the supervisory board of numerous other large industrial and financial companies. Krupp and Krauch were charged with ordering, abetting, taking a consenting part in, and being connected with war crimes and crimes against humanity, while Flick was found guilty of taking a consenting part and aiding and abetting. Krupp received 12 years while Krauch and Flick received 7 years.

3.3.7. Leaders of Non-state Power Structures (Civilian and Military)

For the purposes of this section, non-state power structures will be defined as organisations constituted in opposition to established governments. Such organisations do not, therefore, include government-connected militias, such as those in Rwanda or the former Yugoslavia, or self-proclaimed governments and militias connected to them, such as the Bosnian Serb entity in Bosnia and Herzegovina, the Bosnia Croat entity in the same area, and the Serbian entity of Krajina in Croatia.

Based on this description, seven leaders of non-state structures have been prosecuted: one at the SCSL and six at the ICC. Of these seven, the first three mentioned below were civilians, while the other four were military. To begin with the SCSL, Moimina Fofana, director of war of the Civil Defence Forces, a government-allied militia in Sierra Leone, was sentenced to 25 years' imprisonment for aiding and abetting and command responsibility.

At the ICC, Thomas Lubanga Dyilo, founding member and president of Union des Patriotes Congolais, who was active in Ituri, Democratic Republic of Congo ('DRC'), was sentenced to 14 years' imprisonment as a co-perpetrator. Two high officials of the Forces Démocratiques de Libération du Rwanda ('FDLR'), also active in Kiva, had arrest warrants issued against them. Callixte Mbarushimana, de facto leader and first vice president ad interim of the FDLR, was charged with common purpose, but the PTC refused to confirm the charge. The arrest warrant for Sylvestre Mudacumura, supreme commander of the army of the FDLR, was based on indirect co-perpetration but he is still at large. In addition, a summons to appear was issued against Bahar Idriss Abu Garda, chairman and general coordinator of military operations of the United Resistance Front in Darfur, based on his role as a co-perpetrator and indirect co-perpetrator, but these charges were also not confirmed by the PTC. Charges of being a co-perpetrator were also brought against another leader of the same organisation in Darfur, Abdallah Banda Abakaer Nourain, who was commander-in-chief of the Justice and Equality Movement, a component of the United Resistance Front; the charges were confirmed, but the proceedings against him were terminated due to his death.

Lastly, an arrest warrant was issued for Joseph Kony, leader and commander-in-chief of the Lord's Resistance Army ('LRA') in Uganda, for ordering the commission of war crimes and crimes against humanity but he is also still at large.

3.3.8. Conclusions Regarding High-Level Participants

Section 3.3. has examined the modes of participation of 130 individuals at high levels within their power structures who have been charged with international crimes in the period since the end of World War II. The sentencing patterns of those individuals who were convicted have also been provided. These 130 persons – all but three of them men – were divided into seven categories: heads of state (17 persons), ministers (39), military leaders (33), leaders of other governmental power structures (24), leaders of political parties (5), business leaders (5), and leaders, both military and civilian, in non-state power structures (7). Together they represent 34 per cent of the total number of persons examined in this chapter in all 20 categories (385).

Data on the modes of participation of these individuals are set out in Table 4. A couple of comments on the table are in order. First, all charges against the above persons have been included in the data set, and because of the very regular use of multiple charges,[15] a total of 222 charges were brought against those 130 persons.

Second, the table includes all the charges, whether or not the proceedings resulted in a conviction. Of the proceedings against the 130 persons, 15 resulted in acquittals (three at the IMT, six at ICTY, and six at ICTR); one proceeding was halted at the ICTY due to the death of the accused; nine proceedings were halted at the ICC for various reasons (including death of the accused, non-confirmation of charges by the Pre-Trial Chamber, withdrawal of charges by the prosecutor, and a trial vacated by the Trial Chamber before completion); and two were halted at the ECCC because one accused died and a second was unfit to stand trial. Thus, a total of 27 persons in this group have not faced any sentencing process, meaning that 21 per cent of cases at the leadership level were uncompleted. This number does not take into account the proceedings at the ICC, where charges have been confirmed but no trial has yet begun in the cases of eight persons.

Third, while Table 4 provides the total number of modes of liability per institution, there is a breakdown of each leadership category in the footnotes related to those numbers.

---

[15] Although it is interesting to note that the charges against three heads of state at the ICTY were based on only one charge, namely JCE.

	IMT	IMTFE	CC10	ICTR	ICTY	SCSL	ECCC	ICC	EAC	Total
Class I: Inchoate Liability										
Planning				1[16]			1[17]			2
Conspiracy in crimes against peace	18[18]	21[19]								39
Conspiracy in genocide				7[20]						7
Incitement to genocide			1[21]	7[22]						8

---

[16] A minister.

[17] A minister.

[18] Five ministers, nine military leaders, three other government leaders, and one leader of a political party.

[19] Four heads of state, two ministers, nine military leaders, three business leaders, and three other government leaders.

[20] One head of state and six ministers.

[21] Another government leader.

[22] One head of state and six ministers.

	IMT	IMTFE	CC10	ICTR	ICTY	SCSL	ECCC	ICC	EAC	Total
Class II: Commission Liability										
Co-perpetration								4^{23}		4
Indirect perpetration								1^{24}		1
Indirect co-perpetration								11^{25}		11
JCE	16^{26}		3^{27}	5^{28}	22^{29}	3^{30}	3^{31}	3^{32}	1^{33}	56
Direct partic-ipation				3^{34}				1^{35}	1^{36}	5
Command or superior responsibility		10^{37}		4^{38}	7^{39}		2^{40}	2^{41}	1^{42}	26

---

23 Four non-state leaders.

24 A head of state.

25 Four heads of state, four other government leaders, two leaders of political parties, and one non-state leader.

26 One head of state, five ministers, four military leaders, six other government leaders, and one leader of a political party.

27 Three business leaders.

28 Ministers only.

29 Four heads of state, seven ministers, four military leaders, five other government leaders, and one leader of a political party.

30 Three ministers.

31 One minister, one military leader, and one leader of a political party.

32 One head of state, one military leader, and one non-state leader.

33 A head of state.

34 Two ministers and one other government leader.

35 A military leader.

36 A head of state.

37 Three heads of state, one minister, and six military leaders.

38 Three ministers and one military leader.

39 One minister and six military leaders.

40 One minister and one other government leader.

41 One head of state and one military leader.

42 A head of state.

	IMT	IMTFE	CC10	ICTR	ICTY	SCSL	ECCC	ICC	EAC	Total
Class III: Accomplice Liability										
Aiding and abetting		3^{43}	3^{44}	4^{45}	3^{46}	2^{47}	1^{48}			16
Ordering		3^{49}		2^{50}	1^{51}			1^{52}	1^{53}	8
Instigating				4^{54}			1^{55}	1^{56}		6
Complicity in genocide				2^{57}						2
Participation in crimes against peace	12^{58}	19^{59}								31
Total	46	56	7	39	33	5	19	13	4	222

Table 4: Liability Forms Charged to High-Level Participants.

---

43 Three business leaders.
44 Three business leaders.
45 One head of state, two ministers, and one other government leader.
46 Three military leaders.
47 One head of state and one non-state leader.
48 A minister.
49 Three business leaders.
50 One minister and one other government leader.
51 A military leader.
52 A non-state leader.
53 A head of state.
54 One head of state and three ministers.
55 A minister.
56 A head of state.
57 One head of state and one minister.
58 Five ministers, three military leaders, three other government leaders, and one leader of a political party.
59 Four heads of state, four ministers, nine military leaders, and two other government leaders.

As seen in Table 4, the data support the initial thesis set out in the discussion of heads of state, namely that most institutions gravitated towards the modes of participation prevalent in their constituting documents or their early jurisprudence (such as at the ICTY).

The largest clusters of modes of liability (10 instances or more) can be found in the following areas:

- JCE or its equivalent (at all institutions except the IMTFE, but with the most emphasis at the IMT and ICTY), with a total of 56 instances;

- conspiracy (at the IMT and IMTFE, where this type of inchoate offence was connected to crimes against peace, and at the ICTR, where it was connected to genocide), with a total of 46 instances;

- participation in waging wars of aggression (crimes against peace, only at the IMT and IMTFE), with a total of 31 instances;

- command and superior responsibility (at all institutions except the IMT, the CC10 tribunals, and the SCSL), with a total of 26 instances, 80 per cent of them at the IMTFE, ICTY, and ICTR;

- aiding and abetting (more or less evenly divided between the CC10 tribunals, ICTY, ICTR, SCSL and ECCC), with a total of 16 instances;

- and, lastly, indirect co-perpetration, with 11 instances only at the ICC – but certainly more to follow, as this is the only institution active at the moment.

The seven other modes of indirect liability that have been utilised together account for only 31 instances so far, while surprisingly, five persons, including a head of state, were charged with direct participation. What is less surprising is the prominence of overt preparatory forms of participation, namely planning, instigation, incitement, and conspiracy, in this group of functionaries – 62 instances, or 28 per cent. It is also likely that most instances of JCE and indirect (co-)perpetration in this group are preparatory in nature, as well.

In terms of sentencing, Table 5 sets out the range in each institution. There are nine levels of sentencing, from less than five years' imprisonment all the way to the death penalty.

Sentence	IMT	IMTFE	CC10	ICTR	ICTY	SCSL	ECCC	ICC	EAC	Total
Death	11	6	3							20
Life imprisonment	2	16		6	2		2		1	29
More than 50 years										
40–49 years				1	4					5
30–39 years				3	4					7
20–29 years	2	1		1	7	1				12
10–19 years	2		1		3			2		8
5–9 years		1	2							3
Less than 5 years					2					2
Total	17	24	6	11	18	5	2	2	1	86

Table 5: Sentencing Range for High-Level Participants.

As shown in Table 5, the IMT, IMTFE, ICTR, SCSL, ECCC, and EAC are the six institutions that handed down the largest proportion of high-level sentences (death, life imprisonment, or terms of 40–50 years) relative to the number of accused at those institutions. Overall, there were 54 high-level sentences out of a total of 86, or 62.8 per cent. This is not surprising, given the type and scale of offences committed (in Rwanda and Cambodia) and the extreme cruelty of crimes that were carried out by the organisations of which the accused were in charge (in Sierra Leone and Chad). Moreover, at the IMT and IMTFE, the very high status of the accused persons, combined with the wide territorial range in which crimes were committed, played an important role – as did the fact that the sentencing took place in an era when death sentences were not yet considered objectionable from a human rights perspective. At the other end of the scale, there have only been five sentences of less than 10 years, which should not be surprising in this category of functionaries, which included two business leaders in post-WWII proceedings.

3.4. Mid-Level Participants in Main Power Structures

Unlike the preceding section, where the analysis of power structures took into account the activities of individual perpetrators, this and the following sections will instead look at more general trends, as such an approach will yield similar data sets of interest for this chapter. A total of 117 persons will be examined in this section, divided as follows: 17 at a CC10 tribunal, 28 at the ICTR, 54 at the ICTY, 3 at the SCSL, 4 at the ECCC, and 11 at the ICC.

3.4.1. Senior Military Officers

This swath of the military hierarchy falls between the highest-ranking officers or military leadership, discussed above in Section 3.3.3., and military personnel below the level of officer, who will be addressed in Section 3.5.1. As such, it represents mostly military officials in positions of authority at the regional and local levels, as well as some operating nationally but at a level subordinate to the leadership. Officers attached to the official armed forces of a country as well as in militia aligned with such forces are included in this section.

In all, 44 persons in this category have been subject to judicial scrutiny: three each at the SCSL and ICC, four at the ICTR, and the majority, 34, at the ICTY.

At the SCSL, three senior officers and commanders of the Revolutionary United Front ('RUF') and the RUF/AFRC[60] were prosecuted. All three were convicted in the same joint trial for JCE, but the sentences were different, namely 52, 40, and 25 years.

At the ICC, the three persons charged were a colonel in the armed forces of the Democratic Republic of Congo, for an attack on the village of Bogoro in Ituri, DRC, and two leaders of the Janjaweed militia in Darfur, Sudan. The colonel was charged with co-perpetration but was acquit-

---

[60] Issa Hassan Sesay, Morris Kallon, and Augustine Gbao.

ted.[61] An arrest warrant against the two militia leaders has been issued based on common purpose and inducing, but since they are at large, their trial has not yet begun.[62]

At the ICTR this category included two lieutenant colonels of the Rwandan armed forces[63] as well as two commanders of the Reconnaissance Battalion,[64] namely the commander of the entire unit, who was a major, and the commander of one of its squadrons, who was a captain. Both colonels were convicted of personal participation, with one extra charge each, namely ordering and JCE; both received 25 years' imprisonment. The two commanders were both charged with command responsibility, conspiracy, and complicity; however, the more senior commander was acquitted, while his junior received 15 years.

As indicated, the ICTY has placed a great deal of emphasis on putting military operators on trial. As discussed in the preceding section, the tribunal took action against 14 military leaders, the highest (with the IMTFE) of all the international institutions. Proceedings at the ICTY represent almost 80 per cent of the cases at all institutions at the military intermediate level, the topic of this section.

Within this intermediate level it is possible to distinguish three further tiers, ranged hierarchically from high to low, with 10 persons exercising authority at the regional level or at headquarters below military leaders; 15 persons in a command position at the local level; and another 9 persons exercising some control at the local level but subordinate to the local commanders just mentioned.

The first of these three groups, regional commanders, includes functionaries such as the commander of the Split Military District of the Croatian Army, who was also the overall operational commander of the southern portion of the Krajina region during the military offensive known as Operation Storm;[65] the commander of the Second Operational Group, which was formed by the Yugoslav People's Army ('JNA') to conduct a

---

[61] Ngudjolo Chui.
[62] Ahmad Muhammad Harun and Ali Muhammad Ali Abd-Al-Rahman.
[63] Éphrem Setako and Aloys Simba.
[64] François-Xavier Nzuwonemeye and Innocent Sagahutu.
[65] Ante Gotovina.

military campaign against the Dubrovnik region of Croatia;[66] the commander of the 9th Military Naval Sector ('VPS') of the Yugoslav Navy, which was responsible for attacking Dubrovnik, in the south of Croatia, and the surrounding areas of the Adriatic Sea;[67] the chief of staff to Stanislav Galić, commander of the Sarajevo Romanija Corps of the Bosnian Serb Army, based around Sarajevo, Bosnia and Herzegovina, who then succeeded Galić as corps commander of the Sarajevo Romanija Corps;[68] the chief of the Supreme Command Staff of the Army of the Republic of Bosnia and Herzegovina (ABiH);[69] the commander of the 7th Muslim Mountain Brigade of the ABiH 3rd Corps;[70] the commander of the Kosovo Liberation Army ('KLA') in the Dukagjin operational zone;[71] a member of the KLA General Staff stationed at the headquarters in Jablanica;[72] and the KLA commanders responsible for the operation of the Lapušnik area and the KLA prison camp there.[73]

The modes of participation used for this group were either command responsibility, used five times, or JCE, used three times; two persons, the last ones mentioned, were charged with both. The sentences have ranged from 33 years (reduced on appeal to 29 years for Milošević of the Bosnian Serb Army) to acquittal for all four members of the KLA (either at first instance or after retrial following an appeal), as well as for the chief of staff of the ABiH and for the commander in the Croatian Army (after an appeal, which overturned the original sentence of 24 years). Two other sentences pertained to members of the Yugoslav armed forces (namely 8 years, reduced to seven and a half years on appeal, and 7 years),[74] while the last one was a sentence of 2 years for the other ABiH officer.

The next tier down includes seven of those accused in the joint Bosnian Serb Army ('VRS') or Srebrenica trial (an eighth person in that

---

[66] Pavle Strugar.

[67] Miodrag Jokić.

[68] Dragomir Milošević.

[69] Sefer Halilović.

[70] Amir Kubura.

[71] Ramush Haradinaj.

[72] Lahi Brahimaj.

[73] Fatmir Limaj and Isak Musliu.

[74] Strugar and Jokić, respectively.

trial, Drago Nikolić, will be discussed as part of the third tier below). The seven included the assistant commander for intelligence and security of the VRS Main Staff;[75] a colonel and chief of security of the VRS Main Staff;[76] a lieutenant colonel and commander of the Zvornik Brigade of the Drina Corps of the VRS;[77] a lieutenant colonel and chief of security of the Drina Corps;[78] the commander of a joint force of Bosnian Serb Ministry of the Interior ('MUP') units subordinated to the Drina Corps to participate in the Srebrenica operation;[79] the chief of operations and training administration of the VRS Main Staff;[80] and the assistant commander for moral, legal, and religious affairs of the VRS Main Staff.[81] Other persons connected to the VRS had positions such as chief of staff and deputy commander of the 1st Zvornik Infantry Brigade of the Drina Corps;[82] assistant commander for security and intelligence of the Bratunac Brigade;[83] and commander of the First Tactical Group of the Bosnian Army.[84]

Apart from VRS personnel, this second tier includes the commander of the Bosnian Croat Convicts Battalion (Kažnjenička Bojna);[85] the commander of the Knin garrison of the Croatian Army;[86] the commander of the special KLA unit known as the Black Eagles, in Kosovo;[87] and two militia leaders, one of the Serbian Volunteer Guard (or Arkan's Tigers)[88] and one of the White Eagles or Avengers, a group of local Bosnian Serb paramilitaries in Višegrad, southeastern Bosnia and Herzegovina.[89]

---

[75] Zdravko Tolimir.
[76] Ljubiša Beara.
[77] Vinko Pandurević.
[78] Vujadin Popović.
[79] Ljubomir Borovčanin.
[80] Radivoje Miletić.
[81] Milan Gvero.
[82] Dragan Obrenović.
[83] Momir Nikolić.
[84] Zejnil Delalić.
[85] Mladen Naletilić.
[86] Ivan Čermak.
[87] Idriz Balaj.
[88] Željko Ražnatović.
[89] Milan Lukić.

As in the preceding group, JCE and command responsibility figure prominently here, but in comparison to the preceding group, more often in combination with other forms of liability. There have been six cases in which persons were charged with JCE exclusively, plus two cases of JCE in combination with conspiracy and one in combination with command responsibility. The same pattern can be seen with command responsibility: this form of participation was the sole charge on only one occasion, but it was also charged in combination with aiding and abetting, with complicity, with ordering, and with personal participation, as well as with JCE, as just mentioned. Lastly, one person was convicted of only personal participation and sentenced to life imprisonment.[90]

As expected, there was a range of sentences, but they lean towards the high end, ranging from life imprisonment to acquittal (each on three occasions), with three sentences of 20 years, one of 18 years, two of 17 years, one of 13 years, and one of 5 years (in addition, one person died after being charged but before his trial could begin). The six accused in the joint Srebrenica trial received two of the three life sentences, as well as one sentence each of 18, 17, 13, and 5 years. On the other hand, two of the three acquittals were entered for the Croatian and KLA accused, as well as for the commander of the First Tactical Group of the Bosnian Army. Notable as well is that two persons who pled guilty received lengthy sentences, of 17 and 20 years.[91]

The third tier in this intermediate class consists of the following positions: the assistant commander for logistics within the 4th Detachment (a Yugoslav National Army–organised territorial defence unit) in Bosanski Šamac, Bosnia;[92] the assistant commander for intelligence, reconnaissance, morale, and information in the same 4th Detachment;[93] the commander of the Bratunac Brigade of the VRS;[94] the chief of engineering of the Zvornik Brigade of the VRS;[95] a second lieutenant who served as

---

[90] Lukić.

[91] Momir Nikolić (on appeal after having received 27 years from the Trial Chamber) and Obrenović.

[92] Miroslav Tadić.

[93] Simo Zarić.

[94] Videoje Blagojević.

[95] Dragan Jokić.

chief of security for the Zvornik Brigade;[96] the leader of a reconnaissance unit of the VRS;[97] the commander of the Vitez Brigade of the HVO in Bosnia;[98] the commander of the Mrmak or Vinko Škrobo unit of the Convicts Battalion of the HVO;[99] and the commander of units of Bosnian Croat soldiers of the HVO.[100]

Variations of aiding and abetting figure more prominently in this group than in the two preceding groups. This form of participation was twice charged exclusively, and once each in combination with personal participation and JCE. The other five cases were based on JCE (three times), command responsibility (once), and a combination of command responsibility and personal participation (once).

All persons were convicted and given sentences ranging from 6 to 35 years, with the majority again in the upper range (six of the nine cases resulted in a sentence of over 10 years).[101] The longest sentence was given to the seventh person in the Srebrenica joint trial referred to above, namely Drago Nikolić. Other long sentences (18 and 28 years) were given to persons who had been convicted of a combination of charges, which included personal participation. Notable as well is that the one person who pled guilty, Rajić, still received a 12-year sentence based on command responsibility.

3.4.2. Intermediate Administrators, Including Prison Commanders and Senior Police Officers

Compared to the military category just discussed, the group of 49 civilian administrators is more homogenous. Of the 23 persons adjudicated at the ICTR, 12 were burgomasters or mayors[102] with civil responsibility at the

---

[96]   Drago Nikolić.

[97]   Dragoljub Kunarac.

[98]   Mario Čerkez.

[99]   Vinko Martinović.

[100] Ivica Rajić.

[101] Namely 6, 8, 9, 12, 15 18 (twice), 28, and 35 years' imprisonment.

[102] Jean-Paul Akayesu, burgomaster of Taba; Ignace Bagilishema, Mabanza; Jean Mpambara, Rukara; Grégoire Ndahimana, Kivumu; Paul Bisengimana, Gikoro; Sylvestre Gacumbitsi, Rurumo; Jean-Baptiste Gatete, Murambi; Juvénal Kajelijeli, Mukingo; Joseph Kanyabashi, Ngoma; Élie Ndayambaje, Muganza; Juvénal Rugambarara, Bicumbi; Laurent Semanza, Bicumbi.

local level, and eight were prefectural administrators (six prefects,[103] one subprefect,[104] and one member of a prefectural committee[105]) with civil responsibility at the regional level. The other three functionaries were two councillors[106] and a youth organiser[107] at the local level.

At the ICTY, of the 20 functionaries prosecuted, the majority were either members of a municipal board/crisis staff (6 persons)[108] or were commanders (7)[109] or shift leaders (2)[110] of local prison camps. The remaining five persons included three local police commanders,[111] a high official in the Ministry of the Interior of the Republic of Croatia,[112] and an

---

[103] Emmanuel Bagambiki, prefect in Cyangugu; Sylvain Nsabimana, Butare; Alphonse Ntezi-ryayo, Butare; François Karera, Kigali rural; Clément Kayishema, Kibye; Tharcisse Renzaho, Kigali.

[104] Dominique Ntawukulilyayo, Gisagara.

[105] Michel Bagaragaza, Gisenyi Prefecture.

[106] Mikaeli Muhimana, councillor in Gishyita Commune, Kibuye Prefecture; Vincent Rutaganira, councillor in Mubuga, Gishyita Commune, Kibuye Prefecture.

[107] Joseph Nzabirinda, Butare.

[108] Miroslav Deronjić, president of the Bratunac Municipal Board of the Serb Democratic Party ('SDS') of Bosnia and Herzegovina; Blagoje Simić, president of the Municipal Board of the Serbian Democratic Party and the president of the Serb Crisis Staff (later renamed the War Presidency) in the municipality of Bosanski Šamac; Milomir Stakić, president of the Serb-controlled Prijedor Municipality Crisis Staff and head of the Municipal Council for National Defence; Dusko Tadić, president of the Local Board of the SDS in Kozarac; Stevan Todorović, chief of police and a member of the Serb Crisis Staff in Bosanski Šamac; Stojan Župljanin, member of the Autonomous Region of Krajina ('ARK') Crisis Staff.

[109] Zlatko Aleksovski, commander of the prison facility at Kaonik, near Busovača, Bosnia; Milorad Krnojelac, commander of the Serb-run Kazneno-Popravni Dom (KP Dom) detention camp in Foča, Bosnia; Zdravko Mucić, commander of the Čelebići prison camp, Bosnia; Hazim Delic, deputy commander of the Čelebići camp and then commander of the camp following Mucić's departure; Dragan Nikolić, commander of the Sušica detention camp in the municipality of Vlasenica, Bosnia; Dusko Sikirica, commander of security at the Keraterm detention camp, Prijedor, Bosnia; Goran Jelisić, in a position of authority at the Luka camp, Bosnia.

[110] Damir Došen, shift leader at the Keraterm camp; Dragan Kolundžija, shift commander at the Keraterm camp.

[111] Radomir Kovač, subcommander of the military police of the VRS and a paramilitary leader in the town of Foča, Bosnia; Zoran Vuković, subcommander of the military police of the VRS and a member of the paramilitary in Foča; Vladimir Šantić, local commander of the military police and of the "Jokers", a unit of the Croatian HVO in Bosnia.

[112] Mladen Markač, commander of the special police and assistant minister of the interior.

employee at the Ministry of the Internal Affairs of the Republic of Serbia.[113]

At the ECCC, four officials were charged, namely the secretary of Preah Net Preah District in the North-West Zone of Cambodia,[114] the deputy secretary in the Central Zone,[115] the party secretary of Kirivong District,[116] and the chairman of Phnom Penh's security prison S-21 (Tuol Sleng).[117] Lastly, the ICC charged the communication leader in Kenya's Orange Democratic Movement[118] and the chief of police in Timbuktu, Mali.[119]

A CC10 tribunal sentenced a camp commander, Josef Kramer, who had been in charge of the Belsen concentration camp, to death based on two accusations of aiding and abetting.[120]

The forms of participation varied greatly, both in the number of charges and in the type of liability. With respect to the number of allegations at the ICTR, there were three instances of six charges, two instances of five charges, four instances of four charges, one instance of three charges, two instances of two charges, and 10 cases of only one charge, for a total of 61 charges.

In terms of the types of charges at the ICTR, it is interesting to see the relatively high number that are related to preparatory acts, with nine charges of instigation, five of incitement, two of planning, two of JCE, and one of conspiracy, for a total of 19. There were also 10 charges of ordering and seven of superior responsibility, reflecting the positions of authority of the accused. Lastly, charges related to more immediate involvement included 16 for aiding and abetting, one for complicity, and seven for direct involvement. Of the nine situations with multiple charges, the allegations included both preparatory and executory forms of participation, equally divided between the burgomaster and prefect functions.

---

[113] Franko Simatović, employed in the second administration of the State Security Service.

[114] Im Chaem.

[115] Ao An.

[116] Yim Tith.

[117] Kaing Guek Eav (alias Duch).

[118] Samoei Ruto.

[119] Al Hassan Ag Abdoul Aziz Ag Mohamed Ag Mahmoud.

[120] The Belsen trial is discussed in more detail in Section 3.4.5.

The only charge not laid but known by this institution for this group was attempt.

At the ICTY, seven cases were based on JCE and another five on personal participation; one person was charged with superior responsibility. The other seven cases involved multiple allegations, such as a combination of JCE and superior responsibility (one); personal participation with superior responsibility (one); and aiding and abetting with ordering and superior responsibility (one). In four of these seven cases a general reference to Article 7(1) of the ICTY Statute was made with all its forms of liability, including three with the added allegation of superior responsibility. If one were to assume that Article 7(1) contains five forms of liability (planning, instigating, ordering, committing, and aiding and abetting), then there have been a total of 36 charges in the 20 cases before the ICTY in this group.

At the ECCC, JCE was used against all four defendants, while in the Duch case another five allegations were utilised, namely planning, instigating, ordering, aiding and abetting, and superior responsibility. At the ICC, the charges were indirect co-perpetration, soliciting, and inducing. Only one case at the ECCC resulted in a conviction, namely 35 years' imprisonment for Duch.

With respect to sentencing at the ICTY, there was a wide range. Two persons were sentenced to prison terms between 30 and 40 years, four to between 20 and 30 years, eight to between 10 and 20 years, three to between 5 and 10 years, and one to less than 5 years; two persons were acquitted. It is interesting that some of the highest sentences were meted out to persons who had been charged only with personal participation (40, 28, 23, 18, and 12 years) or with personal participation and command responsibility (15 years). Also of interest is the view of the Appeals Chamber, which disagreed with the Trial Chamber on sentencing in six instances: on four occasions by reducing a sentence, usually by a couple of years (although once from 40 years to an acquittal), and on two occasions by increasing the sentence (in both cases to double or more than double the original sentence). In one instance, a sentence (of 10 years) was pronounced after a guilty plea.

At the ICTR, as at the ICTY, the sentences varied, but on average the sentences imposed tended be higher than at the ICTY. There were six life sentences (including one where the AC increased it from 30 years' imprisonment); three sentences between 40 and 50 years; one sentence between 30 and 40 years; four between 20 and 30 years; three between 10 and 20 years; three between 5 and 10 years; and three acquittals. The AC reduced sentences seven times (including three times from life sentences to terms between 40 and 50 years) and increased them twice. As at the ICTY, the six life sentences all involved a combination of personal partic-ipation and several other charges, except for one, imposed by the AC, which was based on instigation. The shorter sentences were either based on charge of aiding and abetting or entered after a guilty plea (the latter in four instances).

3.4.3. Judges and Justice Officials

There have been only two cases involving judges or justice officials, one at the US military tribunal in Nuremberg immediately after WWII and one at the ICTR. In the trial of Josef Altstötter and others, 16 former German judges, prosecutors, or officials in the Reich Ministry of Justice were charged with being connected (an early version of JCE) with war crimes and crimes against humanity between 1939 and 1945 and with conspiracy in the same crimes between 1933 and 1945; several were also charged with membership in a criminal organisation as defined by the IMT.

Of the 16 accused, one died before the opening of the trial, while a mistrial was declared in respect to a second person. Four accused were acquitted and the remaining 10 were found guilty of war crimes, crimes against humanity, or membership in criminal organisations, or of two or all three of the foregoing charges. The sentences imposed ranged from life imprisonment (four persons) to 10 years (four persons), 7 years (one per-son), and 5 years (one person). Three of the accused had been judges, namely Curt Rothenberger, Oswald Rothaug, and Rudolf Oeschey; Rothaug and Oeschey received life sentences for war crimes and crimes against humanity, while Rothenberger was sentenced to 7 years' impris-onment.

At the ICTR, Siméon Nchamihigo, deputy prosecutor in Cyangugu Prefecture, was sentenced to life imprisonment by the TC, reduced to 40 years on appeal, for instigation, ordering, and aiding and abetting.

3.4.4. Officials, Military and Civilian, in Non-state Power Structures

The only persons charged with international crimes who belonged to non-state power structures at the intermediate level were at the ICC, which charged six people in this context: one in the DRC Ituri situation,[121] one in the Libyan situation,[122] and four in the Ugandan situation.[123] Of these six cases, two proceedings were halted due to the death of the accused,[124] two persons are at large,[125] the trial of one is ongoing,[126] and one was convicted and sentenced to 12 years' imprisonment , reduced to 3 years and 8 months on appeal.[127] The charges in the arrest warrants were more varied than seen before at the ICC and included common purpose (Katanga), direct participation together with ordering (Al-Werfalli), ordering (Lukwiya, Odhiambo, and Otti), and lastly a combination of direct participation, indirect co-perpetration, ordering, and command responsibility (Ongwen).

3.4.5. Conclusions Regarding Mid-Level Participants

With respect to liability forms and sentences, the following results emerge for the intermediate class (as there were no cases in this class at the IMT, IMTFE, or EAC, these three institutions are not included in these tables).

---

[121] German Katanga, highest-ranking commander of the Force de Résistance Patriotique d'Ituri, a rebel militia, during an attack on the village of Bogoro in Ituri.

[122] Mahmoud Mustafa Busayf Al-Werfalli, commander of the Al-Saiqa Brigade.

[123] All four belonged to the Lord's Resistance Army, namely Raska Lukwiya, a deputy leader of the LRA; Okot Odhiambo, also a deputy leader; Vincent Otti, the vice chairman and second-in-command; and Dominic Ongwen, a brigade commander.

[124] Lukwiya and Odhiambo.

[125] Otti and Al-Werfalli.

[126] Ongwen.

[127] Katanga.

	CC10	ICTR	ICTY	SCSL	ECCC	ICC	Total
Class I: Inchoate Liability							
Planning		2			1		3
Conspiracy in war crimes and CAH	16						16
Conspiracy in crimes against peace		3					3
Conspiracy in genocide			1				1
Incitement to genocide		5					5
Class II: Commission Liability							
Co-perpetration						1	1
Indirect co-perpetration						3	3
JCE	16	2	21	3	4	3	49
Direct participa-tion		2	14			2	18
Command or supe-rior responsibility		9	18		1	1	29
Class III: Accomplice Liability							
Aiding and abet-ting	2	17	10		1		30
Ordering		12	6		1	5	24
Instigating		1	4		1		6
Soliciting						1	1
Inducing						3	3
Complicity in genocide		2	1				3
Membership	7						7
Total	41	55	75	3	9	19	202

Table 6: Liability Forms Charged to Mid-Level Participants.

Sentence	CC10	ICTR	ICTY	SCSL	ECCC	ICC	Total
Death	1						1
Life imprisonment	4	6	3				13
More than 50 years				1			1
40–49 years		3		1			4
30–39 years		1	4		1		6
20–29 years		6	8	1			15
10–19 years	3	4	14			1	22
5–9 years	2	3	6				11
Less than 5 years		2					2
Total	10	23	37	3	1	1	75

Table 7: Sentencing Range for Mid-Level Participants.

There have also been 18 acquittals in this group, namely 4 by the CC10 tribunal, 4 by the ICTR, and 10 by the ICTY.

3.5. Low-Level Participants in Power Structures

Given that the international criminal institutions have a mandate to bring the most responsible persons to trial, it is not surprising that relatively few low-level participants have been charged. Of the total of 66 in this class, 45 are guards who were charged in the Belsen trial, which was heard by a CC10 tribunal, the British Military Court in Lüneburg, Germany.[128] The remaining 21, all at the ICTY, included eight guards and 13 persons in three other categories.

3.5.1. Military Personnel

Six low-level soldiers have been tried. Five of them were charged only with JCE, in one joint trial, the Lašva Valley trial,[129] and for the sixth the only charge was personal participation.[130] Of the five in the Lašva Valley trial, four were acquitted, two by the TC and the other two on appeal. The only one convicted, Josipović, was sentenced to 15 years by the TC, reduced to 12 years by the AC. The sixth person received 12 years after a guilty plea.

3.5.2. Other Personnel in Armed Conflict, Such as Members of a Militia

Two people in this category were charged, namely Sredoje Lukić and Mitar Vasiljević. The former, a member of a group of local Bosnian Serb paramilitaries in Višegrad, was charged with aiding and abetting and was sentenced to 27 years' imprisonment. The latter also operated out of Višegrad as a member of the White Eagles, a Bosnian Serb paramilitary unit; he was charged with personal participation and aiding and abetting and was sentenced to 20 years.

---

[128] There have been other trials concerning concentration camps, such as the Dachau trial, the Flossenburg concentration camp trial, and the Mauthausen concentration camp trial, but the Belsen trial has been given the most attention in the reports on the crimes of war criminals. See UNWCC, *Law Reports of Trials of War Criminals*, vol. II, HMSO, London, 1947 (www.legal-tools.org/doc/699fe3/).

[129] Drago Josipović, Zoran Kupreškić, Mirjan Kupreškić, Vlatko Kupreškić, and Dragan Papić; all were members of the Croatian HVO in central Bosnia and Herzegovina.

[130] Dražen Erdemović, who had been a soldier in the 10th Sabotage Detachment of the VRS.

If a militia or paramilitary unit acted in support of a legitimate state government, it could be seen as forming part of a power support structure, and its members could therefore be considered in the fourth class, outlined below. However, because we are speaking of armed personnel in armed conflict, it seems more appropriate to keep this category within the present class.

3.5.3. Policemen

Five policemen were charged, namely Johan Tarčulovski,[131] Miroslav Bralo,[132] Ranko Češić,[133] Darko Mrda,[134] and Dragan Zelenović.[135] The last four were all charged with personal participation (all except Češić after a guilty plea), while Mrda had a charge of JCE added; all received high sentences, namely 20, 18, 17, and 15 years' imprisonment, respectively. Tarčulovski was charged with ordering, planning, and instigation and received a sentence of 12 years.

3.5.4. Guards

In the Belsen trial, Josef Kramer and 44 other men and women were alleged to have been either full members of the staff of the Belsen or Auschwitz concentration camps, or both, or else prisoners elevated by the camp administrators to positions of authority over the other internees. All were charged with being concerned as parties in the maltreatment and murder of inmates in these camps. Of the 45 accused, 44 were charged with this crime for one particular group of victims, while 13 of them were also charged with the same crimes for a second group of victims; one person had accusations levelled against her with respect to the second group only.

---

[131] A police officer acting as an escort inspector in the president's security unit in the Ministry of the Interior; he provided personal security for the president of the former Yugoslav Republic of Macedonia.

[132] A member of the 'Jokers', the anti-terrorist platoon of the 4th Military Police Battalion of the HVO, which operated primarily in the Lašva Valley.

[133] A member of the Intervention Platoon of the Bosnian Serb Police Reserve Corps at the Brčko police station.

[134] A member of an Intervention Squad, a special Bosnian Serb police unit in the town of Prijedor.

[135] A former Bosnian Serb soldier and de facto military policeman in the town of Foča.

Of the 45 accused, 15 were acquitted, while one person did not face trial. The remaining 29 fell into three main categories, namely camp officials, SS guards, and kapos (or in the parlance of the judgment, "prisoner appointed [as] a minor functionary"). Two officials were specifically singled out, namely the commander of the camps, Josef Kramer, and the SS doctor, Fritz Klein; both were sentenced to death. The other 11 camp officials had a broader range, with one person receiving the death penalty, a cluster of six officials each receiving 10 years imprisonment, and the remaining four receiving 1, 3, 5, and 15 years. A majority of the SS guards also received death sentences (six of eight, with the other two receiving 15 years). Among the eight kapos, five received 10-year prison terms, with the other three sentenced to life, 15, and 5 years.

At the ICTY, eight guards became the subjects of proceedings. Five of them served at the same camps, namely the Omarska, Keraterm, and Trnopolje camps, and were part of a joint trial named for those camps, charged with JCE.[136] Another guard at the Keraterm camp was put on trial based on personal participation.[137] The last two persons were guards at different camps, one in Bosnia[138] and one in Kosovo,[139] and were charged respectively with personal participation and personal participation, JCE, and aiding and abetting.

Sentences for the guards in the joint trial ranged from 5 to 25 years (namely 5, 6, 7, 20, and 25 years), with the highest sentences for the two actual guards, reflecting their executory and personal role in the camps, and the lower sentences for those with the more administrative roles, reflecting the preparatory aspects of the JCE charges. The other three guards, all of whom had been at a minimum charged with personal participation, received sentences at the high end of the spectrum as well, with sentences of 13 years and 15 years, as well as one of 8 years after a guilty plea.

---

[136] Miroslav Kvočka, the functional equivalent of the deputy commander of the guard service of the Omarska camp; Dragoljub Prcać, administrative aide to the commander of the Omarska camp; Milojica Kos, guard shift leader in the Omarska camp; Mlađo Radić, guard shift leader in the Omarska camp; and Zoran Žigić, a guard at Keraterm camp who also specifically entered Omarska and Trnopolje camps for the purpose of abusing, beating, torturing, and/or killing prisoners.

[137] Predrag Banović.

[138] Esad Landžo, a guard at the Čelebići camp.

[139] Haradin Bala, a guard at the KLA Lapušnik/Llapushnik prison camp.

3.5.5. Conclusions Regarding Low-Level Participants

Of the 66 persons in this class facing trial at a CC10 tribunal or the ICTY, 19 were acquitted (four at the ICTY and 15 at the CC10 tribunal), while one person was not able to stand trial at the CC10 tribunal due to a medical condition. A total of 84[140] charges were brought against these individuals, of which 58 charges pertained to aiding and abetting in the CC10 tribunal proceeding.

At the ICTY, the majority of the 26 charges against 21 persons consisted of JCE (11) and personal participation (9). There were three charges of aiding and abetting, and one each of planning, ordering, and instigating. The latter three charges were against the same person, one of only two instances when more than two accusations were used (the other involved a combination of personal participation and aiding and abetting). No one has been charged with command or superior responsibility, not surprising for this group of participants at the lower end of the various hierarchies.

In terms of sentencing, the post-WWII tribunal imposed eight death sentences[141] and one sentence of life imprisonment. The other sentences fell into the following ranges: six sentences of 20–30 years, five by the ICTY and one by the CC10 tribunal; 21 sentences of 10–20 years (the largest group), six at the ICTY and 15 at the CC10 tribunal; five sentences of 5–10 years, three at the ICTY and two at the CC10 tribunal; and two sentences below 5 years, both at the CC10 tribunal.

3.6. Participants in Power Support Structures

3.6.1. Religious Leaders

The ICTR put four religious leaders on trial; three were convicted[142] and one acquitted.[143] Those convicted were charged with direct participation and aiding and abetting in combination (two persons) and for aiding and abetting alone (one person); the penalties were 10, 25, and 15 years re-

---

[140] The charges against Josef Kramer are not included here, as they were discussed in the preceding section.

[141] Not including Josef Kramer.

[142] Elizaphan Ntakirutimana, who was a Seventh Day Adventist pastor in Kibuye, Rwanda; Emmanuel Rukundo, who had been a military chaplain; and Athanase Seromba, a Catholic priest in Nyange Parish, Kivumu Commune.

[143] Hormisdas Nsengimana, a Catholic priest and rector of the Collège Christ Roi, a secondary Catholic school in Nyanza, Butare Prefecture.

spectively. The person acquitted had been charged with JCE and superior responsibility.

The SCSL charged one person, Allieu Kondewa, the high priest of the Civil Defence Forces, with aiding and abetting and command responsibility, and sentenced him to 50 years' imprisonment. The ICC also charged one person, Ahmad Al Faqi Al Mahdi, a member of Ansar Eddine, a movement associated with al-Qaeda in the Islamic Maghreb, who was head of the Hisbah (a morality enforcement brigade) in Timbuktu, Mali; he was convicted after a guilty plea and sentenced to 9 years' imprisonment as a co-perpetrator.

3.6.2. Professional Media Personnel: Media Leaders, Publishers, Film Makers, Editors, and Journalists

Professional media personnel may be able to exert substantial influence by fostering a social climate conducive to mass atrocity crimes, especially when acting in groups and when supported by strong media corporations, whether formally state-owned or not. In many cases where universal crimes are committed on a large scale, propaganda and hate speech facilitated by professional media personnel have preceded or accompanied the crimes. In Nazi Germany, for example, a wide range of propaganda tools were employed, including professionally made movies. In 1933 a Propaganda Ministry was established and "charged with controlling and coordinating the content of Germany's press, art, film, music, and literature fields".[144]

At the same time, the actual atrocity crimes committed are often downplayed, covered up, or denied by the same media personnel and/or their colleagues. The contributions and moral blameworthiness of such media acts might be substantial, but the responsibility of professional media personnel is often underestimated and even justified as a form of free speech. However, a few such cases have been brought before international tribunals.

The IMT put two media leaders on trial, namely Julius Streicher, who was the publisher of *Der Stürmer*, an anti-Semitic weekly newspaper, and Walther Funk, the press chief in Nazi Germany. Streicher was con-

---

[144] See, with further references, Gregory S. Gordon, *Atrocity Speech*, Oxford University Press, Oxford, 2017, p. 38.

victed of acting in concert (or JCE) and participation and was sentenced to death, while Funk was convicted of acting in concert and was sentenced to life imprisonment. The IMTFE convicted and sentenced to life imprisonment Kingoro Hashimoto, founder of the Sakurakai publication for conspiracy to wage wars of aggression.

The ICTR put on trial five persons in this category.[145] They were Ferdinand Nahimana, director of Radio Télévision Libre des Mille Collines ('RTLM'); Hassan Ngeze, chief editor of the *Kangura* newspaper; Joseph Serugendo, a member of the steering committee of RTLM; and Georges Ruggiu, a journalist with RTLM. Except for Ngeze, who was charged with aiding and abetting, all of them were accused of incitement, while Serugendo and Ruggiu had counts of direct participation added as well. Nahimana and Ngeze were part of a joint trial,[146] the Media Case, and were sentenced to life imprisonment by the TC, but this was reduced on appeal to 30 and 35 years respectively. Ruggiu received 12 years and Serugendo 6 years, both after a guilty plea.

3.6.3. Authors, Artists, Social Media Actors, and Occasional Public Instigators

While professional media personnel usually operate at traditional outlets such as radio, television, film corporations, newspapers, and publishers, there is another group of people who take part in public social communication that should not be completely forgotten. This somewhat diverse group comprises more or less professional and well-known authors and artists within different fields, social media actors operating on different platforms, and other, more occasional public instigators of hate and propaganda directed at certain groups in society. With the rise of social media, persons within this group who might be considered participants in universal crimes may get more attention in the context of future ICL.

So far, however, only one such case is known to have come before the international tribunals, and it occurred before the social media revolution. It concerned Simon Bikindi, a well-known musician in Rwanda, who contributed to a media campaign organised by the government to foment

---

[145] A sixth person who could be mentioned here, Barayagwiza, has been discussed above in Section 3.3.2.

[146] Together with Barayagwiza.

hatred against the Tutsi people. Bikindi was said to have composed and performed songs aimed at inciting members of the Interahamwe militia and the civilian population to kill Tutsis; his works were widely broadcast by the RTLM radio station. He also participated actively in massacres. He received 15 years' imprisonment for direct and public incitement to commit genocide.

3.6.4. Doctors and Medical Personnel

After World War II, three US military tribunals conducted trials pertaining to medical personnel,[147] of which one, the Hadamar trial,[148] will be discussed in this section. The accused were the chief administrative officer of a small sanatorium in Hadamar, Germany, along with the chief doctor, two chief nurses (including one female), another nurse, a bookkeeper, and the chief caretaker. All seven were charged with direct participation and with aiding and abetting, as well as with being connected with or acting jointly and in pursuance of a common intent. Three of them were sentenced to death, namely the chief administrative officer and the two male nurses, while the chief doctor was sentenced to life imprisonment and the bookkeeper, the caretaker, and the female nurse received 35, 30, and 25 years respectively.

At the ICTR, a medical doctor, Gérard Ntakirutimana, was charged with personal participation and sentenced to 25 years.

---

[147] This does not include Fritz Klein, who was an accused in the Belsen trial, which is discussed above in Section 3.5.4.

[148] The Hadamar trial was conducted by the US Military Commission appointed by the Commanding General Western Military District, USFET, Wiesbaden, Germany. See "The Hadamar Trial: The Trial of Alfons Klein and Six Others", in UNWCC, *Law Reports of Trials of War Criminals*, vol. I, HMSO, London, 1947, pp. 46–54 (www.legal-tools.org/doc/aed83f/). There had been two other trials involving medical personnel, namely the Doctors' Trial or trial of Brandt and Others, as well as the Pohl and Others trial; both were decided by the US military tribunal in Nuremberg. The first of these pertained to Karl Brandt, a senior medical official in the Nazi government. The second concerned Oswald Pohl, chief of the SS Economic and Administrative Main Office, and 17 other civilian officials including doctors, nurses, and medical administrators. However, these two trials are referred to only briefly in the *Law Reports of Trials of War Criminals* but discussed in Chapter 1, Section 1.2.2.

3.6.5. Businessmen

The top leaders of financial and economic institutions and large corporations with close links to the state were discussed above in Section 3.3.6., especially in connection to post-WWII cases. These same cases also involved, in many instances, lower-level associates in those businesses. While we refer to this group of often important economic operators as 'businessmen', persons in this group may have quite different roles and responsibilities.

In the IG Farben case, in addition to the charges against Carl Krauch, the owner of the company, another 22 industrialists and economic leaders were subjected to the same charges of conspiracy, ordering, aiding and abetting, or being connected with war crimes and crimes against humanity. Only 13 of the accused were convicted, and they all received relatively low sentences, with sentences of 8 years (two persons), 7 years (one person), 6 years (two persons), 5 years (one person), 4 years (one person), 3 years (one person), 2 years (three persons), and a year and a half (two persons).

In the Krupp case, the same four charges were laid against 10 other defendants, resulting again in relatively light sentences of 12 years (two persons), 10 years (two persons), 9 years (two persons), 7 years (one person), 6 years (two persons), and 2 years and 10 months (one person). The same happened in the Flick case, where five other industrialists were again accused of these four charges. Three were acquitted, one was sentenced to 5 years, and one received three and a half years.

At the ICTR seven businessmen were put on trial.[149] Five of them were charged with personal participation, four of whom also had other accusations added, namely aiding and abetting (four persons), ordering (two persons), and superior responsibility (two persons); one[150] of these five was charged with all four types of participation just mentioned. The

---

[149] Gaspard Kanyarukiga, a businessman in Kigali and Kivumu Commune; Protais Zigiranyirazo, a businessman in Gisenyi; Yussuf Munyakazi, a businessman and leader of the Bugarama MRND militia in Cyangugu Prefecture; Alfred Musema, director of a tea factory in Gisovu; Georges Rutaganda, a businessman and second vice president of the Interahamwe in Masango commune, Gitarama Prefecture; Obed Ruzindana, a businessman in Kigali; Omar Serushago, a businessman and Interahamwe leader in Gisenyi Prefecture.

[150] Musema.

last two men were charged with planning[151] and a combination of JCE and aiding and abetting.[152] All received high sentences at first instance, namely life imprisonment (two persons), 30 years (one person), 25 years (two persons), 20 years (one person), and 15 years (one person, after a guilty plea). On appeal all the sentences were upheld except for the person who had received 20 years, who was acquitted.[153]

3.6.6. Conclusions Regarding Power Support Structures

Compared to the three classes discussed above, relatively few persons in the support class have been charged. They were mainly involved in post-WWII cases, where 47 persons were put on trial, mostly medical personnel and businessmen (seven and 37 respectively, with another three in the media personnel category). More recently, 17 persons were charged at the ICTR, plus one each at the SCSL and the ICC.

The category of business leaders deserves special mention. As stated above, after World War II, 37 businessmen were charged with international crimes, with each person accused of four different types of participation (resulting in a total of 148 charges); another seven businessmen were charged at the ICTR, for a total of 44 people. Of these 44, 13 were acquitted, including one at the ICTR.

As was noted in Section 3.3.6., the businessmen charged after WWII on the whole received relatively low sentences. Of the 25 persons convicted by the American CC10 tribunals, two persons received sentences above 10 years, 14 received sentences between 5 and 10 years, while nine received sentences of less than 5 years. This stands in stark contrast to the pattern at the ICTR, where of the six businessmen eventually convicted, two received life imprisonment, three received sentences between 20 and 30 years, and one received a sentence between 10 and 20 years. The difference could be explained by the fact at the ICTR, the accused all were at a minimum directly involved in crimes (except one who had been indicted for planning), while the German industrialists carried out their activities far away from the crime scenes and were not directly involved in the preparatory phases of these crimes. Moreover, the German industri-

---

[151] Kanyarukiga.

[152] Zigiranyirazo.

[153] Zigiranyirazo.

alists carried out their crime-related functions as an aspect of their business activities, while in the case of the Rwandan businessmen their involvement in the genocide was not part of their business activities but was carried out in a personal capacity (except in the case of the tea plantation owner, who made equipment and personnel available to assist in commission of the crimes).

3.7. Common Findings and Observations

This conclusion will begin by summarising in three tables some of the salient observations made in the previous four sections of this chapter.

Table 8 will provide for each class of participants the number of persons charged by all the international institutions examined, as well as the number of charges laid, the number of acquittals, and the number of proceedings that were halted or have not yet begun (the latter at the ICC).

Class	Number of persons (% of total)	Number of allegations Average per person (% of total)	Number of acquittals % of persons charged (% of total)	Number of proceedings halted or not yet begun (% of total)
High-level participants	130 (34%)	222 1.7 (31%)	15 12% (26%)	12 (45%)
Mid-level participants	117 (30%)	202 1.7 (29%)	18 16% (18%)	14 (51%)
Low-level participants	76 (20%)	84 1.1 (11%)	19 25% (32%)	1 (4%)
Participants in support structures	62 (16%)	207 3.1 (29%)	14 23% (24%)	
Total	385 (100%)	715 1.8 (100%)	66 18% (100%)	27 (100%)

Table 8: Number of Persons, Allegations, Acquittals, and Proceedings Halted/ Not Yet Begun, by Class of Participants.

Table 9 sets out the forms of liability used in the allegations for the four different classes of participants.

	High-level participants	Mid-level participants	Low-level participants	Participants in support structures	Total
Class I: Inchoate Liability					
Planning	2	3	1	1	7
Conspiracy in war crimes or CAH	39	16		1	56
Conspiracy in crimes against peace		3		37	40
Conspiracy in genocide	7	1			8
Incitement to genocide	8	5		4	17
Subtotal Class I	56	28	1	43	128
Class II: Commission Liability					
Co-perpetration	4	1		1	6
Indirect perpetration	1				1
Indirect co-perpetration	11	3			14
JCE	56	49	11	48	164
Direct participation	5	18	9	17	49
Command or superior responsibility	26	29		6	61
Subtotal Class II	103	100	20	72	295

	High-level participants	Mid-level participants	Low-level participants	Participants in support structures	Total
Class III: Accomplice Liability					
Aiding and abetting	16	30	61	54	161
Ordering	8	24	1	37	70
Instigating	6	6	1		13
Inducing		3			3
Soliciting		1			1
Complicity in genocide	2	3			5
Participation in crimes against peace	31			1	32
Membership		7			7
Subtotal Class III	63	72	63	92	290
Total Classes I–III	222	202	84	207	715

Table 9: Forms of Liability by Class of Participants.

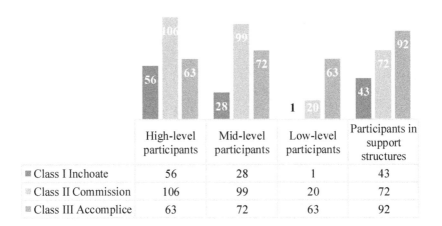

	High-level participants	Mid-level participants	Low-level participants	Participants in support structures
■ Class I Inchoate	56	28	1	43
▨ Class II Commission	106	99	20	72
▨ Class III Accomplice	63	72	63	92

Figure 1: Total Charges in Each Liability Class, by Class of Participants.

Table 10 examines the variations in sentencing ranges within the four classes of participants.

Sentence	High-level participants	Mid-level participants	Low-level participants	Participants in support structures	Total
Death	20	1	8	4	33
Life imprisonment	29	13	1	5	48
More than 50 years		1			1
40–49 years	5	4		1	10
30–39 years	7	6		5	18
20–29 years	12	15	6	5	38
10–19 years	15	22	21	9	67
5–9 years	3	11	5	14	33
Less than 5 years	2	2	2	9	15
Total	93	75	43	52	263

Table 10: Sentencing Range by Class of Participants.

A number of general observations need to be made with respect to the numbers in these tables as well as earlier in the chapter. The first is that all the post-WWII trials mentioned were group trials, whereas only a minority of the modern trials were group trials (with the exception of those at the SCSL, where three of the four trials were group trials, although with only three persons each). Some of the post-WWII group trials discussed above involved dozens of accused (for instance, the IMT trial, the IMTFE trial, the Belsen trial, and the Krauch trial). The fact that the above tables (especially Tables 8 and 9) refer to either numbers of persons or numbers of charges, rather than to number of trials, combined with the fact that in most of the post-WWII trials the accused faced multiple charges, unlike in modern trials, might give the impression that the modern trials are less significant, but this is not the intention; significance cannot be determined from a quantitative analysis alone. Moreover, some of the charges used in the post-WWII cases, specifically the ones related to crimes against peace and conspiracy (except conspiracy in connection with genocide), could no longer be used in modern times. A similar thing can be said for Table 10, in that the post-WWII tribunals tended to hand down more severe sentences than their modern counterparts (including the death penalty, which none of the modern institutions have the jurisdiction to do). As noted in the conclusion to Section 3.3.1., this is a reflection both of the different attitudes in those times and of the duration and intensity of the crimes. However, the conclusions reached below are still valid in general terms, even if the data above would make it possible to draw a distinction between post-WWII and modern practice.

A second general observation relates to the fact that in Table 10, the sentences refer to the final ones handed down after an appeal. At the SCSL, the AC virtually always confirmed the sentences arrived at by the TC, but at the ICTR and ICTY, which share a single AC, this was not always the case. While in the majority of cases the AC confirmed the TC sentences or, rarely, increased the sentence, there have been quite a few occasions on which the AC reduced the original sentence, sometimes drastically – and even, in a few cases, overturning a severe sentence in favour of an acquittal.

Lastly, the narrative above has indicated each time the result of a sentence after a guilty plea. In general, it can be said that persons who pled guilty received lighter sentences than persons with comparable criminal backgrounds who decided to go to trial (with the notable exception of

Kambanda, who received a sentence of life imprisonment after pleading guilty).

Turning now to the information contained in the three tables, the two aspects of most interest in Table 8 are the numbers of persons charged and acquitted in each of the four classes (high-level, mid-level, and low-level participants, and participants in power support structures) relative to the total. While it should not be surprising that the institutions in question would bring to trial and convict the persons most responsible, and have done so in 64 per cent of the cases (34 per cent for high-level and 30 per cent for mid-level participants), one would have thought that the number of 20 per cent for the low-level participants would have been even lower. With respect to the number of acquittals as a percentage of persons charged, which reinforces to some extent what has just been said, this number is highest for the low-level functionaries (25 per cent, compared to 12 per cent and 16 per cent for the high-level and mid-level figures, respectively), although the percentage for power support structures is only slightly less (23 per cent).

In terms of the preferred mode of participation, the observation made in Section 3.2. and repeated at the end of Section 3.3.1. is confirmed when looking at the overall picture. That is, some of the institutions are to some degree captives of their own statutes and the early direction of their appeals chambers. The institutions' statutes go a long way towards explaining the preferences for conspiracy and participation among the post-WWII institutions, as well as the unique forms of participation related to genocide, namely conspiracy, complicity, and incitement, at the ICTR. On the other hand, for JCE at the ICTY, the SCSL, and ECCC, and for the various forms of perpetration at the ICC, the leading and early jurisprudence in those institutions has played a decisive role.

In this context, the repetitive use of certain forms of participation, shown in Table 9, is worth examining in more detail. The direct participation category, with 49 occurrences, shows some counterintuitive results, in that it is surprising to see as many as five occurrences in the high-power group and only nine in the low-power group. Moreover, 17 instances of direct participation for the support group is surprisingly high, as one would expect this group to primarily provide only indirect assistance to the principals in the crimes.

Also surprising is the fact that there are more examples of ordering in total than of command/superior responsibility, 70 versus 61 cases. Even taking into account the high number of businessmen charged with this form of participation after WWII, one would have thought that in most instances of persons in authority prompting others to commit crimes, command/superior responsibility would have been more the legally palatable option, as it operates as a form of omission rather than commission and would therefore be easier to prove. There are two likely reasons for the preference for ordering, especially in the mid-level class. The first is that the element of knowing that an underling had committed crimes would be easier to prove for ordering than for command/superior responsibility. Second, and connected to the first aspect, command/superior responsibility has generally been used for persons further removed, both hierarchically and geographically, from the crime scenes, while the persons charged with giving orders often have a more linear connection with the perpetrators. The latter point is underscored by the fact that 26 of the charges based on command/superior responsibility can be found in the high-level class, and a majority of these 26 pertain to military personnel convicted by the IMTFE.

What is certainly not surprising is the reliance on both JCE and aiding and abetting, both in terms of numbers (with 164 and 161 instances respectively) and in terms of their spread across the four classes of participants. There are some differences: JCE is more prominent in the two higher-ranking groups, indicating that JCE has been used in those two groups as part of the preparatory phase, while aiding and abetting is more frequent in the low-level group, a reminder that persons at that level function mostly in a supporting capacity. The high number of support functionaries charged with both these modes of participation is a reflection of the post-WWII industrialist cases.

With respect to sentencing, even if one excludes the death penalties imposed after WWII, the picture is consistent with the assumption that persons at higher levels of authority should be punished more harshly than those at the lower echelons of a hierarchy. Table 10 shows eight sentencing brackets (excluding death). In the top four brackets, corresponding to prison terms of 30 years or more, high-ranking participants in power structures represent 41 of the 77 sentences, or 53 per cent. Mid-level participants represent 24 of 77, or 31 per cent. Only one low-level participant was in the top four sentencing brackets, while there were 11 such sentences in the support group.

The reverse is also partially true. Close to half of sentences in the four lowest brackets, prison terms below 30 years, were given to low-level participants in power structures, with 34 sentences, and to partici-pants in support structures, with 37 sentences – 22 per cent and 24 per cent, respectively, of the 153 sentences in these four brackets. The fact that these groups together do not exceed the 50 per cent mark is the result of an anomaly in the mid-level group, where 50 persons were sentenced in the lower range, or 34 per cent. In this intermediate group, one might have expected more high-range than low-range sentences, similar to the situa-tion in the group of high-ranking participants, with a breakdown of 41 higher versus 32 lower sentences. But the table instead points to a 24-50 split for the mid-level group.

This unexpected finding regarding sentencing in the mid-level group underscores the fact that sentencing at the international institutions is far from an exact science. While the various tribunals have sentencing guidelines that have played an important role in sentencing patterns over-all, when we look at individual sentences we can detect distinct variations from these guidelines, as well as differences between the various tribunals. That is also why we have not attempted in this chapter to draw a connec-tion between the level of sentencing and the mode of participation, except to note one consistent trend in the modern tribunals: namely, that where a person committed crimes individually in addition to the mode of partici-pation appropriate to the group of which he was part, tribunals are in-clined to impose a higher sentence than for similarly situated persons with similar charges who did not take individual actions to increase the suffer-ing of their victims.

4

Legal Bases of Universal Crimes Norms and Personal Liability

4.1. Methodological Challenges

The subject matter of universal crimes, including personal liability for such crimes, raises special methodological challenges. This is because of the fragmented nature of international criminal law, and because the concept of international crimes is not in itself sufficiently clear to define which crimes and crime elements are included or even what the conditions for inclusion are. These challenges are also of concern to our theory of punishable participation in universal crimes.[1]

In order to provide methodological context to the theory of personal criminal liability outlined in Chapter 2, and further discussed in the next chapters of this book, this chapter includes a broader discussion of legal bases and interpretation of the relevant universal crimes norms under international law. Regardless of the need for theoretical analysis, the ultimate interest of the universal crimes project is in binding international law. With regard to interpretation of treaties, for instance, the general rules set out in the Vienna Convention on the Law of Treaties ('VCLT') are important (see in particular Articles 31–33).[2] For the specific subject matter of this book, the relationship between customary international law and the lawful scope of treaty provisions and court decisions on personal liability is crucial for the scope of possible operational modes of liability in ICL.[3]

This analysis starts from the assumption that the concept of universal crimes in international law is essentially a legal concept, consisting of binding norms of international criminal law. Legal norms are taken to

---

[1] This chapter builds on but is not identical to a similar chapter in the first book of this series; see Terje Einarsen, *The Concept of Universal Crimes in International Law*, Torkel Opsahl Academic Epublisher, Oslo, 2012 (www.legal-tools.org/doc/bfda36/).

[2] See Section 4.3.2. in this chapter.

[3] See in particular Section 4.3.7. in this chapter.

mean rules proscribing a type of conduct, or, conversely, prescribing a kind of conduct that should be followed, which in some way is upheld by sanctions or possible sanctions within a system of law. Following the opinion of the International Law Commission, international law is considered to be a 'system of law'.[4] Therefore, the rules at the operational level of the general theory of criminal law liability of particular interest to this study in ICL are legally binding norms, which originate from specific law-creating sources of international law.[5]

A feature of binding rules is their 'if-then' character: that is, singular norms often form part of a larger structural norm encompassing abstract legal conditions ('if') for certain abstract legal consequences ('then'). Legal norms thus consist of legal conditions and legal consequences that should follow when all the necessary and sufficient conditions are fulfilled ('if a, b, and c, then x and y'). These may concern rights, obligations (duties), procedures, or competences. The simplest legal norms consist of just one condition and one consequence. Other rules may consist of several conditions and one consequence, while the most complex legal norms consist of several cumulative and alternative conditions and a number of consequences. Legal concepts often seek to encompass whole clusters of such legal norms concerned with the same subject matter, such as property rights, freedom of expression, refugee status, and criminal liability.

Because of the complexity of universal crimes and the often-noted fragmentation of international criminal law, a broader theoretical perspective may be needed, consisting of overarching concepts covering the entire field. The concept of universal crimes, it is argued, is the pre-eminent candidate for such a concept. It provides a common legal mega-norm, although, of course, it needs to be analysed and discussed from different perspectives. In a very simplified form, the concept can be shown as follows:

If:

    Universal crime *and*

    Punishable participation

---

4   See International Law Commission ('ILC'), *Conclusions of the Work of the Study Group on Fragmentation of International Law: Difficulties Arising from the Diversification and Expansion of International Law*, 2006, conclusion no. 1, reprinted in *Yearbook of the International Law Commission, 2006*, vol. II, part 2 (www.legal-tools.org/doc/6f7968/).

5   See further Section 4.3. in this chapter.

Then:

Personal criminal liability *and*

Prosecution or extradition *and*

Universal court jurisdiction

There are multiple legal consequences included in this schema, including the issue of jurisdiction. Even so, it is arguably too simple a model, implying that all universal crimes may have legal consequences that are comparable in all respects. That would not be accurate. For example, prosecutorial discretion may insert another layer into the model that needs to be taken into account in relation to the 'duty to extradite or prosecute',[6] raising the broader issue of accountability and jurisdiction.[7] Universal jurisdiction is typically conditioned upon further requirements and limitations. For example, presence in the territory of the prosecuting state is generally required. For sitting heads of state and others enjoying diplomatic immunity, there is the special limitation that they cannot be prosecuted domestically, only before international courts, because of the greater risk of abuse of universal jurisdiction at the domestic level of a single state. The problem could also be that the judicial system of a state, in general, is not independent or set up to guarantee a fair trial; as is well known, this is more or less the case in a number of contemporary states, partly because due process is expensive. It is notable that only a group of Western states are currently prosecuting, on a regular basis, universal crimes cases based on universal jurisdiction, which is an option and not an obligation under international law.[8] On the other hand, prosecution of universal crimes committed within the territory of a state is often an obligation for the territorial state under particular treaties, including the Genocide Convention and human rights conventions – in principle, regardless of the status of the state's judicial system.

In general, there is no doubt that the judicial quality of procedures and judgments in universal crimes cases at the international courts has been better than in the cases prosecuted at the domestic level. For this reason as well, it makes sense to distinguish between personal liability con-

---

6   See also Einarsen, 2012, Chapter 2, Section 2.3.5., *supra* note 1.

7   See the preface to this book.

8   See Chapter 8.

cepts employed in the international jurisprudence and in the jurisprudence of national institutions at the operational fourth level of the general theory of criminal law liability in ICL.[9] It also means that sound development depends on domestic prosecutors and judges learning from their international counterparts, to a greater extent than the reverse, including with respect to personal liability concepts suitable for universal crimes; that is, the internationally established parameters should guide the application of key liability concepts within all levels and subsystems of ICL.[10] This situates international law naturally at the front of our methodological analysis as well.

Before discussing the possible legal bases of universal crimes norms and personal liability, the next section considers the difficulties arising from the diversification and expansion of ICL.

4.2. The Fragmented or Pluralistic Nature of International Criminal Law

Is international criminal law really one body of law that is a coherent subset of public international law? Or, alternatively, is ICL a somewhat artificial term, comprising several more or less integrated and partly conflicting law regimes? Should we view ICL through the lenses of pluralism,[11] rather than upholding the conception of a unified body of law? Or does ICL have a dual nature, consisting of several subsystems (such as, for example, the Rome Statute/ICC) while also being an overarching system? Such a possible dual nature may even extend to ICL being part of the larger system of public international law and simultaneously being a specialised subsystem of 'criminal law'. From a slightly different perspective, ICL and its subsystems may in practice interact and be compared with domestic criminal law systems that have incorporated universal crimes norms and also operate in accordance with certain common fundamental criminal law principles. The dual nature of ICL, as well as this conception of its relationship to domestic criminal law systems, is compatible with

---

[9] See Chapter 7 on liability concepts in the international jurisprudence, and Chapters 8–9 on liability concepts in domestic universal crimes cases.

[10] In fact, this seems to have been the case in recent years, as highlighted in Chapter 10, Section 10.2., based on the findings of Chapters 8–9.

[11] See Elies van Sliedregt and Sergey Vasiliev (eds.), *Pluralism in International Criminal Law*, Oxford University Press, Oxford, UK, 2014.

the general theory of personal criminal law liability as presented in Chapter 2. However, in our opinion it is still useful to highlight the fragmented or pluralistic nature of ICL, although both terms may – depending on their uses – exaggerate differences at the expense of commonality.[12]

In the case of national law within a state, one can expect legislation and criminal courts to form a unified system. Jurisdiction is normally allocated geographically at the lower levels, but a uniform interpretation of the law is made possible through a hierarchical appeal system. In national criminal law, the principles of legality and equality before the law require uniform and foreseeable application of the law. In federal states, distinctions are made between 'state' and 'federal' matters, but otherwise the structures are similar. ICL, on the other hand, does not constitute such a hierarchical and unified system of law.

It may be argued that domestic jurisdiction over universal crimes is inherent in sovereignty and should be applied by all states, at least by those states where the crime scenes have occurred, on the basis of territorial jurisdiction. This is true in theory. In practice, however, ICL has not functioned this way historically, with a few possible exceptions related to post–World War II war crimes trials and, arguably, to more recent transitional and post-transitional justice trials in Latin America.[13] In addition,

---

[12] Some have argued that the term 'pluralism' is more suitable than 'fragmentation' because it more accurately reflects the nature and origin of ICL and also better captures the diversity and complexity of this field. See Elies van Sliedregt and Sergey Vasiliev, "Pluralism: A New Framework for International Criminal Justice", in Van Sliedregt and Vasiliev, 2014, pp. 1–33, *supra* note 11. They argue that fragmentation overstates divergence in reasoning and outcomes and wrongly characterises certain features. We agree that the concept of pluralism may better capture the nuances of substantive and procedural ICL. While we find their critique useful in this regard, some of the same critique might be advanced against the concept of pluralism if used as a core characterisation of ICL. Hence it might not be so much the terms of fragmentation or pluralism that should be considered, but rather how the concepts are being used along with other conceptual tools and characterisations to paint the full picture of ICL.

[13] In 1985 Argentina became the first country in Latin America to bring to court criminal cases for gross human rights violations, comparable to universal crimes, committed during military rule. Argentina was only the second country in the world (after Greece in 1975) to take such action in the period following the World War II cases. The success of this effort was initially limited, since the five junta members convicted were pardoned in 1990 along with other military officials. However, prosecutions of former political and military leaders started again in the mid-1990s, principally in Argentina and Chile. There have subsequently been cases in Bolivia, Guatemala, Haiti, Mexico, Paraguay, Peru, Suriname, and Uru-

some countries have been assisted by the international community in applying their territorial jurisdiction.[14] One key reason is that quite often governments themselves are involved in the universal crimes; another is the lack of adequate mechanisms for judicial implementation of prosecutions of these crimes. Political scientists have pondered why universal crimes trials happen in some countries and not at all (or to a significantly lesser extent) in other countries, even when the violations are much the same.[15] There is no legal remedy for appealing, to an international criminal tribunal, decisions by governments or by domestic prosecutors and courts to prosecute or decline prosecution at the national level. However, there has been positive development with respect to greater use of extraterritorial jurisdiction in universal crimes cases, notably universal jurisdiction, especially among a group of Western states.[16]

With respect to uniformity at the international level, there is no single, authoritative list of universal crimes (or 'international crimes'),[17] nor are there uniform criteria for punishable participation in such crimes. Crimes against humanity have been included in all the statutes of the various international tribunals since World War II, but apart from these, the categories and underlying crimes included, as well as their exact formulations, have varied.[18] In addition to crimes against humanity, genocide, ag-

---

guay. See Elin Skaar, *Judicial Independence and Human Rights in Latin America: Violations, Politics, and Prosecution*, Palgrave Macmillan, New York, 2011, pp. 2–3.

[14] See Chapters 7 and 9 for a comprehensive account.

[15] Skaar, 2011, *supra* note 13, analyses both political and legal structures but emphasises the impact of judicial independence in explaining why some prosecutors and courts in Argentina and Chile eventually took the lead in retributive justice.

[16] See Chapter 8 for a detailed account.

[17] On attempts made to identify 'international crimes', see, for example, Einarsen, 2012, pp. 135–287, *supra* note 1; Kai Ambos, *Treatise on International Criminal Law*, vol. 1, *Foundations and General Part*, Oxford University Press, Oxford, 2013; Robert J. Currie and Joseph Rikhof, *International & Transnational Criminal Law*, 2nd ed., Irwin Law, Toronto, 2013, pp. 107–66 and 290–324; Sarah Wharton, "Redrawing the Line? Serious Crimes of Concern to the International Community beyond the Rome Statute", in *The Canadian Yearbook of International Law*, 2015, vol. 52, pp. 129–83; and Kevin Jon Heller, "What Is an International Crime? (A Revisionist History)", in *Harvard International Law Journal*, 2017, vol. 58, no. 2, pp. 353–420.

[18] An example is the particular jurisdictional limitation of the Nuremberg Charter Article 6 (c), which arguably could be understood as specifying that crimes against humanity come within the tribunal's jurisdiction only when committed "in execution of or in connection with" other crimes – in practice, crimes against peace and war crimes. The English word-

gression, and war crimes have generally been included. Other crimes outside these 'core crimes' have generally not been included, with differing opinions on their legal status in the literature.[19]

Another possible factor leading to fragmentation is court jurisdiction. The International Court of Justice is a general court of international law but not a criminal court. Although it may offer important opinions on legal issues directly relating to universal crimes, its jurisdictional limitations and the fact that it is not directly concerned with individual responsibility for universal crimes makes it unlikely that the ICJ could comprehensively and regularly address universal crimes issues. Historically, the treaty-based Nuremberg and Tokyo tribunals were clearly *ad hoc* courts with confined personal and temporal jurisdiction. The jurisdiction of the International Criminal Tribunal for Rwanda, established by the UN Security Council, was also limited temporarily and territorially. In the case of the International Criminal Tribunal for the former Yugoslavia, also established by the Security Council, the jurisdiction was limited territorially. While no explicit, forward-looking temporal limitation was formally established, it was clear from the beginning that the ICTY would only function for a limited period. The same applies to the Special Court for Sierra Leone and the Extraordinary Chambers in the Courts of Cambodia, arguably the principal hybrid international tribunals.

The only international criminal court with an unlimited forward-looking temporal jurisdiction (covering all crimes committed after 2002) is the treaty-based International Criminal Court. The ICC is therefore potentially the most important international court that has ever been estab-

---

ing of Article 6(c) did not support this interpretation, but the prosecutors at Nuremberg had signed a special common protocol to this effect. See Roger S. Clark, "Crimes against Humanity at Nuremberg", in George Ginsburgs and V.N. Kudriavtsev (eds.), *The Nuremberg Trial and International Law*, Kluwer Academic, Dordrecht, Netherlands, 1990, pp. 190–92. This led the Nuremberg Tribunal to the conclusion that acts before the outbreak of World War II in 1939 were outside its jurisdiction with respect to crimes against humanity. See International Military Tribunal ('IMT'), *Trial of the Major War Criminals before the International Military Tribunal: Nuremberg, 14 November 1945–1 October 1946* (hereafter cited as *Trial of the Major War Criminals*), vol. I, Nuremberg, 1947, p. 254 (www.legal-tools.org/doc/f21343/).

[19] See, for example, Einarsen 2012, pp. 150–68 (with reference to other authors), *supra* note 1. For further viewpoints in the literature, see also the authors mentioned in *supra* note 17.

lished, although it has other jurisdictional limitations.[20] Prosecution usually depends upon a referral by the forum state where the crimes have been committed, as provided in the Rome Statute, Article 13(a), or *proprio motu* upon the forum state being judged unwilling or unable to prosecute.[21] In addition, the limited number of crime types included in operational terms from the start has left other possible universal crimes in limbo, including, for a while, the crime of aggression, which was legally defined for the purpose of the Rome Statute in the 2010 Kampala amendment (see Article 8*bis*) and then finally activated from 17 July 2018.[22]

To date, the ICC has not been able to establish itself as an effective world criminal court for the most serious crimes. It remains to be seen whether it will overcome its legal, political, and financial constraints. Kaye pointed out some years ago that even though "the ICC may seem to have become an indispensable international player", a closer look suggests that it is "still struggling to find its footing almost a decade after its creation". In addition, considering that all six of its investigations involve abuses in Africa, "its reputation as a truly international tribunal is in ques-

---

[20] On the jurisdictional bases of the ICC, see the Rome Statute of the International Criminal Court (hereafter cited as Rome Statute), Articles 13, 14, and 15, including Articles 15*bis* and 15*ter* on the crime of aggression (www.legal-tools.org/doc/7b9af9/).

[21] See Rome Statute, Article 13(c). Two other possibilities exist: referral by the United Nations Security Council, as provided in Rome Statute Article 13(b), and referral by a state party other than the forum state. The latter option has not yet been utilised, but it is clearly part of Article 13(a). See James Crawford, "The Drafting of the Rome Statute", in Philippe Sands (ed.), *From Nuremberg to The Hague: The Future of International Criminal Justice*, Cambridge University Press, Cambridge, 2003, p. 148: "any state party to the Statute can refer a possible crime to the Prosecutor, irrespective of any lack of contact between the referring state and the crime".

[22] See ICC, Resolution ICC-ASP/16/Res.5, adopted by consensus at the 13th plenary meeting, 14 December 2017 (www.legal-tools.org/doc/6206b2/). The interpretation of this resolution, apart from the mere activation of jurisdiction, and its legal impact on the jurisdictional regime agreed upon in Kampala are somewhat contested. See Jennifer Trahan, "From Kampala to New York: The Final Negotiations to Activate the Jurisdiction of the International Criminal Court over the Crime of Aggression", in *International Criminal Law Review*, 2018, vol. 18, no. 2, pp. 197–243. For a broader account of aggression in international law and its political context, see Leila Nadya Sadat (ed.), *Seeking Accountability for the Unlawful Use of Force*, Cambridge University Press, Cambridge, 2018.

tion".[23] Admittedly, the ICC since then has extended its involvement through a broader range of preliminary examinations of situations that may result in concrete investigations of identified suspects. This includes examinations on other continents – in Afghanistan, Colombia, Iraq/UK, Palestine, and Ukraine – but by 2018 the ICC had still only opened actual investigations into 11 situations, of which 10 concern African countries.[24]

Although it is unlikely that the ICC will ever be able to function as a comprehensive world criminal court system for the enforcement of universal crimes, it is nonetheless probable that the court will continue to be the most important institution for consideration of universal crimes issues for decades ahead. It may be able to reinforce a concerted effort by some states to prosecute major leaders and notorious offenders earlier supported or protected by national power structures. If this were accomplished on a regular basis over many years, even for a limited number of cases, that would be a significant step forward in human history. The empirical survey undertaken in Chapters 5–9 of this book suggests that a certain development along these lines is already taking place, and that the international jurisprudence and indirect support of institutions like the ICC has been instrumental in that regard. For this reason, it is understandable that scholarly attention with respect to participation and operational modes of liability has shifted more and more towards the Rome Statute. However, from a theoretical point of view, a general theory of punishable participation in universal crimes needs a broader empirical basis and a different analytical starting point.

As noted earlier, the rise of international institutions in the twentieth century has changed our perceptions of what international law is and how it can serve common interests of the world community as a whole.[25] Within the UN paradigm of international law,[26] partly autonomous regimes have been allowed to operate within frameworks that are not entirely limited by the self-interests of sovereign states and their leaders. Although the

---

[23] David Kaye, "Who's Afraid of the International Criminal Court? Finding the Prosecutor Who Can Set It Straight", in *Foreign Affairs*, May/June 2011, vol. 90, no. 3.

[24] ICC, "The Court Today", updated 21 September 2018, ICC-PIDS-TCT-01-086/18_Eng (www.legal-tools.org/doc/7286c7/).

[25] However, continuous development along the same path is not inevitable, as several more recent events have shown.

[26] On this concept, see Einarsen, 2012, pp. 38–51, *supra* note 1.

distinct character of these regimes also makes it difficult to integrate them within the perspective of a unified international law, each represents a thoughtful response to real-life problems whose solution requires international co-operation. The International Law Commission has identified three types of such 'special' or 'self-contained' regimes:[27]

- Regimes consisting basically of primary rules relating to a special subject matter, for instance, a treaty on the protection of a particular river or the use of a particular weapon.

- Regimes established by secondary rules for the purpose of considering breaches and reactions to breaches of a particular group of primary rules.

- Regimes perceived as a collection of all the rules and principles that regulate a certain problem area, for example, 'law of the seas', 'humanitarian law', 'human rights law', and so on.

Where does international criminal law fit within this analytical framework? Most obviously, it seems to fit well within the last category, as a collection of rules and principles regulating a certain problem area and understood as a distinct field of international law. This is a coherent definition even though the underlying norms proscribing the relevant acts may originate in the related fields of humanitarian law and human rights law. However, each of the various international criminal courts may also fall within the second category, each thus constituting a special regime in its own right. Contemporary ICL thus shows an inherent dualism: from one perspective, it is an almost unified body of law, while from another perspective it comprises several distinct bodies of law. A similar dualism can be found in other parts of international law, such as international human rights law. But these contradictions with respect to the substantive norms become particularly problematic when the law directly concerns attribution of individual criminal liability and enforcement of severe punishment.

At the descriptive level, ICL is a special regime of international law with a polycentric appearance. It can be visualised as several 'circles of law' or 'sub-regimes' functioning independently but also interacting with each other. Earlier in this book we referred to subsystems of criminal law

---

[27] ILC, 2006, conclusions nos. 11 and 12, *supra* note 4.

and distinguished between the international and domestic levels. At the international level, these subsystems are equivalent to 'sub-regimes'. Among these sub-regimes, some are more important than others in the current practice and future development of ICL. For instance, the ICC is now at the centre of gravity, whereas institutions such as the Special Tribunal for Lebanon are at the periphery of the ICL system.[28] The treaty-based ICC regime occupies a central place largely because it was designed to fit well within the main structures of the UN paradigm of international law. Thus its statute clearly envisaged a formal relationship with the United Nations and concrete points of co-operation with several organs of the UN.[29] Of particular importance is the competence of the UN Security Council, under certain circumstances, to extend the operational jurisdiction of the ICC.[30] This effort to 'integrate' the ICC within the core structures of the UN can be seen as an attempt to avoid further fragmentation of international criminal law, but it may arguably also have the effects of politicising the ICC and weakening the independence of the Prosecutor's Office and the court.

In order to counter the negative effects of fragmentation, certain other mechanisms were earlier established as well, such as a common Appeals Chamber for the ICTY and ICTR. There is also an Appeals Division at the ICC and Appeals Chambers within the hybrid special courts such as the SCSL, ECCC, and STL. To the extent that the appeals judges rely on

---

[28] The Special Tribunal for Lebanon ('STL') may still have contributed to the field on several issues, for instance with respect to notions of trials in absentia and corporate liability, and not least a clarification of the legal status of acts of terrorism under international law. In fact, it has made a significant contribution on the status of terrorism under customary international law. See STL, Appeals Chamber, *Interlocutory Decision on the Applicable Law: Terrorism, Conspiracy, Homicide, Perpetration, Cumulative Charging*, STL-11-01/I/AC/ R176bis, 16 February 2011 (www.legal-tools.org/doc/ceebc3/). On international terrorist crimes as universal crimes, see Einarsen, 2012, pp. 266–74, *supra* note 1.

[29] See Rome Statute, Article 2, requiring a formal agreement with the United Nations; Article 13, allowing the Security Council to give the Court jurisdiction and to trigger proceedings; Article 16, providing that the Security Council may suspend or defer proceedings; and Article 119(2), providing a role for the International Court of Justice. In addition, the Rome Statute also assigns a role for the UN Secretary-General (see Articles 121, 123, and 125–28).

[30] This happened in the cases of Darfur, Sudan, in 2005 and Libya in 2011. See UN Security Council Resolution 1593 (2005) (www.legal-tools.org/doc/4b208f/), 31 March 2005, and Resolution 1970 (2011), 26 February 2011 (www.legal-tools.org/doc/00a45e/).

common principles, this could counter fragmentation. But in fact, since the different courts have their own statutes, the appeals judges would normally be expected to respect and give priority to their own constituting instruments, resulting in different jurisprudence regarding the same concepts. There are already some examples of this in differences between ICTY/ICTR case law and ICC jurisprudence in the area of substantive crimes against humanity, and on certain issues of personal liability for participants. This reality comes from the international legality principle, namely, that a court of law must, among other requirements, adhere to the substantive rules in the statutes defining the crimes and thus the jurisdiction of a particular court.

With regard to crimes or penal sanctions not included in the statute of an international or internationalised court, this would be clear enough: they cannot form the basis of prosecution before the court. In that sense, the principle of legality is "a principle of justice whose enforcement is vital to the rule of law".[31] The legality principle provides less guidance with respect to the applicability of crimes under international law generally. Apart from the core crimes, inclusion of a certain crime in a court statute does not guarantee that it is an international or universal crime. Under certain conditions, non-international crimes can also be prosecuted by international or internationalised courts.[32] On the other hand, there might be international crimes that could be prosecuted in conformity with the international legality principle, but that are not. Their possible status under international law is thus not really tested. This arguably allows for a particular kind of fragmentation of ICL: that international prosecution pays attention only to some universal crimes categories.

It is also not clear to what extent the international legality principle may impose limits on the interpretation by judges of the scope of a given crime, including attribution of liability through the modes of punishable

---

[31] Kenneth S. Gallant, *The Principle of Legality in International and Comparative Criminal Law*, Cambridge University Press, Cambridge, 2009, p. 404. Gallant, however, goes one significant step further when he argues that the principle of legality "means that Nuremberg and Tokyo and the rest of the post–World War II prosecutions retroactively creating crimes against peace (aggressive war and conspiracy to wage it) should be a one-time event" (p. 405); he thus implies that the prosecutions were illegitimate and would have been illegal under the current state of international law (pp. 405–6). For a different view, see Section 4.3.4. in this chapter.

[32] See Einarsen, 2012, pp. 145–50, *supra* note 1.

participation, that is, limits that go beyond the generally recognised general principles of treaty interpretation.[33] For example, the VCLT provides for 'systemic integration' in Article 31(3)(c).[34] It requires the interpreter of a treaty to take into account "any relevant rules of international law applicable in the relations between the parties", including other treaties, customary rules, and general principles of law. Furthermore, since the laws of a special regime – and any sub-regime within it – are by definition narrower in scope than the general laws, it might be that a matter is not regulated clearly by a special law. The International Law Commission has therefore suggested that the general law will apply in such cases and fill in the gaps.[35] How far this is possible in international criminal cases will probably always be contested when such issues of interpretation arise, with the international legality principle weighing in favour of more restrictive limits on interpretation.[36]

From the perspective of legal science, a study should aim at the ideal of completeness, considering all material relevant to the topic. Researchers thus are commonly advised to avoid overly broad topics and to narrow the scope to make such completeness possible. However, strict adherence to this ideal would be unfortunate. In contemporary international law, there are many important themes that do not lend themselves to such comprehensive treatment, not only because of their scope but because the legal systems are dynamic and open to new input from different law-creating and interpretative sources, as well as from national systems of law. In such cases there is a need for analysis of broad themes, in both individual monographs and collective projects, in order to counter undesirable and unintended fragmentation of the law. The ideal of completeness must be complemented by consideration of other analytical, inductive, or synthetic approaches.[37] International criminal law is an area particularly in need of such consideration.

---

[33] See further Section 4.3.7.

[34] On 'systemic integration', see also ILC, 2006, conclusions nos. 17 and 18, *supra* note 4.

[35] *Ibid.*, conclusion no. 15.

[36] See Section 4.3.2. on the legality principle as a means of treaty interpretation.

[37] This has long been recognised by some authors. See, for example, Georg Schwarzenberger, *The Inductive Approach to International Law*, Stevens, London, 1965, p. 6, fn. 28: "In the vast majority of cases the classes of objects and events with which science is concerned are

4.3. The Legal Bases of Universal Crimes Norms

4.3.1. The Framework of International Law-Creating Sources

When the UN paradigm of contemporary international law was established after World War II, an important provision was set out in Article 38 of the Statute of the International Court of Justice of 26 June 1945 (hereafter, ICJ Statute), annexed to the UN Charter as Chapter XIV. According to Article 92 of the UN Charter, the ICJ Statute, and thus also its Article 38, was based upon the Statute of the Permanent Court of International Justice under the auspices of the League of Nations, the predecessor of the ICJ. Article 38 codifies the basic norm of international law,[38] as it was already known before the war.

Three law-creating sources are first mentioned in Article 38, paragraphs 1(a–c): (a) "international conventions" (treaties), (b) "international custom", and (c) "the general principles of law recognized by civilized nations". Paragraph 1(d) recognises the importance of two additional kinds of authoritative sources: "judicial decisions" (by independent judges) and "the teachings of the most highly qualified publicists of the various nations". They are both considered as "subsidiary means for the determination of rules of law" that are derived from the published works of scholars and publicly available decisions of courts, often in a dynamic relationship with each other and with the law-creating sources as well as with other law-determining sources. These subsidiary means for the determination of international law are thus important interpretative sources, while other interpretative sources might be relevant as well. This is par-

---

far too numerous to permit anything even distantly approaching exhaustive individual examination of all the members. All the important inductions of science are what used to be called imperfect inductions, that is to say, generalisations based on the examination of a bare sample of the whole class under investigation". Scientists familiar with modern quantitative methods may not fully agree with this statement, but in legal science there is still a lot of truth to it.

38   The term 'basic norm' evokes notions that have been much discussed in legal philosophy. See, for example, the classic but not identical theories of Hans Kelsen, *Pure Theory of Law*, translation from the second German edition by Max Knight, Lawbook Exchange, Clark, NJ, 2008 ('grundnorm'), and H.L.A. Hart, *The Concept of Law*, 2nd ed., Oxford University Press, Oxford, 1994 ('rule of recognition'). Article 38 of the ICJ Statute, however, ought to be understood in more practical terms, as a fundamental direction to the Court (and by implication also to other international jurists) to consider certain compulsory law-creating sources as well as other authoritative sources of international law when deciding legal issues and disputes before it.

---

ticularly clear with respect to interpretation of treaties, where the VCLT applies. Hence Article 38 cannot be interpreted today as exhaustive. This is in fact also true with respect to the law-creating sources, because Article 38 does not mention binding Security Council resolutions; see further below. However, the distinction between law-creating sources and law-determining sources is still important for present-day ICL.[39] Other subsidiary sources for the determination of the content of a rule include a long list of possibly relevant 'interpretative sources', the relevance of which depends both on the primary law-creating source in question and on the factual circumstances of the matter at hand.[40]

What the authors of the ICJ Statute arguably failed to recognise, however, was the full potential of the newly created powers of the UN Security Council ('SC') to take actions and decisions "for the maintenance of international peace and security" (see UN Charter, Chapter V, Article 24(1), and Chapter VII, "Action with Respect to Threats to the Peace, Breaches of the Peace and Acts of Aggression"). By being granted those specific powers to act on behalf of all the members of the UN, the SC has implicitly been vested with a certain power to create binding legal norms, although this may not have been so clear at the outset, and especially not during the Cold War. Since then, the Security Council, acting on behalf of the international community, has repeatedly confirmed the linkage between peace and justice. It has "acted in a number of innovative ways that demonstrate a capacity and willingness to lay down rules and principles of general application, binding on all states, and taking precedence over other legal rights and obligations".[41]

Law making by the SC can take various forms and produce various legal effects. One can distinguish, for example, among determinations with regard to illegality or competences in general,[42] interpretations of the

---

[39] The exact terminology may vary. Thus Schwarzenberger distinguished between "law-determining processes" and "law-determining agencies"; see Schwarzenberger, 1965, pp. 5 and 19, *supra* note 37.

[40] See Section 4.4.1.

[41] Alan Boyle and Christine Chinkin, *The Making of International Law*, Oxford University Press, Oxford, 2007, p. 109.

[42] Two controversial issues are whether the findings by the Security Council are conclusive or not and whether judicial review by the ICJ is possible and can override the opinion of the SC. See, for example, Christine Gray, *International Law and the Use of Force*, 3rd ed., Oxford University Press, Oxford, 2008, pp. 13–17.

UN Charter, establishment of UN courts, and exercise of legislative acts on matters relating to peace and security.[43] It is clear that formal SC resolutions must today be recognised as a fourth possible law-creating source in current international law, and one of particular relevance to the subject matter of universal crimes. Whether or not the decision-making powers of the SC include the power to 'legislate', in the proper sense of the term, has been disputed. But these discussions tend more to concern the definition of 'legislation' than to contest the fact that the SC in some cases has created binding legal norms of a general character within the field of international criminal law.[44]

These different law-creating sources have dynamic and sometimes intricate relationships. Thus a treaty-based rule may reinforce a similar rule that also emerged from the source of international custom, itself often gaining wider acceptance as a result of the treaty. Broadly ratified conventions may provide the necessary "evidence of a general practice accepted as law", in the terms of the ICJ Statute, Article 38(1)(b). In other words, a law-creating source of universal crimes norms may function as an 'interpretative source' with respect to another law-creating source as well, whereas sources other than treaties, international customs, general principles of law, and binding SC resolutions can be legally relevant but not 'law-creating' *per se*.[45]

Legal opinions expressed, for example, in judgments by international courts and/or consistently in the law literature may influence state practice and thus indirectly contribute to new customary rules. Studies and analyses may clarify and in practice further develop the general principles of law. Soft law, such as formulations by the UN General Assembly of norms that are not legally binding, may have similar effects. Thus 'soft' legal materials must also be taken into account in 'hard' law-making processes.

These intricate interrelationships, however, should not be interpreted as eroding the distinction between law-creating sources and law-determining sources (interpretative sources). On the contrary, this distinction is important to maintain as part of the UN paradigm of international

---

[43] In the same vein, see Boyle and Chinkin, 2007, pp. 110–15, *supra* note 41.

[44] See Section 4.3.5.

[45] See Section 4.4.1. on the interpretative sources of international law.

law, and is itself a component of the rule of law. An inherent feature of 'law' is that legal reasoning follows a certain commonly accepted methodology that enables different legal experts to reach the same results, while distinguishing between binding rules and other normative expressions.[46]

The conclusion stands that a binding international rule has to originate from a predefined law-creating source through a process that fulfils certain criteria that are agreed in international law and controllable by a judicial tribunal or supervisory body. This is true even though the content of the rule is affected by other dynamic processes involving additional actors and source materials. Since law is a social construct and is to some extent open-ended, the underlying theories of international law also require ongoing review.[47] This chapter first considers the four separate legal bases: treaties (see Section 4.3.2.), customary law (4.3.3.), general principles of law (4.3.4.), and Security Council legislative resolutions (4.3.5.). A subsequent section (4.3.6.) considers whether several unclear legal bases, taken together, might provide a sufficient legal basis. Finally, the issue of legal bases of personal liability norms is specifically discussed (4.3.7.): What are the requirements of the legality principle and rule of law with respect to criminalisation of participatory conduct and attribution of liability in ICL?

4.3.2. Multilateral Treaties

From a practical point of view, treaties constitute the single most important law-creating source in the history of international law, and a reliable legal means of developing peaceful co-operation among nations. Only through treaties can all recognised states purposely and with a fair amount of certainty create new international law. A 'treaty', according to the definition laid down in Article 2(1)(a) of the VCLT, is "an international agreement concluded between States in written form and governed by international law".

---

[46] See Section 4.5.

[47] See, for example, Brian D. Lepard, *Customary International Law: A New Theory with Practical Applications*, Cambridge University Press, Cambridge, 2010; and Thomas Rauter, *Judicial Practice, Customary International Criminal Law and Nullum Crimen Sine Lege*, Springer International, Cham, Switzerland, 2017.

Many treaties are relevant to the subject matter of universal crimes. Some concern, explicitly or implicitly, the primary material norms proscribing certain acts. Others contain secondary rules for the establishment of international courts, their jurisdiction, and the procedural rules and maybe competences for the courts to enact further rules. As possible legal bases for universal crimes norms, *multilateral treaties* rather than bilateral treaties are the most interesting, especially when adopted by the United Nations and acceded to by many states in different parts of the world. It is not decisive whether a treaty is actually called a 'treaty', a 'convention', or something else. For example, the ICC Rome Statute is a treaty between the states parties although the word 'treaty' is not used in the Rome Statute itself. At the same time, this treaty is among several examples that illustrate that not only states may have treaty-making powers under the UN paradigm of international law. The ICC Rome Statute in Article 4 presupposes that the ICC shall have international legal personality and is thus empowered to conclude agreements in the form of treaties. The general definition of a 'treaty' under international law should therefore rather be corrected to 'an international agreement concluded between entities with legal personality, usually states, in written form and governed by international law'.

A particularly interesting feature of the treaty-based ICC regime is its relationship to the United Nations. According to the Rome Statute in Article 13(b), the Security Council may – acting under Chapter VII of the Charter of the United Nations – refer a 'situation' to the prosecutor of the ICC, typically when crimes within the *ratione materiae* (subject-matter) jurisdiction of the ICC are alleged to have been committed outside the territories of the states parties to the Rome Statute.[48] Such a referral by the SC is a binding decision, for which the competence seems to come from the ICC Rome Statute (treaty) and the UN Charter as legal bases taken in conjunction. However, since a treaty alone cannot directly bind others who are not parties to it,[49] the legal power (competence) in this case must

---

[48] See UN Security Council, Resolution 1593 (2005), 31 March 2005 (Darfur, Sudan) (www.legal-tools.org/doc/4b208f/), and Resolution 1970 (2011), 26 February 2011 (Libya) (www.legal-tools.org/doc/00a45e/).

[49] It should be noted, though, that a treaty may bring norms originating from other legal bases into operation in certain ways that may directly affect the position of third parties. For example, a state with territorial criminal jurisdiction under international law may through a treaty derogate concurrent competence to an international court, which in turn means that

originate in the UN Charter Chapter VII, whereas the specific, practical use of the power is facilitated by the ICC Rome Statute. In addition, the SC has the competence to establish another international criminal tribunal if it so prefers.[50]

Interpretation of treaties is conditioned on well-established method-ological principles, such as those set out in VCLT Articles 31–33, where a distinction is made between principal (Article 31) and supplementary (Ar-ticle 32) means of interpretation. This establishes a certain hierarchy of the interpretative sources specific to treaties. The basic rule is enshrined in Article 31(1), whereby a treaty must be construed "in good faith in ac-cordance with the ordinary meaning to be given to the terms of the treaty in their context and in light of its object and purpose". Although not ex-plicitly mentioned in Article 32 – which refers generally to all "supple-mentary means of interpretation" and especially to "the preparatory work of the treaty" – jurisprudence, in particular international judgments and decisions, and scholarly publications are part of the supplementary means of interpretation. This system is consistent with the general rule of the ICJ Statute, Article 38. It establishes treaties as autonomous legal bases, dif-ferent from other law-creating sources and interpretative sources, which should be interpreted in good faith (VCLT Article 26), and as autonomous international law different from the internal laws of a particular state bound by the treaty (VCLT Article 27). The principles of treaty interpreta-tion are also anchored in customary law and thus are generally binding on all legal subjects of international law. Hence they apply to treaties within international criminal law.[51] Furthermore, they apply to interpretation of

---

the court may have powers to investigate and prosecute crimes committed on the territory of that state even when the crimes are alleged to have been committed by nationals of a third state. This is the case under the Rome Statute with respect to crimes against humanity, genocide, and war crimes, while a special and more limited jurisdictional regime has been established with respect to the crime of aggression, as noted earlier in this chapter.

[50] For instance, an 'International Criminal Court for the Middle East and Northern Africa' with a forward-looking mandate would have several advantages, since few countries in that region have acceded to the ICC Rome Statute. Whether such a court, had it been estab-lished several years ago, could have prevented or decreased certain armed conflicts, we will never know.

[51] See, for example, Gerhard Werle, *Principles of International Criminal Law*, TMC Asser, The Hague, 2005, p. 95. Upheld in Gerhard Werle, *Principles of International Criminal Law*, 2nd ed., TMC Asser, The Hague, 2009, pp. 59–60: "As expressions of customary law, these rules of interpretation must be applied in interpretation not only of the ICC Rome

---

international court statutes created by the Security Council by means of SC resolutions, such as the statutes of the ICTY and ICTR.[52]

Particular issues may arise with respect to special rules of interpretation, such as those set forth in Articles 21 and 22 of the ICC Rome Statute. Article 22(2) prescribes that within the statute the "definition of a crime shall be strictly construed and not extended by analogy". This rule – which had already been applied explicitly at Nuremberg in the Ministries Case[53] and the Justice Case[54] – has been referred to as "the canon of strict construction".[55] In case of ambiguity, the same provision states that "the definition shall be interpreted in favour of the person being investigated, prosecuted or convicted". The latter rule can be credited to the principle of *in dubio pro reo*, which holds that ambiguity or doubt is to be resolved in favour of the accused.[56] These principles of interpretation form part of the legality principle (*nullum crimen sine lege*) and may lead to other results than a plain application of the VCLT principles. However, Rome Statute Article 22(1) applies directly only to cases before the ICC. It is not clear to what extent this provision expresses general principles of international criminal law. As observed by Schabas, it "stands in very marked contrast with the jurisprudence of the *ad hoc* tribunals which has, generally, accorded little significance to principles of strict construc-

---

Statute, but 'any other norm-creating instrument', including the ICTY and ICTR Statutes". For support, see, for example, ICTY, Appeals Chamber, *Prosecutor v. Tadić*, Judgment, IT-94-1-R, 15 July 1999, para. 303 (www.legal-tools.org/doc/8efc3a/).

[52] See, for example, ICTY, Appeals Chamber, *Prosecutor v. Aleksovski*, Judgment, IT-95-14/1, 24 March 2000, para. 98 (www.legal-tools.org/doc/176f05/).

[53] Nuernberg Military Tribunals ('NMT'), "The Ministries Case" [Judgment], in *Trials of War Criminals before the Nuernberg Military Tribunals under Control Council Law No. 10: Nuernberg, October 1946–April 1949*, vol. XIII, US Government Printing Office, Washington, DC, 1952, p. 100 (www.legal-tools.org/doc/eb20f6/): "The principles of strict construction and against retroactive legislation should be applied [...] to words and phrases which are present and which must be interpreted and construed". See also pp. 103 and 115.

[54] NMT, "The Justice Case" [Judgment], in *Trials of War Criminals before the Nuernberg Military Tribunals under Control Council Law No. 10: Nuernberg, October 1946–April 1949*, vol. III, US Government Printing Office, Washington, DC, 1951, p. 982 (www.legal-tools.org/doc/04cdaf/): "We hold that crimes against humanity as defined in C.C. [Control Council] Law 10 must be strictly construed to exclude isolated cases of atrocity or persecution whether committed by private individuals or by a governmental authority".

[55] See William A. Schabas, *The International Criminal Court: A Commentary on the Rome Statute*, Oxford University Press, Oxford, 2010, p. 410.

[56] *Ibid.*

tion".[57] In his opinion, several interpretative results of the ICTY and ICTR would have been impermissible if Article 22(2) had been applied.[58] In any case, both Article 22(1) and the general principles are themselves open to interpretation and further clarification. Note, for instance, that the *in dubio pro reo* principle may primarily concern the facts rather than the law,[59] and that the 'strict construction' principle of Article 22(2) according to its terms is limited to the "definition of a crime", an expression that is itself open to interpretation. For example, it might be arguable whether the principle of strict interpretation applies to the modes of participation that attribute liability for contributions beyond commission of those acts defined as crimes within the jurisdiction of the court.

In terms of *lex ferenda*, it could be argued that although the international legality principle is an important safeguard for the defendant, and thus should be carefully adhered to as far as it applies, it may also serve as an unintended means of creating loopholes in court statutes and arbitrary

---

[57] *Ibid.* Schabas refers to a number of international judgments, which we agree do not support strict interpretation. See ICTY, Appeals Chamber, *Prosecutor v. Tadić*, Judgment, IT-94-1-R, 15 July 1999, para. 80 ff. (www.legal-tools.org/doc/8efc3a/); ICTY, Appeals Chamber, *Prosecutor v. Erdemović*, Judgment, IT-96-22-A, 7 October 1997, Separate and Dissenting Opinion of Judge Cassese, para. 49 (www.legal-tools.org/doc/a7dff6/); ICTR, Trial Chamber, *Prosecutor v. Akayesu*, Judgment, ICTR-96-4-T, 2 September 1998, para. 319 (www.legal-tools.org/doc/b8d7bd/); ICTR, Trial Chamber, *Prosecutor v. Kayishema and Ruzindana*, Judgment, ICTR-95-1, 21 May 1999, para. 103 (www.legal-tools.org/doc/0811c9/); ICTR, Trial Chamber, *Prosecutor v. Rutaganda*, Judgment, ICTR-96-3, 6 December 1999, para. 51 (www.legal-tools.org/doc/f0dbbb/); ICTR, Trial Chamber, *Prosecutor v. Musema*, Judgment, ICTR-96-13-A, 27 January 2000, para. 155 (www.legal-tools.org/doc/1fc6ed/).

[58] Schabas, 2010, pp. 410–11, *supra* note 55.

[59] See, for example, ICTY, Appeals Chamber, *Prosecutor v. Limaj et al.*, Judgment, IT-03-66-A, 27 September 2007, Declaration of Judge Shahabuddeen, para. 2 (www.legal-tools.org/doc/6d43bf/), in which he disagrees but concedes that "the basis of previous jurisprudence of the Tribunal, [...] has held that the principle [of *in dubio pro reo*] does not apply to questions of law". For a broader view in line with the later opinion of Judge Shahabuddeen, see NMT, "The Ministries Case", 1952, p. 100, *supra* note 53: "We stated at the outset that, in any case of real doubt, the language of Law No. 10 should be construed in favour of the defendants". See also ICTY, Trial Chamber, *Prosecutor v. Galić*, Judgment, IT-98-29-T, 5 December 2003, para. 93 (www.legal-tools.org/doc/eb6006/): "The effect of strict construction of the provisions of a criminal statute is that where an equivocal word or ambiguous sentence leaves a reasonable doubt of its meaning which the canons of construction fail to solve, the benefit of the doubt should be given to the subject and against the legislature which has failed to explain itself".

inconsistencies between different parts of ICL that were neither foreseen nor desired when the different court statutes were drafted. In comparison to national criminal legislation, which can more easily be amended based on experience and evaluation, revision of international court statutes is relatively difficult.[60] Judges may accordingly prefer to try to strike a fair balance between the opposing legitimate interests and values, rather than relying mechanically on strict construction principles. In addition, there is a need to clarify the reach of the legality principle, notably with regard to attribution of personal liability and the applicability of modes of participation beyond physical perpetration of universal crimes, which may or may not be explicitly and sufficiently described in the relevant statutes of an international criminal court.

4.3.3. Customary International Law

International custom as law evolves from the practices or customs of entities with legal personality, usually states. Certain conditions must be met before a practice becomes law, as not all acts, practices, or customs of states and other international legal subjects can become binding law. In the ICJ Statute, 'international custom' is explained as evidence of 'a general practice accepted as law'. The common term today for binding international law that originates from practice (custom) is 'customary international law'.

The criteria for distinguishing between customary international law ('CIL') and other practices and conduct have been elaborated by the international law experts and judges at international courts, especially in cases before the ICJ. These criteria have generally been accepted as part of international law throughout the international community. From a logical point of view, this means that the definition of customary international law is circular: the criteria define the relevant customs and the criteria are extracted from that relevant practice. The way to understand this dialectic relationship, therefore, is to take into account the time factor and the development of new customary international law, as well as the readiness of international law judges and experts to uphold and if necessary also refine the criteria in light of new experiences.

---

[60] The Rome Statute, however, provides for amendment procedures that have also resulted in amendments actually being made, most famously with respect to the crime of aggression, as discussed earlier in this chapter, but also by adding more war crimes to Article 8.

There are relatively few limitations on what kinds of customs may be relevant. However, a practice that is incompatible with a broader international custom (a regional custom contrary to a universal custom), or contrary to treaty-based obligations of the state involved, or in conflict with *jus cogens*, can never give rise to customary law. Both the latter two limitations are important with respect to the subject matter of universal crimes. Norms proscribing acts for which direct criminal liability under international law is established are often considered superior to other rules on account of the importance of their content as well as the universal acceptance of their superiority.[61] Hence no derogation is permitted, whether by means of a treaty or a common practice. For example, if torture of alleged terrorists is practised to a certain extent by some states, and *if* state-sponsored torture has already emerged as a discrete universal crime,[62] acts of torture against alleged terrorists, however customary, would simply constitute criminal acts under international law. Furthermore, if a state has agreed to be bound by the UN Convention against Torture, which is a treaty proscribing torture and other cruel, inhuman or degrading treatment or punishment, the state incurs state responsibility for any act of torture within the meaning of the convention that can be attributed to it – regardless of the current status of torture as a discrete crime under international criminal law.

Some norms of customary international law – notably the prohibitions against genocide and slavery – have clearly acquired this higher legal status (*jus cogens*) in the opinion of most commentators. For other norms, arising both nationally and internationally, it is not yet clear that this is the case.[63] There is disagreement on the character and legal status of such norms, "with some authors arguing that all human rights enshrined in international treaties are norms of *jus cogens* while others ad-

---

[61] ILC, 2006, conclusion no. 32, see *supra* note 4.

[62] Torture is clearly a relevant universal crime when committed in the context of crimes against humanity, genocide, or war (whether international or non-international armed conflict).

[63] See, for example, High Court of the Hong Kong Special Administrative Region, Court of First Instance, HCAL 132/2006, 18 February 2008, paras. 126–29 (www.legal-tools.org/doc/52a68d/). See also Inter-American Court of Human Rights ('IACHR'), *Miguel Castro-Castro Prison v. Peru*, Judgment, 25 November 2006, Series C, no. 160, para. 271 (www.legal-tools.org/doc/7d2681/); and IACHR, *Bayarri v. Argentina*, Judgment, 30 October 2008, Series C, no. 187, para. 81 (www.legal-tools.org/doc/be621c/).

vocate a far more stringent approach".[64] It might be recalled here that the general theory of personal criminal law liability outlined in Chapter 2 is premised upon liability being consistent with fundamental human rights and a criminal law subsystem in general compliance with human rights and the rule of law.[65] At the domestic level, the relationship between criminal law and constitutional law is also being discussed more frequently.[66] However, as noted by Einarsen in the first book of this series,[67] the concept and scope of *jus cogens* is not essential to our *study* of universal crimes, since the norms underlying these crimes no doubt have the required character in terms of content and universality. Their superiority thus depends upon their international law status as 'hard' or 'soft' law, and this question needs to be discussed independently of the *jus cogens* concept. In other words, the *jus cogens* concept is not necessary for the discussion of legal bases, although the outcome of that discussion may have implications for the legal consequences of *jus cogens* norms.

When discussing CIL as a source of international law and ICL, it is useful to distinguish between the constitutive elements necessary for the formation of CIL and the evidence for their applicability. The two main criteria, state practice and *opinio juris*, have traditionally both been considered necessary elements. While the element of state practice needs further specification, the second element "is construed either as a belief that the practice is required by law, or a legislative will element by States giving either individual consent or establishing common consensus in order to prove the existence of a customary norm".[68] The principal criteria weighed in determining customary international law, when state practice is considered from a less abstract point of view, seem to be (1) a reasonably consistent practice with regard to the substance of the acts; (2) a fairly general practice (in the sense of being common to a significant number of

---

64 Maarten den Heijer, "Whose Rights and Which Rights? The Continuing Story of Non-Refoulement under the European Convention on Human Rights", in *European Journal of Migration and Law*, 2008, vol. 10, no. 3, pp. 277–314, at p. 299.

65 See Chapter 2, Section 2.1.2.

66 See, for example, Jørn Jacobsen, "Constitutions and Criminal Law Reform", in *Bergen Journal of Criminal Law and Criminal Justice*, 2017, vol. 5, no. 1, pp. 18–36.

67 Einarsen, 2012, p. 9, see *supra* note 1.

68 Rauter, 2017, p. 100, *supra* note 47.

---

states relative to the nature of the issue);[69] (3) a certain number of repetitions or a certain duration of the acts; and (4) *opinio juris*. The latter criterion means that it must be possible to infer from the acts of states (and possibly other relevant entities with legal personality under international law), including from their statements, that the practice is considered legally permissible, or illegal, as the case may be, by the relevant group of actors.[70] As Lepard comments, it is a paradox that the condition of *opinio juris*, as traditionally formulated, requires that states at the critical stage of creating new customary international rules are supposed to believe erroneously that they are legally bound to observe a rule that is not yet legally binding.[71]

Notably, the formulations and application of these cumulative criteria are to some degree flexible. They should be considered in conjunction, as a whole, not as separate and very strict conditions. Requiring the full satisfaction of all criteria simultaneously might unduly obstruct the formation of new customary international law. This is crucial with regard to some issues explored in the universal crimes project. Universal crimes are often committed or condoned by state governments against groups or individuals that should be protected by modern international law. Such crimes are inherently in deep conflict with world community interests and values despite the fact that security and foreign policy concerns, and pos-

---

[69] See Frederic L. Kirgis, "Custom on a Sliding Scale", in *American Journal of International Law*, 1987, vol. 81, no. 1, pp. 146–51. Kirgis assumes a relationship between the amount of practice required and the nature of the norm involved: human rights norms need little state practice, while economic norms need more (pp. 147–48).

[70] The criteria and their content derive primarily from a series of decisions of the ICJ and its predecessor, the Permanent Court of International Justice ('PCIJ'). These include PCIJ, *Case of the S.S. "Lotus"* (France v. Turkey), Judgment, Series A, No. 10, 7 September 1927 (www.legal-tools.org/doc/c54925/); ICJ, *Anglo-Norwegian Fisheries Case* (United Kingdom v. Norway), Judgment, *I.C.J. Reports 1951*, p. 116 (www.legal-tools.org/doc/457811/); ICJ, *North Sea Continental Shelf Cases* (Federal Republic of Germany/Denmark; Federal Republic of Germany/Netherlands), Judgment, *I.C.J. Reports 1969*, p. 3 (www.legal-tools.org/doc /38274a/); and ICJ, *Military and Paramilitary Activities in and against Nicaragua* (Nicaragua v. United States of America), Merits and Judgment, *I.C.J. Reports 1986*, p. 14 (www.legal-tools.org/doc/046698/).

[71] Lepard, 2010, pp. 8–9, *supra* note 47. Instead he argues that a customary law norm arises "when states generally believe that it is desirable now or in the near future to have an authoritative legal principle or rule prescribing, permitting, or prohibiting a certain conduct", and that this belief is sufficient to create the norm. State practice can, however, "serve as one source of evidence" of what states believe.

---

sibly economic calculations as well, may obstruct concerted statements and actions appropriate to their universal criminal character. Hence the typical *jus cogens* character of the relevant substantive norms constituting crimes under international law should be taken into account when interpreting the content of and limitations set by customary international law.[72]

Under these circumstances, the criteria for the formation of international customary law should not be applied in such a manner that states, which are themselves responsible for large-scale human rights violations, can block the emergence of an international rule that would benefit future victims and support responsible behaviour by governments and other powerful actors within a society. This is the underlying reason why an international custom prohibiting certain acts, maybe eventually conferring criminal liability on individual members of political and military leaderships for serious violations, has sometimes been recognised, even if all the conditions for formation of international custom may not have been fully satisfied.

Examples include some of the findings by the Nuremberg Tribunal,[73] especially on the legal status of aggression and criminal liability for aggressive acts before World War II.[74] Another example is the Nicaragua case,[75] where, according to some commentators, the ICJ deviated from "its traditional approach of seeking state practice supported by *opinio juris* by finding first *opinio juris* in the form of UNGA [UN General Assembly] resolutions and then looking for state practice".[76] The critique is that the court did not establish whether the traditional criteria were met to support its opinion that Article 3 of the Geneva Conventions had become

---

[72] One can debate the relevance of such context-specific considerations. However, to take the context into account is, according to Rauter, "in line with a modern understanding of customary international law: that in certain fields of law the context is relevant for ascertaining different requirements for its establishment". Rauter, 2017, p. 137, *supra* note 47. He makes this statement after having discussed ICL judgments by the ICTY Appeals Chamber, the SCSL Appeals Chamber, and the ECCC Supreme Court Chamber.

[73] See IMT, *Trial of the Major War Criminals*, 1947, vol. I, Judgment, pp. 171–341, *supra* note 18.

[74] See also Section 4.3.6.

[75] ICJ, *Military and Paramilitary Activities in and against Nicaragua* (Nicaragua v. United States of America), Merits and Judgment, *I.C.J. Reports 1986*, p. 14 (www.legal-tools.org/doc/046698/).

[76] See Boyle and Chinkin, 2007, p. 280, *supra* note 41.

---

customary international law.[77] Instead of criticising the ICJ for inconsistency, however, and thus challenging its reasoning as unsound or illegitimate, one should recognise that independent judges at a court constituting the highest judicial authority within a legal system will tend to perceive themselves as servants of a broader concept of law that cannot be constrained by a single expectation, whether loyalty to the status quo or to other similar considerations. On balance, judges with effective review powers may over the years advance the essentials of the legal systems of which they are a part. In some cases, this may mean new interpretations of the law. There are also several examples to be found in the jurisprudence of the modern criminal tribunals.[78]

In other words, the general criteria of customary international law are to some extent adjustable depending on the circumstances, including the *jus cogens* character of the emerging substantive norms in question.

4.3.4. General Principles as International Law

The "general principles of law recognised by civilised nations" as a law-creating source of international law (ICJ Statute, Article 38(1)(c)) is an ambiguous notion that has generated much academic debate and confusion, even apart from the unintended ethnocentric connotations of the term 'civilised nations'. There were divergent views already within the committee of jurists that prepared this statute, ranging from a concept based on natural law to one based on the principles demonstrably accepted in the domestic law of those states regarded as civilised,[79] that is, states based on the rule of law. While the precedents in domestic law are surely one valid and important part of the overall concept, fundamental principles of current international criminal law must also be included,[80] especially the norms considered "as overriding principles of *jus cogens* which may qualify the effect of more ordinary rules".[81]

---

[77] *Ibid.* See further Theodor Meron, *Human Rights and Humanitarian Norms as Customary Law*, Clarendon Press, Oxford, 1989, p. 36.

[78] See, for example, Rauter, 2017, pp. 134–37, *supra* note 47 (with respect to deviation from the high frequency and high consistency test under the traditional CIL criteria).

[79] See, *for example*, Ian Brownlie, *Principles of Public International Law*, 4th ed., Clarendon Press, Oxford, 1990, pp. 15–16.

[80] See further Boyle and Chinkin, 2007, pp. 286–88, *supra* note 41.

[81] See Brownlie, 1990, pp. 19, 512–15, *supra* note 79.

This ambiguity has not been resolved, however. While it is commonly recognised that general principles of law are of considerable significance to ICL, the concept is still often exclusively equated with rules originating in domestic law and with the legal principles already recognised by the world's major legal systems.[82] In this context, the ICTY cautioned, "a mechanical importation or transposition from national law into international criminal proceedings has to be avoided".[83] This statement was probably intended to restrict access to the general principles of law, but the formulation could also be used to expand such access, thus facilitating the formation of new general principles of ICL regardless of whether they are already fully recognised domestically. If such an approach is taken, the subject matter of universal crimes might advance a new legal trend of openly acknowledging that it is difficult to distinguish clearly between customary international law and the general principles as law, given that both sources are continuously evolving. On the other hand, we agree with the cautious approach probably intended by the ICTY. The question is, however, whether the general theory of personal criminal law liability indeed contains general principles of criminal law with the necessary merit to be recognised in ICL as general principles. We shall not conclude on the question in this chapter, because it is first necessary to explore the liability concepts that have been used in ICL theory and practice at the international level and also examine how personal liability concepts have been applied in domestic criminal law systems in universal crimes cases. This will in turn provide us with a better empirical basis and understanding of the underlying general principles and thus suggest whether it is possible to reach a well-founded conclusion.

International tribunals might thus rely on multiple legal bases in cases for which their criminal law jurisdiction is not clear, perhaps without taking a definite stand on the exact status of the general principle being invoked.[84] The ICC Rome Statute Article 21(1) is sufficiently flexible for such a position. In the first place, in (1)(a), the *Statute* itself, the particular *elements of crimes*, and the court's *rules of procedure and evidence* apply. Second, in (1)(b), "applicable treaties and the principles and rules

---

[82]   See, *for example*, Werle, 2009, p. 53, *supra* note 51.
[83]   See ICTY, Trial Chamber, *Prosecutor v. Anto Furundžija*, Judgment, IT-95-17/1, 10 December 1998, para. 178 (www.legal-tools.org/doc/e6081b/).
[84]   See also Section 4.3.6.

of international law" may apply, including "the established principles of the international law of armed conflict". Third, in (1)(c), "general principles of law derived by the Court from national laws of legal systems of the world" may also apply, provided that they are not inconsistent with the ICC Rome Statute and with "international law and internationally recognized norms and standards". The latter point implies the existence of some overriding general international norms. Article 21(3), in the same vein, states that the application and interpretation of law pursuant to Article 21 "must be consistent with internationally recognized human rights".[85] In other words, general principles of international law may provide a legal basis for deriving new rules under Articles 21(1)(b) and (c), and may *in addition* serve as a kind of a 'rule of recognition'[86] for evaluation of new 'principles of law' that might be proposed, possibly derived from national laws.[87]

This dual function makes the concept of general principles equivocal. Rules originating from another source may themselves be constituted as general principles. At the same time, general principles, meaning a general rule, a principle, or a fundamental rule, can also be derived from customary international law and expressed in binding treaties. While this may be confusing, it is not in itself contradictory. Specific rules termed 'general principles' can be derived from all the different law-creating sources of international law, including from a particular source called 'general principles of international law' or a similar term. Properly understood, the meaning is that the latter law-creating source is especially concerned with rules characterised as 'general principles', and, by logical inference, that this source, just like treaties and international customary law, may contain substantial rules that have no exact parallel in the binding rules previously derived from the other law-creating sources.

In fact, any legal order necessarily requires general principles of law. This is quite clear when one looks at any given national legal system constituted by law in the profound sense of the term. A written constitution

---

[85] This rule, by advancing the idea that ICL must be compatible with internationally recognised human rights, is fully consistent with the general theory of criminal law liability as set forth in this book; see Chapter 2, Section 2.1.2.

[86] See Hart, 1994, *supra* note 38.

[87] On Article 21(1) of the Rome Statute, see further Schabas, 2010, pp. 381–94, *supra* note 55.

needs to be applied and adapted to changing circumstances, whether or not it is formally amended. If there is no written constitution, there is still a need for constitutive norms that are believed to be binding. Within most areas of substantial law and court procedures, a living body of law cannot do without some general principles that serve the underlying purposes of the legal order and make possible consistent application of specific rules that may conflict with each other. For example, the principles of free consent and good faith, and the *pacta sunt servanda* rule, are universally recognised in contractual law and in international treaty law (as in the preamble to the Vienna Convention on the Law of Treaties, and in its Article 26). Within domestic criminal law, principles such as *in dubio pro reo* (the defendant should have the benefit of reasonable doubt regarding the facts) and the legality principle (*nullum crimen sine lege, nulla poena sine lege*), including the prohibition of *ex post facto* laws, are today generally recognised, at least in states adhering to the rule of law.

Whether they are codified by legislators or not, certain 'constitutive principles' exist in all legal orders, although they might be different in different countries. They are usually familiar to scholars and knowledgeable practitioners working within the various fields of law. Judges may sometimes need to seek interpretative guidance in such principles, especially in difficult cases. In rare cases the principles may be applied directly in a judgment, possibly for lack of more accessible, written sources.

The UN paradigm of international law contains a number of binding general principles. Several of these are expressed in the UN Charter itself and are constitutive of the current legal order. Others may exist more specifically within certain substantive parts of international law; they are what might be termed 'field-specific' constitutive principles, with a content similar to general principles existing internally within the law among 'civilised nations'. As noted earlier, the reference to 'civilised nations' should be taken to mean nations adhering to the rule of law in compliance with fundamental UN principles; the phrase does not point to a state's presumed level of cultural or economic development. Note also that not every rule found in most legal systems adhering to the rule of law is necessarily a general principle of law within the international legal order. The ICTY in the Furundžija case stated that certain criteria must be fulfilled before field-specific national law concepts of criminal law can be applied in international court proceedings:

> (i) [...] [I]nternational courts must draw upon the general concepts and legal institutions common to all the major legal systems of the world [...]; (ii) account must be taken of the specificity of international proceedings when utilising national law notions. In this way a mechanical importation or transposition from national law into international criminal proceedings is avoided.[88]

Among the general principles of international law embodied in the UN Charter and the present order of international law are the principles of equal rights and self-determination of peoples, the sovereign equality and independence of all states, non-interference in the domestic affairs of states for purposes other than those admitted by international law, refraining from the use of force, and observance of human rights and fundamental freedoms for all.

A central question is whether general principles of law on direct criminal liability should also be included. The argument is that individual liability for crimes undermining the international legal order became a constitutive principle of the international legal order established after World War II. Implicit support for this can be found in the first paragraph of the preamble of the UN Charter, where the quest for justice and respect for international law is highlighted and explained:

> We the Peoples of the United Nations, determined to save succeeding generations from the scourge of war, which twice in our lifetime has brought untold sorrow to mankind, and to reaffirm faith in fundamental human rights, in the dignity and worth of the human person, in the equal rights of men and women and of nations large and small, and to establish conditions under which justice and respect for obligations arising from treaties and other sources of international law can be maintained [...].

This statement should be understood in conjunction with the post–World War II tribunals and the adoption of the Universal Declaration of Human Rights and the Genocide Convention, all of which took place

---

88 ICTY, Trial Chamber, *Prosecutor v. Anto Furundžija*, Judgment, IT-95-17/1, 10 December 1998 (www.legal-tools.org/doc/e6081b/).

within the first four years of the formal establishment of the United Nations.[89]

A perhaps more intriguing question is whether general principles on universal crimes existed as part of international law even *before* World War II and the establishment of the UN. The problem for prosecutors at the Nuremberg trials was that the legal basis for criminal liability based upon customary international law and treaties before the war did not seem clear with regard to the crime of aggression and crimes against humanity. The possibility of invoking liability based on general principles of criminal law was also quite doubtful, since the international legal order before the war was much less clear in many respects than the new UN paradigm with regard to alleged existence of universal norms on human rights and the need for individual criminal liability and justice for victims. If relevant general principles of criminal law did not exist, or could not be identified, criminal liability might not be legally established without violating the prohibition of *ex post facto* laws. Prosecutors and judges at Nuremberg would then have had to rely exclusively on prior treaties and customary international law, under which the evidence of existing criminal liability for all the crimes charged was at best doubtful. The defendants were even more dependent upon the existence of general principles of criminal law when invoking the legality principle.

The jurisdiction of the Nuremberg Tribunal was defined in the London Agreement of 8 August 1945 and the Charter of the International Military Tribunal in pursuance of the agreement. The IMT Charter (or Nuremberg Charter) was also based on the assumption that "the countries to which the German Reich unconditionally surrendered [...] [had a right] to legislate for the occupied territories".[90] But one should also note that the Nuremberg Tribunal went further and pointed implicitly to universal jurisdiction over the crimes:

> The Signatory Powers created this Tribunal, defined the law it was to administer, and made regulations for the proper conduct of the Trial. In doing so, they have done together what any one of them might have done singly; for it is not to

---

89   See also Einarsen, 2012, pp. 38–51, *supra* note 1, on the UN paradigm of international law.
90   See IMT, *Trial of the Major War Criminals*, 1947, vol. I, Judgment, p. 219, *supra* note 18.

be doubted that any nation has the right thus to set up special
courts to administer law.[91]

The "law" referred to here is international criminal law, and the implication is that any nation had the right to administer it with regard to the
crimes being committed, that is, on the basis of universal jurisdiction if no
other kinds of jurisdiction existed.

Therefore, a *prima facie* legal basis for the prosecution of crimes
against peace, war crimes, and crimes against humanity, committed by the
German leadership, had been established through international agreements
and presumed international criminal law. The defendants in Nuremberg
thus needed to undermine it by means of other parts of international law.
Paradoxically, perhaps, they resorted to general principles of criminal law.
It was argued on their behalf "that a fundamental principle of all law –
international and domestic – is that there can be no punishment of crime
without a pre-existing [substantive] law".[92] The maxim *nullum crimen
sine lege, nulla poena sine lege* was explicitly invoked.[93] Furthermore,

> It was submitted that ex post facto punishment is abhorrent
> to the law of all civilized nations, that no sovereign power
> has made aggressive war a crime at the time that the alleged
> criminal acts were committed, that no statute had defined
> aggressive war, and that no penalty had been fixed for its
> commission, and no court had been created to try and punish
> offenders.[94]

Under the international legality principle, in general, it is one thing
for a certain conduct to be considered unlawful and criminal in nature,
and another for it to be formally criminalised in international or national
law before the act is committed. A more limited legality requirement, that
formal criminalisation in national legislation or in the statutes of an international or internationalised court enacted after the acts were committed
must be set before indictments are issued and trials starts before the court,
was adhered to in Nuremberg and has been an undisputed element of international criminal law ever since. Within the existing UN paradigm of
international law, it has consistently been upheld that accessibility and

---

[91] *Ibid.*, p. 218.
[92] *Ibid.*, p. 219.
[93] *Ibid.*
[94] *Ibid.*

foreseeability are also elements of the legality principle. But it is *not* a requirement that an act falling within the substantive scope of *international (universal) crimes* must also have been formally criminalised and penalties defined in the relevant court statute *before* the act was committed.[95] This position has also been upheld in international human rights law.[96] The international principle of legality thus "allows for criminal liability over crimes that were either national or international in nature at the time they were committed".[97] It "does not require that international crimes and modes of liability be implemented by domestic statutes in order for violators to be found guilty".[98] A number of domestic courts have thus rendered decisions applying a different standard of the legality principle for ordinary crimes and universal crimes. This is in line not only with the jurisprudence of international criminal courts, but also with international human rights instruments and the jurisprudence of international human rights courts.[99]

---

[95] For a discussion of the requirement of 'double legality' in international universal crimes prosecution, see Terje Einarsen, "New Frontiers of International Criminal Law: Towards a Concept of Universal Crimes", in *Bergen Journal of Criminal Law and Criminal Justice*, 2013, vol. 1, no. 1, pp. 16–20.

[96] See the International Covenant on Civil and Political Rights, Article 15(2): "Nothing in this Article [principle of legality] shall prejudice the trial and punishment of any person for any act or omission which, at the time when it was committed, was criminal according to the general principles of law recognized by the community of nations". At the regional level, the Kononov case decided by the Grand Chamber of the European Court of Human Rights ('ECHR') is instructive; see ECHR, *Kononov v. Latvia*, Grand Chamber Judgment, 36376/04, 17 May 2010 (www.legal-tools.org/doc/ed0506/). The court in this ruling held that the legality principle enshrined in ECHR Article 7 is "an essential element of the rule of law", and that it follows that an offence must be "clearly defined in law" (para. 185). When speaking of 'law', the court explained that this concept "comprises written and unwritten law" and "implies qualitative requirements, notably those of accessibility and foreseeability". The applicant had been convicted in Latvia of war crimes committed in 1944, on the basis of a provision enacted in 1993 (paras. 191–96). The court examined whether there had been a sufficient clear legal basis with respect to the state of international law in 1944. In line with the Nuremberg Judgment, the court concluded that the relevant acts (killing of nine prisoners) were crimes under international law when they were committed, and that the applicant could have foreseen that they constituted war crimes (paras. 234–44). The court thus held by 14 votes to three that there had been no violation of ECHR Article 7.

[97] ECCC, Pre-Trial Chamber, *Decision on Ieng Sary's Appeal against the Closing Order*, 002/19-09-2007-ECCC/OCIJ (PTC75), D427/1/30, 11 April 2011, para. 213 (www.legal-tools.org/doc/d264ce/).

[98] *Ibid.*

[99] *Ibid.* For a thorough overview, see the discussion in paras. 203–65.

The Nuremberg Tribunal, however, faced a significant choice between formal and substantive justice. It was impossible to completely escape the impression, based on facts, that the tribunal applied *ex post facto* laws. It handled the issue in an interesting way. First, it claimed that the Nuremberg Charter was "not an arbitrary exercise of power on the part of the victorious Nations", but an "expression of international law existing at the time of its creation; and to that extent is itself a contribution to international law".[100] It is interesting to note that the tribunal here seems to have relied on the new UN paradigm of international law, although not entirely. Second, the principle of non-retroactive laws was rejected up front as an absolute shield against accountability, referring to morality and the nature of the crimes in question.[101] Due to the grave crimes that had been committed, the defendants could not successfully invoke a principle flowing from the idea of justice, according to the judgment.[102] This latter argument is not immediately convincing from a human rights perspective. It was, however, arguably the best way out of a difficult problem of justification more than anything else.

For the Nuremberg Tribunal, alternative justifications must have appeared less appealing. It could have argued that certain crimes are so grave that they are punishable *ex post facto* within any legal order at any time. That would mean reliance on a far-reaching natural law doctrine. Instead the tribunal emphasised the legal development that had already taken place before World War II. As underscored by the IMT, international law is never static, "but by continual adaptation follows the needs of a changing world".[103] Thus, "in many cases treaties do no more than express and define for more accurate reference the principles of law already

---

[100] IMT, *Trial of the Major War Criminals*, 1947, vol. I, Judgment, p. 218, see *supra* note 18.

[101] *Ibid.*, p. 217, with regard to the crime of aggression: "To assert that it is unjust to punish those who in defiance of treaties and assurances have attacked neighbouring states without warning is obviously untrue, for in such circumstances the attacker must know that he is doing wrong, and so far from it being unjust to punish him, it would be unjust if his wrong were allowed to go unpunished. [...] [T]hey must have known that they were acting in defiance of all international law when in complete deliberation they carried out their designs of invasion and aggression".

[102] *Ibid.*, p. 219: "[T]he maxim *nullum crimen sine lege* is not a limitation of sovereignty, but is in general a principle of justice".

[103] *Ibid.*, p. 221.

existing".[104] Alternatively, the judges could have argued that criminal liability was embodied in general 'constitutive' principles of international law existing already under the classic inter-state period of international law, which could be taken as a reconstruction of former international law.[105] Another alternative could have been to point out that the legality principle was not yet established as a legal rule under international law, which could have prevented or postponed its further development as a fundamental human rights principle.

Given the formation of the United Nations, it turned out not to be necessary for the judges to determine whether criminal liability was clearly established in international law before the war. The *jus cogens* character of the norms in question reinforced the approach taken. Once new rules of justice had been accepted by the international community, and concrete steps taken for implementation through the establishment and Charter of the IMT, the exact content of prior substantive norms became a less decisive consideration. This may be another reason why the Nuremberg Judgment made a fairly general reference to prior treaties, customs, and general principles in justifying the legal basis for the crimes identified in the Nuremberg Charter.[106]

Although it may be doubtful whether individual liability for some universal crimes clearly existed before World War II, such liability was implicitly and instantly part of the constitutive principles of the new UN paradigm of international law established by 1945. The Nuremberg Tribunal was therefore right to apply the Nuremberg Charter and international criminal law in accordance with a substantive notion of justice. In other

---

[104] *Ibid.*

[105] National courts have dealt differently with this issue in cases originating from World War II. Compare, for example, Supreme Court of Canada, *Her Majesty The Queen v. Imre Finta*, 1 *Supreme Court Reports* 701 (24 March 1994) (www.legal-tools.org/doc/f9c23e/); and High Court of Australia, *Polyukhovich v. Commonwealth*, 101 *Australian Law Reports* 545 (1991), 172 *Commonwealth Law Reports* 501, and 91 *International Law Reports* 1 (www.legal-tools.org/doc/b284c2/). The Canadian court took the approach that while crimes against humanity were new, the issue of legality was not important, as the perpetrators must have known that the underlying crimes were wrong. The Australian court held that crimes against humanity had already entered the realm of ICL.

[106] IMT, *Trial of the Major War Criminals*, 1947, vol. I, Judgment, p. 221, *supra* note 18: "The law of war is to be found not only in treaties, but in the customs and practices of states which gradually obtained universal recognition, and from the general principles of justice applied by jurists and practised by military courts".

---

words, a purely formal notion of justice – *nullum crimen sine lege, nulla poena sine lege*, itself a general principle of law – could not take priority without conflicting with other parts of the existing law. It should be recognised, even so, that the Nuremberg Tribunal did in fact prove that most of the criminal acts in question were illegal under any relevant standard. The defendants thus could not have ruled out criminal liability, even when the acts were committed. With regard to most of the war crimes, such responsibility was clearly foreseeable and partly embodied in existing laws before World War II. With regard to crimes against peace, the illegality of the attacks on several countries at the time they occurred cannot be doubted. The same is also true with regard to most of the underlying crimes that constituted crimes against humanity, which to a large extent also overlapped with war crimes. In other words, only a very strict – and for many lawyers and ordinary people, grossly unreasonable – application of the legality principle could potentially exempt the Germans most responsible from justice before the court.

In hindsight, the Nuremberg Principles have been a major contribution to international law and still form an important part of current ICL.[107] The trials and the Judgment should not be regarded as illegitimate or mistaken,[108] or even as a one-time event that cannot serve as a model for emulation.[109] The UN has consistently upheld their legitimacy and importance.[110] Instead of rejecting the precedent, one ought to recognise that a well-founded choice was made after World War II between conflicting principles of justice. The results included support for a universal right un-

---

[107] See ILC, *Principles of International Law Recognized in the Charter of the Nürnberg Tribunal and in the Judgment of the Tribunal*, reprinted in *Yearbook of the International Law Commission, 1950*, vol. II, para. 97.

[108] The Nuremberg and Tokyo trials have "generated much critical literature", as noted by Nina H.B. Jørgensen in *The Responsibility of States for International Crimes*, Oxford University Press, Oxford, 2000, p. 28 (with further references). International lawyers, the UN, and international courts, however, generally regard the results favourably.

[109] See, for example, Gallant, 2009, p. 405, *supra* note 31.

[110] See UN General Assembly, Resolution 95, 11 December 1946, endorsing "the principles of international law recognized by the Charter of the Nuremberg Tribunal and the Judgment of the Tribunal". See also UN General Assembly, Resolution 177 (II), 21 November 1947, urging the ILC to "formulate" the Nuremberg Principles.

der international law of any nation to seek accountability of political and military leaderships for grave crimes on the basis of a fair trial.[111]

A challenge that remains today is to elucidate the content and hierarchical status of the different general principles of international criminal law, including their legal consequences, in settings where parallel rules are founded in different law-creating sources and the jurisdiction of new international courts or national legislation on grave crimes is still being defined. The general theory of personal criminal liability discussed in this book can be seen as a contribution to meeting this challenge. Thus, the four-level theory presented in Chapter 2 reconciles the need for keeping the operational parts of ICL within a common theoretical framework of general principles that can be applied to different subsystems of criminal law.

It should be noted, however, that an international criminal court, once established, cannot abdicate its responsibility for determining guilt because its legal basis does not provide a clear-cut answer to an interpretive issue. When the ICTY and the ICTR were confronted with the problem that the crime of rape had not been defined, the ICTY Trial Chamber, in the Kunarac case, first examined the criminal laws in many different countries in order to ascertain a general principle underlying the crime of rape in national laws.[112] The definition of rape it extracted from these national sources was then accepted as part of international law by the ICTY Appeals Chamber.[113] This indicates that general principles of law are particularly important at this stage of development of international criminal law, and that law-creating mechanisms other than international customary law and treaty law are needed to meet the new legal challenges and seek harmonised universal crimes norms.[114]

---

[111] See UN General Assembly, Resolution 95, *ibid.* Principle I affirms individual responsibility for crimes under international law; Principle III, responsibility of a head of state or government official; and Principle V, the right to a fair trial on the facts and law.

[112] ICTY, Trial Chamber, *Prosecutor v. Kunarac et al.*, Judgment, IT-96-23/IT-96-23/1, 22 February 2001, para. 439 (www.legal-tools.org/doc/fd881d/).

[113] ICTY, Appeals Chamber, *Prosecutor v. Kunarac et al.*, Judgment, IT-96-23/1, 12 June 2002, para. 127 (www.legal-tools.org/doc/029a09/).

[114] This may also include soft law, for example, statements of the law by the ILC and maybe even a comprehensive declaration by the General Assembly on universal crimes; see Einarsen, 2012, pp. 313–18, *supra* note 1.

4.3.5. Legislative Security Council Resolutions

An additional law-creating source, which is still controversial, consists of Security Council resolutions that establish binding rules of a legislative character. This is controversial for reasons relating both to the legal basis of the SC's action under Chapter VII of the UN Charter and to its legitimacy as a law-making organ. Since the end of the Cold War, the SC has interpreted and used its competence in this respect to adopt binding rules and principles of general application. Consequently, "it has asserted and extended its authority where the inadequacies of law-making by treaty might undermine the pursuit of its objectives".[115]

An example of this development, one that has been much discussed, is the comprehensive Security Council Resolution 1373 (2001), aimed at combating terrorism.[116] The point here is that Resolution 1373 lays down universal and binding obligations for states. According to Husabø and Bruce, the content of Resolution 1373 "largely corresponds to what could be expected from a convention, the traditional instrument for creating new obligations under international law".[117] But the legal effects are different, since while states are free to choose whether to sign and accede to or ratify a convention, a resolution adopted under Chapter VII by the SC – made up of a limited number of state representatives, and dominated by the five permanent members – is immediately binding upon all members of the UN without exception. Such a resolution, being imposed on its subjects, has a vertical legislative character, rather than being a horizontal agreement between equal and sovereign states.[118] Furthermore, SC Resolution 1373 provides for an enforcement mechanism, the Counter-Terrorism

---

[115] See Boyle and Chinkin, 2007, pp. 109–10, *supra* note 41.

[116] Whether terrorist crimes are also universal crimes was discussed in the first book of this series (see Einarsen, 2012, *supra* note 1), and not much has changed since then. At that time it had already been concluded that terrorist crimes properly defined are most likely crimes under international law. What has happened in recent years, legally speaking, is that more countries have enacted detailed legislation on terrorist crimes, including participation in terrorist organisations. In Europe, framework legislation enacted by the EU has contributed towards this end.

[117] See Erling Johannes Husabø and Ingvild Bruce, *Fighting Terrorism through Multilevel Criminal Legislation: Security Council Resolution 1373, the EU Framework Decision on Combating Terrorism and their Implementation in Nordic, Dutch and German Criminal Law*, Brill/Martinus Nijhoff, Leiden, 2009, p. 35.

[118] *Ibid.*, p. 36.

Committee, which is a body subordinate to the SC. In SC Resolution 1540 (2005), the SC again legislated in general terms, this time to ensure that non-state actors are prevented from obtaining nuclear, chemical, or biological weapons. These features have led commentators to use the term 'legislation'[119] or 'quasi-legislation'.[120] As Husabø and Bruce observe, from a functional point of view "Resolution 1373 satisfies even the strictest definitions of international legislation".[121] Normatively, they are more sceptical of its legal validity, at least at the time when it was adopted.[122]

Some authors maintain that a systematic interpretation of the UN Charter contradicts the power of the SC to impose general legislative measures on member states.[123] It is true that the decision-making powers of the SC with regard to "measures not involving the use of armed force" are not exhaustively specified or enumerated in the UN Charter (Article 41). But both the text and the context of the Charter support the position that adoptions of binding rules are not *per se* excluded. The limited competences of the General Assembly in Articles 11(1) and 13(1), with regard to the development of general principles of international law, may suggest an underlying assumption that only states can create new general rules of international law, by treaties or the formation of customs. However, the 'threat to the peace', which constitutes both a specific legal basis and a limitation on SC powers (Article 39), read in conjunction with the broad discretion regarding peaceful measures to be employed to that end (Article 41), does not exclude the use of abstract norm creation. Legislative acts are a common way of achieving such goals in national law, and can be presumed to be options within international law as well.

The limitations stem not from any bar to legislation as such by the Security Council, but from the requirement that the measures employed must be sufficiently linked to the specific purpose "to maintain or restore international peace and security" (Article 39); from the limitations flowing from "the purposes and principles of the United Nations" (Article 24, as well as Articles 1 and 2); and from other parts of international law, in-

---

[119] *Ibid.*, pp. 36–39 (with further references).
[120] Boyle and Chinkin, 2007, p. 114, *supra* note 41, use both characterisations.
[121] Husabø and Bruce, 2009, p. 39, *supra* note 117.
[122] *Ibid.*, pp. 40–54.
[123] *Ibid.*, p. 46 (with further references).

cluding the proportionality principle. The UN purposes and principles include, but are not necessarily confined to, "respect for human rights", "the principle of equal rights and self-determination of peoples", "justice", and "settlement of international disputes". It is also important to note that *jus cogens* rules of international law bind the SC in the exercise of its functions. In order for the UN Charter to remain in harmony with the peremptory norms of general international law (*jus cogens*) and not become void as a treaty,[124] the Charter – including its Chapter VII – must be interpreted as not being in conflict with these norms.[125] SC resolutions cannot legitimise grave crimes or any other activity falling within the scope of proscriptive *jus cogens*. The ICTY Appeals Chamber acknowledged such limitations in the Tadić case. It concluded that "neither the text nor the spirit of the Charter conceives of the Security Council as *legibus solutis* (unbound by law)".[126] Whether respect for other binding international rules requires that the Security Council not create new conflicting norms is a more difficult question. A simple answer seems to be that this is unlikely. In their analysis of this issue, Boyle and Chinkin conclude that the jurisprudence of international courts suggests that SC resolutions "override inconsistent international law".[127] SC resolutions thus have great potential significance in future international law, not least within the field of ICL.

Still, it may be that further limitations on SC legislative power should be read into the UN Charter. Some restrictions seem necessary in order to prevent the legislative powers of the SC from expanding beyond peace and security issues. This set of issues, however, often coincides with the concerns of ICL because of the close relationships between peace, security, and justice. Note also that 'peace' and 'security', under current international law, are not narrowly defined terms. The acceptance of basic 'human security' as a fundamental universal value and/or interest, and of

---

[124] See the Vienna Convention on the Law of Treaties, 1969, Articles 53 and 64.

[125] See, for example, Antonios Tzanakopoulos, *Disobeying the Security Council: Countermeasures against Wrongful Sanctions*, Oxford University Press, Oxford, 2011, pp. 70–72 (with further references).

[126] ICTY, Appeals Chamber, *Prosecutor v. Tadić*, ICTY, Judgment, IT-94-1-R, 15 July 1999, para. 28 (www.legal-tools.org/doc/8efc3a/).

[127] Boyle and Chinkin, 2007, pp. 232–33, *supra* note 41.

the complementary notion of a 'responsibility to protect',[128] has expanded the powers of the SC under Chapter VII with respect to measures undertaken with the aim of protecting civilians who are exposed to universal crimes. Alternatively, one may consider that this power is already inherent in Chapter VII but that its use has become politically feasible in the aftermath of the Cold War.[129]

Within this more flexible framework, the SC may be able to rewrite or disregard provisions of international law in particular situations.[130] This is a significant change in traditional perceptions of the limitations of international law. Two SC resolutions on the situation in Libya in 2011 seem to be a case in point. In the first one, the SC considered that "the widespread and systematic attacks currently taking place in the Libyan Arab Jamahiriya against the civilian population may amount to crimes against humanity".[131] It then, in another resolution, authorised member states "to take all necessary measures [...] to protect civilians and civilian populated areas under threat of attack in the Libyan Arab Jamahiriya".[132] For the first time, the United Nations had in practice authorised an international humanitarian intervention, that is, started a regular universally authorised war, for the purpose of protecting human beings against grave (universal) crimes.[133] How successful this concrete intervention was from a humanitarian perspective, and whether the intervention as a whole significantly overstepped its mandate, is another matter that will not be discussed here.

In reference to the resolution on terrorism in 2001, Husabø and Bruce have argued that an "interpretation of Chapter VII as broad as that

---

[128] See, for example, Gareth Evans, *The Responsibility to Protect: Ending Mass Atrocity Crimes Once and For All*, Brookings Institution Press, Washington, DC, 2008.

[129] See, for example, Jennifer M. Welsh, "The Security Council and Humanitarian Intervention", in Vaughan Lowe, Adam Roberts, Jennifer Welsh, and Dominik Zaum (eds.), *The United Nations Security Council and War: The Evolution of Thought and Practice since 1945*, Oxford University Press, Oxford, 2008, pp. 535–62.

[130] Boyle and Chinkin, 2007, pp. 232–33, *supra* note 41.

[131] UN Security Council Resolution 1970 (2011) (www.legal-tools.org/doc/00a45e/).

[132] UN Security Council Resolution 1373 (2011) (www.legal-tools.org/doc/f4d6ad/).

[133] However, under a somewhat narrower definition of 'humanitarian intervention', the Security Council authorised several earlier armed interventions, notably in Northern Iraq (1991), Somalia (1992), Haiti (1993), Rwanda (1994), and East Timor (1999). See Welsh, 2008, pp. 538–53, *supra* note 129.

on which Resolution 1373 is based could easily serve as a precedent for Security Council legislation in other areas", an outcome that could ultimately turn the SC into "a world government".[134] The example of Libya in 2011 might provide additional grounds for such a fear. There are, however, several factors that make such a scenario unlikely in general terms: these include the internal political constraints of the SC, including the veto power held by the five permanent members, as well as the legal reasons mentioned above. In Tadić, the ICTY expressed the view that "there exists no corporate organ formally empowered to enact law directly binding on international legal subjects".[135] Considering that the court in Tadić accepted the legality of Resolution 827 (1993), which established the ICTY itself with such legal effects, this statement might at first seem contradictory. The court probably intended a more limited meaning, namely, that there exists no such organ with a *general* law-creating power, that is, outside the scope of threats to peace and security. Following this interpretation, Tadić confirmed that unrestrained use of legislative powers would not be legally acceptable, although the concrete legislative act establishing the ICTY did fall within the ambit of SC powers.

The case for there being implicit and necessary limitations on SC legislative powers is often linked with the fact that there is only limited scope for judicial review of SC resolutions. Although it might be legally possible for the General Assembly to exercise control of the legality of SC-created rules by means of a request for an advisory opinion from the ICJ,[136] for political reasons this would usually not be an option. Individual states directly affected by an SC resolution could not bring such a complaint themselves, but would be dependent upon the General Assembly to take the initiative. The issue of judicial review of SC resolutions may later arise in a contentious case between two or more states before the ICJ,[137]

---

[134] Husabø and Bruce, 2009, p. 39, *supra* note 117.

[135] ICTY, Appeals Chamber, *Prosecutor v. Tadić*, Judgment, IT-94-1-R, 15 July 1999, para. 43 (www.legal-tools.org/doc/8efc3a/).

[136] See Article 96(1) of the UN Charter and Article 65(1) of the ICJ Statute.

[137] See, for example, Boyle and Chinkin, 2007, pp. 230–31, *supra* note 41, with references to ICJ, *Certain Expenses of the United Nations (Article 17, paragraph 2, of the Charter)*, Advisory Opinion, *I.C.J. Reports 1962*, p. 151 (www.legal-tools.org/doc/72e883/); and ICJ, *Questions of Interpretation and Application of the 1971 Montreal Convention arising from the Aerial Incident at Lockerbie* (Libyan Arab Jamahiriya v. United States of America),

but that would not satisfy a need for an immediate judicial review of a controversial SC resolution.

Other courts, including international criminal courts, may also scrutinise particular Security Council resolutions, as seen in the Tadić case. Another example of indirect court review is the case of Kadi and Al Barakaat before the European Court of Justice ('ECJ'), which held that the European Community judicature does have jurisdiction to review the measures adopted by the Community to give effect to SC resolutions. Although the ECJ declined to expressly "review the lawfulness of a resolution adopted by an international body", it still reviewed norms resulting from the SC resolution by comparing them to "fundamental rights that form an integral part of the general principles of law whose observance the Court ensures".[138] These included the principle of effective judicial protection, which had been infringed on several points.[139] The same principle of judicial review was upheld by the ECJ in the case of Hassan and Ayadi.[140]

The main problem with SC legislative acts, therefore, is arguably not so much the legal basis or legitimacy of the legislative acts *per se*. More importantly, there is little assurance that the SC will act consistently or at all, when it should, and judicial control is uncertain in cases where specific legislative acts may go too far. Despite these problems, it is clear that the law-creating function of the SC needs to be taken into account and further explored, particularly with respect to the concept of universal crimes as part of current international law. In particular, the precedent of SC Resolution 1373 (2001) on terrorism, at least when considered in conjunction with other sources, including other (non-binding) SC resolutions

---

Provisional Measures, Order, *I.C.J. Reports 1992*, p. 114 (www.legal-tools.org/doc/043e5b/).

[138] ECJ, *Yassin Abdullah Kadi and Al Barakaat International Foundation v. Council of the European Union and Commission of the European Communities*, Judgment, C-402/05 P and C-415/05 P, 3 September 2008, paras. 4–5 (www.legal-tools.org/doc/9c3dd5/).

[139] *Ibid.*, para. 8.

[140] ECJ, *Faraj Hassan and Chafiq Ayadi v. Council and Commission of the European Union*, Judgment, C-399/06 P and C-403/06 P, 3 December 2009 (www.legal-tools.org/doc/14b236/).

---

on the same subject matter, may have given birth to a new binding norm on direct criminal liability under international law.[141]

4.3.6. Establishing Universal Crimes Norms with Multiple Legal Bases

The proposition that a binding international rule has to originate from an identifiable law-creating source is closely related to the rule of law in international relations.[142] One may raise the question, however, whether there might be a modification of this clear point of departure that would still be acceptable under international law and particularly relevant for fundamental universal crimes norms. This modification would entail anchoring a legal norm in multiple legal bases, without specifying any one of them as the principal legal basis. While the weight of each specific legal basis might be uncertain, one could still argue that their cumulative weight was sufficient to establish a binding international rule.

At first glance, an approach relying on multiple legal bases might seem questionable, suggesting an arbitrary and subjective mixture of customary international law, treaties, and general principles of law. However, Nuremberg provides a classic illustration of the underlying dilemmas caused by unclear legal status of universal crimes norms and of the consequent need for such a combined approach. The main issues put before the Nuremberg Tribunal were (1) whether aggression was prohibited before and during World War II, and (2) whether individual criminal liability for aggressive acts ('crimes against peace') existed under international law. With regard to the former, the tribunal could rely on a number of international treaties, including several treaties to which Germany was a party and which it clearly had breached,[143] notably the Kellogg-Briand Pact of 1928.[144] In that treaty, the parties had declared "in the names of their respective peoples that they condemn recourse to war for the solution of international controversies, and renounce it, as an instrument of national

---

[141] See Einarsen, 2012, pp. 266–74, *supra* note 1.

[142] *Ibid.*, pp. 28–38.

[143] IMT, *Trial of the Major War Criminals*, 1947, vol. I, Judgment, pp. 216–24, *supra* note 18.

[144] Signed at Paris on 27 August 1928, the Kellogg-Briand Pact was a treaty between several states providing for the renunciation of war as an instrument of national policy.

policy in their relations with another".[145] Although Germany claimed a reservation to the Kellogg-Briand Pact with regard to preventive self-defence, this was dismissed by the tribunal as non-operational on the basis of general principles of law.[146]

The next issue was an even more difficult one, since neither the Kellogg-Briand Pact nor any other treaty explicitly addressed criminal liability for future acts of aggression.[147] The tribunal here seems to have adopted an approach combining different treaties, emerging customary international law, and general principles of law into a single *sui generis* legal basis. What makes the approach particularly innovative and interesting is that the tribunal does not make clear which particular legal basis it regards as the principal law-creating source. The tribunal instead justified its affirmative answer with respect to individual criminal liability by pointing to the dynamic character of international law concerned with fundamental principles, and to the needs of a changing world. In this process it also invoked an analogy, compelling at least in terms of *lex ferenda*, that certain methods of warfare had also first been prohibited and subsequently recognised as war crimes under international law. A longer citation is warranted:

> The Hague Convention of 1907 prohibited resort to certain methods of waging war. These included the inhumane treatment of prisoners, the employment of poisoned weapons, the improper use of flags of truce, and similar matters. Many of these prohibitions had been enforced long before the date of the Convention; but since 1907 they have certainly been crimes, punishable as offences against the laws of war; yet

---

[145] Kellogg-Briand Pact, Article I. See also Article II, stating that the settlement or solution of disputes or conflicts "shall never be sought except by pacific means".

[146] IMT, *Trial of the Major War Criminals*, 1947, vol. I, Judgment, p. 208, *supra* note 18. The court rejected the notion "that Germany alone could decide, in accordance with the reservations made by many of the Signatory Powers at the time of conclusion of the Kellogg-Briand Pact, whether preventive action was a necessity, and that in making her decision, her judgment was conclusive". Instead the court held that "whether action taken under the claim of self-defence was in fact aggressive or defensive must ultimately be subject to investigation and adjudication if international law is ever to be enforced".

[147] In the Versailles Treaty of 28 June 1919, Article 228, the German government after World War I recognised "the right of the Allied and Associated Powers to bring before military tribunals persons accused of having committed acts in violation of the laws and customs of war". This treaty was not directly applicable to crimes committed in World War II.

---

the Hague Convention nowhere designates such practices as criminal, nor is any sentence prescribed, nor any mention of a court to try and punish offenders. [...] In the opinion of the Tribunal, those who wage aggressive war are doing that which is equally illegal, and of much greater moment than a breach of one of the rules of the Hague Convention. [...] The law of war is to be found not only in treaties, but in the customs and practices of states which gradually obtain universal recognition, and from the general principles of justice applied by jurists and practiced by military courts. This law is not static, but by continual adaptation follows the needs of a changing world. Indeed, in many cases treaties do no more than express and define for more accurate reference the principles of law already existing.[148]

The horizontal structure of international law – the systemic fact that "international law is not the product of an international legislature"[149] – may justify a similar approach in other exceptional cases.

The International Law Commission may on certain issues also have proceeded on the implicit basis of such an underlying theory of the legal bases of international criminal law.[150] For example, on the 'obligation to extradite or prosecute' (*aut dedere aut judicare*),[151] the ILC special rapporteur in his first report in 2006 discussed the sources of the obligation. The rapporteur admitted that one of the crucial problems to be solved was to "find a generally acceptable answer to the question if the legal source of the obligation to extradite or prosecute should be limited to the treaties

---

[148] IMT, *Trial of the Major War Criminals*, 1947, vol. I, Judgment, p. 221, *supra* note 18. The prosecutors at Nuremberg often invoked several legal bases for the same crime. See *ibid.*, [Indictment], p. 43, on the legal bases of war crimes norms ("violations of international conventions, of internal penal laws and of the general principles of criminal law"); p. 44, on the crime of murder and ill-treatment of civilians; and p. 51, on the crime of deportation ("contrary to international conventions, in particular to Article 46 of the Hague Regulations 1907, the laws and customs of war, the general principles of criminal law"); p. 53, on murder and ill-treatment of prisoners of war ("contrary to International Conventions, particularly [...] the laws and customs of war, the general principles of criminal law"). See also pp. 54, 56, and 61–65.

[149] *Ibid.*, p. 221.

[150] On various statements by the ILC concerned with international crimes generally, see Einarsen, 2012, pp. 168–202, *supra* note 1. With particular respect to personal liability concepts, see Chapter 5, Section 5.3., of this book.

[151] See also Einarsen, 2012, pp. 202–6, *supra* note 1, on this particular subject matter.

---

which are binding the States concerned, or be extended to appropriate customary norms or general principles of law".[152] As a point of departure, based upon a preliminary analysis, the special rapporteur was "convinced that the sources of the obligation to extradite or prosecute should include general principles of law, national legislation and judicial decisions, and not just treaties and customary rules".[153]

In general, international courts have declined to follow a rigorous methodology that would unduly restrict their freedom to facilitate, if necessary, what seems to be a necessary development of international law in light of world community interests and elementary considerations of justice. Judges of international courts have sometimes been viewed as conservative and restrained in their interpretation of the law in certain fields, while at other times they have been portrayed as radicals. Such a focus on the judges may open interesting debates, but it would be a mistake to lay too much weight on the role of judges while ignoring deeper issues. Because international courts operate within the UN paradigm of international law, they must internalise and be guided by a legal culture compatible with that paradigm, thus including certain basic principles that reflect fundamental, common international interests and values.[154] When differ-

---

[152] ILC, Zdzislaw Galicki, Special Rapporteur, *Preliminary Report on the Obligation to Extradite or Prosecute ('aut dedere aut judicare')*, A/CN.4/571, 2006, p. 12, para. 40 (www.legal-tools.org/doc/59a9ed/).

[153] *Ibid.*, p. 15, para. 48. In the first discussion in the Sixth Committee of the General Assembly on the issue of the legal nature of the obligation, more restricted views were expressed, as also acknowledged by the special rapporteur in his second report. See ILC, Zdzislaw Galicki, Special Rapporteur, *Second Report on the Obligation to Extradite or Prosecute ('aut dedere aut judicare')*, A/CN.4/585, 2007, pp. 8–9 and 12–13, paras. 25–28 and 50 (www.legal-tools.org/doc/ac4038/). Still, the ILC has proceeded on the assumption that several legal bases need to be explored, but in particular treaties and customary international law, including possible "regional principles". See, for example, ILC, *Report of the International Law Commission*, Supplement no. 10, A/64/10, 2009, pp. 344–45, para. 204 (www.legal-tools.org/doc/fc3fe1/).

[154] The same is not necessarily true of politicians concerned with foreign relations and the international community. They typically operate from a domestic platform and represent state interests, which in many concrete cases may contravene long-term common international interests. Thus it may be correct that state representatives comply with international law for instrumental reasons. See Jack L. Goldsmith and Eric A. Posner, *The Limits of International Law*, Oxford University Press, Oxford, 2005, p. 225: "We have argued that the best explanation for when and why states comply with international law is not that states have internalized international law, or have a habit of complying with it, or are drawn by its moral pull, but simply that states act out of self-interest". However, the instrumental

ent fundamental principles, such as justice, effectiveness, and legal certainty, clash, the outcome may then depend upon the concrete circumstances and the individual preferences of the judges.

It is therefore realistic to assume that international courts dealing with universal crimes will sometimes make use of multiple legal bases in a discrete manner, taking one particular legal basis, for instance, customary international law, as the point of departure and using materials from other law-creating sources as interpretative materials to support a conclusion that the norm is legally binding. Under such an approach, the distinction between legal bases and interpretative sources is maintained.

4.3.7. The Legality Principle and Attribution of Personal Criminal Liability

While it is clear that all universal crimes norms at the operational level of any subsystem of ICL require a legal basis in one or more law-creating sources, it is less clear which law-creating source this must be. In principle, the four law-creating sources are equal in the sense that they may all create relevant new universal crimes norms. However, special considerations or norms may modify this point of departure. For example, Rauter has asserted that not all sources of public international law are to be considered adequate sources for the legal basis of individual criminal responsibility. He argues that only customary international law is appropriate in this respect.[155]

Similarly, the question has been raised in the literature, and in several cases before international tribunals, as to whether attribution of all forms of personal liability *must have a legal basis in CIL*. This means that unless the traditional CIL criteria can be proven to apply to a particular mode of liability, attribution of personal liability would be in violation of the legality principle if based on the parameters of that mode. In order to ascertain the scope and limitations of the legality principle, however, it is useful to consider the matter within a broader context of legality and lawfulness.

---

reasons may also include compliance with the fundamental structures of the UN paradigm of international law. Furthermore, from a legal point of view, the motivation for compliance or non-compliance is usually irrelevant.

[155] See Rauter, 2017, p. 85, *supra* note 47.

It is quite clear that the double *nullum sine lege* requirement of the international legality principle applies to the crime description norms identifying a specific universal crime. Hence the existence of such norms is a necessary legal requirement if the jurisdiction to prosecute the crime has been established or is being exercised without the consent of the territorial state where the crime actually occurred. The UN Security Council, for example, established the ICTY without the consent of the former Yugoslavia (or the relevant successor states) to prosecute certain crimes committed in the territory of the former Yugoslavia, namely, "grave breaches of the Geneva Conventions of 1949" (Article 2), "violations of the laws or customs of war" (Article 3), "genocide" (Article 4), and "crimes against humanity" (Article 5). Thus, the written statute of the ICTY clarified which crimes could be prosecuted, in compliance with the first requirement of the *nullum sine lege* principle (legal basis in the written statute).

In addition, these crimes defining the material jurisdiction of the ICTY would also have to be recognised as crimes under general international law at the time they were committed, in compliance with the second requirement of the *nullum sine lege* principle and the non-retroactivity principle (legal basis in a general universal crimes norm existing under international law when the actual offence was committed). In theory, the traditional CIL criteria of state practice and *opinio juris* should then be fulfilled. Another possibility would be a legal basis in the general principles of international law. To anchor the crime description norms only in the general principles of international law is a rather insecure solution; it does not provide sufficient legal security and foreseeability for the offender, and a sole basis in the general principles for these norms has not been accepted. So, with the possible exception of the Nuremberg and Tokyo trials, where the general principles were invoked in conjunction with treaties and customary law, international courts have sought to demonstrate that their own interpretation and application of the material crime description norms in the statutes are in compliance with CIL.[156]

It is not always made clear, though, whether it suffices for the essence or contours of the crime to have a CIL basis or whether it is re-

---

[156] See the extensive study, which also includes examples of personal liability norms, by Rauter, 2017, pp. 125–72, *supra* note 47.

quired that every single element of the crime as defined in the statute be based on CIL. This again might reflect different ways of perceiving the law. Is the function of CIL in this area to create norms of competence (jurisdiction) that enable states and international tribunals to incorporate and perhaps further define the relevant universal crimes in the relevant statutes within certain limits (the essence of the respective crimes being already established under general international law)? Or is the function of CIL to create the exact substantive norm that proscribes a particular and specified conduct in all respects? The first alternative makes sense, since states have discretion with respect to criminalisation, although they must apply the labels of universal crimes in good faith in order to respect international law. Fair trial and fair labelling are necessary to protect the human rights of the accused person, who should not, for example, be convicted for crimes against humanity if he was only guilty of rape. In other words, according to this first alternative, the applicable crime description in the operational statute of an international court must not change the character of the relevant international crime in any essential or unreasonable way that would transform the criminalised conduct into a different kind of act that the accused could not have foreseen as criminal conduct under international law when the act was made. This seems to provide a good solution to the conflicting interests of effective prosecution of universal crimes and lawfulness. The second alternative has, however, often been assumed. And in that case it may seem logical to apply the same strict legality requirements to the modes of liability as well. For example, Rauter seems to take for granted that the same (strict) legality requirements apply to both parts of the law when establishing possible criminal responsibility.[157] The question remains whether that is the correct understanding of ICL and CIL in this area.

When a certain crime X has been established as a crime under international law, it follows from the general theory of personal criminal liability that the *basic type of criminal law liability* for X is established simultaneously.[158] From the perspective of criminalisation and society, to

---

[157] In his generally excellent treatise, Rauter, 2017, see *supra* note 47, discusses international court cases dealing with both matters under the same headings throughout the book. He does not make any distinction between the possibly different requirements relating to the legal basis of the crime description norm and the modes of liability.

[158] See Chapter 2, Sections 2.2.2.4. and 2.2.3.5.

establish a crime without the lawful possibility of attributing criminal liability to persons committing the crime does not make any sense. Therefore, criminal proscription of certain acts must also, by necessary implication, provide for the lawfulness of attributing liability. For this reason, it seems doubtful that all derivative forms of liability must *also* have a *separate* legal basis in CIL.

This ambiguity surrounding, in particular, the requirement of legal specificity and the modes of liability may be one reason why international courts in practice have had difficulties in applying the traditional CIL criteria of state practice and *opinio juris* in this field. Thus, in his detailed analysis of the use of CIL at international criminal courts (especially the ICTY, and to a lesser extent the ICTR), Rauter found that different methodologies are detectable in the tribunals' jurisprudence.[159] From a critical perspective, he noted that the legal basis for the analysis and application of CIL criteria by the tribunals examined has been inconsistent and often in violation of traditional methods for establishing consistent, general, and enduring state practice and *opinio juris*. According to Rauter, the judges have sometimes ignored the CIL requirements or paid lip service to the traditional criteria while actually applying modified versions of them, or applying the traditional criteria without clear proof of state practice and *opinio juris*.[160] While the descriptive part of his study seems well founded, one may ask whether the critique is based on a too-strict conception of what CIL and the international legality principle actually require, in particular with respect to the specificity of all aspects of the crime elements and the modes of liability.

Furthermore, if the jurisdiction of an international (or hybrid international) court is based on prior consent by the territorial state to share its jurisdiction, the crimes specified in the statute of that court may also include crimes that are not necessarily crimes under international law. Consequently, the states parties to the Rome Statute could have decided, if

---

[159] *Ibid.*, p. 172.

[160] *Ibid.*, p. 234: "[A]n analysis of the jurisprudence of international criminal tribunals reveals a hesitation on the part of the chambers to adhere to the traditional method when establishing customary international criminal law. Indeed, it can be stated that the chambers pay lip-service to the traditional two-element approach when elaborating on abstract theory, but they manifestly fail to deliver concrete evidence for State practice and *opinio iuris* in practice when establishing a specific customary international criminal norm".

they deemed it preferable, to include other grave crimes that are not currently recognised universal crimes. The reason is that the ICC itself can only prosecute crimes that are committed in the territory of a state party (territorial jurisdiction) or elsewhere by nationals of a state party (active nationality jurisdiction): in other words, crimes that could also have been prosecuted by a state party in compliance with international law. By virtue of becoming a party to the ICC, a state has agreed that crimes it could have prosecuted may now also be prosecuted by the ICC (with a rather complicated exception for the crime of aggression). For example, since Afghanistan is a state party, the ICC may – if certain conditions are fulfilled – prosecute Rome Statute crimes committed in Afghanistan by US forces even though the United States is not itself a state party. And although Iraq is not a state party, the ICC may prosecute crimes committed by UK forces in Iraq because the UK is a state party. So, if the Rome Statute states parties in the future agree to include another crime that has an uncertain legal basis under CIL, but that is a crime that could have been prosecuted as such domestically by the states parties, it is hard to see why the ICC should have to prove that the newly included crime is also a crime under international law according to the traditional CIL criteria. As long as CIL does not *prohibit* prosecution of that particular crime as formulated (for example, because that would violate fundamental principles of human rights that form part of CIL), the inclusion would be lawful. However, the inclusion of, for example, terrorist crimes – which today still have an uncertain status as crimes under general international law – in the Rome Statute or in the statute of another international criminal court would be a potentially decisive push in the direction of recognised status as crimes under international law. When such status is obtained, the crimes could then be prosecuted by an international court even without prior consent of the territorial state where the crime was committed or of the state of nationality of the alleged offender.

Thus, the point we would like to highlight before considering the personal liability norms is that the exact application of the *nullum sine lege* principle needs quite nuanced analysis. A second point is that the *nullum sine lege* principle has its uncontested and principal application with regard to the crime description norms proscribing the conduct that constitutes a universal crime, for example the crime of genocide. The situation is not so clear with respect to the other fundamental parts of criminal liability. With respect to the principle of culpability including possible defences, we have earlier, in Chapter 2, argued that culpability is an inherent part of the general theory of criminal law: a fundamental criminal law principle at the same level as the legality principle and principle of conduct. For that reason, we have also raised the question in this chapter on the general principles of international law, asking whether, for example, culpability should also be considered an inherent part of ICL as a general principle under international law with a view to personal criminal liability. If this is the case, which we think it is, there is not really a need to prove that the fundamental principle of culpability is (also) part of CIL. The same applies to the various generally recognised defences (both excuses and justifications) that may exculpate the accused. While the exact definitions might be left to statutes (legislation) and judicial decisions, the essence or contours of these universal crimes norms should rather be considered sufficiently anchored in the general principles of ICL.

The same applies to the fundamental principle of fair attribution of personal liability; as defined and discussed in Chapter 2 and as indicated above in this chapter, it should probably also be considered part of general ICL, including its further (third-level) secondary principles. If it is so considered, there is not really a need to prove through the CIL criteria that commission liability as well as inchoate liability and accomplice liability, and relevant derivative forms, lawfully constitute punishable participation at the operational (fourth level) in the kinds of criminal enterprises that are so common in ICL. On the other hand, the fundamental principle of fair attribution of personal liability and the general principles of ICL, or CIL, we would argue, do not close the door on unitary models of attribution if these are considered preferable at the operational level. What is important to underline is that personal criminal liability must also be applied with respect for the principles of conduct and culpability.

Ultimately, this means that the 'hard' version of the legality principle, requiring proof of an-element-for-element legal basis in CIL, is replaced with a softer version, what could be termed a rule of law requirement, which includes consistency with the general principles of ICL and with the general theory of criminal law liability. The more precise content of this norm will be revisited in Chapter 10, after we have explored the use of liability concepts within different parts of ICL and by authors and institutions in Chapters 5–9. This does not mean that there is no legal basis in international law for these universal crimes liability norms (derivative forms of liability); it only means that a legal basis in CIL is not necessarily required apart from the basic form of criminal liability flowing from the relevant crime, since their principal legal basis is the general principles of criminal law that are inherent in the general principles of international law relating to ICL responsibility. One important implication of this systemic order is that juridical entity liability is always a possibility and a policy choice at the operational level in future ICL, with no requirement to first establish proof of such liability already existing under CIL in accordance with the traditional CIL criteria. In other words, if such liability is not *prohibited* by CIL, it will be lawful to implement because such liability is in compliance with the general theory of personal (natural person and juridical entity) criminal law liability.

Finally, however, there is a need for some additional clarification with respect to one particular category of personal liability at the operational level, where we assume that the hard version of the legality principle does apply, at least partly. This concerns liability for what could be termed 'accessorial crimes', related to 'the main crimes'. As compared to attribution of liability for punishable participation in completed, main universal crimes such as genocide, crimes against humanity, war crimes, and aggression, there is also the possible *distinct criminalisation* of certain forms of participatory conduct relating to the main crimes that is meant to apply regardless of the main crime being completed. Such distinct criminalisation typically concerns liability for inchoate offences, but it could in principle also encompass specific forms of accomplice liability. Typical examples of inchoate crimes are attempt, incitement, and conspiracy. Note in this respect that a distinct crime is never only 'attempt', but rather 'attempt to commit genocide', to take just one example. Such criminalisation is fully compatible with the general theory of criminal law liability, which provides the relevant principles at the third level of the theory that in turn can be lawfully made operational at the fourth practical level within any criminal law subsystem – as long as the other parts of the general theory of liability are respected. Hence, distinct, 'accessorial' crimes can be prosecuted whether the relevant main (universal) crime was completed or not, provided the relevant conditions for the accessorial crime were fulfilled. In principle, it is also possible to attribute further accessorial liability to distinct accessorial crimes, for example, complicity in attempt; this will depend on policy considerations.

In our view, the double requirement of the *nullum sine lege* principle also applies to distinct, accessorial crimes. For example, attempt as an inchoate crime can only be prosecuted if there is a legal basis for it in the statute of the relevant international court. For example, the Rome Statute, Article 25(3)(f), allows for the prosecution of attempt as inchoate crimes annexed to all four main crimes of the statute (see, with respect to the crime of aggression, Article 25(3)*bis*, which does not make any exception for attempted crimes of aggression). Attempt was not included in the statutes of the IMT, ICTY, and ICTR, and could thus not have been – and was not – prosecuted before those tribunals. This is again probably legally uncontroversial. In other words, with respect to accessorial crimes, the legal basis in the statutes must be spelled out in accordance with strict legality. Furthermore, if attempt is made accessorial only to the main crimes, it follows that attempt in combination with other forms of attribution cannot lawfully be envisaged. Thus, a person cannot under the Rome Statute be convicted for, for instance, attempt to assist or incite another person to commit genocide.

However, what about the *nullum sine lege* principle relating to the underlying universal crimes norms of criminalising accessorial crimes, for example, attempt to genocide, crimes against humanity, war crimes, and aggression? Must there be a specific, general legal basis for such accessorial norms in CIL? Or is the legal basis on this point sufficiently anchored in the general principles? In this regard, our view is that distinct criminalisation is allowed under the general theory of personal criminal liability and thus might also be considered part of the general principles of ICL, and hence need not be proved under CIL. Again, the legality principle in the strict version is arguably substituted by a softer rule of law requirement, allowing for a legal basis in the general principles insofar as a particular kind of distinct criminalisation is not prohibited in CIL.

These assertions remain to be further investigated in this book. Are the liability concepts applied so far in theory and practice generally in compliance with our theoretical analysis and methodological observations? We will revisit this question in the final chapter of this book.[161]

---

[161] See in particular Chapter 10, Section 10.5.

4.4. Interpretative Sources and Priority Principles

4.4.1. Various Interpretive Sources

In contrast to the law-creating sources discussed above in Section 4.3., an interpretative (law-determining) source of international law as such cannot create binding universal crimes norms. This is true even though the four principal law-creating sources may also be interpretative sources with regard to another possible legal basis. Treaties, customs, general principles, and legislative Security Council resolutions thus each play a double role in the machinery of international criminal law. These roles are, however, distinct.

Among many other possibly relevant interpretative sources, the jurisprudence of international courts is particularly prominent. Others include law literature, UN reports and studies, statements by organs of the UN and other international organisations, as well as state practice of different kinds, including national court decisions on international criminal law issues.[162]

Historically, the commanding position of international courts within this field ('ICL') goes back to the Nuremberg and Tokyo tribunals. In addition, the ICJ has contributed over many years with important judgments and advisory opinions of high quality. This has been followed by the work of more recent international criminal tribunals, which taken together have produced an enormous number of invaluable judgments and interpretations that have developed and reinforced the law. Although some legal reasoning and judgments carry more weight than others, a study of universal crimes should ideally pay attention to any judgment of interpretative force, whether originating from the Nuremberg Tribunal, the ICC, or other international courts, and to some extent should also consider persuasive reasoning by domestic courts applying the same rules.

However, international jurisprudence also has its limitations with respect to some aspects of universal crimes, since courts are dependent upon the cases they receive and their particular jurisdictions. This has es-

---

[162] While interpretive sources apply to all the law-creating sources, their relevance and importance for proving the existence of customary international criminal law has been considered especially important; see *ibid.*, pp. 173–230. Rauter, 2017, see *supra* note 47, discusses in particular national legislation, international conventions, UN resolutions, jurisprudence, the ILC, and legal doctrine.

pecially affected the crime of aggression, which has not been prosecuted internationally since Nuremberg and Tokyo, while this crime can in the future be prosecuted again at the ICC.[163] Furthermore, the somewhat fragmented scheme of modes of liability within ICL as a whole may also have affected their interpretation and applicability at the international level as well as at the domestic level. Hence there is also a need for empirical studies seeking to uncover common trends, and for academic assessment of such possible trends, which in turn might provide theoretical and practical guidance to judges and others in the field. Dynamic development and interaction with other sources is thus not confined to the interpretation of law-creating sources, but includes interaction within the interpretive sources as well.

4.4.2. The Priority Principles: *Lex Superior*, *Lex Specialis*, and *Lex Posterior*

In general, it may not be necessary to prioritise the rules produced on the basis of different law-creating sources. However, if there should be a conflict between two or more rules having incompatible content, principles for prioritisation are needed. This is a general aspect of law, also known in domestic law. The principles of *lex superior* (a superior rule takes priority over an inferior rule), *lex specialis* (a specific rule takes priority over a general rule), and *lex posterior* (a newer rule takes priority over an older rule) are presumably part of the general principles of international law as well as of domestic law.

The impacts of the *lex specialis* and *lex posterior* principles are often uncertain, and the application of these principles should be handled with a great deal of care. Thus, if one rule is newer and the other is more specific, there is no general rule for deciding which should prevail. In general, the scope of the *lex posterior* principle is rather limited,[164] applying to successive multilateral treaties with different parties on the same

---

[163] The activation of jurisdiction for this crime under the Rome Statute has been noted earlier in this chapter. This development may also have the effect that the crime of aggression, despite its continued jurisdictional difficulties, could be taken into account at all stages, including at sentencing, when other crimes are prosecuted at the ICC. See Terje Einarsen, "Prosecuting Aggression through Other Universal Core Crimes at the International Criminal Court", in Leila Nadya Sadat (ed.), *Seeking Accountability for the Unlawful Use of Force*, Cambridge University Press, Cambridge, 2018, pp. 337–85.

[164] See ILC, 2006, conclusion no. 25, *supra* note 4.

---

subject matter. Furthermore, the notion of *lex specialis* does not necessarily imply that the *specialis* rule pre-empts the application of a coexisting more general rule, although this would generally be true.[165] Apart from superior general principles of law (*jus cogens*), there may also be other considerations that provide reasons for concluding that a general law should prevail.[166] For example, one should take into account the nature of the general law and the intentions of the parties, as well as whether the application of special law might frustrate the purpose of the general law or affect the balance of rights and obligations as established in the general law.[167] Such considerations, which are important to note within the fields of international humanitarian law and human rights law, are also relevant for ICL. This is due, in particular, to the general principle of complementary protection in international law, that is, that rules for the protection of fundamental rights and interests of human beings, although originating from different sources of law or different treaties, may supplement each other. Although one substantive rule may be considered the special rule by an adjudicator, the more general substantive rule may apply simultaneously.

For example, the ICJ in the Wall case found that the wall built by Israel within the occupied Palestinian territories violated rules of both international humanitarian law ('IHL')[168] and human rights law ('HRL'),[169] although the court considered IHL to be *lex specialis*.[170] As the ICJ explained, "some rights may be exclusively matters of international humani-

---

[165] *Ibid.*, conclusion no. 5: "The maxim *lex specialis derogat legi generali* is a generally accepted technique of interpretation and conflict resolution in international law. It suggests that whenever two or more norms deal with the same subject matter, priority should be given to the norm that is more specific". See also conclusions nos. 6–8.

[166] *Ibid.*, conclusion no. 10.

[167] *Ibid.*

[168] ICJ, *Legal Consequences of the Construction of a Wall in the Occupied Palestinian Territory*, Advisory Opinion, *I.C.J. Reports 2004*, p. 136, paras. 134–35 (www.legal-tools.org/doc/e5231b/), finding violations of the Fourth Geneva Convention as well as of Security Council resolutions.

[169] *Ibid.*, para. 134, finding violations of the International Covenant on Civil and Political Rights, the International Covenant on Economic, Social and Cultural Rights, and the United Nations Convention on the Rights of the Child.

[170] *Ibid.*, para. 106: "In order to answer the question put to it, the Court will have to take into consideration both these branches of international law, namely human rights law and, as *lex specialis*, international humanitarian law".

tarian law; others may be exclusively matters of human rights law; yet others may be matters of both these branches of international law".[171] The ICJ confirmed its view in its judgment in the Armed Activities case.[172] This debate on the relationship between IHL and HRL has continued in the wake of the Wall case and has been described as "a renewed battle between the proponents of the theories of complementarity and separation".[173] There is only one plausible solution under 'horizontal' international law, where each convention makes up its own legal regime, namely that "IHL and HRL are two distinct, though complementary, branches of law".[174] There is no hierarchical relationship between these and related fields of law like international refugee law and ICL, and the concern should be to seek clarity on the ordinary meaning of the provision at hand, guided by the object and purpose of each regime or instrument or by the particular norm in question.[175] As has been noted, in grey areas such as military occupation, insurgencies, or the 'war on terror', complementary application of different branches of international law not only may be in accordance with law, but "may guarantee the respect of the rule of law".[176]

In an interpretative process where two rules seem to conflict rather than complement each other, the practical way to solve the problem might be to interpret the norms in light of the presumption that a conflict was not intended. As observed by the Appeals Chamber of the ICTY in Tadić, with respect to a possible conflict between customary law and an SC resolution:

---

[171] *Ibid.*

[172] ICJ, *Armed Activities on the Territory of the Congo* (Democratic Republic of Congo v. Uganda), Judgment, *I.C.J. Reports 2005*, p. 166, paras. 216–20 (www.legal- tools.org/doc/ 8f7fa3/).

[173] Noëlle Quénivet, "The History of the Relationship between International Humanitarian Law and Human Rights Law", in Roberta Arnold and Noëlle Quénivet (eds.), *International Humanitarian Law and Human Rights Law: Towards a New Merger in International Law*, Brill/Martinus Nijhoff, Leiden, 2008, p. 12.

[174] Roberta Arnold, "Conclusions", in Arnold and Quénivet, 2008, p. 591, *supra* note 173.

[175] See UN High Commissioner for Refugees and ICTR, *Expert Meeting on Complementarities between International Refugee Law, International Criminal Law and International Human Rights Law: Summary Conclusions*, Arusha, Tanzania, 11–13 April 2011, conclusions nos. 1–4.

[176] Arnold, 2008, p. 592, *supra* note 174.

It is open to the Security Council – subject to peremptory norms of international law (*jus cogens*) – to adopt definitions of crimes in the Statutes which deviate from customary international law. Nevertheless, as a general principle, provisions of the Statute defining the crimes within the jurisdiction of the Tribunal should always be interpreted as reflecting customary international law, unless an intention to depart from customary international law is expressed in the Statute, or from other authoritative sources.[177]

It follows from the same statement that the *lex superior* principle must be adhered to even by the Security Council. Thus a rule seen as possibly conflicting with *jus cogens*, under one interpretation, may be construed under another interpretation as being in compliance with the *jus cogens* norm. In such a case, that alternate interpretation should be preferred. If the conflict between the two rules cannot easily be resolved through interpretation, the superior rule must prevail.

4.5. *Lex Lata* and *Lex Ferenda*

The universal crimes project has among its principal goals to plausibly describe and interpret international universal crimes law as it actually exists (*lex lata*).[178] The rule of law depends on the principle that it is possible to determine the correct interpretation of a rule (*lex lata*) within a legal order. Such an interpretation may be correct even when it is not the preferred legal solution on moral or political grounds. Lawyers adhering to the rule of law must accept a distinction between what the law is (*lex lata*) and what it ought to be (*lex ferenda*). In principle, two independent adjudicators should arrive at the same result with regard to the law if both apply the law at the same time in accordance with the relevant sources and established methodology.

In some cases, however, two different results might be equally plausible and arguable, due to the relative openness of legal judgments. In principle, the favoured interpretation of the law should be arguable in the context of the highest legal authority within the legal order that might de-

---

[177] ICTY, Appeals Chamber, *Prosecutor v. Tadić*, Judgment, IT-94-1-R, 15 July 1999, para. 296 (www.legal-tools.org/doc/8efc3a/).

[178] See the preface to this book, briefly explaining the universal crimes project and the four-part series on universal crimes entitled "Rethinking the Essentials of International Criminal Law and Transitional Justice".

cide on the issue. If a legal solution is only arguable within the context of a power structure or a setting that is closed to independent judicial review, the solution might be *de facto* correct within that structure but still not form part of *lex lata*. In other words, the conception of *lex lata* is closely linked to a substantive conception of the rule of law; that is, 'law' must be distinguishable from political, religious, or military 'power' expressed only formally in judicial disguise by quasi-judicial bodies. As we have pointed out earlier several times already, criminal law – in order to be perceived as criminal law proper – must adhere to certain fundamental principles. If it does not, the criminal law liability inflicted is hardly more than an exercise of power and a violation of *lex lata*.

When two different solutions to a legal question are plausible and arguable, the result will then depend upon the discretion of the adjudicator, guided by community interests and other legally relevant values internalised by the adjudicator. At a given time, it might thus be correct that one solution is as much *lex lata* as the other. This uncertain situation can change, however, when one solution is preferred in practice, as in the jurisprudence of the highest courts within the system. In this sense it is correct that courts, by clarifying a rule, also to some extent create law.

With regard to universal crimes, it is still an open question which court should be 'the highest' or most authoritative court at the international level. The immediate candidates today would seem to be either the ICJ or the ICC. Within the sphere of the ICTY and ICTR, the joint ICTY/ICTR Appeals Chamber was the highest judicial authority. Its jurisprudence was formally not legally subordinated to new jurisprudence originating from the ICC. With regard to the interpretation *lex lata* of a criminal law rule originating from customary international law or the general principles of law, the ICC might in the future be considered 'the highest court'. However, to date, the existing jurisprudence of different international courts provides different interpretative sources rather than being capable in itself of defining *lex lata* of ICL.

Legal authors are not in a position to create law. Their task is to analyse the law and comment on legal developments. In order to do that, they must offer their own views of the law as it is at a given time (*lex lata*). Otherwise, legal discussions become either purely theoretical (which, if well done, may serve legal science if not practice) or meaningless (as the reader will not know what the author is trying to communicate). In some cases authors may criticise the law and suggest better laws for the future (*lex ferenda*), but that too presupposes some conception of what the law actually is. In addition, authors have the option to criticise pronouncements of the law in decisions and other parts of the literature, flagging disagreement with other experts in order to seek the best interpretation when arguments for different views of the law are presented.

The universal crimes project, while basing itself on traditional legal analysis, is intended to explore ways to specify the concept of international crimes and the potential usefulness of a companion concept of universal crimes. The detailed analysis in the remainder of this volume is based on analysis of empirical materials relating to personal liability concepts in different legal documents and decisions that to a large extent are supposed to be general or concrete expressions of *lex lata* within the respective subsystems investigated. But it is also intended to inform debates about criminal law theory, and considerations *lex ferenda*, looking towards the ongoing and future development of international criminal law.

4.6. Concluding Remarks on Personal Criminal Liability

Finally, before we leave the methodological issues for now, we would like to point out that the structure of the general theory of criminal law liability is quite similar to the liability structure set forth in Part III of the Rome Statute. Here the legality principle is made clear in Articles 22–24, while the principle of conduct is set forth in Article 25(2) with reference to the crime descriptions in the statute (Articles 6–8*bis*). The principle of culpability is set forth in general form in Article 30, while some specific elements follow from other provisions, while the defences (excuses and justifications, including some particular jurisdictional limitations) are regulated in Articles 26, 27, 29, and 31–33. The principle of fair attribution of personal liability is applied in Articles 25 (generally) and 28 (command/ superior responsibility) on modes of participation/liability. It is thus interesting to note that Part III is indeed entitled "General Principles of Criminal Law" and closely resembles – at the operational fourth level of the general theory – the second-level fundamental principles and third-level secondary principles of our general theory as developed and explained in Chapter 2 of this book.

In conclusion, although the Rome Statute is not necessarily equivalent to general international law, its structure implies *prima facie* compliance with the general theory of personal criminal law liability, which in turn also may be an indicator that the theory has some merit in the real world. This will, however, become clearer in the next empirical chapters, which examine operational liability concepts in ICL, both historically and recently.

5

___

Personal Liability Concepts in Treaties, Statutes, and Works of the ILC

5.1. Introduction

This chapter will begin with a historical overview of all instruments that have had a bearing on the development of international criminal law, with a specific focus on what these instruments have said about participation in the crimes regulated in this area of international law. These instruments pertain to international treaties, such as the 1948 Convention on the Prevention and Punishment of the Crime of Genocide (the Genocide Convention) and the 1949 Geneva Conventions and their 1977 Additional Protocols, as well as to the statutes of international criminal institutions, ranging from the first such institution after World War II, the International Military Tribunal in Nuremberg, to the most recent one, the Extraordinary African Chambers in Senegal.

However, as the focus of this book is universal rather than international crimes, another category of universal crimes is given attention as well in this chapter, namely transnational crimes such as terrorism and organised crime. The treaties regulating transnational crimes have both inspired forms of participation in international criminal law and provided a parallel historical insight into the thinking of the drafters of these treaties in terms of how to draw the parameters of the circle of persons to be held liable for such crimes. As the initial development with respect to participation in the area of transnational criminal law ('TCL') preceded such development in international criminal law, the overview of this subject matter in TCL will yield valuable information for this book.

Another angle covered in this chapter is the work of the International Law Commission, the legal 'think tank' of the United Nations. The ILC has examined international criminal law notions on a number of occasions and each time has considered not only the crimes to be established under international criminal law but also the means by which they can be committed. This examination, which started very soon after World War II and continues to this day, traces the evolution of the thinking of the most erudite and influential international legal scholars.

5.2. Punishable Participation in Treaties and Statutes of International Institutions

5.2.1. International Criminal Law

There is a conceptual difference between international criminal law and transnational criminal law. The most accepted approach with respect to international criminal law is that it refers to conduct that is prohibited under international law itself, and it is international law that provides for individual liability. The enforcement of this area of law manifests itself either directly, when international institutions apply international law, or indirectly, when states bring perpetrators before national courts through the application of extended forms of jurisdiction, primarily universal jurisdiction.[1] The international crimes discussed in this chapter, namely aggression, genocide, war crimes, and crimes against humanity, are the foremost examples of crimes that are enforced through both direct and indirect means.

5.2.1.1. Early Statements (after WWI and WWII)

The first international document addressing the issue of criminal liability for universal crimes – in this case only war crimes – was developed in 1919 after World War I ('WWI'). The issue of responsibility for the commission of war crimes was of such great importance to the postwar Paris Peace Conference that its Supreme Council in January 1919 established a special Commission on the Responsibility of the Authors of the War and on Enforcement of Penalties, with a dual purpose: to define the legal parameters of responsibility and to charge named individuals for specific war crimes.[2] The final report of this panel provided a lengthy list of behaviours that violated the laws of war, based on the 1907 Hague Convention. It also, for the first time, set out criminal liability for the offence of conducting aggressive war (with respect to Germany) and for violations of the clear dictates of humanity or crimes against humanity (with respect to Turkey). In addition to providing liability for particular crimes, the com-

---

[1]   See Robert Currie and Joseph Rikhof, *International & Transnational Criminal Law*, 2nd ed., Irwin Law, Toronto, 2013, pp. 10–20 and 325–26.

[2]   The commission had 15 members (hence the other name used for it, the Commission of Fifteen): two each from Britain, France, Italy, Japan, and the United States, and one each from Belgium, Greece, Poland, Romania, and Serbia.

mission also recommended the establishment of an international tribunal to prosecute war criminals.[3]

While the majority of the commission clearly intended to develop international law beyond the 1907 confines, this opinion was by no means unanimous. Two members of the commission, Japan and – especially – the United States, expressed concerns about a number of aspects of the majority report, such as the notions of crimes against humanity as a legal concept and of putting on trial a head of state for starting a war. They also opposed the establishment of an international tribunal, preferring instead a union of existing national military tribunals.[4] The final text of the peace treaties represented a compromise between the majority and minority views. The reference to crimes against humanity was maintained, as was a special tribunal to try the German kaiser, Wilhelm II, but the latter only on the charge of "a supreme offence against international morality and the sanctity of treaties", while the tribunals to try lesser war criminals became limited to inter-Allied tribunals or national courts martial of any of the allied countries.[5]

The report of the special commission does not go into any detail on modes of liability, but only states the following in general terms:

> All persons belonging to enemy countries, however high their position may have been, without distinction of rank, including Chiefs of States, who have been guilty of offences against the laws and customs of war or the laws of humanity, are liable to criminal prosecution.[6]

This approach was followed in the peace treaties with Germany (the Versailles Treaty) and Turkey (the Treaty of Sèvres) by stating "persons guilty of criminal acts".[7]

---

[3] See Joseph Rikhof, "The Istanbul and Leipzig Trials: Myth or Reality?", in Morten Bergsmo, CHEAH Wui Ling, and YI Ping (eds.), *Historical Origins of International Criminal Law, Volume 1*, Torkel Opsahl Academic EPublisher, Oslo, 2014, pp. 261–63 (www. legal-tools.org/doc/b75e70/).

[4] *Ibid.*

[5] Articles 227 and 229 of the Versailles Treaty and Article 227 of the Treaty of Sèvres.

[6] "Commission on the Responsibility of the Authors of the War and on Enforcement of Penalties: Report Presented to the Preliminary Peace Conference", in *American Journal of International Law*, 1920, vol. 14, no. 1/2, p. 117. See also ICTY, Trial Chamber, *Prosecutor v. Tadić*, Judgment, IT-94-1-T, 7 May 1997, para. 663 (www.legal-tools.org/doc/0a90ae/).

[7] Articles 227 and 229 of the Versailles Treaty and Article 227 of the Treaty of Sèvres.

While the intention had been to put war criminals on trial before international tribunals, due to the geopolitical situation after WWI only national trials in Germany and Turkey were held, and these countries applied their own laws with respect to liability.[8]

During and after World War II, the issue of how to deal with the atrocities committed during that war came to the fore. On 25 October 1941, US President Franklin D. Roosevelt and British Prime Minister Winston Churchill issued statements condemning German atrocities and affirming that, in Churchill's words, "retribution for these crimes must henceforward take its place among the main purposes of the war". The Soviet minister of foreign affairs, V.M. Molotov, followed with a similar statement on 7 November 1941. The impetus to take action against war criminals gained momentum with the issuance of the St. James Declaration of 13 January 1942, signed by nine occupied countries, and culminated in the Moscow Declaration of 1 November 1943, signed by the United Kingdom, the United States, and the Soviet Union. The latter declaration detailed the modalities of taking legal action against such perpetrators, stating that "they may be judged and punished according to the laws of these liberated countries" and "they will be brought back to the scene of their crimes and judged on the spot by the peoples they have outraged". It ended by saying that "the above declaration is without prejudice to the case of the major criminals whose offences have no particular geographical location and who will be punished by a joint declaration of the Governments of the Allies".

While there had been some discussions at the non-governmental level regarding the establishment of an International Criminal Court dealing with war crimes and other crimes committed during the war, this issue was first raised in a government setting on 20 October 1943 at the newly established United Nations War Crimes Commission ('UNWCC'). Further discussions took place between February and September 1944 and resulted, on 20 September, in a draft Convention for the Establishment of a United Nations Joint Court. Because of British and American concerns that the UNWCC had gone beyond its mandate in terms of defining its jurisdiction, which went as far as to include crimes committed in Germa-

---

[8] See Rikhof, 2014, pp. 263–82, *supra* note 3.

ny against German nationals, the UNWCC on 6 January 1945 made the following recommendations regarding the prosecution of war criminals:

> (1) That the cases should be tried in the national courts of the countries against which the crimes have been committed;
>
> (2) That a convention be concluded providing for the establishment of a United Nations court to pass upon such cases as are referred to it by the Governments;
>
> (3) That pending the establishment of such a court there be established mixed military tribunals to function in addition to the United Nations Court when the latter is established.[9]

The last issue in this recommendation had been the subject of discussion in the UNWCC since August 1944, because it had become clear that the creation of an international court would be subject to long delays and it was considered desirable to have other, interim institutions in place. Articles 228 and 229 of the Versailles Treaty as well as the Allies' national practices were cited as precedents for such a solution.

However, the two tribunals dealing with major war criminals, the International Military Tribunals in Nuremberg ('IMT') and Tokyo ('IMT-FE'), were both initiated by the United States. The first was the product of negotiations with France, the United Kingdom, and the Soviet Union, resulting in the London Agreement of 8 August 1945 and its attachment, the IMT Charter. The second was a result of a Special Proclamation of the Supreme Commander for the Allied Powers, General Douglas MacArthur, on 19 January 1946. The UNWCC only played an indirect part in the drawing up of the London agreement, although the statutes of both institutions incorporated concepts of the draft convention for an international criminal court and the work done on the mixed tribunals.[10]

The IMT Charter contained the following provisions regarding criminal liability:

---

[9] Harry M. Rhea, *The United States and International Criminal Tribunals: An Introduction*, Intersentia, Cambridge, 2012, pp. 63–64.

[10] See Rikhof, 2014, pp. 288–91, *supra* note 3. For a detailed analysis of the negotiations leading to the London Charter, see Lachezar Yanev, "Theories of Co-Perpetration in International Criminal Law", Ph.D. diss., Tilburg University, 2016, pp. 69–81, published as *Theories of Co-Perpetration in International Criminal Law*, Brill/Martinus Nijhoff, Leiden, 2018.

The following acts, or any of them, are crimes coming within the jurisdiction of the Tribunal for which there shall be individual responsibility:

(a) Crimes against Peace: namely, planning, preparation, initiation or waging of a war of aggression, or a war in violation of international treaties, agreements or assurances, or participation in a common plan or conspiracy for the accomplishment of any of the foregoing;

(b) War Crimes: namely, violations of the laws or customs of war. Such violations shall include, but not be limited to, murder, ill-treatment or deportation to slave labor or for any other purpose of civilian population of or in occupied territory, murder or ill-treatment of prisoners of war or persons on the seas, killing of hostages, plunder of public or private property, wanton destruction of cities, towns or villages, or devastation not justified by military necessity;

(c) Crimes against Humanity: namely, murder, extermination, enslavement, deportation, and other inhumane acts committed against any civilian population, before or during the war; or persecutions on political, racial or religious grounds in execution of or in connection with any crime within the jurisdiction of the Tribunal, whether or not in violation of the domestic law of the country where perpetrated.

Leaders, organizers, instigators and accomplices participating in the formulation or execution of a common plan or conspiracy to commit any of the foregoing crimes are responsible for all acts performed by any persons in execution of such plan.[11]

The wording in the constituting document of the IMTFE[12] was very similar: it only added "declared or undeclared" to the notion of war in the crimes against peace segment, while adding a separate sentence on responsibility to the crimes against humanity provision. Control Council Law No. 10 followed the same structure with respect to participation in crimes against peace as was done in the IMT and IMTFE documents, but it took a different approach with respect to the general provision of liability:

---

[11] Charter of the International Military Tribunal, Article 6.
[12] Charter of the International Military Tribunal for the Far East, Article 5.

Any person without regard to nationality or the capacity in which he acted, is deemed to have committed a crime as defined in paragraph 1 of this Article, if he was

(a) a principal or

(b) was an accessory to the commission of any such crime or ordered or abetted the same or

(c) took a consenting part therein or

(d) was connected with plans or enterprises involving its commission or

(e) was a member of any organization or group connected with the commission of any such crime or

(f) with reference to paragraph 1 (a) if he held a high political, civil or military (including General Staff) position in Germany or in one of its Allies, co-belligerents or satellites or held high position in the financial, industrial or economic life of any such country.[13]

There has been very considerable jurisprudence with respect to parameters of criminal liability by the two international tribunals, by the military tribunals operating in occupied Germany under the auspices of Control Council Law No. 10, and by national courts in both Europe and Asia. The types of participation referred to by some of these institutions are discussed in Section 2.1.2., while an overview of the principles can be found in the *Law Reports of Trials of War Criminals*, volume XV.[14]

5.2.1.2. Modern Statements (since 1949)

Between World War II and the establishment of the first international criminal tribunal in 1993, the ICTY, there was a lengthy hiatus in the development of principles of complicity in international criminal law. This gap was interrupted only briefly and early by some provisions in the 1948

---

[13]   Control Council Law No. 10, Article II(2) (www.legal-tools.org/doc/ffda62/). For an analysis of this provision, see Yanev, 2016, pp. 104–8, see *supra* note 10.

[14]   United Nations War Crimes Commission, *Law Reports of Trials of War Criminals*, vol. XV, HMSO, London, 1949, pp. 49–79. See also ICTY, Appeals Chamber, *Prosecutor v. Tadić*, Judgment, IT-94-1-A, 15 July 1999, paras. 195–213 (www.legal-tools.org/doc/8efc3a/); Kai Ambos, *Treatise on International Criminal Law*, vol. 1, *Foundations and General Part*, Oxford University Press, Oxford, 2013, pp. 105–13; Yanev, 2016, pp. 117–29, see *supra* note 10; and Marina Aksenova, *Complicity in International Criminal Law*, Hart, Oxford, 2016, pp. 64–71.

Genocide Convention and the 1949 Geneva Conventions (supplemented by their 1977 Additional Protocols). Article III of the Genocide Convention states:

> The following acts shall be punishable:
>
> (a) Genocide;
>
> (b) Conspiracy to commit genocide;
>
> (c) Direct and public incitement to commit genocide;
>
> (d) Attempt to commit genocide;
>
> (e) Complicity in genocide.[15]

Article V makes it the responsibility of states that ratify the Convention to enact the necessary legislation to give effect to the provisions of the treaty and to provide effective penalties for persons guilty of genocide or any of the other acts enumerated in Article III.

Furthermore, Article VI indicates that persons can be tried for genocide either by the state in whose territory the crime was committed, or by an international penal tribunal whose jurisdiction has been accepted by the states parties to the Convention.

Each of the four Geneva Conventions has only two articles that set out the principles related to individual criminal responsibility for the commission of war crimes (or in the parlance of these conventions, "grave breaches").[16] In each convention, the first[17] of these dual provisions obliges states, as with the Genocide Convention, to enact legislation necessary to provide effective penal sanctions for persons committing, or ordering to be committed, any of the grave breaches of these conventions, and also imposes a prosecution or extradition obligation[18] on these states. The sec-

---

[15] For a brief overview of the negotiations leading to this article, see William A. Schabas, *Genocide in International Law: The Crime of Crimes*, 2nd ed., Cambridge University Press, Cambridge, 2009, pp. 82–83.

[16] For an overview of the background to these articles, see "Geneva Conventions of 1949 and Additional Protocols, and Their Commentaries" on the International Committee of the Red Cross web site.

[17] Article 49 in the First Geneva Convention (www.legal-tools.org/doc/baf8e7/), Article 50 in the Second Geneva Convention (www.legal-tools.org/doc/0d0216/), Article 129 in the Third Geneva Convention (www.legal-tools.org/doc/365095/), and Article 146 in the Fourth Geneva Convention (www.legal-tools.org/doc/d5e260/).

[18] This obligation is expressed as follows in the second paragraph of these articles: "Each High Contracting Party shall be under the obligation to search for persons alleged to have

ond provision sets out the parameters of the grave breaches to which the convention refers.[19]

Additional Protocol I to the Geneva Conventions, dealing with international armed conflicts,[20] contains three articles that expand on the notion of grave breaches, namely Articles 85(1), 86, and 87, which state the following:

> Article 85(1)
>
> 1. The provisions of the Conventions relating to the repression of breaches and grave breaches, supplemented by this Section, shall apply to the repression of breaches and grave breaches of this Protocol.
>
> Article 86
>
> 1. The High Contracting Parties and the Parties to the conflict shall repress grave breaches, and take measures necessary to suppress all other breaches, of the Conventions or of this Protocol which result from a failure to act when under a duty to do so.
>
> 2. The fact that a breach of the Conventions or of this Protocol was committed by a subordinate does not absolve his superiors from penal or disciplinary responsibility, as the case

---

committed, or to have ordered to be committed, such grave breaches, and shall bring such persons, regardless of their nationality, before its own courts. It may also, if it prefers, and in accordance with the provisions of its own legislation, hand such persons over for trial to another High Contracting Party concerned, provided such High Contracting Party has made out a 'prima facie' case".

[19] The most extensive iteration can be found in Article 147 of the Fourth Geneva Convention, which says: "Grave breaches to which the preceding Article relates shall be those involving any of the following acts, if committed against persons or property protected by the present Convention: wilful killing, torture or inhuman treatment, including biological experiments, wilfully causing great suffering or serious injury to body or health, unlawful deportation or transfer or unlawful confinement of a protected person, compelling a protected person to serve in the forces of a hostile Power, or wilfully depriving a protected person of the rights of fair and regular trial prescribed in the present Convention, taking of hostages and extensive destruction and appropriation of property, not justified by military necessity and carried out unlawfully and wantonly". Articles 85(3) and (4) of Additional Protocol I add another 12 grave breaches while Article 85(5) equates grave breaches with the notion of war crimes.

[20] Protocol II, which complements Common Article 3 of the Geneva Conventions, the only article addressing non-international armed conflicts, does not contain any provision in regard to individual criminal responsibility.

may be, if they knew, or had information which should have enabled them to conclude in the circumstances at the time, that he was committing or was going to commit such a breach and if they did not take all feasible measures within their power to prevent or repress the breach.

Article 87

1. The High Contracting Parties and the Parties to the conflict shall require military commanders, with respect to members of the armed forces under their command and other persons under their control, to prevent and, where necessary, to suppress and to report to competent authorities breaches of the Conventions and of this Protocol.

2. In order to prevent and suppress breaches, High Contracting Parties and Parties to the conflict shall require that, commensurate with their level of responsibility, commanders ensure that members of the armed forces under their command are aware of their obligations under the Conventions and this Protocol.

3. The High Contracting Parties and Parties to the conflict shall require any commander who is aware that subordinates or other persons under his control are going to commit or have committed a breach of the Conventions or of this Protocol, to initiate such steps as are necessary to prevent such violations of the Conventions or this Protocol, and, where appropriate, to initiate disciplinary or penal action against violators thereof.

Only at the end of the twentieth century did a number of statutes of international and internationalised tribunals build on the fragmentary nature of the Genocide Convention and Geneva Conventions by also including responsibility for the commission of crimes against humanity, in addition to genocide and war crimes, thereby continuing the tradition started immediately after WWII.

The statute of the ICTY set a precedent in formulating the parameters of the forms of participation, and the ICTR, SCSL, ECCC, and EAC followed suit. The ICC has a more exhaustive enumeration of forms of extended liability.[21]

---

[21]   For a schematic overview of the forms of participation in these statutes, see Tables 1 and 2 in Chapter 3. For the jurisprudence of these tribunals as well as the ICC, see chapter 7.

The ICTY Statute has two provisions on forms of participation, Articles 4(3) and 7. Article 4(3) is identical to Article III of the Genocide Convention, quoted above. Article 7 states the following, using wording, in paragraph 3, that is similar to that in Articles 86(2) and 87(3) of Additional Protocol I above:[22]

> 1. A person who planned, instigated, ordered, committed or otherwise aided and abetted in the planning, preparation or execution of a crime referred to in articles 2 to 5 of the present Statute, shall be individually responsible for the crime. [...]
>
> 3. The fact that any of the acts referred to in articles 2 to 5 of the present Statute was committed by a subordinate does not relieve his superior of criminal responsibility if he knew or had reason to know that the subordinate was about to commit such acts or had done so and the superior failed to take the necessary and reasonable measures to prevent such acts or to punish the perpetrators thereof.[23]

---

[22] While the wording of Article 7 is different from that in the IMT and the IMTFE Statutes, there a similarity in terms of the range of perpetrators, as the three instruments hold liable persons involved in both the preparatory and implementation phases of criminal activity at all levels of a criminal enterprise. However, the ICTY Statute is more limited as it does not include either conspiracy or membership within its parameters; see also the next footnote.

[23] These provisions were inspired by the *Report of the Secretary-General pursuant to paragraph 2 of Security Council Resolution 808 (1993)*, S/25704, 3 May 1993 (www.legal-tools.org/doc/c2640a/). Paragraph 51 of the report indicates that in the view of the secretary-general, the notion of membership should no longer be retained as a source of liability, while paragraph 54 says: "The Secretary-General believes that all persons who participate in the planning, preparation or execution of serious violations of international humanitarian law in the former Yugoslavia contribute to the commission of the violation and are, therefore, individually responsible". Paragraph 56 further states: "A person in a position of superior authority should, therefore, be held individually responsible for giving the unlawful order to commit a crime under the present statute. But he should also be held responsible for failure to prevent a crime or to deter the unlawful behaviour of his subordinates. This imputed responsibility or criminal negligence is engaged if the person in superior authority knew or had reason to know that his subordinates were about to commit or had committed crimes and yet failed to take the necessary and reasonable steps to prevent or repress the commission of such crimes or to punish those who had committed them". See also ICTY, Appeals Chamber, *Prosecutor v. Tadić*, Judgment, IT-94-1-A, 15 July 1999, paras. 186–90 (www.legal-tools.org/doc/8efc3a/).

The wording of the ICTR Statute[24] is identical to that of the ICTY in its provisions on genocide (Article 2) as well as participation (Article 6). The SCSL Statute concurs on the topic of participation (Article 6), although this document makes no reference to genocide. The EAC also has the same language for forms of participation as the ICTY, ICTR, and SCSL (Article 10), but it has no special forms of participation for genocide, even though genocide as a crime falls within its jurisdiction (Article 5). The result is that complicity in genocide has been replaced in the EAC Statute by the general article regarding participation, while there are no inchoate crimes as part of this statute.

The ECCC Statute has very similar language to the above four documents but has deleted the words "in the planning, preparation or execution", while retaining the same general forms of participation in its Article 29(1). It has also added one more requirement to the notion of superior responsibility, compared to the wording in the other documents, namely, "if the superior had effective command and control or authority and control over the subordinate". The connection between forms of participation in genocide and the general forms of participation was clarified by omitting "complicity in genocide" and replacing "genocide" with "participation in acts of genocide". At the same time, of the three inchoate crimes related to genocide set out in the Genocide Convention and the ICTY and ICTR Statutes, namely direct and public incitement, conspiracy, and attempt, only the last two were retained (Article 4).

The ICC Statute uses different language altogether than its predecessors, which is contained in its Article 25(3), as follows:

> 3. In accordance with this Statute, a person shall be criminally responsible and liable for punishment for a crime within the jurisdiction of the Court if that person:
>
> > (a) Commits such a crime, whether as an individual, jointly with another or through another person, regardless of whether that other person is criminally responsible;

---

[24] The *Final Report of the Commission of Experts established pursuant to Security Council resolution 935 (1994)*, S/1994/1125, 4 October 1994, Annex (www.legal-tools.org/doc/4c5f41/), is even more general than the report cited in *supra* note 23. In paragraph 128 it recognised the principle that individuals can be held responsible, while in paragraph 130 it offers a similarly general statement regarding command responsibility.

(b) Orders, solicits or induces the commission of such a crime which in fact occurs or is attempted;

(c) For the purpose of facilitating the commission of such a crime, aids, abets or otherwise assists in its commission or its attempted commission, including providing the means for its commission;

(d) In any other way contributes to the commission or attempted commission of such a crime by a group of persons acting with a common purpose. Such contribution shall be intentional and shall either:

(i) Be made with the aim of furthering the criminal activity or criminal purpose of the group, where such activity or purpose involves the commission of a crime within the jurisdiction of the Court; or

(ii) Be made in the knowledge of the intention of the group to commit the crime;

(e) In respect of the crime of genocide, directly and publicly incites others to commit genocide;

(f) Attempts to commit such a crime by taking action that commences its execution by means of a substantial step, but the crime does not occur because of circumstances independent of the person's intentions. However, a person who abandons the effort to commit the crime or otherwise prevents the completion of the crime shall not be liable for punishment under this Statute for the attempt to commit that crime if that person completely and voluntarily gave up the criminal purpose.

3 bis. In respect of the crime of aggression, the provisions of this article shall apply only to persons in a position effectively to exercise control over or to direct the political or military action of a State.

The latter provision is supplemented by Article 8*bis*, which states, in language identical to that used in the IMT Charter, "For the purpose of this Statute, 'crime of aggression' means the planning, preparation, initiation or execution, by a person in a position effectively to exercise control over or to direct the political or military action of a State, of an act of aggression which, by its character, gravity and scale, constitutes a manifest violation of the Charter of the United Nations".

5.2.2. Transnational Criminal Law

5.2.2.1. Introduction

Transnational criminal law covers the indirect suppression by international law through domestic criminal law of criminal activities that have actual or potential transboundary effects. Enforcement of transnational law is always indirect, accomplished through prosecution by domestic courts. While international criminal law can have as its sources all three forms recognised by general international law, transnational criminal law has only treaties as its sources, although these treaties can be international or regional agreements. These so-called suppression treaties have three essential features that distinguish them from international criminal law arrangements and from other international treaties. The first of these aspects is the obligation of states parties to criminalise within their domestic laws the conduct that is the subject matter of the treaties. Second, these treaties oblige states parties to utilise an expanded version of jurisdiction that goes beyond the one usually utilised at the domestic level, namely territorial or active nationality jurisdiction. They can also include passive nationality jurisdiction or protective jurisdiction; however, the treaties do not go so far as to include universal jurisdiction. The last and most important feature of these treaties is the fact that they oblige states parties either to prosecute perpetrators of the crimes mentioned in the treaties or to extradite such persons (called the *aut dedere aut judicare* obligation).[25]

A number of crimes have had a trajectory from transnational to international crimes. As indicated above, both genocide and war crimes had their genesis in treaties containing some of the just-mentioned features, namely the Genocide Convention and the Geneva Conventions with their Additional Protocols.

There are a number of crimes originating in the transnational sphere which have not been made subject to international jurisdiction, but which have become subject to universal jurisdiction by agreement of the international community; thus they have become part of international criminal law in a broad sense. The crimes in this category are piracy, torture, slavery, and apartheid, while the status of terrorism is uncertain at the moment.[26] To be sure, three of these five crimes (torture, slavery, and apart-

---

[25] Currie and Rikhof, 2013, pp. 327–34, see *supra* note 1.
[26] *Ibid.*, pp. 290–322.

heid) are also part of international criminal law as underlying crimes, but only if they have been committed with certain overarching elements in place: for example, committed during an armed conflict or in a systematic or widespread fashion.

This section will discuss the forms of participation contained in the suppression treaties dealing with all crimes except the core ones discussed above under international criminal law,[27] but only those treaties negotiated at the international level.[28]

5.2.2.2.   Modalities of Participation in Suppression Treaties

Before World War II there were already a number of suppression treaties, the most important of which were the 1910 International Convention for the Suppression of the White Slave Traffic, the 1921 International Convention for the Suppression of the Traffic in Women and Children, the 1929 International Convention for the Suppression of Counterfeiting Currency, the 1936 Convention for the Suppression of the Illicit Traffic in Dangerous Drugs, and the 1937 Convention for the Prevention and Punishment of Terrorism.[29]

The 1910 Trafficking Convention only refers to direct involvement,[30] while the related 1921 Trafficking Convention refers to the obliga-

---

[27]   For an overview of the general aspects of these crimes, see *ibid.*, pp. 337–434.

[28]   For a comprehensive overview of all the treaties, see M. Cherif Bassiouni and Edward M. Wise, *Aut dedere aut judicare: The Duty to Extradite or Prosecute in International Law*, Brill, The Hague, 1995, which mentions over 100 international instruments, divided into 24 groups. The ILC points to 61 such treaties in *Report of the International Law Commission, Sixty-second Session* (2010), A/65/10, p. 332, para. 337. This in turn relied on a document prepared by the ILC Secretariat that set out these treaties, *Survey of Multilateral Conventions which may be of relevance for the work of the International Law Commission on the topic "The obligation to extradite or prosecute (aut dedere aut judicare)": Study by the Secretariat*, A/CN.4/630, 18 June 2010, pp. 79–96 (Annex) (www.legal-tools.org/doc/4eded1/).

[29]   There is also the 1926 Slavery Convention, but as it does not involve any criminalisation it is not further discussed here.

[30]   Article 1 says, "Whoever, in order to gratify the passions of another person, has procured, enticed, or led away, even with her consent, a woman or girl under age, for immoral purposes, shall be punished, notwithstanding that the various acts constituting the offence may have been committed in different countries". Article 2 indicates, "Whoever, in order to gratify the passions of another person, has, by fraud, or by means of violence, threats, abuse of authority, or any other method of compulsion, procured, enticed, or led away a

tion of states to prosecute persons engaged in traffic in children as well as persons who committed offences that were prohibited in the 1910 Convention.[31] In addition, the 1921 Convention provided for punishment of "attempts to commit, and, within legal limits, of acts preparatory to the commission of the offences" prohibited in the 1910 Convention.[32] The 1929 Counterfeiting Convention refers to the commission of particular offences as well as intentional participation and attempt.[33] The 1936 Drugs Convention follows the same structure as the 1929 Counterfeiting Convention by penalising the commission of offences related to the subject matter of the treaty as well as intentional participation and attempt, but it also adds conspiracy.[34]

The last pre-WWII treaty, the 1937 Terrorism Convention, went the furthest in criminalising preparatory acts as well as the circle of perpetrators by including, in addition to attempt:[35]

1) Conspiracy to commit any such act;

2) Any incitement to any such act, if successful;

3) Direct public incitement to any acts mentioned under heads (1), (2) or (3) of Article 2, whether the incitement be successful or not;

4) Wilful participation in any such act;

5) Assistance, knowingly given, towards the commission of any such act.[36]

Since World War II there have been many suppression treaties with similar features in the area of participation, which are shown in Table 11. The table contains 30 treaties in six categories, three of which contain subcategories pertaining to different offences; within each category (and at times each subcategory), the treaties are listed chronologically.

---

woman or girl over age, for immoral purposes, shall also be punished, notwithstanding that the various acts constituting the offence may have been committed in different countries".

[31] Article 2.
[32] Article 3.
[33] Article 3.
[34] Article 2.
[35] Article 2(4).
[36] Article 3. This wording is similar to forms of participation set out in the Genocide Convention.

Category	Offence	Treaty	Direct participation[37]	Other forms of participation
Terrorism[38]	Offences on aircraft	1970 Hague Convention[39]	commits[40]	- attempt - accomplice[41]
		1971 Montreal Convention[42]	commits[43]	- attempt - accomplice[44]
		1988 Montreal Protocol[45]	commits[46]	- attempt[47]

---

[37] 'Commits' in this column indicates that the activity of interest is the one referred to in the subject matter of the treaty.

[38] The 1963 Convention on Offences and Certain Other Acts Committed on Board Aircraft, or Tokyo Convention (www.legal-tools.org/doc/97e04a/), which was amended by the 2014 Protocol to Amend the Convention on Offences and Certain Other Acts Committed on Board Aircraft, does not include criminalisation and is therefore not included in this table. The same is the case for the 1991 Convention on the Marking of Plastic Explosives for the Purpose of Detection (www.legal-tools.org/doc/126466/).

[39] Convention for the Suppression of Unlawful Seizure of Aircraft (www.legal-tools.org/doc/42b7df/).

[40] Article 1(a).

[41] Article 1(b).

[42] Convention for the Suppression of Unlawful Acts against the Safety of Civil Aviation (www.legal-tools.org/doc/c6856a/).

[43] Article 1(1).

[44] Article 1(2).

[45] Protocol for the Suppression of Unlawful Acts of Violence at Airports Serving International Civil Aviation (www.legal-tools.org/doc/bca29e/).

[46] Article II(1).

[47] Article II(2).

Category	Offence	Treaty	Direct participation[37]	Other forms of participation
Terrorism	Offences on aircraft	2010 Beijing Convention[48]	commits[49]	- attempt - organises - directs - participates as an accomplice - assisting after the fact[50] - conspiracy - common purpose[51] - threat[52]
		2010 Beijing Protocol[53]		- attempt - organises - directs - participates as an accomplice - assisting after the fact - conspiracy - common purpose - threat[54]

---

[48] Convention on the Suppression of Unlawful Acts Relating to International Civil Aviation.

[49] Article 1(1).

[50] Article 1(4).

[51] Article 1(5). The text of Article 1(5)(a) reads: "agreeing with one or more other persons to commit an offence set forth in paragraph 1, 2 or 3 of this Article and, where required by national law, involving an act undertaken by one of the participants in furtherance of the agreement". Article 1(5)(b) says: "contributing in any other way to the commission of one or more offences set forth in paragraph 1, 2 or 3 of this Article by a group of persons acting with a common purpose, and such contribution shall either: (i) be made with the aim of furthering the general criminal activity or purpose of the group, where such activity or purpose involves the commission of an offence set forth in paragraph 1, 2 or 3 of this Article; or (ii) be made in the knowledge of the intention of the group to commit an offence set forth in paragraph 1, 2 or 3 of this Article". The language in the latter provision is very similar to Article 25(3)(d) of the Rome Statute.

[52] Article 1(3).

[53] Protocol Supplementary to the Convention for the Suppression of Unlawful Seizure of Aircraft (www.legal-tools.org/doc/1715ac/).

[54] Articles 1(2), 1(3), and 1(4).

Category	Offence	Treaty	Direct participation[37]	Other forms of participation
Terrorism	Protected persons	1973 New York Convention[55]	commits[56]	- threat - attempt - participates as an accomplice[57]
	Hostage taking	1979 New York Convention[58]	commits[59]	- attempt - participates as an accomplice[60]
	Offences on ships and fixed platforms	1988 Rome Conventions[61]	commits[62]	- attempt - abets - threat[63]
	United Nations personnel	1994 New York Convention[64]	commits[65]	- threat - attempt - accomplice - organises - ordering[66]

---

[55] Convention on the Prevention and Punishment of Crimes against Internationally Protected Persons, Including Diplomatic Agents (www.legal-tools.org/doc/514b57/).

[56] Article 2(1)(a) and (b).

[57] Article 2(1)(c), (d), and (e).

[58] International Convention against the Taking of Hostages (www.legal-tools.org/doc/34c06d/).

[59] Article 1(1).

[60] Article 1(2).

[61] Convention for the Suppression of Unlawful Acts against the Safety of Maritime Navigation (www.legal-tools.org/doc/7d6ae4/) and the Protocol for the Suppression of Unlawful Acts against the Safety of Fixed Platforms Located on the Continental Shelf.

[62] Articles 3(1) and 2(1).

[63] Articles 3(2) and 2(2).

[64] Convention on the Safety of United Nations and Associated Personnel (www.legal-tools.org/doc/6bfa73/).

[65] Article 9(1)(a) and (b).

[66] Article 9(1)(c), (d), and (e).

Category	Offence	Treaty	Direct participation[37]	Other forms of participation
Terrorism	Terrorist bombing	1997 New York Convention[67]	commits[68]	- attempt[69] - participates as an accomplice - organises - directs - common purpose[70]
	Terrorist financing	1999 New York Convention[71]	commits[72]	- attempt[73] - participates as an accomplice - organises - directs - common purpose[74]
	Nuclear terrorism	2005 New York Convention[75]	commits[76]	- threat - attempt - participates as an accomplice - organises - directs - common purpose[77]

---

[67] International Convention for the Suppression of Terrorist Bombings (www.legal-tools.org/doc/dda995/).

[68] Article 2(1).

[69] Article 2(2)

[70] Article 2(3). Article 2.3(c) dealing with common purpose inspired Article 25.3(d) of the Rome Statute.

[71] International Convention for the Suppression of the Financing of Terrorism (www.legal-tools.org/doc/fc3fee/).

[72] Article 2(1).

[73] Article 2(4).

[74] Article 2(5).

[75] International Convention for the Suppression of Acts of Nuclear Terrorism (www.legal-tools.org/doc/5891b5/).

[76] Article 2(1).

[77] Articles 2(2), 2(3), and 2(4); regarding common purpose, this is the same text as used above in the Beijing Convention and Protocol. It should be noted that Articles 2(2), 2(3), and 2(4) in the Draft Comprehensive Convention against International Terrorism (A/59/894, Appendix II) use the same language to describe forms of participation.

Category	Offence	Treaty	Direct participation[37]	Other forms of participation
Organised crime	Organised crime	2000 Palermo Convention[78]	commits[79]	- conspiracy - attempt - organises - directs - aids - abets - facilitates - counsels - common purpose[80]
	Trafficking in persons	2000 Palermo Protocol[81]	commits[82]	- attempt - participates as an accomplice - organises - directs[83]
	Smuggling of migrants	2000 Palermo Protocol[84]	commits[85]	- attempt - participates as an accomplice - organises - directs[86]

---

[78] United Nations Convention against Transnational Organized Crime (www.legal-tools.org/doc/a2ce38/).

[79] Article 3(1).

[80] Article 5(1). The text regarding conspiracy and common purpose is the same as in the 2010 Beijing Convention and Protocol above.

[81] Protocol to Prevent, Suppress and Punish Trafficking in Persons, Especially Women and Children, supplementing the United Nations Convention against Transnational Organized Crime.

[82] Article 5(2)(a).

[83] Article 5(2)(b) and (c).

[84] Protocol against the Smuggling of Migrants by Land, Sea and Air, supplementing the United Nations Convention against Transnational Organized Crime.

[85] Article 6(1).

[86] Article 6(1).

Category	Offence	Treaty	Direct participation[37]	Other forms of participation
Organised crime	Manufac-turing and trading in firearms	2000 Palermo Protocol[87]	commits[88]	- attempt - participates as an accomplice - organises - directs - aids and abets - facilitates - counsels[89]
	Corruption	2000 Palermo Convention[90]	commits[91]	- participates as an accomplice[92]
	Proceeds of crime and money laundering	2000 Palermo Convention[93]	commits[94]	- conspiracy - attempt - organises - directs - aids - abets - facilitates - counsels - common purpose[95]

---

87 Protocol against the Illicit Manufacturing of and Trafficking in Firearms, Their Parts and Components and Ammunition, supplementing the United Nations Convention against Transnational Organized Crime (www.legal-tools.org/doc/068977/).

88 Article 5(1).

89 Article 5(2).

90 See above.

91 Article 8(1).

92 Article 8(3).

93 See above.

94 Article 6(1).

95 Article 6(2)(b).

Category	Offence	Treaty	Direct participation[37]	Other forms of participation
Drug trafficking	Drug trafficking	1961 Convention[96]	commits[97]	- intentionally participates - conspiracy - attempt - preparatory acts and financial operations in connexion with offences[98]
		1971 Convention[99]	commits[100]	- intentionally participates - conspiracy - attempt - preparatory acts and financial operations in connexion with offences[101]
		1972 Protocol[102]	commits[103]	- intentionally participates - conspiracy - attempt - preparatory acts and financial operations in connexion with offences[104]

---

96 Single Convention on Narcotic Drugs (www.legal-tools.org/doc/e1d7e5/).
97 Article 36(2)(a)(i).
98 Article 36(2)(a)(ii).
99 UN Convention on Psychotropic Substances (www.legal-tools.org/doc/201b9b/).
100 Article 22(2)(a)(i).
101 Article 22(2)(a)(ii).
102 Protocol Amending the Single Convention on Narcotic Drugs.
103 Article 14.
104 *Ibid.*

Category	Offence	Treaty	Direct participation[37]	Other forms of participation
Drug trafficking	Drug trafficking	1988 Vienna Narcotics Convention[105]	commits[106]	- publicly incites - induces - participates - association - conspiracy - attempt - aids - abets - facilitates - counsels[107]
Human rights	Slavery	1956 Supplementary Convention[108]	commits[109]	- attempt[110] - accessory - conspiracy[111]
	Apartheid	1973 Convention[112]	commits[113]	- participates - directly incites - conspiracy - directly abets - encourages - co-operates[114]

105 United Nations Convention against Illicit Traffic in Narcotic Drugs and Psychotropic Substances. (www.legal-tools.org/doc/e37039/)
106 Article 3(1)(a), (b), (c)(i), and (c)(ii).
107 Article 3(1)(c)(iii) and (iv).
108 Supplementary Convention on the Abolition of Slavery, the Slave Trade, and Institutions and Practices Similar to Slavery (www.legal-tools.org/doc/d038c8/).
109 Articles 3(1), 3(2)(a) (slave trade), and 5 (slavery).
110 Article 3(3) (slave trade).
111 Article 6 (slavery).
112 International Convention on the Suppression and Punishment of the Crime of Apartheid (www.legal-tools.org/doc/d9644f/).
113 Article III(a).
114 Article III(a) and (b).

Category	Offence	Treaty	Direct participation[37]	Other forms of participation
Human rights	Torture	1984 Convention[115]	commits[116]	- attempt - complicity - participates[117]
	Child sexual exploitation	2000 Protocol to the Convention on the Rights of the Child[118]	commits[119]	- attempt - complicity - participates[120]
	Enforced disappearance	2006 Convention[121]	commits[122]	- attempt - orders - solicits - induces - accomplice - participates[123] - superior liability[124]

---

[115] Convention against Torture and Other Cruel, Inhuman or Degrading Treatment or Punishment (www.legal-tools.org/doc/326294/).

[116] Article 4.

[117] Article 4.

[118] Optional Protocol to the Convention on the Rights of the Child on the Sale of Children, Child Prostitution and Child Pornography (www.legal-tools.org/doc/49a0e6/).

[119] Article 3(1).

[120] Article 3(2).

[121] International Convention for the Protection of All Persons from Enforced Disappearance (www.legal-tools.org/doc/33b31f/).

[122] Article 6(1)(a).

[123] Article 6(1)(a).

[124] Article 6(1)(b).

Category	Offence	Treaty	Direct participation[37]	Other forms of participation
Cyber-crime	Cyber-crime	2001 Budapest Convention[125]	commits[126]	- aids and abets - attempt[127]
		2003 Cybercrime Protocol[128]	commits[129]	- aids and abets[130]
Piracy	Piracy	1982 Law of the Sea Convention[131]	commits[132]	- participates - incites - facilitates[133]

Table 11. Forms of Participation in Suppression Treaties.

5.2.3. Conclusions Regarding Treaties and Statutes

This conclusion will look not only at the development of concepts of participation in international criminal and transnational criminal law, but also at possible cross-fertilisation between these two disciplines. With respect to ICL, the pivotal instruments with respect to participation have been the IMT Charter, the Genocide Convention, Additional Protocol I to the Geneva Conventions, the ICTY Statute, and the ICC Statute.

The IMT Charter had a number of unique features that went beyond what had been discussed with respect to participation before WWII, spe-

---

[125] Budapest Convention on Cybercrime.

[126] Articles 2 through 8 (offences against the confidentiality, integrity, and availability of computer data and systems), Article 9 (offences related to child pornography), and Article 10 (offences related to infringements of copyright and related rights).

[127] Article 10.

[128] Additional Protocol to the Convention on Cybercrime, concerning the criminalisation of acts of a racist and xenophobic nature committed through computer systems.

[129] Article 3 (dissemination of racist and xenophobic material through computer systems), Article 4 (racist and xenophobic motivated threat), 5 (racist and xenophobic motivated insult), and Article 6 (denial, gross minimisation, approval, or justification of genocide or crimes against humanity).

[130] Article 7.

[131] United Nations Convention on the Law of the Sea (www.legal-tools.org/doc/c7b2bf/).

[132] Article 101(a).

[133] Article 101(b) and (c).

cifically the preparatory acts of planning, preparation, initiation, and instigation, as well as membership in criminal organisations. Nonetheless, the notions of conspiracy and participation as accomplices had already featured in some of the pre-WWII transnational law treaties, such as the 1936 Drugs Convention and the 1937 Terrorism Convention for conspiracy, and those two conventions plus the 1929 Counterfeiting Convention for indirect participation. The 1921 Trafficking Convention had a general provision with respect to preparatory acts. Interestingly, while all four of these treaties penalise attempt, the IMT Charter does not.

This connection between pre-WWII transnational and post-WWII ICL treaties becomes most obvious when one compares the last treaty before the war and the first one after it, namely the 1937 Terrorism Convention and the 1948 Genocide Convention. The concepts and even the language regarding participation are strikingly similar. Both treaties refer to attempt, conspiracy, and direct and public incitement as inchoate crimes, while the Terrorism Convention is even clearer in explaining the inchoate character of direct and public incitement, adding, "whether the incitement be successful or not"; in this context, the Terrorism Convention goes further than the Genocide Convention by also prohibiting any incitement, successful or not. There is some difference in language when describing indirect participation, which is called "complicity" in the Genocide Convention and "assistance, knowingly given, towards the commission of any such act" in the Terrorism Convention.

While the connection between these two conventions, which on the surface deal with two different areas of international law, might be surprising, it should not be – for two reasons. First, in terms of essential features of ICL and TCL, this distinction was less clear during the WWII era, while some of the aspects of the Genocide Convention, such as national enforcement, would bring it within the character of a transnational treaty. Second, there is no logical reason when drafting a new treaty not to examine best practices from different but related areas of international law that have similar goals in dealing with international and dangerous criminality. In a more recent and compelling example, the drafters of the Rome Statute, when they were trying to define common purpose, found inspiration in the 1997 Terrorist Bombings Convention. Influence can also happen in the reverse direction, as when the 2006 Enforced Disappearance Convention included, for the first time in a transnational criminal law text, a concept that until that time had been within the exclusive domain of international humanitarian law and ICL, namely superior liability.

The ICTY Statute, which became the template for all subsequent international and internationalised tribunals, has a direct link in terms of language with the Genocide Convention when the statute defines that crime, while its wording with respect to command/superior responsibility bears a more than passing similarity to Additional Protocol I. Of the other forms of participation in the ICTY Statute, namely planning, instigating, ordering, committing, or otherwise aiding and abetting, the first two duplicate provisions in the IMT Charter, while aiding and abetting is a more contemporary version of participating accomplices; ordering can also be seen as a more legally accurate, albeit probably more limited, term than the IMT's references to leaders and organisers. There is no reference to JCE in either the IMT Charter or the ICTY Statute, but the ICTY jurisprudence used the term "committed" to infuse a meaning broader than only direct participation; in doing so it relied heavily on the case law developed not by the IMT but by the military tribunals operating in occupied Germany. This was based on Control Council Law No. 10 and its forms of participation, which included, among other aspects, being "connected with plans or enterprises involving [the] commission" of international crimes. This same jurisprudence included explicitly within this concept the notion of accessory after the fact. While this idea is well known in common law jurisdictions, it has also been used in transnational criminal law, such as in the 2010 Beijing Convention and Protocol.

While the IMT Charter, the Genocide Convention, and the ICTY Statute show connections to earlier international law (in the case of the IMT Charter) or to each other, and thus represent an incremental development in the area of ICL, on its face it would appear that the Rome Statute has introduced a number of new concepts not previously known or mentioned. These include committing jointly or through another person, in Article 25(3)(a); soliciting or inducing, in Article 25(3)(b) (in addition to ordering, which was already used in in the ICTY Statute); and common purpose, in Article 25(3)(d). Of the other three provisions in Article 25(3), aiding and abetting in Article 25(3)(c) was already known, albeit in different language in the IMT Charter, the Genocide Convention, and the ICTY Statute, while direct and public incitement to commit genocide in Article 25(3)(e) was contained in the Genocide Convention, as was attempt, which was expanded in Article 25(3)(f).

However, this superficial picture may give an inaccurate impression. Although some terms, especially in Rome Statute Article 25(3)(a), are different expressions of the same underlying concept (soliciting is similar to instigation, which was used in the IMT Charter and the ICTY Statute), and although the parameters of other notions, such as co-perpetration and common purpose, were already discussed in the ICTY jurisprudence, some other concepts can also be found in TCL; one example, that of common purpose in the Terrorist Bombings Convention, has been mentioned above. Other examples are inducing in the 1988 Vienna Narcotics Convention and the 2006 Enforced Disappearance Convention; incitement in the Vienna Narcotics Convention, the 1973 Apartheid Convention, and the 1982 Law of the Sea Convention in relation to piracy; and attempt, which has been a mainstay in virtually all transnational treaties starting from the very beginning with the 1921 Trafficking Convention.

Other forms of participation used in such TCL treaties are co-operation in the Apartheid Convention; association in the 1988 Vienna Narcotics Convention; "preparatory acts and financial operations in connexion" with drug offences in the 1961 and 1971 Drug Trafficking Conventions and the 1972 Drug Trafficking Protocol; and counselling in the 2000 Palermo Convention on organised crime.

Conspiracy is mentioned in the 1961 and 1971 Drug Trafficking Conventions as well as the 1972 Drug Trafficking Protocol and the 1988 Vienna Narcotics Convention; in Articles 5(1) and 6(2)(b) of the 2000 Palermo Convention dealing with organised crime and proceeds of crime and money laundering; in the 2010 Beijing Convention and Protocol on terrorism; and in the 1956 Slavery Convention and the 1973 Apartheid Convention. Lastly, while a number of treaties include issuing threats as a specific offence, some also include threatening as a form of participation. Among them are a number of terrorist conventions, namely the 1973 Convention on Protected Persons, the 1988 Convention and Protocol regarding offences on ships and fixed platforms, the 1994 Convention regarding United Nations personnel, the 2005 Nuclear Terrorism Convention, and the 2010 Beijing Convention and Protocol.

As a final observation, a trend common to both ICL and TCL conventions is that the number of forms of participation has increased over time. While the earlier conventions might refer to four or five types (with aiding and abetting as well as attempt always included), this has increased recently to as many as 10 types of involvement. This started with the 1988

Vienna Narcotics Convention and can also be seen in the 1998 Rome Statute, the 2000 Palermo Convention, the 2006 Enforced Disappearance Convention, and the 2010 Beijing Convention and Protocol.

5.3. Statements of the International Law Commission

5.3.1. Introductory Remarks

The International Law Commission has examined participation in universal crimes on four occasions: in the 1950 Principles of International Law Recognized in the Charter of the Nürnberg Tribunal and in the Judgment of the Tribunal; in the 1954 Draft Code of Offences against the Peace and Security of Mankind; in the 1996 updated Draft Code of Crimes against the Peace and Security of Mankind; and in the ongoing Crimes against Humanity Initiative, which started in 2015.

The last three projects will be examined in detail below, but it will be useful here to briefly set out the references to participation in the first document, which contains seven principles.[134] Principle I states that "any person who commits an act which constitutes a crime under international law is responsible therefor and liable to punishment", while Principle VII says that in general, "complicity in the commission of a crime against peace, a war crime, or a crime against humanity as set forth in Principle VI is a crime under international law". Principle VI with respect to crimes against peace also provides the same forms of participation as the statutes of the IMT and IMTFE, as follows:

> (i) Planning, preparation, initiation or waging of a war of aggression or a war in violation of international treaties, agreements or assurances;
>
> (ii) Participation in a common plan or conspiracy for the accomplishment of any of the acts mentioned under (i).[135]

The explanation of Principle I indicates that the IMT was very clear that individuals can commit international crimes.[136] The commentary on Principle VI states, "The terms 'planning' and 'preparation' of a war of

---

[134] The United Nations General Assembly, in its Resolution 177(II) of 1947, directed the ILC to formulate these principles and also to prepare a draft code of offences against the peace and security of mankind.

[135] *Yearbook of the International Law Commission, 1950*, vol. II, United Nations, New York, 1957, pp. 374–78 (www.legal-tools.org/doc/6465a9/).

[136] *Ibid.*, p. 374, paras. 98–99.

aggression were considered by the Tribunal as comprising all the stages in the bringing about of a war of aggression from the planning to the actual initiation of the war. In view of that, the Tribunal did not make any clear distinction between planning and preparation".[137] It further states, "The Commission understands the expression to refer only to high-ranking military personnel and high State officials, and believes that this was also the view of the Tribunal".[138] With respect to conspiracy the document quotes the IMT, which indicated that "the conspiracy must be clearly outlined in its criminal purpose. It must not be too far removed from the time of decision and of action. … The Tribunal must examine whether a concrete plan to wage war existed, and determine the participants in that concrete plan".[139]

Lastly, with respect to Principle VII, the ILC did not provide its own point of view but only set out what it thought were the views of the IMT regarding its Article 6, which is set out above in Section 5.2.1.2., saying, "the provision did not 'add a new and separate crime to those already listed' … the provision was designed to 'establish the responsibility of persons participating in a common plan' to prepare, initiate and wage aggressive war".

Then the commission comments that "interpreted literally, this statement would seem to imply that the complicity rule did not apply to crimes perpetrated by individual action", but "in practice, therefore, the Tribunal seems to have applied general principles of criminal law regarding complicity. This view is corroborated by expressions used by the Tribunal in assessing the guilt of particular defendants".[140]

The International Law Commission completed its report and submitted it to the General Assembly in 1950. The General Assembly requested that the ILC take into account these principles when preparing the 1954 Draft Code.[141]

---

[137] *Ibid.*, p. 376, para. 116.

[138] *Ibid.*, para. 117.

[139] *Ibid.*, pp. 376–77, para. 118.

[140] *Ibid.*, pp. 377–78, paras. 126–27.

[141] UN General Assembly, Resolution 488(V), 1950 (www.legal-tools.org/doc/af5bdc/).

5.3.2. Draft Codes of Crimes against the Peace and Security of Mankind

5.3.2.1. First Version

The first version of the draft code was completed in 1954, with four articles. It contained the following provision regarding participation in Article 2(13):

> (i) Conspiracy to commit any of the offences defined in the preceding paragraphs of this article; or
>
> (ii) Direct incitement to commit any of the offences defined in the preceding paragraphs of this article; or
>
> (iii) Attempts to commit any of the offences defined in the preceding paragraphs of this article; or
>
> (iv) Complicity in the commission of any of the offences defined in the preceding paragraphs of this article.[142]

The commentary to this provision says the following:

> The notion of conspiracy is found in article 6, paragraph (a), of the Charter of the Nürnberg Tribunal and the notion of complicity in the last paragraph of the same article. The notion of conspiracy in the said Charter is limited to the "planning, preparation, initiation or waging of a war of aggression, or a war in violation of international treaties, agreements or assurances", while the present paragraph provides for the application of the notion to all offences against the peace and security of mankind. The notions of incitement and of attempt are found in the Convention on Genocide as well as in certain national enactments on war crimes. In including "complicity in the commission of any of the offences defined in the preceding paragraphs" among the acts which are offences against the peace and security of mankind, it is not intended to stipulate that all those contributing, in the normal exercise of their duties, to the perpetration of offences against the peace and security of mankind could, on that ground alone, be considered as accomplices in such crimes. There can be no question of punishing as accomplices in

---

[142] *Yearbook of the International Law Commission, 1951*, vol. II, United Nations, New York, 1957, p. 136 (www.legal-tools.org/doc/f8df95/). The acts in question are aggression, genocide, crimes against humanity, and war crimes, the commentaries on which can be found at pp. 135–36 of this document.

such an offence all the members of the armed forces of a State or the workers in war industries.[143]

After transmittal of the report to the General Assembly in 1954, the latter decided to postpone further consideration until the question of defining aggression could be resolved.[144]

5.3.2.2. Second Version

The second attempt to develop a draft code started in 1981, with a request from the General Assembly,[145] and was completed in 1996.

The 20 articles of the 1996 Draft Code contain three provisions dealing with participation: Article 2, addressing individual responsibility in general; Article 6, dealing with the responsibility of the superior; and Article 16, which put a limitation on Article 2 when a crime of aggression has been committed.[146]

Article 2 reads as follows:

> 1. A crime against the peace and security of mankind entails individual responsibility.
>
> 2. An individual shall be responsible for the crime of aggression in accordance with article 16.
>
> 3. An individual shall be responsible for a crime set out in article 17, 18, 19 or 20 if that individual:
>
> (a) Intentionally commits such a crime;
>
> (b) Orders the commission of such a crime which in fact occurs or is attempted;
>
> (c) Fails to prevent or repress the commission of such a crime in the circumstances set out in article 6;
>
> (d) Knowingly aids, abets or otherwise assists, directly and substantially, in the commission of such a crime, including providing the means for its commission;

---

[143] *Ibid.*, pp. 136–37. The final commentaries in 1954 do not address this issue; see *Yearbook of the International Law Commission, 1954*, vol. II, United Nations, New York, 1960, pp. 149–51 (www.legal-tools.org/doc/114616/).

[144] UN General Assembly, Resolution 897(IX), 1954 (www.legal-tools.org/doc/1e2bbe/).

[145] UN General Assembly, Resolution 36/106, 1981 (www.legal-tools.org/doc/617503/).

[146] *Yearbook of the International Law Commission, 1996*, vol. II, part 2, United Nations, New York, 1998, pp. 18, 25, and 47 (www.legal-tools.org/doc/bb5adc/).

(e) Directly participates in planning or conspiring to commit such a crime which in fact occurs;

(f) Directly and publicly incites another individual to commit such a crime which in fact occurs;

(g) Attempts to commit such a crime by taking action commencing the execution of a crime which does not in fact occur because of circumstances independent of his intentions.

Article 6 states, "The fact that a crime against the peace and security of mankind was committed by a subordinate does not relieve his superiors of criminal responsibility, if they knew or had reason to know, in the circumstances at the time, that the subordinate was committing or was going to commit such a crime and if they did not take all necessary measures within their power to prevent or repress the crime". Article 16 says, "An individual who, as leader or organizer, actively participates in or orders the planning, preparation, initiation or waging of aggression committed by a State shall be responsible for a crime of aggression".

The commentaries with respect to those articles are much more detailed than in the 1950 Principles and the 1954 Draft Code.[147] In general, they make clear that the provisions in the 1996 Draft Code are based on or inspired by earlier documents addressing punishable participation. The ILC mentions specifically throughout this part of the document the IMT Charter, the Genocide Convention, the Geneva Conventions and their Additional Protocols, and the statutes of the ICTY and ICTR, as well at times its own earlier work in this area.

The commentary discussing Article 2(3)(a) regarding the actual commission of universal crimes indicates that the notion of 'actual commission' includes both commission and omission – the latter, as long as there is a duty to perform an act. Moreover, commission in general pertains to intentional rather than negligent or accidental conduct.[148]

---

[147] *Ibid.*, pp. 18–22, 25–26, and 42–43.

[148] *Ibid.*, p. 20, para. 7. In an earlier draft of this document, *Report of the International Law Commission on the work of its Forty-second Session* (1990), A/45/10, pp. 12–14, paras. 40–56, there is detailed discussion of the parameters of complicity; on p. 14, para. 52 (www.legal-tools.org/doc/f1e856/), there is a discussion of the perpetrators of a crime, including the observation that indirect perpetrators are not perpetrators in the strict sense but

A number of aspects of ordering in Article 2(3)(b) are noted, such as the fact that the person giving an order must be in a position of authority and must have used this authority to compel a subordinate to commit a crime, thereby contributing significantly to the commission of the crime.[149] While not mentioned in the report, these elements bear significant resemblance to the ICTY/ICTR jurisprudence discussed below, although that jurisprudence requires a substantial and direct effect on the commission of the crime rather than just a significant contribution.

Article 2(3)(c) will be discussed in the context of Article 6 below. Regarding Article 2(3)(d), apart from repeating the wording in the article, the only aspect of the commentary that adds something of significance is the explanation that the accomplice must knowingly provide assistance to the perpetrator of the crime, meaning that an individual who provides some type of assistance to another individual without knowing that this assistance will facilitate the commission of a crime would not be held accountable. It was also mentioned that assisting ex post facto is included in this article as long as the assistance had been agreed upon beforehand.[150] When this provision is compared with the ICTY/ICTR jurisprudence, it is clear that the wording of this provision in the Draft Code, which refers to "direct", was indeed part of the earlier jurisprudence of these institutions at the time the ILC report was written, but this requirement has been abandoned in cases since that time. The notion of accessory after the fact is the same as in the ICTY/ICTR jurisprudence.

The commentary to Article 2(3)(e) makes clear that this provision is meant to "ensure that high-level government officials or military com-

---

accomplices. The same document in its footnote 36 included the following draft article on complicity:

1. Participation in the commission of a crime against the peace and security of mankind constitutes the crime of complicity.

2. The following are acts of complicity: (a) aiding, abetting or provision of means to the direct perpetrator, or making him a promise; (b) inspiring the commission of a crime against the peace and security of mankind by, inter alia, incitement, urging, instigation, order, threat or abstention, when in a position to prevent it; [(c) aiding the direct perpetrator, after the commission of a crime, to evade criminal prosecution, either by giving him refuge or by helping him to eliminate the evidence of the criminal act].

[149] *Ibid.*, p. 20, para. 8.
[150] *Ibid.*, p. 21, paras. 11–12.

---

manders who formulate a criminal plan or policy, as individuals or as co-conspirators, are held accountable for the major role that they play which is often a decisive factor in the commission of the crimes covered by the Code", although "such a plan or policy may require more detailed elaboration by individuals in mid-level positions in the governmental hierarchy or the military command structure who are responsible for ordering the implementation of the general plans or policies formulated by senior officials". The commentary recognised that such a plan needs to be implemented by lower-level individuals, who are covered by the above Article 2(3)(a), while the parameters of orders given by superiors are set out in Article 2(3)(b). Accordingly, the commentary observes that "the combined effect of subparagraphs (a), (b) and (e) is to ensure that the principle of criminal responsibility applies to all individuals throughout the governmental hierarchy or the military chain of command who contribute in one way or another to the commission of a crime...". Lastly, the commentary makes clear that planning in the article is meant to convey criminal responsibility for formulating a plan or participating in a common plan, while the notion of conspiracy is limited to a situation in which the plan is actually carried out.[151]

---

[151] *Ibid.*, p. 21, paras. 13–15. In an earlier draft of this document, *Report of the International Law Commission on the work of its Forty-second Session* (1990), pp. 14–16, paras. 57–67, see *supra* note 148, there was a discussion and eventual disagreement as to whether conspiracy needed a subsequent act or not. The original language for this form of participation was in footnote 36:

The following constitute crimes against the peace and security of mankind:

1. Participation in a common plan or conspiracy to commit any of the crimes defined in this Code.

2. FIRST ALTERNATIVE

Any crime committed in the execution of the common plan referred to in paragraph 1 above attaches criminal responsibility not only to the perpetrator of such crime but also to any individual who ordered, instigated or organized such plan, or who participated in its execution.

2. SECOND ALTERNATIVE

Each participant shall be punished according to his own participation, without regard to participation by others.

In footnote 38 the language had become:

1. Participation in a common plan to commit any of the crimes defined in this Code constitutes conspiracy.

The commentary on Article 2(3)(f) explains that the sources for this provision are the IMT Charter, the Genocide Convention, and the ICTY/ICTR Statutes. For the IMT and the ICTY/ICTR Statutes it emphasises that the word "instigation" is used, but this is not mentioned in relation to the Genocide Convention. This results in some confusion in that this article only refers to incitement if the crime actually occurs and, according to the commentary, the person contributes substantially to that crime. This is indeed instigation as described in the ICTY/ICTR jurisprudence, but it is not the type of incitement set out in the Genocide Convention, which is an inchoate crime according to that same jurisprudence.[152] The commentary explains that incitement must be both direct and public (while the 1954 Draft Code, which is also listed as a source for this article, only requires direct incitement) and notes that private incitement would be covered by Article 3(1)(e) when people jointly plan or conspire to commit a crime. Lastly, it recognises that the public aspect can take place in a public place or by technological means of mass communication, such as radio or television.[153]

With respect to Article 3(2)(f), the commission makes it clear that attempt is the only example of an inchoate crime, in that no subsequent crime is necessary. The reason for including this inchoate crime is as follows: "First, a high degree of culpability attaches to an individual who attempts to commit a crime and is unsuccessful only because of circumstances beyond his control rather than his own decision to abandon the criminal endeavour. Secondly, the fact that an individual has taken a significant step towards the completion of one of the crimes ... entails a threat to international peace and security because of the very serious nature of these crimes".[154]

---

2. Conspiracy means any agreement between the participants to commit jointly a crime against the peace and security of mankind.

[152] See Chapter 7 for this jurisprudence.

[153] *Yearbook of the International Law Commission, 1996*, vol. II, part 2, p. 22, para. 16, see *supra* note 146.

[154] *Ibid.*, p. 22, para. 17. Attempt had already been discussed in *Report of the International Law Commission on the work of its Forty-second Session* (1990), pp. 16–17, paras. 68–76, see *supra* note 148, resulting in the following language:

1. Attempt to commit a crime against the peace and security of mankind constitutes a crime against the peace and security of mankind.

With respect to Article 6, on superior responsibility, the commentary indicates that two requirements must be fulfilled for responsibility to ensue: first, the superior must have known or had reason to know that a subordinate was committing or was going to commit a crime, and second, the superior failed to take all necessary measures to prevent or repress the conduct of his subordinate. For the latter requirement, the commission says that the superior must have had the legal competence to take such measures, which seems to reflect the ICTY/ICTR jurisprudence that a superior must have effective control.[155]

Regarding the first aspect, the commentary has the following to say:

> This criterion indicates that a superior may have the *mens rea* required to incur criminal responsibility in two different situations. In the first situation, a superior has actual knowledge that his subordinate is committing or is about to commit a crime. In this situation, he may be considered to be an accomplice to the crime under general principles of criminal law relating to complicity. In the second situation, he has sufficient relevant information to enable him to conclude under the circumstances at the time that his subordinates are committing or are about to commit a crime. In this situation, a superior does not have actual knowledge of the unlawful conduct being planned or perpetrated by his subordinates, but he has sufficient relevant information of a general nature that would enable him to conclude that this is the case. A superior who simply ignores information which clearly indicates the likelihood of criminal conduct on the part of his subordinates is seriously negligent in failing to perform his duty to prevent or suppress such conduct by failing to make a reasonable effort to obtain the necessary information that will enable him to take appropriate action.[156]

The commentary to Article 16 clarifies the wording "leader or organizer" by stating that criminal responsibility will only attach to those

---

2. Attempt means any commencement of execution of a crime against the peace and security of mankind that failed or was halted only because of circumstances independent of the perpetrator's intention.

[155] *Yearbook of the International Law Commission, 1996*, vol. II, part 2, p. 26, paras. 5–6, see *supra* note 146.

[156] *Ibid.*, p. 26, para. 5.

---

who played a decisive role in planning, preparing, initiating, or waging aggression.[157]

The second draft code was submitted to the General Assembly, which accepted it in 1996[158] and which decided a year later to hold a diplomatic conference for the establishment of an International Criminal Court.[159] The 1996 Draft Code became part of this conference, which was held in 1998.

5.3.3. Crimes against Humanity

In 2014 the ILC decided to add an item dealing with crimes against humanity, based on a 2013 recommendation of its working group on the long-term program of work.[160] Preparation of this item proceeded and in August 2017 the draft articles were submitted to the General Assembly to be forwarded to states for commentary by 1 December 2018.[161]

In 2016, the following was added to the document regarding crimes against humanity:

> Article 5 Criminalization under national law
>
> 1. Each State shall take the necessary measures to ensure that crimes against humanity constitute offences under its criminal law.
>
> 2. Each State shall take the necessary measures to ensure that the following acts are offences under its criminal law:
>
> (a) committing a crime against humanity;
>
> (b) attempting to commit such a crime; and
>
> (c) ordering, soliciting, inducing, aiding, abetting or otherwise assisting in or contributing to the commission or attempted commission of such a crime.

---

[157] *Ibid.*, p. 43, para. 4.

[158] UN General Assembly, Resolution 51/160, 1996 (www.legal-tools.org/doc/297df8/).

[159] UN General Assembly, Resolution 52/160, 1997 (www.legal-tools.org/doc/e7481e/).

[160] It had been commented that this should reflect both progressive development and codification of international law; see *International Law Commission, Sixty-eighth session (first part): Provisional Summary Record of the 3300th Meeting*, Geneva, 18 May 2016, A/CN.4/SR.3300, 3 April 2017, p. 13 (www.legal-tools.org/doc/fcd5db/).

[161] *Report of the International Law Commission, Sixty-ninth Session* (2017), A/72/10, chap. IV, p. 5, para. 14 (www.legal-tools.org/doc/7d6be0/).

3. Each State shall also take the necessary measures to ensure that the following are offences under its criminal law:

(a) a military commander or person effectively acting as a military commander shall be criminally responsible for crimes against humanity committed by forces under his or her effective command and control, or effective authority and control as the case may be, as a result of his or her failure to exercise control properly over such forces, where:

(i) that military commander or person either knew or, owing to the circumstances at the time, should have known that the forces were committing or about to commit such crimes; and

(ii) that military commander or person failed to take all necessary and reasonable measures within his or her power to prevent or repress their commission or to submit the matter to the competent authorities for investigation and prosecution.

(b) With respect to superior and subordinate relationships not described in subparagraph (a), a superior shall be criminally responsible for crimes against humanity committed by subordinates under his or her effective authority and control, as a result of his or her failure to exercise control properly over such subordinates, where:

(i) the superior either knew, or consciously disregarded information which clearly indicated, that the subordinates were committing or about to commit such crimes;

(ii) the crimes concerned activities that were within the effective responsibility and control of the superior; and

(iii) the superior failed to take all necessary and reasonable measures within his or her power to prevent or repress their commission or to submit the matter to the competent authorities for investigation and prosecution.[162]

---

[162] *Report of the International Law Commission, Sixty-eighth Session* (2016), A/71/10, chap. VII, pp. 242–48, para. 84 (www.legal-tools.org/doc/fcd5db/). This became Article 6 in *Report of the International Law Commission, Sixty-ninth Session* (2017), chap. IV, pp. 11–20 for the text and pp. 61–67 for the article about participation; see *supra* note 161.

The ILC explained in its report that both Articles 5(2) and 5(3) had their genesis in the Rome Statute.[163] It then provided the reasons for the difference between the Rome Statute text and its text in Article 5(2), saying:

> (13) In these various international instruments, the related concepts of "soliciting", "inducing" and "aiding and abetting" the crime are generally regarded as including planning, instigating, conspiring and, importantly, directly inciting another person to engage in the action that constitutes the offence. Indeed, the Convention on the Prevention and Punishment of the Crime of Genocide addresses not just the commission of genocide, but also "[c]onspiracy to commit genocide", "[d]irect and public incitement to commit genocide", an "[a]ttempt to commit genocide" and "[c]omplicity in genocide". The Convention on the Non-Applicability of Statutory Limitations to War Crimes and Crimes Against Humanity broadly provides that: "If any of the crimes mentioned in article I is committed, the provisions of this Convention shall apply to representatives of the State authority and private individuals who, as principals or accomplices, participate in or who directly incite others to the commission of any of those crimes, or who conspire to commit them, irrespective of the degree of completion, and to representatives of the State authority who tolerate their commission."
>
> (14) Further, the concept in these various instruments of "ordering" the crime differs from (and complements) the concept of "command" or other superior responsibility. Here, "ordering" concerns the criminal responsibility of the superior for affirmatively instructing that action be committed that constitutes an offence. In contrast, command or other superior responsibility concerns the criminal responsibility of the superior for a failure to act; specifically, in situations where the superior knew or had reason to know that subordi-

---

[163] *Report of the International Law Commission, Sixty-eighth Session* (2016), chap. VII, pp. 250–55, paras. 12 and 21 (the latter indicating that for command responsibility the same text as Article 28 of the Rome Statute was adopted); see *supra* note 162. This was based on the *Second Report on Crimes against Humanity by Sean D. Murphy, Special Rapporteur*, A/CN.4/690, 21 January 2016, pp. 23–35; see also, with same text, *Report of the International Law Commission, Sixty-ninth Session* (2017), chap. IV, pp. 64–65, paras. 13–15, *supra* note 161.

nates were about to commit such acts or had done so, and the superior failed to take necessary and reasonable measures to prevent such acts or to punish the perpetrators.

(15) Treaties addressing crimes other than crimes against humanity typically provide for criminal responsibility of persons who participate in the commission of the offence, using broad terminology that does not seek to require States to alter the preferred terminology or modalities that are well settled in national law. In other words, such treaties use general terms rather than detailed language, allowing States to spell out the precise details of the criminal responsibility through existing national statutes, jurisprudence and legal tradition. For example, the 2006 International Convention for the Protection of All Persons from Enforced Disappearance broadly provides: "Each State Party shall take the necessary measures to hold criminally responsible at least … [a]ny person who commits, orders, solicits or induces the commission of, attempts to commit, is an accomplice to or participates in an enforced disappearance." The language of draft article 5, paragraph 2, takes the same approach.

The confusion in this text with respect to the inchoate offences of incitement and conspiracy in paragraph 13 above – and which is reminiscent of the commentaries on these forms of participation in the 1996 Draft Code in regard to its Article 2(3)(e) and (f) – was already apparent during the plenary debates. The following comment was made:

The Drafting Committee had also discussed the possibility of referring expressly to "incitement" as one of the modes of participation listed in subparagraph (c). It had acknowledged the significance of that particular mode of liability in the context of crimes against humanity, but had eventually decided not to refer to it in paragraph 2, in part because the term "incitement" had not been included in certain international treaties, such as the Rome Statute, and in part because the concept did not exist in some national legal systems. Members of the Drafting Committee had considered that the concept of incitement was covered under the concepts of "soliciting" and "inducing" in subparagraph (c), and that would be reflected in the commentary.[164]

At least one member of the ILC had expressed concern about this approach to incitement, saying, "However, the concept of incitement should not be ignored: the *Radio Télévision Libre des Mille Collines* broadcasts were a prime example of the terrible effects that incitement could have. Even if the Special Rapporteur considered that the concept was covered in draft article 5 (1), she was of the view that it should be listed expressly".[165]

5.3.4. Conclusion Regarding ILC Statements

The aspiration of the ILC, stated as recently as 2016, to reflect both progressive development and codification of international law has not been accomplished in the area of criminal participation in universal crimes – not in the codification aspect and even less so in the progressive development of international law.

This can be seen from the very beginning. While the commission in the commentaries on its 1950 Principles accurately reflected the provisions of the IMT Charter with respect to crimes against peace, its discussion with respect to criminal participation in war crimes and crimes against humanity, where the only form of liability used is complicity, does not explain its own rationale for this choice. Nor does the commission state why the more expanded version in the IMT Charter – that leaders, organisers, instigators, and accomplices participating in the formulation or

---

[164] This latter approach was questioned by one member of the commission. *International Law Commission, Sixty-eighth session (first part): Provisional Summary Record of the 3312th Meeting*, Geneva, 9 June 2016, A/CN.4/SR.3312, 13 April 2016, p. 4. This document goes on to discuss common purpose and command responsibility on the same page in the following manner: "The Drafting Committee had noted that the concept of 'contributing' mentioned in subparagraph (c) covered the possibility of contributing to the commission or attempted commission of a crime against humanity by a group of persons acting with a common purpose. It had considered whether to elaborate further in the draft article on that particular mode of liability, but had considered it preferable to keep a more general reference, again given the differences in national criminal systems". Command responsibility is discussed on pp. 4 and 10–11 of this document.

[165] *International Law Commission, Sixty-eighth session (first part): Provisional summary Record of the 3300th Meeting*, 2016, p. 7, see *supra* note 160. For other criticism about the wording of this article and specifically why the wording of the Rome Statute was not followed more closely, see *ibid.*, pp. 6 and 13.

execution of a common plan or conspiracy to commit any of the foregoing crimes are responsible for all acts performed by any persons in execution of such plan – was not preferable.

While the same can be said in regard to complicity in the first Draft Code of 1954, which used language very similar to that of the Genocide Convention (conspiracy, incitement, complicity, and attempt), that version of the Code was at least progressive in that it extended the inchoate offences of conspiracy, incitement, and attempt to all four international crimes, namely crimes against peace, genocide, war crimes, and crimes against humanity.

The latter comment cannot be made with respect to the 1996 Draft Code. Some of the seven forms of participation, such as command responsibility, ordering, and aiding and abetting, are mostly in accordance with international criminal law as developed by the ICTY and ICTR. On the other hand, the treatment of conspiracy and incitement is at odds not only with this nascent ICTY and ICTR jurisprudence but also with the commission's own 1954 Draft Code, in that the 1996 version required a subsequent act for these forms of participation to be punishable. This is an incorrect understanding of the notions of conspiracy and incitement and also betrays a conceptual confusion between conspiracy and JCE for activities involving agreement for preparatory conduct, as well as between the notions of incitement and instigation.[166] These differences go beyond confusion when the ILC is using the particular terminology related to these concepts and indicate a fundamental lack of understanding of how universal crimes are carried out by collectivities.

It is rather disappointing that 20 years after the finalisation of the second Draft Code, the same conceptual inconsistency persists at the ILC, even with the plethora of jurisprudence from the various international tribunals as well as the ICC. The commission states, in explaining the reason for omitting both conspiracy and incitement from its enumeration of forms of participation, that "the related concepts of 'soliciting', 'inducing' and 'aiding and abetting' the crime are generally regarded as including planning, instigating, conspiring and, importantly, directly inciting another person to engage in the action that constitutes the offence". This, how-

---

[166] See Chapter 7, Sections 7.2.1.1., 7.2.1.3., 7.2.2.4., and 7.2.3.1., for the jurisprudence on these concepts.

ever, is an impoverished view of modes of participation in international criminal law, as was noted to some extent by one of the ILC's own members during the debates in 2016. While a reluctance to transfer the notion of incitement from the crime of genocide, which has been part of ICL since 1948, to crimes against humanity, or to reinstate conspiracy to its status before 1998, would be understandable – and while such an extension would indeed have been a progressive development of international law – it would have been better to state the criminal law policy for declining such an extension rather than to provide a confusing and likely incorrect legal justification for its views.

Apart from this general confusion, the ILC is also not convincing when it explains its choice of modes of participation during its recent debates with respect to crimes against humanity and its Article 5(2), although the iteration in Article 5(3) of command/superior responsibility follows closely the wording of Article 28 of the Rome Statute. In its commentary on Article 5(2), it indicates two sources for its listing of modes of participation, namely committing a crime against humanity, attempting to commit such a crime, and ordering, soliciting, inducing, aiding, abetting or otherwise assisting in or contributing to the commission or attempted commission of such a crime. These two sources are the 1998 Rome Statute and the 2006 International Convention for the Protection of All Persons from Enforced Disappearance. The latter lists the following forms of participation: "any person who commits, orders, solicits or induces the commission of, attempts to commit, is an accomplice to or participates in an enforced disappearance". When comparing the text of Article 5(2) with the text in the Enforced Disappearance Convention and Article 25(3) of the Rome Statute, it becomes clear that all concepts are borrowed from the Enforced Disappearance Convention and that the sequence and wording are borrowed from the ICC – but only for five of the seven forms listed in Article 25(3), as the other two are only partially used. To begin with the latter, the notion of commission in the ILC draft does not mention joint commission or commission through another person, and there is no mention of providing the means for a commission in the aiding and abetting portion. With respect to the two omissions, there is no mention at all of common purpose (except in a brief statement by the Drafting Committee) or, as stated above, of incitement.

There is no explanation, even though a commission member asked why the concepts set out in the Enforced Disappearance Convention are preferred over those in the ICC Statute. While the former is more recent, and its subject matter is one of the crimes against humanity in the ICC Statute, it would be difficult to argue that it has more value as a legal precedent than the ICC Statute.[167] The fact that almost 160 countries were present during the Rome conference, more than 120 of which voted for the Statute's adoption, and the fact that there are 139 signatories to the Statute, with 124 having ratified it, would strongly support the argument that the Rome Statute has become, or is close to becoming, an expression of liability norms that is safely within the parameters of customary international law although not likely expressing the outer limits of lawful forms of personal liability within current ICL.[168] In contrast, the Enforced Disappearance Convention has been signed by 97 countries and ratified by 57. None of this background or its effect on the legal status of either document was discussed by the commission.

Furthermore, with respect to the issue of common purpose, if the rationale was to use the example of the Enforced Disappearance Convention as a justification for the non-inclusion of this concept because of a concern that states would only readily accept forms of liability in this specific transnational treaty, this would represent an incomplete knowledge of the state of transnational law. In this area, there have been four conventions addressing aspects of terrorism between 1997 and 2010 (the earliest of which, the Terrorist Bombings Convention, was actually the inspiration for the notion in the Rome Statute), as well as two 2000 conventions dealing with organised crime. All have been widely accepted by states. As a result, there is a clear familiarity with the concept of common purpose at the domestic level.

---

[167] In addition, the Proposed International Convention on the Prevention and Punishment of Crimes against Humanity of August 2010, a project undertaken by a group of eminent international scholars, refers to Article 25 of the Rome Statute as the appropriate source for individual criminal responsibility in Article 4 on pp. 12–13 and its explanatory note on p. 13; see Leila Nadya Sadat (ed.), *Forging a Convention for Crimes against Humanity*, Cambridge University Press, Cambridge, 2011, Appendix I, pp. 359–402.

[168] See Chapter 4, Section 4.3.7., and Chapter 10, Section 10.6.

In conclusion, the work of the ILC, and especially its most recent effort in the area of punishable participation in international crimes, has been less than helpful for the development of these concepts.[169]

---

[169] For a different view, see Elies van Sliedregt, "The ILC Draft Convention on Crimes Against Humanity: Criminalization Under National Law", 29 April 2018 (available at SSRN web site).

6

_____

Personal Liability Concepts in the Literature

6.1. Introductory Remarks

Previous chapters have touched on the jurisprudence of international criminal institutions as well as academic commentary related to this jurisprudence. Chapters 7 through 9 will discuss liability concepts developed and applied in international as well as domestic jurisprudence. As we will see, the international jurisprudence is starting to play an increasingly important role in these domestic decisions, while courts at the national level have also started to pay more attention to academic writings in this area. At the international level, the criminal courts since the establishment of the ICTY have often made quite extensive use of ICL literature in solving their problems.

This chapter provides a bridge between Chapter 5, which discussed forms of participation in ICL and TCL treaties, statutes of international criminal institutions, and the work of the ILC, and the discussions of jurisprudence in the next three chapters. Academic commentary has provided insights into the relationship between the historical instruments just mentioned and the jurisprudence of the international criminal institutions, and for that reason alone an overview of the academic literature is an essential component of the empirical analysis in this book. However, the valuable contribution of academia does not end there. Books and articles examining the ICL jurisprudence, in particular, have proven indispensable; they not only clarify specific judgments issued by the international criminal institutions, but also either provide conceptual underpinnings for these decisions or propose broader theoretical approaches within which to place these new judicial developments. As this is also an objective of this book, we would be remiss not to include an empirical overview from different angles in order to present as complete a picture as possible.

Our literature review in this chapter begins in 2012. It includes publications spanning a particularly interesting and important period with respect to analysis of personal liability concepts in ICL. In 2012 eminent writers on this subject published two works that reviewed earlier academic contributions in this area of international criminal law. The present book incorporates the views set out in those two books where relevant, but more importantly, explains and builds on the extensive literature published over the six-year period of 2012–17. We conclude the literature review in July 2018. Unlike the treatment of the international jurisprudence, which we will attempt to canvas in a comprehensive manner, the literature review focuses on trends related to the most important aspects of modes of participation as analysed by noted authors in this field in generally well-known publications.

While early scholarly contributions to ICL focused primarily on its historical development, the substantive crimes, and procedural matters,[1] there has more recently been a proliferation of works focusing on personal liability theories and concepts relating to attribution of (individual) liability for participation in universal crimes.

In light of the rapid accumulation of a relatively vast body of research on the latter issues, the following literature survey is not meant to be exhaustive, in terms of either the number of scholarly contributions included or the depth in which each is presented. Rather, we review a representative selection of recent books and articles, ranging in content and scope from comprehensive works dealing with attribution of liability to those focusing on specific concepts or issues. The purpose of the survey is to identify and illustrate current trends, disagreements, and areas of confusion within the scholarly debate relevant to a theory of punishable participation in ICL. The review is primarily descriptive in nature, although some comments and assessments are made when appropriate. Ultimately, the review is meant to be another brick in the foundation for the further assessment of the general theory of personal liability and the autonomous ICL matrix of punishable participation in universal crimes (see Chapter 10).

As the question of attribution of individual liability has proven to be highly controversial, the ongoing discussions touch on a number of interrelated concepts. As a result, this chapter is structured by subtopics in order to best highlight both the trends in the themes discussed and the current scholarly expositions on each subtopic. A central aspect of the review is to demonstrate the need to develop a general theory of personal crimi-

---

[1] See Kai Ambos, *Treatise on International Criminal Law*, vol. 1, *Foundations and General Part*, Oxford University Press, Oxford, 2013, p. 103.

nal law liability in ICL, as called for by several prominent scholars. In particular, both Van Sliedregt, in her book *Individual Criminal Responsibility in International Law*, and Bassiouni, in his *Introduction to International Criminal Law*, stress the fragmented or pluralistic nature of ICL. It comprises not only different legal fields (in particular, criminal law, human rights law, and humanitarian law) and disparate legal traditions and culture (such as common law and civil law), but also several criminal law subsystems.[2] This complex mixture has given rise to a perceived 'identity crisis' in ICL. In particular, the system of imputation or attribution of personal liability has been viewed as under-theorised, or at least as lacking a unifying coherent theory with broad acceptance.[3]

This chapter distinguishes between authors who discuss punishable participation at large by addressing general aspects of personal liability (Section 6.2.) and authors who discuss specific concepts of participation (Section 6.3.). The distinction is not random, since the positions taken by various authors concerning the overarching themes – for example, with respect to methodological issues, fundamental principles of criminal law, or the unitary versus differentiated systems of liability – might be connected to views on specific liability concepts or the appropriate elements of implemented modes of liability, while the relationship is not always (made) clear. Many of the reviewed contributions are relevant to both categories, but often to a different degree.

6.2. Authors Discussing Punishable Participation at Large

6.2.1. Comparative Law versus Autonomous Law Approaches

Various authors advocate markedly different approaches to dealing with the above-noted identity crises of ICL. Some scholars criticise ICL for borrowing too heavily from domestic concepts, while others emphasise the appropriateness of scaling up the reliance on comparative law analysis.

---

[2] See the general discussion of ICL in Chapter 4, Section 4.2.

[3] Elies van Sliedregt, *Individual Criminal Responsibility in International Law*, Oxford University Press, Oxford, 2012, pp. 8–12; M. Cherif Bassiouni, *Introduction to International Criminal Law: Second Revised Edition*, Martinus Nijhoff, Leiden, 2012, p. cxxiv. See also Ambos, 2013, p. 164, *supra* note 1, on the specific category of aiding and abetting; and Kai Ambos, "Individual Liability for Macrocriminality: A Workshop, a Symposium and the Katanga Trial Judgment of 7 March 2014", in *Journal of International Criminal Justice*, 2014, vol. 12, no. 2, pp. 219–29.

Following a symposium on individual criminal law liability for 'macro-criminality' (that is, universal crimes), Ambos identified the comparative law versus autonomous ICL approaches to ICL concepts as one of the main themes in the ongoing scholarly debate.[4]

At one end of the spectrum, a main contribution of the above-mentioned book by Van Sliedregt is to highlight the need to engage in comprehensive comparative law exercises when attempting to define the elements of the various modes of liability. The author, while accepting pluralism with respect to forms of personal liability in international prose-cutions at the domestic (national) level, advocates for limiting the scope of liability pluralism in favour of a uniform approach at the international level, thus supporting autonomous ICL concepts applied with consistency before international criminal tribunals.[5] In extensively surveying the vari-ous forms of criminal responsibility, her book distinguishes between (1) the more traditional forms of liability found in domestic law, and (2) lead-ership liability theories (that is, theories specifically designed for the lead-ership level in universal crimes cases, such as leadership-level JCE and indirect co-perpetration), and (3) some crime-specific modes (that is, complicity in genocide and inchoate crimes of genocide like conspiracy and incitement) developed in ICL. According to Van Sliedregt, a feature of these forms of liability in ICL is that they do not require the establish-ment of a direct link to the subsequent underlying crimes and the physical perpetrators in order for liability to arise. This observation leads her to hold that leadership modes of liability and the relevant crime-specific modes constitute "theories of imputation rather than forms of participating in crime".[6]

This point may justify a brief comment. We agree that modes of lia-bility in the narrow sense are meant for attribution, or imputation, of crim-inal liability, and thus can be seen as theories for connecting persons ex-

---

4   Ambos, 2014, p. 226, *supra* note 3.

5   For details of the arguments, see Van Sliedregt, 2012, pp. 9–12, *supra* note 3. For a less traditional approach, though one that still rejects the usefulness of pluralism, see James G. Stewart and Asad Kiyani, "The Ahistoricism of Legal Pluralism in International Criminal Law", in *American Journal of Comparative Law*, 2017, vol. 65, no. 2, pp. 393–449. They argue, from a historical perspective, that because Western law and legal concepts have been imposed on foreign legal cultures by past colonial regimes, the notion of pluralism does not reflect true cultural diversity anyway.

6   Van Sliedregt, 2012, chaps. 6 and 7, in particular pp. 170 and 181–82, see *supra* note 3.

hibiting different kinds of conduct to a criminal enterprise. This applies in particular to the forms of commission liability at the leadership level. It might, however, be argued, as we have done earlier in this book, that the most important liability distinction from a theoretical perspective is rather between lawful attribution of personal liability for a completed crime A – which may entail labelling the role and position of the accused as well as his or her specific contribution to the criminal enterprise, whether the accused is a leader, an intermediate actor, or a low-level executor of the underlying crimes – and application of distinct (inchoate or even accomplice) liability for an accessorial crime B (formally made a distinct crime) that is closely linked to the main crime A and applicable whether crime A is completed or not. If our point is valid, Van Sliedregt's own distinction might still be very important for its practical utility, but maybe not so much for its theoretical value.

As for the approach underlying Van Sliedregt's contribution, the author particularly stresses the usefulness of a comparative law approach in order to highlight that many of the differences between certain liability concepts and theories are more apparent than real. The employed exercise in comparative law, drawing on domestic law from civil law and Anglo-American jurisdictions, is intended to address the currently under-theorised nature of individual liability by developing a basis for a general part of ICL. The approach is thus claimed to pave the way for developing a "true international theory of criminal responsibility", which additionally could serve to counter the current trend of fragmentation in ICL.[7]

Aksenova, in a book conducting a comprehensive analysis of the merits and proper employment of 'complicity', likewise underlines how an approach based on systematic analysis of its use in domestic jurisdic-

---

[7] *Ibid.*, p. 12. The article by Andrea Carcano, "On Fragmentation and Precedents in International Criminal Law: Possible Lessons from Recent Jurisprudence on Aiding and Abetting Liability", in *Journal of International Criminal Justice*, 2016, vol. 14, no. 4, pp. 771–92, also raises general concern about fragmentation within ICL. To stem further fragmentation, Carcano suggests that international courts and tribunals should adopt a uniform legal methodology focused primarily on identifying customary international law and secondarily on general principles of law, rather than maintaining a strict focus on statutory texts and narrow jurisprudence in that regard. As the identification of CIL and general principles of law at one fundamental level involves consulting state practice and domestic legal doctrines, the approach suggested could be seen as aligned with a fairly strong comparative law component in ICL liability concepts.

tions "may enhance the coherence and legitimacy of international criminal law".[8] More precisely, the comparative law component is emphasised in order to (1) ground complicity as a *general principle of law*, and (2) facilitate a deeper understanding of the distinction between complicity and perpetration. For this purpose, the author analyses the concept of complicity as employed in Germany, France, the United Kingdom, the United States, Italy, Russia, India, and China.[9] Likewise containing a strong comparative law component is Ambos's *Treatise on International Criminal Law*, volume 1, which is a comprehensive contribution focused on the *foundations and general part* of ICL.[10] In dealing with individual liability for international crimes,[11] the author makes extensive use of English, French, German, Italian, Portuguese, and Spanish sources to identify *general principles of law* from both common law and civil law systems, emphasising the goal of "preparing a solid grounding in comparative law for the future ICL".[12]

A contribution by Finnin[13] can be seen as leaning towards an intermediate position. In her book *Elements of Accessorial Modes of Liability*, she sets out to thoroughly analyse and propose the appropriate elements of the modes of perpetration contained in Article 25(3)(b) and (c) of the Rome Statute, which deals with the liability forms of ordering, soliciting, or inducing a crime, as well as aiding and abetting. Unlike Van Sliedregt and Ambos, Finnin explicitly distances her work from a comparative law study, employing general principles only as a secondary source when the primary sources are silent on the matter – in accordance with Article 21 of the Rome Statute.[14] Finnin, however, agrees with Van Sliedregt in acknowledging the need to develop a comprehensive theory of accessorial liability. In this vein, she strongly warns against a jurisprudential lead in the development of the law, stressing the risk of inaccuracy and inconsist-

---

[8] Marina Aksenova, *Complicity in International Criminal Law*, Hart, Oxford, 2016, pp. 5 and 8 ff.

[9] *Ibid.*, chap. 2, parts II and III.

[10] Ambos, 2013, *supra* note 1.

[11] *Ibid.*, chaps. IV–VI.

[12] *Ibid.*, preface.

[13] Sarah Finnin, *Elements of Accessorial Modes of Liability: Article 25(3)(b) and (c) of the Rome Statute of the International Criminal Court*, Martinus Nijhoff, Leiden, 2012.

[14] *Ibid.*, pp. 36–38.

encies in identifying the individual elements of these modes of liability if this is left mostly to the court (the ICC) on a concrete case-to-case basis – as compared to a simultaneous, systematic, and comprehensive approach.[15] What is also true, of course, is that a court cannot easily choose to wait for a comprehensive theory to be developed and must necessarily explain the material and mental elements that need to be fulfilled for a conviction.

The aforementioned book by Bassiouni, on the other hand, represents a move towards a more sceptical position with respect to the usefulness of a comparative law approach. As a historical note, he first highlights how the general part of ICL has developed haphazardly, both because the process has taken place gradually across different judicial bodies – ranging from the IMT to the jurisprudence of *ad hoc* tribunals – and because these bodies often tended to apply perceived general principles of law "without following a method recognized in comparative criminal law technique".[16] As further clarified by the author:

> [t]he haphazard nature of the process, however, did not necessarily exclude the reaching of correct outcomes consonant with what a proper methodology would have reached. But that also meant that the process was unpredictable and the outcomes not always consistent with a given theory of law.[17]

Importantly, this statement also underscores the fact that while the importance of developing a comprehensive theory of individual liability – the point made by Van Sliedregt and Finnin – is a different issue from the merits of a comparative versus an autonomous law approach, they are nonetheless connected. As for the current task of developing a general part of ICL, Bassiouni, however, notes the limitations of a comparative law approach. In particular, he concludes that

> it is impossible, for all practical purposes, to develop a general part of ICL in reliance upon existing sources of international law because of the divergence of national criminal jus-

---

[15] *Ibid.*, p. 5.

[16] Bassiouni, 2012, p. 286, *supra* note 3.

[17] *Ibid.*

tice systems and the methods employed in comparative criminal law approaches.[18]

Therefore, in accordance with this more sceptical view, Bassiouni holds that for the specific purpose of developing a general part of ICL, the contribution of a comparative law approach is restricted to identifying some "common traits" to build upon.[19]

Other authors take the scepticism towards comparative law approaches further, emphasising that the particular nature of universal crimes makes national criminal law concepts ill-suited to deal with personal liability in ICL, or with some aspects of this particular subject matter. Accordingly, several authors stress the need to take an autonomous approach in developing distinct concepts adapted to universal crimes rather than adopting domestic versions that were first developed for different – and less complex – crimes.[20] Among these, Stewart considers the tendencies within ICL jurisprudence to borrow heavily from national criminal law doctrines as unjustified, merely resulting in transferring domestic problems concerning attribution of individual liability to the international level.[21] Rather, he calls for developing an autonomous model specifically adapted for universal crimes. It should be noted, however, that his critique forms part of a general argument in favour of a unitary model of liability attribution in ICL, as further elaborated in the next section of this review. Thus, his scepticism of a comparative law approach must be read as largely reflecting his view with respect to the utility of several different liability modes within ICL. Also with a special focus on complicity, Cryer examines how the question of imputation is dealt with in the common law systems of England and Wales generally, finding them to be un-

---

[18] *Ibid.*, p. 324. The author, however, also notes that in comparison, "comparative criminal procedure has proven much easier for purposes of identifying both general principles and specific norms" (*ibid.*).

[19] *Ibid.* The question of adapting the concepts of attribution to the "particularities of imputation in ICL" is also raised by Ambos, 2013, pp. 177–79, see *supra* note 1.

[20] See, for example, Ambos, 2014, p. 219, *supra* note 3. See also Neha Jain, "The Control Theory in International Criminal Law", in *Chicago Journal of International Law*, 2011, vol. 12, no. 1, pp. 152–200, at p. 196 (although somewhat moderated).

[21] James G. Stewart, "The End of 'Modes of Liability' for International Crimes", in *Leiden Journal of International Law*, 2012, vol. 25, no. 1, pp. 165–219, at pp. 190, 198, 205, and 218.

---

derdeveloped and inappropriate for the international context.[22] Having also briefly noted a similar scepticism of the usefulness of civil law concepts, as represented by German criminal law, Cryer stresses the need to look beyond national concepts of attribution and to seek instead to develop *sui generis* principles and theories of liability that reflect the particular collective nature of universal crimes.[23]

In contrast, Weigend expresses doubts about the possibility of developing new theoretical models tailored to the collective nature of universal crimes.[24] Taking JCE forms of liability as a point of reference, this author is unconvinced by the efforts of the *ad hoc* tribunals to, as he views it, replace the traditional bottom-up analysis of criminal participation as known in domestic doctrines with a top-down approach to attribution of liability through the vehicle of JCE. According to Weigend, a focus on linking participants to the common enterprise rather than on the establishment of a direct connection between these actors and the individuals directly executing the crimes, in order to expand the scope of liability, is the wrong way to go. Rather, the author questions whether mixing individual with collective elements would blur rather than elucidate responsibility for universal crimes, underlining that, despite the particularities of universal crimes, "international criminal law is still in essence criminal law". Thus, rather than inventing new theoretical models of criminal liability for ICL, he recommends following the German model of "cautiously expanding traditional doctrines" when seeking to expand the scope of individual liability for universal crimes.[25]

The contribution made by Robinson,[26] in his article entitled "The Identity Crisis of International Criminal Law", highlights an additional

---

22 Robert Cryer, "Imputation and Complicity in Common Law States: A (Partial) View from England and Wales", in *Journal of International Criminal Justice*, 2014, vol. 12, no. 2, pp. 267–81.

23 *Ibid.*, pp. 279–81. See also Darryl Robinson, "A Cosmopolitan Liberal Account of International Criminal Law", in *Leiden Journal of International Law*, 2013, vol. 26, no. 1, pp. 127–53. This author argues, at least at an intellectual level, for developing a "cosmopolitan approach" to ICL.

24 Thomas Weigend, "Problems of Attribution in International Criminal Law: A German Perspective", in *Journal of International Criminal Justice*, 2014, vol. 12, no. 2, pp. 253–66.

25 *Ibid.*, pp. 264–66.

26 Darry Robinson, "The Identity Crisis of International Criminal Law", in *Leiden Journal of International Law*, 2008, vol. 21, no. 4, pp. 925–63.

aspect beyond the problems of borrowing concepts from national legal doctrines. He argues that the tendency to rely on legal methodology stemming from the related fields of human rights law and humanitarian law serves to undermine adherence to fundamental (liberal) criminal law principles, such as the principles of legality, culpability, and fair labelling.[27] As an example, the author highlights the doctrine of command responsibility, where the conflation of the procedural duties under humanitarian law of the commander with the scope of his or her criminal liability under ICL has caused, in Robinson's opinion, a contradiction between the doctrine and the fundamental principles of criminal law.[28]

In conclusion, the above review demonstrates the existence of a methodological divide within the current scholarly literature as to whether the development of a coherent system of attribution of criminal law liability for participation in universal crimes is best approached from predominantly *comparative* or from more autonomous, *sui generis* perspectives. As the debate concerns how to best to approach issues of liability and attribution at a fundamental level, it carries great potential importance. The preliminary conclusion that can be drawn at this point is that there is not much disagreement among the authors that a comparative perspective often should play a guiding role, while at the same time several authors emphasise the importance of developing autonomous approaches especially adapted to and reflective of the particular ICL context, that is, the special nature of universal crimes. Accordingly, a compromise position might acknowledge the unavoidability and potential usefulness of consulting domestic criminal liability concepts, but stress that it is vital to avoid being either too shallow in the analysis (for instance, relying too heavily on a restricted number of domestic jurisdictions) or insufficiently sensitive to the particular nature of the relevant universal crimes when transplanting domestic concepts to ICL.

---

[27] These three fundamental principles highlighted by Robinson resemble three of the four fundamental principles of criminal law liability earlier identified in this book, with the omission of the principle of conduct. See Chapter 2, Section 2.2.

[28] Robinson, 2008, p. 929, see *supra* note 26.

6.2.2. Unitary versus Differentiated Approaches to Personal Liability

Another ongoing discussion within the scholarly literature relates to which overarching model of attribution applies or should apply within ICL. Views on this question are divided between proponents of a 'unitary' system of attribution and those who favour a countervailing 'differentiated' system.[29] While the distinctions between these two systems, or models, are not always straightforward – a point reflected in the jurisprudence of international courts as well as in the literature – the difference centres on the degree to which the system of attribution clearly distinguishes between the various participants involved. Authors diverge not only with regard to the stand they take on the main issue, but also with respect to their perspective. While some approach the liability system from a pragmatic point of view, basing their arguments on which system offers the best solution in practice, others are mainly concerned with which system best adheres, or fails to adhere, to fundamental principles of criminal law.

In short, a differentiated system typically provides demarcated (derivative) liability categories and, ultimately, operational modes of punishable participation that typically define in sufficient detail the applicable material and mental elements of each form of liability. A unitary system, by contrast, at most distinguishes between, on the one hand, the so-called principals (that is, the physical perpetrators who complete the crime) and on the other hand all kinds of accomplices (that is, other participants). However, on closer inspection it could be argued that one may empirically find that although a large group of participants are labelled accomplices, the liability requirements with respect to several subgroups may actually differ, as subtle distinctions are being applied in practice. For example, while complicity in some jurisdictions is seemingly applied as a broad category in line with the unitary model, there might still exist legally important distinctions, for instance between physical and psychological assistance (aiding *or* abetting).[30]

---

[29] See also our own discussion of the content and limitations of the unitary and differentiated theories or models in Chapter 1, Section 1.2.5.

[30] For a more elaborate and fine-grained discussion of the difference between these models, see Chapter 1, Section 1.2.5.

An even more radical version of the unitary model treats all participants in the relevant criminal enterprise as 'perpetrators' of the crime. This view of what should define a true unitary model is held by Finnin and Stewart.[31]

In her assessment of which of the two systems is actually implemented for the ICC by the Rome Statute, Finnin notes initially that it is unclear whether Article 25(3) reflects a unitary or differentiated model, and furthermore, whether the specific modes under Article 25(3)(b) and (c) are derivative in nature – and thus truly accessorial modes of liability.[32] Some clarification is in order, however, concerning the author's understanding of the term *accessorial liability*. Following Fletcher, Finnin defines it as criminal responsibility derived from the liability of a principal perpetrator; as such it should include liability of instigators as well as of aiders and abettors.[33] Later in her book she confirms that these modes are to be treated as 'derivative' of the principal's liability as well.[34] In advancing this narrow definition of a unitary model, as one that treats all participants as perpetrators, Finnin concludes that a differentiated system of attribution applies under the Rome Statute.

This way of conceptualising the derivation of liability for participants in universal crimes, as deriving from *the act or the liability of a principal perpetrator*, is among the most commonly employed within the existing ICL literature.[35] It places the executors of the underlying crimes in the centre and has the effect of seemingly requiring a linkage between

---

[31] See Finnin, 2012, pp. 12–13, *supra* note 13, and Stewart, 2012, *supra* note 21.

[32] See discussion in Finnin, 2012, chap. 2, *supra* note 13.

[33] Finnin, 2012, p. 3, n. 12, and p. 93, see *supra* note 13. Citing George Fletcher, *Rethinking Criminal Law*, Oxford University Press, Oxford, 2000, pp. 636–37, Finnin further explains that she prefers the term "accessorial liability" over "complicity", as the latter is sometimes understood more broadly to incorporate also forms of group liability, an issue with which her book is not concerned.

[34] *Ibid.*, chap. 4, parts II–IV.

[35] See Aksenova, 2016, p. 22, *supra* note 8; Hans Vest, "Problems of Participation: Unitarian, Differentiated Approach, or Something Else?", in *Journal of International Criminal Justice*, 2014, vol. 12, no. 2, pp. 295–309, at pp. 305–7; Van Sliedregt, 2012, pp. 67–70, *supra* note 3; and Alicia Gil Gil and Elena Maculan, "Current Trends in the Definition of 'Perpetrator' by the International Criminal Court: From the Decision on the Confirmation of Charges in the *Lubanga* Case to the *Katanga* Judgment", in *Leiden Journal of International al Law*, 2015, vol. 28, no. 2, pp. 349–71, at p. 363.

those who complete the crime and all others who might be responsible for their contributions to the criminal enterprise.

It does, however, differ from the definition of derivative criminal liability as employed in the present book under the proposed general theory of personal criminal law liability. As explained in Chapter 2, Section 2.2.3.5., rather than conceptualising this as liability for the criminal offences committed by other persons, criminal responsibility for a certain form of participation should be seen as derived from *the basic form of liability for the relevant crime* (for example, 'liability for crimes against humanity'), thus making each participant's own contribution to the crime the focus of liability assessment in a principled manner.

This proposed theory on the correct object of 'liability derivation', which seems to be quite similar to the 'accessorial object' in Finnin's terminology, conveniently bypasses the problems noted by Van Sliedregt concerning whether accessorial liability also depends on the full culpability (guilt) of the principal perpetrator. The latter issue raises complex new questions, for instance, through a possible need to introduce a set of main rules and exceptions with respect to the consequences of different defences and excuses applicable to the principal, or to some of the principals. For example, when there are several executors on the ground ('principals'), as is often the case when universal crimes are committed, some but not all of them may have legitimate or excusable reasons for their acts. From which actors' culpability or non-culpability should the liability position of accomplices then be derived from? These problems become superfluous under the general theory, because the question with respect to completed crimes is always the same: provided that an operational mode of liability matches the requirements of the general theory, does the conduct of the suspect or accused fulfil the culpability (mental) and material requirements of the relevant mode?

Illustrative of the complications ensuing from the 'principal-driven' derivative and accessorial liability theory is that the topic is found worthy of extensive consideration as part of Finnin's own contribution. More precisely, after having concluded on the derivative nature of liability under Article 25(3)(b) and (c) of the Rome Statute, Finnin continues her discussion by noting that both strictly and partially derivative approaches must be considered. Under the strictly derivative approach, there is no distinction between justifications and excuses, and consequently the principal perpetrator must not be entitled to *any defence* in order to impose liability for the acts of the accessory. A partially derivative approach incorporates the distinction between justifications and excuses, whereby only the presence of the former for the benefit of the principal perpetrator would also rule out holding the accessory liable for his actions in relation to the crime (that is, the fact that the principal perpetrator is entitled to an excuse because of mental incapacity does not rule out accessorial liability for other participants).[36]

These kinds of complications, or at least a need for secondary liability rules, are also a reason why Stewart – who advocates a unitary model of autonomous liability, as further elaborated below – is critical of the whole notion of the derivative nature of complicity liability under ICL, ultimately questioning whether this may be one of the instances in which ICL inappropriately and counterproductively borrows too heavily from domestic doctrines.[37]

The underlying real-world problem, magnified in ICL as compared to lesser crimes prosecuted domestically, is that the executors often only participate at the last phase and at the lowest level of a large criminal enterprise when universal crimes are completed, while many other persons have played quite different and often much more important roles. Therefore, putting the fungible personnel of executors at the centre of criminal law liability analysis, especially derivative analysis, may create a number of problems that could be solved by other analytical means in theory and practice. This theoretical weakness is accompanied by a highly artificial representation of universal crimes in legal communication, implying that the crimes somehow *originate* from the underlying offences being committed by – in sociological terms – not particularly powerful individuals within a social context that is created and maintained by high-level leaders and others with significant powers. The question, then, is whether a renewed theory of derivative criminal law liability, like the one we are proposing in this book, will better capture the reality as well solving the above-mentioned legal problems, an issue on which we shall draw conclusions later in the book.

Compared to Finnin, Ambos takes a midway position, arguing that the system of attribution implemented by the Rome Statute is most appro-

---

[36] Finnin, 2012, chap. 4, part IV, see *supra* note 13.
[37] Stewart, 2012, pp. 188–90, see *supra* note 21.

priately labelled a "functional unitary system" with elements of a differentiated system.[38] In a similar vein, Vest contends that the Rome Statute represents a kind of mixed model, in that Article 25(3) adheres to a differentiated model while the rule on sentencing reflects a unitary model.[39] Vest further argues the advantages of treating it as a flexible system. He suggests that the ICC could accommodate this mixed model, when determining the sentence in accordance with Rule 145(1)(c) of the Rules of Procedure and Evidence, by considering first the 'mode' of perpetration and second the accused's 'degree' of participation.[40]

While nearly all authors so far mentioned acknowledge, either fully or partially, a differentiated component to attribution of liability under the Rome Statute, one of the strongest opponents of a differentiated model of attribution is Stewart. In his article, appropriately entitled "The End of 'Modes of Liability' for International Crimes",[41] the author argues *lex ferenda* for collapsing all existing modes into a pure unitary model whereby all participants who causally contribute to a universal crime with the requisite mental elements are considered 'perpetrators', without differentiation between principals and accessories. Drawing on earlier scholarly critique of the theory of command/superior responsibility and joint criminal enterprise, an essential component of Stewart's argument in favour of a unitary model is that the concept of complicity[42] – although having largely so far escaped similar scholarly criticisms – equally falls short of meeting two crucial requirements for being theoretically sustainable.[43] First, the author argues that liability for 'complicity' is theoretically unjustifiable as it does not consistently satisfy the conceptual necessity of establishing congruence between the mental element in the completed crime(s) and the mental element required for the relevant mode of liability.

---

[38] Ambos, 2013, pp. 145–46 and n. 379, see *supra* note 1.

[39] Vest, 2014, see *supra* note 35. See also the discussion in Chapter 1, Section 1.2.5., of this book.

[40] *Ibid.*, pp. 307–9.

[41] Stewart, 2012, see *supra* note 21.

[42] Stewart employs the term "complicity" as equivalent to the notion of "accessorial liability", thus encompassing such specific modes as soliciting, inducing, and aiding and abetting. As for its scope, his understanding of the concept of complicity thus coincides with Finnin's understanding of the concept of accessorial liability (Finnin, 2012, see *supra* note 13), the difference apparently being a question of preferred terminology.

[43] Stewart, 2012, pp. 185–204, see *supra* note 21.

Whenever the mental element required for an accomplice (for example, knowledge or recklessness) is lower than the one that applies for the crime (for instance, the principal perpetrator is required to act with intent), complicity magnifies the accomplice responsibility contrary to the principle of culpability. By the same logic, when the mental element for complicity is stricter than for the crime itself, it induces impunity. Stewart therefore concludes:

> All fixed mental elements for accessorial liability (i.e., purpose, knowledge or recklessness) violate basic principles of blame attribution since in each, there will occasionally be a marked departure from culpability when the elements of the crime do not match those of the mode of liability.[44]

Second, Stewart takes notice of the not-so-clear status of causation within the current ICL doctrine on complicity. The core of his argument is somewhat hard to fully grasp, but it largely goes as follows. As a point of departure, the author recognises that the doctrine, as applied in ICL, does not require proof that a cause-effect relationship existed between the conduct of an aider and abettor and the commission of the crime, nor that such conduct served as a precondition for the commission of the crime. According to Stewart, this understanding of complicity, by not requiring a *causal link*, is in direct defiance of the principle of culpability. At the same time, the author notes, the case law has required – as part of the *actus reus* – some action *related to* the criminal harm, namely that an aider and abettor's act exerted a substantial effect on the commission of the crime. This again, Stewart claims, merely adds new layers of ambiguity. He therefore reasons that a causal contribution is nonetheless required via the substantial effect element, despite any confusion that may exist in the complicity doctrine, since there is, in his opinion, no alternative way to contribute to a crime other than causally.[45]

Taken together, these two points lead to the main argument of his article. Given that the same mental element as well as a causal contribu-

---

[44] *Ibid.*, p. 198. See also James G. Stewart, "Complicity", in Markus Dubber and Tatjana Hörnle (eds.), *Oxford Handbook of Criminal Law*, Oxford University Press, Oxford, 2014. The latter contribution provides an analysis of complicity theory, drawing on a comparison of, particularly, Anglo-American and German law; the author makes a similar point when reviewing recklessness as a mental standard for complicity, at pp. 557–58.

[45] Stewart, 2012, pp. 199–200, see *supra* note 21.

tion are required for both principals and accomplices in order to satisfy the principle of personal culpability, Stewart concludes that differentiating perpetrators and accomplices becomes obsolete. This makes a unitary model of attribution, whereby accomplices are treated as a subset of perpetrators, the natural solution.[46] A unitary model, he argues, also reduces the concern that the current set of ill-defined modes of liability may violate the principle of legality.[47] Furthermore, he claims that these principled reasons are compounded by practical advantages, as such a model would relieve ICL of the overly complicated and seriously inefficient system of modes of liability that is currently in use.[48] Lastly, while Stewart recognises that there often will be a difference in moral blameworthiness between a principal offender and an accomplice, his response is that this aspect can be sufficiently addressed at the sentencing stage.[49]

This last point coincides with that made by Sadat and Jolly, who reject any hierarchical order of the modes of liability under Rome Statute Article 25(3), based on a canon of seven interpretive principles developed by the authors. In their opinion, the provision rather contains "overlapping forms of criminal participation, any one of which may give rise to criminal responsibility under the Statute, responsibility that will then be assessed in terms of culpability at the sentencing stage of the proceedings".[50] Their use of the term "culpability" in the quotation is arguably a bit confusing, as the language is close to suggesting that culpability should not be considered when assessing personal liability at the conviction stage (whether the accused is guilty or not). Probably the correct way

---

[46] *Ibid.*, p. 205.

[47] *Ibid.*, p. 214.

[48] See also James G. Stewart, "The Strangely Familiar History of the Unitary Theory of Perpetration", in Bruce Ackerman *et al.* (eds.), *Visions of Justice: Essays in Honor of Professor Mirjan Damaska*, Duncker & Humblot, Berlin, 2016 (www.legal-tools.org/doc/23a652/). In this follow-up article, the author draws on the historical experiences of five countries to argue that their shifts from a differentiated to a unitary model largely reflected conscious choices based on the principled and practical arguments highlighted in his own current reasoning.

[49] Stewart, 2012, pp. 170–71, *supra* note 21.

[50] See Leila Sadat and Jarrod M. Jolly, "Seven Canons of ICC Treaty Interpretation: Making Sense of Article 25's Rorschach Blot", in *Leiden Journal of International Law*, 2014, vol. 27, no. 3, pp. 755–88, at p. 758. See also Marjolein Cupido, "Common Purpose Liability Versus Joint Perpetration: A Practical View on the ICC's Hierarchy of Liability Theories", in *Leiden Journal of International Law*, 2016, vol. 29, no. 3, pp. 897–915.

to read the authors, evident also when they discuss the "degree of an accused's culpability", is that the level of blameworthiness *also* forms part of the overall *gravity* of the accused's act, which is to be assessed at the sentencing stage rather than expressed through the labels attached at the stage of attribution.[51]

At the other pole of the scholarly debate, some authors make both principled and practical arguments in favour of the differentiated model of attribution. Directly addressing the point made by Stewart concerning non-congruence of elements in relation to the fundamental principle of culpability, Aksenova calls for a more sophisticated understanding of the principle itself:

> I understand the principle of culpability as not requiring the modes of liability to match the crime; rather, it presupposes holding a person accountable for his contribution to the crime if it is done culpably.[52]

In accordance with this understanding, the author maintains that it is perfectly reasonable to attribute criminal liability to those who intentionally make a contribution to the criminal enterprise, although the occurrence of the criminal outcome (completion of the crime) is merely foreseen as a possibility. Thus, Aksenova emphasises:

---

[51] See Cupido, 2016, *supra* note 50. Interestingly in this regard, she assesses the alleged inferior status, in terms of level of blameworthiness, of common purpose liability under Article 25(3)(d) of the Rome Statute as compared to joint perpetration in subparagraph (a). The author concludes that while the former in theory stipulates a lower *actus reus* and *mens rea* standard, in practice the ICC has tended to apply the requirements of both forms of liability in a "context-dependent way", in relation to the specific case, thus not allowing for accepting in general terms that common purpose liability is a less serious type of liability than joint perpetration. For a somewhat different account, see Marina Aksenova, "The Modes of Liability at the ICC: The Labels that Don't Always Stick", in *International Criminal Law Review*, 2015, vol. 15, no. 4, pp. 629–64. Aksenova argues that the established and, in her view, misguided position at the ICC – that Article 25(3) offers a value-based hierarchy of modes of participation – has led the court to over-utilise the modes of commission liability under subparagraph (a) in seeking to best reflect the gravity of the crimes. In her opinion, this has caused a displacement of the different forms of complicity in (b) through (d), despite the latter forms of liability being more appropriate in many instances, as they are specifically designed to deal with cases of multiple offenders in different roles.

[52] Aksenova, 2016, p. 17, see *supra* note 8.

> What matters is that the underlying act is wrongful and that
> the assistance is provided on the basis of a choice available
> to an accomplice and in the absence of legal excuses.[53]

At this point in the literature survey, it seems appropriate to make clear that we agree with Aksenova on this important issue, and that the general theory of criminal law liability sketched out in Chapter 2, designed to be usefully applicable to the field of ICL as well, is in line with her view.

In the extension of this view, a major value of her book is the presentation of clear arguments in favour of maintaining a differentiated system of attribution within ICL. The author explicitly rejects Stewart's argument that culpability can be sufficiently addressed at the sentencing stage, insisting instead that a clear distinction between perpetrators and accessories at the stage of attribution is "dictated by the principle of fairness".[54] In Aksenova's opinion, the principle of individual criminal responsibility requires the accused's involvement in the crimes to be established as precisely as possible in legal terms – and retaining the concept of complicity is indispensable in this regard.[55] In particular, she stresses that if ICL does not actively ensure *fair labelling*, that is, an accurate description of the accused's acts, this "undermines the cause of international criminal law by creating an image of 'collective punishment'".[56] Accordingly, fair labelling (and fair attribution) is vital in maintaining the legitimacy of international criminal law.

There is a specific assumption behind this line of reasoning, namely that Aksenova conceives of the main function of labelling and thus the attribution of specific forms of personal liability as expressive. In her view, the question of attribution of liability (with regard to identified participants in the criminal enterprise) implies a distinct set of norms set apart from the other essential question, that of "wrongdoing", meaning that a relevant universal crime has been committed (by someone or by a group of people) according to a crime description in compliance with the legali-

---

[53]   *Ibid.*, p. 18.

[54]   *Ibid.*, pp. 17 and 238.

[55]   *Ibid.*, p. 237.

[56]   *Ibid.*, p. 238.

ty principle.[57] This is also clear from her discussion of the merits of legal sentencing discretion, where the author proclaims that the overall assessment of degree of blameworthiness should itself not be fixed by the specific label attached to the conduct. Rather, at the sentencing stage, the mode of liability is just one of multiple elements that could inform the gravity of the criminal conduct, where the focus should be on overall assessment of the factual circumstances of the actual crime and the concrete act (or omission) of the convicted person.[58]

As a natural consequence of the above, Aksenova, although not explicitly rejecting the substance of the argument as invalid, is also unconvinced by Stewart's asserted practical reasons for dismissing the differentiated approach. Partly, this may expose different views as to what are practical, real problems for the legal actors involved, in particular for judges at international tribunals, and how difficult or time-consuming they are to handle. In addition, the distinct value of a public appearance of justice is probably more important to Aksenova. Hence, she underlines:

> The expressive function of international criminal justice is based not only on the outcome, namely convictions, but also on the way in which the administration of justice is carried out.[59]

In another article, intended as a direct criticism of Stewart's proposal to collapse all categories and modes into one broad category of perpetrators, Jackson portrays this argument as inherently flawed.[60] Starting from the premise that a fundamental basis for criminal responsibility under the principle of culpability is the recognition of individuals as moral agents, capable of free choice, the author argues that only a differentiated model can sufficiently capture the different contributions individuals

---

[57] The line of argument rests on an approach that differentiates the question of attribution of responsibility, on the one hand, from that of wrongdoing, on the other. The former is primarily seen as representing norms at a separate level that are primarily addressed to judges and jurors, not to potential violators. This point is further elaborated below as part of the review of the scope of the legality principle.

[58] Aksenova, 2016, p. 259, *supra* note 8. See also Aksenova, 2015, *supra* note 51. This is also more in line with our views as expressed in Chapter 10, Section 10.7.3., on the relationship between forms of personal liability and proportionate punishment.

[59] *Ibid.*, p. 19.

[60] Miles Jackson, "The Attribution of Responsibility and Modes of Liability in International Criminal Law", in *Leiden Journal of International Law*, 2016, vol. 29, no. 3, pp. 879–95.

---

make to a crime, particularly in collective crime contexts.[61] Jackson further explicitly rejects a unitary model, viewing it as having neither practical nor expressive benefits as compared to the differentiated model.

The practical difficulties of assessing individual acts within a larger context, Jackson argues, are simply moved to the sentencing stage under Stewart's unitary model. Furthermore, although a unitary model would have some expressive benefits in linking the accused more directly to the crime, or rather, the criminal enterprise, the elimination of all forms of complicity would, more importantly, violate the principle of fair labelling.[62] Similarly, while the majority of his article concerns the usefulness of a "control theory" for co-perpetration, Wirth also takes a principled stand in favour of the differentiated model.[63] In his opinion, it provides better consistency with the legality principle, at least in the context of Article 25(3) of the Rome Statute. More generally, the author stresses:

> Clear and distinguishable modes of liability are especially important in international criminal law, where the link between the accused and the crimes [is] often more in issue than the occurrence of the crimes themselves.[64]

A contribution by Ohlin adds another dimension to the debate by taking into account the human rights of the accused. In contrast to Stewart's unitary proposal, Ohlin stresses the need to develop even more subtle modes of liability than those currently in use in order to permit finer gradations of culpability before the sentencing stage.[65] Ohlin makes reference to Megret[66] and to human rights theory of criminal law, suggesting that the principle of culpability and the expressive function of modes of liabil-

---

[61] *Ibid.*, p. 884.

[62] *Ibid.*, p. 887 ff.

[63] Steffen Wirth, "Co-Perpetration in the *Lubanga* Trial Judgment", in *Journal of International Criminal Justice*, 2012, vol. 10, no. 4, pp. 971–95.

[64] *Ibid.*, p. 979.

[65] Jens David Ohlin, "Joint Intentions to Commit International Crimes", in *Chicago Journal of International Law*, 2011, vol. 11, no. 2, pp. 693–753, at p. 718. His proposal of a more differentiated system, based on joint intentions, is further addressed later in this chapter.

[66] Frédéric Mégret, "Prospects for 'Constitutional' Human Rights Scrutiny of Substantive International Criminal Law by the ICC, with Special Emphasis on the General Part" (paper presented at Washington University School of Law, Whitney R. Harris World Law Institute, International Legal Scholars Workshop, Roundtable in Public International Law and Theory, 4–6 February 2010).

ity could be seen as part of an accused's human right to fair labelling. Thus, Ohlin holds:

> The criminal process owes an obligation to criminal defendants to properly label their criminal conduct, and this obligation is more basic and foundational than the obligation to limit punishment to the level of their culpability. Indeed, one might even *generate* the constraint against punishment as initially deriving from the constraint against labeling.[67]

It should be noted that Ohlin's attempt to link the notion of fair labelling to human rights norms is a novel and thus also quite recent approach, and that the precise content or function of fair labelling is not always consistently expressed in the literature. It appears common among scholars, however, to view fair labelling as a matter of individual fairness in the criminal law process, closely related to the concept of a fair trial. In addition, the communicative function of ICL, broadly speaking, has also been emphasised: that is, to externally convey, as accurately as possible, the wrongdoing of the accused for purpose of general deterrence as well as to ensure legitimacy of ICL and the international criminal tribunals in the eyes of the wider public.[68] A link here can be made to the argument put forth by Vest in his contribution mentioned above: that an approach to liability that does not clearly distinguish between principal perpetration and secondary participation would provide insufficient guidance both to potential new perpetrators and to the legal profession that gets involved in such cases.[69] On the other hand, other authors, notably Stewart,[70] question whether fair labelling even exists as a distinct legal principle, separate from the principle of culpability.

At this point a brief comment seems warranted. In our view, 'fair labelling' is not a core human rights principle as such. It concerns, rather, the content and application of the more specific fundamental principles of criminal law liability set forth in Chapter 2 of this book, in particular the

---

[67] Ohlin, 2011, p. 751, see *supra* note 65.
[68] See, for example, Aksenova, 2016, p. 7, *supra* note 8; Robinson, 2008, p. 925, *supra* note 26; and Jackson, 2016, p. 888, *supra* note 60.
[69] See Vest, 2014, pp. 307–9, *supra* note 35.
[70] Stewart, 2012, p. 176, *supra* note 21. Stewart recognises, however, the notion of fair labelling as being useful in the effort to explain and reflect an accused's guilt; it is just that this might be done more effectively at sentencing.

principle of fair attribution of personal liability and the secondary principles of personal liability that provide guidance as to how liability for different kinds of punishable participation in criminal enterprises should be attributed to individuals under a general theory. Fair attribution of liability, of which fair labelling is one important aspect, means essentially that liability must reflect the role and actual contribution as well as the culpability of the accused.[71] A clear and principled conception of 'derivative' criminal law liability is also important in this regard, as pointed out earlier. In short, derivation of specific liability categories and creation of operational modes of liability must be fair in the sense of complying with all the fundamental criminal law liability principles, including the principle of culpability.

A different, basically *lex ferenda* parameter is the effectiveness for external communicative purposes when considering the usefulness of differentiated, lawful modes. However, there is also the rule of law consideration that applies to the internal legal process, namely that the application of operational modes must provide sufficiently detailed reasons in the judgment as to (1) why a particular labelling of personal criminal liability is justified, and (2) why the material and culpability (mental) elements in the case against the accused have been met (the two questions may converge if the labelling is clear according to established practice). This requirement, which in our opinion is linked to the fundamental criminal law principle of fair attribution of personal liability rather than to the fundamental legality principle concerned with the abstract crime description norm,[72] necessitates a concrete judicial assessment of the factual circumstances in light of the specific (universal) crime charged as well as the alleged punishable participation of the accused.

Despite the heated scholarly discussions that emerge from the above reviews, some authors downplay the importance of the unitary versus differentiated model distinction. Van Sliedregt, for example, agrees with Ambos that many practical problems of criminal participation have been solved within ICL through the use of mixed models without coherent doctrinal grounding. In addition, her comparative law perspective reveals that

---

[71] See Chapter 2, Section 2.2.2.4. As noted earlier, under the general theory of personal criminal liability a distinction is made between liability (determination of responsibility/guilt) and proportionate sentencing. See also Chapter 10, Section 10.7.3.

[72] See Chapter 2, Section 2.2.2.1., and Chapter 4, Section 4.3.7.

the conceptual distinction between unitary and differentiated models is also fading across the legal systems of the world.[73] Although she also thoroughly discusses the criteria for distinguishing between principals and accessories, by way of the naturalistic and normative approach, the decreasing importance of differentiating between the unitary and differentiated models leads her to note that the principals/accessories divide is also of less practical importance today. As already discussed, moreover, differentiating principals and accessories might not be the most sophisticated approach in the context of serious mass crimes where the social and broader contextual element, rather that the physical execution of the underlying crimes, is the core definitional feature of the criminal activity.

6.2.3. Combining Modes of Liability: Acceptable Legal Creativity?

A related question concerns possible extension of criminal law liability versus absolute limits on the scope of liability for universal crimes: that is, whether 'new' categories or modes of participation can or should be invented, and in particular whether different operational modes within a specific criminal law subsystem can lawfully be combined. The purpose would be to cast a wider net by attributing liability to an even broader class of participants in the relevant criminal enterprises. Unsurprisingly, various policy perspectives seem to influence authors' stances on this complex and important issue. Most of the contributions to the literature have focused on the ICC, where the court has combined committing a crime "jointly with another" with committing a crime "through another person" in Article 25(3)(a) of the Rome Statute, thus creating a new mode of 'indirect co-perpetration'. This example will be further discussed below, together with so-called 'interlinked JCE', which has served a similar attributional purpose at the *ad hoc* tribunals.[74]

It would be useful at this point to briefly sketch out the factual scenarios and essential features of the two just-mentioned 'combined' forms of liability. At a general policy level, the problem concerns the possibility of effectively holding the most powerful leadership-participants behind the scene accountable for mass crimes that are physically executed by

---

[73] Van Sliedregt, 2012, p. 73, see *supra* note 3.

[74] The topic of interlinked JCE forms part of the more general, and longstanding, scholarly debate on JCE liability, which is considered below. See also Chapter 7, Sections 7.2.2.2.–7.2.2.4., on the international jurisprudence in this regard.

---

subordinate participants in what may constitute large or multiple crime scenes that are often far removed, geographically and/or in time, from the daily lives and concrete acts of the masterminds. Importantly, as recognised by both Ohlin and Van Sliedregt, the task of combining the two modes of liability under the Rome Statute, Article 25(3)(a), is structurally almost identical to the problem faced by the *ad hoc* tribunals in cases of interlinked JCE.[75] However, they differ somewhat in their specific elements as well as with respect to the underlying principle of attribution employed ('control theory' versus 'common plan').[76]

The essential features of *indirect co-perpetration* can simplistically be described as follows: collaboration ("jointly with another") between high-level leaders A and B, each leader vertically controlling a separate power structure (or a clearly separate part of the same structure). Liability is imposed on both A and B (and possibly on others who participate at the leadership level) for crimes physically committed by subordinates in one or the other power structure ("through another person") who are controlled by *either* A *or* B (the co-perpetrators). Graphically speaking, this form of liability draws a diagonal liability line between A and crimes committed under the command or leadership of B, and vice versa.

As for scenarios of *interlinked JCE*, the essentials are as follows: a 'leadership JCE' is linked to an 'execution JCE' that may pursue partly different criminal and policy goals, and thus they cannot be considered parts of one integrated JCE. Liability is imposed on participants in the leadership JCE for crimes physically committed by one or several members of the execution JCE: that is, the leadership participants and physical executors are not considered members of the same JCE, but the execution JCE is still used as a tool by at least one member of the leadership JCE to execute the crime in pursuance of a common plan of the leadership JCE.[77]

Among those accepting such combinations of modes as largely unproblematic at a fundamental level, Ambos expresses the view concerning indirect co-perpetration that "[i]n principle, this is not a new mode of re-

---

[75] See Jens David Ohlin, "Second-Order Linking Principles: Combining Vertical and Horizontal Modes of Liability", in *Leiden Journal of International Law*, 2012, vol. 25, no. 3, pp. 771–97. Also see Van Sliedregt, 2012, p. 170, *supra* note 3.

[76] Van Sliedregt, 2012, pp. 170–71, see *supra* note 3.

[77] For details of the jurisprudential development of these forms of liability, see Chapter 7, Section 7.2.2.4.

sponsibility but only the 'factual coincidence of two recognized forms of perpetration'".[78] This view is also shared by Weigend in one of his works.[79] As a consequence, no direct or potential conflict exists with the fundamental principles of criminal law.

On the contrary, Ohlin, Van Sliedregt, and Weigend (in another work)[80] consider indirect co-perpetration to represent a new mode of liability under the Rome Statute, by combining "other modes of liability" already in existence. One key observation leading them (unlike Ambos) to treat it as a new mode is that the ICC has occasionally not required that each distinct element of the two original modes of liability be satisfied for each defendant to be held liable as an indirect co-perpetrator. On this basis they are sceptical about the possibility of (the ICC) combining modes at will in the absence of a liability theory that may justify such legal creativity. In other words, the legitimacy of combining modes of perpetration cannot simply be assumed.[81]

It might be added to this, however, that while the *categories* of acting "jointly with another person" and "through another person" are explicitly grounded in Article 25(3)(a) of the Rome Statute, the required specific material and mental criteria of fully *operational modes* of liability are not sufficiently expressed in this provision.[82] Consequently, these criteria necessarily had to be, and have been, developed in the jurisprudence into true operational modes, sometimes with and sometimes without general support in the literature. This means that the *modes* of co-perpetration and perpetration through another are to a large extent judge-made. Hence the invention of indirect co-perpetration can also be viewed as part of the task imposed upon the ICC, namely to develop judicially the naked categories

---

[78] Ambos, 2013, p. 157, see *supra* note 1.

[79] Thomas Weigend, "Perpetration through an Organization: The Unexpected Career of a German Legal Concept", in *Journal of International Criminal Justice*, 2011, vol. 9, no. 1, pp. 91–111. According to this author, the real challenge is not to define modes of liability, but to better define the substantive meaning of the criterion 'control' by the co-perpetrators.

[80] Jens David Ohlin, Elies van Sliedregt, and Thomas Weigend, "Assessing the Control-Theory", in *Leiden Journal of International Law*, 2013, vol. 26, no. 3, pp. 725–46.

[81] *Ibid.*, p. 736.

[82] This is different with respect to some other categories of liability in Article 25(3), for example, Article 25(3)(c) on complicity and Article 25(3)(f) on attempt (inchoate liability). These latter provisions are more detailed and define both necessary material and mental elements; they thus constitute statutory-made, operational modes from the beginning.

of letter (a) into operational modes. These modes must be lawful and thus in compliance with the fundamental principles of criminal law liability, but they must also be explained in the concrete judgment when applied.[83] The warning by Ohlin, and by Van Sliedregt and Weigend above, that a liability theory needs to be developed – in order to circumscribe unwarranted expansion of ICL liability and better assess the work of the ICC – is most appropriate in this regard. However, it could well be that the additional and specific mode of 'indirect co-perpetration' is perfectly lawful under such a general theory, and that its lawfulness may not depend on whether it rests on full "factual coincidence" (Ambos) of two other modes already developed by the ICC.

With respect to interlinked JCE, Van Sliedregt takes issue with linking leadership JCE to execution JCE, which she sees as risking guilt by association, contrary to the principle of personal culpability. She also points out that the underpinning theory of liability suffers from an "imputational shortcoming" because it insufficiently specifies the criteria for linking at the leadership (horizontal) level.[84] In a related article, Ohlin attempts to address this "missing link" by proposing a specific criminal law liability theory that is able to stipulate *how* and *when* different forms of perpetration can be combined for the purpose of attributing justified individual liability.[85] His theory would apply to instances of combining vertical and horizontal modes of perpetration for leadership-level participants, most notably by means of indirect co-perpetration and interlinked (leadership-level) JCE, as explained above.

Ohlin then stresses – along the lines of Van Sliedregt's critique of interlinked JCE liability – that the control theory, as so far applied by the ICC, only justifies vertical liability for a predominant leader. It is thus insufficient to justify the imposition of indirect perpetration liability to all participating members at the horizontal leadership level. As an alternative option, the author presents what he calls a second-order linking principle labelled the "personality principle". It serves to justify combining various first-order (vertical) linking principles. This principle recognises the (of-

---

[83] See earlier discussions in Chapter 2 and Chapter 4 on the rule of law requirements related to the imposition of criminal law liability.
[84] Van Sliedregt, 2012, pp. 163–64, see *supra* note 3.
[85] Ohlin, 2012, see *supra* note 75.

ten) collective nature of the leadership group, where the decisive criterion is the degree of collectivity – a common mindset, constituted by rational integration, plans, and subplans within the leadership group.

The personality principle thus in effect serves to establish liability for contribution to a relevant crime through collective indirect control of a power structure. According to Ohlin, "the co-perpetrators at the leadership level constitute a joint agent", which might also be referred to as a "collective agent", or "a legal person, a group agent, or an organization".[86] The proposed linking principle thus allows the imposition of indirect perpetration liability on all the leadership members, because the indirect perpetration by one leader is attributable to the collective agent.[87] Ohlin emphasises that explicit recognition of this collectivist aspect at the theoretical level is essential in order to abide by the principle of personal culpability,[88] and that for all instances where individuals at the leadership level cannot be established as constituting a true collective entity, liability for the leadership participants in these settings would be unjustifiable.

How one frames this issue affects not only the preferred solution, but whether the issue is even seen as a problem that needs to be further addressed. If combining modes of liability is viewed primarily as a response to overlapping modes, given the factual circumstances, then such a solution would present itself as largely uncontroversial; but if it is viewed as an exercise in combining some, but not all, elements of originally distinct modes of perpetration that have been sufficiently defined, for example, in the Rome Statute, questions arise as to the legitimacy of such legal creativity.

Importantly, the issue of combining modes also has clear links to other fundamental questions addressed in this book that would help determine which solution is lawful or most appropriate, such as the scope and function of the legality principle in relation to the task of attribution (see next section). For example, some forms of participation might be criminalised as distinct accessorial (B) crimes, whether the main (A)

---

[86] *Ibid.*, p. 786.

[87] *Ibid.*, pp. 786–87.

[88] See also Jens David Ohlin, "Searching for the Hinterman: In Praise of Subjective Theories of Imputation", in *Journal of International Criminal Justice*, 2014, vol. 12, no. 2, pp. 325–43.

crime is completed or not. But if the main crime is completed (for instance, crimes against humanity), commission liability will instead *assimilate* all forms of inchoate and accomplice liability of the accused for the same main crime. This is in line with the general theory of personal criminal liability as presented in Chapter 2.[89] And commission by omission liability will defer to commission liability through perpetration.

The fact that the issue of combining modes has been explicitly raised in some of the most recent contributions to the ICL literature also shows that scholars are increasingly acknowledging the importance of the question. Although the above contribution by Ohlin offers one possible route to theoretically justifying the combination of certain modes, the question is still in need of further analysis, preferably as part of a broader theory of criminal law liability. In Chapter 10, Section 10.7.2., we shall quite briefly return to this issue.

6.2.4. The Legality Principle: Does It Extend to Modes of Liability?

A further important issue – one frequently taken up in the scholarly discussions of specific concepts relating to individual lability for participation in universal crimes – is whether the principle of legality is applicable beyond the relevant substantive crimes and the crime descriptions provided in customary international law and in the written statutes of the international criminal tribunals. A more precise question, in our context, is whether the legality principle also restricts the discretionary freedom of the tribunals in attributing liability for some kind of participation in the substantive crime project (the criminal enterprise), typically through the application of various operational modes of liability that may provide a normative linkage between the conduct of the accused and a completed crime.

As pointed out earlier in this chapter, and in preceding chapters, it is useful to distinguish in this regard between liability for distinct inchoate offences (and possibly also for distinct accomplice offences) and for completed offences, since there is presumably no disagreement among scholars of ICL that the legality principle applies to all offences that are made punishable as distinct crimes. For example, attempted war crimes cannot be punishable in compliance with the legality principle before an interna-

---

[89]   See Chapter 2, Section 2.2.3.6.

tional criminal tribunal if there is no provision in its statute clarifying that such attempts are punishable.[90] In the Rome Statute, Article 25(3)(f), a general provision to this effect has been included, making punishable not only attempt to commit war crimes, but also attempt to commit genocide, crimes against humanity, and aggression.[91]

The particular question with respect to the possible application of the legality principle to acts of attribution of liability for completed crimes is only rarely addressed directly. Rather, it seems often to be an implicit assumption, in some of the discussions of specific concepts of individual criminal liability in the literature, that the legality principle applies or must be taken into account, without further analysis as to why.

Various scholars thus assume, either directly or indirectly, that the legality principle applies equally to judicial attribution of liability, linking an individual to a crime through the modes of participation. But some admit to uncertainty. One prominent author, Bassiouni, underscores the uncertainty that is often involved in identifying the scope of personal criminal law liability:

> [I]t may not satisfy the principles of legality that apply not only to the content of the specific crimes (*i.e., nullum crimen sine lege*), but also extend to the principles of criminal responsibility and penalties (*i.e., nulla poena sine lege*).[92]

---

[90] See also Chapter 4, Sections 4.3.4. and 4.3.7. It is not sufficient that criminal law liability for attempted war crimes (or attempted universal crimes generally) have a legal basis in customary international law or in the general principles of criminal law and general international law; in addition, the legality principle requires a specific legal basis in the written rules concerned with the material jurisdiction of the relevant tribunal, in other words, through the material crime descriptions in the statute or charter of the tribunal. These requirements are inherent in the international legality principle and have been referred to as 'double legality'. See Terje Einarsen, "New Frontiers of International Criminal Law: Towards a Concept of Universal Crimes", in *Bergen Journal of Criminal Law and Criminal Justice*, vol. 1, no. 1, 2013, pp. 16–20.

[91] This follows clearly from the wording of Article 25(3)(f) with respect to the first three crimes, where "such a crime" refers back to "a crime within the jurisdiction of the Court" in the introductory clause to paragraph (3). The same solution follows just as clearly with respect to aggression from the new Article 25(3)*bis*, including its placement, read also in the conjunction with paragraphs (2) and (3), which remained unchanged when the crime of aggression was included in the Rome Statute.

[92] Bassiouni, 2012, p. 292, see *supra* note 3.

In a similar vein, Ambos make a comparable statement on the legality principle in relation to modes of perpetration:

> The nullum crimen principle does not only apply to the specific offence covering a certain conduct but also to the *general conditions of liability*, including the grounds excluding criminal responsibility (*'defences'*).[93]

Such strong statements on the reach of the international legality principle may on their face seem convincing and supportive of the rule of law in light of the often-asserted need for increased protection of the accused in international criminal law procedures against expansive liability doctrines. From a *lex lata* perspective, however, the statements are not clearly grounded in legal sources and reasoning. They are also problematic statements *lex ferenda* with respect to their apparently sweeping implications for international criminal justice and the criminal law liability that has been imposed on individuals at international tribunals prior to the formation of the ICC.

In effect, they imply that the legality principle has been systematically violated, not only at Nuremberg but at all international and hybrid criminal tribunals, with the possible exception of the ICC. For example, it is only in the Rome Statute that grounds for excluding criminal responsibility ('defences') are spelled out; similarly, the Rome Statute marks the first time in the history of ICL that a provision on mental elements has been included in the statute of an international tribunal.[94] The absences in earlier court statutes do not mean, however, that defences and mental elements were not considered in the practice of those other tribunals. Furthermore, it can surely be argued that the fundamental principles of criminal law liability were generally adhered to (the fundamental principles of conduct, culpability, fair attribution of personal liability, *and* the legality principle properly understood).

Hence it is a bit hard to digest the implications of such broad statements on the reach of the legality principle that are based mostly on assertions. Could it be, then, that the whole subject matter has not been sufficiently thought through in the scholarly literature, not even by such prominent authors of ICL? However, other authors actively invoke the legality

---

[93] Ambos, 2013, p. 90, *supra* note 1.
[94] See Rome Statute, Article 30.

principle as well when discussing specific modes of liability. For example, Manacorda and Meloni caution against the adoption of a JCE doctrine outside the international *ad hoc* tribunals because the JCE doctrine is regarded as challenging the legality principle, considering the questionable status of JCE under customary international law as well as its asserted ambivalent application by the *ad hoc* tribunals. This again raises questions, in their opinion, with respect to the requisite of clarity and precision as a subcomponent of the legality principle.[95] Concerning the jurisprudence prior to the Lubanga judgment, Gil and Maculan argue that the wide interpretive route adopted by the ICC has caused an expansion of principal liability that in their view runs contrary to both the principle of legality and individual criminal responsibility.[96] Based on the same assumption regarding the scope of the legality principle, Stewart, as mentioned above, uses as one of his arguments in favour of a unitary system that the lack of clear definitions of the various modes of liability makes a differentiated system less compatible with an ICL that strives to comply with the legality principle.[97]

One of the few contributions to the scholarly literature that explicitly raises the question of whether the legality principle correctly extends to modes of perpetration is the article by Sadat and Jolly.[98] The authors, as noted above, develop an interpretative canon of seven principles for interpreting the Rome Statute's Article 25. The idea is to aid the court in developing a uniform and consistent application of the modes of liability. This interpretive framework is based on the assumption that the principle of legality, in particular the subcomponent of strict construction, extends to *interpreting* the modes of liability, but the authors also concede that "an argument can certainly be made that Article 25 is not part of the crime's definition and therefore not subject to Article 22(2)'s application".[99] In a footnote, the authors further remark:

---

[95] Stefano Manacorda and Chantal Meloni, "Indirect Perpetration *versus* Joint Criminal Enterprise: Concurring Approaches in the Practice of International Criminal Law?", in *Journal of International Criminal Justice*, 2011, vol. 9, no. 1, pp. 159–78, at p. 165 ff.

[96] Gil Gil and Maculan, 2015, p. 350, see *supra* note 35. The authors also argue that the ICC Katanga judgment marks an important shift in this regard.

[97] Stewart, 2012, p. 214, see *supra* note 21.

[98] Sadat and Jolly, 2014, see *supra* note 50.

[99] *Ibid.*, pp. 759–60.

[I]t is perhaps useful to observe that some legal systems would not treat modes of criminal responsibility in the same manner as the substantive criminal law to which they apply, and it is not obvious from the Rome Statute itself that this was the drafters' intent. A full treatment of this question, therefore, is left for another day.[100]

As discussed in Chapter 2, the conceptual distinction between the substantive crime and the attribution of liability is also highlighted by Aksenova,[101] with particular reference to an older work by Fletcher. While Sadat and Jolly leave the question open, Fletcher takes the explicit stand that the issue of attribution belongs under a distinct set of norms directed primarily towards judges and jurors, not potential violators.[102] According to this perspective, the foreseeability purpose underlying the legality principle does not apply as much to the modes of liability as to the substantive crimes and the crime definitions. This argument is closely aligned with our own view on the matter. However, it is also important to underline that the absence of an either lawful or unlawful attribution of liability *dichotomy*, as generally instituted by the legality principle, does not leave courts free to impose liability at will. Thus we may recall that three sets of other requirements apply, according to the proposed general theory of criminal law liability:[103] (1) compliance with fundamental human rights principles;[104] (2) compliance with fundamental criminal law principles (which may overlap to some extent with human rights principles, notably with respect to the legality principle);[105] and (3) compliance with a broad-

---

[100] *Ibid.*, p. 760.

[101] Aksenova, 2016, p. 30, see *supra* note 8.

[102] George P. Fletcher, *Rethinking Criminal Law*, Little, Brown, Boston, 1978, pp. 491–92.

[103] See Chapter 2, Sections 2.1.2. and 2.2.2.1.

[104] They include, of course, the legality principle; see International Covenant on Civil and Political Rights, Article 15. Although the legality principle according to Article 15(3) is a bit limited in the context of universal crimes being prosecuted domestically, by requiring a legal basis in *either* "national or international law", the international legality principle in our view is directly applicable to *inchoate crimes* (and to distinct accomplice crimes such as membership or participation in a criminal/terrorist organisation) prosecuted before international tribunals, exactly because they are made distinct (accessorial) crimes and thus require a written legal basis in court statutes, as do all distinct crimes. See also Chapter 4, Section 4.3.7.

[105] Notably, inchoate liability must be based on the appearance of distinct inchoate crimes in the respective statutes, either explicitly or through interpretation of the relevant legal basis.

er notion of rule of law, which notably requires that courts of law provide sufficient reasons in their judgments as to why a conviction for attributable, punishable participation in a criminal enterprise is actually justified.

Overall, the role and scope of the legality principle with respect to the linking of individual participants to the crime, that is, attribution through the vehicles of derivative theoretical categories and operational modes of perpetration, is a crucial question that is currently insufficiently addressed in the scholarly literature – and as such, is in need of further theoretical scrutiny. As elaborated in Chapter 2 and discussed also in Chapter 4, an attractive and arguably more correct solution is to instead apply a broader perspective of the rule of law as a different and softer, yet principled and well-defined part of a more comprehensive approach to evaluating lawfulness of attribution of criminal law liability for completed crimes within ICL. This approach can still satisfy the legality principle, provided that legality in this regard is not limited to a clear legal basis in customary international law but also extends to a legal basis in the general principles of criminal law and international law.[106] However, the final conclusion on the matter shall be drawn at the end of this book, when the theory has been tested and reconsidered.[107]

6.3. Authors Discussing Specific Concepts of Participation

6.3.1. Different Forms of Commission Liability

Based on his comprehensive analysis of the modes of liability under Article 25(3) of the Rome Statute, Ambos highlights the fact that a system of different, potentially attributable modes of participation leaves as a vital task in future theory and practice to develop ICL into a sufficiently refined system that allows for precise delimitation of all distinct modes.[108] On the question of which specific theory of imputation would be best suited to differentiate between participants in criminal enterprises, however, he notes that the scholarly literature is divided: some authors favour a subjective theory of the JCE type, while others prefer the more objective test of

---

International tribunals, it seems, have always adhered to this rule and the underlying distinction between inchoate crimes and attribution of liability for completed crimes. See summary of the empirical findings in Chapter 10, Sections 10.2. and 10.5.

[106] See Chapter 4, Section 4.3.7.

[107] See Chapter 10, Section 10.8.

[108] Ambos, 2013, pp. 176–79, see *supra* note 1.

---

the control theory underlying indirect perpetration at the ICC, and still others advocate alternative theories.

While the review here focuses on recent scholarship, it should be noted that the notion of JCE liability, and its merits as a possibly distinct liability theory, has been subject to a longstanding and at times intense debate within the scholarly community, as well as disagreements among judges at international tribunals. As a brief background note in this regard, JCE liability was first developed, at least with respect to its constituent elements, in the Tadić appeal judgment.[109] Its most prominent feature is the existence of a common purpose or plan among those considered members of the relevant criminal enterprise.

As confirmed and further developed in the case law of the *ad hoc* tribunals, the broader notion of JCE embraces three distinct liability categories that are primarily distinguished by the required mental element.[110] The first, JCE I, requires that participants all share the same intent to commit the crime, including any specific intent required by the crime in question. JCE II, the so-called systemic variant of JCE I, applies to participation in a criminal plan, although this plan need not be express but may rather take the form of willing participation in a larger institutionalised system of criminality (concentration camp scenario). The accused is required to have had knowledge of the common plan and intent to further the system of ill-treatment. The last variant, JCE III or extended JCE liability, imposes liability on all members for acts (for instance, killing) committed by one or more members of the JCE that, although outside the common plan or purpose, were foreseeable in the ordinary course of events. The required mental element is akin to *dolus eventualis*. By his continuous participation in the JCE, the accused willingly accepted the risk that these foreseeable crimes would take place; or alternatively, he acted recklessly, that is, opted to remain indifferent to the risk of such foreseeable crimes.[111]

---

[109] See ICTY, Appeals Chamber, *Prosecutor v. Tadić*, Judgment, IT-94-1-A, 15 July 1999 (www.legal-tools.org/doc/8efc3a/).

[110] See Antonio Cassese, *Cassese's International Criminal Law*, 3rd ed., revised by Antonio Cassese, Paola Gaeta, Laure Baig, Mary Fan, Christopher Gosnell, and Alex Whiting, Oxford University Press, Oxford, 2013, p. 163.

[111] For a more detailed elaboration of the various categories of JCE liability, see *ibid.*, pp. 161–75.

The scholarly community has raised a number of objections against JCE liability at various levels. It has been suggested that the doctrine lacks the required specificity, concerning, among other things, the level of contribution required;[112] that with respect to extended JCE III in particular, the doctrine is at odds with the principle of personal culpability because it allows for guilt by association through a lower foreseeability standard as compared to intent;[113] that it does not sufficiently differentiate between the various members' level of participation;[114] and that questions can be raised about its statutory basis in the ICTY Statute Article 7(1) (commission liability) and about the legal status of extended JCE III under customary international law.[115]

This latter concern, regarding lack of both statutory and CIL basis, has also been raised as an objection against the control theory under the Rome Statute. In contrast to the more subjective focus on common plans and mental elements, the control theory is focused on the objective and essential contribution to the crime by a person in 'control' of the criminal enterprise, in the sense that the person accused of commission liability, although removed from the crime scene, could have chosen not to make his or her contribution to the crime, typically from the top level of the rel-

---

[112] See, for example, Allison M. Danner and Jenny Martinez, "Guilty Associations: Joint Criminal Enterprise, Command Responsibility, and the Development of International Criminal Law", in *California Law Review*, 2005, vol. 93, no. 1, pp. 75–169; Ciara Damgaard, *Individual Criminal Responsibility for Core International Crimes: Selected Pertinent Issues*, Springer, Berlin-Heidelberg, 2008; George P. Fletcher and Jens David Ohlin, "Reclaiming Fundamental Principles of Criminal Law in the Darfur Case", in *Journal of International Criminal Justice*, 2005, vol. 3, no. 3, pp. 539–61; and Robinson, 2008, see *supra* note 26.

[113] See, for example, Ambos, 2013, pp. 172–76, *supra* note 1; Danner and Martinez, 2005, *supra* note 112; Mark Osiel, "The Banality of Good: Aligning Incentives against Mass Atrocity", in *Columbia Law Review*, 2005, vol. 105, no. 6, pp. 1751–1862; Steven Powles, "Joint Criminal Enterprise: Criminal Liability by Prosecutorial Ingenuity and Judicial Creativity?", in *Journal of International Criminal Justice*, 2004, vol. 2, no. 2, pp. 606–19; Damgaard, 2008, *supra* note 112; Fletcher and Ohlin, 2005, *supra* note 112; and Robinson, 2008, *supra* note 26.

[114] See Ohlin, 2011, *supra* note 65; Van Sliedregt, 2012, p. 142, *supra* note 3; and Jens David Ohlin, "Three Conceptual Problems with the Doctrine of Joint Criminal Enterprise", in *Journal of International Criminal Justice*, 2007, vol. 5, no. 1, pp. 69–90, especially pp. 76–77.

[115] See, for example, Powles, 2004, *supra* note 113; Danner and Martinez, 2005, *supra* note 112; and Damgaard, 2008, *supra* note 112.

---

evant power structure, and in so choosing would have prevented the crime from being completed. However, Clarke can be understood to downplay the importance of the critique against JCE as well as the control theory; he argues that in contrast to the common objection that the control theory rests too heavily on only a few domestic systems, the basis for the control theory is also firmly grounded in the jurisprudence of the IMT and the subsequent Nuremberg cases' application of Control Council Law No. 10.[116] According to this account, what are now known as the doctrines of JCE and control theory were little more than two sides of the same coin in the early jurisprudence.[117]

In other words, Clarke implicitly makes the argument that both doctrines may be implemented in parallel. This is an interesting point from the perspective of our general theory of personal criminal law liability as set forth in Chapter 2, because the fundamental and secondary principles it contains provide for the possibility of different levels and forms of derivative liability at the operational fourth level of the theory. The implication is that the principles are mainly rules of competence within certain limits to criminalise different forms and to attribute liability through broader categories or more specific modes of liability setting out the required material and mental elements, rather than strict act-based rules addressed to the person concerned (the accused). This allows for certain variations at the operational level within and between different criminal law subsystems under a common theoretical umbrella applicable in ICL, so that different doctrines and rules may compete with or complement each other even though all or some are lawful and possible within a *specific* subsystem. We shall return to this latter point in Chapter 10, after having explored the jurisprudence of international and domestic courts, which should make clearer whether the general theory in fact is able to explain outcomes at the fourth operational level where it ultimately counts the most: in the criminal trials of persons accused of universal crimes.

While the debate sketched above is still ongoing, especially following the ICC's adoption of the control theory but (so far) not JCE liability for commission liability under Article 25(3)(a) of the Rome Statute, some

---

[116] Robert C. Clarke, "Together Again? Customary Law and Control over the Crime", in *Criminal Law Forum*, 2015, vol. 26, no. 3, pp. 457–95, in particular pp. 466–89.

[117] *Ibid.*, pp. 487 and 495.

parts of the recent debate have focused on the *relative* merits of these two alternative theories of liability. Yanev and Kooijmans are among those who reject the notion of control theory as a suitable approach to differentiating between principals and accessories under the Rome Statute, citing both principled and practical grounds for their objection.[118] Based on an analysis of the wording of Article 25(3)(a), the *travaux préparatoires*, as well as asserted CIL and select national law, they conclude that there is no statutory basis for the control theory at the ICC. Second, they also object to the court's adoption of the control theory, as it constitutes an impractical approach to co-perpetration – in particular, in the opinion of these authors, because of the "essential contribution" requirement employed by the ICC, which they consider to be "unreasonably restrictive and leading to 'hypothetical and abstract value judgments'".[119] Rather, Yanev and Kooijmans concur with Ohlin (elaborated below) that "intentionality", instead of objective control, should be at the centre of any doctrine of group criminality.[120] Sadat and Jolly also are critical of the control theory of commission liability under the Rome Statute. Applying their interpretative framework, they proclaim the adoption of the control theory to violate each of the seven-part canon, concluding that its inclusion under the Rome Statute is improper regardless of its usefulness at a theoretical level.[121]

On the other side of the debate, Wirth argues that the control theory, with its objective criterion for differentiating between principal and accessorial liability, is preferable to any subjective approach.[122] In particular, Wirth asserts that, considering that damage to the values that criminal law strives to protect (for example, life, physical integrity, property) is caused through the *actus reus*, rules of attribution should "focus on the damage and the actor's objective contribution to it [...] not on the – sometimes subtle – distinction as to whether the damage caused was the actor's pur-

---

[118] See Lachezar Yanev and Tijs Kooijmans, "Divided Minds in the Lubanga Trial Judgment: A Case against the Control Theory", in *International Criminal Law Review*, 2013, vol. 13, no. 4, pp. 789–828.

[119] *Ibid.*, p. 827.

[120] *Ibid.*, p. 828.

[121] Sadat and Jolly, 2014, p. 756, see *supra* note 50.

[122] Wirth, 2012, pp. 977–78, see *supra* note 63.

pose or 'merely' the (probable) result of his/her conduct".[123] The author further highlights practical and prosecutorial policy reasons for preferring the control standard. Although the article does present several objections to some of the specific elements, as defined by the ICC for co-perpetration under the control theory, Wirth highlights the theory's advantages over JCE,[124] including simplicity and the fact that the overall approach taken by the ICC makes it well suited to meet future challenges in attribution of liability.[125]

In a similar vein, Manacorda and Meloni praise the control theory for avoiding the at times confusing differentiation of the gravity of the contributions of members of a JCE, as compared to the contribution by others who are not included as members, thus providing a clearer and more precise definition of the concept of perpetration as commission liability. They do, however, recognise weaknesses of the current control formula, particularly with respect to its application to scenarios featuring more informal power structures.[126] Nevertheless, the authors favour the control theory over JCE on the basis of the fundamental principles of criminal law liability. First, the status of JCE under CIL, and thus its adherence to the legality principle, is questioned; and second, the particular mix of objective and subjective factors when determining the threshold of the control theory is considered to be more in line with the principle of culpability – in particular when compared to JCE III.[127]

---

[123] *Ibid.*, p. 978.

[124] For some of the more specific critique that has been forwarded against the JCE doctrine, see further below, in particular regarding the contribution by Ohlin, 2011, see *supra* note 65.

[125] Wirth, 2012, p. 977, see *supra* note 63.

[126] Manacorda and Meloni, 2011, pp. 164, 171 ff., see *supra* note 95. For a comparison of the common plan requirement in the JCE III jurisprudence and its consequences for crimes beyond the original plan at the ICTY/ICTR with the judgments in this area at the SCSL/ECCC and the caselaw regarding joint perpetration at the ICC, see Lachezar Yanev, "On Common Plans and Excess Crimes: Fragmenting the Notion of Co-Perpetration in International Criminal Law", in *Leiden Journal of International Law*, 2018, vol. 31, no. 3, pp. 693-718. Manacorda and Meloni, 2011, pp. 164, 171 ff., see *supra* note 95.

[127] *Ibid.*, pp. 166–67 and 174. For a similar critique of the doctrine of JCE being contrary to the principle of culpability as well as fair labelling, see Robinson, 2008, *supra* note 26. Note, however, that some authors argue that the ICC has in fact required a relatively weak *mens rea*, and that this introduces a form of liability akin to JCE III under the Rome Stat-

The theoretical contribution in the book by Ambos is also largely in line with a control theory approach to attribution of commission liability, although – recalling the discussion on comparative law versus autonomous law approaches to ICL in Section 6.2.1. – he stresses the need for the theory employed to be adapted to the particularities of imputation in the ICL context. In particular, Ambos holds:

> [T]he discussion of the organizational control theory (*Organisationsherrschaftslehre*) shows that the *system of individual attribution of responsibility*, as used for ordinary criminality, must be modified in ICL, aiming at the development of a mixed system of individual-collective responsibility in which the overall act or criminal situation (*Gesamttat*) and the criminal enterprise or organization which controls this situation take centre stage and serve as the points of reference for imputation.[128]

As for each individual participant, his or her criminal contribution must be assessed based on its effect on the overall criminal plan or purpose pursued by the criminal enterprise or organisation. In this regard, Ambos points out:

> The control criterion, especially in its variant of a functional, mutual domination of the commission as required in the context of co-perpetration, may lose importance because of the collective or systemic dimension of the criminal events.[129]

The author himself describes this as a system of "organizational domination in stages", where domination would require "at least some form of control over part of the organization".[130] More precisely, according to this model, which we may refer to as 'the combined individual-collective liability theory', the distinction between principals and accessories should be determined by means of a descriptive three-level hierarchy within a power structure, based on domination/control of the act.[131]

---

ute and the control theory. See Ohlin, Van Sliedregt, and Weigend, 2013, *supra* note 80; and Gil Gil and Maculan, 2015, *supra* note 35.

[128] Ambos, 2013, p. 177, *supra* note 1.

[129] *Ibid.*, p. 178.

[130] *Ibid.*,

[131] *Ibid.*, pp. 177–79.

The highest, leadership level includes persons qualifying as possible indirect perpetrators, based on their capacity to exercise total and undisturbed control over the organisation and its criminal activities. The second level is populated by mid-level actors responsible for implementing the top-level decisions and policies through further planning and organisational activities. While these persons often possess control over the practical implementation, they typically lack capacity to exercise the sort of total control that characterises the top-level perpetrators, rendering the mid-level actors as possible co-perpetrators or accomplices rather than indirect perpetrators. The third level consists of the ground-level executors. Under the control paradigm presented by Ambos, they qualify only as accomplices in the universal crimes being committed,[132] despite being the physical perpetrators of the underlying offences at the relevant crime scenes.[133]

While the contributions discussed so far focus on the merits of the JCE versus control theory doctrines, Ohlin by contrast rejects the suitability of both.[134] He develops instead an alternative approach for distinguishing between the various forms of participation based on a modification of the JCE doctrine. This third approach or theory is labelled 'joint intention'. As we understand it, the key is a shared mental state of mind among the relevant participants, one that is profound, resulting in a common plan with respect to the successful completion of certain crimes. According to Ohlin, the proposed new theory downplays the objective element of the control theory in favour of the collective mental framework of the participants. Ohlin also stresses the existence of a common plan as a critical

---

[132] See *ibid.*, n. 74.

[133] Whether a physical perpetrator (executor) of an underlying crime – for example, someone who commits the murder of a civilian in the context of a widespread or systematic attack against a civilian population constituting a crime against humanity, or in the context of a specific intent to destroy a protected group amounting to genocide – is liable for commission liability or accomplice liability seems to depend on the personal intent of the executor. While the Rome Statute's Article 25(3)(a), read in conjunction with Article 30 ('Mental element'), on its face applies to all physical perpetrators acting with the required *mens rea*, including intent to commit an offence and knowledge of the relevant social context, the question seems more open-ended with respect to the crime of genocide, where executors of the underlying crimes may act with intent and knowledge, but maybe not with specific genocidal intent. Hence, accomplice liability seems to be an alternative to commission liability if the specific intent is lacking or cannot be sufficiently proven.

[134] See Ohlin, 2011, *supra* note 65. See also Ohlin, 2014, *supra* note 88.

commonality between the current JCE doctrine and the IMT doctrine of conspiracy. The common plan thus represents an externalisation of a deeper common intent among the relevant participants for the crime(s) to occur. In consequence, it must be assumed, the group members who might be liable for commission liability become fewer and more clearly defined than in the current doctrines. This feature, he argues, also unites the (objective) control theory and (subjective) JCE into a single doctrine, centred on the concept of collective intent.[135]

Ohlin praises the current JCE doctrine for at least implicitly building on the participants' joint intentions, but he is at the same time highly critical of JCE III for extending vicarious liability to crimes that fall outside the scope of the common plan.[136] The insistence on equal culpability for all members of the JCE, regardless of the scope of their participation (their actual contribution), is seen by Ohlin as a major weakness of JCE liability in that it insufficiently differentiates the blameworthiness of each JCE participant.

With respect to the doctrine of co-perpetration, Ohlin acknowledges its merits in avoiding the problems resulting from JCE III but criticises it for exaggerating the importance of control through the "essential contribution" requirement and for simultaneously undervaluing the importance of common intent as the crucial element in attributing commission liability for group criminality. According to Ohlin, the joint intention theory resolves these problems by eliminating over-expansive vicarious liability and offering a subtler differentiation of the participants' culpability, which the author sees as a crucial task. Under the joint intention theory, principal liability is only appropriate for those who share a clear common intent to commit the crimes, while those falling short of this intention are to be considered accessories. In terms of labelling, a more subtle system of liability in line with this theory, Ohlin argues, could be achieved by revising and spitting the current JCE doctrine into "two more specific and accurate modes of liability" in which individuals acting with intention are considered as co-perpetrators of the JCE, while those acting without similar intention but with knowledge that they assist in the criminal enterprise are

---

[135] See to the contrary, however, Lachezar Yanev, "A Janus-faced Concept: Nuremberg's Law on Conspiracy *vis-à-vis* the Notion of Joint Criminal Enterprise", in *Criminal Law Forum*, 2015, vol. 26, no. 3, pp. 419–56.

[136] Ohlin, 2011, p. 747, *supra* note 65.

considered aiders and abettors of the JCE.[137] By applying both the control theory and the proposed joint intention theory to hypothetical cases, the author further claims to demonstrate the shortcomings of the former and the superiority of the latter.

Ohlin's joint intention theory has been subject to critique, however, in particular by authors rushing to defend the merits of the control theory. Countering Ohlin's argument in favour of a subjective approach, Granik, for example, emphasises the need for a theory adapted to attribution of liability for high-level leaders removed from the crime scene.[138] She argues that the most appropriate course of action is to employ the theory that best balances a subjective focus on intention and an objective requirement for action.[139]

Thus, Granik criticises Ohlin's proposal as suffering from the opposite of what he argues is wrong with the control theory: the joint intention approach, she contends, unduly shifts the balance too far by overemphasising the requirement for an existing collective mental framework. Rather, she holds the control theory to better adhere to the principle of culpability and fair labelling through its more balanced mix of objective and subjective criteria. Although she acknowledges the usefulness of the joint intention theory in differentiating the level of culpability in the five scenarios offered by Ohlin in his discussion of hypothetical cases, the objective component of the control theory, an essential contribution to the criminal enterprise, better reflects the degree of culpability for the most responsible, high-level co-perpetrators who orchestrate the commission of crimes from a distance.

Differentiating perpetrators and accomplices exclusively on whether or not they have joint intention does not, according to Granik, do justice to the differences in degree of responsibility between the true masterminds of the crime and the foot soldiers.[140] We would like to point out, however, that the latter critique might arise from a misunderstanding of Ohlin's theory, which is not concerned with foot soldiers who have not

---

[137] *Ibid.*, pp. 714–15.

[138] Maria Granik, "Indirect Perpetration Theory: A Defence", in *Leiden Journal of International Law*, 2015, vol. 28, no. 4, pp. 977–92, at p. 978.

[139] *Ibid.*, p. 978.

[140] *Ibid.*, p. 986.

taken part in the common plan. It still seems to be a valid point, though, that at least in some factual circumstances the control theory, in line with Granik's point of view, better reflects that prominent masterminds are particularly culpable. Granik also highlights the legitimacy of the control theory following its use in domestic jurisdictions, citing, among others, Ambos on its usefulness in convicting the former Peruvian president Fujimori,[141] and Muñoz-Conde and Olásolo on its employment in several other Latin American countries.[142]

Similarly, Jain offers a comprehensive analysis of the potential merits of the control theory based on its application in German domestic law.[143] She primarily sides with Granik, although she strongly warns that an uncritical adoption of the German concepts of co-perpetration and indirect perpetration based on control theory, without adaptation to the specific nature of universal crimes, would be a disastrous path to follow.

In this regard, we would like to point out that the German concepts based on the control theory have been influenced by Roxin, who discussed the notion of indirect perpetration to leaders in a seminal article in 1963.[144] Roxin was concerned with the relationship between organised power structures and collective crimes. In his opinion, one may understand the acts of leaders from the point of view of criminal law in two ways, as collective crimes or as individual acts, but "[n]either of the two viewpoints can, in isolation, entirely encompass the substantive criminality of the occurrences".[145] He highlighted in particular the feature of control over an organised power structure by actors who remain behind the scenes, suggesting that an absence of proximity to the crime in question might be "compensated by an increasing degree of organizational control

---

[141] Kai Ambos, "The *Fujimori* Judgment: A President's Responsibility for Crimes Against Humanity as Indirect Perpetrators by Virtue of an Organized Power Apparatus", in *Journal of International Criminal Justice*, 2011, vol. 9, no. 1, pp. 137–58.

[142] Francisco Muñoz-Conde and Héctor Olásolo, "The Application of the Notion of Indirect Perpetration through Organized Structures of Power in Latin America and Spain", in *Journal of International Criminal Justice*, 2011, vol. 9, no. 1, pp. 113–35.

[143] Jain, 2011, see *supra* note 20.

[144] Claus Roxin, "Crimes as Part of Organized Power Structures", *Journal of International Criminal Justice*, 2011, vol. 9, no. 1, pp. 193–205. Originally published in German in 1963; republished in 2011 in an English translation by Belinda Cooper.

[145] *Ibid.*, p. 194.

by the leadership positions in the apparatus".[146] In other words, according to Roxin, the farther removed such a punishable participant is, in structural terms, from the victim and the direct criminal act, the more responsibility he bears for the crimes committed.[147] Roxin underlined that the number of victims is not conclusive in determining perpetration at the highest level: "[if] only a single person has been persecuted, the person behind the scenes would still have to be convicted as a perpetrator". These observations and assumptions are in our opinion important for a proper understanding of the general theory of personal criminal liability as well, especially when applied to responsibility for universal crimes.

So, although we agree with Jain that adaption to the specific nature of universal crimes is warranted, Roxin's thoughts underlying the control theory are in fact in line with the nature of these crimes. This does not mean, however, that a particular version of the control theory is the only relevant – or always the best – theory for attributing liability to leaders of the relevant power structures, as the similar but still different notion of JCE liability at the *ad hoc* tribunals later has indicated.

In particular, Jain points out some features of the control doctrine in its domestic or strict form that are less suitable for some current realities of mass atrocity. Among others, they include Roxin's notion of a tightly structured hierarchical organisation that often is not reflected in the more informal power structures found in real life, as well as the related criterion of fungible subordinates, a scenario that is not likely in the context of all specific offences and is also less suited to smaller organisations where members are more difficult to replace.[148] Jain's main point, however, is that the control of the crime concept still offers the best starting point for building a coherent theory of criminal participation in ICL – which, according to the author, is currently lacking.[149]

Furthermore, Jain argues that the control theory subsumes several forms of conduct under a single concept of 'control', thus providing a

[146] *Ibid.*, p. 200.

[147] *Ibid.* "We can see that the objective elements of organizational control are very clearly delineated here: whereas normally, the farther removed a participant is from the victim and the direct criminal act, the more he is pushed to the margins of events and excluded from control over the acts, in this case the reverse is true".

[148] Jain, 2011, see *supra* note 20, pp. 194–95.

[149] *Ibid.*, p. 196 ff.

framework for a nuanced theory of perpetration as well as tying attribution to the elements of the crime rather than to the blameworthiness of a person's internal attitude.[150] Concerning Ohlin's alternative theory, Jain holds his criticism of the control theory to be based on an unsatisfactory analysis of its application in domestic jurisdictions, and hence a misconstruction of its proper nature. First, most of Ohlin's critique, she argues, is limited to the 'co-perpetration' component of the control theory. He thus also mistakenly uses co-perpetration to demonstrate the insufficiencies of the control theory in his hypothetical concentration camp scenario, which is better dealt with under the concept of indirect co-perpetration, according to Jain. More importantly, perhaps, she questions his claim that the control theory is excessively focused on the objective elements. She also thinks Ohlin's argument that the control theory has nothing to add to his 'joint intention' theory is flawed. On the contrary, the notion of joint intention constitutes at best only a necessary, but not a sufficient, account of perpetration liability for collective crimes. Unlike the control theory, Ohlin's theory says nothing on the *actus reus* requirement.[151] Therefore, Jain largely agrees with Granik in stressing the virtues of the control theory as a doctrine based on a successful mix of subjective and objective elements, as demonstrated in judicial practice.

In sum, while the merits of the doctrine of JCE have been widely debated among ICL scholars since its emergence in the ICTY Tadić appeal judgment, the alternative control theory of attribution embraced by the ICC under the Rome Statute has further shaped the debate within the scholarly community. Scholars writing more recently tend to position themselves either as proponents of a subjective approach, similar to that taken by the *ad hoc* tribunals through the vehicle of JCE, or as proponents of the control theory adopted by the ICC. Although many scholars favouring the control theory also recognise the importance of a subjective component, they find the mix of objective and subjective criteria under the control theory preferable. An important modification to the general trend, however, is that proponents of both sides express some ambivalence, either warning against an uncritical elevation of a particular domestic doctrine to the level of international law (albeit with some dissent, pointing to

---

[150] *Ibid.*, p. 162.
[151] *Ibid.*, p. 193.

predecessors also at the subsequent Nuremberg cases) or advocating a subjective theory based on a modified version of the current JCE doctrine. Consequently, the literature has not reached a consensus on attribution of commission liability for chief participants in criminal enterprises who are often removed from the crime scenes where universal crimes are carried out, but there are scholarly contributions and trends pointing towards a possible consensus in the future.

Ultimately the question is how the general theory of criminal law liability may be helpful in this regard. In line with our thinking, part of the answer seems to be that the control theory and the JCE doctrine are not mutually exclusive, in principle not even in a particular criminal law subsystem. They are, rather, complementary concepts and both fall within the lawful range of fair attribution of commission liability. Thus a court of law may, depending on the relevant legal sources, find space for the coexistence of both liability concepts.

6.3.2. Different Kinds of Liability for Omission

The question of general omission liability in ICL has been sporadically addressed in various works, with no clear consensus emerging. Ambos, in an earlier contribution, for example, asserts that as the Rome Conference failed to include a general rule on omission in the final version, the legality principle in Article 22 of the Rome Statute thus blocks the ICC from employing this form of liability in its general form.[152] This sounds perhaps a bit surprising, since omission liability is presumably well known in most criminal law subsystems and thus may also be inherent in the norms of attribution of ICL liability. Hence, Van Sliedregt, on the other hand, holds it as doubtful that the legality principle prohibits the inclusion of omission liability under Article 25, as she considers participation by omission to form part of CIL and the general principles of international law inherent in ICL. Its applicability under the Rome Statute should therefore, in her opinion, follow through Article 21(1)(b) and (c).[153] In the more re-

---

[152] Kai Ambos, "Article 25", in Otto Triffterer (ed.), *Commentary on the Rome Statute of the International Criminal Court: Observers' Notes, Article by Article*, C.H. Beck, Munich, 2008, p. 770, margin no. 51. The question here of *general* omission liability is different from that of specific forms of omission liability such as command and superior responsibility, which of course Ambos recognises.

[153] Van Sliedregt, 2012, p. 94, see *supra* note 3.

cent book by Ambos, as already mentioned on several occasions, his elaborated position is more nuanced and possibly changed. While maintaining that there exists no specific rule on liability for commission by omission *in general* in ICL amounting to customary law or principles of international law, he now concurs that there might exist a "traditional general principle of law" for omission liability if a legal duty and material ability to act exists. Ambos also argues *lex ferenda*:

> [F]rom a policy perspective, it is difficult to understand why the ICC should not be in a position to prosecute a commission by omission if this is done, by one way or the other, in most criminal justice systems of the world and by the ad hoc tribunals.[154]

Even more relevant for the present purpose, Ambos further underlines that the underlying rationale and specific elements of commission by omission liability "still need to be further developed".[155] Again, there is an obvious link here to the general discussion of whether the international legality principle extends its applicability to attribution of liability for completed crimes. More commonly, the literature has tended to discuss omission liability with respect to specific modes of liability. For example, an article by Ingle addresses the incoherencies in the ICTY and ICTR jurisprudence on liability for aiding and abetting (complicity) by omission, reflecting how the tribunals have struggled to develop a coherent doctrine.[156] Based on these observations, the author stresses the need for an analysis of the fundamental philosophical (theoretical) principles underlying liability for aiding and abetting by omission, which she argues centre on the critical distinction between positive acts and negative omissions. In particular, given that this mode of liability is premised on the criminal acts of a third party, such as the physical perpetrator of the completed crime, and on a failure to act by the accomplice, a sound theoretical grounding of its application is held to be critical.

Ingle specifically highlights two problems with the jurisprudence of the *ad hoc* tribunals, which she portrays as posing a risk of an unwarrant-

---

[154] Ambos, 2013, pp. 189–97, see *supra* note 1.

[155] *Ibid.*, p. 197.

[156] Jessie Ingle, "Aiding and Abetting by Omission before the International Criminal Tribunals", in *Journal of International Criminal Justice*, 2016, vol. 14, no. 4, pp. 747–69.

ed expansion of liability for aiding and abetting by omission.[157] First, some judgments have simply transposed the elements of aiding and abetting by positive acts to the act of omission, without any profound analysis or comparison of the scope of liability for omissions and positive acts for an aider and abettor. This, the author argues, should be avoided – both to guard against collective punishment, and thus adhere to the principle of individual liability and culpability, as well as to ensure consistency with the principle of legality. In her view, the doctrine of aiding and abetting liability must clearly and accurately separate instances of acts and omissions.[158]

Second, and closely related, while the *ad hoc* tribunals have required a causal link in the form of a "substantial effect" for positive acts, Ingle holds that the accompanying counterfactual analysis is problematic with respect to commission and complicity by omission – in particular when also including a punishable third party such as the physical perpetrator in the context of aiding and abetting. In order to overcome this expansion of omission liability, imposing such liability should hinge on a so-called 'duty of guarantee'.[159] This means, according to Ingle, that the duty must be such that it can be established by meticulous counterfactual analysis that the criminal result would not have taken place – or at least would have been substantially less likely to have taken place – if the accused had properly acted in accordance with the duty. In order to adhere to the principles of legality and personal culpability, the author recommends that the duty to act must be a real duty under criminal law as opposed to a duty under other parts of law, and that liability for the acts of a third party should only arise where a special relationship exists beyond that of pure omissions.[160]

---

[157] See also Ines Peterson, "Open Questions Regarding Aiding and Abetting Liability in International Criminal Law: A Case Study of ICTY and ICTR Jurisprudence", in *International Criminal Law Review*, 2016, vol. 16, no. 4, pp. 565–612. Based on a comprehensive analysis of the ICTY and ICTR jurisprudence on aiding and abetting with a special focus on imposing liability for high-ranking politicians and military leaders remote from the crime scene, this author suggests that the *ad hoc* tribunals occasionally have over-expanded the scope of liability for aiding and abetting in general (that is, not only in the specific context of omissions).

[158] Ingle, 2016, pp. 747, 763, see *supra* note 156.

[159] *Ibid.*, p. 764.

[160] *Ibid.*, p. 153 ff.

Although one may not agree with Ingle on all aspects of her analysis, for our purpose it is interesting to note her call to think through the underlying theoretical principles in this regard – in effect, reinforcing the call by many others for a possible general theory of attribution of liability for punishable participation in completed universal crimes.[161]

The question of omission liability has been further addressed in the literature in the context of command and superior responsibility, often focusing on the problems of establishing some kind of sufficient normative linkage between the asserted omission and the completed crime, often cast in terms of a causal requirement. It should be noted from the outset, however, that the issue of such a linkage might be challenging, depending on the concrete factual circumstances, with respect to all potential criminal conduct consisting primarily of inaction or omission.

Still, there might be particular sub-issues connected to this form of liability within ICL. Thus, as part of building his argument in favour of a unitary system, Stewart reviews among others the previous scholarly critique of command responsibility as a step towards establishing a benchmark by which to assess the merits of the complicity doctrine. In this vein, Stewart analyses the criticism of the practice of convicting superiors for the failure to punish subordinates, highlighting what he describes as the majority view that "using failure to punish as a vehicle for convicting the

---

[161] Another topic that has often been debated with respect to aiding and abetting liability is the possible requirement for 'specific direction' as an element of this mode of liability. See, for example, Janine Clark, "'Specific Direction' and the Fragmentation of International Jurisprudence on Aiding and Abetting: Perišić and Beyond", in *International Criminal Law Review*, 2015, vol. 15, no. 3, pp. 411–51. She provides a comprehensive analysis of the Perišić appeal judgment, arguing that the Appeals Chamber's elevation of the "specific direction" requirement is unsupported and has contributed to fragmentation of the international jurisprudence on aiding and abetting – which in turn is held to undermine legal certainty, at least in the short run. See also Leila Sadat, "Can the ICTY *Šainović* and *Perišić* Cases Be Reconciled?", in *American Journal of International Law*, 2014, vol. 108, no. 3, pp. 475–85; Shane Darcy, "Assistance, direction and control: Untangling international judicial opinion on individual and State responsibility for war crimes by non-State actors", International Review of the Red Cross (2014), vol. 96, no. 893, pp. 243–273475–85; and Frédéric Mégret and Sienna Anstis, "The Taylor Case; Aiding and Abetting, 'Specific Direction' and the Possibility of Negligence Liability for Remote Offenders", in Charles Jalloh and Alhagi Marong (eds.), *Promoting Accountability for Gross Human Rights Violations in Africa under International Law: Essays in Honour of Prosecutor Hassan Bubacar Jallow*, Brill/Martinus Nijhoff, Leiden, 2015.

superior of the same offence as the subordinate is 'largely disproportion-ate'".[162] In sum, Stewart contends:

> If international criminal justice is to become coherent not harsh, causation is an indispensable element for the perpetra-tion of all harm-type offences.[163]

This specific issue is more comprehensively addressed in an article by Robinson, who argues that the current state of law on command responsibility in ICL jurisprudence is too complicated and should be simplified in order to better adhere to the principle of culpability.[164] In particular, by claiming causation as an indispensable component of the principle of personal culpability, the author finds that the tribunal jurisprudence has underplayed and in effect erroneously dismissed causation as a material element of this mode – that is, as irreconcilable with the "failure to pun-

---

[162] Stewart, 2012, pp. 183–84, see *supra* note 21. The claim that it is "the same crime" does not seem accurate, however. Even if it is so constructed, we have difficulty seeing why different actors cannot be held liable for their own contributions to a criminal enterprise, just because the contribution formally is an omission *ex post*. If soldiers have a reason to believe they will not be punished for atrocities, it is more likely that atrocities will be committed in the first place, and it is the duty of commanders to make clear that impunity will not follow atrocities at any time. Hence, lack of punishment is tantamount to accepting crimes committed and tacitly encouraging new crimes. Such conduct is extremely socially dangerous and thus clearly worthy of punishment, for preventive reasons and for justice to be reinstated.

[163] *Ibid.*, p. 184.

[164] Darryl Robinson, "How Command Responsibility Got So Complicated: A Culpability Contradiction, Its Obfuscation, and a Simple Solution", in *Melbourne Journal of International Law*, 2012, vol. 13, no. 1, pp. 1–58. See also Robinson, 2008, p. 949 ff., *supra* note 26. See also Darryl Robinson, "A Justification of Command Responsibility", in *Criminal Law Forum*, 2017, vol. 28, no. 4, pp. 633-668, in which he examines the "mens rea" aspect of command responsibility and comes to the conclusion that the "should have known" standard as set out in the ICC Statute, which in his view incorporates criminal negligence and the duty to inquire is a sound approach from a doctrinal perspective. Although this chapter is concerned with the literature, it is perhaps interesting to note that the discussion of command responsibility by Judge Eboe-Osuji in the Bemba appeals judgment resembles a law journal article seeking to clarify principled aspects of the law on command responsibility, including the approach to causation, and may be read as such. See ICC, Appeals Chamber, *Prosecutor v. Bemba*, Judgment, Concurring Separate Opinion of Judge Eboe-Osuji, ICC-01/05-01/08 A, 8 June 2018, para. 151 ff. (www.legal-tools.org/doc/b31f6b/). See also Kazuya Yokohama, "The Failure to Control and the Failure to Prevent, Repress and Submit: The Structure of Superior Responsibility under Article 28 ICC Statute", in *International Criminal Law Review*, 2018, vol. 18, no. 2, pp. 275-303 although this article was published before the decision of the Appeal Chamber in the Bemba case.

---

ish" category.[165] To ensure compliance with fundamental principles of criminal law liability, Robinson proposes what he calls a "simple and elegant solution", categorising command responsibility as an accessorial mode of liability where an omission, also in the form of failure to have crimes investigated and prosecuted, is construed as perfectly reconcilable with a causation element.[166] More precisely, while he holds "failure to prevent" as posing no particular problem, the "failure to punish" branch of command responsibility is reconciled with causation when being applied only to instances of a "series of crimes".[167]

Liability for failure to punish, under Robinson's liability theory, thus cannot be retroactively imposed for the first crime in the series since there is an absence of causal contribution to these completed crimes. Liability can, however, legitimately be imposed for the ensuing crimes under the logic that the commander's culpable omission in relation to the first crime contributed to the scenario of new crimes.[168] While Robinson recognises the unavoidable impunity for single-crime cases under his proposal, this in his view is a consequence of taking the principle of personal culpability seriously.[169] The author finds this solution preferable, as it also serves to reconcile the early case law with command responsibility under the Rome Statute.[170] As for a theory of what satisfies the causality standard under command responsibility, Robinson argues for an elastic "risk aggravation" theory under which it suffices that the commander's omission increased the risk of subsequent crimes taking place.[171] Lastly, Robinson notes that an alternative could be to recognise command responsibility as a separate (distinct) crime, rather than as a mode linking the superior to other crimes, but he rejects this option on grounds that it is currently blocked under ICL due to the legality principle.[172]

---

[165] Robinson, 2012, pp. 3, 16, and 25–29, see *supra* note 164.

[166] *Ibid.*, pp. 16–17.

[167] *Ibid.*

[168] *Ibid.*, p. 17.

[169] *Ibid.*

[170] See Rome Statute, Article 28, which requires that the crimes committed by subordinates were "a result of his or her [the commander's] failure to exercise control properly".

[171] Robinson, 2012, pp. 44–46, and 53–56, see *supra* note 164.

[172] *Ibid.*, pp. 4–5 and p. 30 ff.

While we agree that the legality principle requires a legal basis in the Rome Statute for distinct crimes – whether these are the main crimes (genocide, crimes against humanity, war crimes, crime of aggression), or inchoate crimes punishable whether the main crimes are completed or not, or distinct accessorial crimes otherwise annexed to the main crimes – the legality principle, in our view, is satisfied in any case with respect to criminal law liability for command responsibility and superior responsibility under Article 28 of the Rome Statute. Just as the conduct element and the culpability element are set forth in some detail for the inchoate crime of attempt in Article 25(3)(f), both elements are also sufficiently described in Article 28 and thus clearly satisfy the legality principle in that regard. Furthermore, since command and superior responsibility for conduct constituting a serious breach of duty no doubt is potentially punishable under customary international law, the legality principle is also satisfied in this regard.[173]

In our view, moreover, commission liability for acts of omission or inaction in criminal law generally may also have something in common with criminal liability for culpable acts of negligence resulting in harm as well as with criminal liability for acts or omissions creating an unacceptable risk of harm. Hence the underlying reasons for command and superior responsibility in ICL are grounded in the social expectation under the rule of law that persons with great power are able to both direct and inflict *and* prevent and punish criminal acts through their control over subordinates in situations involving armed conflict and mass violence. Such situations are inherently dangerous to civilians and especially to vulnerable groups in society and thus call for responsible commanders and superiors to do the right thing, even when confronted with difficult choices. The concept of causation is not mechanical in these contexts. The legal issue of the leader's culpability focuses on a possible failure to take necessary, reasonable, and timely measures to prevent or punish the criminal conduct that likely or surely would be, was being, or had been committed by subordinates. However, commission by omission requires that it be proven beyond a reasonable doubt that the commander or superior in effect could have prevented, or could have investigated and punished, the criminal acts committed by subordinates – and that the commander knew, or should

---

[173] For further discussion of the legality principle generally with respect to the crime description under CIL, see Chapter 4, Sections 4.3.3. and 4.3.7.

have known, about these acts based upon reasonable and sufficient information available to him.

This standard of culpability also implies that the commander or superior should be expected to act proactively to prevent serious crimes and should not wait until he is told about crimes being planned or being committed. For instance, with regard to crimes against civilians typically committed during armed conflict – such as wilful killing, torture, pillage, and sexual violence, including rape – it would be expected that the commander or superior clearly makes known to his subordinates, by means of instruction, order, or a compulsory code of conduct, that these are prohibited criminal acts that will be punished. This would be a practical and important first step before employing the troops or armed group and may not be too much to expect from a military or civilian leader. Second, oversight and monitoring mechanisms should be in place to provide relevant information to the commander or superior about the actual conduct of his subordinates. Third, it should be expected that the commander or superior will make use of the information and oversight mechanisms for assessment of possible crimes before, during, and after operations. Failure in these respects may indicate that the commander or superior has not taken his responsibility seriously, although other measures taken, to some degree at least, may have compensated for an initial failure. However, it should not matter whether the commander or superior operates a highly professional army or a private militia, or was close to or remote from an actual crime scene, because a person who chose to take on the role of a commander or superior already knew or should have known the social expectations of such a role with respect to prevention and prosecution of universal crimes. Hence, as urged by Robinson, cited above, it should be possible to simplify the culpability assessment of command and superior responsibility in compliance with the general theory of personal liability – without resorting to new liability theories of command responsibility in particular.

Thus, whether the Rome Statute does or does not allow for liability for a failure to have 'first-time crimes' investigated and prosecuted depends on the interpretation of the Rome Statute and Article 28 as a whole, including a literal and contextual interpretation of the term "as a result of" in relation to such a failure. There is also the consideration that lack of investigation and prosecution of serious crimes is tantamount to accepting the crimes committed and tacitly encouraging new similar crimes. Such conduct by omission of leaders is extremely socially dangerous and thus clearly worthy of punishment, for preventive reasons and for justice to be reinstated.

Another interesting contribution concerning possible omission liability has been provided by Heller, who argues for revival of the mode of taking 'a consenting part' in universal crimes, as employed in the Nuremberg trials by military courts in occupied Germany.[174] Under this mode, which was set forth in Control Council Law No. 10, Article II(2)(c), and further defined in the jurisprudence, a participant was liable for the relevant crimes if the accused (1) had knowledge that such a crime had been or was about to be committed, and (2) occupied a sufficiently high-level place within the relevant power structure to put the accused *in a position to influence by objecting* to the occurrences of the crimes, *despite not being* a military commander in the chain of command or a leader with direct powers to decide on the matter, and (3) failed to object. Hence, taking 'a consenting part' is clearly distinguishable from command and superior liability. Taking 'a consenting part' is, however, close to responsibility for bystanders, which generally has not been recognised *lex lata* in ICL.[175] In fact, it fits the definition of (non-innocent) 'bystanders', proposed by Botte-Kerrison, as persons "who were aware that the crimes were being perpetrated but chose not to react" and, at the same time, "indirectly contributed to their perpetration".[176] However, the 'bystanders' and mode of liability Heller refers to has an additional element, namely that the person enjoys a certain status and authority (although not in the direct chain of command) within the power structure employed to commit the crimes. This distinguishes these persons from other bystanders and thus may impose on them a qualified duty to act.

Hence, the justification for this form of liability rested on the logic that the combination of knowledge and position of influence imposed on a

---

[174] Kevin Jon Heller, "'Taking a Consenting Part: The Lost Mode of Participation", in *Loyola of Los Angeles International & Comparative Law Review*, 2017, vol. 39, no. 1, pp. 247–58. See also Kevin Jon Heller, *The Nuremberg Military Tribunals and the Origins of International Criminal Law*, Oxford University Press, Oxford, 2012, pp. 259–62.

[175] See Chapter 2, Section 2.2.2.2., of this book.

[176] Auriane Botte-Kerrison, "Responsibility for Bystanders in Mass Crimes: Towards a Duty to Rescue in International Criminal Justice", in *International Criminal Law Review*, 2017, vol. 17, no. 5, pp. 879–908, at p. 880. Botte-Kerrison credits other authors as well when identifying these elements of her definition.

sufficiently high-level individual a duty to use his or her authority to prevent serious crimes, or at least reduce the severity of the crimes, and that failure to do so amounts to criminal culpability. Heller advocates for the practical advantages of this mode of liability under current ICL, and he claims that it has the potential to become a vibrant tool for international prosecutors and courts.[177] A question, then, is whether attribution of liability on this basis is lawful under the general theory of criminal law liability and may exist as a residual category within ICL generally, and thus in principle might again be made operational within a specific criminal law subsystem, for example through the Rome Statute of the ICC. We shall return to this issue in the concluding chapter of the book.[178] If the answer is yes, this then raises two further questions: (1) whether this form of liability might somehow be applicable through interpretation of the terms of Article 25(3) of the Rome Statute (probably not), and (2) whether the Rome Statute in the future ought to be amended to include this earlier used mode of liability.

6.3.3. Ordering and Different Forms of Accomplice Liability

The review so far has demonstrated several ongoing discussions in the literature, stretching across a range of central concepts relating to liability for participation in universal crimes. This last section shall broaden the picture a bit by reviewing selected contributions to the literature with respect to some other forms of liability, in particular the mode of 'ordering', as well as an interesting attempt to provide a new comprehensive liability theory applicable to different kinds of so-called 'atrocity speech' in ICL. The purpose is to highlight disagreements and critiques of the current state of law or ICL practice in order to further prove the apparent need for a new common theory on attribution of individual liability.

We start by recalling an article by Vest mentioned earlier, in which the author notes that indirect perpetration, 'perpetration through another', in the Rome Statute, Article 25(3)(a), and ordering ('orders') in subparagraph (b) largely overlap. In his opinion, the "difference between these two modes seems minimal". On this observation, the author holds that ordering could be equated with indirect perpetration, for which "perpetra-

---

[177] Heller, 2017, p. 256, see *supra* note 174.
[178] See Chapter 10, Section 10.6.

tion through another person would be the appropriate label".[179] As a possibly more elegant solution, however, Vest recalls the simplified definition included in the 1991 Draft Code of Crimes against the Peace and Security of Mankind,[180] defining principal perpetration of all crimes under the following formula: "An individual who commits or orders the commission of ...".[181]

Under this solution, perpetration is restricted to what he calls "classical scenarios qualified by the agent's innocence or lack of *mens rea*": in other words, scenarios where the intermediate ordering agent is not punishable while the person ordering from the top is considered a perpetrator. As a consequence, however, Vest acknowledges, "the provision on intermediary perpetration would become obsolete in cases in which the direct perpetrators remain criminally responsible".[182] The logic seems to be, in fact, that intermediate ordering liability would be ruled out either if a person at the top is considered an indirect perpetrator or if a physical executor is considered a direct perpetrator. This solution, however, appears difficult to reconcile with the inclusion of 'order' as a distinct mode of liability in subparagraph (b), *complementing* liability for perpetration through another in subparagraph (a).

Ambos nonetheless expresses an opinion similar to Vest's, arguing that 'orders', although provided for under subparagraph (b) in Article 25(3) of the Rome Statute, structurally belongs to the form of perpetration provided for in subparagraph (a). Thus, 'orders' in reality represents a form of commission through another person.[183] Yanev and Kooijmans also concur with this opinion.[184] In the course of making the case against the appropriateness of the 'control theory' under the Rome Statute, they note that under an approach that differentiate principals and accessories, based on 'control', it is difficult to see how indirect perpetration (through anoth-

---

[179] Vest, 2014, p. 304, see *supra* note 35, referencing some of his earlier work.

[180] *Report of the International Law Commission, Forty-third Session* (1991), A/46/10, Supp. No. 10, chap. IV.

[181] Vest, 2014, pp. 303–4, see *supra* note 35. The author also mentions the alternative option of applying ordering as a form of instigation.

[182] *Ibid.*, p. 304.

[183] Ambos, 2013, p. 163, see *supra* note 1.

[184] Yanev and Kooijmans, 2013, pp. 799–800, see *supra* note 118.

er) differs from ordering. Consequently, they argue that ordering is most appropriately construed as a form of indirect perpetration.

On the other side of the debate, Finnin,[185] in her above-mentioned book on accessorial (accomplice) liability, treats ordering as an accessorial-type mode. In the same vein, in directly opposing the view held by Ambos, Van Sliedregt holds that ordering under the Rome Statute is most appropriately classified as an accessorial form of liability distinct from those provided for in subparagraph (a). As stated by Van Sliedregt, "ordering is provided for in subparagraph (b) and there seems to be no compelling reason for subsuming it under indirect perpetration in (a)".[186]

What is particularly notable is that, along with their diverging views on the correct classification of ordering, either as a form of commission (principal) liability or as accomplice (accessorial) liability, Ambos and Finnin also back different mental elements for ordering. Ambos, as a consequence of structurally classifying ordering as a form of perpetration, concludes that a conviction for ordering requires the accused to share the respective subjective element of the crime, for instance, specific intent to destroy a protected group with a view to liability for ordering genocide.[187] On the contrary, Finnin, with reference to Article 30, deliberately departs from the jurisprudence of the *ad hoc* tribunals in proposing that the accused, as an accessory, needs only knowledge that the physical perpetrator(s) harbour such intent.[188]

From the perspective of a possibly common liability theory, the point made by Bassiouni on the importance of an accused's position within the relevant power structure introduces an additional nuance to the debate, demonstrating the complexities involved when one seeks to define the proper elements of a specific mode such as ordering. As a general point, Bassiouni stresses that a characteristic of ICL is a (roughly) tripartite distinction between high-level decision makers, intermediary planners and organisers, and the low-level participants who carry out the criminal plans physically. Thus, Bassiouni holds that it might be necessary to develop different liability criteria for persons at different levels:

---

[185] Finnin, 2012, see *supra* note 13.
[186] Van Sliedregt, 2012, pp. 108–9, see *supra* note 3.
[187] Ambos, 2013, p. 163, see *supra* note 1.
[188] Finnin, 2012, pp. 191–97, in particular pp. 193–94, see *supra* note 13.

A criminal justice policy judgment is therefore needed to distinguish between these strata of responsibility for purposes, *inter alia*, of determining a form of mental element (specific or general intent, or recklessness) as may be required for each strata of perpetrators.[189]

In line with this point of view, when the person ordering a crime holds a high-level position and exercises overall control, ordering might more easily be equated with commission liability for indirect perpetration, while similar acts of a person at an intermediary level without such control suggest accomplice liability. This logic would actually also resonate with the general view of Ambos himself, as he stresses the importance of the accused's degree of overall control/domination of a criminal enterprise in considering whether it can be classified as commission liability.[190]

Another complication involves instances of multiple, interlinked power structures.[191] Part of this issue concerns the delimitation of the relevant structures and whether certain entities constitute distinct organisations or are different parts of the same organisation. Beyond this, one may further consider the possibility of differentiating between different 'crime scenes', defined in space and time, where the underlying universal crimes are committed. This gives rise to the possibility that individuals at the middle levels of a relevant power structure may, in relation to one specific crime scene, be closely directed by orders from a higher level and unable to exercise much discretion or control, while with respect to a different specific crime scene they may exercise powers equivalent to overall control or dominance. Following the above logic, mid-level actors would in the first instance be more akin to accomplices and in the second instance more akin to perpetrators. Hence, in our view, instead of trying to solve such problems conceptually, another option would be to resolve them on the basis of the relevant facts of the individual case. This would be condi-

---

[189] Bassiouni, 2012, p. 291, see *supra* note 3. While this point is not further addressed in this book, Bassiouni also holds that this differentiation of the accused's position in the power structure has specific implications as to which *defences* should be available to different strata of participants.

[190] Ambos, 2013, pp. 177–79, see *supra* note 1; see also Section 6.3.1. of this chapter.

[191] For authors who discusses the implication of instances of multiple interlinked power structures, see, for example, Van Sliedregt, 2012, pp. 158–71, *supra* note 3; Ohlin, 2012, pp. 775–76 (on JCE), *supra* note 75; and Ambos, 2013, p. 157 (on indirect co-perpetration), *supra* note 1.

tioned upon recognising that 'ordering', depending on the circumstances, might either rise to commission liability ('perpetration through another') or be considered an activity within a larger structure more akin to accomplice liability.

Furthermore, Bassiouni has highlighted some practical, mainly evidentiary considerations with respect to the appropriate *mental* elements required for each stratum of participants. While Ambos would require one who orders a crime, if seen as a special form of indirect perpetration, to share the specific intent for the crime (genocide or persecution-type crimes against humanity), Bassiouni underlines the difficulties of proving specific intent on the part of high-level actors, as they often will manage to sustain plausible deniability. Therefore, he argues, general intent should be sufficient for high-level decision makers even for special intent crimes, allowing the mental element to be more easily established by inferential evidence.[192]

With respect to perhaps the most frequent instances of complicity, aiding and abetting, Aksenova highlights how the application of such accomplice liability represents an "intricate balancing act".[193] She admits that the absence of a requirement that the conduct of the accomplice *caused* the principal to act unlawfully may expand liability too broadly. However, the balance is restored through an elevated mental requirement in the form of *knowledge of the criminal outcome*, and *intent to aid or encourage*.[194] According to the author, this balancing act has some specific evidentiary implications, where the means of upholding the necessary balance is to take into account each individual accused's physical proximity to the crime(s), in effect placing limitations on the use of inferential analysis in establishing an accomplice's culpability. She suggests that where the accomplice is in immediate proximity to the physical crime scene, his or her culpable mind may be inferred from the circumstances of the unfolding events, while the objective contribution must be established in detail. This would be different if the accomplice operated quite removed from the actual crime scene, where the elevated culpability "become[s]

---

[192] Bassiouni, 2012, p. 315, see *supra* note 3.
[193] Aksenova, 2016, p. 258, see *supra* note 8.
[194] *Ibid.*

dispositive for attaching responsibility to the accomplice". As Aksenova underlines:

> This consideration is particularly relevant in the context of mass atrocities – the gap between the accomplice and the crime is often very wide, and the only way to compensate for this distance is to focus on individual culpability.[195]

Overall, this illustration clearly should demonstrate the complexities of the scholarly debate on attribution of personal liability when large criminal enterprises unfold. In our opinion, all the interlinked factors can only be addressed simultaneously, through a comprehensive theory of punishable participation in universal crimes.

6.3.4. Different Kinds of Liability for Atrocity Speech

This brings us to the last scholarly contributions reviewed in this chapter, namely the recent books by Gordon on ICL liability for so-called atrocity speech and by Wilson on incitement and other speech crimes.[196] We start with Gordon, who argues that the law governing the relationship between speech and universal crimes has been broken. According to the author, (1) incitement to genocide has not been adequately defined; (2) it is questionable why incitement to other universal crimes such as war crimes and crimes against humanity has not been criminalised; (3) the law on hate speech as persecution is split between the ICTR and the ICTY; (4) instigation is often confused with incitement;[197] (5) the scope of ordering is too circumscribed; and (6) the modalities do not function properly in relation to each other. Hence the law on punishable speech has become too fragmented.

Gordon first undertakes a thorough historical and legal analysis of the different kinds of possible criminal law liability for "atrocity speech"

---

[195] *Ibid.*

[196] See Gregory S. Gordon, *Atrocity Speech Law: Foundation, Fragmentation, Fruition*, Oxford University Press, Oxford, 2017; Richard Ashby Wilson, *Incitement on Trial: Prosecuting International Speech Crimes*, Cambridge University Press, Cambridge, 2017.

[197] Gordon, 2017, p. 246, see *supra* note 196. Gordon refers to the ICTR Media Case and the flawed analysis of 'instigation' by Agbor in different publications, for example, Avitus A. Agbor, "The Substantial Contribution Requirement: The Unfortunate Outcome of an Illogical Construction and Incorrect Understanding of Article 6(1) of the Statute of the ICTR", in *International Criminal Law Review*, 2012, vol. 12, no. 2, pp. 155–92.

in ICL.[198] This concept and its twin concept, "atrocity speech law", are proposed and employed by Gordon as collective terms in the book in order to better capture some common features of liability-relevant speech (law) and the relationship of different forms when criminal liability is to be assessed for socially dangerous speech linked to actual or potential other universal crimes. Although Gordon also proposes a set of specific solutions to deal with each of the above-mentioned modalities and deficiencies,[199] a particularly interesting feature of the book for our project is his proposal for a comprehensive "Unified Liability Theory".[200] For this purpose he even proposes a new treaty on the matter, the "Convention on the Classification and Criminalization of Atrocity Speech Offenses",[201] as well as amendment of the Rome Statute in the form of a new Article 25*bis*, to be titled "Liability Related to Speech".[202]

As the titles clearly indicate, however, Gordon's unified liability theory – although comprehensive for its particular subject matter – is not a general theory on personal criminal law liability, either for (rule of law–aspiring) domestic criminal law subsystems in general or for ICL liability generally. For this reason, we shall not go further into the details of his liability theory and proposals in this chapter. What is important to note here is that Gordon provides yet another example of scholars who are dissatisfied with the current state of liability theories and, consequently, with some parts of operational liability law within ICL. His book thus reinforces the idea that the time is ripe for a more general liability theory as well.

This is also the case with Wilson's book, in which one chapter is entitled "A New Model for Preventing and Punishing International Speech Crimes".[203] His analysis of speech crimes in law and practice is undertaken with a view to developing a more workable approach to preventing and

---

[198] Gordon, 2017, pp. 29–182 ("Foundation") and pp. 185–269 ("Fragmentation"), see *supra* note 196.

[199] *Ibid.*, pp. 273–365 ("Fruition").

[200] *Ibid.*, pp. 367–95 ("Fruition" – "Restructuring: A Unified Theory for Atrocity Speech Law").

[201] *Ibid.*, pp. 378–81.

[202] *Ibid.*, pp. 381–82.

[203] Wilson 2017, pp. 248–304, see *supra* note 196.

punishing such crimes.[204] Wilson proposes specifically that "prosecutors, in the first instance, ought to consider charging two inchoate crimes – direct and public incitement to genocide or hate speech as a form of persecution – as preventative measures". And if the moment for prevention has passed, "then international prosecutors ought to consider two modes of liability for completed crimes; ordering and aiding and abetting".[205]

Wilson does not recommend charging instigation as the mode of liability for prosecuting speech crimes, even though instigation may appear to be the natural charge for speech seeking to convince or encourage others to commit universal crimes that are subsequently completed. His rationale is closely related to the problems and failures of speech cases before international tribunals, and here Wilson provides a thorough analysis. In particular, he analyses the issue of causation and evidentiary matters in speech crimes cases from different scientific perspectives, as well as the causation standards that have been applied by courts. It is thus interesting to our project here that he finally also provides "three hopefully constructive recommendations".[206] The first one is to distinguish in a clear manner between material causation and legal causation. With respect to legal causation, he advises:

> International courts need to be explicit that the attribution of responsibility is determined by the "scope of liability," that is, the conduct that the defendant should have taken reasonable steps to avoid since an offence was a foreseeable consequence of their act or omission, acknowledging that the scope of liability is a policy decision derived from the statutes and the case law.[207]

Earlier in the book, Wilson also makes clear the useful distinction between physical and mental causation. While mental causation involves human subjectivity and psychological state of mind, the properties of physical objects are mind-independent.[208] The point is – and here Wilson

---

[204] See also Richard Ashby Wilson and Matthew Gillett, *The Hartford Guidelines on Speech Crimes in International Criminal Law*, Peace and Justice Initiative, The Hague, 2018.

[205] Wilson 2017, p. 248, see *supra* note 196.

[206] *Ibid.*, p. 300.

[207] *Ibid.*, p. 301.

[208] *Ibid.*, p. 162.

references Aristotle – that the use of persuasive language is intended to lead to decisions.

Since decisions are taken before the act to complete the crime (which is typically completed by executors on the ground in universal crimes cases), atrocity speech typically influences the mindsets of other people who participate in the criminal enterprise in indirect ways. What is contributed to the crime by an act of instigation is often only a causal factor in the whole criminal enterprise and only indirectly a causal factor in the crime eventually perpetrated. The core issue is thus whether such a (limited) causal factor can be established, whether the person with intent and knowledge contributed to the further events including the occurrence of the crime, and, ultimately, whether the speech should be considered sufficiently dangerous and blameworthy under the circumstances. With this addition to Wilson's recommendation, the concept of instigation would seem to be not only workable, but also in compliance with the general theory of personal liability applied to universal crimes.

This becomes even more clear in light of his second recommendation, namely to admit that "the classifications of essential, substantial and significant contribution often represent distinctions without a [real] difference".[209] Wilson thus suggests that we "abandon the ornate framework of levels of causal contribution and utilize a single test of causation across all forms of criminal responsibility".[210] To Wilson, a relevant contributing factor is one that is neither necessary nor sufficient but contributes to the crime by increasing the likelihood of its occurrence.[211] We will eventually

---

[209] *Ibid.*, p. 302.

[210] *Ibid.* It is, however, noteworthy that international judges continue to use such qualifications, as evidenced by a recent speech case judgment; see MICT, Appeals Chamber, *Prosecutor v. Šešelj*, Judgment, MICT-16-99-A, 11 April 2018 (www.legal-tools.org/doc/96ea58/). In para. 153 of this judgment the language of a factor contribution is adopted with a view to *actus reus* causation, but still with the caveat that "the instigation was a factor substantially contributing to the conduct of another person committing the crime". With respect to the *mens rea* of the accused, the Appeals Chamber in para. 154 held that Šešelj "intended to prompt the commission of the crimes, or at the very least, was aware of the substantial likelihood that the crimes of deportation, persecution (forcible displacement), and other inhuman acts (forcible transfer) as crimes against humanity would be committed in execution of his instigation".

[211] *Ibid.*, p. 303. His third and final recommendation refers to how international criminal tribunals are not fully benefitting from certain types of expertise, a topic outside the scope of this book.

---

take this into account when presenting our own recommendable criteria for punishable participation in universal crimes.[212]

6.4. Conclusion

The preceding review testifies to our initial assertion, made in the introduction to this chapter, that attribution of personal criminal liability for participation in universal crimes has been a highly controversial topic. It has caused a number of disagreements, and at times confusion, within the scholarly literature, which often gives rise to comments on ICL cases and trends in the case law with respect to the same subject matter. The scholarly disputes, however, have not been confined to specific concepts of participation at the micro level, but also concern the more general, macro-level theoretical questions of criminalisation and imputation, including the meaning and scope of the fundamental principles of criminal law.

As for the latter, Section 6.2. illustrated the different positions of various authors with respect to several fundamental issues: whether the question of attribution is best approached from a comparative law perspective or an autonomous, *sui generis*, understanding of ICL concepts; the relative merits and suitability of a unitary versus differentiated system of attribution in ICL; the scope of discretion and boundaries of the legitimacy of combining modes of liability in order to cast the net of criminal liability further; as well as the uncertain applicability of the legality principle to new operational modes of liability for completed crimes, as compared to inchoate and distinct crimes where the legality principle applies with certainty. Next, Section 6.3. explored some of the discussions and various positions taken on specific concepts of criminal participation, starting with the debate on subjective versus objective approaches to attribution of liability and then providing some other illustrative examples of disagreements, as well as potential explanations and solutions. This section discussed different forms of omission liability, ordering, and (to some extent) aiding and abetting. Finally, the special liability problems and the newly proposed unified liability theory proposed by Gordon with regard to atrocity speech were briefly explained, and Wilson's proposals to approach and reconsider the framework of causal contribution were briefly presented as well.

---

[212] See Chapter 10 and Appendix I in this volume.

The last and vital point we would like to highlight is that the two levels of the topic – the more general and the more specific – are closely connected. Thus, the positions taken on the fundamental questions often inform solutions to questions concerning the applicability of specific liability concepts. The implication, we assume, is that there is an urgent need to situate the smaller but often important subtopics within a larger theory of attribution, capable of addressing all issues simultaneously. The approach taken in this book, as set out first in Chapter 2, therefore, may offer a more comprehensive assessment of punishable participation beyond what currently exists in the literature. It remains to be seen whether our effort in that regard comes to fruition, to use Gordon's expression. This might become clearer, however, in the next chapters and finally in Chapter 10.

7

Liability Concepts in
the International Jurisprudence

7.1. Introductory Remarks

Since the beginning of international criminal law, a number of concepts have been used to hold persons liable for the commission of universal (international) crimes,[1] in addition to liability for singular commission of such crimes. While singular commission of crimes is usually the starting point for analysis of criminal law liability with respect to domestic criminal law, cases of singular commission of universal crimes are the exception rather than the rule, and thus within ICL a different point of departure might be required. Since juridical entity liability has not been implemented within ICL, the international jurisprudence revisited in this chapter only deals with individual liability for physical persons.

Here we will basically follow the same approach and sequence as developed in Chapter 2, Section 2.2.2.5., and refined in Section 2.2.3.1., where we combined at a general level the three relevant classes of personal liability (direct participation, indirect participation, and incomplete participation) with the three phases of a typical universal criminal enterprise (pre-execution phase, execution phase, and post-execution phase). The pre-execution phase of a universal criminal enterprise may involve several stages, typically starting with an initial mental plan; this is followed by initiation and incitement, a conspiracy or common plan, further planning and preparation, and, finally, the attempt stage. So-called incomplete or inchoate crimes might in principle be applicable to each stage – with the exception of the initial mental plan not expressed in the physical world – if the law has opted to criminalise preparatory forms of participation in criminal enterprises as distinct crimes. The relevant candidates in our context are conspiracy, incitement, and attempt. However, whether these are

---

[1] For a general overview of the principles in Article 25(3) of the ICC Statute, including the notion of a hierarchy of blameworthiness, see ICC, Trial Chamber, *Prosecutor v. Katanga*, Judgment, ICC-01/04-01/07, 7 March 2014, paras. 1383–87 (www.legal-tools.org/doc/f74b4f/).

made distinct inchoate crimes or not, liability for participation at the pre-execution phase may incur liability at the fourth level of the criminal law liability theory through specific modes of participation when the crime is actually completed. This is important with respect to complex mass crimes, where different people often are involved at the different stages and phases of the criminal enterprise. While liability for incomplete participation is typically assimilated for those also participating directly at the execution phase (the perpetrator, joint perpetrators, perpetrators through another, and persons liable by omission), for the others, distinct liability for their pre-execution contributions to the criminal enterprise is crucial. Hence, if the enterprise leads to completed crimes, additional liability categories come into the picture, for instance, joint perpetration and forms further derived, like JCE or indirect co-perpetration, and this factual circumstance also casts a retrospective light on earlier contributions to the enterprise, especially those outside the scope of applicable distinct inchoate crimes.

What needs to be added, and recalled on the basis of Chapter 2, Section 2.2.3.1., is that the class of indirect participation (instigating, ordering, complicity, and, possibly, membership) might be relevant to all three phases – although again, the people who participate only indirectly may be different at the different phases, even with respect to the same category of participation. On the other hand, to take one example, the same person who instigates the crime at the pre-execution level may also physically assist in the crime at the execution level and thus be liable for both instigation and complicity in concurrence when the crime has been committed.

As discussed earlier in Chapter 2, Section 2.2.3.6., personal criminal law liability might be derived at different analytical levels (derivation orders) and enacted and applied in more or less specified forms in actual law. Both factors apply to ICL liability discourse. Combining a theoretical and a practical approach, this chapter deals first with the possible inchoate crimes (conspiracy, incitement, and attempt), followed by the further preparatory and indirect forms of participation relevant to the pre-execution phase (planning and preparation, ordering, and instigation).[2] Next, atten-

---

[2]   Ordering and instigation, as well as various forms of complicity, and participation or membership in a criminal organisation, are also relevant to the execution phase.

tion will be given to direct forms of participation, such as perpetration, joint perpetration, perpetration through another person, and further derivative forms such as JCE and command/superior responsibility. Lastly, the chapter turns to aspects of accessoryship, often ranging from the pre-execution phase to the execution phase and beyond, such as aiding and abetting, accessoryship after the fact, and membership.

This chapter provides a brief and overarching description of the *lex lata* elements of the modes of participation as discussed in the jurisprudence of the international(ised) tribunals and the ICC since 1993. The limitations with respect to the type of institutions examined and the time period covered are linked, as the first international tribunal, the ICTY, was established in 1993. The institutions of interest since then are the two international criminal tribunals, the International Criminal Tribunal for the former Yugoslavia ('ICTY') and International Criminal Tribunal for Rwanda ('ICTR'); the two internationalised tribunals, namely the Special Court for Sierra Leone ('SCSL') and the Extraordinary Chambers in the Courts of Cambodia ('ECCC'); the regional internationalised tribunal in Senegal, the Extraordinary African Chambers ('EAC'); and the ICC. The background, structure, and jurisdiction of the tribunals have been explained in Chapter 5, Section 5.2.1.2. The jurisprudence of the three other national court systems with some international aspects, namely the ones in Bosnia and Herzegovina, East Timor, and Kosovo, will not be discussed here, as their background, structure, jurisdiction, and jurisprudence will be examined in Chapter 9.

As a brief overview, the discussion in this chapter will not incorporate academic commentary or criticisms, as the academic literature has been examined in Chapter 6 and will also become a part of the analysis in Chapter 10. Lastly, this overview will only examine the legal parameters of the liability concepts without addressing the underlying facts of the cases in question, which were addressed to some extent in Chapter 3 and will be revisited in Chapter 10. However, the conclusion to the present chapter will point to the general direction of the jurisprudence of the six international institutions.

7.2. Punishable Modes of Participation

7.2.1. Forms of Inchoate Liability

7.2.1.1. Conspiracy

Liability for conspiracy as such in international criminal law beyond Nuremberg[3] has only been possible with respect to genocide, and then only under the Statutes of the ICTY, ICTR, and ECCC. However, it is noteworthy that participation in a conspiracy or a common agreement and plan to commit other universal crimes, such as crimes against humanity and war crimes, may be implicitly criminalised within ICL as involvement in a joint criminal enterprise – when such crimes are actually completed – through modes of liability such as JCE and (indirect) co-perpetration.

To the extent that international terrorism has also currently emerged as a possible crime under international law, conspiracy to commit acts of terror might even be punishable as an inchoate crime under customary international law, although this question falls outside the scope of this survey since no international court has ruled on the matter. In addition, there is the issue of whether conspiracy to commit, for example, CAH or the crime of aggression is allowed as a residual category within customary international law or should be considered prohibited within ICL and thus need not be included in future treaties or international court statutes. This issue, however, also falls outside the scope of the present chapter.[4]

Conspiracy to commit genocide is an agreement between two or more persons to commit the crime of genocide. The act of entering into an agreement to commit genocide constitutes the *actus reus* of conspiracy to commit genocide. The individuals involved in the conspiracy must possess the same *mens rea* as for genocide, namely, the specific intent to destroy, in whole or in part, a national, ethnical, racial, or religious group, as such. As an inchoate crime, it is the agreement itself that is punishable, regardless of whether genocide is actually committed as a result of the agreement.[5]

---

[3] See discussion of the Nuremberg judgment and conspiracy in Chapter 2, Section 2.2.3.1.

[4] For a discussion of ICL liability for conspiracy *lex lata* under general international law, notably customary international law, in particular in relation to the legality principle, see Chapter 4, Section 4.3.7., and Chapter 10, Section 10.8.

[5] ICTR, Appeals Chamber, *Prosecutor v. Nahimana, Barayagwiza and Ngeze* (the Media Case), Judgment, ICTR-99-52-A, 28 November 2007, paras. 894–98 (www.legal-tools.org/

Conspiracy is a continuing crime in the sense that individuals are capable of joining a conspiracy even after the initial agreement and may be held liable for such conspiracy as though they were original conspirators.[6]

7.2.1.2. Planning of the Criminal Enterprise

Liability for planning requires that one or more persons plan or design the criminal conduct constituting one or more crimes, which are later actually perpetrated with at least the awareness of the substantial likelihood that a crime will be committed in the execution of that plan.[7] Planning does not require a finding of a position of authority.[8] It implies that one or several

---

doc/4ad5eb/); ICTR, Appeals Chamber, *Prosecutor v. Seromba*, Judgment, ICTR-2001-66-A, 12 March 2008, paras. 218 and 221 (www.legal-tools.org/doc/b4df9d/); ICTY, Trial Chamber, *Prosecutor v. Tolimir*, Judgment, IT-05-88/2-T, 12 December 2012, paras. 785–86 (www.legal-tools.org/doc/445e4e/) (which also indicate that since this offence was based on a common law concept, common law principles can be used to define its parameters); ICTR, Appeals Chamber, *Prosecutor v. Nzabonimana*, Judgment, ICTR-98-44D-A, 29 September 2014, para. 391 (www.legal-tools.org/doc/a1abb4/); ICTR, Appeals Chamber, *Prosecutor v. Karemera*, Judgment, ICTR-98-44-A, 29 September 2014, para. 643 (www.legal-tools.org/doc/372a64/); ICTY, Appeals Chamber, *Prosecutor v. Popović et al.*, Judgment, IT-05-88-A, 30 January 2015, para. 544 (www.legal-tools.org/doc/4c28fb/); ICTY, Appeals Chamber, *Prosecutor v. Tolimir*, Judgment, IT-05-88/2-A, 8 April 2015, para. 582 (www.legal-tools.org/doc/010ecb/); ICTR, Appeals Chamber, *Prosecutor v. Nyiramasuhuko et al.*, Judgment, ICTR-98-42-A, 14 December 2015, paras. 469, 473, and 649 (www.legal-tools.org/doc/b3584e/).

6   ICTY, Trial Chamber, *Prosecutor v. Popović et al.*, Judgment, IT-05-88-T, 10 June 2010, paras. 870–76 (www.legal-tools.org/doc/481867/); ICTY, Trial Chamber, *Prosecutor v. Tolimir*, Judgment, IT-05-88/2-T, 12 December 2012, para. 785 (www.legal-tools.org/doc/445e4e/).

7   ICTR, Appeals Chamber, *Prosecutor v. Nahimana, Barayagwiza and Ngeze* (the Media Case), Judgment, ICTR-99-52-A, 28 November 2007, para. 479 (www.legal-tools.org/doc/4ad5eb/); SCSL, Appeals Chamber, *Prosecutor v. Brima, Kamara and Kanu* (the AFRC Case), Judgment, SCSL-2004-16-A, 22 February 2008, para. 301 (www.legal-tools.org/doc/4420ef/); ICTR, Appeals Chamber, *Prosecutor v. Kanyarukiga*, Judgment, ICTR-02-78-A, 8 May 2012, para. 258 (www.legal-tools.org/doc/e6e1c9/); SCSL, Appeals Chamber, *Prosecutor v. Taylor*, Judgment, SCSL-04-01-T, 26 September 2013, paras. 491–94 (www.legal-tools.org/doc/3e7be5/); ECCC, Trial Chamber, Case 002/01, Judgment, 002/19-09-2007/ECCC/TC, 7 August 2014, para. 698 (www.legal-tools.org/doc/4888de/); ICTY, Trial Chamber, *Prosecutor v. Karadžić*, Judgment, IT-95-5/18-T, 24 March 2016, para. 571 (www.legal-tools.org/doc/173e23/).

8   ICTR, Appeals Chamber, *Prosecutor v. Kanyarukiga*, Judgment, ICTR-02-78-A, 8 May 2012, para. 258 (www.legal-tools.org/doc/e6e1c9/); ICTY, Trial Chamber, *Prosecutor v.*

---

persons contemplate designing the commission of a crime at both the preparatory and execution phases.[9]

The accused must have a substantial level of participation in the planning, such as actually formulating the criminal plan or endorsing a plan proposed by another.[10] The person who perpetrated the *actus reus* of the offence must have acted in furtherance of the plan.[11] In that respect, it will be sufficient to demonstrate that the planning was a factor substantially contributing to the criminal enterprise.[12] Presence at the scene of the crime is not required for this type of criminal responsibility.[13]

7.2.1.3. Incitement

A person may be found guilty of direct and public incitement to commit genocide if he or she directly and publicly incited the commission of genocide (the *actus reus*) and had the intent to directly and publicly incite others to commit genocide (the *mens rea*). In order to be direct, the incitement must be a specific appeal to commit a genocidal act and not merely a vague or indirect suggestion. However, implicit language may be direct because incitement does not have to involve an explicit appeal to

---

Haradinaj et al., Judgment, IT-04-84bis-T, 29 November 2012, para. 622 (www.legal-tools. org/doc/1bad7b/).

[9] ICTY, Appeals Chamber, *Prosecutor v. Kordić and Čerkez*, Judgment, IT-95-14/2-A, 17 December 2004, para. 26 (www.legal-tools.org/doc/738211/).

[10] ICTR, Trial Chamber, *Prosecutor v. Seromba*, Judgment, ICTR-2001-66-I, 13 December 2006, para. 303 (www.legal-tools.org/doc/091a66/); SCSL, Appeals Chamber, *Prosecutor v. Brima, Kamara and Kanu* (the AFRC Case), Judgment, SCSL-2004-16-A, 22 February 2008, para. 301 (www.legal-tools.org/doc/4420ef/); ICTR, Trial Chamber, *Prosecutor v. Hategekimana*, Judgment, ICTR-00-55B-T, 6 December 2010, para. 643 (www.legal-tools. org/doc/6082dd/); ICTR, Trial Chamber, *Prosecutor v. Gatete*, Judgment, ICTR-2000-61-T, 31 March 2011, para. 573 (www.legal-tools.org/doc/f6c347/); ICTR, Trial Chamber, *Prosecutor v. Nyiramasuhuko et al.*, Judgment, ICTR-98-42-T, 24 June 2011, para. 5591 (www.legal-tools.org/doc/e2c881/); ICTY, Trial Chamber, *Prosecutor v. Tolimir*, Judgment, IT-05-88/2-T, 12 December 2012, para. 900 (www.legal-tools.org/doc/445e4e/).

[11] ICTY, Trial Chamber, *Prosecutor v. Galić*, Judgment, IT-98-29-T, 5 December 2003, para. 168 (www.legal-tools.org/doc/eb6006/).

[12] ICTY, Trial Chamber, *Prosecutor v. Popović et al.*, Judgment, IT-05-88-T, 10 June 2010, para. 1006 (www.legal-tools.org/doc/481867/); ICTR, Trial Chamber, *Prosecutor v. Kanyarukiga*, Judgment, ICTR-02-78, 1 November 2010, para. 618 (www.legal-tools.org/doc/415384/).

[13] ICTY, Appeals Chamber, *Prosecutor v. Boškoski and Tarčulovski*, Judgment, IT-04-82-A, 19 May 2010, para. 125 (www.legal-tools.org/doc/54398a/).

---

commit genocide. In order to determine whether a speech act is direct, it should be viewed in light of its cultural and linguistic context, its audience and how the speech was understood by its intended audience, and the political and community affiliations of the inciter.[14] As an inchoate crime, direct and public incitement to commit genocide is punishable even if no act of genocide has resulted from the incitement or if the effects of the incitement are extended in time.[15]

When assessing the public element of incitement, factors such as the place where the incitement occurred and whether the attendance was selected or limited can be taken into account, but the number of persons present is not an essential factor in this assessment.[16] It should be noted that the international jurisprudence so far only concerns cases featuring traditional forms of public communication, such as gatherings in public places, speech over television and radio, and speech in print publications of different kinds. Some additional issues may arise with respect to the public factor when the communication takes place through various kinds of social media with restricted access or limited use. On the other hand, the effectiveness and thus the potential dangerousness of the use of social media for the purpose of incitement to commit serious crimes may weigh in favour of liability for incitement being extended beyond genocide to all categories of recognised international crimes.

---

[14] ICTR, Appeals Chamber, *Prosecutor v. Nahimana, Barayagwiza and Ngeze* (the Media Case), Judgment, ICTR-99-52-A, 28 November 2007, paras. 698–701 (www.legal-tools. org/doc/4ad5eb/); ICTR, Trial Chamber, *Prosecutor v. Bikindi*, Judgment, ICTR-01-72-T, 2 December 2008, paras. 387–89 (www.legal-tools.org/doc/a7213b/) (including the possibility of songs amounting to incitement); ICTR, Appeals Chamber, *Prosecutor v. Nyiramasuhuko et al.*, Judgment, ICTR-98-42-A, 14 December 2015, para. 2678 (www.legal-tools. org/doc/b3584e/).

[15] ICTR, Appeals Chamber, *Prosecutor v. Nahimana, Barayagwiza and Ngeze* (the Media Case), Judgment, ICTR-99-52-A, 28 November 2007, paras. 678, 692, and 720 (www. legal-tools.org/doc/4ad5eb/); ICTR, Appeals Chamber, *Prosecutor v. Nzabonimana*, Judgment, ICTR-98-44D-A, 29 September 2014, para. 234 (www.legal-tools.org/doc/a1abb4/); ICTR, Appeals Chamber, *Prosecutor v. Nyiramasuhuko et al.*, Judgment, ICTR-98-42-A, 14 December 2015, paras. 2335, 2676–77, 2781, 3338, and 3345 (www.legal-tools.org/ doc/b3584e/).

[16] ICTR, Appeals Chamber, *Prosecutor v. Nzabonimana*, Judgment, ICTR-98-44D-A, 29 September 2014, para. 231 (www.legal-tools.org/doc/a1abb4/); MICT, Appeals Chamber, *Prosecutor v. Ngirabatware*, Judgment, MICT-12-29-A, 18 December 2014, para. 52 (www.legal-tools.org/doc/16b4ef/).

The crime of incitement is completed as soon as the discourse in question is uttered or published, even though the effects of the incitement may extend over time.[17]

The *mens rea* required for the crime of direct and public incitement to commit genocide presupposes a genocidal intent, that is, the person who is inciting to commit genocide must have himself or herself the specific intent to commit genocide.[18]

7.2.1.4. Attempt

There has been no jurisprudence regarding the content of this inchoate crime or form of liability at the ICTY/ICTR,[19] but the ICC Statute gives the following detailed description:

> Attempts to commit such a crime by taking action that commences its execution by means of a substantial step, but the crime does not occur because of circumstances independent of the person's intentions. However, a person who abandons the effort to commit the crime or otherwise prevents the completion of the crime shall not be liable for punishment under this Statute for the attempt to commit that crime if that

---

17 ICTR, Appeals Chamber, *Prosecutor v. Nahimana, Barayagwiza and Ngeze* (the Media Case), Judgment, ICTR-99-52-A, 28 November 2007, para. 723 (www.legal-tools.org/doc/4ad5eb/); ICTR, Trial Chamber, *Prosecutor v. Muvunyi*, Judgment, ICTR-00-55A-T, 11 February 2010, para. 24 (www.legal-tools.org/doc/d2df88/); ICTR, Trial Chamber, *Prosecutor v. Nzabonimana*, Judgment, ICTR-98-44D-T, 31 May 2012, para. 1752 (www.legal-tools.org/doc/00cb8e/); MICT, Appeals Chamber, *Prosecutor v. Ngirabatware*, Judgment, MICT-12-29-A, 18 December 2014, para. 52 (www.legal-tools.org/doc/16b4ef/).

18 ICTR, Appeals Chamber, *Prosecutor v. Rutaganda*, Judgment, ICTR-96-3-A, 26 May 2003, para. 524 (www.legal-tools.org/doc/40bf4a/); ICTR, Appeals Chamber, *Prosecutor v. Nyiramasuhuko et al.*, Judgment, ICTR-98-42-A, 14 December 2015, para. 3338 (www.legal-tools.org/doc/b3584e/).

19 Except to say that attempt is by definition an inchoate crime, inherent in the criminal conduct *per se*, and as such it is punishable as a separate crime irrespective of whether or not the intended crime is accomplished. See ICTR, Appeals Chamber, *Prosecutor v. Akayesu*, Judgment, ICTR-96-4-A, 1 June 2001, para. 473 (www.legal-tools.org/doc/c62d06/); ICTR, Trial Chamber, *Prosecutor v. Rutaganda*, Judgment, ICTR-96-3-T, 6 December 1999, paras. 34–35 (www.legal-tools.org/doc/f0dbbb/); ICTR, Trial Chamber, *Prosecutor v. Musema*, Judgment, ICTR-96-13-T, 27 January 2000, paras. 115–16; ICTR, Trial Chamber, *Prosecutor v. Semanza*, Judgment, ICTR-97-20-T, 15 May 2003, para. 378 (www.legal-tools.org/doc/7e668a/).

person completely and voluntarily gave up the criminal purpose.[20]

Subsequent rulings have elaborated on this provision by saying that
attempt to commit a universal crime is a crime in which the objective elements are incomplete, while the subjective elements are complete.[21] The
more specific conditions of a criminal attempt, for instance the notion of a
"substantial step", have thus far not been further developed. However, it is
clear from the wording that liability includes not only a 'complete attempt', where the potential perpetrator has done everything to complete
the crime but still fails in the execution, but also an 'incomplete attempt',
where there are still some steps to be taken towards execution of the crime
although other steps have been taken that move the criminal enterprise
beyond the preparatory (pre-execution) phase and close to execution.

7.2.2. Forms of Commission and Omission Liability

7.2.2.1. Singular Perpetration

Before discussing the parameters of direct perpetration by a single person,
it would be useful to iterate the classification of various types of perpetration as set out in the ICC jurisprudence.

ICC jurisprudence has provided the following three forms of committing a crime as a perpetrator, in which a person:

- physically carries out the objective elements of the offence (commission of the crime in person, or direct perpetration); or

- has, along with others, control over the offence by reason of the essential tasks assigned to him or her (commission of the crime jointly
  with others, or co-perpetration); or

---

[20] See Rome Statute, Article 25(3)(f).

[21] See ICC, Pre-Trial Chamber, *Prosecutor v. Katanga and Chui*, Decision on Confirmation
of Charges, ICC-01/04-01/07, 30 September 2008, paras. 458–60 (www.legal-tools.org/
doc/67a9ec/); ICC, Pre-Trial Chamber, *Prosecutor v. Ntaganda*, Decision on Confirmation
of Charges, ICC-01/04-02/06, 9 June 2014, para. 175 (www.legal-tools.org/doc/5686c6/);
ICC, Pre-Trial Chamber, *Prosecutor v. Gbagbo*, Decision on Confirmation of Charges,
ICC-02/11-01/11, 12 June 2014, para. 201 (www.legal-tools.org/doc/5b41bc/); ICC, Pre-
Trial Chamber, *Prosecutor v. Blé Goudé*, Decision on Confirmation of Charges, ICC-02/
11-02/11, 11 December 2014, para. 121 (www.legal-tools.org/doc/0536d5/).

- controls the will of those who carry out the objective elements of the offence (commission of the crime through another person, or indirect perpetration).[22]

Moreover, in a situation with a plurality of participating persons, it is possible to locate principals and accessories along a spectrum that emphasises different aspects of the involvement. The point would be, then, to distinguish those who should be considered perpetrators rather than accomplices, based on an overall assessment of their contributions. As we will see later, in Chapters 8 and 9 on national jurisprudence, this approach has been quite common in domestic ICL cases.

If the objective manifestation of the crime is the focal point of investigation, because all elements of the crime were carried out by the same person, this can be called an objective approach: a single accused potentially is liable both as a principal and as single perpetrator. The subjective approach does not primarily examine the level of contribution but instead looks at the shared intent to carry out a crime, which is done in the further derivative JCE or common purpose doctrine. Indirect co-perpetration – sometimes labelled just co-perpetration in order to distinguish it from a particular kind of 'diagonal' indirect perpetration – focuses on the degree of control exercised by a person who is removed from the scene of the crime but has control of or is the mastermind behind the commission of the offences, while the crime is typically completed jointly at the physical crime scene by several other persons.[23]

---

[22] ICC, Pre-Trial Chamber, *Prosecutor v. Lubanga*, Decision on Confirmation of Charges, ICC-01/04-01/06, 29 January 2007, paras. 329–37 (www.legal-tools.org/doc/b7ac4f/); ICC, Pre-Trial Chamber, *Prosecutor v. Katanga and Chui*, Decision on Confirmation of Charges, ICC-01/04-01/07, 30 September 2008, paras. 480–88 (www.legal-tools.org/doc/67a9ec/).

[23] ICC, Pre-Trial Chamber, *Prosecutor v. Lubanga*, Decision on Confirmation of Charges, ICC-01/04-01/06, 29 January 2007, paras. 327–31 (www.legal-tools.org/doc/b7ac4f/); ICC, Pre-Trial Chamber, *Prosecutor v. Bemba*, Decision on Confirmation of Charges, ICC-01/05-01/08, 15 June 2009, paras. 346–47 (www.legal-tools.org/doc/07965c/); ICC, Pre-Trial Chamber, *Prosecutor v. Nourain and Jamus*, Corrigendum of the Decision on Confirmation of Charges, ICC-02/05-03/09, 7 March 2011, para. 126 (www.legal-tools.org/doc/5ac9eb/); ICC, Pre-Trial Chamber, *Prosecutor v. Ruto, Kosgey and Sang*, Decision on Prosecutor's Application for Summons to Appear for William Samoei Ruto, Henry Kiprono Kosgey, and Joshua Arap Sang, ICC-01/09-01/11, 8 March 2011, para. 39 (www.legal-tools.org/doc/6c9fb0/). However, see also ICC, Trial Chamber, *Prosecutor v. Chui*, Judgment, Concurring Opinion of Judge Christine Van den Wyngaert, ICC-01/04-02/12,

---

In light of this general overview, it is relevant now to indicate that singularly committing an offence has been defined both by international tribunals and by the ICC as "the physical perpetration of a crime by the offender himself or the culpable omission of an act that was mandated by a rule of criminal law",[24] provided that the person acted with the intent to commit the crime, or with an awareness of the substantial likelihood that the crime would occur as a consequence of his or her conduct.[25]

In other words, singular perpetration requires that the accused person alone fulfil all material and mental elements of the crime description at the execution phase. This does not mean that the perpetrator must have acted alone; to the contrary, he or she would, in most cases of universal crimes, be part of a much larger criminal enterprise that involves many crime scenes and locations. Furthermore, singular perpetration at the execution phase at one particular crime scene does not exclude the possibility that other persons could be liable for other forms of perpetration for the same crime at the same crime scene – typically the person or persons who have used a power structure to have the criminal acts committed.

Outside the ICC context it has also been said that direct participation can be found in a situation where the conduct of the accused was as much an integral part of the crimes as the acts it enabled,[26] in the sense

---

18 December 2012, para. 6 (www.legal-tools.org/doc/7d5200/); ICC, Trial Chamber, *Prosecutor v. Katanga*, Judgment, ICC-01/04-01/07, 7 March 2014, paras. 1390–97 (www. legal-tools.org/doc/f74b4f/); ICC, Appeals Chamber, *Prosecutor v. Lubanga*, Judgment, ICC-01/04-01/06 A5, 1 December 2014, paras. 460–73 (www.legal-tools.org/doc/585c75/); ICC, Trial Chamber, *Prosecutor v. Bemba, Musamba, Kabongo, Wandu and Arido*, Judgment, ICC-01/05-01/13, 19 October 2016, para. 62 (www.legal-tools.org/doc/fe0ce4/).

24 ICTY, Appeals Chamber, *Prosecutor v. Tadić*, Judgment, IT-94-1-A, 15 July 1999, para. 188 (www.legal-tools.org/doc/8efc3a/).

25 ECCC, Trial Chamber, *Kaing Guek Eav alias Duch*, Judgment, 001/18-07-2007/ECCC/ TC, 26 July 2010, paras. 480–81 (www.legal-tools.org/doc/dbdb62/); EAC, Trial Chamber, *Prosecutor v. Habré*, Judgment, 30 May 2016, para. 1820 (www.legal-tools.org/doc/ 98c00a/); ICC, Trial Chamber, *Prosecutor v. Bemba, Musamba, Kabongo, Wandu and Arido*, Judgment, ICC-01/05-01/13, 19 October 2016, para. 58 (www.legal-tools.org/doc/ fe0ce4/).

26 ICTR, Appeals Chamber, *Prosecutor v. Gacumbitsi*, Judgment, ICTR-2001-64-A, 7 July 2006, para. 161 (www.legal-tools.org/doc/aa51a3/); ICTR, Appeals Chamber, *Prosecutor v. Ndindabahizi*, Judgment, ICTR-01-71-A, 16 January 2007, para. 123 (www.legal-tools. org/doc/0f3219/); ICTR, Appeals Chamber, *Prosecutor v. Kalimanzira*, Judgment, ICTR-05-88-A, 20 October 2010, para. 219 (www.legal-tools.org/doc/fad693/); ICTR, Appeals

that the accused approved and embraced as his own the decision to commit the crime.[27]

7.2.2.2. Joint Perpetration

The *actus reus* of joint perpetration has usually been considered twofold: (1) the existence of an agreement or common plan,[28] which was temporarily replaced by the requirement of shared intent,[29] between two or more persons, and (2) the coordinated, essential contribution[30] by each of these

---

Chamber, *Prosecutor v. Munyakazi*, Judgment, ICTR-97-36A-A, 28 September 2011, para. 135 (www.legal-tools.org/doc/48cbd6/).

[27] ICTR, Trial Chamber, *Prosecutor v. Seromba*, Judgment, ICTR-2001-66-I, 13 December 2006, para. 161 (www.legal-tools.org/doc/091a66/).

[28] ICC, Pre-Trial Chamber, *Prosecutor v. Lubanga*, Decision on Confirmation of Charges, ICC-01/04-01/06, 29 January 2007, paras. 343–48 (www.legal-tools.org/doc/b7ac4f/); ICC, Pre-Trial Chamber, *Prosecutor v. Katanga and Chui*, Decision on Confirmation of Charges, ICC-01/04-01/07, 30 September 2008, paras. 519–26 (www.legal-tools.org/doc/67a9ec/); ICC, Pre-Trial Chamber, *Prosecutor v. Bemba*, Decision on Confirmation of Charges, ICC-01/05-01/08, 15 June 2009, para. 350 (www.legal-tools.org/doc/07965c/); ICC, Pre-Trial Chamber, *Prosecutor v. Garda*, Decision on Confirmation of Charges, ICC-02/05-02/09, 8 February 2010, para.160 (www.legal-tools.org/doc/cb3614/); ICC, Pre-Trial Chamber, *Prosecutor v. Nourain and Jamus*, Corrigendum of Decision on Confirmation of Charges, ICC-02/05-03/09, 7 March 2011, paras. 128–29 and 136 (www.legal-tools.org/doc/5ac9eb/); ICC, Pre-Trial Chamber, *Prosecutor v. Muthaura, Kenyatta and Ali*, Decision on Prosecutor's Application for Summons to Appear for Francis Kirimi Muthaura, Uhuru Muigai Kenyatta, and Mohammed Hussein Ali, ICC-01/09-02/11, 8 March 2011, para. 36 (www.legal-tools.org/doc/df8391/); ICC, Pre-Trial Chamber, *Prosecutor v. Ruto, Kosgey and Sang*, Decision on Prosecutor's Application for Summons to Appear for William Samoei Ruto, Henry Kiprono Kosgey, and Joshua Arap Sang, ICC-01/09-01/11, 8 March 2011, para. 40 (www.legal-tools.org/doc/6c9fb0/); ICC, Trial Chamber, *Prosecutor v. Lubanga*, Judgment, ICC-01/04-01/06, 14 March 2012, paras. 989–99 (www.legal-tools.org/doc/677866/); ICC, Pre-Trial Chamber, *Prosecutor v. Gbagbo*, Decision on Confirmation of Charges, ICC-02/11-01/11, 12 June 2014, para. 230 (www.legal-tools.org/doc/5b41bc/); ICC, Pre-Trial Chamber, *Prosecutor v. Blé Goudé*, Decision on Confirmation of Charges, ICC-02/11-02/11, 11 December 2014, para. 134 (www.legal-tools.org/doc/0536d5/).

[29] ICC, Trial Chamber, *Prosecutor v. Chui*, Judgment, Concurring Opinion of Judge Christine Van den Wyngaert, ICC-01/04-02/12, 18 December 2012, paras. 32–35 (www.legal-tools.org/doc/7d5200/).

[30] ICC, Trial Chamber, *Prosecutor v. Lubanga*, Judgment, ICC-01/04-01/06, 14 March 2012, paras. 989–99 (www.legal-tools.org/doc/677866/); ICC, Pre-Trial Chamber, *Prosecutor v. Gbagbo*, Decision on Confirmation of Charges, ICC-02/11-01/11, 12 June 2014, para. 230 (www.legal-tools.org/doc/5b41bc/); ICC, Pre-Trial Chamber, *Prosecutor v. Blé Goudé*, Decision on Confirmation of Charges, ICC-02/11-02/11, 11 December 2014, paras. 134–36 (www.legal-tools.org/doc/0536d5/); ICC, Pre-Trial Chamber, *Prosecutor v. Al Mahdi*, De-

---

persons, resulting in the commission of a crime. With respect to the first of these requirements, the agreement does not have to be explicit, as implicit consent to be part of the joint criminal enterprise will suffice. Nor does the plan have to be specifically directed at committing a crime, as long as its implementation embodies a sufficient risk that, in the ordinary course of events, a crime will be committed.[31] The agreement or common plan need not be specifically directed at the commission of offence(s), and it may include non-criminal goals; however, it is necessary that the agreement or common plan involve a critical element of criminality.[32]

As to the requirement of an 'essential contribution', it has not been considered necessary to establish that the accused was present at the scene of the crime or that there was a direct and physical link between the essential contribution and the commission of the crime.[33] This requirement was apparently replaced within certain parts of ICL, for a short period of time, by a different element, namely 'direct contribution',[34] but the original approach was restored by the first appeal decision in this area. That ruling also clarified that this kind of contribution is supposed to take place at a level where the co-perpetrator had the power to frustrate the commission

---

cision on Confirmation of Charges, ICC-01/12-01/15, 24 March 2016, para. 24 (www.legal-tools.org/doc/bc8144/); ICC, Trial Chamber, *Prosecutor v. Gombo, Musamba, Kabongo, Wandu and Arido*, Judgment, ICC-01/05-01/13, 19 October 2016, para. 65 (www.legal-tools.org/doc/fe0ce4/).

[31] ICC, Trial Chamber, *Prosecutor v. Lubanga*, Judgment, ICC-01/04-01/06, 14 March 2012, paras. 983–88 (www.legal-tools.org/doc/677866/); ICC, Appeals Chamber, *Prosecutor v. Lubanga*, Judgment, ICC-01/04-01/06 A5, 1 December 2014, paras. 445–51 (www.legal-tools.org/doc/585c75/); ICC, Trial Chamber, *Prosecutor v. Gombo, Musamba, Kabongo, Wandu and Arido*, Judgment, ICC-01/05-01/13, 19 October 2016, para. 66 (www.legal-tools.org/doc/fe0ce4/).

[32] ICC, Trial Chamber, *Prosecutor v. Gombo, Musamba, Kabongo, Wandu and Arido*, Judgment, ICC-01/05-01/13, 19 October 2016, para. 67 (www.legal-tools.org/doc/fe0ce4/).

[33] ICC, Trial Chamber, *Prosecutor v. Lubanga*, Judgment, ICC-01/04-01/06, 14 March 2012, paras. 1004–5 (www.legal-tools.org/doc/677866/); ICC, Appeals Chamber, *Prosecutor v. Lubanga*, Judgment, ICC-01/04-01/06 A5, 1 December 2014, para. 469 (www.legal-tools.org/doc/585c75/); ICC, Trial Chamber, *Prosecutor v. Gombo, Musamba, Kabongo, Wandu and Arido*, Judgment, ICC-01/05-01/13, 19 October 2016, para. 69 (www.legal-tools.org/doc/fe0ce4/).

[34] ICC, Trial Chamber, *Prosecutor v. Chui*, Judgment, Concurring Opinion of Judge Christine Van den Wyngaert, ICC-01/04-02/12, 18 December 2012, paras. 40–48 (www.legal-tools.org/doc/7d5200/).

of the crime.[35] Since persons at a high level of a power structure who hold such power are not usually present at the crime scene, and since they typically use the structure to have the relevant criminal acts committed for some political, ideological, or economic purpose, this interpretation tends to combine joint perpetration at the execution phase with perpetration through another ('indirect perpetration'). Hence, 'indirect joint perpetration' would perhaps have been a more appropriate label in order to distinguish this scenario, which includes masterminds and leaders removed from the crime scenes, from liability for 'joint multiple perpetration' and 'joint functional perpetration', where all the perpetrators in a particular case participated directly at the crime scene (although possibly with different roles and functions). In other words, 'joint perpetration' is a flexible concept, but this may also give rise to some confusion and a need for further and presumably more precise derivative concepts of criminal law liability within ICL.

The *mens rea* of joint perpetration liability generally has been considered to comprise three aspects: (1) the subjective element of the joint perpetrators with respect to the underlying crime; (2) the fact that the joint perpetrators all are mutually aware and mutually accept that implementing their common plan may result in the realisation of the material elements of the crime; and (3) that the joint perpetrators are aware of the factual circumstances enabling them to jointly control the crime.[36]

---

[35] ICC, Appeals Chamber, *Prosecutor v. Lubanga*, Judgment, ICC-01/04-01/06 A5, 1 December 2014, paras. 469 and 473 (www.legal-tools.org/doc/585c75/); ICC, Trial Chamber, *Prosecutor v. Al Mahdi*, Judgment, ICC-01/12-01/15, 27 September 2016, para. 19 (www.legal-tools.org/doc/042397/).

[36] ICC, Pre-Trial Chamber, *Prosecutor v. Lubanga*, Decision on Confirmation of Charges, ICC-01/04-01/06, 29 January 2007, paras. 349–50 (www.legal-tools.org/doc/b7ac4f/); ICC, Pre-Trial Chamber, *Prosecutor v. Katanga and Chui*, Decision on Confirmation of Charges, ICC-01/04-01/07, 30 September 2008, paras. 527–28, 533–34, and 538–39 (www.legal-tools.org/doc/67a9ec/); ICC, Pre-Trial Chamber *Prosecutor v. Bemba*, Decision on Confirmation of Charges, ICC-01/05-01/08, 15 June 2009, para. 351 (www.legal-tools.org/doc/07965c/); ICC, Pre-Trial Chamber, *Prosecutor v. Garda*, Decision on Confirmation of Charges, ICC-02/05-02/09, 8 February 2010, para. 161 (www.legal-tools.org/doc/cb3614/); ICC, Pre-Trial Chamber, *Prosecutor v. Nourain and Jamus*, Corrigendum of Decision on Confirmation of Charges, ICC-02/05-03/09, 7 March 2011, paras. 150–53 (www.legal-tools.org/doc/5ac9eb/); ICC, Pre-Trial Chamber, *Prosecutor v. Ruto, Kosgey and Sang*, Decision on Confirmation of Charges, ICC-01/09-01/11, 23 January 2012, paras. 286–92, 306, 313, 333–36, and 348 (www.legal-tools.org/doc/96c3c2/); ICC, Trial Chamber, *Pros-*

7.2.2.3. Perpetration through Another

Just as the notion of essential contribution as an element of joint perpetration was the subject of debate at the trial level at the ICC, perpetration through another person was also debated. The points of contention were (1) whether committing a crime through a physical person, as Rome Statute Article 25(3)(a) appears to indicate, can be expanded to commission of the crime through an organisation, and (2) whether Article 25(3)(a) would also allow judges to combine two of the specifically mentioned types of perpetration, namely joint perpetration and perpetration through another person, into a combined form and use the notion of indirect co-perpetration.[37]

In short, it would appear that a majority of the judges, including the appeal judges, have favoured an approach that would make it possible to apply the broadest forms of liability under this article.

With respect to perpetration through an organisation, it has been generally acknowledged, at least within the Rome Statute subsystem, that the notion of the perpetrator behind the perpetrator – a device to capture leaders in an organisation who utilise not only persons who cannot be held responsible for their crimes, but also persons who were involved and responsible for the execution of crimes themselves – can be applied in the international sphere to certain types of organisations,[38] provided that the following criteria are met:

---

ecutor v. Lubanga, Judgment, ICC-01/04-01/06, 14 March 2012, paras. 1012–13 (www.legal-tools.org/doc/677866/); ICC, Trial Chamber, *Prosecutor v. Gombo, Musamba, Kabongo, Wandu and Arido*, Judgment, ICC-01/05-01/13, 19 October 2016, para. 70 (www.legal-tools.org/doc/fe0ce4/).

[37] As discussed in Chapter 2, Section 2.2.3.6., such a combination of liability categories is not prohibited under the general theory of criminal law liability. However, legislators and treaty makers may still opt for a more limited version of criminal liability, at least as long as the liability scheme as a whole within the relevant subsystem does not provide certain groups of persons with impunity from universal crimes liability.

[38] ICC, Appeals Chamber, *Prosecutor v. Lubanga*, Judgment, ICC-01/04-01/06 A5, 1 December 2014, para. 465 (www.legal-tools.org/doc/585c75/). This approach has not found uniform agreement among the ICC judiciary; see ICC, Trial Chamber, *Prosecutor v. Chui*, Judgment, Concurring Opinion of Judge Christine Van den Wyngaert, ICC-01/04-02/12, 18 December 2012 (www.legal-tools.org/doc/7d5200/); ICC, Trial Chamber, *Prosecutor v. Katanga*, Judgment, Minority Opinion of Judge Christine Van den Wyngaert, ICC-01/04-01/07, 7 March 2014, paras. 277–79 (www.legal-tools.org/doc/9b0c61/); ICC, Trial Chamber, *Prosecutor v. Blé Goudé*, Partially Dissenting Opinion of Judge Christine Van den

- the leader must have control over the organisation;

- the organisation must consist of an organised and hierarchical apparatus of power; and

- the execution of crimes must be secured by an almost automatic compliance with the orders issued by the leader.[39]

These elements have been subject to some elaboration. With respect to the criterion that the organisation must be based on hierarchical relations between superiors and subordinates, judges have held that the organisation must also comprise sufficient subordinates to guarantee that superiors' orders will be carried out, if not by one subordinate, then by another. This means that the leader must use his control over the apparatus to execute crimes, and that he, as the perpetrator behind the perpetrator, can mobilise the authority and power within the organisation to secure compliance with his orders.[40]

With respect to the requirement that the execution of the crimes be secured by almost automatic compliance with the orders, it has been said that the organisation must be structured in a manner that enables the leader to actually secure the commission of crimes. This means that the leader's control over the apparatus allows him to utilise his subordinates as a mere gear in a giant machine in order to produce the criminal result automatically. It also means that the successful execution of the plan will not be compromised by any particular subordinate's failure to comply with an order. Any one subordinate who does not comply can simply be replaced by another who will carry out the order. This can be accomplished, for instance, through intensive, strict, and violent training regimens.[41]

Wyngaert, ICC-02/11-02/11-186-Anx, 11 December 2014, para. 5 (www.legal-tools.org/doc/7485d0/).

[39] ICC, Pre-Trial Chamber, *Prosecutor v. Katanga and Chui*, Decision on Confirmation of Charges, ICC-01/04-01/07, 30 September 2008, paras. 511–18 (www.legal-tools.org/doc/67a9ec/); ICC, Trial Chamber, *Prosecutor v. Katanga*, Judgment, ICC-01/04-01/07, 7 March 2014, paras. 1404–13 (www.legal-tools.org/doc/f74b4f/).

[40] ICC, Pre-Trial Chamber, *Prosecutor v. Katanga and Chui*, Decision on Confirmation of Charges, ICC-01/04-01/07, 30 September 2008, paras. 512–14 (www.legal-tools.org/doc/67a9ec/); ICC, Trial Chamber, *Prosecutor v. Katanga*, Judgment, ICC-01/04-01/07, 7 March 2014, paras. 1408–9 (www.legal-tools.org/doc/f74b4f/).

[41] ICC, Pre-Trial Chamber, *Prosecutor v. Katanga and Chui*, Decision on Confirmation of Charges, ICC-01/04-01/07, 30 September 2008, paras. 515–17 (www.legal-tools.org/doc/

This form of control, where there is almost automatic compliance with the orders of the leaders, is different from the 'ordering' model of liability in that the leader does not merely order the commission of a crime, but through his control over the organisation essentially decides whether and how the crime will be committed.[42] If the leader is acting in concert with other leaders, one may ask whether the same form of liability is applicable. Here, the answer is presumably 'why not?', as long as the same requirements are met. Otherwise a leader could arrange to escape liability by co-operating at the leadership level, and this form of liability would not be applicable to the leaders of most states simply because of the way the leadership level is organised. It should be recalled that this kind of defence was raised at Nuremberg but did not excuse persons acting jointly at the top leadership level under the dictates of Hitler.

With respect to the *mens rea* of this type of liability, the indirect perpetrator must be aware of the elements fundamental to his or her exertion of control over the crime: that is, the indirect perpetrator must be aware of the position he or she held within the organisation and of the essential features of the organisation that secured the functional automatism.[43]

The expansion of perpetration to certain organisations led to the development of a new form of perpetrator liability, called 'indirect co-perpetration'. This is a specific term of art in the jurisprudence of the ICC, which describes it as follows:

> a new axis for the attribution of criminal responsibility: in addition to the horizontal axis (joint perpetration) and the vertical axis (perpetration through another person), a new *diagonal axis* ("indirect co-perpetration") was created.[44]

67a9ec/); ICC, Trial Chamber, *Prosecutor v. Katanga*, Judgment, ICC-01/04-01/07, 7 March 2014, paras. 1411–12 (www.legal-tools.org/doc/f74b4f/).

[42] ICC, Pre-Trial Chamber, *Prosecutor v. Katanga and Chui*, Decision on Confirmation of Charges, ICC-01/04-01/07, 30 September 2008, para. 518 (www.legal-tools.org/doc/67a9ec/).

[43] ICC, Trial Chamber, *Prosecutor v. Katanga*, Judgment, ICC-01/04-01/07, 7 March 2014, paras. 1414–15 (www.legal-tools.org/doc/f74b4f/).

[44] ICC, Trial Chamber, *Prosecutor v. Chui*, Judgment, Concurring Opinion of Judge Christine Van den Wyngaert, ICC-01/04-02/12, 18 December 2012, para. 59 (www.legal-tools.org/doc/7d5200/) (italics added).

This form of further derivative liability is tailored to cover situations where leaders of different, autonomous power structures choose to co-operate by using their forces or subordinates in a joint operation for a common purpose that involves committing universal crimes. The leaders will then be liable also for the crimes committed by the other structure. The elements of this form of liability are as follows:

- the perpetrator must be part of a common plan or an agreement with one or more persons;

- the perpetrator and the other co-perpetrator(s) must carry out essential contributions in a coordinated manner which result in the fulfilment of the material elements of the crime;

- the perpetrator must have control over the organisation;

- the organisation must consist of an organised and hierarchical apparatus of power;

- the execution of the crimes must be secured by almost automatic compliance with the orders issued by the perpetrator.[45]

These criteria have been further explained by saying that this form of liability still rests on the notion of reciprocal imputation of coordinated actions performed by each co-perpetrator. The only difference compared to so-called 'direct co-perpetration' is that the objective (material) elements of the crime are executed by other persons who are utilised by the (other) co-perpetrators for the commission of the crime. This form of responsibility combines the commission of a crime jointly with another (each of a plurality of persons has the capacity to frustrate the commission of the crime by not performing his or her coordinated contributive acts within the framework of an agreement among the persons) with the commission of a crime through another person (a person commits the crime by subjugating another person's will, rather than by personally and directly executing the objective elements of the crime).[46]

---

[45] ICC, Pre-Trial Chamber, *Prosecutor v. Ntaganda*, Decision on Confirmation of Charges, ICC-01/04-02/06, 9 June 2014, para.104 (www.legal-tools.org/doc/5686c6/).

[46] ICC, Pre-Trial Chamber, *Prosecutor v. Ongwen*, Decision on Confirmation of Charges, ICC-02/04-01/15, 23 March 2016, para. 39 (www.legal-tools.org/doc/74fc6e/).

7.2.2.4. Joint Criminal Enterprise

The derivative liability category of 'joint criminal enterprise' ('JCE') and its predecessor 'common design' was developed in ICL jurisprudence, first through the concept of common design in post–World War II cases and later by UN-established criminal tribunals. It can be considered as derived from conspiracy in conjunction with perpetration or from joint perpetration in combination with complicity. In essence, JCE constitutes liability for a group of persons who successfully complete a crime together at the execution stage, or through the use of one or several other participants, according to and in agreement with a common criminal plan or policy made or agreed to by the group of persons, and the planned crime or a similar crime is in fact completed. In general, the ICTY and ICTR jurisprudence has distinguished three types of JCE.[47] They can be seen as further derived from the liability category of JCE.

In the first form of joint criminal enterprise, JCE I, all of the persons committed to the JCE possess the same intent to effect the common purpose, namely the crime.[48] The second form of joint criminal enterprise, JCE II, the 'systemic' form, is a variant of the first form and is characterised by the existence of an organised criminal system, in particular in the

---

[47] ICTY, Appeals Chamber, *Prosecutor v. Tadić*, Judgment, IT-94-1-A, 15 July 1999, para. 227 (www.legal-tools.org/doc/8efc3a/); ICTY, Appeals Chamber, *Prosecutor v. Vasiljević*, Judgment, IT-98-32-A, 25 February 2004, para. 100 (www.legal-tools.org/doc/e35d81/); ICTY, Appeals Chamber, *Prosecutor v. Stakić*, Judgment, IT-97-24-A, 22 March 2006, para. 64 (www.legal-tools.org/doc/09f75f/). It is worth noting that in one of the first cases in which JCE was used, namely the Tadić case, the accused had been acquitted by the Trial Chamber since it could not be proven that he, as part of a larger group of five men, had played any part in the commission of murder. The Appeals Chamber found that there was criminal liability based on JCE even if there was no proof of personal commission by any of the members in the JCE. For a subsequent detailed analysis holding that the Tadić case had correctly considered JCE to be part of customary international law, see ICTY, Appeals Chamber, *Prosecutor v. Đorđević*, Judgment, IT-05-87/1-A, 27 January 2014, paras. 32–58 (www.legal-tools.org/doc/e6fa92/); ICTY, Appeals Chamber, *Prosecutor v. Popović et al.*, Judgment, IT-05-88-A, 30 January 2015, paras. 1440 and 1672–74 (www.legal-tools.org/doc/4c28fb/); ICTY, Appeals Chamber, *Prosecutor v. Tolimir*, Judgment, IT-05-88/2-A, 8 April 2015, paras. 280–84 (www.legal-tools.org/doc/010ecb/); ICTY, Appeals Chamber, *Prosecutor v. Prlić et al.*, Judgment, IT-04-74-A, 29 November 2017, paras. 587–91 (www.legal-tools.org/doc/941285/); see also EAC, Trial Chamber, *Prosecutor v. Habré*, Judgment, 30 May 2016, paras. 1865–85 (www.legal-tools.org/doc/98c00a/).

[48] ICTY, Trial Chamber, *Prosecutor v. Haradinaj et al.*, Judgment, IT-04-84bis-T, 29 November 2012, para. 620 (www.legal-tools.org/doc/1bad7b/).

---

case of concentration or detention camps. This form of joint criminal enterprise requires personal knowledge of the organised system and intent to further the criminal purpose of that system. The third, 'extended' form of joint criminal enterprise, JCE III, entails responsibility for crimes committed that go beyond the common purpose, but that are nevertheless a natural and foreseeable consequence of the common purpose. The requisite *mens rea* for the extended form is twofold. First, the accused must have the intention to participate in and contribute to the common criminal purpose. Second, in order to be held responsible for crimes that were not part of the common purpose but that were nevertheless a natural and foreseeable consequence of it, the accused must also know that such a crime might be perpetrated by a member of the group, and must willingly take the risk that the crime might occur by joining or continuing to participate in the enterprise.[49]

The general and more specific requirements for this type of responsibility are as follows:

- There must be a plurality of persons, who do not need to be organised in a military, political, or administrative structure.

- There must exist a common plan, design, or purpose that amounts to or involves the commission of a crime. There is no necessity for this plan, design, or purpose to have been previously arranged or formulated. The common plan or purpose may materialise extemporaneously and be inferred from the fact that a plurality of persons act in unison to put into effect a joint criminal enterprise.

- The accused must participate in the common design involving the perpetration of one of the international crimes. This participation need not involve commission of a specific crime, but may take the form of assistance in, or contribution to, the execution of the common plan or purpose. The participation in the enterprise must be significant, meaning an act or omission that makes an enterprise ef-

---

[49] ICTY, Appeals Chamber, *Prosecutor v. Đorđević*, Judgment, IT-05-87/1-A, 27 January 2014, paras. 468 and 474 (www.legal-tools.org/doc/e6fa92/); ICTY, Appeals Chamber, *Prosecutor v. Stanišić and Simatović*, Judgment, IT-03-69-A, 9 December 2015, para. 77 (www.legal-tools.org/doc/198c16/); ICTY, Trial Chamber, *Prosecutor v. Karadžić*, Judgment, IT-95-5/18-T, 24 March 2016, para. 570 (www.legal-tools.org/doc/173e23/); ICTY, Trial Chamber, *Prosecutor v. Mladić*, Judgment, IT-09-92-T, 22 November 2017, paras. 3558–60 (www.legal-tools.org/doc/96f3c1/).

ficient or effective, for instance, a participation that enables the system to run more smoothly or without disruption.[50]

More recently, some refinements and clarifications have been made to these general principles.

In general, the doctrine of joint criminal enterprise can be used against high-level functionaries[51]; it is not restricted to small-scale cases but can also apply to large criminal enterprises.[52] Where the common purpose includes crimes committed over a wide geographic area, a person may be found criminally responsible for his participation in the whole enterprise, even if his contributions to the enterprise occurred only in a much smaller geographic area.[53]

With respect to the first two categories of JCE, it has been made clear that mere membership in the group having a common criminal purpose is not sufficient,[54] although an omission can amount to JCE partici-

---

[50] ICTY, Appeals Chamber, *Prosecutor v. Tadić*, Judgment, IT-94-1-A, 15 July 1999, para. 227 (www.legal-tools.org/doc/8efc3a/); ICTY, Appeals Chamber, *Prosecutor v. Vasiljević*, Judgment, IT-98-32-A, 25 February 2004, para. 100 (www.legal-tools.org/doc/e35d81/); ICTY, Appeals Chamber, *Prosecutor v. Stakić*, Judgment, IT-97-24-A, 22 March 2006, para. 64 (www.legal-tools.org/doc/09f75f/); ICTR, Appeals Chamber, *Prosecutor v. Gatete*, Judgment, ICTR-2000-61-A, 9 October 2012, paras. 239 and 241 (www.legal-tools.org/doc/1d0b08/); ECCC, Trial Chamber, Case 002/01, Judgment, 002/19-09-2007/ECCC/TC, 7 August 2014, paras. 692–94 (www.legal-tools.org/doc/4888de/); ICTR, Appeals Chamber, *Prosecutor v. Karemera*, Judgment, ICTR-98-44-A, 29 September 2014, paras. 145–46 (www.legal-tools.org/doc/372a64/); ICTY, Trial Chamber, *Prosecutor v. Karadžić*, Judgment, IT-95-5/18-T, 24 March 2016, paras. 562 and 564–66 (www.legal-tools.org/doc/173e23/); ICTY, Appeals Chamber, *Prosecutor v. Stanišić and Župljanin*, Judgment, IT-08-91-A, 30 June 2016, paras. 136 and 154 (www.legal-tools.org/doc/e414f6/); ICTY, Trial Chamber, *Prosecutor v. Mladić*, Judgment, IT-09-92-T, 22 November 2017, paras. 3558–60 (www.legal-tools.org/doc/96f3c1/); EAC, Trial Chamber, *Prosecutor v. Habré*, Judgment, 30 May 2016, paras. 1893–1904 (www.legal-tools.org/doc/98c00a/).
[51] ICTY, Appeals Chamber, *Prosecutor v. Krajišnik*, Judgment, IT-00-39-A, 17 March 2009, para. 194 (www.legal-tools.org/doc/770028/).
[52] ICTY, Appeals Chamber, *Prosecutor v. Brđanin*, Judgment, IT-99-36-A, 3 April 2007, para. 425 (www.legal-tools.org/doc/782cef/).
[53] ICTY, Appeals Chamber, *Prosecutor v. Tadić*, Judgment, IT-94-1-A, 15 July 1999, para. 199 (www.legal-tools.org/doc/8efc3a/); ICTY, Trial Chamber, *Prosecutor v. Popović et al.*, Judgment, IT-05-88-T, 10 June 2010, para. 1024 (www.legal-tools.org/doc/481867/).
[54] ICTY, Trial Chamber, *Prosecutor v. Brđanin*, Judgment, IT-99-36, 1 September 2004, para. 263 (www.legal-tools.org/doc/4c3228/); ICTR, Trial Chamber, *Prosecutor v. Karemera et al.*, Judgment, ICTR-98-44-T, 2 February 2012, para. 1437 (www.legal-tools.org/doc/5b9068/).

pation for which it is not necessary to establish a duty to act.[55] However, it is not required that each member in the JCE be identified by name; it can be sufficient to refer to categories or groups of persons.[56]

The common criminal objective of the JCE may also evolve over time, as long as the committed group members have agreed on this expansion. It means that the crimes that make up the common purpose may evolve and change over time, and for this reason the JCE may have different participants at different times.[57]

It is not necessary that the persons carrying out the *actus reus* of the crime forming part of the common purpose have been participants in or members of the JCE. Consequently, persons carrying out the crime need not share the intent of the crime with the participants committed to the common plan or policy. Nor is the mental state of persons carrying out the crime a determinative factor in finding the requisite intent for the participants in a JCE. But if a JCE used a non–group member to commit a crime,

---

[55] ICTR, Trial Chamber, *Prosecutor v. Ndahimana*, Judgment, ICTR-01-68, 30 December 2011, paras. 810–11 (www.legal-tools.org/doc/d8e4f2/); ICTY, Trial Chamber, *Prosecutor v. Haradinaj et al.*, Judgment, IT-04-84bis-T, 29 November 2012, para. 619 (www.legal-tools.org/doc/1bad7b/); ICTY, Appeals Chamber, *Prosecutor v. Stanišić and Župljanin*, Judgment, IT-08-91-A, 30 June 2016, para. 111, 732–33 (www.legal-tools.org/doc/e414f6/).

[56] ICTY, Appeals Chamber, *Prosecutor v. Krajišnik*, Judgment, IT-00-39-A, 17 March 2009, para. 156 (www.legal-tools.org/doc/770028/); ICTY, Trial Chamber, *Prosecutor v. Đorđević*, Judgment, IT-05-87/1, 23 February 2011, para. 1862 (www.legal-tools.org/doc/653651/); ICTY, Appeals Chamber, *Prosecutor v. Đorđević*, Judgment, IT-05-87/1-A, 27 January 2014, paras. 127–30 (www.legal-tools.org/doc/e6fa92/); ICTR, Appeals Chamber, *Prosecutor v. Karemera*, Judgment, ICTR-98-44-A, 29 September 2014, para. 605 (www.legal-tools.org/doc/372a64/); ICTY, Trial Chamber, *Prosecutor v. Karadžić*, Judgment, IT-95-5/18-T, 24 March 2016, para. 562 (www.legal-tools.org/doc/173e23/).

[57] ICTY, Appeals Chamber, *Prosecutor v. Krajišnik*, Judgment, IT-00-39-A, 17 March 2009, para. 163 (www.legal-tools.org/doc/770028/); STL, Appeals Chamber, Interlocutory Decision on the Applicable Law: Terrorism, Conspiracy, Homicide, Perpetration, Cumulative Charging, STL-II-OI/I/AC/RI76bis, 16 February 2011, paras. 246–48; SCSL, Trial Chamber, *Prosecutor v. Taylor*, Judgment, SCSL-03-01-T, 18 May 2012, para. 464 (www.legal-tools.org/doc/8075e7/); ICTY, Appeals Chamber, *Prosecutor v. Šainović et al.*, Judgment, IT-05-87-A, 23 January 2014, paras. 609–11 (www.legal-tools.org/doc/81ac8c/); ICTY, Trial Chamber, *Prosecutor v. Karadžić*, Judgment, IT-95-5/18-T, 24 March 2016, para. 563 (www.legal-tools.org/doc/173e23/); ICTY, Trial Chamber, *Prosecutor v. Mladić*, Judgment, IT-09-92-T, 22 November 2017, para. 3561 (www.legal-tools.org/doc/96f3c1/); MICT, Appeals Chamber, *Prosecutor v. Šešelj*, Judgment, MICT-16-99-A, 11 April 2018, paras. 95–96 (www.legal-tools.org/doc/96ea58/).

---

that crime must be traced back to the JCE.[58] For persons in a criminal enterprise to be liable it must be shown that they acted together, or in concert with each other, in the implementation of a common objective,[59] but is not a legal requirement that they acted in unison.[60]

With respect to the contribution factor, the actual participation or contribution of an accused to a crime committed with relevance to the common purpose need not be substantive or criminal, but it should at least be a significant contribution to the crimes committed;[61] routine duties can amount to such a contribution.[62] The fact that different persons might have different levels of involvement does not negate the existence of a

---

58 ICTY, Appeals Chamber, *Prosecutor v. Krajišnik*, Judgment, IT-00-39-A, 17 March 2009, paras. 225–26 (www.legal-tools.org/doc/770028/); ICTY, Appeals Chamber, *Prosecutor v. Karadžić*, Judgment (Rule 98bis), IT-95-5/18-AR98bis.1, 11 July 2013, para. 79 (www.legal-tools.org/doc/84001b/); ICTY, Appeals Chamber, *Prosecutor v. Đorđević*, Judgment, IT-05-87/1-A, 27 January 2014, paras. 165, 169, and 171 (www.legal-tools.org/doc/e6fa92/); ICTY, Appeals Chamber, *Prosecutor v. Šainović et al.*, Judgment, IT-05-87-A, 23 January 2014, paras. 1256–57 (www.legal-tools.org/doc/81ac8c/); ICTR, Appeals Chamber, *Prosecutor v. Karemera*, Judgment, ICTR-98-44-A, 29 September 2014, para. 153 (www.legal-tools.org/doc/372a64/); ICTY, Appeals Chamber, *Prosecutor v. Popović et al.*, Judgment, IT-05-88-A, 30 January 2015, paras. 1050 and 1065 (www.legal-tools.org/doc/4c28fb/); ICTY, Appeals Chamber, *Prosecutor v. Stanišić and Župljanin*, Judgment, IT-08-91-A, 30 June 2016, paras. 119 and 994–96 (www.legal-tools.org/doc/e414f6/); ICTY, Trial Chamber, *Prosecutor v. Mladić*, Judgment, IT-09-92-T, 22 November 2017, para. 3561 (www.legal-tools.org/doc/96f3c1/); EAC, Trial Chamber, *Prosecutor v. Habré*, Judgment, 30 May 2016, paras. 1905–8 (www.legal-tools.org/doc/98c00a/).
59 ICTY, Trial Chamber, *Prosecutor v. Stanišić and Simatović*, Judgment, IT-03-69-T, 30 May 2013, para. 1259 (www.legal-tools.org/doc/066e67/); ICTY, Appeals Chamber, *Prosecutor v. Popović et al.*, Judgment, IT-05-88-A, 30 January 2015, para. 1050 (www.legal-tools.org/doc/4c28fb/).
60 ICTY, Appeals Chamber, *Prosecutor v. Đorđević*, Judgment, IT-05-87/1-A, 27 January 2014, paras. 138–42 (www.legal-tools.org/doc/e6fa92/).
61 ICTY, Appeals Chamber, *Prosecutor v. Krajišnik*, Judgment, IT-00-39-A, 17 March 2009, para. 215 (www.legal-tools.org/doc/770028/); ICTY, Appeals Chamber, *Prosecutor v. Šainović et al.*, Judgment, IT-05-87-A, 23 January 2014, paras. 985 and 987 (www.legal-tools.org/doc/81ac8c/). This implies a lesser level of contribution for JCE as compared to aiding and abetting according to ICTY, Appeals Chamber, *Prosecutor v. Gotovina and Markač*, Judgment, IT-06-90-A, 16 November 2012, paras. 147 and 149 (www.legal-tools.org/doc/03b685/); ICTY, Appeals Chamber, *Prosecutor v. Popović et al.*, Judgment, IT-05-88-A, 30 January 2015, para. 1378 (www.legal-tools.org/doc/4c28fb/); ICTY, Judgment, Trial Chamber, *Prosecutor v. Mladić*, Judgment, IT-09-92-T, 22 November 2017, para. 3561 (www.legal-tools.org/doc/96f3c1/).
62 ICTY, Appeals Chamber, *Prosecutor v. Stanišić and Župljanin*, Judgment, IT-08-91-A, 30 June 2016, para. 253 (www.legal-tools.org/doc/e414f6/).

JCE, and differing levels of involvement can be dealt with at the sentencing stage.[63] A person's position of authority and silent approval count in favour of a finding that his or her participation was significant,[64] which includes a failure to ensure the investigation and punishment of crimes committed.[65]

With respect to the third category of JCE, a person

can only be held responsible for a crime outside the common purpose, if under the circumstances of the case: (i) it was foreseeable that such a crime might be perpetrated by one or other members of the group and (ii) the accused willingly took that risk (*dolus eventualis*). The crime must be shown to have been foreseeable to the accused in particular.[66]

[63] ICTY, Appeals Chamber, *Prosecutor v. Brđanin*, Judgment, IT-99-36-A, 3 April 2007, para. 432 (www.legal-tools.org/doc/782cef/); ICTY, Trial Chamber, *Prosecutor v. Đorđević*, Judgment, IT-05-87/1, 23 February 2011, para. 1863 (www.legal-tools.org/doc/653651/); ICTY, Appeals Chamber, *Prosecutor v. Stanišić and Župljanin*, Judgment, IT-08-91-A, 30 June 2016, para. 121 (www.legal-tools.org/doc/e414f6/).

[64] ICTY, Appeals Chamber, *Prosecutor v. Šainović et al.*, Judgment, IT-05-87-A, 23 January 2014, paras. 1242 and 1368 (www.legal-tools.org/doc/81ac8c/); ICTY, Appeals Chamber, *Prosecutor v. Popović et al.*, Judgment, IT-05-88-A, 30 January 2015, para. 1385 (www.legal-tools.org/doc/4c28fb/); ICTY, Appeals Chamber, *Prosecutor v. Stanišić and Župljanin*, Judgment, IT-08-91-A, 30 June 2016, para. 752 (www.legal-tools.org/doc/e414f6/).

[65] ICTY, Appeals Chamber, *Prosecutor v. Đorđević*, Judgment, IT-05-87/1-A, 27 January 2014, paras. 454 and 460 (www.legal-tools.org/doc/e6fa92/); ICTY, Appeals Chamber, *Prosecutor v. Šainović et al.*, Judgment, IT-05-87-A, 23 January 2014, paras. 1233–34 (www.legal-tools.org/doc/81ac8c/); ICTY, Appeals Chamber, *Prosecutor v. Stanišić and Župljanin*, Judgment, IT-08-91-A, 30 June 2016, paras.121 and 734 (www.legal-tools.org/doc/e414f6/).

[66] ICTY, Appeals Chamber, *Prosecutor v. Brđanin*, Judgment, IT-99-36-A, 3 April 2007, para. 365 (www.legal-tools.org/doc/782cef/). See also ICTY, Appeals Chamber, *Prosecutor v. Đorđević*, Judgment, IT-05-87/1-A, 27 January 2014, para. 906 (www.legal-tools.org/doc/e6fa92/); ICTY, Appeals Chamber, *Prosecutor v. Šainović et al.*, Judgment, IT-05-87-A, 23 January 2014, paras. 1281–82, 1525, 1538, and 1557 (www.legal-tools.org/doc/81ac8c/); ICTR, Appeals Chamber, *Prosecutor v. Karemera*, Judgment, ICTR-98-44-A, 29 September 2014, paras. 623, 627, 630, and 634 (www.legal-tools.org/doc/372a64/); ICTY, Appeals Chamber, *Prosecutor v. Popović et al.*, Judgment, IT-05-88-A, 30 January 2015, paras. 1431–32 and 1701 (www.legal-tools.org/doc/4c28fb/); ICTY, Appeals Chamber, *Prosecutor v. Stanišić and Župljanin*, Judgment, IT-08-91-A, 30 June 2016, paras. 614, 621, 958, and 967–76 (www.legal-tools.org/doc/e414f6/); ICTY, Appeals Chamber, *Prosecutor v. Prlić et al.*, Judgment, IT-04-74-A, 29 November 2017, paras. 2836, 2891–93, 2896, and 3022–29 (www.legal-tools.org/doc/941285/).

Willingly taking a risk means deciding to participate in a JCE with the awareness that crime was a possible (not probable) consequence of the implementation of that enterprise.[67] For third-category JCE liability, the accused does not need to be present at the scene of the crime,[68] nor does he need to possess intent for the crime falling outside the common purpose, nor is there an express time frame for the foreseeability criterion. The mental state of the person or persons carrying out the extended crime is not relevant to the finding of the mental state of the accused but is determinative to the finding of which extended crime was committed.[69]

JCE, including third-category JCE, can also be a basis for liability in genocide and other specific intent crimes.[70] It is, however, always re-

---

[67] ICTY, Appeals Chamber, *Prosecutor v. Brđanin*, Judgment, IT-99-36-A, 3 April 2007, para. 411 (www.legal-tools.org/doc/782cef/); ICTY, Appeals Chamber, *Prosecutor v. Gotovina and Markač*, Judgment, IT-06-90-A, 16 November 2012, paras. 90 and 97 (www.legal-tools.org/doc/03b685/); ICTY, Appeals Chamber, *Prosecutor v. Đorđević*, Judgment, IT-05-87/1-A, 27 January 2014, paras. 907, 911–13, and 926–27 (www.legal-tools.org/doc/e6fa92/); ICTY, Appeals Chamber, *Prosecutor v. Tolimir*, Judgment, IT-05-88/2-A, 8 April 2015, para. 514 (www.legal-tools.org/doc/010ecb/); ICTY, Appeals Chamber, *Prosecutor v. Stanišić and Župljanin*, Judgment, IT-08-91-A, 30 June 2016, para. 1055 (www.legal-tools.org/doc/e414f6/); ICTY, Appeals Chamber, *Prosecutor v. Prlić et al.*, Judgment, IT-04-74-A, 29 November 2017, para. 2836 (www.legal-tools.org/doc/941285/).

[68] ICTY, Appeals Chamber, *Prosecutor v. Tolimir*, Judgment, IT-05-88/2-A, 8 April 2015, para. 549 (www.legal-tools.org/doc/010ecb/).

[69] ICTY, Trial Chamber, *Prosecutor v. Popović et al.*, Judgment, IT-05-88-T, 10 June 2010, para. 1031 (www.legal-tools.org/doc/481867/); ICTY, Appeals Chamber, *Prosecutor v. Popović et al.*, Judgment, IT-05-88-A, 30 January 2015, para. 1696 (www.legal-tools.org/doc/4c28fb/); ICTY, Appeals Chamber, *Prosecutor v. Stanišić and Simatović*, Judgment, IT-03-69-A, 9 December 2015, para. 81 (www.legal-tools.org/doc/198c16/).

[70] ICTY, Appeals Chamber, *Prosecutor v. Brđanin*, Decision on Interlocutory Appeal, IT-99-36-A, 19 March 2004, paras. 5–10 (www.legal-tools.org/doc/acb003/). However, see STL, Appeals Chamber, Interlocutory Decision on the Applicable Law: Terrorism, Conspiracy, Homicide, Perpetration, Cumulative Charging, STL-11-OI/I/AC/RI76bis, 16 February 2011, para. 249, with respect to specific intent offences in general, as well as, in this respect, ICTR, Trial Chamber, *Prosecutor v. Ndahimana*, Judgment, ICTR-01-68, 30 December 2011, para. 722 (www.legal-tools.org/doc/d8e4f2/); ICTY, Appeals Chamber, *Prosecutor v. Đorđević*, Judgment, IT-05-87/1-A, 27 January 2014, paras. 77–84 (www.legal-tools.org/doc/e6fa92/); ICTY, Appeals Chamber, *Prosecutor v. Popović et al.*, Judgment, IT-05-88-A, 30 January 2015, paras. 1440 and 1708 (www.legal-tools.org/doc/4c28fb/); ICTY, Trial Chamber, *Prosecutor v. Karadžić*, Judgment, IT-95-5/18-T, 24 March 2016, para. 549 (www.legal-tools.org/doc/173e23/); ICTY, Appeals Chamber, *Prosecutor v. Stanišić and Župljanin*, Judgment, IT-08-91-A, 30 June 2016, paras. 595–600 (www.legal-tools.org/doc/e414f6/); ICTY, Trial Chamber, *Prosecutor v. Mladić*, Judgment, IT-09-92-T, 22 November 2017, para. 3435 (www.legal-tools.org/doc/96f3c1/).

quired that the extended, underlying crime committed (for example, murder) also fall within the enumerated offences of the relevant crime category charged (for instance, genocide, or crimes against humanity).

The Appeals Chamber of the ICTY has provided a number of indicators to differentiate between aiding and abetting and JCE:

- Aiding and abetting generally involves a lesser degree of individual criminal responsibility than co-perpetration in a joint criminal enterprise.[71]

- The aider and abettor is always an accessory to a crime perpetrated by another person, the principal (the 'principal' is here synonymous with a perpetrator, which could also be a group of persons constituting a JCE).

- In the case of aiding and abetting, no proof is required of the existence of a common concerted plan, let alone of the pre-existence of such a plan. No plan or agreement is required: indeed, the principal may not even know about the accomplice's contribution.[72]

- The aider and abettor carries out acts directed to assist, encourage, or lend moral support to the perpetration of a certain specific crime (murder, extermination, rape, torture, wanton destruction of civilian property, and so on), and this support has a substantial effect upon the perpetration of the crime. By contrast, in the case of (committed group members) acting in pursuance of a common purpose or design constituting a successful joint criminal enterprise, it is sufficient for the participant to perform acts that in some way are directed to the furthering of the common plan or purpose in at least a significant manner.[73]

---

[71] ICTY, Appeals Chamber, *Prosecutor v. Krnojelac*, Judgment, IT-97-25-A, 17 September 2003, para. 75 (www.legal-tools.org/doc/46d2e5/); ICTY, Appeals Chamber, *Prosecutor v. Vasiljević*, Judgment, IT-98-32-A, 25 February 2004, para. 102 (www.legal-tools.org/doc/e35d81/); ICTY, Appeals Chamber, *Prosecutor v. Kvočka*, Judgment, IT-98-30/1-A, 28 February 2005, para. 92 (www.legal-tools.org/doc/006011/).

[72] ICTY, Appeals Chamber, *Prosecutor v. Tadić*, Judgment, IT-94-1-A, 15 July 1999, para. 229 (www.legal-tools.org/doc/8efc3a/).

[73] ICTY, Appeals Chamber, *Prosecutor v. Tadić*, Judgment, IT-94-1-A, 15 July 1999, para. 229 (www.legal-tools.org/doc/8efc3a/); ICTY, Appeals Chamber, *Prosecutor v. Krnojelac*, Judgment, IT-97-25-A, 17 September 2003, paras. 31–33 (www.legal-tools.org/doc/46d2e5/); ICTY, Appeals Chamber, *Prosecutor v. Vasiljević*, Judgment, IT-98-32-A, 25

- In the case of aiding and abetting, the requisite mental element is the knowledge that the acts performed by the aider and abettor assist the commission of a specific crime by the principal. By contrast, in the case of common purpose or design more is required, namely the intent to pursue a common purpose (which can be inferred from circumstantial evidence).[74]

JCE has been used outside the ICTY/ICTR context in the proceedings of the Special Court for Sierra Leone,[75] as well in the ECCC, although in the latter institution it was decided that the third category was not part of customary international law,[76] nor was it included in the law of Cambodia during the time period for which the Chambers had jurisdiction, the 1970s.[77]

February 2004, para. 89 (www.legal-tools.org/doc/e35d81/); STL, Appeals Chamber, Interlocutory Decision on the Applicable Law: Terrorism, Conspiracy, Homicide, Perpetration, Cumulative Charging, STL-II-OI/I/AC/RI76bis, 16 February 2011, para. 227.

[74] ICTY, Appeals Chamber, *Prosecutor v. Tadić*, Judgment, IT-94-1-A, 15 July 1999, para. 229 (www.legal-tools.org/doc/8efc3a/); ICTY, Appeals Chamber, *Prosecutor v. Krnojelac*, Judgment, IT-97-25-A, 17 September 2003, paras. 31–33 (www.legal-tools.org/doc/46d2e5/); ICTY, Appeals Chamber, *Prosecutor v. Vasiljević*, Judgment, IT-98-32-A, 25 February 2004, para. 102 (www.legal-tools.org/doc/e35d81/); ICTY, Appeals Chamber, *Prosecutor v. Kvočka*, Judgment, IT-98-30/1-A, 28 February 2005, para. 89 (www.legal-tools.org/doc/006011/); ICTY, Appeals Chamber, *Prosecutor v. Popović et al.*, Judgment, IT-05-88-A, 30 January 2015, para. 1369 (www.legal-tools.org/doc/4c28fb/); ICTY, Appeals Chamber, *Prosecutor v. Stanišić and Župljanin*, Judgment, IT-08-91-A, 30 June 2016, paras. 375, 480, 486, 915, and 917–22 (www.legal-tools.org/doc/e414f6/).

[75] SCSL, Appeals Chamber, *Prosecutor v. Brima, Kamara and Kanu* (the AFRC Case), Judgment, SCSL-2004-16-A, 22 February 2008, paras. 72–86 (www.legal-tools.org/doc/4420ef/); SCSL, Appeals Chamber, *Prosecutor v. Sesay, Kallon and Gbao* (the RUF Case), Judgment, SCSL-04-14-A, 26 October 2009, paras. 295–306 and 312–18 (www.legal-tools.org/doc/133b48/).

[76] In this book we argue that attribution of personal criminal liability is not governed by the international legality principle. Hence, a specific form of personal liability need not be part of customary international law in the sense of requiring a specific CIL legal basis. It would be sufficient under general international criminal law that the relevant kind of liability form not be prohibited by CIL and not violate the general principles of criminal law liability.

[77] ECCC, Trial Chamber, *Prosecutor v. Kaing Guek Eav alias Duch*, Judgment, 001/18-07-2007/ECCC/TC, 26 July 2010, paras. 504–13 (www.legal-tools.org/doc/dbdb62/); ECCC, Trial Chamber, Case 002/01, Judgment, 002/19-09-2007/ECCC/TC, 7 August 2014, para. 691 (www.legal-tools.org/doc/4888de/); ECCC, Supreme Court Chamber, Case 002/01, Judgment, 002/19-09-2007-ECCC/SC, 23 November 2016, paras. 773–810, 980–83 (re.

The ICC Statute includes a concept similar to JCE, namely common purpose,[78] the formulation of which was based on the 1997 International Convention for the Suppression of Terrorist Bombings; it is generally seen as encompassing JCE I and II but not the 'outer limits' of JCE III.[79] This concept was first explored in 2011,[80] with the jurisprudence since that time providing the following parameters:

- Common purpose requires a common plan, the ingredients of which are the same as in the common plan for perpetration.[81]

- The level of contribution should be significant,[82] which means the contribution is of a type that influences the commission of the crime

---

contribution), 986–87 (re. contribution by omission), 1030–31 (examples of contribution), and 1053–55 (re. intent) (www.legal-tools.org/doc/e66bb3/).

[78] Article 25(3)(d).

[79] ICC, Trial Chamber, *Prosecutor v. Chui*, Judgment, Concurring Opinion of Judge Christine Van den Wyngaert, ICC-01/04-02/12, 18 December 2012, para. 61, n. 77 (www.legal-tools. org/doc/7d5200/).

[80] ICC, Pre-Trial Chamber, *Prosecutor v. Mbarushimana*, Decision on Confirmation of Charges, ICC-01/04-01/10, 16 December 2011, paras. 268–74 (www.legal-tools.org/doc/ 63028f/). For a general reference to this mode of liability see ICC, Pre-Trial Chamber, *Prosecutor v. Ntaganda*, Decision on Confirmation of Charges, ICC-01/04-02/06, 9 June 2014, para. 158 (www.legal-tools.org/doc/5686c6/); ICC, Pre-Trial Chamber, *Prosecutor v. Gbagbo*, Decision on Confirmation of Charges, ICC-02/11-01/11, 12 June 2014, para. 252 (www.legal-tools.org/doc/5b41bc/).

[81] ICC, Pre-Trial Chamber, *Prosecutor v. Mbarushimana*, Decision on Confirmation of Charges, ICC-01/04-01/10, 16 December 2011, para. 271 (www.legal-tools.org/doc/ 63028f/); ICC, Pre-Trial Chamber, *Prosecutor v. Ruto, Kosgey and Sang*, Decision on Confirmation of Charges, ICC-01/09-01/11, 23 January 2012, paras. 353–54 (www.legal-tools. org/doc/96c3c2/); ICC, Trial Chamber, *Prosecutor v. Katanga*, Judgment, ICC-01/04-01/07, 7 March 2014, paras. 1620–42 (www.legal-tools.org/doc/f74b4f/).

[82] ICC, Pre-Trial Chamber, *Prosecutor v. Mbarushimana*, Decision on Confirmation of Charges, ICC-01/04-01/10, 16 December 2011, paras. 276–83 (www.legal-tools.org/doc/ 63028f/). This issue was addressed but not decided upon in ICC, Appeals Chamber, *Prosecutor v. Mbarushimana*, Judgment on the Appeal of the Prosecutor against the Decision of Pre-Trial Chamber I of 16 December 2011 entitled 'Decision on the Confirmation of Charges', ICC-01/04-01/10 OA 4, 30 May 2012, paras. 64–69 (www.legal-tools.org/doc/ 6ead30/) (except in the separate opinion of Judge Fernández de Gurmendi at paras. 5–15). It was discussed in ICC, Trial Chamber, *Prosecutor v. Chui*, Judgment, Concurring Opinion of Judge Christine Van den Wyngaert, ICC-01/04-02/12, 18 December 2012, para. 44 (www.legal-tools.org/doc/7d5200/). See also ICC, Pre-Trial Chamber, *Prosecutor v. Ruto, Kosgey and Sang*, Decision on Confirmation of Charges, ICC-01/09-01/11, 23 January 2012, paras. 353–54 (www.legal-tools.org/doc/96c3c2/); ICC, Trial Chamber, *Prosecutor v. Prosecutor v. Katanga*, Judgment, ICC-ICC-01/04-01/07, 7 March 2014, paras. 1620–42

---

as to its occurrence and mode of commission, but the crime does not depend on the contribution and is not conditioned by it.[83]

- Contributions after the fact can also be part of this mode of liability.[84]

- Whether a person is part of the group carrying out (completing) the agreed crime or not is not an element of this mode of liability.[85]

- There is no need for a direct link between the contribution and the crime, nor for spatial proximity.[86]

- The *mens rea* of this type of liability requires that the person (1) means to engage in the relevant conduct that allegedly contributes to the crime, and (2) is at least aware that his or her conduct contributes to the activities of the group of persons for whose crimes he or she is alleged to bear responsibility.[87]

(www.legal-tools.org/doc/f74b4f/); ICC, Trial Chamber, *Prosecutor v. Katanga*, Judgment, Minority Opinion of Judge Christine Van den Wyngaert, ICC-01/04-01/07, 7 March 2014, para. 38 (www.legal-tools.org/doc/9b0c61/) (this judgment also indicates in para. 287 that there is no need to incorporate a specific direction requirement for contribution and in the same paragraph that both the *mens rea* and *actus rea* thresholds for this type of liability are "extremely low"); ICC, Pre-Trial Chamber, *Prosecutor v. Ongwen*, Decision on Confirmation of Charges, ICC-02/04-01/15, 23 March 2016, para. 44 (www.legal-tools.org/doc/74fc6e/); ICC, Pre-Trial Chamber, *Prosecutor v. Al Mahdi*, Decision on Confirmation of Charges, ICC-01/12-01/15, 24 March 2016, para. 27 (www.legal-tools.org/doc/bc8144/), which also said that the contribution does not need to be significant or reach a certain minimum degree (as was also the case in the Ongwen decision).

83 ICC, Trial Chamber, *Prosecutor v. Katanga*, Judgment, ICC-01/04-01/07, 7 March 2014, paras. 1632–33 (www.legal-tools.org/doc/f74b4f/).

84 ICC, Pre-Trial Chamber, *Prosecutor v. Mbarushimana*, Decision on Confirmation of Charges, ICC-01/04-01/10, 16 December 2011, paras. 286–87 (www.legal-tools.org/doc/63028f/); ICC, Pre-Trial Chamber, *Prosecutor v. Ruto, Kosgey and Sang*, Decision on Confirmation of Charges, ICC-01/09-01/11, 23 January 2012, paras. 353–54 (www.legal-tools.org/doc/96c3c2/).

85 ICC, Trial Chamber, *Prosecutor v. Katanga*, Judgment, ICC-ICC-01/04-01/07, 7 March 2014, para.1631 (www.legal-tools.org/doc/f74b4f/); ICC, Trial Chamber, *Prosecutor v. Katanga*, Judgment, Minority Opinion of Judge Christine Van den Wyngaert, ICC-01/04-01/07, 7 March 2014, para. 286; with respect to the notion of group in this context, see the latter judgment, paras. 191–93 (www.legal-tools.org/doc/9b0c61/).

86 ICC, Trial Chamber, *Prosecutor v. Katanga*, Judgment, ICC-01/04-01/07, 7 March 2014, paras. 1635–36 (www.legal-tools.org/doc/f74b4f/).

87 ICC, Pre-Trial Chamber, *Prosecutor v. Mbarushimana*, Decision on Confirmation of Charges, ICC-01/04-01/10, 16 December 2011, para. 288 (www.legal-tools.org/doc/

- Knowledge is sufficient to incur liability for contributing to a group of persons acting with a common purpose.[88]

7.2.2.5. Command/Superior Responsibility

The important and specific liability category of command/superior liability in ICL can be considered to derive from the more general category of omission liability for direct participation in universal crimes (any form of perpetration liability). Such liability typically requires a duty to act based upon established norms flowing from the specific position, competence, or power of a person that is different from mere moral obligations to act in a specific situation.

Hence, a superior will be subject to individual criminal liability if all of the following requirements are met:

- a superior-subordinate relationship exists; and

- the superior knew or had reason to know that a criminal act was about to be, was being, or had been committed; and

- the superior failed to take necessary and reasonable measures to prevent or punish the conduct in question.[89]

63028f/); ICC, Pre-Trial Chamber, *Prosecutor v. Ruto, Kosgey and Sang*, Decision on Confirmation of Charges, ICC-01/09-01/11, 23 January 2012, paras. 353–54 (www.legal-tools. org/doc/96c3c2/); ICC, Trial Chamber, *Prosecutor v. Katanga*, Judgment, Minority Opinion of Judge Christine Van den Wyngaert, ICC-01/04-01/07, 7 March 2014, para. 24 (www. legal-tools.org/doc/9b0c61/).

[88] ICC, Pre-Trial Chamber, *Prosecutor v. Mbarushimana*, Decision on Confirmation of Charges, ICC-01/04-01/10, 16 December 2011, para. 289 (www.legal-tools.org/doc/ 63028f/); ICC, Pre-Trial Chamber, *Prosecutor v. Ruto, Kosgey and Sang*, Decision on Confirmation of Charges, ICC-01/09-01/11, 23 January 2012, paras. 353–54 (www.legal-tools. org/doc/96c3c2/); ICC, Trial Chamber, *Prosecutor v. Katanga*, Judgment, Minority Opinion of Judge Christine Van den Wyngaert, ICC-01/04-01/07, 7 March 2014, para. 288 (www.legal-tools.org/doc/9b0c61/).

[89] ICTY, Appeals Chamber, *Prosecutor v. Orić*, Judgment, IT-03-68-A, 3 July 2008, para. 18 (www.legal-tools.org/doc/e053a4/); ICTR, Trial Chamber, *Prosecutor v. Nizeyimana*, Judgment, ICTR-2000-55C, 19 June 2012, para. 1475 (www.legal-tools.org/doc/f8cdd9/); SCSL, Trial Chamber, *Prosecutor v. Taylor*, Judgment, SCSL-03-01-T, 18 May 2012, para. 490 (www.legal-tools.org/doc/8075e7/); ICTY, Appeals Chamber, *Prosecutor v. Gotovina and Markač*, Judgment, IT-06-90-A, 16 November 2012, para. 128 (www.legal-tools.org/ doc/03b685/); ECCC, Trial Chamber, Case 002/01, Judgment, 002/19-09-2007/ECCC/TC, 7 August 2014, para. 715 (www.legal-tools.org/doc/4888de/); ICTY, Trial Chamber, *Prosecutor v. Karadžić*, Judgment, IT-95-5/18-T, 24 March 2016, para. 579 (www.legal-tools. org/doc/173e23/); ICTY, Trial Chamber, *Prosecutor v. Mladić*, Judgment, IT-09-92-T, 22

A superior-subordinate relationship exists where a superior has effective command and control over a subordinate, which means that the superior has the material ability to prevent or punish the subordinate's criminal conduct.[90] Superior responsibility can arise by virtue of the supe-

---

November 2017, para. 3568 (www.legal-tools.org/doc/96f3c1/); ICTY, Appeals Chamber, *Prosecutor v. Prlić et al.*, Judgment, IT-04-74-A, 29 November 2017, para. 313 (www.legal-tools.org/doc/941285/). For a more detailed description see Article 28 of the ICC Statute and its interpretation in ICC, Pre-Trial Chamber, *Prosecutor v. Bemba*, Decision on Confirmation of Charges, ICC-01/05-01/08, 15 June 2009, paras. 408–48 (www.legal-tools.org/doc/07965c/) (following closely the ICTY/ICTR jurisprudence); ICC, Pre-Trial Chamber, *Prosecutor v. Ntaganda*, Decision on Confirmation of Charges, ICC-01/04-02/06, 9 June 2014, para. 164 (www.legal-tools.org/doc/5686c6/); ICC, Trial Chamber, *Prosecutor v. Bemba*, Judgment, ICC-01/05-01/08, 21 March 2016, para. 170 (www.legal-tools.org/doc/edb0cf/) (with a discussion on the nature of this form of liability at paras. 171–74). Given that this form of liability is one of omission, the ICC has expressed some doubt as to whether it should be charged if the evidence discloses that a person was involved in deliberate conduct that resulted in the commission of crimes; see ICC, Pre-Trial Chamber, *Prosecutor v. Ongwen*, Decision on Confirmation of Charges, ICC-02/04-01/15, 23 March 2016, para. 147 (www.legal-tools.org/doc/74fc6e/). Regarding the various theories of command/superior responsibility, see ICC, Appeals Chamber, *Prosecutor v. Bemba*, Judgment, ICC-01/05-01/08A, 8 June 2018, Concurring Separate Opinion of Judge Eboe-Osuji, paras. 187–269, which includes a discussion of the difference between complicity and command/superior responsibility at paras. 217–31 (www.legal-tools.org/doc/b31f6b/).

90 ICTY, Appeals Chamber, *Prosecutor v. Orić*, Judgment, IT-03-68-A, 3 July 2008, para. 20 (www.legal-tools.org/doc/e053a4/); ICTR, Appeals Chamber, *Prosecutor v. Bagosora and Sengiyumva*, Judgment, ICTR-98-41-A, 14 December 2011, para. 642 (www.legal-tools.org/doc/52d501/); ICTR, Appeals Chamber, *Prosecutor v. Ndindiliyimana et al.*, Judgment, ICTR-00-56-A, 29 September 2014, para. 378 (www.legal-tools.org/doc/4c5065/); ICTR, Appeals Chamber, *Prosecutor v. Nizeyimana*, Judgment, ICTR-00-55C-A, 29 September 2014, para. 342 (www.legal-tools.org/doc/e1fc66/); ICTY, Appeals Chamber, *Prosecutor v. Popović et al.*, Judgment, IT-05-88-A, 30 January 2015, para. 1857 (www.legal-tools.org/doc/4c28fb/); ICTR, Appeals Chamber, *Prosecutor v. Karemera*, Judgment, ICTR-98-44-A, 29 September 2014, paras. 254 and 258 (www.legal-tools.org/doc/372a64/); ICTR, Appeals Chamber, *Prosecutor v. Nyiramasuhuko et al.*, Judgment, ICTR-98-42-A, 14 December 2015, para. 995 (www.legal-tools.org/doc/b3584e/); ICTY, Trial Chamber, *Prosecutor v. Karadžić*, Judgment, IT-95-5/18-T, 24 March 2016, paras. 580–82 (www.legal-tools.org/doc/173e23/); ICC, *Pre-Trial Chamber, Prosecutor v. Bemba*, Decision on Confirmation of Charges, ICC-01/05-01/08, 15 June 2009, para. 418 (www.legal-tools.org/doc/07965c/); ICC, Trial Chamber, *Prosecutor v. Bemba*, Judgment, ICC-01/05-01/08, 21 March 2016, paras.176, 178, and 180–90 (www.legal-tools.org/doc/edb0cf/); EAC, Trial Chamber, *Prosecutor v. Habré*, Judgment, 30 May 2016, paras. 2175–90 (www.legal-tools.org/doc/98c00a/). In the Rwandan context it was held that a priest can have effective control; see ICTR, Trial Chamber, *Prosecutor v. Nsengimana*, Judgment, ICTR-01-69-T, 17 November 2009, paras. 819–28 (www.legal-tools.org/doc/b3866c/).

rior's *de jure* or *de facto* power over the relevant subordinate.[91] The possession of *de jure* power may not suffice for the finding of superior responsibility if it does not manifest itself in effective control[92] or if it only amounts to influence.[93] A superior cannot, it has been held, incur responsibility for crimes committed by a subordinate before the superior assumed his position as such.[94] The latter proposition, however, with respect to investigation and prosecution of crimes committed under the command or superiority of a former commander or superior, is open to abuse within any kind of power structure and is difficult to reconcile with the purpose of command/superior liability. It also raises the question as to whether this particular kind of omission to investigate and prosecute former serious

---

[91] ICTR, Trial Chamber, *Prosecutor v. Nizeyimana*, Judgment, ICTR-2000-55C, 19 June 2012, para. 1476 (www.legal-tools.org/doc/f8cdd9/); SCSL, Trial Chamber, *Prosecutor v. Taylor*, Judgment, SCSL-03-01-T, 18 May 2012, para. 493 (www.legal-tools.org/doc/8075e7/); ICTY, Trial Chamber, *Prosecutor v. Prlić et al.*, Judgment, IT-04-74, 29 May 2013, para. 242 (www.legal-tools.org/doc/2daa33/); ICTY, Trial Chamber, *Prosecutor v. Karadžić*, Judgment, IT-95-5/18-T, 24 March 2016, para. 580 (www.legal-tools.org/doc/173e23/); ICTY, Trial Chamber, *Prosecutor v. Mladić*, Judgment, IT-09-92-T, 22 November 2017, para. 3569 (www.legal-tools.org/doc/96f3c1/).

[92] ICTY, Appeals Chamber, *Prosecutor v. Halilović*, Judgment, IT-01-48-A, 16 October 2007, para. 204 (www.legal-tools.org/doc/d97ef6/); ICTY, Trial Chamber, *Prosecutor v. Perišić*, Judgment, IT-04-81-T, 6 September 2011, paras. 142–44 (www.legal-tools.org/doc/f3b23d/); ICTR, Trial Chamber, *Prosecutor v. Bizimungu et al.*, Judgment, ICTR-99-50-T, 30 September 2011, para. 1873 (www.legal-tools.org/doc/7077fa/); ICTY, Trial Chamber, *Prosecutor v. Stanišić and Župljanin*, Judgment, IT-08-91-T, 27 March 2013, paras. 112–13 (www.legal-tools.org/doc/2ed57f/).

[93] ICTR, Trial Chamber, *Prosecutor v. Bizimungu et al.*, Judgment, ICTR-99-50-T, 30 September 2011, paras. 1891–93 (www.legal-tools.org/doc/7077fa/); ICTR, Trial Chamber, *Prosecutor v. Nizeyimana*, Judgment, ICTR-2000-55C, 19 June 2012, para. 1476 (www.legal-tools.org/doc/f8cdd9/); SCSL, Trial Chamber, *Prosecutor v. Taylor*, Judgment, SCSL-03-01-T, 18 May 2012, para. 493 (www.legal-tools.org/doc/8075e7/).

[94] ICTY, Appeals Chamber, *Prosecutor v. Hadžihasanović et al.*, Decision on Interlocutory Appeal Challenging Jurisdiction in Relation to Command Responsibility, IT-01-47-AR72, 16 July 2003, paras. 37–56 (www.legal-tools.org/doc/608f09/); ICTY, Appeals Chamber, *Prosecutor v. Halilović*, Judgment, IT-01-48-A, 16 October 2007, para. 67 (www.legal-tools.org/doc/d97ef6/); ICTR, Trial Chamber, *Prosecutor v. Karemera et al.*, Judgment, ICTR-98-44-T, 2 February 2012, para. 1492 (www.legal-tools.org/doc/5b9068/); ICTY, Trial Chamber, *Prosecutor v. Stanišić and Župljanin*, Judgment, IT-08-91-T, 27 March 2013, para. 114 (www.legal-tools.org/doc/2ed57f/). For the opposite view, see SCSL, Trial Chamber, *Prosecutor v. Sesay, Kallon and Gbao* (the RUF Case) Judgment, SCSL-04-15-T, 2 March 2009, paras. 294–306 (www.legal-tools.org/doc/7f05b7/); this was overruled on appeal in SCSL, Appeals Chamber, *Prosecutor v. Sesay, Kallon and Gbao* (the RUF Case), Judgment, SCSL-04-14-A, 26 October 2009, para. 874 (www.legal-tools.org/doc/133b48/).

---

crimes in *prima facie* violation of human rights at least amounts to *ex post* complicity liability under ICL.

The superior-subordinate relationship need not be of a permanent nature, but instead could arise on an *ad hoc* or temporary basis,[95] such as when one commander acts for another.[96] A superior may, however, incur superior responsibility no matter how far down the chain of authority the subordinate may be, and even if the subordinate has participated in the crimes through intermediaries.[97] A superior does not need to know the exact identity of the subordinates who perpetrated the crimes in order to incur liability.[98]

With respect to the second requirement, this element is fulfilled if a superior knew or had reason to know that a subordinate's criminal act had been carried out, was taking place, or was about to happen.[99] In the case

---

[95] ICTR, Trial Chamber, *Prosecutor v. Nyiramasuhuko et al.*, Judgment, ICTR-98-42-T, 24 June 2011, para. 5648 (www.legal-tools.org/doc/e2c881/); ICTY, Trial Chamber, *Prosecutor v. Perišić*, Judgment, IT-04-81-T, 6 September 2011, para. 138 (www.legal-tools.org/doc/f3b23d/); ICTY, Trial Chamber, *Prosecutor v. Stanišić and Župljanin*, Judgment, IT-08-91-T, 27 March 2013, para. 114 (www.legal-tools.org/doc/2ed57f/).

[96] ICC, Trial Chamber, *Prosecutor v. Bemba*, Judgment, ICC-01/05-01/08, 21 March 2016, para. 177 (www.legal-tools.org/doc/edb0cf/); ICC, Appeals Chamber, *Prosecutor v. Bemba*, Judgment, ICC-01/05-01/08A, 8 June 2018, Separate Opinion of Judge Van den Vyngaert and Judge Morrison, paras. 33–36 (www.legal-tools.org/doc/c13ef4/).

[97] ICTY, Appeals Chamber, *Prosecutor v. Orić*, Judgment, IT-03-68-A, 3 July 2008, para. 20 (www.legal-tools.org/doc/e053a4/); SCSL, Trial Chamber, *Prosecutor v. Taylor*, Judgment, SCSL-03-01-T, 18 May 2012, para. 494 (www.legal-tools.org/doc/8075e7/); ICTY, Appeals Chamber, *Prosecutor v. Popović et al.*, Judgment, IT-05-88-A, 30 January 2015, para. 1892 (www.legal-tools.org/doc/4c28fb/); ICC, Trial Chamber, *Prosecutor v. Bemba*, Judgment, ICC-01/05-01/08, 21 March 2016, para. 179 (www.legal-tools.org/doc/edb0cf/).

[98] ICTR, Appeals Chamber, *Prosecutor v. Bizimungu*, Judgment, ICTR-00-56B-A, 30 June 2014, para. 79 (www.legal-tools.org/doc/2a4ad3/).

[99] ICTY, Appeals Chamber, *Prosecutor v. Kordić and Čerkez*, Judgment, IT-95-14/2-A, 17 December 2004, para. 839 (www.legal-tools.org/doc/738211/); ICTR, Appeals Chamber, *Prosecutor v. Bagosora and Sengiyumva*, Judgment, ICTR-98-41-A, 14 December 2011, para. 642 (www.legal-tools.org/doc/52d501/); ICTR, Appeals Chamber, *Prosecutor v. Ntabakuze*, Judgment, ICTR-98-41A-A, 8 May 2012, para. 248 (www.legal-tools.org/doc/281406/); SCSL, Trial Chamber, *Prosecutor v. Taylor*, Judgment, SCSL-03-01-T, 18 May 2012, paras. 497–98 (www.legal-tools.org/doc/8075e7/); ICTR, Appeals Chamber, *Prosecutor v. Karemera*, Judgment, ICTR-98-44-A, 29 September 2014, para. 307 (www.legal-tools.org/doc/372a64/); ICTY, Trial Chamber, *Prosecutor v. Mladić*, Judgment, IT-09-92-T, 22 November 2017, para. 3570 (www.legal-tools.org/doc/96f3c1/); ICC, Appeals Chamber, *Prosecutor v. Bemba*, Judgment, ICC-01/05-01/08A, 8 June 2018, Separate Opinion of

of specific intent crimes such as genocide, this requires proof that the superior was aware of the criminal intent of the subordinate.[100]

A superior had reason to know if information was available to him that would have put him on notice of offences committed by subordinates.[101] The 'reason to know' standard is met if the superior possessed information sufficiently alarming to justify further inquiry.[102]

With respect to the third requirement, 'necessary measures' means appropriate actions by which the superior genuinely tried to prevent the criminal act of the subordinate before its commission or to punish the crime after its commission,[103] while 'reasonable measures' are those rea-

Judge Van den Vyngaert and Judge Morrison, paras. 38–47 (www.legal-tools.org/doc/c13ef4/).

100 ICTR, Appeals Chamber, *Prosecutor v. Karemera*, Judgment, ICTR-98-44-A, 29 September 2014, para. 307 (www.legal-tools.org/doc/372a64/).

101 ICTY, Appeals Chamber, *Prosecutor v. Krnojelac*, Judgment, IT-97-25-A, 17 September 2003, para. 156 (www.legal-tools.org/doc/46d2e5/); ICTR, Appeals Chamber, *Prosecutor v. Ndindiliyimana et al.*, Judgment, ICTR-00-56-A, 11 February 2014, paras. 396–97 (www.legal-tools.org/doc/4c5065/); ICC, Trial Chamber, *Prosecutor v. Bemba*, Judgment, ICC-01/05-01/08, 21 March 2016, paras. 191–96 (www.legal-tools.org/doc/edb0cf/).

102 ICTY, Appeals Chamber, *Prosecutor v. Strugar*, Judgment, IT-01-42A, 17 July 2008, para. 298 (www.legal-tools.org/doc/981b62/); ICTR, Trial Chamber, *Prosecutor v. Hategekimana*, Judgment, ICTR-00-55B-T, 6 December 2010, paras. 655–56 (www.legal-tools.org/doc/6082dd/); ICTY, Appeals Chamber, *Prosecutor v. Popović et al.*, Judgment, IT-05-88-A, 30 January 2015, para. 1910 (www.legal-tools.org/doc/4c28fb/); ICTY, Trial Chamber, *Prosecutor v. Karadžić*, Judgment, IT-95-5/18-T, 24 March 2016, para. 586 (www.legal-tools.org/doc/173e23/); ICTY, Trial Chamber, *Prosecutor v. Mladić*, Judgment, IT-09-92-T, 22 November 2017, para. 3570 (www.legal-tools.org/doc/96f3c1/).

103 ICTR, Appeals Chamber, *Prosecutor v. Ndahimana*, Judgment, ICTR-01-68-A, 16 December 2013, para. 79 (www.legal-tools.org/doc/7034a5/); ICC, Pre-Trial Chamber, *Prosecutor v. Gbagbo*, Decision on Confirmation of Charges, ICC-02/11-01/11, 12 June 2014, para. 264 (www.legal-tools.org/doc/5b41bc/); ICTR, Appeals Chamber, *Prosecutor v. Bizimungu*, Judgment, ICTR-00-56B-A, 30 June 2014, para. 133 (www.legal-tools.org/doc/2a4ad3/); ECCC, Trial Chamber, Case 002/01, Judgment, 002/19-09-2007/ECCC/TC, 7 August 2014, para. 716 (www.legal-tools.org/doc/4888de/); ICTY, Appeals Chamber, *Prosecutor v. Popović et al.*, Judgment, IT-05-88-A, 30 January 2015, para. 1927 (www.legal-tools.org/doc/4c28fb/); ICC, Trial Chamber, *Prosecutor v. Bemba*, Judgment, ICC-01/05-01/08, 21 March 2016, paras. 202–4 (www.legal-tools.org/doc/edb0cf/); ICTY, Trial Chamber, *Prosecutor v. Karadžić*, Judgment, IT-95-5/18-T, 24 March 2016, para. 589 (www.legal-tools.org/doc/173e23/); ICTY, Trial Chamber, *Prosecutor v. Mladić*, Judgment, IT-09-92-T, 22 November 2017, para. 3571 (www.legal-tools.org/doc/96f3c1/).

sonably falling within the material powers of the superior.[104] A superior is not expected to perform the impossible but must use every means within his ability.[105] Such measures may include carrying out an investigation, transmitting information in a superior's possession to the proper administrative or prosecutorial authorities, issuing special orders aimed at bringing unlawful practices of subordinates into compliance with the rules of war, protesting against or criticising criminal action, reporting the matter to the competent authorities, or insisting before a superior authority that immediate action be taken.[106]

7.2.3. Forms of Accomplice Liability

7.2.3.1. Ordering

Personal liability for 'ordering' – through command, instruction, or directive – other persons to participate in a crime or criminal enterprise is a

---

[104] ICTY, Appeals Chamber, *Prosecutor v. Orić*, Judgment, IT-03-68-A, 3 July 2008, para. 177 (www.legal-tools.org/doc/e053a4/); ICTR, Appeals Chamber, *Prosecutor v. Bagosora and Sengiyumva*, Judgment, ICTR-98-41-A, 14 December 2011, para. 683 (www.legal-tools.org/doc/52d501/); ICTY, Appeals Chamber, *Prosecutor v. Popović et al.*, Judgment, IT-05-88-A, 30 January 2015, paras. 1927–31 (www.legal-tools.org/doc/4c28fb/); ICC, Trial Chamber, *Prosecutor v. Bemba*, Judgment, ICC-01/05-01/08, 21 March 2016, para. 198 (www.legal-tools.org/doc/edb0cf/); ICTY, Trial Chamber, *Prosecutor v. Karadžić*, Judgment, IT-95-5/18-T, 24 March 2016, para. 588 (www.legal-tools.org/doc/173e23/).

[105] ICTY, Trial Chamber, *Prosecutor v. Popović et al.*, Judgment, IT-05-88-T, 10 June 2010, para. 1043 (www.legal-tools.org/doc/481867/); ICTY, Trial Chamber, *Prosecutor v. Đorđević*, Judgment, IT-05-87/1, 23 February 2011, para. 1887 (www.legal-tools.org/doc/653651/); ICTY, Trial Chamber, *Prosecutor v. Perišić*, Judgment, IT-04-81-T, 6 September 2011, para. 157 (www.legal-tools.org/doc/f3b23d/); ICTY, Trial Chamber, *Prosecutor v. Stanišić* and *Prosecutor v. Župljanin*, Judgment, IT-08-91-T, 27 March 2013, para. 116 (www.legal-tools.org/doc/2ed57f/); ICC, Appeals Chamber, *Prosecutor v. Bemba*, Judgment, ICC-01/05-01/08A, 8 June 2018, Majority Opinion, paras. 167–70 (www.legal-tools.org/doc/40d35b/), Separate Opinion of Judge Van den Wyngaert and Judge Morrison, paras. 51–56 (on causation) (www.legal-tools.org/doc/c13ef4/), Concurring Separate Opinion of Judge Eboe-Osuji, paras. 270–82 (with a discussion on causation at paras. 156–86) (www.legal-tools.org/doc/b31f6b/).

[106] ICTR, Trial Chamber, *Prosecutor v. Karemera et al.*, Judgment, ICTR-98-44-T, 2 February 2012, para. 1501 (www.legal-tools.org/doc/5b9068/); SCSL, Trial Chamber, *Prosecutor v. Taylor*, Judgment, SCSL-03-01-T, 18 May 2012, para. 502 (www.legal-tools.org/doc/8075e7/); ICTY, Appeals Chamber, *Prosecutor v. Popović et al.*, Judgment, IT-05-88-A, 30 January 2015, paras. 1932–33 (www.legal-tools.org/doc/4c28fb/); ICC, Trial Chamber, *Prosecutor v. Bemba*, Judgment, ICC-01/05-01/08, 21 March 2016, paras. 199–201 and 205–9 (www.legal-tools.org/doc/edb0cf/); ICTY, Trial Chamber, *Prosecutor v. Karadžić*, Judgment, IT-95-5/18-T, 24 March 2016, para. 588 (www.legal-tools.org/doc/173e23/).

---

liability form derived from the class of indirect participation in universal crimes. It might be applicable at different levels of a power structure; however, at the top level an order that in fact uses the structure to commit crimes, for example, for some larger political, ideological, or economic purpose, might instead amount to perpetration through another, or its further derivative forms JCE or (indirect) co-perpetration.

Ordering implies that a person in a position of authority uses that authority to convince another person to commit an offence,[107] with the intent that a crime be committed in the realisation of that act or omission or with the awareness of the substantial likelihood that a crime would be committed in the realisation of that act or omission.[108]

For the person ordering the crime to be held responsible, it is also required that the person who received the order actually proceed to commit the offence.[109] In addition, a causal link between the act of ordering

---

[107] ICTR, Appeals Chamber, *Prosecutor v. Nahimana, Barayagwiza and Ngeze* (the Media Case), Judgment, ICTR-99-52-A, 28 November 2007, para. 481 (www.legal-tools.org/doc/4ad5eb/); ICTR, Appeals Chamber, *Prosecutor v. Kalimanzira*, Judgment, ICTR-05-88-A, 20 October 2010, para. 213 (www.legal-tools.org/doc/fad693/); ICTR, Appeals Chamber, *Prosecutor v. Bagosora and Sengiyumva*, Judgment, ICTR-98-41-A, 14 December 2011, para. 277 (www.legal-tools.org/doc/52d501/); ICTR, Appeals Chamber, *Prosecutor v. Ndindiliyimana et al.*, Judgment, ICTR-00-56-A, 11 February 2014, para. 365 (www.legal-tools.org/doc/4c5065/); ICC, Pre-Trial Chamber, *Prosecutor v. Gbagbo*, Decision on Confirmation of Charges, ICC-02/11-01/11, 12 June 2014, para. 244 (www.legal-tools.org/doc/5b41bc/); EAC, Trial Chamber, *Prosecutor v. Habré*, Judgment, 30 May 2016, paras. 1841–44 (www.legal-tools.org/doc/98c00a/); ICTY, Trial Chamber, *Prosecutor v. Mladić*, Judgment, IT-09-92-T, 22 November 2017, para. 3566 (www.legal-tools.org/doc/96f3c1/).

[108] ICTY, Appeals Chamber, *Prosecutor v. Blaškić*, Judgment, IT-95-14-A, 29 July 2004, paras. 41–42 (www.legal-tools.org/doc/88d8e6/); SCSL, Appeals Chamber, *Prosecutor v. Taylor*, Judgment, SCSL-04-01-T, 26 September 2013, para. 589 (www.legal-tools.org/doc/3e7be5/); ICC, Pre-Trial Chamber, *Prosecutor v. Ntaganda*, Decision on Confirmation of Charges, ICC-01/04-02/06, 9 June 2014, para. 145 (www.legal-tools.org/doc/5686c6/); ICC, Pre-Trial Chamber, *Prosecutor v. Gbagbo*, Decision on Confirmation of Charges, ICC-02/11-01/11, 12 June 2014, para. 244 (www.legal-tools.org/doc/5b41bc/); ECCC, Trial Chamber, Case 002/01, Judgment, 002/19-09-2007/ECCC/TC, 7 August 2014, para. 702 (www.legal-tools.org/doc/4888de/).

[109] ICTR, Appeals Chamber, *Prosecutor v. Nahimana, Barayagwiza and Ngeze* (the Media Case), Judgment, ICTR-99-52-A, 28 November 2007, para. 481 (www.legal-tools.org/doc/4ad5eb/); ICTY, Trial Chamber, *Prosecutor v. Đorđević*, Judgment, IT-05-87/1, 23 February 2011, para. 1871 (www.legal-tools.org/doc/653651/); ICTY, Trial Chamber, *Prosecutor v. Tolimir*, Judgment, IT-05-88/2-T, 12 December 2012, para. 906 (www.legal-tools.org/doc/445e4e/).

---

and the physical perpetration of a crime needs to be demonstrated, inasmuch as the order must have had direct and substantial effect on the commission of the illegal act.[110]

While ordering entails a superior-subordinate relationship between the person giving the order and the person carrying it out,[111] effective control will not have to be proven, as it is not a necessary element of this mode of criminal participation. Nor is a formal superior-subordinate relationship required for a finding of ordering so long the person possessed the authority to order, including *de facto* authority. [112] The superior-subordinate relationship can be informal and of a purely temporary nature.[113] It is not necessary that an order be given in writing or in any particular form.[114] Presence at the scene of the crime is not required for this type of criminal responsibility.[115]

---

[110] ICTR, Appeals Chamber, *Prosecutor v. Kamuhanda*, Judgment, ICTR-99-54A-A, 19 September 2005, para. 76 (www.legal-tools.org/doc/8ff7cd/); ICTR, Appeals Chamber, *Prosecutor v. Hategekimana*, Judgment, ICTR-00-55B-A, 8 May 2012, para. 67 (www.legal-tools.org/doc/885b2c/); ICTR, Appeals Chamber, *Prosecutor v. Ndindiliyimana et al.*, Judgment, ICTR-00-56-A, 11 February 2014, para. 291 (www.legal-tools.org/doc/4c5065/); ICC, Pre-Trial Chamber, *Prosecutor v. Gbagbo*, Decision on Confirmation of Charges, ICC-02/11-01/11, 12 June 2014, para. 244 (www.legal-tools.org/doc/5b41bc/); ICTR, Appeals Chamber, *Prosecutor v. Nyiramasuhuko et al.*, Judgment, ICTR-98-42-A, 14 December 2015, para. 1895 (www.legal-tools.org/doc/b3584e/).

[111] ICTR, Appeals Chamber, *Prosecutor v. Semanza*, Judgment, ICTR-97-20-A, 20 May 2005, para. 360 (www.legal-tools.org/doc/a686fd/); ICTY, Trial Chamber, *Prosecutor v. Haradinaj et al.*, Judgment, IT-04-84bis-T, 29 November 2012, para. 624 (www.legal-tools.org/doc/1bad7b/).

[112] ICTR, Appeals Chamber, *Prosecutor v. Semanza*, Judgment, ICTR-97-20-A, 20 May 2005, para. 361 (www.legal-tools.org/doc/a686fd/); ICTY, Appeals Chamber, *Prosecutor v. Boškoski and Tarčulovski*, Judgment, IT-04-82-A, 19 May 2010, para. 164 (www.legal-tools.org/doc/54398a/); ICTR, Appeals Chamber, *Prosecutor v. Nyiramasuhuko et al.*, Judgment, ICTR-98-42-A, 14 December 2015, paras. 1904 and 1915 (www.legal-tools.org/doc/b3584e/).

[113] ICTR, Trial Chamber, *Prosecutor v. Nizeyimana*, Judgment, ICTR-2000-55C, 19 June 2012, para. 1464 (www.legal-tools.org/doc/f8cdd9/); ICTR, Trial Chamber, *Ngirabatware*, Judgment, ICTR-99-54-T, 20 December 2012, para. 1292 (www.legal-tools.org/doc/393335/).

[114] ICTR, Appeals Chamber, *Prosecutor v. Kamuhanda*, Judgment, ICTR-99-54A-A, 19 September 2005, para. 76 (www.legal-tools.org/doc/8ff7cd/); ICTY, Appeals Chamber, *Prosecutor v. Boškoski and Tarčulovski*, Judgment, IT-04-82-A, 19 May 2010, para. 160 (www.legal-tools.org/doc/54398a/); ICTY, Trial Chamber, *Prosecutor v. Popović et al.*, Judgment, IT-05-88-T, 10 June 2010, para. 1012 (www.legal-tools.org/doc/481867/); ICTY, Trial

7.2.3.2.   Instigating

Instigating,[116] also derived from the class of indirect participation liability, entails prompting another person to commit an offence[117] with the intent that a crime be committed, or prompting an act or omission with the awareness of the substantial likelihood that a crime would be committed in the realisation of that act or omission.[118] A causal relationship between

---

Chamber, *Prosecutor v. Stanišić and Župljanin*, Judgment, IT-08-91-T, 27 March 2013, para. 98 (www.legal-tools.org/doc/2ed57f/).

[115] ICTY, Appeals Chamber, *Prosecutor v. Boškoski and Tarčulovski*, Judgment, IT-04-82-A, 19 May 2010, para. 125 (www.legal-tools.org/doc/54398a/).

[116] For a comparison with the ICC notions of soliciting and inducing, see ICC, Trial Chamber, *Prosecutor v. Gombo, Musamba, Kabongo, Wandu and Arido*, Judgment, CC-01/05-01/13, 19 October 2016, paras. 73–82 (www.legal-tools.org/doc/fe0ce4/).

[117] ICTR, Appeals Chamber, *Prosecutor v. Nahimana, Barayagwiza and Ngeze* (the Media Case), Judgment, ICTR-99-52-A, 28 November 2007, para. 440 (www.legal-tools.org/doc/4ad5eb/); ICC, Pre-Trial Chamber, *Prosecutor v. Ntaganda*, Decision on Confirmation of Charges, ICC-01/04-02/06, 9 June 2014, para. 153 (www.legal-tools.org/doc/5686c6/); MICT, Appeals Chamber, *Prosecutor v. Ngirabatware*, Judgment, MICT-12-29-A, 18 December 2014, para. 162 (www.legal-tools.org/doc/16b4ef/); ICTY, Trial Chamber, *Prosecutor v. Karadžić*, Judgment, IT-95-5/18-T, 24 March 2016, para. 572 (www.legal-tools.org/doc/173e23/); ICTY, Trial Chamber, *Prosecutor v. Šešelj*, Judgment, IT-03-67-T, 31 March 2016, para. 295 (www.legal-tools.org/doc/9a8e36/); MICT, Appeals Chamber, *Prosecutor v. Šešelj*, Judgment, MICT-16-99-A, 11 April 2018, para. 124 (www.legal-tools.org/doc/96ea58/).

[118] ICTY, Appeals Chamber, *Prosecutor v. Kordić and Čerkez*, Judgment, IT-95-14/2-A, 17 December 2004, paras. 27 and 30 (www.legal-tools.org/doc/738211/); ICTR, Appeals Chamber, *Prosecutor v. Gacumbitsi*, Judgment, ICTR-2001-64-A, 7 July 2006, para. 107 (www.legal-tools.org/doc/aa51a3/); SCSL, Appeals Chamber, *Prosecutor v. Fofana and Kondewa* (the CDF Case), Judgment, SCSL-04-14-A, 28 May 2008, para. 51 (www.legal-tools.org/doc/b31512/); SCSL, Trial Chamber, *Prosecutor v. Taylor*, Judgment, SCSL-03-01-T, 18 May 2012, paras. 471–72 (www.legal-tools.org/doc/8075e7/); ICTR, Trial Chamber, *Prosecutor v. Ngirabatware*, Judgment, ICTR-99-54-T, 20 December 2012, para. 1291 (www.legal-tools.org/doc/393335/); ICTY, Trial Chamber, *Prosecutor v. Stanišić and Župljanin*, Judgment, IT-08-91-T, 27 March 2013, paras. 95–96 (www.legal-tools.org/doc/2ed57f/); ICTY, Trial Chamber, *Prosecutor v. Prlić et al.*, Judgment, IT-04-74, 29 May 2013, para. 226 (www.legal-tools.org/doc/2daa33/) (although this decision departs from previous Trial Chamber decisions in requiring a positive act in para. 229); SCSL, Appeals Chamber, *Prosecutor v. Taylor*, Judgment, SCSL-04-01-T, 26 September 2013, para. 589 (www.legal-tools.org/doc/3e7be5/); ICC, Pre-Trial Chamber, *Prosecutor v. Ntaganda*, Decision on Confirmation of Charges, ICC-01/04-02/06, 9 June 2014, para. 153 (www.legal-tools.org/doc/5686c6/); ECCC, Trial Chamber, Case 002/01, Judgment, 002/19-09-2007/ECCC/TC, 7 August 2014, para. 700 (www.legal-tools.org/doc/4888de/); MICT, Appeals Chamber, *Prosecutor v. Ngirabatware*, Judgment, MICT-12-29-A, 18 December 2014, para. 166 (www.legal-tools.org/doc/16b4ef/); ICTY, Trial Chamber, *Prosecutor v. Šešelj*,

---

the instigation and the physical perpetration of the crime is required in the sense that the instigation contributed substantially to the conduct of the person committing the crime.[119] Hence, instigation, properly understood as a term of art within ICL discourse, is different from atrocity speech[120] in the form of incitement at the pre-execution phase that does not lead to a completed crime but might still be punishable as an inchoate crime, notably with respect to incitement to commit genocide. However, it will not be necessary to prove that the crime would not have been perpetrated without the instigation.[121]

Both express and implied conduct may constitute instigation.[122] Presence at the scene of the crime is not required for this type of criminal responsibility,[123] nor is any authority on the part of the instigator required.[124]

Judgment, IT-03-67-T, 31 March 2016, para. 296 (www.legal-tools.org/doc/9a8e36/); ICTY, Trial Chamber, *Prosecutor v. Mladić*, Judgment, IT-09-92-T, 22 November 2017, para. 3565 (www.legal-tools.org/doc/96f3c1/).

[119] ICTR, Appeals Chamber, *Prosecutor v. Nahimana, Barayagwiza and Ngeze* (the Media Case), Judgment, ICTR-99-52-A, 28 November 2007, para. 678 (www.legal-tools.org/doc/4ad5eb/); ICTY, Trial Chamber, *Prosecutor v. Šešelj*, Judgment, IT-03-67-T, 31 March 2016, para. 295 (www.legal-tools.org/doc/9a8e36/) (which also adds the elements that the instigator must have used different forms of persuasion such as threats, enticement, or promises to the physical perpetrators of the crimes and that the incriminating statements must be clearly identifiable with their existence firmly established).

[120] On the concept of 'atrocity speech', see Gregory S. Gordon, *Atrocity Speech Law: Foundation, Fragmentation, Fruition*, Oxford University Press, Oxford, 2017.

[121] ICTY, Appeals Chamber, *Prosecutor v. Kordić and Čerkez*, Judgment, IT-95-14/2-A, 17 December 2004, para. 27 (www.legal-tools.org/doc/738211/); ICTR, Appeals Chamber, *Prosecutor v. Nyiramasuhuko et al.*, Judgment, ICTR-98-42-A, 14 December 2015, para. 3327 (www.legal-tools.org/doc/b3584e/).

[122] ICTR, Appeals Chamber, *Prosecutor v. Kamuhanda*, Judgment, ICTR-99-54A-A, 19 September 2005, para. 593 (www.legal-tools.org/doc/8ff7cd/); ICTY, Appeals Chamber, *Prosecutor v. Boškoski and Tarčulovski*, Judgment, IT-04-82-A, 19 May 2010, para. 157 (www.legal-tools.org/doc/54398a/).

[123] ICTY, Appeals Chamber, *Prosecutor v. Boškoski and Tarčulovski*, Judgment, IT-04-82-A, 19 May 2010, para. 125 (www.legal-tools.org/doc/54398a/); ICTY, Trial Chamber, *Prosecutor v. Haradinaj et al.*, Judgment, IT-04-84bis-T, 29 November 2012, para. 623 (www.legal-tools.org/doc/1bad7b/); ICTR, Appeals Chamber, *Prosecutor v. Nyiramasuhuko et al.*, Judgment, ICTR-98-42-A, 14 December 2015, para. 3327 (www.legal-tools.org/doc/b3584e/).

[124] ICTY, Trial Chamber, *Prosecutor v. Stanišić and Župljanin*, Judgment, IT-08-91-T, 27 March 2013, para. 96 (www.legal-tools.org/doc/2ed57f/).

7.2.3.3. Complicity (Aiding and Abetting)

Complicity or accessoryship to universal crimes constitutes a form of liability for assisting or facilitating a criminal enterprise or individual perpetrators of such crimes. The acts may take place before, at, or after the execution phase. The terminology has not been fully consistent within ICL,
and in many cases 'aiding and abetting'[125] has been used interchangeably
or as the main concept comprising the different kinds of relevant physical
or psychological assistance that might be possible. In this book we use
complicity as the most general term, while also using the terms to some
extent interchangeably. In this particular chapter, 'aiding and abetting' is
the appropriate term since it has been the more common phrase in the relevant jurisprudence.

The *actus reus* of aiding and abetting consists of carrying out acts
(specifically directed)[126] to provide practical assistance, encouragement,
or moral support, which has a substantial effect on the perpetration of an

---

[125] While the terms 'aiding' and 'abetting' are usually used conjunctively, as one concept, the
two notions within this concept are slightly different: aiding refers to some form of physical assistance in the commission of the crime, while abetting connotes encouragement or
another form of moral suasion. See William A. Schabas, *The International Criminal Court:
A Commentary on the Rome Statute*, Oxford University Press, Oxford, 2010, p. 434.

[126] There was some uncertainty about this requirement that the acts be specifically directed,
which appeared to have been confirmed by ICTY, Appeals Chamber, *Prosecutor v. Perišić*,
Judgment, IT-04-81-A, 28 February 2013, paras. 25–42 and 73 (www.legal-tools.org/doc/
f006ba/); see also ICTY, Trial Chamber, *Prosecutor v. Stanišić and Simatović*, Judgment,
IT-03-69-T, 30 May 2013, para. 1264 (www.legal-tools.org/doc/066e67/). However, the
Appeals Chamber of the SCSL took issue with this jurisprudence and held that there was
no such requirement; see SCSL, Appeals Chamber, *Prosecutor v. Taylor*, Judgment, SCSL-
04-01-T, 26 September 2013, paras. 471–81 and 486 (www.legal-tools.org/doc/3e7be5/).
This was followed later by the ICTY Appeals Chamber itself in a comprehensive and detailed decision in *Prosecutor v. Šainović et al.*, Judgment, IT-05-87-A, 23 January 2014,
paras. 1617–51 (www.legal-tools.org/doc/81ac8c/); see also ECCC, Trial Chamber, Case
002/01, Judgment, 002/19-09-2007/ECCC/TC, 7 August 2014, para. 710 (www.legal-tools.
org/doc/4888de/); ICTY, Appeals Chamber, *Prosecutor v. Popović et al.*, Judgment, IT-05-
88-A, 30 January 2015, para. 1764 (www.legal-tools.org/doc/4c28fb/); ICTY, Appeals
Chamber, *Prosecutor v. Stanišić and Simatović*, Judgment, IT-03-69-A, 9 December 2015,
paras. 104–6 (www.legal-tools.org/doc/198c16/); ICTY, Trial Chamber, *Prosecutor v.
Karadžić*, Judgment, IT-95-5/18-T, 24 March 2016, para. 576 (www.legal-tools.org/doc/
173e23/); ICTY, Trial Chamber, *Prosecutor v. Mladić*, Judgment, IT-09-92-T, 22 November 2017, para. 3564 (www.legal-tools.org/doc/96f3c1/).

international crime.[127] Substantial effect has been defined as meaning that "the criminal act most probably would not have occurred in the same way had not someone acted in the role that the suspect in fact assumed".[128] Either aiding or abetting alone is sufficient to render the perpetrator crimi-

---

[127] ICTR, Appeals Chamber, *Prosecutor v. Nahimana, Barayagwiza and Ngeze* (the Media Case), Judgment, ICTR-99-52-A, 28 November 2007, para. 482 (www.legal-tools.org/doc/4ad5eb/); STL, Appeals Chamber, Interlocutory Decision on the Applicable Law: Terrorism, Conspiracy, Homicide, Perpetration, Cumulative Charging, STL-II-OI/I/AC/RI76bis,16 February 2011, para. 226; SCSL, Appeals Chamber, *Prosecutor v. Taylor*, Judgment, SCSL-04-01-T, 26 September 2013, paras. 362, 368–85, 390–92, and 401 (www.legal-tools.org/doc/3e7be5/); ECCC, Trial Chamber, Case 002/01, Judgment, 002/19-09-2007/ECCC/TC, 7 August 2014, para. 704 (www.legal-tools.org/doc/4888de/); ICTY, Appeals Chamber, *Prosecutor v. Popović et al.*, Judgment, IT-05-88-A, 30 January 2015, paras. 1758 and 1812 (www.legal-tools.org/doc/4c28fb/).

There had been disagreement at the Trial Chamber level in early jurisprudence as to whether the effect had to be direct and substantial, but the directness requirement was eliminated in ICTY, Appeals Chamber, *Prosecutor v. Tadić*, Judgment, IT-94-1-A, 15 July 1999, para. 229 (www.legal-tools.org/doc/8efc3a/); see also ICTR, Appeals Chamber, *Prosecutor v. Kayishema and Ruzindana*, Judgment, ICTR-95-1-A, 1 June 2001, paras. 191–94 (www.legal-tools.org/doc/9ea5f4/); ICTY, Trial Chamber, *Prosecutor v. Karadžić*, Judgment, IT-95-5/18-T, 24 March 2016, para. 575 (www.legal-tools.org/doc/173e23/); ICTY, Trial Chamber, *Prosecutor v. Šešelj*, Judgment, IT-03-67-T, 31 March 2016, para. 353 (www.legal-tools.org/doc/9a8e36/); ICTY, Trial Chamber, *Prosecutor v. Mladić*, Judgment, IT-09-92-T, 22 November 2017, para. 3567 (www.legal-tools.org/doc/96f3c1/).

At the ICC, see Pre-Trial Chamber, *Prosecutor v. Ruto, Kosgey and Sang*, Decision on Confirmation of Charges, ICC-01/09-01/11, 23 January 2012, para. 354 (www.legal-tools.org/doc/96c3c2/); Trial Chamber, *Prosecutor v. Lubanga*, Judgment, ICC-01/04-01/06, 14 March 2012, para. 997 (www.legal-tools.org/doc/677866/); Trial Chamber, *Prosecutor v. Chui*, Judgment, Concurring Opinion of Judge Christine Van den Wyngaert, ICC-01/04-02/12, 18 December 2012, para. 44 (www.legal-tools.org/doc/7d5200/); Pre-Trial Chamber, *Prosecutor v. Ongwen*, Decision on Confirmation of Charges, ICC-02/04-01/15, 23 March 2016, para. 43 (www.legal-tools.org/doc/74fc6e/); Pre-Trial Chamber, *Prosecutor v. Al Mahdi*, Decision on Confirmation of Charges, ICC-01/12-01/15, 24 March 2016, para. 26 (www.legal-tools.org/doc/bc8144/), which indicated that the contribution does not need to be substantial (as the Ongwen decision also did); Trial Chamber, *Prosecutor v. Bemba, Musamba, Jean-Kabongo, Wandu and Arido*, Judgment, ICC-01/05-01/13, 19 October 2016, paras. 87–96 (www.legal-tools.org/doc/fe0ce4/), which goes even further and indicates that aiding and abetting 'does not require the meeting of any specific threshold' in para. 93.

[128] ICTY, Appeals Chamber, *Prosecutor v. Tadić*, Judgment, IT-94-1, 7 May 1997, para. 688 (www.legal-tools.org/doc/0a90ae/).

---

nally liable.[129] Aiding and abetting can be committed at a time and place removed from the actual crime.[130]

The *actus reus* of aiding and abetting may be perpetrated through an omission, provided that this failure to act had a decisive effect on the commission of the crime. The *actus reus* and *mens rea* requirements for aiding and abetting by omission are the same as for aiding and abetting by a positive act. The critical issue to be determined is whether, on the particular facts of a given case, it is established that the failure to discharge a legal duty assisted, encouraged, or lent moral support to the perpetration of the crime, and had a substantial effect on it. [131]

Furthermore, the mere presence at the scene of a crime can be an example of an omission. While such presence of an individual in a position of superior authority does not provide sufficient grounds to conclude that he encouraged or supported the crime, the presence of a person with

---

[129] ICTY, Appeals Chamber, *Prosecutor v. Vasiljević*, Judgment, IT-98-32-A, 25 February 2004, para. 102 (www.legal-tools.org/doc/e35d81/); ICTY, Trial Chamber, *Prosecutor v. Haradinaj et al.*, Judgment, IT-04-84bis-T, 29 November 2012, para. 625 (www.legal-tools. org/doc/1bad7b/); ICTY, Appeals Chamber, *Prosecutor v. Lukić*, Judgment, IT-98-32/1-A, 4 December 2012, para. 424 (www.legal-tools.org/doc/da785e/).

[130] SCSL, Appeals Chamber, *Prosecutor v. Fofana and Kondewa* (the CDF Case), Judgment, SCSL-04-14-A, 28 May 2008, para. 72 (www.legal-tools.org/doc/b31512/); ICTY, Appeals Chamber, *Prosecutor v. Lukić*, Judgment, IT-98-32/1-A, 4 December 2012, para. 425 (www.legal-tools.org/doc/da785e/); ICTY, Trial Chamber, *Prosecutor v. Karadžić*, Judgment, IT-95-5/18-T, 24 March 2016, para. 576 (www.legal-tools.org/doc/173e23/).

[131] ICTY, Appeals Chamber, *Prosecutor v. Orić*, Judgment, IT-03-68-A, 3 July 2008, paras. 42–46 (www.legal-tools.org/doc/e053a4/); ICTY, Appeals Chamber, *Prosecutor v. Mrkšić et al.*, Judgment, IT-95-13/1-A, 5 May 2009, paras. 145–59 (www.legal-tools.org/doc/ 40bc41/); SCSL, Trial Chamber, *Prosecutor v. Taylor*, Judgment, SCSL-03-01-T, 18 May 2012, para. 483 (www.legal-tools.org/doc/8075e7/); ICTR, Appeals Chamber, *Prosecutor v. Ndahimana*, Judgment, ICTR-01-68-A, 16 December 2013, para. 147 (www.legal-tools. org/doc/7034a5/); ICTY, Appeals Chamber, *Prosecutor v. Šainović et al.*, Judgment, IT-05-87-A, 23 January 2014, paras. 1677–79 (www.legal-tools.org/doc/81ac8c/); ECCC, Trial Chamber, Case 002/01, Judgment, 002/19-09-2007/ECCC/TC, 7 August 2014, para. 706 (www.legal-tools.org/doc/4888de/); ICTY, Appeals Chamber, *Prosecutor v. Popović et al.*, Judgment, IT-05-88-A, 30 January 2015, paras. 1740–41 and 1812 (www.legal-tools.org/ doc/4c28fb/); ICTR, Appeals Chamber, *Prosecutor v. Nyiramasuhuko et al.*, Judgment, ICTR-98-42-A, 14 December 2015, paras. 2206 and 2255 (www.legal-tools.org/doc/ b3584e/); ICTY, Trial Chamber, *Prosecutor v. Karadžić*, Judgment, IT-95-5/18-T, 24 March 2016, para. 575 (www.legal-tools.org/doc/173e23/); ICTY, Trial Chamber, *Prosecutor v. Mladić*, Judgment, IT-09-92-T, 22 November 2017, para. 3567 (www.legal-tools.org/ doc/96f3c1/).

superior authority, such as a military commander, can be a probative indication for determining whether that person encouraged or supported the perpetrators of the crime.[132] Where the presence of a person bestows legitimacy on, or provides encouragement to, the actual perpetrator, that may be sufficient to constitute aiding and abetting.[133]

Moreover, responsibility for having aided and abetted a crime by omission may arise, regardless of whether the person's presence at the crime scene provided encouragement to the perpetrators, if the person was under a duty to prevent the commission of the crime but failed to act, provided his failure to act had a substantial effect on the commission of the crime.[134]

Aiding and abetting is also possible where a commander allows the use of resources under his or her control, including personnel, to facilitate the perpetration of a crime.[135]

The *mens rea* required for aiding and abetting is the knowledge or awareness of the substantial likelihood that the practical assistance, encouragement, or moral support assists or facilitates the commission of the offence, although the accused does not need to have the intent to commit the crime.[136] It is not necessary that the aider and abettor know the precise

---

[132] ICTY, Trial Chamber, *Prosecutor v. Boškoski and Tarčulovski*, Judgment, IT-04-82, 10 July 2008, para. 402 (www.legal-tools.org/doc/939486/); ICTR, Trial Chamber, *Prosecutor v. Seromba*, Judgment, ICTR-2001-66-I, 13 December 2006, para. 308 (www.legal-tools.org/doc/091a66/); ICTR, Trial Chamber, *Prosecutor v. Ngirabatware*, Judgment, ICTR-99-54-T, 20 December 2012, para. 1295 (www.legal-tools.org/doc/393335/).

[133] MICT, Appeals Chamber, *Prosecutor v. Ngirabatware*, Judgment, MICT-12-29-A, 18 December 2014, para. 150 (www.legal-tools.org/doc/16b4ef/).

[134] ICTY, Appeals Chamber, *Prosecutor v. Mrkšić et al.*, Judgment, IT-95-13/1-A, 5 May 2009, para. 49 (www.legal-tools.org/doc/40bc41/); ICTR, Trial Chamber, *Prosecutor v. Karemera et al.*, Judgment, ICTR-98-44-T, 2 February 2012, para. 1431 (www.legal-tools.org/doc/5b9068/).

[135] ICTR, Trial Chamber, *Prosecutor v. Bagosora, Kabiligi, Ntabakuze and Nsengiyumva*, Judgment, ICTR-98-41-T, 18 December 2008, para. 2009 (www.legal-tools.org/doc/6d9b0a/); ICTR, Trial Chamber, *Prosecutor v. Ndindiliyimana et al.*, Judgment, ICTR-00-56-T, 17 May 2011, para. 1914 (www.legal-tools.org/doc/c71b24/); ICTY, Trial Chamber, *Prosecutor v. Perišić*, Judgment, IT-04-81-T, 6 September 2011, para. 128 (www.legal-tools.org/doc/f3b23d/).

[136] ICTY, Appeals Chamber, *Prosecutor v. Brđanin*, Judgment, IT-99-36-A, 3 April 2007, para. 484 (www.legal-tools.org/doc/782cef/); ICTY, Appeals Chamber, *Prosecutor v. Lukić*, Judgment, IT-98-32/1-A, 4 December 2012, para. 428 (www.legal-tools.org/doc/da785e/); SCSL, Appeals Chamber, *Prosecutor v. Taylor*, Judgment, SCSL-04-01-T, 26 September

crime that was intended and that was committed, but he must be aware of the essential elements of the crime committed by the principal offender, including the principal offender's state of mind.[137]

However, the aider and abettor does not need to share the intent of the principal offender,[138] nor does he even need to know who is committing the crime.[139]

2013, paras. 414–40 and 451 (www.legal-tools.org/doc/3e7be5/); ICTR, Appeals Chamber, *Prosecutor v. Ndahimana*, Judgment, ICTR-01-68-A, 16 December 2013, para. 157 (www.legal-tools.org/doc/7034a5/); ICTY, Appeals Chamber, *Prosecutor v. Šainović et al.*, Judgment, IT-05-87-A, 23 January 2014, para. 1172 (www.legal-tools.org/doc/81ac8c/); MICT, Appeals Chamber, *Prosecutor v. Ngirabatware*, Judgment, MICT-12-29-A, 18 December 2014, para. 155 (www.legal-tools.org/doc/16b4ef/); ICTY, Trial Chamber, *Prosecutor v. Karadžić*, Judgment, IT-95-5/18-T, 24 March 2016, para. 577 (www.legal-tools.org/doc/173e23/); ICTY, Trial Chamber, *Prosecutor v. Šešelj*, Judgment, IT-03-67-T, 31 March 2016, para. 353 (www.legal-tools.org/doc/9a8e36/); ICTY, Trial Chamber, *Prosecutor v. Mladić*, Judgment, IT-09-92-T, 22 November 2017, para. 3576 (www.legal-tools.org/doc/96f3c1/).

Article 25(3)(c) of the ICC Statute imposes a higher level of *mens rea* by adding the words "for the purpose of facilitating the commission". See, at the ICC, Pre-Trial Chamber, *Prosecutor v. Mbarushimana*, Decision on Confirmation of Charges, ICC-01/04-01/10, 16 December 2011, paras. 274 and 289 (www.legal-tools.org/doc/63028f/); Pre-Trial Chamber, *Prosecutor v. Blé Goudé*, Decision on Confirmation of Charges, ICC-02/11-02/11, 11 December 2014, para. 167 (www.legal-tools.org/doc/0536d5/); Trial Chamber, *Prosecutor v. Bemba, Musamba, Kabongo, Wandu and Arido*, Judgment, ICC-01/05-01/13, 19 October 2016, paras. 97–98 (www.legal-tools.org/doc/fe0ce4/); although Trial Chamber, *Prosecutor v. Chui*, Judgment, Concurring Opinion of Judge Christine Van den Wyngaert, ICC-01/04-02/12, 18 December 2012, para. 25 (www.legal-tools.org/doc/7d5200/), seems to suggest that this additional wording might be jurisdictional rather than substantive.

[137] ICTR, Appeals Chamber, *Prosecutor v. Nahimana, Barayagwiza and Ngeze* (the Media Case), Judgment, ICTR-99-52-A, 28 November 2007, para. 482 (www.legal-tools.org/doc/4ad5eb/); SCSL, Appeals Chamber, *Prosecutor v. Brima, Kamara and Kanu* (the AFRC Case), Judgment, SCSL-2004-16-A, 22 February 2008, paras. 242–43 (www.legal-tools.org/doc/4420ef/); SCSL, Appeals Chamber, *Prosecutor v. Fofana and Kondewa* (the CDF Case), Judgment, SCSL-04-14-A, 28 May 2008, para. 367 (www.legal-tools.org/doc/b31512/); STL, Appeals Chamber, Interlocutory Decision on the Applicable Law: Terrorism, Conspiracy, Homicide, Perpetration, Cumulative Charging, STL-II-OI/I/AC/RI76bis, 16 February 2011, para. 227; ICTY, Appeals Chamber, *Prosecutor v. Popović et al.*, Judgment, IT-05-88-A, 30 January 2015, paras. 1751, 1754, and 1794 (www.legal-tools.org/doc/4c28fb/); ICTY, Trial Chamber, *Prosecutor v. Karadžić*, Judgment, IT-95-5/18-T, 24 March 2016, para. 577 (www.legal-tools.org/doc/173e23/); ICTY, Trial Chamber, *Prosecutor v. Mladić*, Judgment, IT-09-92-T, 22 November 2017, para. 3567 (www.legal-tools.org/doc/96f3c1/).

[138] ICTR, Trial Chamber, *Prosecutor v. Seromba*, Judgment, ICTR-2001-66-I, 13 December 2006, para. 309 (www.legal-tools.org/doc/091a66/); ICTY, Appeals Chamber, *Prosecutor v.*

With respect to aiding and abetting genocide, the international tribunals have found that this form of commission is present if a person knowingly aided or abetted one or more persons in the commission of genocide, while knowing that such person or persons were committing genocide, even though the aider and abettor himself did not have the specific intent to destroy, in whole or in part, a national, ethnical, racial, or religious group, as such.[140]

Aiding and abetting has been found to be present in the following circumstances: provision of arms and ammunition; provision of military personnel; provision of operational support such as communications equipment and training, logistical support, safe haven in the form of a guest house, financial support, medical support, herbalists to bolster confidence of fighters, and security escorts for arms, ammunition, diamonds, drivers, messengers, and liaison personnel; and providing advice and direction in military strategy.[141]

Popović et al., Judgment, IT-05-88-A, 30 January 2015, para. 1794 (www.legal-tools.org/doc/4c28fb/); ICTY, Trial Chamber, *Prosecutor v. Šešelj*, Judgment, IT-03-67-T, 31 March 2016, para. 353 (www.legal-tools.org/doc/9a8e36/); ICTY, Trial Chamber, *Prosecutor v. Mladić*, Judgment, IT-09-92-T, 22 November 2017, para. 3567 (www.legal-tools.org/doc/96f3c1/).

[139] ICTY, Appeals Chamber, *Prosecutor v. Brđanin*, Judgment, IT-99-36-A, 3 April 2007, paras. 108 and 355 (www.legal-tools.org/doc/782cef/); MICT, Appeals Chamber, *Prosecutor v. Ngirabatware*, Judgment, MICT-12-29-A, 18 December 2014, para. 149 (www.legal-tools.org/doc/16b4ef/).

[140] ICTY, Appeals Chamber, *Prosecutor v. Krstić*, Judgment, IT-98-33-A, 19 April 2004, para. 140 (www.legal-tools.org/doc/86a108/); ICTR, Appeals Chamber, *Prosecutor v. Rukundo*, Judgment, ICTR-2001-70-A, 20 October 2010, paras. 52 and 61 (www.legal-tools.org/doc/d5b969/); ICTR, Appeals Chamber, *Prosecutor v. Kalimanzira*, Judgment, ICTR-05-88-A, 20 October 2010, para. 220 (www.legal-tools.org/doc/fad693/); SCSL, Trial Chamber, *Prosecutor v. Taylor*, Judgment, SCSL-03-01-T, 18 May 2012, para. 487 (www.legal-tools.org/doc/8075e7/); MICT, Appeals Chamber, *Prosecutor v. Ngirabatware*, Judgment, MICT-12-29-A, 18 December 2014, para. 155 (www.legal-tools.org/doc/16b4ef/); ICTY, Trial Chamber, *Prosecutor v. Karadžić*, Judgment, IT-95-5/18-T, 24 March 2016, para. 577 (www.legal-tools.org/doc/173e23/). See ICTY, Appeals Chamber, *Prosecutor v. Lukić*, Judgment, IT-98-32/1-A, 4 December 2012, paras. 458–59 (www.legal-tools.org/doc/da785e/), re persecution, while indirectly see STL, Appeals Chamber, Interlocutory Decision on the Applicable Law: Terrorism, Conspiracy, Homicide, Perpetration, Cumulative Charging, STL-II-OI/I/AC/RI76bis, 16 February 2011, para. 249.

[141] SCSL, Trial Chamber, *Prosecutor v. Taylor*, Judgment, SCSL-03-01-T, 18 May 2012, paras. 6918, 6927, 6937–43, and 6950 (www.legal-tools.org/doc/8075e7/). For a number of other examples, some historical, see SCSL, Appeals Chamber, *Prosecutor v. Taylor*,

Table 12 sets out the differences between aiding and abetting, JCE, and co-perpetration with respect to their *actus reus* and *mens rea*.

	Actus reus	*Mens rea*
Aiding and abetting	• substantial contribution	• knowledge of commission of act
JCE (only basic and systemic forms)	• common plan • significant contribution	• intent to further common plan
Co-perpetration	• common plan • coordinated essential contribution	• mutual awareness and acceptance of plan resulting in a crime • awareness of the factual situation

Table 12: Differences between Aiding and Abetting, JCE, and Co-perpetration.

7.2.3.4. Accessory after the Fact

Indirect participation through aiding and abetting may also occur after the act is committed.[142] If the aiding and abetting occurs after the crime, it must be established that a prior agreement existed between the principal

---

Judgment, SCSL-04-01-T, 26 September 2013, para. 369 (www.legal-tools.org/doc/3e7be5/).

[142] ICTR, Appeals Chamber, *Prosecutor v. Nahimana, Barayagwiza and Ngeze* (the Media Case), Judgment, ICTR-99-52-A, 28 November 2007, para. 482 (www.legal-tools.org/doc/4ad5eb/); SCSL, Appeals Chamber, *Prosecutor v. Fofana and Kondewa* (the CDF Case), Judgment, SCSL-04-14-A, 28 May 2008, para. 71 (www.legal-tools.org/doc/b31512/); SCSL, Trial Chamber, *Prosecutor v. Taylor*, Judgment, SCSL-03-01-T, 18 May 2012, para. 484 (www.legal-tools.org/doc/8075e7/); ICC, Pre-Trial Chamber, *Prosecutor v. Mbarushimana*, Decision on Confirmation of Charges, ICC-01/04-01/10, 16 December 2011, para. 286 (www.legal-tools.org/doc/63028f/); ICTY, Appeals Chamber, *Prosecutor v. Lukić*, Judgment, IT-98-32/1-A, 4 December 2012, para. 425 (www.legal-tools.org/doc/da785e/); ICC, Trial Chamber, *Prosecutor v. Bemba, Musamba, Kabongo, Wandu and Arido*, Judgment, ICC-01/05-01/13, 19 October 2016, para. 96 (www.legal-tools.org/doc/fe0ce4/); ICTY, Trial Chamber, *Prosecutor v. Mladić*, Judgment, IT-09-92-T, 22 November 2017, para. 3567 (www.legal-tools.org/doc/96f3c1/).

and the person who subsequently aided and abetted in the commission of the crime.[143]

7.2.3.5. Complicity as Different from Aiding and Abetting

While the terms complicity and aiding and abetting appear to be similar,[144] they have been the subjects of debate in the ICTY/ICTR jurisprudence. Since the ICTY and ICTR Statutes contain a specific provision with respect to complicity in genocide,[145] while at the same time having a general provision of extended liability that includes aiding and abetting for genocide,[146] the question arose as to whether these two notions fully overlap.

The answer given was that aiding and abetting is only one aspect of the larger notion of complicity, and that for genocide the *mens rea* for complicity, which goes beyond aiding and abetting, could possibly be the narrower, specific intent of genocide.[147] It has also been said that complicity in genocide requires a positive act, while with aiding and abetting, the

---

[143] SCSL, Trial Chamber, *Prosecutor v. Sesay, Kallon and Gbao* (the RUF Case), Judgment, SCSL-04-15-T, 25 February 2009, para. 278 (www.legal-tools.org/doc/7f05b7/); ECCC, Trial Chamber, Case 002/01, Judgment, 002/19-09-2007/ECCC/TC, 7 August 2014, para. 713 (www.legal-tools.org/doc/4888de/).

[144] ICTY, Trial Chamber, *Prosecutor v. Blagojević*, Judgment, IT-02-60-T, 27 January 2005, para. 777.

[145] Articles 4(3)(e) and 2(3)(e), respectively.

[146] Articles 7(1) and 6(1), respectively.

[147] ICTY, Appeals Chamber, *Prosecutor v. Krstić*, Judgment, IT-98-33-A, 19 April 2004, paras. 137–39 (www.legal-tools.org/doc/86a108/); ICTR, Appeals Chamber, *Prosecutor v. Ntakirutimana*, Judgment, ICTR-96-10-A and ICTR-96-17-A, 13 December 2004, para. 371 (www.legal-tools.org/doc/af07be/); ICTY, Trial Chamber, *Prosecutor v. Blagojević & Jokić*, Judgment, IT-02-60, 17 January 2005, paras. 679 and 784 (www.legal-tools.org/doc/7483f2/); ICTY, Trial Chamber, *Prosecutor v. Krajišnik*, Judgment, IT-00-39-T, 27 September 2006, paras. 864–66 (www.legal-tools.org/doc/62a710/); ICTR, Trial Chamber, *Prosecutor v. Ngirabatware*, Judgment, ICTR-99-54-T, 20 December 2012, para. 1347 (www.legal-tools.org/doc/393335/). See, however, ICTY, Appeals Chamber, *Prosecutor v. Krstić*, Judgment, Partial Dissenting Opinion of Judge Shahabuddeen, IT-98-33-A, 19 April 2004, paras. 59–68 (www.legal-tools.org/doc/86a108/); ICTY, Trial Chamber, *Prosecutor v. Milošević*, Decision on Motion for Judgment of Acquittal, IT-02-54-T, 16 June 2004, paras. 290–97 (www.legal-tools.org/doc/d7fb46/); ICTR, Trial Chamber, *Prosecutor v. Karemena, Ngirumpatse and Nzirorera*, Decision on Defence Motions Challenging the Pleading of a Joint Criminal Enterprise in a Count of Complicity in Genocide in the Amended Indictment, ICTR-98-44-T, 18 May 2006, para. 6 (www.legal-tools.org/doc/5bc554/); ICTR, Trial Chamber, *Prosecutor v. Nyiramasuhuko et al.*, Judgment, ICTR-98-42-T, 24 June 2011, para. 5980 (www.legal-tools.org/doc/e2c881/).

same crime can be accomplished by failing to act or refraining from taking action (omission).[148]

The question remained unresolved at the ICTY and ICTR,[149] but it has been dealt with in the Rome Statute by separating the crime of genocide from the means of committing such a crime and by deleting the term 'complicity'.

7.2.3.6. Membership/Participation in Universal Crimes Organisations

Membership was both a form of accessory liability and an inchoate offence after World War II. The Statute of the IMT allowed it to declare any organisation criminal, and four organisations were so designated: the Leadership Corps of the Nazi Party, the Gestapo, the SD, and the SS.[150] The membership concept was also applied to other organisations in national legislation and jurisprudence.[151] Under this system, a person was held liable if he belonged to a designated organisation and had knowledge that the organisation was used for criminal purposes – or as the IMT put it:

> A criminal organization is analogous to a criminal conspiracy in that the essence of both is co-operation for criminal purposes. There must be a group bound together and organized for a common purpose. The group must be formed or used in connection with the commission of crimes denounced by the Charter. Since the declaration with respect to the organizations and groups will, as has been pointed out,

---

[148] ICTR, Trial Chamber, *Prosecutor v. Akayesu*, Judgment, ICTR-96-4-T, 2 September 1998, paras. 547–48 (www.legal-tools.org/doc/b8d7bd/); ICTR, Trial Chamber, *Prosecutor v. Musema*, Judgment, ICTR-96-13-T, 27 January 2000, para.183.

[149] ICTR, Appeals Chamber, *Prosecutor v. Krstić*, Judgment, IT-98-33-A, 19 April 2004, para. 142, n. 247 (www.legal-tools.org/doc/86a108/).

[150] International Military Tribunal ('IMT'), *Trial of the Major War Criminals before the International Military Tribunal: Nuremberg, 14 November 1945–1 October 1946* (hereafter cited as *Trial of the Major War Criminals*), vol. XXII, Nuremberg, 1947, pp. 505, 511, and 516–17 (www.legal-tools.org/doc/d1427b/).

[151] Elies van Sliedregt, *Individual Criminal Responsibility in International Law*, Oxford University Press, Oxford, 2012, pp. 26–33; Shane Darcy, *Collective Responsibility and Accountability under International Law*, Transnational Publishers, Leiden, 2007, pp. 26–28, referring to legislation in Norway, France, and the Netherlands and to decisions by Polish courts and US military courts in occupied Germany with respect to concentration camps as criminal organisations.

fix the criminality of its members, that definition should exclude persons who had no knowledge of the criminal purposes or acts of the organization and those who were drafted
by the state for membership, unless they were personally im-
plicated in the commission of acts declared criminal by Article 6 of the Charter as members of the organization. Membership alone is not enough to come within the scope of
these declarations.[152]

This concept has fallen into disuse since that time, but the judicial
reasoning for not applying it is unclear. The discussion of membership
was part of developing the JCE approach, and in that context it has been
made clear that mere membership in a JCE without further plan or activities is not sufficient to attract liability.[153]

There has been one unequivocal comment about the notion of
membership in the ICTY, namely in the Stakić case, where the following
was said:

The Trial Chamber emphasises that joint criminal enterprise
can not be viewed as membership in an organisation because
this would constitute a new crime not foreseen under the
Statute and therefore amount to a flagrant infringement of the
principle *nullum crimen sine lege*.[154]

This judgment refers to a previous decision by the Appeals Chamber, which came to the same conclusion but in doing so made mention of
the explanatory report of the UN secretary-general establishing the ICTY,
including the following sentence: "the Secretary General believes that this
concept should not be *retained* in regard to the International Tribunal".[155]

---

[152] IMT, *Trial of the Major War Criminals*, vol. XXII, p. 500, see *supra* note 150.

[153] ICTY, Trial Chamber, *Prosecutor v. Kvočka*, Judgment, IT-98-30/1, 2 November 2001,
para. 281 (www.legal-tools.org/doc/34428a/); ICTY, Trial Chamber, *Prosecutor v. Simić*,
Judgment, IT-95-9-T, 17 October 2003, para. 158 (www.legal-tools.org/doc/aa9b81/); IC-
TY, Trial Chamber, *Prosecutor v. Brđanin*, Judgment, IT-99-36, 1 September 2004, para.
263 (www.legal-tools.org/doc/4c3228/).

[154] ICTY, Trial Chamber, *Prosecutor v. Stakić*, Judgment, IT-97-24-T, 31 July 2003, para. 433
(www.legal-tools.org/doc/32ecfb/).

[155] ICTY, Appeals Chamber, *Prosecutor v. Milutinović*, Decision on Dragoljub Ojdanić's Motion Challenging Jurisdiction – Joint Criminal Enterprise, IT-99-37-AR72, 21 May 2003,
paras. 24–26 (www.legal-tools.org/doc/d6110d/), italics added. The report referred to is
*The Report of the Secretary General Pursuant to Paragraph 2 of Security Council Resolu-
tion 808*, UN Doc. S/25704, 3 May 1993, which makes this comment in para. 51.

This could be interpreted as an acknowledgment that membership in criminal organisations was part of international criminal law in 1993, but that for jurisdictional reasons it was deemed not desirable to include it in the Statute of the ICTY.[156] From a principled point of view, the difference is potentially crucial. As we have already pointed out in Chapter 2, Section 2.2.3.6., and shall return to in Chapter 10, while liability for having committed an inchoate, distinct crime is indeed governed by the legality principle, which is also concerned with the crime description when the crime in question has the character of an inchoate crime from another perspective, attribution of personal liability for contribution to a completed crime is a different matter. Attribution of liability is not *per se* prohibited by ICL customary international law or by the fundamental principles of criminal law liability. Notably, the Stakić decision does not refer to the jurisdictionally oriented part of the Appeals Chamber's decision and does not provide any further analysis of the relevant statement, nor does it make any reference to the practice in this regard after World War II.[157]

During the negotiations for the ICC Statute, France made a proposal to include a provision dealing with criminal organisations as part of the debate about whether legal persons should fall within the jurisdiction of the ICC, but there was not sufficient support to make either variation part of the Statute.[158]

7.3. Conclusion

Examining the jurisprudence of the six international institutions – the ICTY, ICTR, SCSL, ECCC, EAC, and ICC – one can detect a general tendency to use several derivative categories and operational modes of participation to capture a large number of perpetrators linked both horizontally (perpetrators at the same level of a hierarchy but occupying a wide variety of functions) and vertically (perpetrators at lower or higher levels of a hierarchy). While the earliest cases in the first institutions, the ICTY and

---

[156] *Ibid. (Prosecutor v. Milutinović)*, para. 26.

[157] Moreover, the judgment is not clear on whether membership is a crime or a mode of liability; although in the excerpt it speaks of membership as a crime, it also equates this notion with JCE, which is generally equally unclear in terms of classification. However, the Appeals Chamber of the Special Court for Sierra Leone is quite unequivocal that membership is not included in its Statute; see SCSL, Appeals Chamber, *Prosecutor v. Taylor*, Judgment, SCSL-04-01-T, 26 September 2013, para. 398 (www.legal-tools.org/doc/3e7be5/).

[158] Schabas, 2010, pp. 425–27, see *supra* note 125.

ICTR, pertained to a low-level and a mid-level operator, respectively (a soldier in the first ICTY case, Tadić, and a burgomaster in the first ICTR case, Akeyasu), both institutions quickly initiated prosecutions involving persons higher up in the various hierarchies in the former Yugoslavia and Rwanda. This came to be known as the policy of prosecuting persons who bear the greatest responsibility, and it was later enshrined in the constitutive documents of the SCSL[159], the ECCC,[160] and the ICC.[161]

In order to implement such a policy of holding responsible only persons who had very important functions in the preparation and/or execution of universal crimes, a number of legal devices were employed. In some cases, these devices were legal concepts known at the domestic level, in both common and civil law countries, and then applied at the international level in circumstances different than those at the domestic level, primarily in terms of scale, but without changing the legal parameters. The prime example of this approach has been liability for complicity in the crimes, operationalised especially through the concept of 'aiding and abetting'.

Another approach has been to use existing forms of liability and then adapt the legal parameters drastically to put on trial persons with important functions in large organisations. From a theoretical perspective, what has happened might be described as a development through derivation of individual liability at different levels or orders, sometimes even by combining categories of liability into new and more specific subcategories and ultimately into fully operational modes of liability at the fourth level of the general theory of criminal law liability.[162] This has been the case for JCE as a subcategory and mode of liability in three forms (I through III) at the ICTY, ICTR, SCSL, ECCC, and EAC, where prosecutors and judges have relied also on the common law concept of common purpose or common intention; while at the ICC the civil law notion of joint perpetration or perpetration through another person has become very prominent and has resulted in derivative concepts of personal liability such as indirect co-perpetration. While the connections to domestic criminal law tra-

---

[159] Article 1 of the Statute the Special Court for Sierra Leone.
[160] Article 1 of the Law on the Establishment of the Extraordinary Chambers.
[161] Implicit in Article 52(2)(c) of the Rome Statute.
[162] See Chapter 2, Sections 2.2.2.5. and 2.2.4.

ditions of certain groups of states have presumably been important from the perspective of individual actors, because the terms employed have been familiar to some of the judges, it is interesting to note that this development, which has included steps towards more autonomous ICL liability concepts as well, also seems to be fully compatible with the general theory of personal criminal law liability set forth in Chapter 2.

Other forms of liability, for the most part in the preparatory phase of committing crimes, such as planning, ordering, inducing, soliciting, and instigation, bear a strong resemblance to notions at the national level, in both civil and common law, with similar or the same terms as well as substantive content, such as counselling, inducing, and instigating. The same can be said for the typically inchoate offences of conspiracy, attempt, and incitement,[163] with the caveat that apart from attempt, these offences are more prevalent in common law countries, while at the international level they are only made applicable in a limited manner; these three offences had only been used for the crime of genocide before the entry into force of the Rome Statute, where attempt has been generalised, incitement remains applicable only to genocide, and conspiracy has been abandoned. However, it should be added in this context that although conspiracy has not been recognised in current ICL as an attributable mode of liability with respect to completed crimes, as we have seen in this chapter, from a theoretical point of view conspiracy might be considered to have merged with categories of perpetration into further derivative liability concepts such as common design and JCE.

Lastly, there are the forms of liability that have been developed specifically for international law purposes, such as command/superior responsibility and membership. Command/superior responsibility was not known at the national level except when states implemented the grave breaches regime of the Geneva Conventions or ratified the Rome Statute (or more recently when ratifying the Forced Disappearance Convention). Membership liability was utilised at the ICL level immediately after WWII but has fallen into disuse at the international level; it has seen a

---

163 The offence of incitement to commit genocide is different from the commission of a hate crime, which has been subsumed within the underlying crime of persecution as a crime against humanity and can be committed before and during other crimes against humanity; there is jurisprudential disagreement between the ICTY and the ICTR regarding the level of intensity required to meet the threshold of this crime.

comeback at the national level in some countries recently when courts have addressed the issue of organised crime and terrorist organisations.

8

Personal Liability Concepts in
Domestic Universal Crimes Cases
Based on Nationality and Universal Jurisdiction

8.1. Introduction to Chapters 8 and 9

While Chapter 7 addressed the parameters of forms of participation as discussed at the international level, Chapters 8 and 9 will examine the jurisprudence at the domestic level.

There has been a long and abiding interaction between the work done internationally, on the one hand, and legislative and jurisprudential developments at the local level, on the other. This has been most apparent with respect to the criminal activities (such as murder, imprisonment, property damage, and persecution) that underlie war crimes and crimes against humanity. When the newly established international criminal institutions, such as the ICTY and ICTR, were asked for the first time to provide definitional content of underlying crimes that were also known at the domestic level, such as rape,[1] they would typically engage in a detailed comparative analysis of the definitions of such crimes in a large number of countries from various legal traditions. After such an inquiry, the judges at the ICTY and ICTR would extract the most common approach with respect to such a crime and apply that to the situation at hand. Subsequent decisions at the international level would then refer to the definition or concept developed in the initial cases and, following precedent, would either use the same definition or provide additional reasoning to support a change in the definition. This exercise was often undertaken under the rubric of customary international law to conform to at least one of the two requirements of this source of international law, namely state practice. This recourse to customary international law is most notable in a decision

---

[1] ICTY, Trial Chamber, *Prosecutor v. Kunarac et al.*, Judgment, IT-96-23/IT-96-23/1, 22 February 2001, paras. 439–60 (www.legal-tools.org/doc/fd881d/).

of the Special Tribunal for Lebanon that sought to define the crime of terrorism.[2]

This influence goes in both directions, however. The interpretations by the international criminal institutions of the underlying crimes have had an impact on subsequent jurisprudence at the national level, even for crimes already known in the domestic context. Domestic courts have been called upon to adjudicate cases involving international crimes for which special legislation has often been enacted to make criminal prosecution possible, especially for crimes against humanity.[3]

Interactions between the international and domestic levels are even more prevalent in the area of modes of liability, as these forms of participation when set out in international criminal legal instruments resembled very closely the language and conceptual approaches of domestic notions of liability. This can be seen in the statutes of the IMT and IMTFE, where common law notions of conspiracy, aiding and abetting, and 'being concerned with', among others, were included; these three concepts subsequently played an important role in the jurisprudence of these two tribunals.[4] These trends continued with the establishment of the international tribunals, beginning in 1993. The drafters of the Rome Statute attempted to chart a more independent course but still included some modes of liability that are similar, at least in language, to domestic approaches, although compared to the international tribunals the Rome Statute gave more attention to civil law forms of liability.[5]

As with the underlying crimes, during the discussion at the international level with respect to forms of participation the judges would regularly canvass national jurisdictions as to the meaning of these forms of liability, then afterwards begin developing their own independent interpre-

---

[2] Special Tribunal for Lebanon, Appeals Chamber, Interlocutory Decision on the Applicable Law: Terrorism, Conspiracy, Homicide, Perpetration, Cumulative Charging, STL-II-OI/I/AC/RI76bis, 16 February 2011, paras. 93–102.

[3] In a number of countries, this special legislation provides for more serious sentencing provisions when the underlying crime is treated as an international crime than when it is treated as an ordinary crime. In Canada, in its first modern war crimes trial, it was decided that murder as a war crime or crime against humanity has different legal implications than murder under the Criminal Code; see Superior Court of Montreal, *Her Majesty the Queen v. Munyaneza*, 500-73-002500-052, 20 November 2006 (www.legal-tools.org/doc/a15d98/).

[4] For more detail on the modes at the international level, see Chapter 7.

[5] *Ibid.*

tations. And, as with the underlying crimes, this new international jurisprudence would be noticed and over time incorporated into the judgments
of the domestic courts. However, given the fact that domestic jurisdictions
had a long history of interpretation of their own forms of liability, the use
of international jurisprudence was not as readily or easily accepted as had
been the case for underlying crimes.[6]

Because of this ongoing interaction and mutual reliance between the
international and domestic spheres, we felt that it was important to incorporate the development of the jurisprudence by national courts into these
two empirical chapters. These chapters include jurisprudence emanating
from countries that put people on trial for crimes committed within their
respective territories, as well as that from countries that have utilised extra-territorial jurisdiction to try people for crimes committed abroad.[7]

Before beginning our examination of the jurisprudence, we should
briefly explain the methodology we have employed, which is different for
the chapters dealing with extra-territorial jurisdiction (Chapter 8) and territorial jurisdiction (Chapter 9). With respect to the former, we have tried
to be as exhaustive as possible by discussing in detail legislation as well
as the individual court decisions in the 15 counties that have prosecuted
persons for the commission of crimes outside the country where they were
put on trial. An exhaustive approach was possible because there are relatively few such decisions and because in the vast majority of these cases,
the relevant legislation and the judgments could be found online or were
made available by national authorities.

The situation is different for the jurisprudence in countries exercising territorial jurisdiction, that is, those that have prosecuted persons for
international crimes committed in those countries. For one thing, there are
more than twice as many countries in this category as in the extra-
territorial category mentioned above. Moreover, it is more difficult to find
the original decisions and, in some cases, to digest them, given the large
number of languages employed in (often untranslated) decisions.[8] For

---

[6] An example can be found below in Section 8.16.2.

[7] For more details on these forms of jurisdiction, see Section 8.2. below.

[8] In some cases translations of decisions can be found, as was the case for some Rwandan
judgments in the UK extradition case of *Government of Rwanda v Nteziryayo & Ors*
(2017), EWHC 1912 (Admin), paras. 156–207 (www.legal-tools.org/doc/c4b49e/), but
modes of liability were not discussed and thus the rulings are of limited value for this

these reasons, the jurisprudence discussed in Chapter 9 is drawn from a mix of primary and secondary sources; primary sources, that is, the jurisprudence of the courts themselves, are utilised for the situation of Bangladesh, while for the other countries discussed (Ethiopia, East Timor, and selected countries in Latin America and Europe), we rely on secondary sources.

Because of the large number of cases in the territorial jurisdiction countries and the use of secondary sources for most of them, Chapter 9 examines overarching trends relevant to modes of participation rather than making an assessment of each individual case. Moreover, because of the use of secondary sources, the examination of the jurisprudence is not as up to date as is the case for the countries using extra-territorial jurisdiction, where case law is current as of July 2018.

8.2. Introduction to This Part of the Survey

This chapter addresses the efforts made at the national level in using forms of liability to bring persons accused of universal crimes to justice, based on extra-territorial jurisdiction.

The most common type of criminal jurisdiction is based on the principle of sovereignty, meaning that a state is entitled to prosecute crimes that have taken place within its territory – hence the name territorial jurisdiction. However, international law also recognises the ability of a state to exercise extra-territorial jurisdiction for crimes committed outside its territory, provided that there is some link between the state and the commission of the crime. Such links are found in the nationality of persons: the active nationality or active personality principle stipulates that a state can prosecute crimes committed by its nationals abroad, while the passive nationality or passive personality principle allows a state to prosecute a crime committed abroad in which its national has been a victim. Lastly, a prosecution can be based on universal jurisdiction: this applies in a situation where the crime was not committed in the state wanting to prosecute, nor is the perpetrator or victim a national of that state, but the perpetrator of the crime abroad has subsequently relocated to that state. In some instances, this type of jurisdiction has also been used in circum-

---

chapter. See also "Activity Report 2017" under "Democratic Republic of the Congo", *TRIAL International*, 28 May 2018.

---

stances where there is no perpetrator present in the state, but investigations have been undertaken because the crimes are sufficiently serious that any country is entitled to initiate a prosecution. This is frequently referred to as absolute jurisdiction or universal jurisdiction *in absentia*.[9]

The countries that have carried out prosecutions based on extra-territorial jurisdiction are all in Europe and North America. In Europe, between 1994 and July 2018, 13 countries initiated criminal prosecutions for crimes committed outside the respective countries. These resulted in 64 indictments in which 68 persons were convicted (with one person in two countries) and seven persons were acquitted (including one on appeal) in 51 cases, some of which involved multiple accused. In North America, two countries, Canada and the United States, completed four criminal trials for such crimes: three in Canada (with one acquittal) and one in the United States.

It should be kept in mind that most countries initially based their investigations and prosecutions on charges of war crimes (and then only the ones committed in international armed conflicts), or genocide, or torture, in the period before ratifying and implementing the Rome Statute; once in force, that statute made it possible also to include crimes against humanity within the range of allegations. Before the Rome Statute, the only treaties that gave countries such jurisdiction were the grave breaches provisions in the 1949 Geneva Conventions and Additional Protocol I, the 1948 Genocide Convention, and the 1984 Torture Convention. As a result, as will be seen in this chapter, the older cases at the national level are al-

---

[9]   See Council of the European Union, *The AU-EU Expert Report on the Principle of Universal Jurisdiction*, 8672/1/09/REV 1, 16 April 2009, pp. 7–11, paras. 8–14 (with examples of various national approaches at pp. 12–30, paras. 15–27); United Nations, *The Scope and Application of the Principle of Universal Jurisdiction*, Report of the Secretary-General prepared on the basis of comments and observations of Governments, UN Doc. A/65/181, 29 July 2010, pp. 5–6, paras. 12–17; and REDRESS/FIDH, *Extraterritorial Jurisdiction in the European Union: A Study of the Laws and Practice in the 27 Member States of the European Union*, December 2010, pp. 16–27, with a table of the types of jurisdictions available in the countries of the European Union at p. 17. See also four reports by TRIAL International: *Make Way for Justice #1: Universal Jurisdiction Annual Review 2015* (www.legal-tools.org/doc/ef5d31/); *Make Way for Justice #2: Universal Jurisdiction Annual Review 2016* (www.legal-tools.org/doc/4223e4/); *Make Way for Justice #3: Universal Jurisdiction Annual Review 2017* (www.legal-tools.org/doc/17bef2/); and *Make Way for Justice #4: Momentum Towards Accountability: Universal Jurisdiction Annual Review 2018* (www.legal-tools.org/doc/b01bcf/).

most always based on the provisions implementing these three treaties, while the more recent cases take their guidance from the Rome Statute, utilising both crimes against humanity and an expanded range of war crimes, whether committed in an international armed conflict or a non-international armed conflict.

Finally, this chapter only examines completed criminal cases and the judgments rendered in those cases. A number of countries, especially in Europe, have been and continue to be very active in investigating universal crimes in cases that have not come to fruition yet (France, Germany and Spain come to mind), or they have extradited persons to other countries (for instance, Sweden, the Netherlands, and Canada have extradited to countries such as Rwanda).

8.3. The Netherlands

8.3.1. Overview of Cases

The Netherlands has become the main centre of international criminal justice, both internationally and domestically. Internationally, the ICC, the ICTY and the STL are located in The Hague, while the SCSL has conducted its most high-profile case, that of former Liberian president Charles Taylor, in that city as well.

On the domestic side, the activities of the Dutch government have been equally impressive in that 14 persons (two based on active personality rather than universal jurisdiction) in nine cases have been made subject to criminal trials. The cases are discussed below.

8.3.1.1. Participation in Torture in Afghanistan

Former Zairian army officer Sebastien Nzapali was convicted of torture on 7 April 2004 for his participation in severely beating persons in 1996. He received two and half years' imprisonment.[10]

---

[10] Netherlands, District Court, The Hague, Case LJN AO7178, 7 April 2004 (www.legal-tools. org/doc/6a9117/). See also Menno T. Kamminga, "Netherlands Judicial Decisions Involving Questions of International Law: First Conviction under the Universal Jurisdiction Provisions of the UN Convention against Torture", in *Netherlands International Law Review*, 2004, vol. 51, no. 3, pp. 439–44 (with an English translation of the decision at pp. 444–49).

8.3.1.2. Participation in War Crimes and Torture in Afghanistan

Heshamuddin Hesam and Habibullah Jalalzoy were convicted in 2005 for war crimes and torture due to their involvement in the KhAD (the main state security and intelligence agency in Afghanistan at the time) in Kabul between 1979 and 1989. They received prison sentences of 9 and 12 years, respectively,[11] which was upheld by a Court of Appeal on 29 January 2007[12] and again by the Supreme Court of the Netherlands on 8 July 2008.[13]

8.3.1.3. Providing Chemicals to Saddam Hussein

Frans van Anraat, a Dutch national, was convicted at the trial level of complicity in war crimes on 23 December 2005 and sentenced to 15 years' imprisonment for having provided chemicals used by the Saddam Hussein regime in attacks against Kurds within Iraq in 1988 and against the Iranian army during the Iraq-Iran war in 1980–88. He was acquitted of complicity in genocide, as it was not established that he had actual knowledge of the genocidal intent of the Saddam government.[14] During the appeal of this case the court increased his sentence to 17 years on 9 May 2007,[15] even though the Court of Appeal stated that there had been no evidence of genocide during the Anfal campaign.[16] This verdict was

---

[11] Netherlands, District Court, The Hague, Cases LJN AU4373 and LJN AV1163, 14 October 2005 (www.legal-tools.org/doc/94c8b1/). See also Guénaël Mettraux, "Dutch Courts' Universal Jurisdiction over Violations of Common Article 3 *qua* War Crimes", in *Journal of International Criminal Justice*, 2006, vol. 4, no. 2, pp. 362–71 (and further discussion as a result of this article in the same journal, vol. 4, no. 3, pp. 878–89).

[12] Netherlands, Court of Appeal, The Hague, Cases LJN AZ9365 and LJN AZ9366, 29 January 2007 (www.legal-tools.org/doc/7a6292/).

[13] Netherlands, Supreme Court, Case LJN BG1476, 8 July 2008 (www.legal-tools.org/doc/5f70ca/).

[14] Netherlands, District Court, The Hague, Case LJN AX6406, 23 December 2005 (www.legal-tools.org/doc/35538e/). See also Erwin van der Borght, "Prosecution of International Crimes in the Netherlands: An Analysis of Recent Case Law", in *Criminal Law Forum*, 2007, vol. 18, no. 1, pp. 87–136.

[15] See Harmen van der Wilt, "Genocide, Complicity in Genocide and International v. Domestic Jurisdiction: Reflections on the *van Anraat* Case", in *Journal of International Criminal Justice*, 2006, vol. 4, no. 2, pp. 239–57, and "Genocide v. War Crimes in the *Van Anraat* Appeal", in *Journal of International Criminal Justice*, 2008, vol. 6, no. 3, pp. 557–657.

[16] Netherlands, Court of Appeal, The Hague, Case LJN BA6734, 9 May 2007 (www.legal-tools.org/doc/1e1b4b/).

confirmed by the Supreme Court on 30 June 2009,[17] and a complaint on the latter decision to the European Court of Human Rights ('ECHR') was declared inadmissible on 6 July 2010.[18]

8.3.1.4. Arms Sale to Liberia

On 6 June 2006 another Dutch national, Guus van Kouwenhoven, was convicted for violating a United Nations arms embargo in Liberia and sentenced to 8 years' imprisonment. There was insufficient evidence of his knowledge or direct involvement to convict him of war crimes.[19] The verdict was overturned by an appeals court on 10 March 2008 and an acquittal substituted instead.[20] On 19 April 2010, the Supreme Court overturned the acquittal and ordered a re-trial by another Court of Appeal.[21] On 21 April 2017, he was convicted and sentenced to 19 years' imprisonment for aiding and abetting in war crimes and violating the United Nations arms embargo.[22]

8.3.1.5. Acquittal on Charges of War Crimes and Torture

In another case, a general in the Afghan Military Intelligence Service during the Najibullah regime, Abdoullah Faqirzada, was acquitted on charges of war crimes and torture on 25 June 2007.[23] This was confirmed on ap-

---

[17] Netherlands, Supreme Court, Case LJN BG4822, 30 June 2009 (www.legal-tools.org/doc/ ae408d/). See also Marten Zwanenburg and Guido Den Dekker, "Prosecutor v. Frans van Anraat", *American Journal of International Law*, 2010, vol. 104, no. 1, pp. 86–94.

[18] ECHR, *Van Anraat v. The Netherlands*, 65389/09, 6 July 2010 (www.legal-tools.org/doc/ 567d90/).

[19] Netherlands, District Court, The Hague, Case LJN AY5160, 6 June 2006 (www.legal-tools. org/doc/b13477/). There was no discussion related to liability by any of the three courts, apart from mentioning co-perpetration as the basis for liability at the court of first instance. See also Larissa van den Herik, "The Difficulties of Exercising Extraterritorial Criminal Jurisdiction: The Acquittal of a Dutch Businessman for Crimes Committed in Liberia", in *International Criminal Law Review*, 2009, vol. 9, no 1, pp. 211–26.

[20] Netherlands, Court of Appeal, The Hague, Case LJN BC7373, 10 March 2008 (www.legal-tools.org/doc/5990af/).

[21] Netherlands, Supreme Court, Case LJN BK8132, 19 April 2010 (www.legal-tools.org/doc/ 40296a/).

[22] Netherlands, Court of Appeal, The Hague, Case ECLI:NL:GHSHE:2017:1760, 21 April 2017 (www.legal-tools.org/doc/4211df/).

[23] Netherlands, District Court, The Hague, Case LJN BA9575, 25 June 2007 (www.legal-tools.org/doc/cac017/).

peal on 16 July 2009[24] and again by the Supreme Court on 8 November 2011.[25]

8.3.1.6. Life Imprisonment for War Crimes in Rwanda

A Rwandan national, Joseph Mpambara, was arrested in August 2006 on charges of direct participation in murder during the genocide in Rwanda. Jurisdiction was denied on 24 July 2007 by the court of first instance on the basis that neither the perpetrator nor any victim had Dutch nationality.[26] This judgment was confirmed on appeal on 18 December 2007[27] and again by the Supreme Court on 21 October 2008.[28] (Legislation to remedy this jurisdictional problem was adopted by the Dutch parliament on 18 November 2011 and came into force on 1 April 2012, with retroactive application to 24 October 1970.[29]) A trial against Mpambara on different charges, namely torture and war crimes, began on 13 October 2008; he was convicted and sentenced to 20 years' imprisonment on the torture charges only (because of a lack of nexus with respect to the war crimes charges) on 23 March 2009.[30] This was increased on appeal to life imprisonment on 7 July 2011, in part because the court set aside the ruling re-

---

[24] Netherlands, Court of Appeal, The Hague, Case LJN BJ2796, 16 July 2009 (www.legal-tools.org/doc/dc714e/).

[25] Netherlands, Supreme Court, Case LJN BR6598, 8 November 2011 (www.legal-tools.org/doc/35f07b/). See also *Yearbook of International Humanitarian Law, Volume 14, 2011*, Correspondents' Reports, TMC Asser Press, The Hague, 2012, pp. 5–6 (www.legal-tools.org/doc/d79048/).

[26] Netherlands, Case LJN BB0494. See also *International Justice Tribune*, no. 78, 19 November 2007, p. 2; and Elies van Sliedregt, "International Crimes before Dutch Courts: Recent Developments", in *Leiden Journal of International Law*, 2007, vol. 20, no. 4, pp. 895–908.

[27] Netherlands, Court of Appeal, The Hague, Case LJN BC1757, 18 December 2007 (www.legal-tools.org/doc/cec56c/).

[28] Netherlands, Supreme Court, Case, ECLI:NL:HR:2008:BD6568, 21 October 2008 (www.legal-tools.org/doc/cb3eae/).

[29] For a similar problem regarding retroactive application, see Section 8.10.1. below on Norway.

[30] Netherlands, District Court, The Hague, Case LJN BI2444, 23 March 2009 (www.legal-tools.org/doc/5071f2/). See also Larissa van den Herik, "A Quest for Jurisdiction and an Appropriate Definition of Crime: Mpambara before the Dutch Courts", in *Journal of International Criminal Justice*, 2009, vol. 7, no. 5, pp. 1117–31; and *Yearbook of International Humanitarian Law, Volume 14, 2011*, pp. 1–3, see *supra* note 25.

garding lack of nexus and found the accused guilty of war crimes rather than torture.[31]

8.3.1.7. Liability for Involvement in Organisation Responsible for Terrorist Crimes in Sri Lanka

On 21 October 2011, a Dutch trial court issued sentences of between 2 and 6 years in the case of five members of the LTTE (Liberation Tigers of Tamil Eelam) for involvement in an organisation that had been accused of having carried out terrorist activities, war crimes, and crimes against humanity. The convictions and sentences were for the terrorist offences, as the court was of the view that:

> Considering that count 1.A. concerns charges which are all related to the non-international armed conflict there can be no question of participation in an organisation, the object of which was to commit terrorist crimes. Although it is possible that incidentally certain violent actions carried out by members of the LTTE bear all the marks of a terrorist crime, and at the same time are not or insufficiently related to armed conflict (such actions have not been established on the basis of the case file), so that such actions may constitute terrorist crimes, but such incidental actions do not entail that the LTTE should be considered a terrorist organisation for that reason alone. If this were otherwise then the rights conferred by the Geneva Conventions and Protocol II could be withheld from persons wrongfully. The defendant must therefore be acquitted of count 1.A. of the summons.[32]

The court also indicated that there was no factual basis for the charge of crimes against humanity as there had been no widespread or systematic attack on the civilian population during the time period of the charges. Both the prosecution and the defence appealed the decisions to the Court of Appeal[33] and then to the Supreme Court, which issued five

---

[31] Netherlands, Court of Appeal, The Hague, Case LJN BR0686, 7 July 2011 (www.legal-tools.org/doc/b7a8c9/).

[32] Netherlands, District Court, The Hague, Cases LJN BU9716 and BU7200, 21 October 2011 (www.legal-tools.org/doc/255180/). These are the two most important cases from a legal perspective.

[33] Netherlands, Court of Appeal, Case ECLI:NL:GHDHA:2015:1082, 30 April 2015 (www. legal-tools.org/doc/fd647c/).

similar decisions on 4 April 2017,[34] none of which discussed the issue of personal liability. The case arguably provides an illustration of *de facto* individual liability for 'membership in an organisation' responsible for concurrent war crimes and terrorist crimes, being *de jure* prosecuted solely as terrorist crimes on the basis of organisational status because the relevant form of liability (membership) was considered not applicable to war crimes under international law.

8.3.1.8.   Instigation to Genocide in Rwanda

On 22 June 2010, a woman of Rwandan nationality who later became a Dutch citizen was arrested on suspicion of involvement in the 1994 Rwandan genocide. The suspect, Yvonne Ntacyobatabara (Basebya), 63 years old at the time of her arrest, was said to have led a group of young men in the mass murder of Tutsis and moderate Hutus. On 17 November 2011, the District Court in The Hague ruled that she should remain in custody while investigation in her case was still ongoing. In a trial that started in October 2012, she was convicted for incitement (instigation) to genocide and sentenced to 6 years and 8 months' imprisonment on 1 March 2013.[35] The judgment was appealed by the prosecutor, but the appeal was later withdrawn.

8.3.1.9.   War Crimes in Ethiopia

On 15 December 2017 the trial of Eshetu Alemu came to an end. There is a connection between the Mengistu case in Ethiopia[36] and the Alemu case in the Netherlands in that Alemu was one of the co-accused in the Mengistu case and had received the death penalty *in absentia*. Alemu had been a senior official in the Derg with responsibility for the Gojjam region, where he was in charge of two prison camps, at Debre Marcos and at Metekel, between 1 February 1978 and 31 December 1981.

The investigation by the Dutch police and investigative judge produced a large amount of documentary evidence (even though co-operation by the Ethiopian government was limited), as well as the evidence of al-

---

[34]   Netherlands, Supreme Court, Cases ECLI:NL:HR:2017:574 through 2017:578, 4 April 2017 (www.legal-tools.org/doc/032ef2/).

[35]   Netherlands, District Court, The Hague, Case ECLI:NL:RBDHA:2013:8710, 1 March 2013 (www.legal-tools.org/doc/3f41c2/).

[36]   See Chapter 9, Section 9.4.3.1.

most 20 witnesses located in the Netherlands, Canada, and the United States.

The court convicted Alemu of indirect participation in a number of war crimes against 637 civilians, namely arbitrary imprisonment, killing, torture, and cruel treatment. The latter was based on the deplorable conditions in the prison camps, while the first was based on prison sentences imposed by the accused without any fair trial guarantees. He received a life sentence.[37]

8.3.2. Forms of Liability: Common Analysis

The main forms of liability are contained in Articles 45–48 of the Dutch Criminal Code,[38] which include the following provisions, among others:

> Article 45
>
> An attempt to commit a serious offence shall be punishable if the intention of the offender has revealed itself by a commencement of the performance of the criminal act. […]
>
> Article 46
>
> Preparation to commit a serious offence which, by statutory definition, carries a term of imprisonment of eight years or more, shall be punishable, if the offender intentionally obtains, manufactures, imports, conveys in transit, exports or has possession of objects, substances, information carriers, spaces or means of transport intended for the commission of that serious offence. […]
>
> Article 47 [participation]
>
> 1. The following persons shall be criminally liable as offenders of a criminal offence:
>
> 1°. any persons who commit the offence, either personally or jointly, or who cause an innocent person to commit the offence;
>
> 2°. any persons who, by means of gifts, promises, abuse of authority, use of force, threat or deception or by providing opportunity, means or information, intentionally solicit the commission of the offence.

---

[37] Netherlands, District Court, Case ECLI:NL:RBDHA:2017:16383, 15 December 2017 (www.legal-tools.org/doc/412f02/).

[38] The Netherlands Criminal Code, 3 March 1881 (www.legal-tools.org/doc/e70992/).

2. With regard to the last category, only those acts they intentionally solicited, and their consequences, shall be taken into account.

Article 48 [aiding and facilitation]

1. The following persons shall be criminally liable as accomplices to a criminal offence:

1°. any persons who intentionally aid and abet the commission of the serious offence;

2°. any persons who intentionally provide opportunity, means or information for the commission of the serious offence.

Conspiracy is set out in Article 80, which states, "a conspiracy shall exist as soon as two or more persons agree to commit the serious offence".[39]

In the first case, Nzapali, the person was charged and convicted of indirect forms of liability. While there is very little analysis of the law of indirect involvement in this short decision, joint perpetration is mentioned and superior responsibility is alluded to by the court when it states

> that he, the accused [...] jointly and in conjunction with others, as civil servant, i.e. as member of the Garde Civile (specifically as head of the Garde Civile for the province of Bas-Zaïre) and in the performance of his duties, repeatedly and intentionally inflicted (grievous) bodily harm to someone who was deprived of his freedom [...] As commander of the Garde Civile, the accused had the victim [...] arrested by his subordinates/bodyguards. [...] The accused watched all this from his balcony.

The brief discussion of the forms of liability might indicate that the court only needed to be satisfied that attribution of liability to the accused, for the relevant acts of torture and war crimes, was justified.

The two cases involving members of the KhAD were based on the notion of co-perpetration (joint perpetration). Without much analysis, the Court of Appeal agreed with the first instance court that the charge of carrying out international crimes was justified because the accused "jointly

---

[39] Both conspiracy and incitement are also set out in the Wet internationale misdrijven (International Crimes Statute), Article 3.2 (www.legal-tools.org/doc/1bea26/).

and in conjunction with others, (again and again) [...] violated the laws and customs of the war".[40] It added that one of the suspects had been "the head of the interrogations department of the military KhAD [...] from 1979 till [...] 1990 and that in that position he had to control the work of the interrogators, among other things by being present for some time during those interrogations and, if necessary, to instruct the interrogator how to do the work".[41] With respect to the second suspect, the observation was made that

> the accused was in the period [from] the end of 1983 up to and including May 1990 in Kabul, in Afghanistan, at the time of the communist regime supported by the Soviets, head of the military intelligence service, the KhAD-e-Nezami and deputy minister of the ministry of state security (WAD) and he was therefore a powerful and influential person. During the exercise of this duty/these duties the accused has been guilty, as can be proven, of very serious crimes with regard to three victims: being a co-perpetrator to torture and the violation of the laws and practices of war.[42]

The Supreme Court did not further discuss the issue of extended liability, although the words "in conjunction" in the lower decisions were translated in this decision as "in association". Again, it seems that the court only needed to be satisfied that attribution of liability for the perpetration of torture and war crimes was justified.

In the van Anraat case, the court of first instance, when acquitting the accused of genocide, held that for principles of extended liability the primary source of interpretation should be international criminal law rather than Dutch law. International criminal law requires *knowledge* of the special intention of genocide for aiders and abetters of this crime,[43] a requirement that appears to be narrower than the Dutch version of this type of liability (which allows conditional intent, in other words, willingly and knowingly accepting the reasonable chance that a certain consequence or a circumstance will occur). Therefore, the court held that international law

---

[40] Netherlands, Case LJN AZ9366 (2005), para. 8; also see Case LJN AZ9365 (2005), para. 8.
[41] Netherlands, Case LJN AZ9366 (2005), para. 10.2.2.
[42] Netherlands, Case LJN AZ9365 (2005), para. 13.
[43] See for example Rome Statute, Article 30, read in conjunction with Articles 6 and 25(3)(c).

should be followed on this point.[44] On the other hand, the court indicated that for war crimes, international criminal law and Dutch law were very similar in spite of the different language used, namely a substantial contribution to the crime in international law versus the intentional facilitation of the offences in Dutch law. In the words of the court,

> this subject is of a more factual nature, and presently does not form a substantial element of liability under international criminal law, so it is not a matter of a clear deviation from international rules and therefore the court will proceed on the application of Dutch law.[45]

The court continued,

> It has been established that the accused, consciously and solely acting in pursuit of gain, has made an essential contribution to the chemical warfare program of Iraq during the nineteen eighties. His contribution has enabled, or at least facilitated, a great number of attacks with mustard gas on defenceless civilians.[46]

The appeals court in the same case agreed with the conclusion with respect to being an accessory to genocide but added the refinement that based on the facts, neither the international nor the Dutch variant of this type of liability was established.[47] With respect to aiding and abetting war crimes by providing the opportunity for the commission of the offences, the court said,

> From case law administered by the Supreme Court it appears that it is not a requirement that the assistance offered should be indispensable [...] or should have made an adequate causal contribution to the main offence [...]. It is sufficient when the assistance offered by the accessory has indeed promoted the offence or has made it easier to commit that offence. [...] From international criminal law perspective, these requirements for the contribution of the so-called 'aider or abettor' are not essentially more severe.[48]

---

[44] Netherlands, Case LJN AX6406 (2005), paras. 6.2, 6.5, 6.5.1, and 8.

[45] *Ibid.*, paras. 6.5.2 and 6.6.

[46] *Ibid.*, para. 17.

[47] Netherlands, Case LJN BA6734 (2007), para. 7.

[48] *Ibid.*, para. 12.4.

The court agreed with the original decision that the accused had made a substantial contribution.[49] The Supreme Court agreed with the Court of Appeal but made one clarification regarding the notion of intention with respect to aiding and abetting, namely that this form of intent could be *dolus directus* in either the first or second degree, that is, a full intent or conditional intent.[50] The ECHR did not discuss the issue of liability.[51]

The final decision in the van Kouwenhoven case by the Court of Appeal in Den Bosch in 2017 addressed the issue of participation in war crimes and crimes against humanity. He was charged with 14 counts and convicted of five of these charges. Of the nine charges of which he was acquitted, three dealt with co-perpetration (joint perpetration), three with soliciting, and three with superior responsibility. The court acquitted him of these nine counts without much explanation, except to say that there was insufficient evidence of a coordinated contribution or of carrying out activities with respect to war crimes.[52] The court also said, in the context of the charges dealing with superior responsibility, that the accused did not have effective control to prevent the crimes in question.[53] The five remaining charges, those on which he was convicted, were based on the concept of aiding and abetting. He was also convicted on two counts of subverting the UN arms embargo.

The court noted that in order to be held liable as an aider or abettor under Dutch law, an accused must have contributed to or facilitated the commission of war crimes by a third party; such assistance must have been directed at the commission of crimes by the third party. The assistance did not have to have been indispensable, in the sense that the crimes would not have been committed without it; it is sufficient for the aiding

---

[49] *Ibid.*, para. 16.

[50] Netherlands, Case LJN BG4822 (2009), para. 6.2.

[51] ECHR, *Anraat v. The Netherlands*, Judgment, 65389/09, 6 July 2010 (www.legal-tools.org/doc/567d90/).

[52] Netherlands, Case ECLI:NL:GHSHE:2017:1760 (2017), sec. L1.

[53] *Ibid.*, sec. D.2.1.

and abetting to have promoted or otherwise facilitated the commission of crimes.[54]

The court did not find that van Kouwenhoven was part of a common plan (conspiracy) to commit war crimes, or knew that the weapons and ammunition he supplied were going to be used by others for their commission. Instead, the court held that by providing weapons and ammunition, by allowing his armed personnel to join the Liberian combined armed forces, by violating the UN arms embargo, and by allowing the Royal Timber Company camp at Bomi Wood to be used as a collection and distribution site, Van Kouwenhoven must have been aware that "in the ordinary course of events" those weapons and ammunition would be used.[55] In other words, the court concluded that van Kouwenhoven knowingly exposed himself to the substantial chance that the weapons and ammunition he provided would be used by others to commit war crimes and/ or crimes against humanity. Importantly, the court held that this included both those crimes for which the weapons and ammunition were used directly (such as shooting civilians) and those for which they were used indirectly, that is, when the threat of the presence of weapons and/or armed forces was used to commit war crimes, such as rape or pillage. The court further held that the accused was aware of the cruel nature of the armed conflict being fought by Charles Taylor, and that he knowingly accepted the risk that his assistance would facilitate the commission of war crimes and/or crimes against humanity. Van Kouwenhoven was thus held liable as an aider or abettor.

Being convicted as an aider and abettor, however, did not in any way diminish his responsibility; in fact, the court specifically noted the seriousness of his contribution to the crimes in sentencing him to 19 years' imprisonment. In doing so, the court reiterated the preventative or deterrent value of this judgment by saying that international businessmen, such as the accused, who do not hesitate to do business with regimes like Charles Taylor's are firmly put on notice that they can become involved in,

---

[54] *Ibid.*, sec. L.2. While the court does not refer here to international jurisprudence (as it does in its discussion regarding war crimes in section K), it does say in this section that the requirements just stated are not out of step with international law.

[55] *Ibid.*, secs. L.2.1 and L.2.5. This language is similar to the *mens rea* requirement in Article 30(2)(b) of the Rome Statute.

and be held criminally liable for, (international) crimes (against humanity).[56]

The van Kouwenhoven case and the van Anraat case thus illustrate that individual liability for universal crimes committed or facilitated through juridical entity participation might be possible to identify and prosecute successfully in domestic proceedings, even when the crimes have a transnational character. Prosecution of individual businessmen may thus fill part of the impunity gap relating to the frequent lack of complementary prosecution of corporations involved in war crimes.[57]

With respect to the Faqirzada case, the charge was based on the notion of superior responsibility, which, according to the court of first instance, meant that the requirements of international criminal law had to be incorporated in assessing this form of liability.[58] The accused was acquitted because he

> was one of the deputies to the Director of the Military Khad (Khad-e-Nezami), an organisation that in those days committed violations of human rights on a large scale, like torturing prisoners. It can be assumed that the defendant was closely involved in these practices. Nevertheless, it cannot be established with adequate certainty that the defendant was in a position to exercise effective command and control over the Head of the Investigation and Interrogation Department in all cases and under all circumstances. Although in the chain of command he was superior to [P4], there is still a lack of clarity about [...] whether the defendant was at any point in time in a position to exercise 'effective command and control' over the Military Khad as deputy to [P3] and likewise over the Investigation and Interrogation Department, a position that was undeniably held by [P3]. For that reason it cannot

---

[56] *Ibid.*, sec. Q. For commentaries, see the following two blog posts: Dieneke De Vos, "Corporate Accountability: Dutch Court Convicts Former 'Timber Baron' of War Crimes in Liberia", European University Institute, 24 April 2017 (available on EUI web site); and James G. Stewart, "The Historical Importance of the Kouwenhoven Trial", blog of James G. Stewart, 5 May 2017 (available on its web site).

[57] See Chapter 4, Section 4.3.7., and Chapter 10, Section 10.3.

[58] See Netherlands, Case LJN BA9575 (2007) under "Considerations regarding count 2: Superior responsibility". This notion has been incorporated in Dutch law in the Wet internationale misdrijven (International Crimes Statute), Article 9 in conjunction with Article 1(b) (www.legal-tools.org/doc/1bea26/).

---

be excluded that the defendant was not in a position to take disciplinary action against the responsible persons for the acts of violence committed against the victims referred to in the charges. In other words: the Court is of the opinion that the question [of] whether the defendant had 'effective control' cannot be answered affirmatively with a sufficient degree of certainty. Therefore, the Court believes that one of the most important requirements necessary to be able to give an affirmative answer to the question [of] whether the defendant carried 'superior responsibility' for the war crimes he is charged with, has not been fulfilled.[59]

This concept of command and superior responsibility was canvassed in detail by the Court of Appeal,[60] which concluded that this form of liability existed in customary international law for war crimes committed in both international as well as non-international armed conflicts. The reasoning with respect to the latter form of armed conflict was based on the fact that the crimes in question had been committed between 1985 and 1986, a time period very close to the establishment of the ICTY in 1993, which allowed for this form of liability.[61] An interesting question, however, is whether it was really necessary from an ICL point of view, also taking into account the legality principle, to prove that this particular form of liability *existed* within CIL at the relevant time, or whether it had been sufficient to make sure that this form of liability was not *prohibited* by CIL at that time.[62]

The court, while relying heavily on ICTY and ICTR jurisprudence with respect to content,[63] stated that the essential characteristic of command/superior responsibility is the notion of 'subordinate'. This concept

> must be interpreted within the context of a hierarchical relationship between superior and subordinate. Here it is necessary to consider de facto relations between superior and subordinate, as well as the de jure relationship – the hierarchical

---

[59] *Ibid.* under "Conclusion".

[60] Netherlands, Case LJN BJ2796 (2009), paras. 22–39.

[61] *Ibid.*, para. 40.

[62] Although this would not have made any practical difference in this case because of the conclusion entered by the court, it might be an important question under other circumstances.

[63] Netherlands, Case LJN BJ2796 (2009), paras. 136–44.

> relations based on laws and decrees within the organisation within which these persons are employed. In addition, the superior must be actually capable of intervening on the basis of this hierarchical relationship if his subordinate misbehaves, in any event if the latter commits criminal offences [...].[64]

Applying the law to the facts, the Court of Appeal was of the view that a *de jure* relationship existed between the accused and his staff who had committed the war crimes,[65] but that the element of effective control was not proven beyond reasonable doubt.[66] The Supreme Court upheld the acquittal while confirming the reasoning with respect to command/ superior responsibility,[67] again relying heavily on ICTY jurisprudence and specifically quoting the Orić case.[68]

Mpambara was convicted of co-perpetration of both physical and mental torture, at first instance;[69] this was upheld on appeal but on the basis of co-perpetration in the commission of war crimes, without any further legal explanation at both levels with respect to the mode of liability.[70]

The Ntacyobatabara case presents the most detailed analysis of the various forms of indirect participation in relation to genocide. Dutch national law has incorporated the Genocide Convention, allowing Dutch prosecutors to use the following forms of liability: 'complicity', 'conspiracy', and 'direct and public incitement', in addition to 'co-perpetration' (joint perpetration) and 'solicitation' (instigation). According to the court:

> Co-perpetration refers to a situation when two or more persons together jointly commit a criminal offence. Co-perpetration is based on the assumption that there is an intentional and close collaboration between two or more persons. This means that the co-perpetrators collaborate knowingly, thus intentionally, to commit the criminal act. The intention

---

[64] *Ibid.*, para. 135.

[65] *Ibid.*, para. 159.

[66] *Ibid.*, paras. 173–75.

[67] Netherlands, Case LJN BR6598 (2011), paras. 2.6 and 2.7. The English translation of the decision follows the Dutch text.

[68] *Ibid.*, para. 2.4.2.

[69] Netherlands, Case LJN BI2444 (2009), chap. 16, paras. 58–61, and chap. 19, para. 11.

[70] Netherlands, Case LJN BR0686 (2011), para. 21.1.

should not only be aimed at their mutual collaboration but also at the commission of the criminal offence. It is not required that all co-perpetrators carry out overt acts or that they are personally present when the criminal offences are committed. Their collaboration needs to be intensive and aimed at the unlawful act, whereas the participation of the co-perpetrator who does not carry out the overt acts should be substantial. In this manner it is possible that the co-perpetrator who does not carry out the overt acts is involved in the planning and/or organisation [of] the criminal offence. Their close collaboration may appear among other matters from – explicit or tacit – agreements and assignment of responsibilities.[71]

The legal requirement for solicitation (instigation),[72] according to the court,

is defined as a situation whereby a person, by using one or more means of solicitation provided in article 47 [of the Criminal Code] (gifts, promises, abuse of authority, violence, threat or deception, or by providing the opportunity, means or information) has intentionally solicited another person to commit a criminal offence because of which the person who was solicited can personally be held liable to punishment. Those actions must have been solicited intentionally and the intention of the person doing the solicitation must have been aimed at both soliciting the other to commit the crime and at the component parts of the crime which the other person was solicited to commit. The person soliciting must put the idea into the other person's head to commit the criminal offence, "awaken the other person's will" to commit a certain crime. A charge of solicitation cannot be brought if the other person already had the idea to commit the crime before the person doing the solicitation started his actions. However, a person can be held liable for solicitation if the intention to commit a certain offence already existed in the mind of the incited person, but only materialised after the actions of the person doing the solicitation. The psychological change must have

---

[71] Netherlands, Case ECLI:NL:RBDHA:2013:8710 (2013), chap. 13, para. 2.

[72] The translated version of the judgment refers to incitement rather than solicitation, but from the Dutch text it is clear that solicitation or inducement is the correct legal expression. We have made adjustments to the quoted excerpt to reflect this.

been caused by the latter and the means that person used to solicit the other to commit the criminal offence. A charge of completed solicitation can only be brought if the crime has been committed or if a punishable attempt was made to commit that crime.[73]

With respect to complicity, the court held that

persons are liable as accessories if they intentionally assist during the commission of a crime (simultaneous complicity) [or if they] intentionally provide the opportunity, means or information necessary to commit the crime (consecutive complicity). The intention of the accessory should not only be aimed at providing assistance or the opportunity, means or information to the perpetrator, but also at the crime itself. The actions of the accessory somehow must have promoted or facilitated the commission of the crime. Different from the situation of being a co-perpetrator, the charge of being an accessory does not require the condition of close and intentional collaboration. A charge of being an accessory can only be brought if the crime that was promoted or facilitated has indeed been committed or if a punishable attempt was made to commit that crime.[74]

Conspiracy has the following elements, according to the court:

From the moment two or more persons agree to commit a serious offence, this constitutes conspiracy. The agreement is not bound by a certain form and does not necessarily mean that the crime should be committed by all conspirators. It is sufficient that one of them undertakes to commit the crime himself. However, the agreement should include an explicit intention, i.e. it should be aimed at a specific crime.[75]

While the requirement that at least one of the conspirators must personally execute the crime was based on domestic law, this may not be a necessary requirement in other contexts. The same is true with respect to

---

[73] *Ibid.*, chap. 13, paras. 3–5. The court also said in chap. 15, para. 12, that "incitement to commit a crime does not equal being a co-perpetrator of a crime committed afterwards, even if this was the same crime as the one that was incited".

[74] *Ibid.*, chap. 13, paras. 6–7.

[75] *Ibid.*, chap. 18, para. 5.

some of the more specific requirements relating to the other forms of liability discussed by the court.

For the parameters of the offence of incitement to genocide, however, the court relied explicitly on ICTR jurisprudence, stating:

> the distinctive element of genocide is the aim to entirely or partly destroy a protected group as such. For the qualification of incitement to genocide it is required that the inciter himself/herself had the aim of creating a genocide. The inciter must have had the intention that the persons who were incited indeed went on to commit genocide.[76]

Again, this does not necessarily mean that the whole statement is applicable as *lex lata* within other domestic jurisdictions or other parts of ICL, since different formulations of liability ('modes of liability') for incitement to genocide may apply within different subsystems of criminal law liability.

The court acquitted the accused of all the charges[77] except that of 'direct and public incitement' (instigation), which the accused carried out by publicly performing a hateful song encouraging violence against Tutsis. The court provided the following reasoning:

> That she, at several moments in time in the period from 22 February 1992 up to 6 April 1994, in the direct vicinity of her house (in the Gikondo district and in the municipality of Kicukiro) in the Kigali Prefecture (Rwanda), in public, being: in the street in the direct vicinity of her house and in the compound of her house and at the bar next to her house and in the compound of the house of Bucyana, which could be heard and seen from the public road, each time orally incited to commit a criminal offence, being genocide. For then and there, on multiple occasions, she was the lead singer of the Tubatsembesembe song in the presence of a group of persons (including youngsters and porters of the local market and women).[78]

---

[76] *Ibid.*, chap. 12, para. 9.

[77] *Ibid.*, chap. 14, paras. 41 and 48–50 for the charge of solicitation, as well as chap. 14, para. 13; chap. 14, para. 51 for the charge of complicity; chap. 18, paras. 5–7 for the charge of conspiracy.

[78] *Ibid.*, chap. 12, para. 33.

With respect to the Alemu case, the forms of liability charged were instigation, co-perpetration, aiding and abetting, and superior responsibility. The court relied on previous Dutch and international jurisprudence to provide the parameters of these forms of participation without going into much detail. The exception was with respect to the concept of superior responsibility, where reference was made to ICTY and ICC case law because the court was of the view that this form of liability found its origins in customary international law, which had been applied by the ICTY, as a result of which the jurisprudence of that tribunal should be taken into consideration for this type of liability under Dutch law.[79]

8.4. Germany

8.4.1. Overview of Cases

In Germany, courts have prosecuted and convicted 11 individuals in nine cases on the basis of universal jurisdiction, as well as one person on the basis of active personality jurisdiction.[80]

Four were convicted of involvement in crimes committed in the former Yugoslavia.[81] Novislav Đajić,[82] Maksim Sokolović,[83] Đurađ Kušljić[84] and Nicala Jorgić[85] were all found guilty in first instance between 1997 and 1999.

---

[79] Netherlands, Case ECLI:NL:RBDHA:2017:16383 (2017), para. 13.5.2.

[80] See Amnesty International, *Germany: End Impunity through Universal Jurisdiction*, London, 2008, pp. 93–98 (www.legal-tools.org/doc/6c4702/).

[81] For an overview of the legal issues involved, see Ruth Rissing-van Saan, "The German Federal Supreme Court and the Prosecution of International Crimes Committed in the Former Yugoslavia", in *Journal of International Criminal Justice*, 2005, vol. 3, no. 2, pp. 381–99.

[82] See TRIAL International page on Đajić (available on its web site); and Amnesty International, 2008, p. 93, *supra* note 80.

[83] See TRIAL International page on Sokolović (available on its web site); and Amnesty International, 2008, p. 97, *supra* note 80.

[84] See TRIAL International page on Kušljić (available on its web site); and Amnesty International, 2008, p. 98, *supra* note 80.

[85] See TRIAL International page on Jorgić (available on its web site); and Amnesty International, 2008, pp. 93–97, *supra* note 80.

8.4.1.1. Shooting Incident in Bosnia

Đajić, a former member of the Bosnian Serb forces, had been involved in a shooting incident with 15 Bosnian Muslims on a bridge in his hometown of Trnovace near Foca on 22 June 1992, when 15 Muslims were taken prisoner, executed, and then thrown in the river Drina. He was convicted on 23 May 1997 and sentenced to 5 years' imprisonment on 14 counts of aiding murder and one count of attempted murder, although he had been charged with genocide.

8.4.1.2. Ethnic Cleansing in Bosnia

Sokolović took part in May 1992 in a Serb campaign against the Muslim population of Osmaci. This campaign was part of systematic plan to displace or eliminate this population; for this purpose, the houses of the Muslim inhabitants were raided, while the women and children were deported or sent to the border. The male population was physically mistreated or murdered and many of them were sent to detention camps. Sokolović personally oversaw the displacement of the inhabitants of Osmaci; he personally persecuted the Muslim men and physically mistreated five prisoners. In addition, he took part in the surveillance of the building where the prisoners were detained overnight and where the worst mistreatments were carried out. From this first detention camp, the prisoners that had not been selected for execution were transported by bus to confinement camps. Sokolović personally oversaw the transfer of 56 men: he took the necessary steps to prevent them from escaping as they were led to the waiting buses, while inflicting kicks and blows. He was convicted to 9 years' imprisonment on 29 November 1999 for aiding and abetting genocide in conjunction with grave breaches of the Geneva Conventions (namely 56 counts of unlawful imprisonment and five counts of aggravated assault). This was upheld on appeal on 21 February 2001.[86]

8.4.1.3. Killing in Bosnia

In June 1992 the Serbs took power in Vrbànjci, a municipality in northern Bosnia. Kušljić, a Bosnian Serb, was appointed chief of the police station and also held a leading position in the local army contingent. He ordered

---

[86] Germany, Bundesgerichtshof, Case 3 StR 372/00, 21 February 2001 (www.legal-tools.org/doc/89fb79/).

his subordinates to kill six Muslims in the vicinity of a sawmill and took part in the killings himself. In August 1992 he supervised the expulsion of the Muslim population from the town of Dabovci, but his direct involvement in the killings of 18 men, which happened in this context, could not be proven. He was convicted of genocide in December 1999 and received a life sentence, upheld on appeal in February 2001, but on the basis of grave breaches rather than genocide.[87]

8.4.1.4. Murder and Ill-Treatment in Bosnia

Jorgić was the leader of a paramilitary group that took part in acts of terror against the Muslim population. Jorgić arrested Muslims and put them in prison camps where they were tortured. In June 1992, he took part in the execution of 22 inhabitants of Grabska (among them disabled and elderly people), who had gathered in the open in order to escape fighting; three other Muslims had to carry the dead to a mass grave. A few days later, Jorgić ordered the expulsion of the village of Ševarlije and the brutal ill-treatment of 40 to 50 of its inhabitants, six of whom were shot dead; the seventh victim, who was not fatally wounded, died later when he was burned together with the six bodies. In September 1992, Jorgić put a tin bucket on the head of a prisoner in the central prison of Doboj and hit it with such force that the victim died as a consequence of the blow. Jorgić was convicted on 11 counts of genocide and 30 counts of murder[88] and received a life sentence on 26 September 1997.[89] This was upheld by an appeals court on 30 April 1999 (in a decision that reduced the counts of genocide to one)[90] and on 12 December 2000,[91] and later by the ECHR on 12 July 2007.[92]

---

[87] Germany, Bundesgerichtshof, Case 3 StR 244/00, 21 February 2001 (www.legal-tools.org/doc/bb9913/).

[88] The counts of murder were reduced to eight counts on 21 June 2004 during a rehearing at first instance, but it resulted in the same sentence.

[89] Germany, Oberlandesgericht Dusseldorf, Case 2 StE 8/96, 26 September 1997 (www.legal-tools.org/doc/853a97/).

[90] Germany, Bundesgerichtshof, Case 3 StR 215/98, 30 April 1999 (www.legal-tools.org/doc/85b784/).

[91] Germany, Bundesverfassungsgericht, Case 2 BvR 1290/99, 12 December 2000 (www.legal-tools.org/doc/5ef246/).

[92] ECHR, *Jorgic v. Germany*, Judgment, 74613/01, 12 July 2007 (www.legal-tools.org/doc/812753/).

8.4.1.5. Genocide in Rwanda

Onesphore Rwabukombe was arrested on 25 April 2008 and indicted on 3 June 2008 for crimes against humanity and genocide committed in Rwanda in 1994. He was released in 2008 but arrested for the second time in December 2008, then released again in May 2009 due to insufficient evidence. Finally, he was arrested again as a result of new information and his trial started on 18 January 2011 in the Higher Regional Court of Frankfurt am Main. The allegations against him were that in 1994 Rwabukombe was a member of the local executive committee of the Rwandan governing party MRND (Mouvement Républicain National pour la Démocratie et le Développement) and mayor of the Muvumba commune in the north of Rwanda. During the genocide against the Tutsi ethnic minority, which took place between April and July 1994, Rwabukombe was alleged to have incited the Hutu residents of Muvumba to kill Tutsis and was said to have actively participated in the killings in the nearby Murambi district. In particular, he was accused of being responsible for the deaths of more than 3,730 people when, on 11 April 1994, he reportedly participated in the massacre in the Kiziguro church. He was convicted on 18 February 2014 and sentenced to 14 years' imprisonment for the massacre in Kiziguro, but not for the killings in Kibungo and Kabarondo, due to a lack of evidence.[93] On 21 May 2015, on appeal, the Federal Supreme Court ordered a partial retrial because the federal court found that evidence showed Rwabukombe took an active role in genocide, rather than just aiding and abetting it as found by the lower court.[94] On 29 December 2015 he was convicted on retrial by the Higher Regional Court of Frankfort am Main and given life imprisonment for being a co-perpetrator in the genocide, as he had the required specific intent for this crime;[95] the appeal of this case was dismissed on 26 July 2016.

---

[93] Germany, Oberlandesgericht Frankfurt am Main, Case 5-3 StE 4/10-4-3/10, 18 February 2014 (www.legal-tools.org/doc/8c79bc/).

[94] Germany, Bundesgerichtshof, Case 3 StR 575/14, 21 May 2015 (www.legal-tools.org/doc/368fdd/).

[95] Germany, Oberlandesgericht Frankfurt am Main, Case 4-3 StE 4/10-4-1/15, 29 December 2015 (www.legal-tools.org/doc/bd14c5/).

8.4.1.6. Crimes against Humanity in the Democratic Republic of Congo

On 16 November 2009, police in Germany arrested two Rwandan militia leaders on suspicion of crimes committed in the eastern Democratic Republic of Congo between January 2008 and July 2009. Ignace Murwanashyaka, the leader of the Forces Démocratiques de Libération du Rwanda ('FDLR') rebel group, and his aide Straton Musoni were held on suspicion of crimes against humanity and war crimes. They were accused in their roles as president and vice president of the FDLR of having ordered and coordinated the FDLR's crimes from Germany and of not preventing these crimes. They were charged with 26 counts of crimes against humanity and 39 counts of war crimes. The charges related to the killings of more than 200 people as well as the commission of rape, the use of child soldiers, the use of civilians as human shields, and the pillage and burning down of villages during fighting in the areas of Kipopo, Mianga, Busurungi, Kubua, and Manje. The trial started on 5 May 2011, and they were convicted on 28 September 2015; during the proceedings, several charges of war crimes and crimes against humanity, including the recruitment of child soldiers, were dropped for lack of evidence. Murwanashyaka was convicted for aiding and abetting war crimes on five counts and for leading a foreign terrorist organisation; he received a 13-year prison term. Musoni, who received 8 years, was convicted for leading a foreign terrorist organisation but acquitted of war crimes and crimes against humanity because of a lack of sufficient evidence of his direct involvement in the commission of any of these crimes.[96] He was subsequently released, as he had already been in pre-trial detention for almost six years and therefore qualified for conditional release for good behaviour.[97]

---

[96] Germany, Oberlandesgericht Stuttgart, Case 5-3 StE 6/10, 28 September 2015 (www.legal-tools.org/doc/af8e31/).

[97] See TRIAL International page on Musoni (available on its web site).

8.4.1.7.   War Crimes in Syria[98]

On 24 October 2015, a 20-year-old German citizen, Aria Ladjedvardi, was arrested and his apartment in the Frankfurt area was searched on suspicion that he committed war crimes in Syria. He was accused of having posed next to two severed heads spiked on sticks while he was fighting in the Syrian civil war with a rebel group against President Bashar Assad's army. He was convicted on 12 July 2016 and sentenced to 2 years in prison for the desecration of a dead body as part of the war crime of outrages upon personal dignity, in particular humiliating and degrading treatment, as set out in the Rome Statute. The sentence was upheld on appeal on 27 July 2017.[99]

On 31 May 2016 Abdelkarim El B., a German national, was charged with the war crime of treating in a gravely humiliating or degrading manner a person who is required to be protected under international humanitarian law. The trial began on 22 August 2016 before the Higher Regional Court in Frankfurt. On 8 November 2016, Abdelkarim El B. was found guilty of committing a war crime, of being member of a terrorist organisation (the Islamic State), and of violation of the Military Weapons Control Law ('KWKG') and sentenced to 8 years and 6 months' imprisonment.[100] The war crimes conviction was based on the fact that he had been directly involved in the desecration of a corpse of a captured soldier, including the cutting of the nose and ears, while other indignities to the corpse such as kicking it and shooting it in the head were attributed to him as a 'joint principal' (joint perpetrator) on account of him belonging to the

---

[98]   For a general overview of the investigations and prosecutions with respect to atrocities committed in Syria, see Human Rights Watch, *These Are the Crimes We Are Fleeing: Justice for Syria in Swedish and German Courts*, October 2017 (www.legal-tools.org/doc/6bfe43/). See also Wolfgang Kaleck and Patrick Kroker, "Syrian Torture Investigations in Germany and Beyond: Breathing New Life into Universal Jurisdiction in Europe?", in *Journal of International Criminal Justice*, 2018, vol. 16, no. 1, pp. 165–91.

[99]   Germany, Oberlandesgericht Frankfurt am Main, Case 5-3 StE 2/16-4-1/16, 12 July 2016, parts CIII and CIV (www.legal-tools.org/doc/f44466/). For appeals decision, Germany, Bundergerichthof, Case StR 57/17, 27 July 2017 (www.legal-tools.org/doc/5d2ee7/).

[100]   Germany, Oberlandesgericht Frankfurt am Main, Case 5-3 StE 4/16-4-3/16, 8 November 2016 (www.legal-tools.org/doc/57c158/).

group whose members carried out these acts and having formulated a joint decision to participate through his statements.[101]

8.4.1.8.   War Crimes in Iraq

On 22 February 2017 the trial against Rami K., a member of the Iraqi Armed Forces, started before the Higher Regional Court in Berlin. Rami K. was accused of war crimes for having treated persons in a humiliating or degrading manner by posing for a photo while holding the severed heads of two Islamic State fighters who had been killed in battle. The photo was later published on social media. He had confessed to the crime.[102]

8.4.1.9.   Beheading in Syria

On 17 February 2013, the Canadian national Carl Campeau, who had been working as a legal adviser to the UN forces (UNDOF) in the Golan Heights, was abducted by the terrorist organisation Jabhat al-Nusra in the Damascus area. Suliman Al-S. participated in his abduction by keeping the victim under surveillance between March and June 2013. Campeau was held captive for eight months but escaped in October 2013. While he was in detention, his captors issued death threats against him and tried unsuccessfully to obtain a ransom for his release. On 20 September 2017, the Higher Regional Court of Stuttgart found Suliman Al-S. guilty of aiding and abetting the kidnapping of an employee of the United Nations in Syria in February 2013. He was sentenced to 3 years and 6 months in prison. The charges of membership in a terrorist organisation were dropped.[103]

8.4.2.   Forms of Liability: Common Analysis

The main forms of liability are contained in Articles 22, 25–27, and 30 of the German Criminal Code,[104] which state the following:

---

[101] *Ibid.*, part IIIB.

[102] Kammergericht Berlin, Case of Rami K., 1 March 2017 (www.legal-tools.org/doc/d994aa/); TRIAL International, *Make Way for Justice #4*, 2018, p. 58, see *supra* note 9.

[103] *Ibid.*, p. 56; Oberlandesgericht Stuttgart, Case of Suliman Al-S., 20 September 2017 (www.legal-tools.org/doc/c123aa/).

[104] German Criminal Code, 1998 (www.legal-tools.org/doc/e71bdb/).

22 Attempt

A person attempts to commit an offence if he takes steps which will immediately lead to the completion of the offence as envisaged by him.

25 Perpetration

(1) Any person who commits the offence himself or through another shall be liable as a principal.

(2) If more than one person commits the offence jointly, each shall be liable as a principal (joint principals).

26 Abetting

Any person who intentionally induces another to intentionally commit an unlawful act (abettor), shall be liable to be sentenced as if he were a principal.

27 Aiding

(1) Any person who intentionally assists another in the intentional commission of an unlawful act shall be convicted and punished as an aider.

(2) The sentence for the aider shall be based on the penalty for a principal. It shall be mitigated pursuant to section 49(1).

30 Conspiracy

(1) A person who attempts to induce another to commit a felony or abet another to commit a felony shall be liable according to the provisions governing attempted felonies. The sentence shall be mitigated pursuant to section 49 (1). Section 23 (3) shall apply mutatis mutandis.

(2) A person who declares his willingness or who accepts the offer of another to commit or abet the commission of a felony shall be liable under the same terms.

With respect to the four early Bosnian cases, only two addressed forms of personal liability from a legal perspective at the appeal level, and then only very briefly.[105] The case of Sokolović discussed the notion of aiding and abetting in genocide, and the Bundesgerichtshof (Federal Supreme Court) agreed with the lower court, the Oberlandesgericht in

---

[105] In the Jorgić case it was only said that the accused carried out genocide by himself or together with others as a co-perpetrator, without further analysis. See Germany, Case 2 StE 8/96 (1997), pp. 163–64 and 167–68, and Case 3 StR 215/98 (1999), p. 33.

Dusseldorf, that for the aider and abettor to attract this type of liability it is sufficient that he knew that the principal offender had the specific intent to commit genocide; it is not necessary to show that the aider and abettor shared that intent.[106] This approach was confirmed by the same court on the same day in the Kušljić case.[107]

While the Rwabukombe and Murwanashyaka judgments went into some detail with respect to a number of forms of extended liability, the three subsequent cases, namely the Aria L. case, the Abdelkarim El B. case, and the Suliman Al-S. case, did not have much to add to the debate. The Aria L. case involved direct involvement in crimes, as did the Rami K. case. The Abdelkarim El B. case was for the most part based on direct involvement, with a brief reference to joint perpetration, and the Suliman Al-S. case was based on aiding and abetting.[108]

In the Rwabukombe case the Federal Supreme Court discussed two forms within the class of 'direct participation', namely direct and indirect perpetration.

The court began by setting out the general requirements for co-perpetration ('joint perpetration'). They included the following criteria: (1) the activity goes beyond merely promoting criminal acts and is part of a joint effort in terms of a division of labour; (2) the participant makes an essential contribution to this activity and intends to have his contribution

---

[106] Germany, Case 3 StR 372/00 (2001), paras. 2–4.

[107] Germany, Case 3 StR 244/00 (2001), p. 10, para. 3.

[108] On the general principles regarding joint perpetration, another war crimes case, this one dealing with a WWII situation, namely the case of Oskar Gröning, states in part IV, para. 56: "An accomplice is a person who does not only abet someone else's actions, but rather also contributes his own act to a common criminal enterprise so that his contribution is viewed as part of the activities of the other and conversely the other's actions as an endorsement of his own criminal contribution. Whether or not a participant had a close nexus to the crime must be judged upon taking into account the overall circumstances from his subjective point of view. Material for an assessment could be the degree to which a person has an interest in seeing the crime committed, the scope of participation in the crime, and control over the commission of the crime or at least a desire to control the commission of the crime". Germany, Landgericht Lüneburg, Case 27 Ks 1191 Js 98402113 (9/14), 15 July 2015 (www.legal-tools.org/doc/057092/). This decision was confirmed on appeal in Germany, Bundergerichthof, Case 3 StR 49/16, 20 September 2016 (www.legal-tools.org/doc/4abce8/). For a commentary, see Pavlos Andreadis-Papadimitriou, "Assistance in Mass Murder under Systems of Ill-treatment: The Case of Oskar Gröning", in *Journal of International Criminal Justice*, 2017, vol. 15, no. 1, pp. 157–74.

---

be part of the joint effort; (3) whether the participant has such a close relationship to the group carrying out the criminal activity is based on a number of circumstances, such as his own interest in the successful outcome of the enterprise, the extent of his participation, and his influence on the activity in the sense that the conduct and outcome of the enterprise depend decisively on the will of the participant. In addition, it is not necessary for the defendant to have taken part in the stage during which the act was carried out; instead, a contribution to the act during the preparatory stages can be sufficient.[109]

Applying this approach to the facts of the case, the lower court had not given sufficient consideration to the fact that the defendant, who was an eminent person of authority commanding respect by virtue of his position and role, was already involved in the preparations for the massacre and had carried out further activities that were significant for the act's execution. These included his exhortation of armed persons to kill the victims, his query concerning the killings' progress, his transport of other Hutu attackers to the church, and finally the moving of other Tutsi victims from the neighbouring hospital to the church grounds at his request. This resulted in his participation being labelled as direct (co-)perpetration ('joint functional perpetration')[110] because of his essential contribution. The court rejected indirect perpetration ('perpetration through another') by means of Organisationsherrschaft (domination through an organisation), the approach suggested by the prosecutor.[111]

The subsequent judgment by the Higher Regional Court repeated the legal parameters of co-perpetration as determined by the Supreme Court,[112] while also applying these legal principles to the facts in much the same manner.[113]

---

[109] Germany, Case 3 StR 575/14 (2015), para. 10.

[110] See Chapter 2, Section 2.2.3.2., on the principle of direct participation.

[111] Germany, Case 3 StR 575/14 (2015), paras. 11–12. See also Kai Ambos, "The German Rwabukombe Case: The Federal Court's Interpretation of Co-perpetration and the Genocidal Intent to Destroy", in *Journal of International Criminal Justice*, 2016, vol. 14, no. 5, pp. 1221–34.

[112] Germany, Oberlandesgericht Frankfurt am Main, Case 4-3 StE 4/10 4 1/15, 29 December 2015, part III, A.3 (www.legal-tools.org/doc/bd14c5/).

[113] *Ibid.*

The Murwanashyaka judgment discussed both the notions of command responsibility and of aiding and abetting, finding him only guilty of the latter, and for the former relying on literature to ascertain the international jurisprudence in this regard.[114] With respect to command responsibility,[115] the judgment states that it is sufficient to attract liability if a commander can influence the action of the military units by means of subordinate persons of the military leadership through a chain of command. But the defendant did not have such a possibility of influence because he did not have sufficient information about the activities of Abacunguzi Fighting Forces ('FOCA') in the Kivu provinces of DRC to enable effective control, and furthermore, he did not have the actual means to prevent the war crimes committed by the FOCA soldiers against the will of their military leadership.[116] In addition, the superior can only be punishable if he could indeed have prevented the act in a manner made possible by the required and reasonable use of his command or leadership; it is not sufficient to conclude that the superior could have made the execution of the subordinate act more difficult or less likely. In this case, the accused was only formally the chief military leader of the FDLR and was in fact dependent on the military branch, without any commanding power in military affairs against the military. The court observes that on this point, German law is stricter than international criminal law.[117]

With respect to aiding and abetting,[118] the court stated that the accused had mainly provided what it termed 'moral assistance' to the war crimes committed. Moral assistance can be provided, in some circumstances, in the form of technical advice or knowledge that results in im-

---

[114] Germany, Case 5-3 StE 6/10 (2015) (www.legal-tools.org/doc/af8e31/).

[115] This form of liability is not contained in the regular Criminal Code but in special legislation dealing with international crimes, namely the Völkerstrafgesetzbuch (www.legal-tools.org/doc/fa8c3f/). It states the following in Section 4 (while Section 13 of the same act provides more detail): "(1) A military commander or civilian superior who omits to prevent his or her subordinate from committing an offence pursuant to this Act shall be punished in the same way as a perpetrator of the offence committed by that subordinate. Section 13 subsection (2) of the Criminal Code shall not apply in this case. (2) Any person effectively giving orders or exercising command and control in a unit shall be deemed equivalent to a military commander. Any person effectively exercising command and control in a civil organisation or in an enterprise shall be deemed equivalent to a civilian superior".

[116] See Germany, Case 5-3 StE 6/10 (2015), part 4, sec. A.2.c.

[117] *Ibid.*, part 4, secs. A.2.d and A.4.

[118] For the general principles regarding aiding and abetting, see *supra* note 108.

proved prospects for a successful execution of the act, but that was not the case here. However, the case law also recognises the possibility of psychological assistance, which reinforces the will and decision of the principal actor to commit the act. The accused provided such psychological assistance by declaring, in interviews, memoranda, and press releases, that he was prepared to deny or minimise the war crimes ordered by the FOCA leadership. Through this public propaganda, he helped the FOCA leadership conceal the war crimes in order to prevent stronger intervention by the United Nations against the FDLR and the punishment of those responsible for the war crimes.[119]

8.5.   Sweden

8.5.1.   Overview of Cases

In Sweden, 11 persons have been convicted and imprisoned in 10 cases, seven of those cases based on universal jurisdiction and the other three based on active personality jurisdiction.

8.5.1.1.   Torture in Bosnia

On 18 December 2006, Jackie Arklöv, a Swedish national, was sentenced to 8 years in prison for crimes committed in Bosnia and Herzegovina in 1993.[120] He was found guilty of the torture of 11 prisoners of war and civilians and was ordered to pay compensation to the victims. The acts of torture and mistreatment that Arklöv admitted to included, among others, seriously abusing a man and later forcing him to walk through a minefield littered with dead bodies, and forcing a pregnant woman down on her knees and placing his gun barrel into her mouth, threatening to kill both her and her unborn baby while the other soldiers kicked her in the back repeatedly. Earlier, on 8 September 1995, he had been convicted by a Bosnian court for war crimes committed against prisoners of war and civilians and sentenced to 13 years in prison. However, this sentence was later reduced to 8 years due to Arklöv's young age. In an exchange of prisoners, organised by the Swedish Red Cross, he returned to Sweden, where he was acquitted for lack of evidence. However, in 2004 the Swedish authorities reopened the investigations regarding the alleged war

---

[119]   See Germany, Case 5-3 StE 6/10 (2015), part 4, sec. 5.b.

[120]   District Court of Stockholm, Case of Arklöv, Judgment, 18 December 2006 (www.legal-tools.org/doc/9672e6/).

crimes in Bosnia thanks to new testimonies, and on 10 November 2006 new proceedings began in which Arklöv pleaded guilty. A new investigation was carried out in 2007 regarding further alleged war crimes committed by Arklöv in Bosnia, but due to lack of evidence no new charges were brought against him.[121]

8.5.1.2.   Inhuman Treatment in Bosnia

On 12 January 2010, a 43-year-old man from Bosnia and Herzegovina, Ahmet Makitan, was apprehended on suspicion of having committed grave breaches of the 1949 Geneva Conventions in Bosnia and Herzegovina in 1992. Makitan, a Swedish citizen by the time of his arrest, had been a camp guard at the Dretelj detention camp, which was established by the Croat armed forces in May 1992 for Serb prisoners in Dretelj near Èapljin; he participated in the detention, torture, and murder of civilian Bosnian Serbs between May and August 1992. His trial began on 13 October 2010 and ended on 21 March 2011, and he was sentenced to 5 years' imprisonment on 8 April 2011 for being a perpetrator. His acts consisted of complicity in hostage taking and complicity in creating brutal and unlawful conditions for the prisoners, as well having exposed them to torture and inhuman and degrading treatment by violating their personal human dignity.[122]

8.5.1.3.   Crimes against Humanity in Kosovo

On 7 September 2011, Milić Martinović, a 34-year-old Serb arrested in Sweden, was charged with aggravated crimes against humanity against 29 civilians, namely murder, attempted murder, aggravated robbery, and aggravated arson, in connection with a massacre in Ćuška in Kosovo. He was sentenced to life imprisonment on 20 January 2012, but this was overturned on 19 December 2012 by an appeals court, which held there was no proof that he had been involved in the massacre.[123]

---

[121]   See TRIAL International page on Arklöv (available on its web site).

[122]   See District Court of Stockholm, Case of Makitan, Judgment, 8 April 2011 (www.legal-tools.org/doc/e83399/); TRIAL International page on Makitan (available on its web site).

[123]   District Court of Stockholm, Case of Martinović, Judgment, 20 January 2012 (www.legal-tools.org/doc/be8892/); Svea Court of Appeal, Case of Martinović, Judgment, 19 December 2012 (www.legal-tools.org/doc/be8892/); TRIAL International page on Martinović (available on its web site).

8.5.1.4. Genocide in Rwanda

On 22 December 2011, a suspect in the Rwandan genocide, Stanislas Mbanenande, was arrested, and trial proceedings began in November 2012. Mbanenande was accused of having participated in killings that formed part of the genocide between 12 and 16 April 1994, when over 100 persons fled up Ruhiro mountain in the southern part of Kibuye. In relation to some of the charges surrounding the massacres in a neighbour-hood in Kibuye, the court held that the prosecutor had not presented enough evidence for a conviction. Mbanenande received a life sentence after being convicted on 20 June 2013, which was upheld on appeal on 19 June 2014.[124]

8.5.1.5. Genocide, Murder, Attempted Murder, and Kidnapping in Rwanda

On 24 September 2014, Claver Berinkindi and another suspect, both originally from Rwanda, were arrested in Sweden for their alleged participation in the genocide in southern Rwanda. On 26 September 2014 the other suspect was released, while Berinkindi was held in prison awaiting trial. Between 18 April and 31 May 1994, Berinkindi allegedly led attacks and participated in the killings of ethnic Tutsis. He was involved in attacks in five different locations, including the village of Nyamiyaga and the surrounding area in the prefecture of Butare in Rwanda. Berinkindi was one of the leaders of attacks on a municipal building in the municipality of Muyira and a nearby school that killed thousands: some of the victims were buried alive, and others were killed with guns, spears, clubs, and machetes. Berinkindi also was involved in attacks on Nyamure mountain that killed families who had sheltered people fleeing the mass violence. On that basis, Berinkindi was accused of murder, incitement to murder, attempted murder, and abduction as genocide. His trial started on 16 September 2015, and he was convicted and given a life sentence on 16 May 2016 for genocide and gross crimes under international law consisting of

---

[124] See District Court of Stockholm, Case of Mbanenande, Judgment, 20 June 2013 (www. legal-tools.org/doc/51756c/); Svea Court of Appeal, Case of Mbanenande, Judgment, Case Nr B 6659-13, 19 June 2014 (www.legal-tools.org/doc/66279c/); also see TRIAL International page on Mbanenande (available on its web site).

murder, kidnapping, and attempted murder.[125] His conviction was upheld on 15 February 2017.[126]

8.5.1.6. War Crimes in Syria[127]

On 26 February 2015, Mouhannad Droubi, who had received asylum in Sweden in 2013, was sentenced to 5 years in prison after being convicted of the war crime of attacking an enemy who is *hors de combat*, as well as of particularly grave assault by abusing a captured member of the armed forces of the Assad government. Droubi was part of a group connected to the Free Syrian Army, and he and other members beat a prisoner and posted a video of the abuse on Facebook. On 26 February 2016, the court of appeals overturned the decision of first instance and ordered a new trial, after the previously unknown victim had been tracked down by a Swedish journalist and had brought new evidence before the court. On 11 May 2016, the district court overturned the war crime conviction after it emerged that the victim was not a pro-regime soldier, as previously thought, but a member of the Free Syrian Army, like Droubi himself. Since there appeared to be no link between the beatings and the ongoing armed conflict in Syria, Droubi was sentenced under Swedish law instead of international law. The court sentenced Droubi to 7 years' imprisonment for aggravated assault. It also ordered his deportation as soon as he had served his sentence and banned him from Sweden for life.[128] On 5 August 2016, the court of appeals overturned this decision, holding that the crime in question should be characterised as a war crime and as aggravated assault. It sentenced Droubi to 8 years in prison, to be followed by deportation and banning from the country for life.[129]

---

[125] See District Court of Stockholm, Case of Berinkindi, Judgment, 16 May 2016 (www.legal-tools.org/doc/baac2c/). Also see TRIAL International page on Berinkindi (available on its web site).

[126] Svea Court of Appeal, Case of Berinkindi, Judgment, 15 February 2017 (www.legal-tools.org/doc/3936b6/).

[127] For a general overview of the investigations and prosecutions with respect to atrocities committed in Syria, see Human Rights Watch, 2017, *supra* note 98.

[128] See District Court of Huddinge, Case of Droubi, Judgment, 11 May 2016 (www.legal-tools.org/doc/59def0/).

[129] See Svea Court of Appeal, Case of Droubi, Judgment, 5 August 2016 (www.legal-tools.org/doc/a3f045/); TRIAL International, *Make Way for Justice #3*, 2017, pp. 50–51, see *supra* note 9.

8.5.1.7. Terrorist Crimes in Syria

On 14 December 2015, two Swedish nationals, Hassan al-Mandlawi, 32, and Al-Amin Sultan, 30, were sentenced to life in prison for terrorist crimes in Syria in 2013 and for assisting in illegitimate executions. They were found guilty of a number of terror offences, including taking part in the beheading of two prisoners in the Syrian city of Aleppo in April 2013. Although the two did not wield the knife used in the executions, the court ruled that evidence demonstrated they were instrumental in the killings. Al-Mandlawi is alleged to have held down the legs of one of the victims in the video, while the pair instructed others to go ahead with the killings in Swedish.[130]

8.5.1.8. War Crimes in Iraq

In September 2016, Iraqi national Raed Abdulkareem was charged with committing a war crime for allegedly posing with dead bodies of Islamic State fighters in Iraq. The authorities had discovered incriminating photos during a separate investigation into a robbery, for which he was serving a 42-month sentence; he admitted to being in the photos but denied any wrongdoing, claiming he had been forced to pose for them. On 6 December 2016, he was found guilty of war crimes and sentenced to 6 months' imprisonment, which was increased to 9 months on appeal.[131]

8.5.1.9. Murder and War Crimes in Syria

On 16 February 2017, the Stockholm District Court sentenced a 46-year-old Syrian citizen, Haisam Omar Sakhanh, for participation in a mass execution of seven people that took place in Idlib Province in northwestern Syria in May 2012. The defendant had been a member of the Islamist armed group Suleiman Company (Firqat Suleiman el-Muqatila) and had shot one of the victims with an assault rifle. The defendant's objection, that the execution was carried out by order and related to the enforcement

---

[130] See District Court of Gothenburg, Case of al-Mandlawi and Sultan, Judgment, 14 December 2015 (www.legal-tools.org/doc/4f54c1/); "ISIS Syria Beheading Video: Two Swedish Nationals Jailed for Islamic State Execution in Aleppo", *International Business Times*, 14 December 2015 (available on its web site).

[131] See District Court of Blekinge, Case of Abdulkareem, Judgment, 6 December 2016 (www.legal-tools.org/doc/860452/); TRIAL International, *Make Way for Justice #3*, 2017, p. 52, see *supra* note 9. For the appeal decision, see Sweden, Scania and Blekinge Court of Appeal, B-3187-16, 11 April 2017 (www.legal-tools.org/doc/897810/).

of an adjudicated death sentence by a legitimate court following a fair trial, was not accepted by the Swedish court. The execution, undertaken in violation of international humanitarian law, was held to be a serious crime against the law of nations. The defendant was sentenced to life imprisonment, which was upheld on appeal.[132]

8.5.1.10. War Crimes in Syria

On 14 September 2017, Swedish prosecutors brought charges against Mohamed Abdoullah for violating the personal dignity of five dead and severely injured persons in Syria. On 25 September 2017, he was sentenced to 8 months in prison.[133]

8.5.2. Forms of Liability: Common Analysis

In Sweden, there is no general provision setting out all the different forms of liability for participation, but liability for direct perpetration is implicitly described in the specific descriptions of crimes. However, Chapter 23 of the Swedish Criminal Code[134] contains provisions related to most forms of 'partial' participation, which relate both to the preparatory phases of a crime, such as attempt,[135] preparation,[136] and conspiracy,[137] and to

---

[132] See Stockholms Tingsrätt, "Mass Execution in Syria Is Assessed to Be a Serious Crime against the Law of Nations and Results in Life Imprisonment", 16 February 2017 (available on its web site). For the appeal decision, see Sweden, Stockholm City Court, B3787-16, 16 February 2017 (www.legal-tools.org/doc/e5c4ef/). See also "On the Establishment of Courts in Non-international Armed Conflict by Non-state Actors: Stockholm District Court Judgment of 16 February 2017", in *Journal of International Criminal Justice*, 2018, vol. 16, no. 2, pp. 403–424. Also see TRIAL International, *Make Way for Justice #4*, 2018, p. 73, *supra* note 9.

[133] See District Court of Södertörn, Case of Abdullah, Judgment, 25 September 2017 (www.legal-tools.org/doc/6a513a/). TRIAL International, *Make Way for Justice #4*, 2018, p. 74, *supra* note 9. See also Network for Investigation and Prosecution of Genocide, Crimes against Humanity and War Crimes, *Prosecuting War Crimes of Outrage upon Personal Dignity Based on Evidence from Open Sources: Legal Framework and Recent Developments in the Member States of the European Union*, The Hague, February 2018, pp. 15–16 (www.legal-tools.org/doc/2424e4/).

[134] Swedish Criminal Code, 21 December 1962 (www.legal-tools.org/doc/996a70/).

[135] Chapter 23, sec. 1.

[136] Chapter 23, sec. 2, which refers to "a person who, with the intention of committing or promoting a crime, presents or receives money or anything else as pre-payment or payment for the crime or who procures, constructs, gives, receives, keeps, conveys or engages in any other similar activity with poison, explosive, weapon, picklock, falsification tool or other such means".

'indirect participation' that might take place both before and at the completion stage, such as instigation[138] and complicity. The latter form of personal liability is explained in the sentencing provision, which states:

> Punishment as provided for an act in this Code shall be imposed not only on the person who committed the act but also on anyone who furthered it by advice or deed.[139]

Most universal crimes cases in Sweden have attributed personal liability under provisions dealing with violations of international humanitarian law (Chapter 22, section 6) combined with specific crimes, such as murder or assault (Chapter 3) or crimes involving public danger (Chapter 13). The last sentence of Chapter 22, section 6, also contains an abbreviated form of command responsibility.

Of the 10 cases mentioned above, liability for participation was discussed in six of them, almost all of which dealt with perpetration or joint perpetration at the execution phase.

In the Martinović case, it was found that all the soldiers/policemen had participated in upholding the atmosphere of violence, threats, and control necessary for executing the crimes. They acted jointly and in concert. Martinović was one of the soldiers, and he participated with knowledge of the common criminal plan and himself executed concrete parts of the plan; as a result he was considered a perpetrator responsible for murder and attempted murder, in addition to hostage taking, grave robbery, and grave fire for the purpose of murder.

In the Mbanenande case, the court of first instance considered the accused to be a person with a minor and informal leadership role, who acted in collaboration with others in the attacks against Tutsis. He had participated in the attacks by, for example, commanding and organising groups of perpetrators and encouraging them to attack Tutsis. He had committed these crimes jointly and in collusion with other perpetrators, and as a result of these actions he was considered a direct perpetrator for murder and attempted murder when shooting at people, as well as being

---

[137] *Ibid.*, with the following definition: "by conspiracy is meant that someone decides on the act in collusion with another as well as that someone undertakes or offers to execute it or seeks to incite another to do so".

[138] Chapter 23, sec. 4.

[139] *Ibid.*

complicit in murder, attempted murder, incitement to murder, and abduction.

In the al-Mandlawi and Sultan case, the accused were both present at the killing event, although they did not execute the beheading themselves. The judgment at first instance discussed whether they should be perceived as perpetrators, inciters, or accomplices. Based upon a holistic assessment, they were considered joint perpetrators in accordance with the extended notion of perpetration under Swedish law. The court considered their concrete forms or factors of participation according to the three films of the event, which were central to the facts of the case. Taking into account that they assisted and abetted the executors and played an active role in the criminal enterprise, the court concluded that they were (joint) perpetrators. This reasoning provides at the same time a good illustration of the often quite pragmatic or practical way of attributing specific forms of personal liability in domestic universal crimes cases.

In the same vein, in the Berinkindi case, the first-level court came to the conclusion that the accused through his acts played such an active and central role in the execution of the criminal acts that he was to be considered a co-perpetrator. In the Droubi case, the August 2016 court of appeals did not discuss modes of participation in great detail, as it was clear that Droubi was a direct executor (perpetrator) of the violence and acted together with others who also were direct executors, which was the same conclusion reached in the 2015 judgment at first instance.

Lastly, in the Sakhanh case, the accused was considered to have taken part in the execution squad jointly with others and to have fired at least six shots with an automatic gun, hitting one of the victims in body and head. He was also held responsible for the prior ill-treatment of the victims, although it is not clear from the judgment whether the accused personally had ill-treated anybody. He thus seems to have been held, in reality, responsible for 'joint perpetration' of international crimes that could well have been classified as war crimes, consisting of murder and ill-treatment of prisoners.

8.6. France

8.6.1. Overview of Cases

In France, there have been six convictions in five cases for international crimes, all based on universal jurisdiction.

8.6.1.1.   Torture in Mauritania

On 1 July 2005, Ely Ould Dah, a Mauritanian army captain, was sentenced *in absentia* to 10 years' imprisonment for torture in Mauritania in 1990 and 1991. Ould Dah had been in France when the investigation was opened, but he managed to flee to Mauritania during a conditional release. His complaint against this conviction to the European Court of Human Rights was declared inadmissible on 30 March 2009. The background of the case was that his crimes were conducted in the context of clashes between Mauritanians of Arab-Berber origin and others belonging to black African ethnic groups; some servicemen from these ethnic groups, accused of mounting a coup d'état, were taken prisoner, and some of them were subjected to acts of torture or barbarity by their guards. Among these guards was Ould Dah, an intelligence officer at the Nouakchott army headquarters in Mauritania, holding the rank of lieutenant. He was found to be responsible for having been complicit by ordering or instructing the torture of two black Mauritanian soldiers, Mamadou Diagana and Ousmane Dia, and to have participated in these acts.[140]

8.6.1.2.   Torture and Disappearances in Argentina

The second person convicted was Alfredo Astiz, an Argentine captain, convicted *in absentia* to life imprisonment for aiding and abetting and ordering the torture and disappearance of two French nuns, Alice Domon and Léonie Duquet, in 1990, based on application of the passive personality principle rather than universal jurisdiction.[141]

8.6.1.3.   Torture in Tunisia

On 15 December 2008, Khaled Ben Saïd, the former vice consul of Tunisia based in Strasbourg and a former police superintendent in Jendouba, Tunisia, was sentenced *in absentia* to 8 years' imprisonment for complici-

---

[140] For the first instance decision, see Fédération internationale des ligues des droits de l'homme ('FIDH'), "Mauritanie: Affaire Ely Ould Dah", 2005, pp. 49–55 (www.legal-tools.org/doc/858813/). For the decision by the Court of Cassation, see Cour de cassation chambre criminelle, no. de pourvoi 02-85379 (www.legal-tools.org/doc/cb459b/). For the ECHR decision, see ECHR, *Ould Dah v. France*, Decision, 13113/03, 17 March 2009 (www.legal-tools.org/doc/6c588a/).

[141] See Cour d'Assises de Paris, Case of Astiz, Judgment, 16 March 1990 (www.legal-tools.org/doc/888d10/); also see TRIAL International page on Astiz (available on its web site).

ty by giving instructions to commit torture.[142] The appeal resulted in his term of imprisonment being increased to 12 years on 24 September 2010.[143]

8.6.1.4.   Genocide and Crimes against Humanity in Rwanda

Pascal Simbikangwa was convicted on 14 March 2014 for his involvement in the Rwanda genocide and sentenced to 25 years' imprisonment for the commission of genocide and complicity in crimes against humanity. It was shown that he supplied arms to the Interahamwe, an extremist Hutu militia, as they were manning the barriers in Kigali, and gave instructions to them to kill Tutsis.[144] This ruling was upheld on appeal on 3 December 2016.[145]

On 30 May 2014, the case of Octavien Ngenzi and Tito Barahira, two former Rwandan mayors, was referred by the investigative judge to the criminal court; this referral was appealed by the suspects but was dismissed on 28 January 2015. They were eventually convicted, on 6 July 2016, of direct participation in genocide and crimes against humanity, committed in Kabarondo in the prefecture of Kibungo.[146]

---

[142] Cour d'Assises du Bas-Rhin, Case of Ben Saïd, Judgment, 15 December 2008 (www.legal-tools.org/doc/48acce/).

[143] See Cour d'Assises de la Meurthe et Moselle, Case of Ben Saïd, Judgment, 24 September 2010 (www.legal-tools.org/doc/682080/); TRIAL International page on Ben Saïd (available on its web site). Also see FIDH, *Condamnation de Khaled Ben Saïd: Une victoire contre l'impunité en Tunisie*, 2010 at pp. 67–69 for the first instance decision (as well as report by investigative judge at pp. 51–66), and pp. 70–72 for the appeal decision (www.legal-tools.org/doc/f63173/).

[144] Paris Cour d'assises, Judgment 13/0033, *Affaire Pascal Senyamuhara Safari alias Pascal Simbikangwa* (www.legal-tools.org/doc/c04bcc/). For an analysis of the case, see Helen L. Trouille, "France, Universal Jurisdiction and Rwandan *génocidaires*: The *Simbikangwa* Trial", in *Journal of International Criminal Justice*, 2016, vol. 14, no. 1, pp. 202–8.

[145] Cour d'Assises de la Seine-Saint-Denis, *Affaire Pascal Senyamuhara Safari alias Pascal Simbikangwa*, Judgment, 3 December 2016 (www.legal-tools.org/doc/07161c/).

[146] See TRIAL International page on Ngenzi (available on its web site); Cour d'Assises de Paris, Case of Ngenzi and Barahirwa, Judgment, 7 July 2016 (www.legal-tools.org/doc/b74c0f/). The verdict as well as the sentence of life imprisonment was upheld on appeal on 6 July 2018; see "Paris Court Hands Life Sentence to Ngenzi and Barahira", *KT Press*, 7 July 2018.

8.6.2. Forms of Liability: Common Analysis

The provisions with respect to liability are set out in Article 121 of the French Criminal Code,[147] of which the most relevant sections are as follows:

> Article 121-4
>
> The perpetrator of an offence is the person who:
>
> 1° commits the criminally prohibited act;
>
> 2° attempts to commit a felony or, in the cases provided for by Statute, a misdemeanour.
>
> Article 121-5
>
> An attempt is committed where, being demonstrated by a beginning of execution, it was suspended or failed to achieve the desired effect solely through circumstances independent of the perpetrator's will.
>
> Article 121-6
>
> The accomplice to the offence, in the meaning of article 121-7, is punishable as a perpetrator.
>
> Article 121-7
>
> The accomplice to a felony or a misdemeanour is the person who knowingly, by aiding and abetting, facilitates its preparation or commission.
>
> Any person who, by means of a gift, promise, threat, order, or an abuse of authority or powers, provokes the commission of an offence or gives instructions to commit it, is also an accomplice.

France has also penalised membership acts as part of a concerted plan to commit the international crimes of genocide,[148] crimes against humanity,[149] and war crimes,[150] while doing the same for participation in a group formed or in an agreement established with a view to the preparation for committing a crime, as demonstrated by one or more material actions.[151]

---

[147] French Penal Code, 1 March 1994 (www.legal-tools.org/doc/01ab1f/).

[148] Article 211-1.

[149] Article 212-1.

[150] Article 212-2.

[151] Article 212-3.

None of the very short judgments above provides any analysis of forms of liability beyond stating the facts of the involvement as mentioned above. All of the cases – except the last one, based on direct participation in genocide and crimes against humanity – grounded the liability of the accused in Article 121-7, second paragraph, on various forms of basically indirect participation. This provision states that

> any person who, by means of a gift, promise, threat, order, or an abuse of authority or powers, provokes the commission of an offence or gives instructions to commit it, is also an accomplice.

It is noteworthy, however, that Article 121-6 qualifies an "accomplice" to be just as punishable as a "perpetrator".

Again, as observed in cases from other countries as well, domestic courts seem to take a quite pragmatic approach to attribution of liability, in this case also facilitated by broad, enumerative provisions on personal liability that make complicity and perpetration more or less equal.

8.7. Belgium

8.7.1. Overview of Cases

Since 2001, there have been four cases in Belgium, all related to the Rwandan genocide and all based on universal jurisdiction, which have led to eight people being convicted.

8.7.1.1. War Crimes in Rwanda

On 8 June 2001, the first universal jurisdiction case in Belgium resulted in the conviction of the "Butare Four" for war crimes. Sentences of between 12 and 20 years were handed down to Julienne Mukabutera, Consolata Mukangango, Vincent Ntezimana, and Alphonse Higaniro.[152] The charges all related to the commission of homicide, directly or indirectly, or attempted homicide of a number of named and unnamed persons.

---

[152] Cour d'Assises de Bruxelles, Case of Mukabutera, Mukangango, Ntezimana and Higaniro, Judgment, 8 June 2001 (www.legal-tools.org/doc/a70d94/).

On 29 June 2005, the half-brothers Etienne Nzabonimana and Samuel Ndashyikirwa were sentenced to 12 and 10 years respectively for murders as war crimes of Tutsis in Kirwa.[153]

8.7.1.2. Failed Trial in Case Concerned with War Crimes in Rwanda

The trial of Major Bernard Ntuyahaga began in April 2007. He was found guilty of the murder as a war crime of 10 Belgian peacekeepers and a number of civilians in Rwanda and was sentenced to 20 years in prison on 5 July 2007, although he was acquitted of the murder of the former prime minister of Rwanda, Agathe Uwilingiyimana, and of involvement in other massacres. His appeal was rejected on 12 December 2007.[154]

On 9 December 2009, Ephrem Nkezabera was convicted and sentenced to 30 years in prison on charges of violating international criminal law and committing war crimes for his role within the Interahamwe militia. On 6 January 2010, Nkezabera appealed this verdict but the sentence was upheld in his absence. On 1 March 2010, a higher court ruled that there should be a complete retrial in order to allow Nkezabera to attend the proceedings. He died of liver cancer on 24 May 2010, which put an end to all proceedings against him.[155]

8.7.2. Forms of Liability: Common Analysis

Articles 66–67 in the Belgian Criminal Code deal with liability as follows:[156]

> Article 66. Shall be punished as perpetrators of a crime or offence:
>
> Those who have completed or have directly cooperated in its execution;

---

[153] Cour d'Assises de l'Arrondissement Administratif de Bruxelles-Capitale, Case of Nzabonimana and Samuel Ndashyikirwa, Judgment, 29 June 2005 (www.legal-tools.org/doc/51c5bb/).

[154] Cour d'Assises de l'Arrondissement Administratif de Bruxelles-Capitale, Case of Ntuyahaga, Judgment, 5 July 2007 (www.legal-tools.org/doc/cd8233/).

[155] Cour d'Assises de Bruxelles, Case of Nkezabera, Judgment, 1 December 2009 (www.legal-tools.org/doc/cbb892/).

[156] Belgian Criminal Code, 8 June 1867 (www.legal-tools.org/doc/fda528/).

Those who, by any act whatsoever, have lent support to the execution such that, without their assistance, the crime or offence had not been committed;

Those who, by gifts, promises, threats, abuse of authority or power, machinations or culpable artifice, directly incited the crime or the offence;

(Those who, whether through speeches at meetings or in public places, or through written or printed texts, or any images or emblems, which have been displayed, distributed or sold, offered for sale or exposed to public view, have led directly to its commission, without prejudice to the penalties provided by law against the perpetrators of incitement to crime or offences, even if these provocations were not implemented).

Article 67. Shall be punished as accomplices to a crime or misdemeanour:

Those who have given instructions to commit it;

Those who procured weapons, instruments, or any other means used to commit the offence, knowing that they were to be used;

Those who, except as specified in paragraph 3 of Article 66, knowingly aided or abetted the perpetrator or perpetrators of the crime or offence in preparing, facilitating, or committing the offence.

The accused in the Butare Four case were all convicted of all the modes of liability set out in Articles 66 and 67 without further explanation of the legal parameters of these modes. The same approach was used in the Nzabonimana and Ndashyikirwa case and in the Ntuyahaga judgment. In the latter it was noted that the accused held military authority due to his superior rank in the Rwandan army and that he was respected in Rwanda's highly hierarchised society, but that in spite of this, he did not take any action within the limits of his authority as a senior officer to oppose the criminal acts to which he was a witness. The court held that he could not have been unaware, given his professional position and his presence at the scene, that Belgian soldiers were subjected to a veritable lynching, which lasted several hours.

The Ntuyahaga case provides yet another indication that domestic courts want to make sure that liability is attributable to the accused for the crimes that have taken place, but that detailed discussions of forms of liability may not be considered necessary under the factual circumstances of a given case.

8.8. Finland

8.8.1. Overview of Cases

8.8.1.1. Genocide in Rwanda

A Rwandan citizen, François Bazaramba, was arrested in Finland on 14 April 2007 and remanded in custody on suspicion of genocide. On 20 February 2009, the Finnish government decided not to extradite him to Rwanda, and on 1 June 2009 he was charged with genocide and murder. His trial started on 1 September 2009, and he was convicted on the genocide charge on 11 June 2010, receiving a life sentence. The court found that Bazaramba had facilitated the acquisition and distribution of materials used in torching Tutsi homes; in addition, the court said he had spread anti-Tutsi propaganda and incited killings by fomenting anger and contempt towards Tutsis. The court also agreed with the prosecution's claims that Bazaramba had organised roadblocks and night patrols to oppress the Tutsi population. Lastly, the court indicated that Bazaramba had directly ordered or urged others to kill five Tutsis.[157]

On 31 December 2010, another court decided there was no reason to order a retrial, and on 22 August 2011 the appeals hearing began. On 30 March 2012, the court of appeals found Bazaramba guilty of genocide and sentenced him to life imprisonment, which was confirmed again on appeal by the Supreme Court on 22 October 2012.[158]

8.8.1.2. Degrading a Corpse as a War Crime in Iraq

On 18 March 2016, an Iraqi man, Jebbar Salman Ammar, was given a 16-month suspended sentence in a rare war crime case where the defendant was found personally guilty of degrading the corpse of a deceased enemy soldier. The 29-year-old former member of an Iraqi paramilitary unit had posted pictures of himself and the severed head of an alleged Islamic State militant on his public Facebook page. Four days later, in an unrelated case,

---

[157] See Finland, District Court of Porvoos, Case of Basaramba, Judgment, Case R 09/404, 11 June 2010 (www.legal-tools.org/doc/f266fe/).

[158] See Supreme Court of Finland, Case of Basaramba, Judgment, 22 October 2012 (www.legal-tools.org/doc/00b95b/).

an Iraqi Shi'ite militiaman, Hadi Habeeb Hilal, was given a 13-month suspended sentence for the same crime.[159]

8.8.1.3. War Crimes, Murder, and Aggravated Assault in Iraq

In June 2014, 1,700 unarmed Iraqi army recruits were arrested at Camp Speicher near Tikrit, Iraq, by members of the Islamic State. The victims were laid on the ground and shot one by one. Two Iraqi twin brothers are alleged to have murdered 11 of them. On 24 May 2017, the District Court of Pirkanmaa acquitted the Iraqi twin brothers for lack of evidence.[160] They were granted compensation for their pre-trial detention and were allowed to reside in Finland. The prosecution has appealed this judgment.[161]

8.8.2. Forms of Liability: Common Analysis

Participation is regulated in the Finnish Criminal Code[162] in Chapter 5, sections 1 and 3–6, as follows:

> Section 1 – Attempt
>
> (1) An attempt of an offence is punishable only if the attempt has been denoted as punishable in a provision on an intentional offence.
>
> (2) An act has reached the stage of an attempt at an offence when the perpetrator has begun the commission of an offence and brought about the danger that the offence will be completed. An attempt at an offence is involved also when such a danger is not caused, but the fact that the danger is not brought about is due only to coincidental reasons.
>
> Section 3 – Complicity in an offence
>
> If two or more persons have committed an intentional offence together, each is punishable as a perpetrator.
>
> Section 4 – Commission of an offence through an agent

---

[159] See Finland, District Court of Pirkanmaa, Judgment, R 16/1304, 18 March 2016 (www.legal-tools.org/doc/96a1b2/) and Finland, District Court of Kanta-Häme, Judgment R 16/214, 22 March 2016 (www.legal-tools.org/doc/546cd9/).

[160] See Finland, District Court of Pirkanmaa, Judgment, 24 May 2017 (www.legal-tools.org/doc/b01bcf/).

[161] TRIAL International, *Make Way for Justice #4*, 2018, p. 20, see *supra* note 9.

[162] Finnish Criminal Code (www.legal-tools.org/doc/4b1a65/).

A person is sentenced as a perpetrator if he or she has committed an intentional offence by using, as an agent, another person who cannot be punished for said offence due to the lack of criminal responsibility or intention or due to another reason connected with the prerequisites for criminal liability.

Section 5 – Instigation

A person who intentionally persuades another person to commit an intentional offence or to make a punishable attempt of such an act is punishable for incitement to the offence as if he or she was the perpetrator.

Section 6 – Abetting

(1) A person who, before or during the commission of an offence, intentionally furthers the commission by another of an intentional act or of its punishable attempt, through advice, action or otherwise, shall be sentenced for abetting on the basis of the same legal provision as the perpetrator.

(2) Incitement to punishable aiding and abetting is punishable as aiding and abetting.

Command/superior responsibility is set out in Chapter 11, section 12.

Bazaramba was convicted for direct participation (perpetration) in the genocide, based on the following reasoning by the court:

[He] inflicted on Tutsis living in Maraba sector and its surroundings conditions of life calculated to bring about the physical destruction of the Rwandan Tutsis in whole or in part between 15 April 1994 and 31 May 1994 with the following acts:

(i) By giving a speech of incitement against the Tutsis in Birambo market square on Friday, 15 April 1994, Bazaramba disseminated anti-Tutsi propaganda and incited Hutus to kill by fomenting hatred and contempt of the Tutsi;

(ii) Bazaramba organised road blocks and night patrols established for the purpose of controlling the Tutsi and led this activity;

(iii) Bazaramba forced Tutsis to leave their homes;

(iv) Bazaramba acquired and distributed the supplies such as matches used in burning residential and other buildings owned by Tutsi, and incited and ordered Hutus to burn these buildings; and

(v) Bazaramba distributed among the Hutu movable and immovable property which had been left behind by the Tutsi or forcibly taken from them.[163]

The court also held that Bazaramba ordered and incited the murder of various other Tutsis.[164] There was no further legal discussion of these or other forms of participation. This indicates that the court was satisfied on the facts that the accused could be held responsible for participation in genocide and deserved a life sentence, and did not find it necessary to specify and distinguish in much detail the applicable forms of liability.

8.9. Austria

8.9.1. Overview of Cases

8.9.1.1. Acquittal of Murder and Genocide in Bosnia

Duško Cvjetković, a Bosnian Serb who had been charged with murder and genocide in Bosnia and Herzegovina, was acquitted by a jury of all charges on 13 July 1994. He had been charged with participating in the forcible transfer of two Muslim civilians to a detention camp in Kamenica, where they were repeatedly mistreated and subsequently murdered, and with assisting in the pillage and arson of houses in the Muslim part of Kućice.[165]

8.9.1.2. Murder/Attempted Murder/Arson in Bosnia

On 6 July 2016, a Bosnian Muslim with Austrian citizenship was convicted on 16 counts of murder, attempted murder, and arson and sentenced to 10 years' imprisonment for attacking the village of Serdari as part of a large group of Bosnian Muslims in September 1992. They killed 20 people, including six children, and set fire to six houses, apparently in revenge for Serb attacks.[166]

---

[163] See Finland, District Court of Porvoos, Case of Basaramba, Judgment.

[164] *Ibid.*, pp. 111–12.

[165] Supreme Court of Austria, Case of Cvjetković, Decision, Case 15Os99/94, 13 July 1994 (www.legal-tools.org/doc/44d3dc/).

[166] Regional Court of Linz, Judgment, 6 July 2016 (www.legal-tools.org/doc/d03778/). Associated Press, "Austrian Court Convicts Man of Murder during Bosnian War", 6 July 2016 (available on Fox News web site).

8.9.1.3. Membership in Rebel Group Committing Murder in Syria

On 10 November 2016, Austrian prosecutors charged a member of a Syrian rebel group with 20 counts of murder for allegedly executing wounded government soldiers in his home country; he was convicted on 11 May 2017 and sentenced to life imprisonment.[167]

8.9.2. Forms of Liability: Common Analysis

Participation is regulated by Sections 12 and 13 of the Austrian Criminal Code,[168] which states:

> § 12. Not only the immediate perpetrator commits the offense, but also anyone who induces another to carry it out, or who otherwise contributes to its execution.

> § 13. If several persons were involved in the act, each of them is to be punished according to his guilt.

Attempt is set out in Section 15, which states:

> § 15. (1) Criminal liability for intentional crimes is not only applicable for the completed act, but also for attempt and for every participation in an attempt.

> (2) The act is attempted as soon as the perpetrator has made his decision to execute it or to induce another (Section 12) through an act immediately preceding the execution.

There was no discussion of participation in the Cvjetković case, as the charges were dismissed on jurisdictional grounds.

8.10. Norway

8.10.1. Overview of Cases

8.10.1.1. War Crimes in Bosnia

On 10 July 2008, charges of rape, torture, illegal internment of civilians, and crimes against humanity were laid against Mirsad Repak, a 41-year-old Norwegian citizen who came from Bosnia and Herzegovina as an asylum seeker in 1993. According to the charges, in 1992 Repak was a member of the paramilitary Croatian Defence Forces ('HOS'), in the Dretelj detention camp in Bosnia and Herzegovina, holding a middle leader posi-

---

[167] Regional Court of Innsbruck, Judgment, 11 May 2017 (www.legal-tools.org/doc/abee9a/); TRIAL International, *Make Way for Justice #4*, 2018, p. 14, see *supra* note 9.

[168] Austrian Criminal Code, 23 January 1974 (www.legal-tools.org/doc/15e0cd/).

tion in the unit. Serbian civilians were detained in the Dretelj camp and held in inhuman conditions, suffering mistreatment and rape; Repak assisted in depriving civilian Serbs of their liberty and was also involved in the interrogation and torture of a woman detained in the camp. The court came to the following conclusion:

> At the Dretelj camp the number of detainees increased gradually. In August 1992 there were some 130 male and some 90 female detainees in the camp, with an average age of about 50 years. Many of the detainees in the camp were subjected to very serious physical and psychological abuse. At least two killings took place. Several of the female detainees were subjected to rape – some of them a number of times. There was also sexual abuse committed against male detainees. A number of detainees were subjected to torture and other kinds of abuse during their stay there. Many suffered persistent injury. Degrading acts also took place, like detainees having to crawl on their hands and feet, eat grass and make animal sounds.[169]

Repak's trial started on 27 August 2008, and he was convicted and sentenced to 5 years' imprisonment on 2 December 2008, although the recently amended universal crimes legislation was held to be partially unconstitutional, with respect to retroactivity. Instead the ordinary provisions on serious common crimes were applied to the facts of the case.

On 8 March 2010, an appellate court found Repak guilty again of most of the war crimes committed, but he was acquitted on one count while the unconstitutionality of the legislation was upheld. He was sentenced to four and a half years' imprisonment on 12 April 2010. The Supreme Court confirmed the unconstitutionality of the retroactive universal crimes legislation on 3 December 2010 but still increased the sentence to 8 years on 14 April 2011 based on applicable common crimes provisions.[170] It is, however, noteworthy that the Supreme Court only decided that retroactive application of the 2008 universal crimes legislation would be contrary to Section 97 of the Norwegian Constitution, not that such

---

[169] Norway, Oslo District Court, Case 08-018985MED-OTIR/08, 2 December 2008, para. 115 (www.legal-tools.org/doc/19cd6d/).

[170] Borgarting Court of Appeal, Case of Repak, Judgment, Case LB-2009-24039, 12 April 2010 (www.legal-tools.org/doc/6fd75f/). Supreme Court of Norway, Case of Repak, Judgment, Case HR-2010-2057-P, 3 December 2010 (www.legal-tools.org/doc/188d4b/).

retroactive application would be contrary to ICL or international human rights, including the European Convention on Human Rights and the International Covenant on Civil and Political Rights. (It would clearly not have been contrary to international law to apply recognised law on war crimes, crimes against humanity, and genocide.)

8.10.1.2. Genocide in Rwanda

On 4 May 2011 Sadi Bugingo was arrested for acts relating to genocide and complicity to commit genocide in Rwanda. His trial started on 25 September 2012, and he was convicted to 21 years' imprisonment on 14 February 2013 for complicity to multiple instances of murder (he could not be convicted for genocide due to the non-applicability of the retroactive universal crimes legislation). The ruling was upheld on appeal on 16 January 2015.[171]

8.10.2. Forms of Liability: Common Analysis

Like Sweden, Norway does not have a general overarching provision dealing with forms of participation in the executive phase, as such forms, mostly aiding and abetting, are set out for each individual crime in the Norwegian Criminal Code.[172] There is a general provision addressing attempt in Section 49. However, in the new Criminal Code of 2005, in force from 1 October 2015, there is a general, brief provision on complicity,[173] which states that "a criminal law provision applies also to a person who contributes to the crime, unless otherwise provided".[174] In addition, as in Sweden, there is an overarching provision dealing with one aspect of preparatory commission, namely attempt,[175] as well a section dealing in general with superior responsibility[176] and instigation.[177]

---

[171] Borgarting Court of Appeal, Case of Bugingo, Judgment, Case LB-2013-41556, 16 January 2015 (www.legal-tools.org/doc/d0cc92/).

[172] Norwegian Criminal Code, 22 May 1902 (www.legal-tools.org/doc/a15cdd/). See also Marina Aksenova, *Complicity in International Criminal Law*, Hart, Oxford, 2016, p. 47.

[173] Section 15. For an overview, see Jorn Jacobson, "Norway: Three Codes, Three (Somewhat) Different Solutions", blog of James G. Stewart, 8 October 2017 (www.legal-tools.org/doc/4d020e/).

[174] Authors' translation.

[175] Sections 49–51.

[176] Section 139, third subsection.

[177] Section 140.

In the Repak case, where the common criminal law provisions were applied, the court found that the defendant had contributed to an unlawful arrest leading to a deprivation of liberty, resulting in liability under Criminal Code Section 223, second subsection, which holds liable a person who unlawfully deprives another a person of his liberty or aids or abets in such deprivation of liberty.[178] The court also found that he arrested and participated in the transport of another victim, resulting in a violation of the same provision.[179] He was acquitted of the other charges, including torture and rape, because he had neither the intention to carry out the torture nor any knowledge of a rape subsequent to the unlawful arrest.

With respect to the Bugingo case, the court was of the view that the accused

> contributed to the killing of about 1,000 people who had sought refuge in the municipality of Birenga, that he contributed to the killing of hundreds of people who had applied for refuge at Economat, and that he contributed to killing at least eight people who had applied for refuge at the hospital in Kibungo. The killings were carefully planned and the defendants undoubtedly acted in concert. He was one of several local leaders in Kibungo who supported and participated in the genocide. The killings were committed at short intervals, and were part of the genocide in Rwanda. The accused will subsequently be convicted of violation of Section 233 of the Criminal Code, first and second paragraphs.[180]

Section 233 deals with homicide either directly or as an aider or abettor. Neither case reviewed here provides more details on the legal nature of 'aiding and abetting' (complicity) as applied to the facts. Again, we see that domestic courts are either not aware of or do not find it necessary to engage in legal discussions of what may – or may not – constitute (different forms of) punishable participation in international criminal law.

---

[178] Judgment, paras. 126, 132, and 149 (www.legal-tools.org/doc/19cd6d/).

[179] *Ibid.*, paras. 155, 163, 180, 187, 194, 201, 233, and 248.

[180] Norway, Oslo District Court, Case 12–106377MED-OTIR/03, 15 February 2013, p. 26, section 5.7, Authors' translation (www.legal-tools.org/doc/e6c9be/).

8.11. Switzerland

8.11.1. Overview of Cases

In Switzerland, two cases went to trial in the late 1990s, resulting in one conviction.

8.11.1.1. Acquittal of War Crimes in Bosnia

Goran Grabez was charged with having committed war crimes against prisoners of the Omarska and Keratem camps in Bosnia and Herzegovina between May and August 1992, by personally severely beating prisoners and by offending their human dignity. He was acquitted on 18 April 1997 for lack of evidence,[181] which was upheld on appeal on 5 September 1997. The appeal ruling only discussed the issue of damages to be awarded to the accused.[182]

8.11.1.2. Genocide in Rwanda

In July 1998, Fulgence Niyonteze was charged with war crimes, crimes against humanity, and genocide for his involvement in Rwandan genocide. He had been the burgomaster of Mushubati, Rwanda, in 1994, and he was charged with inciting the population to kill Tutsis and moderate Hutus, ordering military personnel to kill civilians, and encouraging refugees to go back to their homes, with the intention of having them killed and taking their property. The Military Court of First Instance found the defendant guilty of murder, attempted murder, and grave breaches of the Geneva Conventions and sentenced him to life imprisonment.[183] On 26 May 2000 an appeals court reduced the sentence to 14 years,[184] which was upheld on a further appeal on 27 April 2001.[185]

---

[181] Switzerland, Lausanne Military Tribunal Division I, Case of "G", Judgment, 18 April 1997 (www.legal-tools.org/doc/d3c048/).

[182] Switzerland, Tribunal Militaire de Cassation, Case of "G", Judgment, 5 September 1997 (www.legal-tools.org/doc/08fb2f/).

[183] Lausanne Military Tribunal Division II, Case of Niyonteze, Judgment, 30 April 1999 (www.legal-tools.org/doc/bb9da0/).

[184] Geneva Military Appeals Tribunal, Case of Niyonteze, Judgment, 26 May 2000 (www.legal-tools.org/doc/fe2edc/).

[185] High Military Appeals Court, Case of Niyonteze, Judgment, 27 April 2001 (www.legal-tools.org/doc/ac0342/). See TRIAL International page on Niyonteze (available on its web site).

8.11.2. Forms of Liability: Common Analysis

Criminal liability is regulated in Articles 22 and 24–25 of the Swiss Criminal Code,[186] as follows:

> Article 22
>
> 1. If, having embarked on committing a felony or misdemeanour, the offender does not complete the criminal act or if the result required to complete the act is not or cannot be achieved, the court may reduce the penalty.
>
> 2. If the offender fails to recognise through a serious lack of judgement that the act cannot under any circumstances be completed due to the nature of the objective or the means used to achieve it, no penalty is imposed.
>
> Article 24
>
> 1. Any person who has wilfully incited another to commit a felony or a misdemeanour, provided the offence is committed, incurs the same penalty as applies to the person who has committed the offence.
>
> 2. Any person who attempts to incite someone to commit a felony incurs the penalty applicable to an attempt to commit that felony.
>
> Article 25
>
> Any person who wilfully assists another to commit a felony or a misdemeanour is liable to a reduced penalty.
>
> Article 26
>
> If criminal liability is established or increased by a special obligation on the part of the offender, a participant is liable to a reduced penalty.

In the Grabez case,[187] no forms of liability were discussed, as the allegations were based on personal involvement while the accused was also acquitted.

While in the Niyonteze case there was an iteration of the facts leading to the legal conclusion that he had incited persons to kill Tutsis, there was no legal discussion with respect to the parameters of forms of liability at the two appeal stages.

---

[186] Swiss Criminal Code, 21 December 1937 (www.legal-tools.org/doc/8204e0/).

[187] Switzerland, Tribunal Militaire de Cassation, Case of "G", Judgment, 5 September 1997.

8.12. United Kingdom

8.12.1. Overview of Cases

8.12.1.1. Conspiracy to Torture and Hostage Taking in Afghanistan

The first prosecution using universal jurisdiction in the UK was against Afghan militia leader Faryadi Zardad.[188] On 18 July 2005, a jury convicted him of conspiracy to torture and hostage taking committed in Afghanistan between 1992 and 1996 and sentenced him to 20 years' imprisonment. Zardad had been in charge of a checkpoint between Kabul and Pakistan where his subordinates committed torture, murder, and other atrocities for which he was found to be responsible; his appeal was rejected on 7 February 2007.[189]

8.12.1.2. Acquittal of Conspiracy to Torture during Civil War in Nepal

On 4 January 2013, a Nepalese army officer, Colonel Kumar Lama, was arrested and charged with two counts of conspiracy to torture during his country's civil war in 2005. His trial began on 24 February 2015, but he was acquitted of all charges on 7 September 2016.[190]

8.12.2. Forms of Liability: Common Analysis

The main forms of liability applicable are aiding and abetting, counselling, procuring, incitement, and conspiracy, although British law also knows notions such as co-perpetrator (including through another person, called innocent agency) and common purpose/joint enterprise.[191]

Aiding and abetting is described as follows:

> Whosoever shall aid, abet, counsel, or procure the commission of any indictable offence, whether the same be an offence at common law or by virtue of any Act passed or to be

---

[188] In general, see Aegis Trust, *Suspected War Criminals and Génocidaires in the UK: Proposals to Strengthen Our Laws*, Laxton, UK, June 2009; and UK Parliament, Joint Committee on Human Rights, *Closing the Impunity Gap: UK Law on Genocide (and Related Crimes) and Redress for Torture Victims*, 11 August 2009.

[189] United Kingdom, Court of Appeal, Criminal Division, Case 200505339/D3, Judgment, 7 February 2007 (www.legal-tools.org/doc/e047b9/).

[190] Central Criminal Court of England and Wales, Case of Lama, Judgment, 7 September 2016 (www.legal-tools.org/doc/03b2c8/).

[191] Aksenova, 2016, pp. 30–36, see *supra* note 168.

passed, shall be liable to be tried, indicted, and punished as a principal offender.[192]

Accessory after the fact is also criminalised in the following terms:

> Where a person has committed a relevant offence, any other person who, knowing or believing him to be guilty of the offence or of some other relevant offence, does without lawful authority or reasonable excuse any act with intent to impede his apprehension or prosecution shall be guilty of an offence.[193]

Attempt is described as follows:

> If, with intent to commit an offence to which this section applies, a person does an act which is more than merely preparatory to the commission of the offence, he is guilty of attempting to commit the offence.[194]

Conspiracy is defined as follows:

> If a person agrees with any other person or persons that a course of conduct shall be pursued which, if the agreement is carried out in accordance with their intentions, either—
>
> (a) will necessarily amount to or involve the commission of any offence or offences by one or more of the parties to the agreement, or
>
> (b) would do so but for the existence of facts which render the commission of the offence or any of the offences impossible,
>
> he is guilty of conspiracy to commit the offence or offences in question.[195]

Forms of incitement are set out in the Serious Crime Act in Sections 44–46, with the following wording:

> Section 44: Intentionally encouraging or assisting an offence
>
> (1) A person commits an offence if—

---

[192] Accessories and Abettors Act 1861, Section 8, as amended by the Criminal Law Act 1977, section 65(4) (www.legal-tools.org/doc/804a64/).

[193] Criminal Law Act 1967, Section 4(1) (www.legal-tools.org/doc/d7959f/).

[194] Criminal Attempts Act 1981, Section 1(1) (www.legal-tools.org/doc/4387c5/).

[195] Criminal Law Act 1977, Section 1.

(a) he does an act capable of encouraging or assisting the commission of an offence; and

(b) he intends to encourage or assist its commission.

(2) But he is not to be taken to have intended to encourage or assist the commission of an offence merely because such encouragement or assistance was a foreseeable consequence of his act.

Section 45: Encouraging or assisting an offence believing it will be committed

A person commits an offence if—

(a) he does an act capable of encouraging or assisting the commission of an offence; and

(b) he believes—

(i) that the offence will be committed; and

(ii) that his act will encourage or assist its commission.

Section 46: Encouraging or assisting offences believing one or more will be committed

(1) A person commits an offence if—

(a) he does an act capable of encouraging or assisting the commission of one or more of a number of offences; and

(b) he believes—

(i) that one or more of those offences will be committed (but has no belief as to which); and

(ii) that his act will encourage or assist the commission of one or more of them.

(2) It is immaterial for the purposes of subsection (1)(b)(ii) whether the person has any belief as to which offence will be encouraged or assisted.

(3) If a person is charged with an offence under subsection (1)—

(a) the indictment must specify the offences alleged to be the "number of offences" mentioned in paragraph (a) of that subsection; but

(b) nothing in paragraph (a) requires all the offences potentially comprised in that number to be specified.[196]

Command/superior responsibility in set out in Article 65 of the International Criminal Court Act 2001 with the same language as Article 28
of the Rome Statute, while Article 55 of the ICC Act provides applicable
forms of liability in common law, namely aiding, abetting, counselling,
accessory after the fact, procuring, incitement, attempt, and conspiracy to
the international offences of genocide, war crimes, and crimes against
humanity.

As there were no reasons delivered in either of the two cases noted
above, there is no further information available as to the parameters of the
charge of conspiracy used in both cases involving persons in a position of
authority.

8.13. Denmark

8.13.1. Overview of Cases

8.13.1.1. Grave Breaches of the Geneva Conventions in Bosnia

On 25 November 1994, Refik Sarić was convicted for personally severely
beating and torturing over a dozen detainees in 1993 at a prison in Bosnia
and Herzegovina and sentenced to 8 years' imprisonment for grave
breaches of the Geneva Conventions.[197] This was upheld on appeal on 15
August 1995,[198] while an appeal to the European Court of Human Rights
was held to be inadmissible on 2 February 1999.[199]

8.13.2. Forms of Liability: Analysis

Attempt and complicity are regulated by Sections 21–24 of the Danish
Criminal Code,[200] as follows:

---

[196] For a critical review of these provisions, see Jeremy Horder, *Ashworth's Principles of Criminal Law*, 8th ed., Oxford University Press, Oxford, 2016, pp. 500–1.

[197] Denmark, Eastern Division of the Danish High Court, Case of Sarić, 25 November 1994 (www.legal-tools.org/doc/b65c87/).

[198] Denmark, Supreme Court, Case of Sarić, 15 August 1995 (www.legal-tools.org/doc/a8de3a/).

[199] ECHR, Decision as to the Admissibility of Application no. 31913/96 by Refik Sarić against Denmark (www.legal-tools.org/doc/978814/).

[200] Danish Criminal Code, 15 April 1930 (www.legal-tools.org/doc/606ecd/). For an overview, see Iryna Marchuk, "The Unitary Form of Participation in Danish Criminal Law

Section 21

(1) Acts which aim at the promotion or accomplishment of an offence shall be punished as an attempt when the offence is not completed.

(2) The punishment prescribed for the offence may be reduced in the case of attempt, particularly where the attempt gives evidence of little strength or persistence in the criminal intention.

(3) Unless otherwise provided, an attempt shall only be punishable when a penalty exceeding imprisonment for 4 months can be imposed for the offence.

Section 22

Attempts shall not be punishable if, voluntarily and not because of fortuitous obstacles to the completion of the offence or to the fulfillment of his purpose, the perpetrator desisted from implementing his intention and prevented the offence's completion, or took steps which would have prevented its completion had it not, without his knowledge, already been unsuccessful or averted in some other way.

Section 23

(1) The penalty in respect of an offence shall apply to any person who has contributed to the execution of the wrongful act by instigation, advice or action. The punishment may be reduced for any person who has only intended to give assistance of minor importance, or to strengthen an intention already existing and if the offence has not been completed or an intended assistance has failed.

(2) The punishment may similarly be reduced for a person who has contributed to the breach of a duty in a special relationship in which he himself had no part.

(3) Unless otherwise provided, the penalty for participation in offences that are not punishable more severely than with imprisonment for 4 months may be remitted where the accomplice only intended to give assistance of minor importance or to strengthen an intention already existing, or where his complicity is due to negligence.

(and Its Potential Use in International Criminal Law)", blog of James G. Stewart, 5 October 2017 (available on its web site).

Section 24

The accomplice shall not be punished if, under the conditions laid down in Section 22 of this Act, he prevents the completion of the offence or takes steps which would have prevented its completion had it not, without his knowledge, already been unsuccessful or averted in some other way.

In the Sarić case there was no discussion of extended liability, as the accused had committed the impugned acts in his personal capacity ('direct perpetration').

8.14. Spain

8.14.1. Overview of Cases

8.14.1.1. Crimes against Humanity in Argentina

On 19 April 2005, Adolfo Scilingo was convicted by the Spanish National Court, the Audiencia Nacional ('AN'), and sentenced to 640 years' imprisonment for attempted genocide and other crimes committed during Argentina's 'dirty war' between 1976 and 1983. The main charge against him was related to his participation in two death flights during which 30 persons, who had been drugged beforehand, were thrown into the sea from an airplane. Scilingo had had an active hand in these acts.[201] On 4 July 2007, the Supreme Court of Spain increased Scilingo's prison sentence to 1,084 years (but effective for only 25 years). At the same time it altered the conviction to the specific penalties provided in the current Criminal Code for the crimes of murder and unlawful detention, but held that these crimes constituted crimes against humanity according to international law.[202]

---

[201] For general comments regarding this case, see three articles in *Journal of International Criminal Justice*, 2005, vol. 3, no. 5: Christian Tomuschat, "Issues of Universal Jurisdiction in the Scilingo Case", pp. 1074–81; Alicia Gil Gil, "The Flaws of the *Scilingo* Judgment", pp. 1082–91; and Giulia Pinzauti, "An Instance of Reasonable Universality: The Scilingo Case", pp. 1092–1105. Audiencia Nacional, Case of Scilingo, Judgment, Case No. 16/2005, 19 April 2005 (www.legal-tools.org/doc/d042b3/).

[202] Supreme Court of Spain, Case of Scilingo, Judgment, 3 July 2007 (www.legal-tools.org/doc/7eb774/).

8.14.2. Forms of Liability: Analysis

The following forms of liability exist in the Spanish Criminal Code,[203] Articles 27–29:

> Article 27
>
> Those criminally responsible for felonies and misdemeanours are the principals and their accessories.
>
> Article 28
>
> Principals are those who perpetrate the act themselves, alone, jointly, or by means of another used to aid and abet.
>
> The following shall also be deemed principals:
>
> (a) Whoever directly induces another or others to commit a crime;
>
> (b) Whoever co-operates in the commission thereof by an act without which a crime could not have been committed.
>
> Article 29
>
> Accessories are those who, not being included in the preceding Article, co-operate in carrying out the offence with prior or simultaneous acts.

Attempt is recognised in the articles dealing with punishment, namely Articles 62 and 63.

Command responsibility is regulated in Article 615*bis*, which indicates that a commander or superior in breach of his obligations shall be punished in the same manner as those actually committing the offence in question.

There is no discussion about the exact form of liability in the Scilingo case, which resulted in the following criticism in the literature:

> It is also somewhat surprising that in this decision, the AN fails to provide any argument regarding the accused's actual participation in the facts. Spanish law distinguishes between perpetrator and accomplice, assigning different punishments to each category in accordance with their contribution to the commission of the crime. Scilingo is, however, charged with 30 murders, one case of torture and one illegal detention, all making up a crime against humanity. ... It sentences the de-

---

[203] Spanish Criminal Code, 23 November 1995 (www.legal-tools.org/doc/c5acd0/).

fendant as a perpetrator for 'his direct and personal involvement in the facts', which is inadmissible under Spanish law. The Court must prove the direct commission of the elements of the crime by the accused, or his personal control over the commission, in order to be able to sentence him as a perpetrator. Otherwise, in accordance with Spanish criminal law, it must decide whether he participated in the crime as a principal accomplice or merely as an accomplice, pursuant to the criteria developed by legal commentators and the case law. Alternatively, he might have merely committed the offence of failing to prevent or to report the commission of a crime, due to the fact that he was present whilst his superiors were engaging in torture.[204]

8.15. Italy

8.15.1. Overview of Cases

8.15.1.1. Illegal Detention, Torture, and Disappearances in Argentina

Alfredo Astiz, who was tried in France (see above), was also tried *in absentia* in Italy. On 14 March 2007, he was convicted of illegal detention, torture, and forced disappearance by the Corte di Assise of Rome. On 24 April 2008, the Corte di Assise di Appello confirmed this verdict and sentenced Astiz to life imprisonment.[205]

8.15.1.2. 'Operation Condor' in Chile, Uruguay, and Argentina

On 17 January 2017, at a tribunal in Rome, two former heads of state, two ex-chiefs of security forces, and a former foreign minister were tried *in absentia* and sentenced to life imprisonment for their involvement in the 1970s in the cross-border system of repression in South America known as Operation Condor. The Rome trial examined the disappearance of 42 dual citizens: 33 Italian-Uruguayans, 5 Italian-Argentinians, and 4 Italian-

---

[204] Gil Gil, 2005, p. 1082 under heading D, see *supra* note 196.

[205] See Corte di Assise di Roma, Case of Astiz, Judgment, 14 March 2007 (www.legal-tools. org/doc/e7a51f/). Also see appeal judgment (in Italian) Corte di Assise di Appello, Case of Astiz, Judgment, 24 April 2008 (www.legal-tools.org/doc/c4eda1/). On 26 February 2009, the Corte Suprema di Cassazione confirmed this verdict, La Corte Supreme Di Cassazione, Case of Astiz, Judgment, no. 39.595/2008, 26 February 2009 (www.legal-tools.org/doc/ e3b717/).

Chileans. Sentenced to life in prison were former military dictator Francisco Morales Bermúdez and former prime minister Pedro Richter Prada of Peru; former dictator Luis García Meza and former minister of interior Luis Arce Gómez of Bolivia; and former foreign minister Juan Carlos Blanco of Uruguay. Two Chilean military men, Hernán Jerónimo Ramírez and Rafael Ahumada Valderrama, also received life terms. The former head of the Uruguayan National Security Council, Gregorio Alvarez, was also one of the initially accused, along with the head of the Chilean secret police ('DINA'), Manuel Contreras, and DINA operative Sergio Arellano Stark; all three died after the charges were laid but before the verdict was announced. On the other hand, the tribunal acquitted an infamous trio of Uruguayan intelligence operatives, Nino Gavazzo, José Arab, and Jorge Silveira, and a Uruguayan marine intelligence officer, Jorge Troccoli, all of whom were operating in Argentina during the mid-1970s. Ten other Uruguayan military figures were acquitted as well. Relatives of the Uruguayan victims have indicated they will appeal.[206]

8.15.2. Forms of Liability: Common Analysis

Complicity in Italy is primarily regulated by Article 110 of the Italian Criminal Code,[207] which says that when more than one person participated in the same offence, each of them shall be subject to the punishment described, except as provided in the subsequent articles.[208]

---

[206] See National Security Archive, "Operation Condor: Condemned to Life!", 17 January 2017 (www.legal-tools.org/doc/602989/). Corte di Assise di Roma, Case of Bermúdez *et al.*, Judgment, 17 January 2017 (www.legal-tools.org/doc/785768/).

[207] Codice Penale, R.D. 1398/1930, 19 October 1930 (www.legal-tools.org/doc/46945d/).

[208] See Aksenova, 2016, p. 37, *supra* note 168. For further discussion regarding complicity and the jurisprudence in this regard, see *ibid.* pp. 38–39, where it is said that "to qualify as a party to crime in Italy, it is sufficient that the person willingly contributes to the commission of the offence with the general knowledge about the factual situation and that his input constitutes necessary support for carrying out the crime" (p. 38), while the distinction between (co-)perpetrators and accomplices is that "co-perpetrators take the decision to carry out the offence, while accomplices aim at the realisation of the decision taken by others" (p. 38). Also see Filippo de Minicis, "A Unitary Theory Is Both Viable and Preferable", blog of James G. Stewart, 11 October 2017 (available on its web site).

Italy has also regulated the inchoate crime of attempt,[209] while conspiracy and incitement are not punishable if a crime has not been committed.[210]

In the Astiz case, the highest appeals court confirmed the general approach set out in Article 110[211] while also indicating that Astiz, with a subordinate role in the chain of command, had played a role in the detention of the three victims and had made a contribution to their fate.[212]

The Operation Condor judgment does not discuss modes of liability.

8.16. Canada

8.16.1. Overview of Cases

8.16.1.1. Hostage Taking of UN Personnel in Bosnia

Nicholas Nikola Ribic, a Canadian citizen of Yugoslavian origin, was charged in February 1999 with the personally taking three unarmed UN military observers as hostages in Bosnia and Herzegovina in 1995. His first trial began in October 2002 but ended on 20 January 2003 with the declaration of a mistrial. On 12 June 2005, following a second trial, he was convicted, and on 14 September 2005 he was sentenced to 3 years' imprisonment; this verdict was upheld on appeal on 24 November 2008.[213]

8.16.1.2. Genocide, Crimes against Humanity, and War Crimes in Rwanda

Désiré Munyaneza was charged on 19 October 2005 with genocide, war crimes, and crimes against humanity for his involvement in Butare during the Rwandan genocide, with the underlying crimes of murder, sexual violence, and looting. The trial began in May 2007 and he was convicted on

---

[209] See Astolfo Di Amato, *Criminal Law in Italy*, Kluwer International, Alphen aan den Rijn, 2011, pp. 105–6.

[210] Article 115.

[211] At para. 4.3.

[212] At para. 2.6.

[213] Canada, *R. v. Ribic*, 2008 ONCA 790 (www.legal-tools.org/doc/d93112/).

all counts on 22 May 2009. He was sentenced to life imprisonment on 29 October 2009,[214] with the ruling upheld on appeal on 8 May 2014.[215]

8.16.1.3. Acquittal of Genocide and Crimes against Humanity in Rwanda

On 6 November 2009, a second Rwandan, Jacques Mungwarere, was arrested and charged with the commission of genocide and crimes against humanity, namely murder, but he was eventually acquitted on 5 July 2013.[216]

8.16.2. Forms of Liability: Common Analysis

Criminal liability is for the most part set out in Sections 21 and 22 of the Canadian Criminal Code,[217] which state the following:

> Section 21
>
> (1) Every one is a party to an offence who
>
> (a) actually commits it;
>
> (b) does or omits to do anything for the purpose of aiding any person to commit it; or
>
> (c) abets any person in committing it.
>
> (2) Where two or more persons form an intention in common to carry out an unlawful purpose and to assist each other therein and any one of them, in carrying out the common purpose, commits an offence, each of them who knew or ought to have known that the commission of the offence would be a probable consequence of carrying out the common purpose is a party to that offence.
>
> Section 22

---

[214] Canada, *R. v. Munyaneza*, 2009 QCCS 4865 (www.legal-tools.org/doc/81e956/). Also see Robert Currie and Joseph Rikhof, *International and Transnational Criminal Law*, Irwin Law, Toronto, 2013, pp. 272–75. See, for comments, Fannie Lafontaine, "Canada's Crimes against Humanity and War Crimes Act on Trial: An Analysis of the Munyaneza Case", in *Journal of International Criminal Justice*, 2010, vol. 8, no. 1, pp. 269–88; and Robert Currie and Ion Stancu, "*R. v. Munyaneza*: Pondering Canada's First Core Crimes Conviction", in *International Criminal Law Review*, 2010, vol. 10, no. 3, pp. 829–53.

[215] Canada, *Munyaneza v. R*, 2014 QCCA 906 (www.legal-tools.org/doc/9d2707/).

[216] Canada, *R. v. Mungwarere*, 2013 ONSC 4594 (www.legal-tools.org/doc/f68e84/); see also Currie and Rikhof, 2013, pp. 275–78, *supra* note 209.

[217] Canadian Criminal Code, 1985 (www.legal-tools.org/doc/35111a/).

---

(1) Where a person counsels another person to be a party to an offence and that other person is afterwards a party to that offence, the person who counselled is a party to that offence, notwithstanding that the offence was committed in a way different from that which was counselled.

(2) Every one who counsels another person to be a party to an offence is a party to every offence that the other commits in consequence of the counselling that the person who counselled knew or ought to have known was likely to be committed in consequence of the counselling.

(3) For the purposes of this Act, counsel includes procure, solicit or incite.

Other sections deal with the inchoate offences of conspiracy,[218] attempt,[219] and counselling/inciting an offence that was not committed.[220]

The Crimes against Humanity and War Crimes Act[221] repeats the offences of conspiracy, attempt, and counselling for the crimes of genocide, war crimes, and crimes against humanity,[222] while also adding accessory after the fact in the same sections and adding the offences of command and superior responsibility in Sections 5 and 7, including the possibility of conspiracy, attempt, counselling, and accessory after the fact in relation to command/superior responsibility.[223]

The first two cases concerning extra-territorial jurisdiction did not discuss forms of personal liability because the accused had been involved in the commission (execution) of the crimes as direct perpetrator.

However, the most recent case, that of Mungwarere, did provide a fairly detailed discussion of the specific notions of 'co-perpetration' and 'aiding and abetting'. With respect to co-perpetration, the judge repeated the dictum of an earlier decision by the Supreme Court of Canada in the case, saying that when there is uncertainty about the killing of a person

---

[218] Section 465.

[219] Section 463.

[220] Section 464.

[221] Crimes Against Humanity and War Crimes Act, 2000 (www.legal-tools.org/doc/0d3078/).

[222] Sections 4(1.1) and 6(1.1). There are two divisions in this act with respect to the crimes and participation, one division for such crimes being committed in Canada and another for commission outside Canada.

[223] Section 5(2.1) and 7(2.1).

involving more than one perpetrator, any one of whom could have delivered the fatal blow, any person whose conduct constituted "a significant contributing cause" of the death is guilty of manslaughter or murder in general, provided that the two or more persons together formed an intention to commit the offence, were present at the commission of the crime, and contributed to it, although each does not personally have to have committed all of the essential elements of that offence.[224]

In regard to aiding and abetting, the judge again referred to that Supreme Court decision in setting out its essential requirements, namely that the act relied upon must in fact aid or abet, and that this must also have been done with the particular intention to facilitate or encourage the principal's commission of the offence, with knowledge that the principal intends to commit the crime.

Applying these general principles to the crimes under consideration in this case, the judge expressed the view that the Crown, in order to be successful on the charge of commission of genocide under Section 21(1)(a) of the Criminal Code, must show that the accused formed with other people the intention to kill Tutsis, was present when the killings of Tutsis were committed, and committed acts that contributed significantly to the death of those Tutsis. There is no need for a direct causal link between the acts of the accused and the killing, provided that the acts of the accused were a significant contributing cause of the deaths of the victims. The accused and other participants must share the same criminal intent, namely to eliminate, in whole or in part, the Tutsi ethnic group.[225]

With respect to Section 21(1)(b) and the charge of aiding and abetting genocide, the evidence must show that one or more individuals, with the intention to do so, caused the death of one or more Tutsis in order to eliminate this ethnic group, and that the accused committed one or more acts that had the effect of aiding in the commission of the murders, that he intended to facilitate the murders, and that he knew the genocidal intent of the author or authors of the murders. It is not necessary for the accused himself to have been motivated by a desire to destroy the Tutsi ethnic

---

[224] Canada, *R. v. Mungwarere*, 2013 ONSC 4594, para. 52.
[225] *Ibid.*, para. 53.

group, as long as he knew that this was the purpose of the perpetrators of the offense when they committed the intentional killings of Tutsis.[226]

The judgment explains the difference between a co-perpetrator and an aider and abetter (accomplice) by referring to two ICTY Appeals Chamber decisions. It comes to the conclusion that the *mens rea* for co-perpetration is higher because a co-perpetrator shares the intent of the other perpetrators in carrying out the criminal intent, while an aider and abetter only needs to be aware that his contribution assists or facilitates the crime com-mitted by other participants. With respect to the *actus reus*, the judge is more hesitant to set the level of contribution required for aiding and abetting, as the international jurisprudence relied upon by both parties concerned 'joint criminal enterprise', a concept broader than either co-perpetration (joint perpetration) or aiding and abetting (complicity). The conclusion reached is that the terminology with respect to aiding and abetting used by the Supreme Court could be utilised, that is, the acts must in fact aid the crime in the sense of providing practical or tangible help. In order to provide meaning to these words while also using an international criminal law interpretation when dealing with international crimes, the judge holds that the phrase "significantly contributing to the crime" ("largement facilité le crime"),[227] used by the ICTY Appeals Chamber in the Kvočka case,[228] fulfils both objectives.

8.17. United States

8.17.1. Overview of Cases

8.17.1.1. Conspiracy to Torture and Other Crimes in Liberia

In the United States,[229] Charles "Chuckie" Taylor, the son of Liberia's ex-president Charles Taylor, was charged on 6 December 2006 with, among

---

[226] *Ibid.*, para. 55.

[227] *Ibid.*, paras. 56–61.

[228] ICTY, Appeals Chamber, *Prosecutor v. Kvočka et al.*, Judgment, IT-98-30/1-A, 28 February 2005 (www.legal-tools.org/doc/006011/). The other case is ICTY, Appeals Chamber, *Prosecutor v. Vasiljević*, Judgment, IT-98-32-A, 25 February 2004 (www.legal-tools.org/doc/e35d81/).

[229] The United States has also arrested a number of persons for involvement in atrocities in their homelands, but these prosecutions are launched under US legislation related to immigration or citizenship fraud. See, on the US Immigration and Customs Enforcement web site, "Human Rights Violators Investigations", and "Human Rights Violators & War Crimes Unit" (available on its web site).

other things, conspiracy to commit torture. He was the leader of the elite Anti-Terrorist Unit from approximately 1997 through at least 2002, a period in which that unit committed torture,[230] including violent assaults, rapes, beating people to death, and burning civilians alive.[231] He was convicted on 30 October 2008 and sentenced to 97 years of incarceration on 9 January 2009. The appeal of this decision was upheld on 15 July 2010.[232]

8.17.2. Forms of Liability: Analysis

In the United States participation is regulated in Title 18 of the United States Code,[233] where Section 2 says:

> (a) Whoever commits an offense against the United States or aids, abets, counsels, commands, induces or procures its commission, is punishable as a principal.

> (b) Whoever willfully causes an act to be done which if directly performed by him or another would be an offense against the United States, is punishable as a principal.[234]

Section 3 says:

> Whoever, knowing that an offense against the United States has been committed, receives, relieves, comforts or assists the offender in order to hinder or prevent his apprehension, trial or punishment, is an accessory after the fact.

The inchoate offences of conspiracy, attempt, and incitement are included within the description of a number of individual offences but not as general concepts.[235]

In the Taylor case at the appeal level, there was no discussion of the notion of conspiracy.

---

[230] He was charged with this crime because he was a US national, although US law does provide universal jurisdiction for torture, genocide, and the war crime of child recruitment.

[231] See Human Rights Watch, "US: Justice Dept. Brings First Charges for Torture Abroad", 6 December 2006 (www.legal-tools.org/doc/8d10e0/).

[232] United States Court of Appeals for the Eleventh Circuit, *United States of America v. Roy M. Belfast*, Case 09-10461-AA, 18 September 2009 (www.legal-tools.org/doc/221838-1/).

[233] The Code of Laws of the United States of America (Title 18 - Crimes and Criminal Procedure) (www.legal-tools.org/doc/d49f73/).

[234] See also Aksenova, 2016, p. 36, *supra* note 168.

[235] See, for instance, incitement to commit genocide in Section 1091(c), while in Section 1091(d) there is a reference to attempt and conspiracy; another example is conspiracy to commit torture in Section 2340A(c).

8.18. Concluding Remarks

8.18.1. Legislation

When we examine the legislation of the 15 countries with universal jurisdiction discussed in this chapter, a confusing picture with respect to participation emerges. All the countries entertain various types of liability (with the exception of Italy, which has a very general provision setting out criminal liability), and the most common forms are known in all jurisdictions.[236] Overall, there appears to be a general attempt at the domestic level to base forms of liability on somewhat similar conceptual notions, at least with respect to some forms of personal liability. However, the precise parameters of liability are often drawn differently in different countries, and at times the language used to express the same type of liability also varies. One notable difference is that the three common law countries in this study – the United Kingdom, Canada, and the United States – tend to use more forms of inchoate liability, such as attempt, incitement, and conspiracy, than their 12 civil law counterparts (though it should be noted that attempt is set out in the legislation of all the countries, while incitement can be found in the Netherlands and Finland).[237]

Direct singular perpetration is criminalised in all the jurisdictions examined. With respect to the notion of joint perpetration, this is mentioned explicitly without further definitional description in the criminal codes of the Netherlands, Germany, Austria, Finland, and Spain. Some countries specify what is required to be a joint perpetrator or 'co-perpetrator', usually saying in essence that without the assistance of the perpetrator the offences would not have been committed, as is the case in Belgium and Spain.[238]

Another aspect of perpetration, namely 'perpetration through another person' (indirect perpetration), is present in the legislation of the Netherlands, Germany, Finland, and Spain. This concept is also known (albeit

---

[236] See, in general terms, Aksenova, 2016, pp. 45–52 and especially pp. 47–48, *supra* note 168.

[237] See Elies van Sliedregt, *Individual Responsibility in International Law*, Oxford University Press, Oxford, 2012, pp. 147–50.

[238] *Ibid.*, p. 95.

only developed in the jurisprudence) as 'innocent agency' in common law countries, such as the UK and Canada.[239]

Some legislation makes reference to means to convince a third person to commit a criminal act, such as threat, abuse of power, deception, use of force, gifts, or promises. This can be found in the Netherlands as part of the perpetration section, while in France it is included under aiding and abetting. In Belgium it comes within the provision dealing with incitement as part of perpetration (although in the French-language version of the Belgian law the word 'provoquer' is used for incitement, the meaning of which is closer to causing or instigating; this is confirmed by the Dutch-language version of the law, which uses the term 'uitgelokt', the same term used in the Netherlands law).[240] In the UK, procuring is generally seen as using deception in this context.[241] It has furthermore been postulated in the literature that in the UK the abuse of power aspect can be considered a form of ordering.[242]

In common law countries, such as Canada and the UK, the notion of common purpose or common intention is used to delineate forms of group liability where more than one person partakes in the commission of an offence.[243]

The definition of 'aiding and abetting' (complicity) also has a number of variants in domestic legislation.[244] In some countries, such as Austria, Switzerland, Canada, the United Kingdom, and the United States, as well as in the most recent version of the Criminal Code of Norway, this form of participation is set out as a form of liability without further clarification.

Other countries have provided some definition with respect to the notion of aiding and abetting, usually by indicating that a person has provided assistance to the commission of the crime; this is the case in Germany, France, Belgium, Finland, Denmark, and Spain. Lastly, some countries have added, to the general description of aiding and abetting, exam-

---

[239] *Ibid.*, pp. 90–91.

[240] *Ibid.*, p. 102.

[241] Aksenova, 2016, p. 31, see *supra* note 168.

[242] Van Sliedregt, 2012, pp. 102 and 131–32, *supra* note 232.

[243] Aksenova, 2016, p. 96, see *supra* note 168.

[244] For background, see Van Sliedregt, 2012, pp. 112–17, *supra* note 232.

ples of the means, by which the assistance can be accomplished; this is the case in the Netherlands, Belgium, and Sweden (as part of the section dealing with preparatory acts). These references can be general in nature, such as providing opportunity, means, or information (the Netherlands); providing instructions or procuring weapons, instruments, or other means (Belgium); or presenting or receiving money or anything else as prepayment or payment for the crime or procuring, constructing, giving, receiving, keeping, conveying, or engaging in any other similar activity with poison, explosive, weapon, picklock, falsification tool, or other such means (Sweden).

Both the Canadian and US legislation mention accessory after the fact as a form of participation.[245]

Other forms of indirect participation using persuasion in the preparatory phase, which resulted in the commission of crime, have been penalised under various expressions, such as inducing, soliciting, counselling, encouraging, and instigation, namely in Germany, Spain, Sweden, Switzerland, Finland (both for participation and aiding and abetting), Canada, the United Kingdom, and the United States.[246]

Command responsibility is known in the Swedish Criminal Code, but in more general language than that used in the Rome Statute, while the US Code lists command responsibility within its iteration of forms of adding and abetting. Some countries discussed in this chapter have included command responsibility within their criminal codes, such as Finland and Spain, but most have implemented the substantive provisions of the Rome Statute, including the command/superior responsibility concepts, in specific legislation, as is the case with the Netherlands, Germany, the UK, and Canada. There appear to be different approaches with respect to this notion in Germany and Canada, which treat command/superior responsibility as a distinct offence ('crime'), while the Netherlands, Finland, Spain, and the UK treat it as a form of indirect participation. The former approach extends the parameters of participation, as it allows both regular forms of indirect approaches as well as inchoate offences to be combined with command/superior responsibility as a distinct crime.

---

[245] *Ibid.*, pp. 119–20.
[246] *Ibid.*, pp. 102–4.

With respect to contributions before the execution stage of the crime,[247] such as 'conspiracy', further 'planning and preparation', 'attempt', and 'incitement' (as a form of instigation before the execution stage), attempt is known in all countries, while the UK and Canada have a general provision regulating conspiracy and incitement. The United States uses these types of liability only in relation to specific crime types. While in theory it would be possible in such countries to have double inchoates by combining, for instance, attempt with conspiracy or incitement with conspiracy, national courts at least in some cases have frowned upon drawing the circle of perpetration too wide.[248]

The Netherlands also has a provision dealing with conspiracy, but the jurisprudence appears to require that at least one of the co-conspirators commits the crime envisaged in the original agreement, which makes it more akin to some variants of joint criminal enterprise than to a common law–type 'conspiracy'. In Sweden, the translated provision in the Criminal Code dealing with conspiracy says, "By conspiracy is meant that someone decides on the act in collusion with another as well as that someone undertakes or offers to execute it or seeks to incite another to do so", which appears to also resemble notions of co-perpetration and incitement.

This latter observation may also bring out some more general points, namely that the same or similar concepts of personal liability employed within different (domestic) subsystems of criminal law liability may not contain the same content, while on the other hand different concepts within different systems may contain similar content. In addition, the same or similar concepts within different jurisdictions may also contain more or less the same content. Although that picture may look confusing, it is not really surprising since there has not been much international coordination of criminal law liability concepts at domestic levels, and there have also been inconsistencies within ICL. Furthermore, this state of law at the 'fourth level' is not incompatible with our proposed general theory. To the contrary, it is to be expected that specific provisions on criminal law liability differ and are applied differently within different jurisdictions. The

---

[247] If the crime is not completed, punishable contributions before the execution stage are often referred to as 'inchoate crimes'.

[248] See, for instance, in Canada, *R. v. Déry*, 2006 SCC 53 (www.legal-tools.org/doc/96e28e/), where attempt to conspire to commit an offence was not accepted as a form of liability.

challenge of this book is to determine the scope of discretion in this regard with respect to universal crimes.

8.18.2. Jurisprudence

8.18.2.1. Statistical Information

With respect to the jurisprudence in the 15 countries under consideration, it would be useful to point to some general statistical information first. As noted in the introduction to this chapter, in Europe, between 1994 and July 2018, 13 countries initiated criminal prosecutions for crimes committed outside their borders. These resulted in 64 indictments in which 68 persons were convicted (with one person indicted in two countries) and seven persons were acquitted (including one on appeal) in 51 cases, some of which involved multiple accused. In North America, two countries, Canada and the United States, completed four criminal trials for such crimes: three in Canada (with one acquittal) and one in the United States.

Some observations can be made with respect to the efforts in Europe and North America. The first is that most cases taken to court pertained to situations arising from the conflicts in the former Yugoslavia and Rwanda. A smaller number of prosecutions were launched in relation to crimes committed in other countries in Africa (Liberia, DRC, Mauritania, Tunisia) and Asia (Afghanistan, Nepal, Syria, Sri Lanka), while two cases were related to South America (Argentina). It is likely that the preponderance of cases related to the former Yugoslavian countries and Rwanda is a result of the cooperation with those countries at the national level as well with the two international tribunals established for those situations (the latter form of co-operation often preceded and facilitated the former).

In terms of the international crimes pursued, the majority of the allegations were based on torture, genocide, and war crimes. More recent cases also charged crimes against humanity. This may be explained by the fact that most countries under consideration only formally introduced the concept of crimes against humanity after having ratified the Rome Statute, raising the prospect of retroactivity for the prosecution of those crimes committed before 1998.

The sentences imposed varied, even for the most serious crimes such as genocide and torture. Most sentences were in the upper range: five persons received sentences of less than 5 years' imprisonment; 17 received prison terms between 5 and 9 years; 12 received terms between 10 and 19 years; eight received 20 years or more; and 19 received life imprisonment. There were two outliers with extremely high sentences, namely the United States, where a term of 97 years was imposed, and Spain, where a person was sentenced to 1,084 years.

In terms of perpetrators, one can arrange them on a scale by level, from low to high. As outlined in Chapter 3, Section 3.2., low-level participants hold positions at the bottom rung of a military or civilian hierarchy, with nobody reporting to them. Those at the intermediate level include military officers, local or regional civilian administrators, and functionaries in the middle ranks of a civilian organisation; they supervise persons at lower levels and report to persons at higher levels. High-level perpetrators are at the apex of their organisation or carry out important functions at the national level in their country. There is a fourth class of people who belong to power support structures, such as media or business organisations; for the purpose of this chapter, we will subsume these support figures into the low-level class.

Based on this distinction, the jurisprudence dealt with low-level perpetrators in 22 cases (five in Sweden, four in Germany, three each in Austria and Canada, two in Belgium, and one each in the Netherlands, Norway, France, Switzerland, and Finland). There were 19 cases with mid-level perpetrators (four in France, three in the Netherlands, two each in Sweden, Norway, Belgium, and Germany, and one each in Finland, Denmark, Spain, and Italy). Finally, 11 cases featured high-level perpetrators (four in the Netherlands, two each in Germany and the UK, and one each in Belgium, the United States, and Italy).

The jurisprudence in the above countries utilised three types of punishable participation most frequently: direct perpetration (in 15 cases, with four in Germany, three in Sweden, two each in France and Canada, and one each in Finland, Switzerland, Denmark, and Spain); co-perpetration or joint perpetration (11 cases, with five in Sweden, four in the Netherlands, and one each in Germany and Canada); and aiding and abetting or complicity (14 cases, with three each in the Netherlands and Belgium, two each in Germany, France, and Norway, and one each in Italy and Canada). Other forms of liability used are command/superior responsibility (two cases in the Netherlands and one each in Germany, Italy, and Belgium, the latter indirectly); conspiracy (the Netherlands, the UK, and the United States); incitement (the Netherlands, Finland, and Switzerland); solicitation/instigation (the Netherlands); and ordering (Finland). Some cases discuss more than one form of liability, such as a few cases in the Netherlands, Germany, Finland, and Canada.

On the relationship between international and domestic criminal law, it is noteworthy that courts in only *three* countries have explicitly examined their domestic legislation in the context of ICL, namely the Netherlands (with respect to the concepts of command/superior responsibility, aiding and abetting, and incitement), Germany (in relation to command/ superior responsibility, albeit indirectly), and Canada (regarding aiding and abetting). Again, this seems to suggest – consistent with earlier observations – that domestic courts are generally not putting much emphasis on specific forms of liability when they are satisfied on the facts of the case that personal criminal law liability is attributable to the accused for the crimes in question.

8.18.2.2. Co-perpetration (Joint Perpetration)

Moving from the statistical realm to the substantive discussion of forms of perpetration (direct participation), Germany and the Netherlands have discussed this notion in the most detail, with some passing references in judgments in Sweden and Canada.

In the Netherlands, co-perpetration was used in six cases. The Ntacyobatabara judgment explained this concept in most detail, as follows:

> Co-perpetration refers to a situation when two or more persons together jointly commit a criminal offence. Co-perpetration is based on the assumption that there is an intentional and close collaboration between two or more persons. This means that the co-perpetrators collaborate knowingly, thus intentionally, to commit the criminal act. The intention should not only be aimed at their mutual collaboration but also at the commission of the criminal offence. It is not required that all co-perpetrators carry out overt acts or that they are personally present when the criminal offences are committed. Their collaboration needs to be intensive and aimed at the unlawful act, whereas the participation of the co-perpetrator who does not carry out the overt acts should be substantial. In this manner, it is possible that the co-perpetrator who does not carry out the overt acts is involved in the planning and/or organisation the criminal offence. Their close collaboration may appear among other matters

from – explicit or tacit – agreements and assignment of responsibilities.[249]

Of the other five cases, only the van Kouwenhoven judgment addressed one aspect of co-perpetration, saying that the accused had not been part of a common plan to commit war crimes.[250]

In Germany, the general principles of co-perpetration were expressed as follows in a WWII case, that of Oskar Gröning:

> [a co-perpetrator] is a person who does not only abet someone else's actions, but rather also contributes his own act to a common criminal enterprise so that his contribution is viewed as part of the activities of the other and conversely the other's actions as an endorsement of his own criminal contribution. Whether or not a participant had a close nexus to the crime must be judged upon taking into account the overall circumstances from his subjective point of view. Material for an assessment could be the degree to which a person has an interest in seeing the crime committed, the scope of participation in the crime, and control over the commission of the crime or at least a desire to control the commission of the crime.[251]

This was further elaborated by the Federal Supreme Court in the Rwabukombe case, when it described co-perpetration as an activity that goes beyond merely promoting criminal acts and is part of a joint effort in terms of a division of labour. The participant makes an essential contribution to this activity and intends to have his contribution be part of the joint effort; whether the participant has such a close relationship to the group carrying out the criminal activity is based on a number of circumstances, such as his own interest in the successful outcome of the enterprise, the extent of his participation, and his influence on the activity in the sense that the conduct and outcome of the enterprise depend decisively on the will of the participant. In addition, it is not necessary for the defendant to have taken part in the stage during which the act was carried out; instead, a contribution to the act during the preparatory stages can be sufficient.[252]

---

[249] Netherlands, Case ECLI:NL:RBDHA:2013:8710 (2013), chap. 13, para. 2.

[250] Netherlands, Case ECLI:NL:GHSHE:2017:1760 (2017), sec. L2.1.

[251] Germany, Case 27 Ks 1191 Js 98402113 (9/14) (2015).

[252] Germany, Case 3 StR 575/14 (2015), para. 10.

While there is no extended legal reasoning in the Swedish case law, some aspects of co-perpetration can be gleaned from the more general comments with respect to the three decisions with the most detail. It was said that the accused acted jointly and in concert with other soldiers and that he participated with knowledge of the common criminal plan and himself executed concrete parts of the plan (Martinović); that the accused had participated in attacks by commanding and organising groups of perpetrators and encouraging them to attack Tutsis, as a result of which he had committed these crimes jointly and in collusion with other perpetrators (Mbanenande); and that the accused played an active and central role in the execution of criminal acts (Berinkindi).

In Canada, it was said that when there is uncertainty about a killing that involved more than one perpetrator, any one of whom could have delivered the fatal blow, any person whose conduct constituted a significant contributing cause of the death is guilty of manslaughter or murder in general, provided that the two or more persons together formed an intention to commit the offence, were present at the commission of the crime, and contributed to it, although each does not personally have to have committed all of the essential elements of that offence.[253]

While none of the European cases refer to international criminal law jurisprudence, the contours of co-perpetration ('joint functional perpetration')[254] as set out at the international level within ICL are clearly recognisable in the judgments of the Netherlands, Germany, and Sweden. Elements such as very close co-operation between perpetrators; an agreement between the perpetrators, either explicitly or implicitly; a division of labour at the preparatory or executive phase of the crime or both; and a contribution that can be described as essential are all present in the jurisprudence of both the ICC and the three mentioned European countries.

---

[253] *R. v. Mungwarere*, 2013 ONSC 4594, para. 52.

[254] Joint perpetration comes in several versions, namely 'joint multiple perpetration' (when the same contributions are made by several persons in accordance with a common plan) and 'joint functional perpetration' (when different contributions are made by several persons in accordance with a common plan); see Chapter 2, Section 2.2.3.2. Both are applicable within ICL, but the latter is the most practical – and dangerous – form with respect to universal crimes committed through power structures. Both versions might be combined with 'perpetration through another'.

Their rulings also make clear that this type of involvement can be utilised against perpetrators at all levels within an organisation.

While the concept of co-perpetration is discussed in the Canadian cases (and similarly in the UK), it has a different conceptual starting point. In Canada, when there is uncertainty as to who exactly executed the crime or the underlying offence of a universal crime such as a crime against humanity – that is, who completed the crime on the ground – *but* there was shared intention to commit the crime and all persons were present at the scene of the crime, where they all made a significant contribution, then all share the same responsibility for the whole outcome of the criminal enterprise. This approach seems more akin to JCE in the early ICTY jurisprudence than to co-perpetration in the ICC jurisprudence.

This kind of inconsistency in the jurisprudence at the domestic level is, however, unproblematic from the perspective of the general theory of international criminal law liability, although consistency is always preferable, all else being equal.

8.18.2.3. Aiding and Abetting (Complicity)

Another form of participation that has been discussed or alluded to in the national jurisprudence is aiding and abetting. In Belgium and France there is no discussion of the parameters of aiding and abetting apart from referring to the exact text of the legal provisions regulating this form of liability. In Norway, the Repak case indicates that arresting and participating in the transport of victims, resulting in criminal acts against them, amounts to aiding and abetting (complicity), while contributing to the killing of victims in Rwanda had the same result in the Bugingo case.

More food for thought can be found in the Dutch, German, and Canadian judgments. In the Dutch jurisprudence, complicity was discussed in four cases, those of van Anraat, van Kouwenhoven, Ntacyobatabara, and Alemu. The first of these, the van Anraat judgment, makes clear that ICL should be the primary source for interpretation of principles of liability. However, if Dutch law is broader than ICL in its scope of liability, there is still no problem in applying Dutch law. This issue was raised in the context of *mens rea*, where Dutch law knows the concept of *dolus eventualis*, or conditional intent, meaning that a person accepts a reasonable chance that a certain consequence or circumstance will occur, which can be seen as another manner of saying that not only harm but also the risk of harm is incorporated in this notion. The court of first instance in van Anraat held that the more limited *mens rea* concept of ICL should prevail over Dutch law in such a situation, but it was overruled by the Supreme Court. Under the general theory of criminal law liability, the judgment of the Dutch Supreme Court is unproblematic because the theory predicts that different results might be reached within different parts of the 'fourth level', which are all compatible with the fundamental principles of criminal law liability. In this case, application of the concept of *dolus eventualis* was compatible with the fundamental principle of culpability, while the judgment was also compatible with the fundamental principles of legality, conduct, and personal liability.[255]

In the same case, the appeals court agreed with the court of first instance regarding the influence of international law, but it found that the lower court had not followed that area of law when it required a form of contribution that was too high, that is, 'essential' rather than 'substantial'. A substantial contribution is present where the accused has promoted the offence or made it easier to commit that offence. This last point was confirmed in the Ntacyobatabara decision, which also indicated that aiding and abetting can occur during the commission of a crime (simultaneous complicity) or by providing the opportunity, means, or information necessary to commit the crime (consecutive complicity). Most recently, the approach with respect to the notion of substantial contribution as well as the notion of a conditional *mens rea* test were confirmed in the most recent court of appeals decision in the van Kouwenhoven case.

In Germany, the general precepts with respect to aiding and abetting (complicity) were given as follows:

> aiding and abetting is generally interpreted to mean any act that objectively promotes or facilitates the successful commission of the crime by the principal with no causal link of any act of assistance needing to be specifically established for the crime committed.[256]

Especially noteworthy is the negative statement with respect to the often-alleged 'causal link requirement' in the literature.[257]

---

[255] See Chapter 2, Section 2.2.3.4.

[256] See the case of Oskar Gröning in Germany, Case 27 Ks 1191 Js 98402113 (9/14) (2015).

[257] See Chapter 6, Section 6.2.3.1.

This complicity doctrine was further elaborated in the Murwanashyaka judgment, where the court indicated than any relevant act can also include 'moral assistance'; such assistance can take two forms. The first consists of technical advice, which imparts knowledge that results in improved prospects for a successful execution of the criminal act. Secondly, moral assistance can be provided through psychological assistance, such as propaganda, that is intended to influence the will of the principal actor by reinforcing the decision to act and, as in the case in the Netherlands, can be seen as an extension from harm to risk of harm as an underlying criminal concept.

In Canada, the Mungwarere judgment indicated that Canadian law in general requires that the act relied upon must in fact aid or abet, and that this must also have been done with the particular intention to facilitate or encourage the principal's commission of the offence, with knowledge that the principal intends to commit the crime. The court explained that the *mens rea* for aiding and abetting is lower than for coperpetration in that the aider and abettor only needs to be aware that his contribution assists or facilitates the crime committed by other participants, rather than necessarily sharing the intent of the other perpetrators. The judge in this case balanced the requirements of Canadian law with the case law of the ICTY by adding 'significant contribution' to the other elements of the Canadian provision of aiding and abetting.

Assessing the jurisprudence in the three countries just discussed, it appears that all three, either directly (as in the Netherlands and Canada) or indirectly (as in Germany), seek a well-founded linkage to ICL. In Canada, this led a court to overlay national law with an international component, thereby possibly limiting the reach of the concept of aiding and abetting for universal crimes as compared to national offences. In the Netherlands, adhering to international law was seen as a starting point for interpretation, with the caveat that if Dutch law is broader, it takes precedence, as in the case of conditional intent. The German courts, while not referring to ICL in this area, appear to have taken a broader approach to moral assistance than has been the case so far in ICL jurisprudence. However, this Dutch and German jurisprudence, when utilizing the concept of risk of harm, cannot necessarily be said to be contrary to international law in this respect, as the basic requirements for aiding and abetting in ICL are similar, while the particular fact situations underlying the domestic cases have not yet been addressed at international criminal tribunals; judges there might very well utilise the domestic case law in their deliberations. For instance, the description of *mens rea* in international criminal law, which includes awareness of the substantial likelihood that the practical assistance, encouragement, or moral support assists or facilitates the commission of the offence, does not appear that far removed from the concept of conditional intent in the Netherlands. And as already noted above, a certain inconsistency does not necessarily imply that one of the solutions must be incompatible with the general theory of criminal law liability.

8.18.2.4. Command/Superior Responsibility

This form of liability has been discussed in the Netherlands, Germany, and Belgium. It was alluded to briefly in the Belgian Ntuyahaga case, as part of the iteration of aiding and abetting, when the court noted that the accused had held military authority due to his superior rank but did not, however, take any action within the limits of his authority as a senior officer to oppose the criminal acts that he witnessed and of which he must have been aware.

In the Netherlands three cases have discussed the concept of command/superior responsibility. In the first one, the Faqirzada case, the court of appeals sets out the elements of this notion in some detail by relying heavily on ICTY/ICTR jurisprudence:

> [T]he essential characteristics of command/superior responsibility are the notion of "'subordinate", which [...] must be interpreted within the context of a hierarchical relationship between superior and subordinate. Here it is necessary to consider de facto relations between superior and subordinate, as well as the de jure relationship – the hierarchical relations based on laws and decrees within the organisation within which these persons are employed. In addition, the superior must be actually capable of intervening on the basis of this hierarchical relationship if his subordinate misbehaves, in any event if the latter commits criminal offences [...].[258]

The Supreme Court confirmed the reasoning with respect to command/superior responsibility[259] while again relying heavily on ICTY ju-

---

[258] Netherlands, Case LJN BJ2796 (2009), para. 135.
[259] Netherlands, Case LJN BR6598 (2011), paras. 2.6 and 2.7. The English translation of the decision follows the Dutch text.

risprudence, specifically quoting the Orić case.[260] This same reliance on international jurisprudence can be found in the Alemu case.[261]

While the elements for this form of responsibility were made clear, in practice only one person has been held liable, namely Alemu, because in the other two cases, Faqirzada and van Kouwenhoven, the person did not have effective control.

In Germany, the Murwanashyaka judgment of the Federal Appeals Court discussed command/superior responsibility while relying on academic literature that in turn had examined international jurisprudence on this point. The main elements of the judgment regarding this form of responsibility are that it is sufficient to attract liability if a commander can influence the action of the military units by means of subordinate persons in the military leadership through the chain of command. In addition, the superior can only be punishable if he indeed could have prevented the act through the required and reasonable use of his command or leadership; it is not sufficient to conclude that the superior could have made the subordinate's execution of the act more difficult or less likely. In the Murwanashyaka case, the accused was only formally the chief military leader of the FDLR and was in fact dependent on the military branch, without any commanding power in military affairs against the military. The court observes that on this point, German law is stricter than international criminal law.[262] As in the Netherlands, the accused was acquitted of this charge.

Courts in the Netherlands and Germany, where command/superior responsibility has been discussed in some detail, have drawn significantly on the international jurisprudence in developing the parameters of the concept while still keeping close to the national jurisprudence. This is not surprising, since neither country had this type of responsibility in its legislation until it incorporated the provisions of the Rome Statute in its criminal legislation, utilising the detailed language of Article 28 of that instrument.

---

[260] ICTY, Appeals Chamber, *Prosecutor v. Orić*, Judgment, IT-03-68-A, 3 July 2008 (www. legal-tools.org/doc/e053a4/).

[261] Netherlands, Case ECLI:NL:RBDHA:2017:16383 (2017), para. 13.5.2.

[262] Germany, Case 5-3 StE 6/10 (2015), part 4, secs. A.2.d and A.4.

8.18.2.5. Conspiracy

Conspiracy has been used in the United Kingdom, the United States, and the Netherlands. In the Netherlands, as indicated above, it does not appear to be treated as a full 'inchoate offence'. The judgment in the Ntacyobata-bara case states that

> From the moment two or more persons agree to commit a se-
> rious offence, this constitutes conspiracy. The agreement is
> not bound by a certain form and does not necessarily mean
> that the crime should be committed by all conspirators. It is
> sufficient that one of them undertakes to commit the crime
> himself. However, the agreement should include an explicit
> intention, i.e. it should be aimed at a specific crime.[263]

Conspiracy has been the only form of liability used in the two UK judgments and the one US case, both in situations where the facts pertained to a person high up in a military or civilian hierarchy. None of the decisions provides reasons with respect to this form of responsibility, but it would appear that conspiracy in these cases was used as a possible substitute for command/superior responsibility. This could have been the case in the US context because the reference to command responsibility is part of an enumeration under the general heading of accessoryship and as such appears to be more akin to ordering. In the UK, the first case had been started and completed successfully with this approach before the amendments implementing the Rome Statute, so this form of liability was not available at that time. It is likely that with the success in the first case, it was decided that either conspiracy has been established as a viable form of liability or that the evidence to prove all the elements for command/ superior responsibility was not available. Given the problems in the Netherlands and Germany on that account, the approach taken was certainly justified.

8.18.2.6. Preparatory Acts

Criminal charges based on other preparatory acts at stages before completion and attempted completion of the crime, such as 'solicitation' and 'incitement', have been used in the Netherlands, Finland, and Switzerland.

---

[263] Netherlands, Case ECLI:NL:RBDHA:2013:8710 (2013), chap. 18, para. 5.

In the Netherlands, in the Ntacyobatabara case, the legal require-ment for solicitation,[264] according to the court

> is defined as a situation whereby a person, by using one or
> more means of solicitation provided in article 47 [of the
> Criminal Code] (gifts, promises, abuse of authority, violence,
> threat or deception, or by providing the opportunity, means
> or information) has intentionally solicited another person to
> commit a criminal offence because of which the person who
> was solicited can personally be held liable to punishment.
> Those actions must have been solicited intentionally and the
> intention of the person doing the solicitation must have been
> aimed at both soliciting the other to commit the crime and at
> the component parts of the crime which the other person was
> solicited to commit. The person soliciting must put the idea
> into the other person's head to commit the criminal offence,
> "awaken the other person's will" to commit a certain crime.
> A charge of solicitation cannot be brought if the other person
> already had the idea to commit the crime before the person
> doing the solicitation started his actions. However, a person
> can be held liable for solicitation if the intention to commit a
> certain offence already existed in the mind of the incited per-
> son, but only materialised after the actions of the person do-
> ing the solicitation. The psychological change must have
> been caused by the latter and the means that person used to
> solicit the other to commit the criminal offence. A charge of
> completed solicitation can only be brought if the crime has
> been committed or if a punishable attempt was made to
> commit that crime.[265]

The same case also discussed the requirements of incitement to commit genocide by relying on the ICTR jurisprudence:

> For the qualification of incitement to genocide it is required
> that the inciter himself/herself had the aim of creating a gen-
> ocide. The inciter must have had the intention that the per-

---

[264] The translated version of the judgment refers to incitement rather than solicitation, but from the Dutch text it is clear that solicitation or inducement is the correct legal expression.

[265] Netherlands, Case ECLI:NL:RBDHA:2013:8710 (2013), chap. 13, paras. 3–5. The court also said at chap. 15, para. 12, that "incitement to commit a crime does not equal being a co-perpetrator of a crime committed afterwards, even if this was the same crime as the one that was incited". See also the Alemu case, Netherlands, ECLI:NL:RBDHA:2017:16383 (2017).

sons who were incited indeed went on to commit geno-cide.[266]

In Finland, the Bazaramba case indicates that the accused gave a speech amounting to incitement to kill Tutsis in Rwanda in 1994, without providing further details, while the same was done in Switzerland in the Niyonteze case in similar circumstances.

Ordering as a legal concept has also been alluded to in Finland in the Bazaramba case, again without further details.

8.18.2.7. Final Observations

We conclude this chapter with two short observations regarding the application of domestic criminal law in the area of participation for universal crimes. The first is that if the same situations that we have seen adjudicated at the national level had been the subject of judicial consideration at the international level, the result would not necessarily have been different in terms of finding personal liability, although the reasoning or even the concrete form of liability might have been different.[267] With respect to the latter, one could contrast the approach of the UK and US courts when using conspiracy, which is not available under the Rome Statute, with the use of command/superior liability in the Netherlands and Germany, where international jurisprudence was closely adhered to.

Secondly, and this relates to the first point, the sophistication of personal liability analysis at the national level has to some extent improved over time, especially since 2010. Before that date, the jurisprudence was more concerned with jurisdictional issues and the parameters of international crimes. It is quite possible that because these issues needed to be resolved first and because of prosecutorial discretion, which had to take into account resources for such expensive cases, only the most straight-forward cases were selected for investigation and prosecution. These cases were invariably based either on direct involvement (perpetration) or on a close connection with other perpetrators carrying out the underlying crimes, so that attribution of personal liability was quite easily resolved under the existing national laws. As time went on, the jurisprudence developed at both the international and domestic levels, and with it the

---

[266] Netherlands, Case ECLI:NL:RBDHA:2013:8710 (2013), chap. 12, para. 9.
[267] See Ambos, 2016, pp. 1221–34, sec. 4A, *supra* note 111.

knowledge and experience of national specialist prosecution teams, which in turn increased their comfort level in bringing forward cases with more complex liability issues. Whether this will continue might be up for debate, though: for instance, none of the cases based on command/superior responsibility has yielded success as yet. This, however, might have more to do with the need to provide the courts with sufficient evidence than with the law as such, since cases prosecuted on the basis of universal jurisdiction often take place quite a distance from the relevant crime scenes and the social context of the universal crimes committed.

9

Personal Liability Concepts in
Domestic Universal Crimes Cases
Based on Territorial Jurisdiction

9.1. Introduction

While the preceding chapter dealt with domestic prosecutions based on universal or extraterritorial jurisdiction, this chapter examines efforts by countries to utilise ICL concepts regarding modes of participation in attributing criminal liability, based on territorial jurisdiction, for universal crimes that have taken place in their own territory.

As noted in Chapter 8, under international law the most common type of criminal jurisdiction is based on the territoriality principle. The exercise of this type of jurisdiction is a direct function of statehood and, by extension, an affirmation of territorial sovereignty.[1] The vital role of territorial jurisdiction as the default rule of criminal jurisdiction was explicitly expressed in the widely known 1927 Lotus Case, in which the Permanent Court of International Justice ('PCIJ') stated that "in all systems of law the principle of the territorial character of criminal law is fundamental".[2]

The decisive criterion under the territorial principle is the granting of jurisdiction over a criminal offence to the state in whose territory the act or omission took place. Accordingly, any state has jurisdiction over all types of conduct in its territory, irrespective of the nationality of the alleged offender.[3] Territory includes the land mass, internal waters, and ter-

---

[1] Antonio Cassese, *Cassese's International Criminal Law*, 3rd ed., revised by Antonio Cassese, Paola Gaeta, Laurel Baig, Mary Fan, Christopher Gosnell, and Alex Whiting, Oxford University Press, Oxford, 2013, p. 274; and Robert J. Currie and Joseph Rikhof, *International and Transnational Criminal Law*, 2nd ed., Irwin Law, Toronto, 2013, pp. 61–62.

[2] PCIJ, *Case of the S.S. Lotus* (France v. Turkey), Judgment, Series A, No. 10, 7 September 1927, p. 20 (www.legal-tools.org/doc/c54925/), cited in Cassese, 2013, p. 274, see *supra* note 1.

[3] Currie and Rikhof, 2013, pp. 61–62, see *supra* note 1.

ritorial sea extending 12 nautical miles from the coastal baseline.[4] The territorial land is also considered under international law to encompass other land under the control of the state, such as any occupied territory.[5]

Concerning the more precise determination of territorial jurisdiction, the PCIJ in the Lotus Case added that "the territoriality of criminal law [...] is not an absolute principle of international law and by no means co-incides with territorial sovereignty".[6] As noted by Cassese, this statement suggests a corollary of the territoriality principle, namely that a criminal offence is subject to a state's jurisdiction even if committed outside its national territory, provided the effects are felt in that territory.[7] Taking into consideration the complexities of universal crimes, then, as well as the fact that a criminal act often has several stages corresponding to different modes of participation, it is not always straightforward to determine territorial jurisdiction and which state has prioritised jurisdiction over the crime. An obvious example would be a criminal offence that is planned in one country and executed in another, a situation that is particularly relevant to, among others, war crimes pertaining to an international armed conflict. The territorial principle may thus lead to dual jurisdiction for both the state where a crime is planned and the state where it is executed (and/or where its effects are directly felt).

The systematic and large-scale nature of universal crimes, which implies either the direct involvement of or, alternatively, the corrosion of state institutions, often tends to render the authorities of the territorial state either unwilling or unable to prosecute these crimes. Nonetheless, number of national prosecutions for previous atrocities based on territorial jurisdiction is quite impressive. In total, over 30 countries have engaged in prosecuting universal crimes on the basis of territorial jurisdiction, including countries in Latin America, Africa, Europe, and Asia.[8]

---

[4] A state also has limited jurisdiction over the contiguous zone and the exclusive economic zone.

[5] Cassese, 2013, p. 275, see *supra* note 1; Currie and Rikhof, 2013, pp. 62–63, see *supra* note 1.

[6] PCIJ, *Case of the S.S. Lotus* (1927), p. 20 (www.legal-tools.org/doc/c54925/), cited in Cassese, 2013, p. 274, see *supra* note 1.

[7] Cassese, 2013, p. 274, see *supra* note 1.

[8] Joseph Rikhof, "Fewer Places to Hide? The Impact of Domestic War Crimes Prosecutions on International Impunity", in Morten Bergsmo (ed.), *Complementarity and the Exercise of*

In Europe, most of the countries that have carried out prosecutions of universal crimes are those of the former Yugoslavia, namely Bosnia and Herzegovina, Kosovo, Serbia, Croatia, Montenegro, Macedonia, and Slovenia, but also Romania, Hungary, and Lithuania. The Latin American countries include Chile, Peru, Colombia, Argentina, Uruguay, Bolivia, Guatemala, Haiti, Mexico, and El Salvador. Examples in Asia involve proceedings first and foremost in East Timor and Bangladesh, but also one case in Afghanistan as well as some in Indonesia, although those in the latter country have been widely considered sham proceedings. In Africa, prosecutions have been initiated in the Republic of Congo, the Democratic Republic of Congo, Rwanda, Ethiopia, Chad, Guinea, Burundi, Uganda, Libya, and Côte d'Ivoire. In addition, Israel, Paraguay, and Brazil have been involved in cases turning on extraditions of individuals for these types of crimes.[9]

In the course of these processes, over 16,000 individuals have been prosecuted for their involvement in crimes, a number that is particularly impressive if compared to the total of just 204 persons convicted by the international tribunals and national courts on the basis of universal jurisdiction.[10] At the same time, as will be shown in this chapter, some of these national convictions have occurred in mass trials and/or in proceedings of questionable legal quality.

There is considerable variation with respect to the character of the judicial institutions that have utilised territorial jurisdiction to prosecute universal crimes or similar types of atrocity crimes. They range from strongly internationalised institutions (for instance, in East Timor and Bosnia and Herzegovina) to primarily domestic institutions with international facets (for example, Iraq) or with certain special courts (for instance, Bangladesh, Rwanda) or prosecutors (for example, Ethiopia), to purely domestic judicial bodies. Many of these institutions can also be described as 'mixed tribunals' because of their combined national-international legal

---

Universal Jurisdiction for Core International Crimes, Torkel Opsahl Academic EPublisher, Oslo, 2010, pp. 32 and 112.

[9]   Rikhof, 2010, pp. 32, 39, 56 ff., and 59, see *supra* note 8.
[10] *Ibid.*, p. 112.

framework and/or mixed composition in employing both national and international judges and prosecutors.[11]

The institutions towards the strongly internationalised end of the scale include the East Timor Special Panels for Serious Crimes, which came into being following the promulgation of a constituting instrument by the United Nations Transitional Administration in East Timor ('UNTAET') on 6 June 2000.[12] Accordingly, the Special Panels were formally established through national legislation rather than through an agreement between the UN and the national authorities of East Timor.[13] Set up as specialised chambers within the Dili District Court, the Serious Crimes regime is best characterised as a domestic undertaking with strongly internationalised facets. One such feature relates to the composition of judges, where the regulation provided that each Special Panel would be staffed by one Timorese judge and two international judges appointed by the UN.[14] The UNTAET also established a special prosecutor's office, the Serious Crimes Unit, which was funded and staffed by the UN.[15]

A similar institution is the War Crimes Chamber ('WCC') in the Criminal and Appellate Divisions of the Court of Bosnia and Herzegovina (BiH). The WCC was set up as a joint initiative, in co-operation with the UN Security Council, between the ICTY and the High Representative in BiH.[16] Applying primarily the BiH Criminal Code of 2003, the WCC has jurisdiction over the core crimes of genocide, crimes against humanity,

---

[11] Kai Ambos is one author who applies this label to some of these institutions; see *Treatise on International Criminal Law*, vol. 1, *Foundations and General Part*, Oxford University Press, Oxford, 2013, pp. 40 ff. See also Joseph Rikhof, "Analysis: A History and Typology of International Criminal Institutions", in *PKI Global Justice Journal*, 2017, vol. 1, no. 15.

[12] UNTAET was established by the UN Security Council acting under the UN Charter, Chapter VII, in Resolution 1272 (1999) as the successor to the United Nations Mission to East Timor ('UNAMET'), and effectively exercised all legislative and executive authority, including the administration of justice; see UNTAET 1272 (1999) (1). For the purpose of the latter, the UNTAET established the SPSC by UNTAET Regulation 2000/15 of 6 June 2000; see UNTAET Regulation 2000/11, Section 10.3, of 6 March 2000.

[13] Rikhof, 2010, p. 9, see *supra* note 8.

[14] UNTAET Regulation 2000/15, Section 22.1.

[15] See UNTAET Regulation 2000/16.

[16] Cassese, 2013, p. 264, see *supra* note 1; Currie and Rikhof, 2013, pp. 222–23, see *supra* note 1.

---

and war crimes that have occurred in Bosnian territory.[17] While the WCC concerns itself with the most serious war crimes, BiH entity-level courts (including cantonal and district-level courts) also handle other war crime prosecutions.[18] Up to the end of 2012, international judges and prosecutors were also recruited to adjudicate and prosecute cases before the chamber.[19]

In the states that have primarily domestic institutions with various international facets, the judicial institutions display either less pronounced international aspects or only some of the components that are present in their more strongly internationalised counterparts. For example, the Iraqi Special Tribunal, later renamed the Iraqi High Criminal Court, was established by the US Coalition Provisional Authority. The Iraqi Transitional National Assembly approved its statute in 2005.[20] Although it constitutes a separate judicial organ outside the regular Iraqi judicial system,[21] its predominantly national character is evident in that both the judges and the prosecutors are exclusively Iraqi nationals. Despite this, the court also has some distinctly international elements: for instance, its daily operations are supported by international advisors, and under specific circumstances international judges may also be appointed.[22]

Other institutions in this category include those of Bangladesh, Rwanda, and Ethiopia. In Bangladesh, the prosecutions of alleged war crimes during the liberation struggle against Pakistan are conducted on the basis of a primarily domestic process under domestic law. However, the Bangladesh authorities established the specialised International Crimes Tribunal for the purpose of adjudicating these crimes.[23] A similar arrangement is found in Rwanda, where the High Council of the Judiciary in February 2012 established a chamber for universal crimes within the

---

[17] We say "primarily" because, as explained in Section 9.6.2. below, the Court of BiH under certain circumstances may also employ the provisions of the old Socialist Federal Republic of Yugoslavia ('SFRY') Criminal Code.

[18] Cassese, 2013, p. 264, see *supra* note 1.

[19] Currie and Rikhof, 2013, pp. 222–23, see *supra* note 1.

[20] *Ibid.*, pp. 223–24.

[21] Ambos, 2013, pp. 46–47, see *supra* note 11.

[22] Articles 4(3) and 28 of the Statute of the Iraqi Special Tribunal. See Currie and Rikhof, 2013, p. 223, n. 296, *supra* note 1.

[23] Rikhof, 2010, p. 56, see *supra* note 8.

High Court of Kigali, specifically for the purpose of adjudicating cases transferred from the ICTR and other countries.[24]

Ethiopia represents a third variant. The transitional Ethiopian government in 1992 established the Office of the Special Prosecutor, which was tasked with prosecuting participants allegedly involved in the crimes that occurred during the Derg regime. These proceedings were to take place before ordinary, domestic courts under the existing provisions of the national Penal Code of 1957.[25]

In the remainder of this chapter, we analyse how ICL concepts related to modes of participation have been employed within the jurisprudence of a sample of countries that have conducted trials involving serious crimes on the basis of territorial jurisdiction. Considering the relatively high number of states that have undertaken this task, the chapter is not intended to be exhaustive, but presents a representative sample of states from each major region for which there is accessible jurisprudence involving aspects of legal analysis relevant to our investigation. The following jurisdictions are included in the analysis: Bosnia and Herzegovina, Croatia, and Serbia in Europe; East Timor and Bangladesh in Asia; Ethiopia in Africa; and Argentina, Colombia, Chile, Guatemala, Peru, and Uruguay in Latin America.

9.2. East Timor

9.2.1. Overview and Historical Background

Following its declaration of independence in May 2002, the new nation of Timor-Leste, formerly East Timor, opted for a two-track path to deal with the crimes that took place towards the end of Indonesia's occupation of the territory. This dual approach included criminal proceedings through the Special Panels for Serious Crimes ('SPSC') as well as the transitional justice mechanism of the Commission for Reception, Truth and Reconciliation ('CAVR'). Both were established by the United Nations Transition-

---

24 *Ibid.*, p. 63.

25 Proclamation 22/1992 establishing the Office of the Special Prosecutor, 8 August 1992, issued by the House of Representatives of the Transitional Government of Ethiopia; see in particular Articles 6 and 7. For a more detailed account, see S. Vaughan, "The Role of the Special Prosecutors Office", in Kjetil Tronvoll, Charles Schaefer, and Girmachew Alemu Aneme (eds.), *The Ethiopian Red Terror Trials: Transitional Justice Challenged*, James Currey, Woodbridge, UK, 2009, pp. 51–67.

al Administration in East Timor,[26] which was tasked with facilitating East Timor's transition to independence.

This section is exclusively concerned with the SPSC. We will show that although there was considerable variation in the quality of the trials conducted as part of the Serious Crimes process,[27] both the prosecutors of the Serious Crimes Unit ('SCU') and the judges of the SPSC faced significant difficulties in attempting to employ the complex crimes and legal concepts of ICL. They faced particular challenges in attempting to link the individual accused to the crimes, as the legal analysis in the application of the various modes of participation tended to be inconsistent and at times confused. We illustrate some of the difficulties encountered by judges when conducting internationalised prosecutions at the domestic level.[28] The population of cases includes those up until May 2005, when the UN mandate of the SCU was formally terminated.[29]

The historical context for the crimes that took place in East Timor started with the Indonesian invasion of East Timorese territory in December 1975. This initiated a 24-year occupation under which large-scale atrocities and human rights abuses were perpetrated against both Timorese resistance groups and the civilian population, including periodic massa-

[26] See *supra* note 12. The CAVR was established by UNTAET Regulation 2001/10 of 13 July 2001.

[27] The variation in quality of the judgments persisted for the entire lifetime of the SPSC. In fact, one author concludes that "[t]he quality of a Judgment depended more on who wrote it than at what point in the Special Panels' evolution it was written". David Cohen, *Indifference and Accountability: The United Nations and the Politics of International Justice in East Timor*, Special Report 9, East-West Center, Honolulu, 2006, p. 42.

[28] The literature that has evaluated the Serious Crimes process in East Timor also generally finds inadequate legal analysis and a poor conceptual understanding of fundamental ICL doctrines. See, for example, Cohen, 2006, pp. 89–90, *supra* note 27. Also see Alexander Zahar, "Commentary on Trial Judgments of the East Timor Special Panels in the Case of Jose Cardoso Ferreira and Agustinho Atolan", in Andre Klip and Göran Sluiter (eds.), *Annotated Leading Cases of International Criminal Tribunals: Timor Leste: The Special Panels for Serious Crimes, 2001–2003*, Intersentia, Antwerp, 2008, pp. 762–65.

[29] On the termination of the SCU mandate and the path ahead for the remaining cases not yet investigated, see Caitlin Reiger and Marieke Wierda, *The Serious Crime Process in Timor Leste: In Retrospect*, Prosecutions Case Studies Series, International Center for Transitional Justice, 2006, pp. 36–37.

cres of unarmed civilian protesters.[30] In total, an estimated one-third of the population of East Timor, about 200,000 people, perished.[31] The atrocities culminated in 1999 in the aftermath of a UN-initiated referendum on independence for East Timor, which resulted in a clear pro-independence majority of 78.5 per cent.[32] After the vote, the Indonesian military and the civilian administration in East Timor pursued a strategy of escalated violence to suppress the demand for independence. This strategy included the establishment and arming of Timorese militia groups tasked with carrying out a scorched earth policy.[33] Eventually, at the end of September 1999, Indonesia withdrew from East Timor after strong international pressure.

Established by national legislation as an initiative of the UNTAET administration, the SPSC had temporal jurisdiction restricted to these final events, namely the atrocities carried out between 1 January and 25 October 1999.[34] The details of the institutional setup of the SPSC, including its mixed composition of Timorese and international judges, and its jurisdiction over universal crimes (genocide, crimes against humanity, war crimes) are set out in the introductory section of this chapter.

Before turning to the SPSC's application of specific modes of participation, several aspects of these trials must be noted. These speak to the merits of the Serious Crimes process as well as to some serious legal shortcomings that affect the value of these trials from an ICL perspective.[35]

---

[30] Judicial System Monitoring Programme, *Digest of the Jurisprudence of the Special Panels for Serious Crimes*, Dili, Timor Leste, April 2007, p. 6 (hereafter cited as *SPSC Digest*); and Reiger and Wierda, 2006, pp. 4–8, see *supra* note 29.

[31] Reiger and Wierda, 2006, p. 4, see *supra* note 29.

[32] *SPSC Digest*, 2007, p. 6, see *supra* note 30.

[33] Reiger and Wierda, 2006, pp. 4–8, see *supra* note 29.

[34] UNTAET Regulation 2000/11, Section 10, and UNTAET Regulation 2000/15, Section 2. The procedural aspects of the trials are set out in UNTAET Regulation 2000/30, the Transitional Rules of Criminal Procedure ('TRCP').

[35] In addition to the aspects mentioned in this section, the Serious Crimes process has also been strongly criticised in relation to the right to fair trial and adequate defence counsel for the accused. See, for example, Reiger and Wierda, 2006, pp. 26–28, *supra* note 29. See also, as an illustration of an apparent blatant violation of the right to fair trial, East Timor, Dili District Court, Trial Chamber, *Prosecutor v. Maubere*, Judgment, Case 23/2003, 27 May 2004 (www.legal-tools.org/doc/9cf6f5/). The accused was convicted of murder as a crime against humanity although he was never charged with this underlying crime, effectively undermining his opportunity to properly prepare his defence. The Court of Appeal

---

First, those prosecuted in the East Timorese Serious Crimes trials were for the most part relatively low-level perpetrators.[36] Most of the participants who occupied high-level positions within the relevant power structures were sheltered by Indonesia, which refused to extradite them. Some early prosecutions that took place before the Indonesian Ad Hoc Human Rights Court have likewise been widely criticised as primarily designed to shield perpetrators rather than to ensure criminal responsibility for the crimes.[37] Thus, those most responsible for the atrocities have largely avoided criminal responsibility.[38]

Second, while the applicable law provided for jurisdiction over universal crimes, the majority of the cases (in particular in the early stages of the Serious Crimes process) were prosecuted as ordinary domestic crimes, most often in the form of murder.[39] The decisions by the SCU to pursue many of these crimes as domestic rather than universal crimes have been a source of controversy. An example is *Prosecutor v. Joao Fernandes*,[40] in which the accused was indicted and convicted for a single murder for his participation in a massacre in a police station in Maliana. At trial, the dissenting Timorese judge strongly criticised the prosecution's decision, arguing that the facts of the case indicated that the more correct indictment would have been one of crime against humanity.[41] Linton also demon-

---

changed the conviction to an ordinary crime of murder under the Indonesian Penal Code – an offence also not included in the indictment. For an extended critique of this judgment, see Cohen, 2006, pp. 77–79, *supra* note 27.

[36] Reiger and Wierda, 2006, p. 28, see *supra* note 29.

[37] *Ibid.*, p. 10. Also see Megan Hirst and Howard Varney, *Justice Abandoned? An Assessment of the Serious Crimes Process in East Timor*, Occasional Paper Series, International Center for Transitional Justice, 2005, pp. 11–12.

[38] Hirst and Varney, 2005, p. 16, see *supra* note 37. As noted by Reiger and Wierda, 2006, pp. 1–2, *supra* note 29, the predicted inability of a domestic Timorese process to ensure the surrender of the most responsible participants was one of the main reasons that several actors, including the UN-appointed International Commission of Inquiry, favoured the establishment of an international tribunal similar to the ICTY and ICTR rather than a hybrid-type tribunal like the SPSC.

[39] For a critical evaluation of this practice, see Suzannah Linton, "Prosecuting Atrocities at the District Court of Dili", in *Melbourne Journal of International Law*, 2001, vol. 2, no. 2, pp. 414–58.

[40] East Timor, Dili District Court, Trial Chamber, *Prosecutor v. Fernandes*, Judgment, Case 1/2000, 25 January 2000 (www.legal-tools.org/doc/e2e6d6/).

[41] Dissenting Opinion of Judge Maria Pereira, in Cohen, 2006, p. 47, see *supra* note 27.

---

strates the possibility of prosecuting this case under CAH, although she concludes that prosecuting it instead as a domestic crime of murder was not inappropriate, given that the grossly inadequate resources available to the SCU would have limited its ability to conduct the necessary investigations to obtain a conviction for the more complex universal crime of CAH. .[42]

A third, and for our purpose perhaps even more important, aspect of the Serious Crimes proceedings relates to the competence of the judges. While the international judges who served on the Special Panels represented a rather wide range of national jurisdictions,[43] none had any prior experience with ICL or IHL, and some even lacked experience with criminal law in general.[44] A similar pattern of limited experience with complex universal crimes also characterised the SCU's investigative body, the United Nations Civilian Police ('CIVPOL'),[45] which may help explain why simple domestic crimes were the ones most often charged.

This lack of experience among the SPSC judges was reflected in often inaccurate and sometimes confused application of ICL concepts and theories. Thus, while the applicable law at the SPSC largely incorporates the provisions of the Rome Statute, there are many instances in which the SPSC's application of the concepts fell short of adhering to international standards.

A related problem is that in the early judgments, at least, the judges made limited reference to existing international jurisprudence. Recourse to this jurisprudence, in particular to the often quite elaborate jurisprudence of the *ad hoc* tribunals, arguably could have aided the SPSC judges in a more sophisticated elucidation of complex ICL concepts.[46] This can be seen in, among other cases, *Prosecutor v. Umbertus Ena and Carlos Ena*. Upon appeal of the conviction of the former defendant, the Court of

---

[42] Linton, 2001, pp. 437–55 and 456–58, see *supra* note 39.

[43] Including, among others, the United States, Germany, Italy, Burundi, Uganda, Portugal, Brazil, and Cape Verde.

[44] Reiger and Wierda, 2006, pp. 14–15, see *supra* note 29. This was the case even though UNTAET Regulation 2000/15, Section 23.2, emphasised previous experience in criminal law, international law, IHL, and human rights law as among the required qualifications for judges of the Special Panels.

[45] Reiger and Wierda, 2006, pp. 16–17, see *supra* note 29.

[46] Cohen, 2006, p. 46, see *supra* note 27.

Appeal issued a somewhat confused ruling that an accused could not be convicted of multiple counts of one underlying crime (for instance, multiple murder) as CAH, nor of several *different underlying crimes* (for example, murder, torture, enforced disappearance) as CAH, despite the existing jurisprudence of the *ad hoc* tribunals supporting the opposite.[47]

That said, the SPSC did gradually increase its examination of the jurisprudence of the *ad hoc* tribunals, leading to more sophisticated legal analyses in some judgments. An example is the case of *Prosecutor v. Abilio Mendes Correia*,[48] in which the Special Panel quite cogently analysed the elements of CAH and the underlying offences by carefully (at least by SPSC standards) consulting a number of ICTY and ICTR cases.

However, despite increased reliance on international jurisprudence, great variation persisted in the quality of the Special Panels' efforts to apply such jurisprudence, and by extension the substantive law of ICL. This is illustrated by *Prosecutor v. Jose Cardoso*, in which the Special Panel copy-pasted from another judgment that exclusively cited the Trial Chamber judgments of the ICTY and ICTR, despite their common Appeals Chamber having ruled on the same cases.[49] As noted by Zahar, this had direct implications for the application of the law. The Special Panel's reliance on older Trial Chamber judgments led it to erroneously require a state policy context for CAH, even though this requirement had already been rejected as a legal element in subsequent jurisprudence of the ICTY Appeals Chamber.[50] There are also some instances in which the SPSC conflated two separate universal crimes – on at least two occasions, by

---

[47] East Timor, Dili District Court, Trial Chamber, *Prosecutor v. Umbertus Ena and Carlos Ena*, Judgment, Case 5/2002, 23 March 2004 (www.legal-tools.org/doc/ec8173/), cited in Cohen, 2006, pp. 66–68, see *supra* note 27.

[48] East Timor, Dili District Court, Trial Chamber, *Prosecutor v. Abilio Mendes Correia*, Judgment, Case 19/2001, 9 March 2004 (www.legal-tools.org/doc/6b03bf/), cited in Cohen, 2006, p. 60, see *supra* note 27.

[49] East Timor, Dili District Court, Trial Chamber, *Prosecutor v. Cardoso*, Judgment, Case 04/2001, 5 April 2003, para. 306 (www.legal-tools.org/doc/272392/).

[50] Zahar, 2008, pp. 763–64, see *supra* note 28. However, as the author also notes, the existence of a state policy or plan may be of evidential value in proving the other elements of the crime.

convicting an accused of "crime against humanity in the form of genocide".[51]

This pattern of inaccuracies and inconsistencies in the application of legal concepts and theories is, as will be shown in the next section, repeated with respect to the SPSC's application of the law on individual criminal liability in terms of the various modes of participation linking the accused to the crime.

9.2.2. Legal Basis of Personal Liability

The applicable law before the SPSC on modes of participation is set out in UNTAET Regulation 2000/15, Section 14(3), which reads as follows:

> Section 14: Individual criminal responsibility
>
> 14.3 In accordance with the present regulation, a person shall be criminally responsible and liable for punishment for a crime within the jurisdiction of the panels if that person:
>
> (a) commits such a crime, whether as an individual, jointly with another or through another person, regardless of whether that other person is criminally responsible;
>
> (b) orders, solicits or induces the commission of such a crime which in fact occurs or is attempted;
>
> (c) for the purpose of facilitating the commission of such a crime, aids, abets or otherwise assists in its commission or its attempted commission, including providing the means for its commission;
>
> (d) in any other way contributes to the commission or attempted commission of such a crime by a group of persons acting with a common purpose. Such contribution shall be intentional and shall either:
>
> (i) be made with the aim of furthering the criminal activity or criminal purpose of the group, where such activity or purpose involves the commission of a crime within the jurisdiction of the panels; or

---

[51] See East Timor, Court of Appeal, *Prosecutor v. dos Santos*, Judgment, Case 16/2001, 15 July 2003 (www.legal-tools.org/doc/d8d11e/), and East Timor, Dili District Court, Trial Chamber, *Prosecutor v. Bere*, Judgment, Case 10/2000, 15 May 2001 (www.legal-tools.org/doc/7f265a/), cited in Cohen, 2006, pp. 84–88, *supra* note 27.

(ii) be made in the knowledge of the intention of the group to commit the crime;

(e) in respect of the crime of genocide, directly and publicly incites others to commit genocide;

(f) attempts to commit such a crime by taking action that commences its execution by means of a substantial step, but the crime does not occur because of circumstances independent of the person's intentions. However, a person who abandons the effort to commit the crime or otherwise prevents the completion of the crime shall not be liable for punishment under the present regulation for the attempt to commit that crime if that person completely and voluntarily gave up the criminal purpose.

In addition, Section 16 of the same regulation provides for the mode of command responsibility:[52]

Section 16: Responsibility of commanders and other superiors

In addition to other grounds of criminal responsibility under the present regulation for serious criminal offences referred to in Sections 4 to 7 of the present regulation, the fact that any of the acts referred to in the said Sections 4 to 7 was committed by a subordinate does not relieve his superior of criminal responsibility if he knew or had reason to know that the subordinate was about to commit such acts or had done so and the superior failed to take the necessary and reasonable measures to prevent such acts or to punish the perpetrators thereof.

The question of the existence of a hierarchy of modes of participation, which also has been the subject of much debate at the ICC in its interpretation of the identical wording of Article 25(3) of the Rome Statute,[53] was addressed by the SPSC in the case of *Prosecutor v. Anton Lelan*

---

[52] As is evident, while Section 14 is based on Article 25 of the Rome Statute, Section 16 on command responsibility is instead more akin to the *ad hoc* tribunal model. As stated by the SPSC in East Timor, *Cardoso* (2003), para. 507: "The concept of command responsibility [...] follows the examples set out in the ICTY and ICTR Statutes [...]". The panel did, however, also reference Article 28 of the Rome Statute when interpreting Section 16, although it relied primarily on ICTY jurisprudence; see in particular paras. 519–21.

[53] The ICC has taken the position that Article 25(3) does express a hierarchy of modes of participation, reflecting different degrees of blameworthiness, and is closely linked to the

Sufa. Phrasing it in terms of primary and subsidiary forms of liability, the SPSC directly addressed this question in considering whether the mode of command responsibility would be assimilated by that of ordering in instances where the facts of the case satisfied the elements of both. On the specific subject matter at hand, the Special Panel took the position that

> [t]he more indirect form of liability (of being merely a superior who did not prevent the criminal acts or punish his subordinates) is subsidiary to the more direct form of participation (ordering the killings).[54]

Having taken notice thereafter of examples of different solutions employed by the ICTY and ICTR, the panel further reasoned that

> [i]n "civil law" jurisdictions, a person who intentionally participates in the commission of a crime by ordering it, is regarded as a perpetrator of that crime himself, whereas a superior who fails to prevent a crime by his subordinates is not regarded as the perpetrator of that crime but of a separate crime of omission (failure to supervise). In such a case it is an undisputed principle that the separate crime of omission (by negligence) is subsidiary to the (intentionally) ordered crime. This principle also applies to international criminal law (Ambos in Cassese et al, The Rome Statute (Oxford, 2002), 843).
>
> This view is supported by the following: Since a superior who orders a crime (Sec.14.3(b) Reg.2000/15) must also be regarded as committing it "through another person" in the

---

theory of control of the crime. See, among others, Trial Chamber, *Prosecutor v. Katanga*, Judgment, ICC-01/04-01/07, 7 March 2014, paras. 1383–87 (www.legal-tools.org/doc/f74b4f/); Pre-Trial Chamber, *Prosecutor v. Mbarushimana*, Confirmation of Charges, ICC-01/04-01/10, 16 December 2011, para. 279 (www.legal-tools.org/doc/63028f/); and Trial Chamber, *Prosecutor v. Lubanga*, Judgment, ICC-01/04-01/06, 14 March 2012, para. 999 (www.legal-tools.org/doc/677866/). This issue has also been widely discussed in the scholarly literature; see, for example, Leila Sadat and Jarrod M. Jolly, "Seven Canons of ICC Treaty Interpretation: Making Sense of Article 25's Rorschach Blot", in *Leiden Journal of International Law*, 2014, vol. 27, no. 3, pp. 755–88; and Marjolein Cupido, "Common Purpose Liability Versus Joint Perpetration: A Practical View on the ICC's Hierarchy of Liability Theories", in *Leiden Journal of International Law*, 2016, vol. 29, no. 3, pp. 897–99. See further Chapter 6, Section 6.2.2.2.

54 East Timor, Dili District Court, Trial Chamber, *Prosecutor v. Sufa*, Judgment, Case 4a/2003, 25 November 2004, para. 18 (www.legal-tools.org/doc/48777b/), cited in *SPSC Digest*, 2007, pp. 96–97, see *supra* note 30.

sense of Sec.14.3(a) Reg.2000/15, and since the various forms of individual responsibility enumerated in Sec.14.3 have a distinct ranking – from the most direct form of commission in *lit.* (a) to the most indirect form of participation in *lit.* (d) – the more indirect form of responsibility incurred for the same conduct must be subsidiary to the more direct one, if violation of the principle *ne bis in idem* is to be avoided.

[…] Finally, it is widely held that no necessity is apparent to make use of superior responsibility for other purposes than as a "fall back liability" in the event that the ordering of a crime ("direct command responsibility") cannot be proven.[55]

The Special Panel thus considers that there exists a distinct ranking of the modes of liability, seemingly differentiated by the degree of direct (causal) link between the acts of the accused and the crime in each mode. This case is also one in which the SPSC judges actively consulted existing *ad hoc* jurisprudence and engaged in comparative law analysis, at least to some extent, when addressing problems relating to modes of participation.

As for the indictment stage, the Special Panels also considered how and to what extent an indictment must specify the specific mode of participation on which criminal liability is based. In this regard, the SPSC at times expressed the view that the modes of participation are not part of the elements of the substantive crimes, and therefore need not be specified in the indictment – at least not, apparently, beyond whether liability is based on Section 14 of UNTAET Regulation 2000/15 or under the separate provision on command responsibility under Section 16:

An "insufficient" indictment would be one that fails to indicate whether a person's criminal responsibility is individual (TRCP Sec. 14) or as a commander or superior (TRCP Sec. 16). In the present case, the defendant is informed in each count that he is alleged to be individually responsible as described in Sec. 14 of UNTAET Reg. 2000/15. […] Although the Prosecutor could have chosen to further specify the basis for the defendant's individual criminal responsibility with reference to a particular subsection of the regulation, it is not required that he do so.

---

[55] *Ibid.*, paras. 19–22.

> The subsections of TRCP Sec. 14.3 are not elements of an offense that must be specifically articulated. Rather, they merely describe the forms of conduct that are incorporated within the concept of individual criminal responsibility set out in TRCP Sec. 14. An indictment is not defective should it fail to specify a particular subsection of TRCP Sec. 14, and individual criminal responsibility can be demonstrated by evidence satisfying any of the subsections in TRCP Sec. 14.3. Consequently, proof that a person conducted himself as described in any one of the subsections in TRCP Sec. 14.3 will be sufficient to establish individual criminal responsibility on the count involved.[56]

In the case of *Prosecutor v. Francisco Pedro*, the Special Panel further expressed the opinion that the prosecution is not permitted to include charges of both direct perpetration and accessorial liability in a single indictment:

> As opposite, to the commission of a crime, *aiding, abetting* and *assisting* is a form of accessory liability. "The act of assistance need not have caused the act of the principal offender". The distinction between participation in a common criminal plan or enterprise, on one hand, and aiding and abetting a crime, on the other, is also supported by the Rome Statute for an International Criminal Court. Its Article 25 distinguishes between a person who "contributes to the commission or attempted commission of (...) a crime", where the contribution is intentional and done with the purpose of furthering the criminal activity or criminal purpose of the group or in the knowledge of the intention of the group to commit the crime; from a person who, "for the purpose of facilitating the commission of such a crime, aids, abets or otherwise as-

---

[56] East Timor, *Abilio Mendes Correia* (2004), pp. 2–3, in *SPSC Digest*, 2007, p. 28, see *supra* note 30. (Authors' note: It would appear that the references to TRCP in this quotation are in error and that instead a reference to UNTAET Regulation 2000/15 was intended; see *supra* note 34.) See also East Timor, Dili District Court, *Prosecutor v. de Carvalho*, Interlocutory Decision on Indictment, Case 10/2001, 27 January 2004, paras. 15–16 (www.legal-tools.org/doc/4bd0d3/); East Timor, Dili District Court, *Prosecutor v. Amati and Matos*, Decision on the Defendants' Motion on Defects in the Indictment, Case 12/2003, 11 November 2004, pp. 4–5 (www.legal-tools.org/doc/47ea51/); and East Timor, Dili District Court, Trial Chamber, *Prosecutor v. Da Costa and Punef*, Judgment, Case 22/2003, 27 April 2005, pp. 13–14 (www.legal-tools.org/doc/8acf9a/).

---

sists in its commission or its attempted commission, including providing the means for its commission". Therefore the action of one perpetrator who commits or of more co-perpetrators who participate in the commission stands separate from the conduct of abettors and aiders. So different that they cannot belong to the same person when committing the same crime. They are antithetical.[57]

On these grounds, the court dismissed the indictment.[58] The indictment charged that the accused had himself stabbed the victim (direct perpetration) or, alternatively, aided and abetted the stabbing,[59] and it might seem that the judges of the Special Panel here are confusing two stages of the criminal proceedings. However, while it is undisputed that an accused cannot be convicted both as a principal and as an accessory to the same offence, it seems strange that the prosecution should not have the opportunity to include alternative charges of, for instance, aiding and abetting in case it should turn out that the evidence does not suffice to elevate the accused's liability to that of a direct perpetrator. If such alternative, or subsidiary, charges are barred, this may lead to impunity for blameworthy acts of assistance or even to an underutilisation of commission forms of liability due to the more demanding elements of such modes of participation.

In sum, it seems that at the indictment stage the SPSC has required an indictment merely to specify whether an accused is alleged criminally responsible either under the mode of command responsibility or generically under Section 14. Beyond this, the Special Panels have repeatedly accepted that an indictment need not further specify the precise mode of participation linking the individual to the crime in question.

9.2.3. Application of the Modes of Liability

As noted above, those prosecuted before the SPSC were primarily low-level perpetrators. This aspect of the Serious Crimes process had direct

---

[57] East Timor, Dili District Court, *Prosecutor v. Pedro*, Interlocutory Decision to Dismiss Amended Indictment, Case 1/2001, 22 May 2001, pp. 5–6 (www.legal-tools.org/doc/547fd0/), cited in *SPSC Digest*, 2007, p. 27, see *supra* note 30.

[58] After a period of multiple amended indictments, this case was left dormant for almost two years, and eventually began in December 2004; see Cohen, 2006, p. 54, *supra* note 27.

[59] *Ibid.* In fact, in an amended indictment the prosecution, at one point in the course of the initial stages of the proceedings, also added a second defendant.

implications for the modes of participation utilised, in that attribution was based most frequently on singular or joint perpetration.[60] The various modes intended to capture the high-level organisers and instigators typically removed from the crime scene were less frequently employed, especially when compared to what is typically the case at the international tribunals.

Despite the emphasis on direct commission–type liability, the prosecutor over the course of the trials invoked a relatively wide range of modes, which to a varying degree were analysed by the SPSC. In addition to singular or joint perpetration, this include such modes as ordering,[61] aiding and abetting,[62] command responsibility,[63] and, rather frequently, JCE.[64] As further discussed below, however, many judgments are inherently unclear as to the specific mode of participation under which criminal liability is imputed, partly owing to the SPSC's inability to sufficiently differentiate the elements of the substantive crimes from the elements of the mode of participation in the course of the legal analysis and its application to the facts of the case.[65] Therefore, it is difficult to give a more

---

[60] Gideon Boas, James L. Bischoff, and Natalie L. Reid, *Forms of Responsibility in International Criminal Law, Volume I*, Cambridge University Press, Cambridge, 2007, p. 377. For examples of cases involving singular or joint perpetration, see East Timor, Dili District Court, Trial Chamber, *Prosecutor v. da Costa Nunes*, Judgment, Case 1/2003, 10 December 2003 (www.legal-tools.org/doc/493119/); East Timor, Dili District Court, Trial Chamber, *Prosecutor v. Pedro*, Judgment, Case 1/2001, 14 April 2005 (www.legal-tools.org/doc/99146b/); and East Timor, *de Carvalho* (2004).

[61] See, for example, East Timor, Dili District Court, Trial Chamber, *Prosecutor v. Rudolfo Alves Correia*, Judgment, Case 27/2003, 25 April 2005 (www.legal-tools.org/doc/4941ef/).

[62] For one case that considers aiding and abetting, see East Timor, Dili District Court, Trial Chamber, *Prosecutor v. Marques et al.*, Judgment, Case 09/2000, 11 December 2001 (www.legal-tools.org/doc/9e43e1/).

[63] See, for example, East Timor, Dili District Court, Trial Chamber, *Prosecutor v. Franca Da Silva*, Judgment, Case 4a/2001, 5 December 2002 (www.legal-tools.org/doc/f1b9e9/); and East Timor, *Cardoso* (2003).

[64] See, for example, East Timor, Dili District Court, Trial Chamber, *Prosecutor v. Martins and Goncalves*, Judgment, Case 11/2001, 13 November 2003 (www.legal-tools.org/doc/b77869/); East Timor, Dili District Court, Trial Chamber, *Prosecutor v. Barros and Mendonca*, Judgment, Case 1/2004, 12 May 2005 (www.legal-tools.org/doc/43c772/); East Timor, Dili District Court, Trial Chamber, *Prosecutor v. Perreira*, Judgment, Case 34/2003, 27 April 2005 (www.legal-tools.org/doc/5ce1a8/); and East Timor, *Cardoso* (2003).

[65] See Boas, Bischoff, and Reid, 2007, p. 134, *supra* note 60, citing as an example the specific case of East Timor, *Marques et al.* (2001).

elaborate and precise account of the range and relative frequency of the SPSC's utilisation of the various modes of participation, and even more difficult to pinpoint the elements defined for the respective modes.

Upon closer examination, there is significant variation within the jurisprudence of the Special Panels with respect to the thoroughness and accuracy of legal analysis, including the degree to which the judges made use of international jurisprudence in specifying the elements and scope of the various modes of participation. In fact, in various instances the Special Panels made little or no effort to develop a theory of liability or even establish the fundamental elements of the mode(s) of participation in question. An example is *Prosecutor v. Damiao da Costa Nunes*. While the court found the accused guilty of crimes against humanity in the form of murder and persecution as a co-perpetrator, the judges made no attempt to identify the elements of co-perpetration or to engage in any other form of substantive legal analysis of the law on individual criminal responsibility.[66]

The judges' approaches to analysing modes of liability often reflect a casual or careless attitude, similar to that expressed by the Special Panel concerning the required specification of liability modes in the indictment in the Pedro case, discussed in the preceding section. On occasion, such superficial analysis has caused not only inaccurate but also downright confused application of modes of participation in specific cases. The following examples, while not exhaustive, serve to illustrate some of the confusion that has occurred in the course of the Special Panels' application of the law on criminal participation.

First, there are inconsistencies in the application of specific elements of some of the modes of participation. With respect to the required mental element for ordering, soliciting, or inducing a crime under Section 14(3)(b), for example, the court in *Prosecutor v. Joni Marques et al.* indicated a knowledge standard:

---

[66] See the extremely abbreviated discussion on the legal aspects in East Timor, *da Costa Nunes* (2003), paras. 62–63, in Cohen, 2006, p. 71, see *supra* note 27. Other cases that illustrate incomplete treatments of the law on individual criminal responsibility and failure to establish the elements of the modes employed include East Timor, Dili District Court, Trial Chamber, *Prosecutor v. Lao*, Judgment, Case 10/2003, 3 December 2004 (www.legal-tools.org/doc/17309a/), and Trial Chamber, *Prosecutor v. Tacaqui*, Judgment, Case 20/2001, 12 September 2004 (www.legal-tools.org/doc/864bbe/).

> His *mens rea* arises from the evidence that, by participating in the decision-making for ordering the killing of the victim, he really knew that it would occur by other expeditious means. For him, the death was an expected result.[67]

In a later judgment, the panel elevated the required *mens rea* to one of intent for the criminal outcome:

> Regardless of the term which best defines a particular defendant's actions, criminal responsibility under Section 14.3(b) requires more than a mere causal relationship between the actions of a defendant and the resulting offense. Even in circumstances where a defendant's action <u>in fact</u> caused another to commit a crime or attempt to do so, a defendant can be held criminally responsible only if he acted <u>with the intent that the resulting crime be committed.</u> Were we to conclude otherwise, a defendant could be held responsible for the criminal actions of others even in circumstances where the defendant had neither the intent nor a reasonable expectation that his own actions would lead to the commission of the crime. This view is consistent with the provisions of Section 18.1 of UNTAET Regulation 2000/15, which states that an accused shall be criminally responsible only if the material elements of his crime "are committed with intent and knowledge." As defined in Section 18.2 of the same regulation, the meaning of intent "in relation to a consequence" is "that person means to cause that consequence or is aware that it will occur in the ordinary course of events." Similarly, the requirement of "knowledge" is met when a defendant has "awareness that a circumstance exists or a consequence will occur in the ordinary course of events.[68]

While such inconsistencies may at least partly reflect a natural development in the interpretation of the law, there are several examples of more serious confusion within the SPSC jurisprudence.

A telling example is found in *Prosecutor v. Francisco Perreira*,[69] where the judges' lack of conceptual understanding of fundamental doc-

---

[67] East Timor, *Marques et al.* (2001), para. 717, in *SPSC Digest*, 2007, p. 101, see *supra* note 30.

[68] East Timor, *Abilio Mendes Correia* (2004), para. 65, in *SPSC Digest*, 2007, p. 100, emphasis in original, see *supra* note 30.

[69] East Timor, *Perreira* (2005).

trines of individual criminal liability led to an erroneous conviction of attempted murder as a CAH in a case where the victim was actually killed. Perreira, along with several of his fellow militia guards, chased down a fugitive, after which the accused stabbed the victim in the back with a machete before one of the other guards shot the victim in the head. In applying JCE to this scenario, the majority of the Special Panel considered that liability under JCE requires that all participants share a common intent to achieve the criminal outcome in question, in this case murder. Having concluded that the evidence was insufficient to support such a finding, the judges instead convicted the accused of attempted murder.[70] Considering that attempt is an inchoate offence, it is logically incoherent to convict Perreira for attempted murder when the crime was in fact completed by the accused.[71]

Furthermore, at no point does the majority assess the applicability of the third form of JCE, also known as extended liability JCE. This form is specifically designed for scenarios where a specific crime fell outside the scope of the common plan but was nonetheless a foreseeable possibility, and where the accused accepted the outcome should it occur (that is, *dolus eventualis*) or willingly took that risk by his participation in the common design (that is, recklessness).[72] This oversight on the part of the judges indicates a fundamental lack of insight into the law of JCE liability.[73]

Another example demonstrates how insufficiently establishing the elements of the doctrine of command responsibility resulted in an unclear, at best, application of the law to the facts of the case. In *Prosecutor v. Marcelino Soares*,[74] the accused was convicted of CAH based on the notion of command responsibility, among other modes of liability. However,

---

[70] The dissenting judge strongly disagreed with the manner in which the majority applied the doctrine of JCE to the case, concluding instead that the appropriate conviction for count one would be murder as CAH rather than attempted murder. East Timor, *Perreira* (2005), Separate Opinion of Judge Phillip Rapoza, paras. 18–34.

[71] Cohen, 2006, p. 80, see *supra* note 27.

[72] For a detailed account of the three versions of JCE and their respective elements, see Chapter 7, Section 7.2.2.2. For attempt, see Chapter 7, Section 7.2.1.4.

[73] Cohen, 2006, p. 81–82, see *supra* note 27.

[74] East Timor, Dili District Court, Trial Chamber, *Prosecutor v. Soares*, Judgment, Case 11/2003, 11 December 2003 (www.legal-tools.org/doc/96331a/).

the Special Panel failed to elaborate on the specific elements required in order to establish criminal liability under this mode of participation, and thus also by implication to convincingly demonstrate that the facts of the case supported a finding of guilt.[75]

On appeal, the appellate court's treatment of the accused's liability under the doctrine of command responsibility was not much more convincing. While the Court of Appeal offered some sporadic factual findings relevant to proving some of the elements of command responsibility,[76] it did not do so in a systematic manner, thus causing confusion as to which exact elements it did consider necessary for a conviction.[77] Similarly perplexing is the court's conclusion: "The accused knew he was participating in the acts and he wanted to participate [...]".[78] As noted by Cohen, this statement might be consistent with a finding of criminal liability under the modes of singular or co-perpetration, but it has no obvious relevance for the doctrine of command responsibility as a special form of omission liability.[79]

9.2.4. Concluding Remarks

While the UNTAET regulations provide the SPSC with a legal framework mirroring that of the International Criminal Court, with respect to both the substantive crimes and modes of perpetration, the Special Panel has struggled to apply the law in a coherent way, often falling short of international standards of criminal law analysis.

Although there is some variation in the quality of the judgments, the SPSC never managed to develop a sound theory of individual criminal liability. On the contrary, as the above review illustrates, the Special Panels on many occasions made little effort even to establish the elements of the various modes, often resulting in inaccuracies and at times outright confusion when applying the modes to the facts of the case at hand. In

---

[75] Cohen, 2006, p. 74, see *supra* note 27.

[76] *Ibid.*, p. 75.

[77] *Ibid.*

[78] East Timor, Dili District Court, Court of Appeal, *Prosecutor v. Soares*, Judgment, Case 11/2003, 17 February 2005 (www.legal-tools.org/doc/105fc2/), in Cohen, 2006, p. 75, see *supra* note 27.

[79] Cohen, 2006, p. 75, see *supra* note 27. For a detailed account of the elements of command responsibility under international law, see Chapter 7, Section 7.2.2.5.

some cases they made little or no recourse to international jurisprudence, despite the fact that such recourse could have provided the inexperienced judges of the Special Panels with invaluable guidance. Even when international jurisprudence was consulted, it was often done in a less than satisfactory manner.

As some authors have concluded, the SPSC in general did not develop a jurisprudence of a sufficient standard to make a significant contribution to the further development of ICL.[80]

9.3. Bangladesh

9.3.1. Overview and Historical Background

The Bangladesh International Crimes Tribunal is charged with prosecuting universal crimes that were mainly committed from 25 March to 16 December 1971, during Bangladesh's War of Liberation.[81] The court is developing and applying comprehensive interpretations of extended liability in some areas. A number of different forms of extended liability have been invoked in a majority of the 34 trial-level decisions published between January 2013 and July 2018. There has so far been a 100 per cent conviction rate, with most cases resulting in sentences of death or, less commonly, life imprisonment. Earlier cases lacked a clear universal theory of punishable participation, set a low bar for findings of guilt through extended liability beyond singular perpetration, and introduced domestic modifications to international standards that increased the probability of guilty verdict. More recent precedents and methods of analysis have been of a higher quality in this respect and provide a better comparative basis for analysing the domestic Bangladeshi approaches and other domestic and international jurisdiction.

9.3.2. The Legal Basis of Modes of Liability

The constituting legislation provides jurisdiction for crimes against peace, crimes against humanity, and genocide. It uses wording derived from the IMT Charter for crimes against peace; from Control Council Law No. 10 (which is broader than the IMT Charter, while adding two more underly-

---

80 Reiger and Wierda, 2006, p. 26, see *supra* note 29.
81 See International Crimes (Tribunals) Act, 1973, Section 3(1) (www.legal-tools.org/doc/c09a98/).

ing crimes, namely abduction and confinement) for crimes against human-ity; and from the Genocide Convention for genocide.[82] The definition of war crimes used the wording of the IMT Charter while adding a "violation of any humanitarian rules applicable in armed conflicts laid down in the Geneva Conventions of 1949".[83] The statute finishes by providing juris-diction for "any other crimes under international law".[84]

Extended liability is set out in two provisions. Section 3, which provides jurisdiction for the four above-mentioned crimes, goes on to say that the following are also crimes within the jurisdiction of the tribunal: "attempt, abetment or conspiracy to commit any such crimes" and "com-plicity in or failure to prevent commission of any such crimes".[85] Section 4 then says:

> 4. (1) When any crime as specified in section 3 is committed by several persons, each of such person is liable for that crime in the same manner as if it were done by him alone.
>
> (2) Any commander or superior officer who orders, permits, acquiesces or participates in the commission of any of the crimes specified in section 3 or is connected with any plans and activities involving the commission of such crimes or who fails or omits to discharge his duty to maintain disci-pline, or to control or supervise the actions of the persons under his command or his subordinates, whereby such per-sons or subordinates or any of them commit any such crimes, or who fails to take necessary measures to prevent the com-mission of such crimes, is guilty of such crimes.

9.3.3. Application of the Modes of Liability

9.3.3.1. Lack of a General Theory of Personal Liability

Several of the more recent Bangladeshi cases, particularly the Sakhawat Hossain decision,[86] have presented sophisticated and comprehensive in-

---

[82] *Ibid.*, Section 3(2)(a), (b), and (c).

[83] *Ibid.*, Section 3(2)(e).

[84] *Ibid.*, Section 3(2)(f).

[85] *Ibid.*, Section 3(2)(g).

[86] Bangladesh International Crimes Tribunal, *Chief Prosecutor v. Md. Sakhawat Hossain, Md. Billal Hossain Biswas, Md. Lutfor Morol [died during trial], Md. Ibrahim Hossain alias Ghungur Ibrahim [absconded], Sheikh Mohammad Mujibur Rahman alias Mujibur Rahman [absconded], Md. A. Aziz Sardar son of late Ful Miah Sardar [absconded], Abdul*

---

terpretations of extended liability. For example, the court in Sakhawat Hossain presented an extended and thorough review of command responsibility based on varied sources such as the works of Sun Tzu, the practice of the Holy Roman Empire, the US Civil War, The Hague Conventions, the Leipzig War Crimes Trials, the Tokyo Trials, the Geneva Conventions, and the statutes and case law of the ICTY, ICTR, SCSL, and ICC.[87]

Other cases present a nuanced treatment of the elements of command and superior responsibility, such as analysis in the Sobhan case on whether "substantial influence" constitutes "effective control". [88] The Sakhawat Hossain case also presented a similarly extensive history and description of the concept of JCE, including careful separation of the concepts of JCE, conspiracy, and mere membership in an organisation.[89] Persuasive analysis of the concept of aiding and abetting and its distinction from other forms of liability has also been shown by the court in the cases of Abdul Jabbar Engineer as well as Shamsul Haque.[90]

At trial, defendants were often found criminally liable for universal crimes through a multitude of modes of liability. The terminology was sometimes not used clearly and consistently, and modes of liability were sometimes applied with minimal analysis of concepts or legal analysis.

Aziz Sardar son of late Ahmmad Sardar [absconded], Kazi Ohidul Islam alias Kazi Ohidus Salam [absconded], and Md. Abdul Khaleque Morol [absconded], Judgment, Case ICT-BD 04 of 2015, 10 August 2016 (www.legal-tools.org/doc/b1bbc7/).

[87] *Ibid.*, paras. 759–93.

[88] Bangladesh International Crimes Tribunal, *Chief Prosecutor v. Moulana Abdus Sobhan*, Judgment, Case ICT-BD 01 of 2014, 18 February 2015, paras. 190 and 543 (www.legal-tools.org/doc/100a3b/).

[89] Bangladesh, *Sakhawat Hossain* (2015), paras. 734–48. See also Bangladesh International Crimes Tribunal, *Chief Prosecutor v. Syed Md. Qaiser*, ICT-BD 04 of 2013, Judgment, 23 December 2014, paras. 916–20 (www.legal-tools.org/doc/f2e9a8/), for a sound analysis and discussion of JCE I and JCE II.

[90] Bangladesh International Crimes Tribunal, *Chief Prosecutor v. Md. Abdul Jabbar Engineer*, ICT-BD 01 of 2014, Judgment, 24 February 2015, paras. 136–43 and 154 (www.legal-tools.org/doc/40deae/); Bangladesh International Crimes Tribunal, *Chief Prosecutor v. Advocate Md. Shamsul Haque, S. M. Yusuf Ali, Md. Ashraf Hossain [absconded], Professor Sharif Ahamed alias Sharif Hossain [absconded], Md. Abdul Mannan [absconded], Md. Abdul Bari [absconded], Harun [absconded] and Md. Abul Hashem [absconded]*, ICT-BD 02 of 2015, Judgment, 18 July 2016, paras. 384–85 (www.legal-tools.org/doc/f11183/).

For example, in the Abdul Alim case, the defendant was alleged to have "abetted, aided, instigated, encouraged, facilitated and substantially contributed to" crimes against humanity, with the following subsequent allegations: JCE as a form of co-perpetration, complicity, being substantially concerned, substantial contribution, guilt through associate organisations, superior responsibility, aiding and abetting, abetting and contributing, and inciting.[91] In the case of Mir Quasem Ali, the court considered aiding, abetting, complicity, JCE, inducement and assistance, encouragement and instigation, ordering, substantially facilitating and assisting, co-perpetration, planning superior responsibility, culpable and effective association, common policy and purpose, instance, and being concerned with universal crimes.[92] Such concepts were frequently not fully explained or defined as they were being applied.

The court also sometimes made findings of guilt through a number of forms of liability with minimal analysis. For example, in the Ashrafuzzaman case, after a statement of the facts and evidence, the accused was found to be guilty through the modes of common plan and purpose, abetting, complicity, superior responsibility, JCE, and personal participation in the space of several paragraphs.[93] In Mir Quasem Ali, while the court did explain and analyse some key legal concepts,[94] in four paragraphs the accused was found to be guilty through the modes of participation, aiding, abetting, inducement, encouragement, facilitation, contribution, association, instigation, assisting, complicity, culpable affiliation, and common policy and purpose. There was generally little discussion and application of legal tests or separation of concepts.[95]

---

[91] Bangladesh International Crimes Tribunal, *Chief Prosecutor v. Md. Abdul Alim @ M. A Alim*, ICT-BD 01 of 2012, Judgment, 9 October 2013, paras. 17 and 269 (www.legal-tools.org/doc/907c69/).

[92] Bangladesh International Crimes Tribunal, *Chief Prosecutor v. Mir Quasem Ali*, ICT-BD 03 of 2013, Judgment, 2 November 2014 (www.legal-tools.org/doc/2b3071/).

[93] Bangladesh International Crimes Tribunal, *Chief Prosecutor v. (1) Ashrafuzzaman Khan @ Naeb Ali Khan [absconded] & Chowdhury Mueen Uddin [absconded]*, ICT-BD 01 of 2013, Judgment, 3 November 2013, paras. 241–45 (www.legal-tools.org/doc/2538dc/).

[94] Bangladesh, *Mir Quasem Ali* (2014), paras. 641–59.

[95] *Ibid.*, paras. 237–40.

9.3.3.2. Definition of Concepts without Clear Legal Tests

Several cases defined modes of liability as including or not including other modes of liability instead of invoking clear legal tests. For example, in Azam, complicity was defined in broad terms as encompassing aiding and abetting, procurement (for example, of weapons), instigation (for instance, giving instructions), "accessorial liability", "accomplice liability", and "conspiratorial liability". These concepts were not further clarified.[96]

In the Syed case, the court stated that "the act of abetting encompasses 'inciting', 'soliciting', 'inducing', 'influencing', 'encouraging' the principal perpetrators". The court then stated that "participation refers to the act of ordering, soliciting, inducing, aiding, abetting, or otherwise assisting the commission of a crime or the facilitation thereof".[97] This creates conceptual confusion because "participation" is defined as including abetting, soliciting, and inducing, whereas abetting itself is also defined as including soliciting and inducing. In a subsequent case, "abetting" was given a different definition: "Abetting involves no more than encouraging of a particular act by conduct and act. Abettor assists the principal perpetrator or perpetrators in committing the crime".[98]

9.3.3.3. Modes Interpreted with a Low Bar for Findings of Guilt

The court interpreted various modes of liability in such a way that a low bar was set for findings of guilt, particularly with regard to the qualitative nature of a defendant's contribution to a crime. For example, in Ashrafuzzaman the court stated that "physical participation or involvement of the accused in any manner, either even by a single act or omission … inevitably and lawfully may make them criminally liable".[99] The court in Kamaruzzaman similarly found that JCE includes contribution to a crime "in any manner", and that it is enough to be "related to a scheme or sys-

---

[96] Bangladesh International Crimes Tribunal, *Chief Prosecutor v. Professor Gholam Azam*, ICT-BD 06 of 2011, Judgment, 15 July 2013, paras. 218–20 (www.legal-tools.org/doc/436ed9/).

[97] Bangladesh, *Syed Md. Qaiser* (2014).

[98] Bangladesh International Crimes Tribunal, *Chief Prosecutor v. Md. Forkan Mallik @ Forkan*, ICT-BD 03 of 2014, Judgment, 16 July 2015, para. 92 (www.legal-tools.org/doc/55a064/).

[99] Bangladesh, *Ashrafuzzaman* (2013), para. 66.

tem which had a criminal outcome".[100] In Zahid, the court relied on ICTY jurisprudence to conclude that it is not necessary to show that a contribution to JCE is "substantial" or "significant".[101]

A number of decisions also relied on the ICTY Tadić case to invoke the standard of "concerned with the killing" as distinct from other modes of extended liability. This was interpreted in Mujahid as requiring that the accused took "consenting part" in the crime, that the accused was "connected with plans or enterprise", and that the accused "belonged to" the criminal organisation.[102] Standards such as "concerned with", "connected with", and "belonged to" were not clearly defined and appear to have been treated expansively.

9.3.3.4. Concepts Not Clearly Based on International Standards

The court also considered modes of extended liability that are not clearly rooted in international standards. For example, in Molla the court found that the accused's "prior conduct and 'culpable association' were sufficient to connect him" to an attack and therefore constitute complicity, but there was little explanation of what "culpable association" means or how it is to be applied.[103] In Abul Alim, the defendant was accused of leading an "associate organization" to an organisation that committed crimes, but there was little definition of "associate organization" or discussion of the nature of the required links and individual contribution between the asso-

---

[100] Bangladesh International Crimes Tribunal, *Chief Prosecutor v. Mohammed Kamaruzzaman*, ICT-BD 03 of 2012, Judgment, 9 May 2013, paras. 241 and 244 (www.legal-tools.org/doc/65ed5a/).

[101] Bangladesh International Crimes Tribunal, *Chief Prosecutor v. Zahid Hossain Khokon @ M. A. Zahid @ Khokon Matubbar @ Khokon*, ICT-BD 04 of 2013, Judgment, 13 November 2014 (www.legal-tools.org/doc/2e7b53/). But in the Azad case, the court found that it is necessary to establish that the accused "substantially contributed or facilitated" an offense. Bangladesh International Crimes Tribunal, *Chief Prosecutor v. Moulana Abdul Kalam Azad*, ICT-BD 05 of 2012, Judgment, 21 January 2013, para. 209 (www.legal-tools.org/doc/3fdb60/).

[102] Bangladesh International Crimes Tribunal, *Chief Prosecutor v. Ali Ahsan Muhammad Mujahid*, ICT-BD 04 of 2012, Judgment, 17 July 2013, paras. 445–46 and 626 (www.legal-tools.org/doc/77d0d6/).

[103] Bangladesh International Crimes Tribunal, *Chief Prosecutor v. Abdul Quader Molla*, ICT-BD 02 of 2012, Judgment, 5 February 2013, paras. 212 and 215 (www.legal-tools.org/doc/42e4c8/).

---

ciate organisation and the criminal organisation.[104] In Mir Quasem Ali, the concept of "instance" was introduced as encompassing signalling, providing moral support, encouragement, and approval of crimes.[105] These terms are not themselves defined, nor was there discussion of how "instance" relates to other forms of liability such as aiding and abetting. The use of these novel terms, often without definitions, increased the probability of findings of guilt.

9.3.3.5. Application of Domestic Legal Rules and Interpretation to Lower the Threshold for Guilt

The court in Mujahid also significantly reduced or eliminated the requirement that a defendant have knowledge of the crime under the command responsibility doctrine:

> [T]he prosecution is not required to prove that the accused superior either had any 'actual knowledge' (knew) or 'constructive knowledge' (should have known) about commission of the subordinate's crime. The 'knowledge' requirement is not needed to prove [the] accused's superior position within the ambit of the Act of 1973. However an individual's superior position *per se* is a significant *indicium* that he had knowledge of the crimes committed by his subordinates.[106]

9.3.4. Concluding Remarks

While recent decisions have presented examples of comprehensive analysis and application of modes of extended liability, the development of such standards has been inconsistent. There has been in several cases an excessive invocation of modes of liability without consistent definitions or explanation of how these concepts differ from each other. There has also been a substantive lowering of the threshold of guilt through expansive interpretation of liability concepts, introduction of novel concepts without clear definitions, and application of domestic legal rules that are not in line with international standards. Such trends show a divergence between the approach of the courts in Bangladesh and the approach in international tribunals and other domestic jurisdictions.

---

[104] Bangladesh, *Abdul Alim* (2013), para. 663.

[105] Bangladesh, *Mir Quasem Ali* (2014), para. 256.

[106] Bangladesh, *Ali Ahsan Muhammad Mujahid* (2013).

9.4. Ethiopia

9.4.1. Overview and Historical Background

In order to address its history of mass atrocities, Ethiopia opted in 1992 for criminal prosecutions before its domestic courts in order to end impunity for those responsible for the crimes that occurred between 1974 and 1991. It chose this path rather than dealing with the atrocities through a national reconciliation process of the type undertaken elsewhere in the world.

Following a popular revolution in Ethiopia in 1974, a military junta that became known as the Derg (meaning 'Council' in the Geez language[107]) exploited the upheaval to seize control of the state apparatus. The regime remained in power until it was overthrown by the military forces of the Ethiopian People's Democratic Force in 1991. During its reign, the Derg actively sought to eliminate anyone who posed a threat to their incumbency and Marxist-oriented ideology, employing their security forces to eliminate, torture, or otherwise impose grave suffering on individuals and groups whom they labelled as either "subversives", "anti-revolutionaries", or generally "anti-people".[108]

9.4.2. The Legal Basis of Personal Liability

While the exact figures are controversial, the court documents give an idea of the scale of the atrocities. The charges filed indicate that at least 12,315 individuals were killed, while the trials found sufficient evidence to establish that 9,546 of them were direct victims of crimes.[109]

---

[107] Firew Kebede Tiba, "The *Mengistu* Genocide Trial in Ethiopia", in *Journal of International Criminal Justice*, 2007, vol. 5, no. 2, pp. 513–28, at p. 515.

[108] For more details see Firew Kebede Tiba, "The Trial of Mengistu and Other Derg Members for Genocide, Torture and Summary Executions in Ethiopia", in Chacha Murungu and Japhet Biegon (eds.), *Prosecuting International Crimes in Africa*, Pretoria University Press, Pretoria, 2011, pp. 163–65; and Firew Kebede Tiba, "Mass Trials and Modes of Criminal Responsibility for International Crimes: The Case of Ethiopia", in Kevin Jon Heller and Gerry Simpson (eds.), *The Hidden Histories of War Crimes Trials*, Oxford University Press, Oxford, 2013, pp. 307–10.

[109] Tiba, 2011, pp. 163–65, see *supra* note 108. These figures are, however, likely quite conservative given the total number of deaths associated with the regime's repression, which by some estimates are as high as 1.5 million dead, disappeared, or injured on all sides; see Tiba, 2007, p. 516, *supra* note 107.

As noted in the introduction to this chapter, the Ethiopian proceedings are more domestic in nature than those in some other countries, but they nonetheless have certain international facets.

The first of these relates to the prosecutorial strategy and nature of the proceedings. The Office of the Special Prosecutor ('OSP') developed a prosecutorial strategy similar to that known from international tribunals and discussed extensively in the specialised ICL literature,[110] namely one of differentiating offenders based on their position in the hierarchical power structure of the criminal apparatus. The OSP placed offenders in three categories: (1) high-level policy makers and decision makers; (2) mid-level officials and commanders in charge of implementing and further passing down orders; and (3) low-level executors on the ground, who most often physically carried out the crimes.[111]

On the other hand, the Ethiopian cases are unprecedented in the nature of their proceedings, in that they prosecuted universal crimes by utilising mass trials. The case of Mengistu and Others had a total of 106 defendants, while other cases have joined up to 200 accused in a single trial.[112] Given their mass nature, it is perhaps not surprising that the trials have been criticised for several weaknesses. These are primarily related to the rights of the accused, including the right to a free, fair, and expeditious trial, the right of access to adequate counsel of one's choice, and the right to be present (as many were convicted *in absentia*). Issues have also been raised in relation to 'victor's justice'.[113]

The second aspect relates to the substantive crimes under the 1957 Penal Code, which are different in two respects from the prevailing standards under customary international law. First, the Penal Code does not clearly separate the crime of genocide from CAH, but lumps them together under its Article 281. When ruling on a preliminary objection raised by

---

[110] See the discussion in Chapter 6, Section 6.2.3.1.

[111] Girmachew Alemu Aneme, "The Anatomy of *Special Prosecutor v. Colonel Mengistu Hailemariam et al.* (1994–2008)", in *International Journal of Ethiopian Studies*, 2009, vol. 4, no. 1/2, pp. 1–53, at p. 3; Tiba, 2011, p. 169, see *supra* note 108.

[112] These last figures are reported by Tiba, 2007, p. 514, n. 2, see *supra* note 107. He cites as representative cases those of *Special Prosecutor v. Kassayie Aragaw et al.*, File 923/89 (www.legal-tools.org/doc/f36eb2/), and *Special Prosecutor v. Debela Dinsa et al.*, File 912/89 (www.legal-tools.org/doc/5d99af/), heard at the Ethiopian Federal High Court.

[113] For more details, see Tiba, 2007, pp. 172–80, *supra* note 107.

the defence in the Mengistu and Others case on the argument that the charges did not sufficiently distinguish these crimes, the Central High Court took the view that CAH was, under Ethiopian law, to be understood more as an elucidation of the concept of genocide than as an independent crime.[114] Second, the definition of protected groups in relation to the crime of genocide is extended under Ethiopian law to cover political groups. This is a broader interpretation than that found in most international instruments,[115] although such expansion became more prevalent after 1998, when countries started to incorporate the Rome Statute into domestic law and increased the number of protected groups.[116]

This aspect caused some controversies during the trials; however, in an interlocutory decision in 1995, the Federal High Court held it not to be inconsistent with international law, as the court considered the international Genocide Convention to lay down only a minimum standard.[117] This extended scope is key to the possibility of employing the crime of genocide in the Ethiopian trials, as the victims of the Derg were mostly political opponents rather than ethnic, racial, national, or religious groups.

9.4.3. Application of the Modes of Liability

9.4.3.1. Charges in the Trial against Mengistu and Others

In the case of Mengistu and Others, the defendants were collectively and individually charged with over 200 counts of genocide, relating to both the preparatory and execution stages, with aggravated homicide, and with several other crimes under the Ethiopian Penal Code.[118]

---

[114] Ruling of the court as cited in Aneme, 2009, pp. 17–18, see *supra* note 111.

[115] Compare: Convention on the Prevention and Punishment of the Crime of Genocide, Article 2; ICTY Statute, Article 4; Rome Statute, Article 6; and ICTR Statute, Article 2.

[116] Rikhof, 2010, pp. 21–81, see *supra* note 8.

[117] Aneme, 2009, pp. 16 and 32, see *supra* note 111. There was, however, dissent on this issue. In particular, Judge Nuru Seid held that the acts of the accused were lawful under Ethiopian law at the time of commission, accepting that the unlawfulness of attacking political groups had been repealed early in the Derg regime; and as political groups were not protected under international law, the judge reasoned that the accused could not be convicted under the heading of genocide. See Tiba, 2007, pp. 519–21, *supra* note 107.

[118] Aneme, 2009, p. 3, see *supra* note 111.

With respect to the universal crime of genocide, the Special Prosecutor filed two main charges, which appear differentiated by the mode of perpetration invoked. The relevant articles of the Penal Code provide:

Art. 281. Genocide; Crimes against Humanity

Whosoever, with intent to destroy, in whole or in part, a national, ethnic, racial, religious or political group, *organizes*, *orders* or *engages* in, be it in time of war or in time of peace:

(a) killings, bodily harm or serious injury to the physical or mental health of members of the group, in any way whatsoever; or [...]

(c) the compulsory movement or dispersion of peoples or children, or their placing under living conditions calculated to result in their death or disappearance,

is punishable with rigorous imprisonment from five years to life, or, in cases of exceptional gravity, with death.[119]

Art. 32. Principal Act: Offender and Co-offenders.

(1) A person shall be regarded as having committed an offence and punished as such if:

(a) he actually commits the offence either directly or indirectly, for example by means of an animal or a natural force; or

(b) he without performing the criminal act itself fully associates himself with the commission of the offence and the intended result; or

(c) he employs a mentally deficient person for the commission of an offence or knowingly compels another person to commit an offence.

(2) Where the offence committed goes beyond the intention of the offender he shall be tried in accordance with Article 58(3).

(3) Where several co-offenders are involved they shall be liable to the same punishment as provided by law.

The Court shall take into account the provisions governing the effect of personal circumstances (Art. 40) and those gov-

---

[119] Article 281 of the 1957 Ethiopian Penal Code (emphasis added), cited in Tiba, 2013, p. 314, see *supra* note 108.

erning the award of punishment according to the degree of individual guilt. (Art. 86).[120]

The first charge of preparation and public provocation (that is, incitement) to commit genocide reads as follows:

> The defendants in violation of Articles 32(1)(a) and 286(a)[121] of the then 1957 Penal Code of Ethiopia beginning from 12 September 1974 by establishing the Provisional Military Administration Council, organising themselves as the general assembly, standing and sub-committees; while exclusively and collectively leading the country, agreed among themselves to commit and caused to be committed crimes of genocide against those whom they identified as members of anti-revolution political groups. In order to assist them [to] carry out these, they recruited and armed various *kefitegna* and *kebele* [administrative units] leaders, revolutionary guards, cadres and revolutionary comrades whom as accomplices, they incited and emboldened in public meeting halls, over the media by calling out the names of members of political groups calling for their elimination using speeches, drawings and writings until 1983 in various months and dates thereby causing the death of thousands of members of political groups.[122]

The second charge held that the accused as co-perpetrators (that is, joint perpetration) either directly or indirectly committed the crime of genocide:

> The defendants in violation of Articles 32(1)(a) and 281 of the 1957 Penal Code of Ethiopia, beginning from 12 September 1974 while exclusively and collectively leading the country by establishing the Provisional Military Administration Council or government, organising themselves as the general assembly, standing and sub-committees, planned, participated, and ordered the destruction in whole or in part

---

[120] Article 32 of the 1957 Ethiopian Penal Code, cited in *ibid.*

[121] Article 286 as referred to in the indictment is a special provision of the Ethiopian Penal Code dealing specifically with preparation and incitement of crimes of an international character. See *ibid.*, p. 313.

[122] Ethiopian Federal Supreme Court, *Special Prosecutor v. Mengistu and Others*, File 30181, 26 May 2008 (www.legal-tools.org/doc/60031b/), translated by and cited in Tiba, 2011, p. 169, see *supra* note 108.

[of] members of politically organised socio-national groups, [and] thereby committed genocide. To accomplish this goal, they created various investigation, torturing and execution institutions, hit squads and *Nebelbal* army divisions; carried out campaign 'clearing fields', 'free measures' and 'red terror' to kill or cause the killings of members of political groups and cause injury to their physical and mental health or cause their total disappearance by banishing them in a manner calculated to cause them social harm or cause their death.[123]

As is evident from the quoted text of the first charge, the defendants were alleged to be responsible for collectively having agreed on a common plan to commit and cause to be committed the crime of genocide. This seems to suggest something akin to what is known under international law as joint perpetration or JCE, involving the organising and arming as well as inciting publicly, through speeches, drawings, and writings, lower-level officials, cadres, and security personnel to execute the underlying crimes.[124]

Under the second charge, the defendants were charged with having committed genocide. Three separate modes appear to be utilised, namely that they planned, ordered, and participated in genocide.[125] While the defence early on objected that it was incorrect to charge the defendants with both incitement and commission concurrently for the same fact, the Central High Court accepted the charges by saying that they were not referring to the same acts, but rather that the defendants were involved in the crimes in different ways, at different crime scenes, and at different times.[126]

As the above quotes indicate, the charges appear to mix several modes of participation without clearly separating them or providing any definitions of these concepts and their elements. Unfortunately, as will be further demonstrated, the impression from the final judgment is that the

---

[123] *Ibid.*, p. 170. For both charges, see also Aneme, 2009, pp. 3–6, *supra* note 111.

[124] On the elements of joint perpetration, JCE, and incitement under international law, see Chapter 7, Sections 7.2.2.2., 7.2.2.4., and 7.2.1.3.

[125] On the elements of the mode of planning and ordering under international law, see Chapter 7, Sections 7.2.1.2. and 7.2.3.1.

[126] Aneme, 2009, pp. 13 and 17, see *supra* note 111.

judges also largely failed to clarify the elements of the various modes and what separates one from another, or to establish with sufficient clarity the links between the individual accused and the crimes.

9.4.3.2. Incoherent Conceptual Approach in the Judgment

In its verdict on 12 December 2006, the Federal High Court convicted all except one defendant on each of the two main charges, and the convictions were upheld by the Federal Supreme Court on appeal.[127] The following makes reference to both court decisions in discussing the judges' approach to the modes of participation.

The judgments were largely characterised by a lack of substantive legal analysis with respect to the various modes that serve to link the individual defendant to the crime(s). In general, the courts did not develop a substantive theory of criminal liability, nor did they provide any clear conceptual definitions of the elements required for liability to arise under each of the modes. This again served to muddle the legal tests applied in attributing liability, where simple membership in the Derg appears to have been the decisive criterion for establishing culpability of the defendants as a collective.[128] The judgments also make minimal reference to customary international law and to the existing body of international jurisprudence.[129]

More concretely, as the charges included notions akin to both joint perpetration (or co-perpetration) and ordering, a vital task of legal analysis would have been to clearly establish the unique elements of each of these modes in order to assess their applicability to the specific case at hand.[130] This is particularly so because, as noted in Chapter 7, Section 7.2.3.1., in cases involving high-level officials who use a power structure to commit crimes for political or ideological purposes, there will often be a fine line between the mode of ordering, on the one hand, and of (indirect) co-perpetration (or, alternatively, JCE liability), on the other. By not engaging in substantive analysis of a theory of criminal liability capable of elucidating these modes of participation, the courts did not manage to

---

[127] *Ibid.*, pp. 22 and 32.

[128] Tiba, 2013, p. 306, see *supra* note 108.

[129] Tiba, 2011, p. 184, see *supra* note 108.

[130] For the details on the elements of these modes as applied at the international tribunals, see Chapter 7, Sections 7.2.2.2. and 7.2.3.1.

clarify the distinction and ground the imposition of liability in sufficiently convincing legal analysis; instead they muddled the application of these modes.

Turning to the courts' application of the specific mode of joint perpetration, there are also cases in which aspects relating to the elements of this mode were insufficiently elucidated. For example, the judges in Mengistu and Others could have benefited from consulting the jurisprudence of international tribunals, in particular the ICC, since, as Tiba notes, the notion of joint perpetration (or co-perpetration) set out in the Ethiopian Penal Code is similar to that of Article 25(3)(a) under the Rome Statute.[131] As detailed in Chapter 7, Section 7.2.2.2., the *actus reus* of joint perpetration in international law is held to consists of two elements: (1) the existence of an agreement or common plan between two or more persons, and (2) a coordinated essential contribution by each participant resulting in the commission of the crime.

As for the first element, a key argument of the defence was that there did not exist any plan or agreement to commit genocide among the Derg members. The Federal High Court reasoned as follows:

> [A]s is clearly known, when a government is in power, it does not have only one objective or task. It has many objectives and tasks. The evidence submitted by the parties demonstrates this. However, even if many of its objectives were good, the existence of good deeds does not wipe out responsibility for the criminal acts. One cannot say that there was no criminal intention. The main question is whether the accused had the intention to eliminate politically affiliated groups.[132]

As pointed out by Tiba,[133] at this point the court's reasoning appears to be at least partly in line with current ICC jurisprudence, which has emphasised that the plan need not be explicit, nor specifically directed at committing a crime, and it may involve non-criminal goals, but nonetheless must contain a critical element of criminality.[134]

---

[131] Tiba, 2013, pp. 323–24, see *supra* note 108.

[132] Translated and cited in Tiba, 2013, p. 319, see *supra* note 108.

[133] *Ibid.*, p. 319.

[134] For the relevant international jurisprudence, see Chapter 7, Section 7.2.2.2.

Concerning the second element, that of an essential contribution, the OSP's charges as well as the judgment of the Federal High Court and the appeal judgment of the Federal Supreme Court all failed to clearly establish the relevant contribution of each of the defendants to the crime(s).[135] Following the international jurisprudence, this element of an essential contribution does not require the accused to have been present at the crime scene, nor does it require each individual contribution to have had a direct physical link to the commission of the crime; rather, it turns on an accused's ability to frustrate the commission of the crime by refraining from carrying out his assigned task.[136] This reasoning as developed at the ICC rests on the underlying theory of control over the crime, and it presupposes a certain high-level position within a power structure. The lack of legal analysis and elucidation on this element in the Mengistu and Others case is particularly problematic because the defendants assumed quite different leadership roles, and the court failed to sufficiently establish whether all, including those with more peripheral roles within the Derg, had the material ability to frustrate the commission of the crime(s). Rather, both the Federal High Court and the Federal Supreme Court appear to have based the attribution of criminal liability to the various defendants primarily on mere membership in the Derg.[137] In fact, the Supreme Court reasoned that the members should be seen as having accepted the criminal outcome by virtue of their continued membership in the Derg, which applied even to those being dispatched to provincial regions far removed from the centre of decision making.[138]

The Federal High Court seems to lay down a form of expanded liability for both types of charges, reasoning that all members were liable for the Derg's actions by directly supporting or not opposing the regime, manifested through continued membership in the organisation.[139]

It should be mentioned, however, that there are some discernible similarities between this application of the law on criminal attribution by the Federal High Court and the form of omission liability known as 'tak-

---

[135] Tiba, 2013, p. 320, see *supra* note 108.

[136] For details and references to relevant international jurisprudence, see Chapter 7, Section 7.2.2.2.

[137] Tiba, 2013, p. 322, see *supra* note 108.

[138] *Ibid.*

[139] *Ibid.*, p. 318.

ing a consenting part', a mode of participation set forth in Control Council Law No. 10, Article II(2)(c), and employed in the subsequent Nuremberg trials by military courts in occupied Germany.[140] According to the post-WWII jurisprudence, a willing participant would incur criminal liability for the crime if he (1) had knowledge that such a crime had been or was about to be committed, and (2) occupied a sufficiently high-level place within the relevant power structure to enable him to exert influence by objecting to the occurrences of the crimes, despite not being a military commander in the chain of command or a leader with direct powers to decide on the matter, and (3) failed to do so.[141] However, the Ethiopian judges made no attempt to ground the attribution of criminal liability to the Derg members in the relevant post-WWII jurisprudence in regard to this mode of participation. Moreover, it is also questionable whether the more peripheral or lower-level members of the Derg who were convicted would satisfy the element of retaining a sufficiently influential position in order to be included under this type of liability.

9.4.4. Concluding Remarks

The overall impression of the legal analysis employed with respect to modes of participation in the Mengistu and Others case is that the Ethiopian courts involved did not make much of an attempt to develop a theory of criminal liability, which again led to either a lack of a sufficient differentiation between the various modes of participation invoked or an absence of a clear elucidation of their respective material elements.

Rather, the Federal High Court and the Supreme Court appear to have considered mere membership in the Derg as the main criterion for attributing individual liability to the various participants. Liability for mere membership in a criminal organisation may lawfully lead to attribution of individual liability – at least this was assumed at Nuremberg, and is a principle currently applied in transnational criminal law with respect to membership in terrorist organisations. However, there is a significant difference between attribution of liability for membership as such, constituted as a distinct crime (the rule applied at Nuremberg) that may itself

---

[140] For a more detailed account of the jurisprudence on this mode of participation, see Kevin Jon Heller, "'Taking a Consenting Part': The Lost Mode of Participation", in *Loyola of Los Angeles International & Comparative Law Review*, vol. 39, no. 1, 2017, pp. 247–58.

[141] See also Chapter 7, Section 7.2.2.5.

justify a certain amount of punishment, and attribution of liability for the specific crimes committed by other members of the organisation, simply through the fact of membership. In particular, not sufficiently establishing the individual contribution of each defendant gives the impression of a process akin to collective responsibility or guilt by association, which challenges the fundamental principle of personal culpability. As emphasised by Tiba, recourse to the existing jurisprudence of the international tribunals in order to better ground the imposition of liability for the individual defendant in a theory of criminal participation would have made the convictions more convincing and more resilient to much of the critique they have faced.[142]

9.5. Latin American Countries: Selected Features

9.5.1. Common Aspects of the Latin American Trials

In prosecuting individuals accused of serious human rights violations, a number of Latin American courts, including those in Argentina, Chile, Colombia, Guatemala, Peru, and Uruguay, have conducted trials that have relied on ICL concepts. As the Latin American region encompasses many autonomous jurisdictions, each with its own distinctive legal framework, the jurisprudence on modes of criminal participation has not evolved in a consistent manner across the various jurisdictions.[143] Latin American jurisprudence in this area has also developed in a variety of legal contexts, including trials for universal crimes, appeal cases, and constitutional cases, with international criminal law sometimes being referred to contextually rather than being the principal issue in each case.

Despite this, there are certain regional commonalities that make the emerging jurisprudence from this region highly relevant in a broader ICL context. The most important is that most of the domestic jurisdictions have undertaken the task of developing an appropriate liability theory for attributing criminal responsibility to high-level officials operating far removed from the actual crime scenes. This aspect will be the focus of the present narrative, and as will be demonstrated, incorporating ICL concepts

---

[142] Tiba, 2013, pp. 323–24, see *supra* note 108.

[143] Due Process of Law Foundation, *Digest of Latin American Jurisprudence on International Crimes*, *Volume I*, Washington, DC, 2010, p. 75 (hereafter cited as *DPLF Digest, Vol. I*).

into the pre-existing domestic legal frameworks has not been without challenges.

In some of the Latin American trials, perpetrators have been prosecuted for domestic-type offences (such as murder, serious bodily injury, and so on) because the universal crimes were not incorporated into the domestic criminal codes. However, in many of the trials mentioned in this narrative the factual scenarios of the cases involve serious human rights violations that otherwise would amount to universal crimes, such as crimes against humanity. Illustrative in this regard is the case of former Peruvian president Alberto Fujimori, where the court explicitly qualified the acts as CAH because the individual crimes of murder and aggravated assault had taken place as part of a wider pattern of systematic human rights violations.[144] Upon appeal, the Supreme Court reasoned that despite CAH not having been incorporated into the Peruvian Criminal Code, the classification of the crimes as such did not violate the principle of legality. The court found that the formal basis for the conviction remained that of the domestic crimes of murder, serious bodily injury, and aggravated kidnapping, and that the notion of CAH simply served to highlight the gravity and international dimension of the criminal complex in which these crimes took place.[145]

9.5.2. Application of the Modes of Liability

9.5.2.1. The Range of Modes Applied in the Latin American Jurisdictions

In the course of the Latin American trials, the applications of modes of participation largely coincide with the attributional doctrines and legal concepts currently being developed by the International Criminal Court, while the jurisprudence of the *ad hoc* tribunals has been relied upon to a

---

[144] Peru, Corte Superior de Justicia de Lima, Sala Penal Especial, Cases of Barrios Altos, La Cantuta, and SIE Basements (*Alberto Fujimori Fujimori*), Judgment, Expediente AV 19-2001, 7 April 2009 (www.legal-tools.org/doc/571949/).

[145] Peru, Corte Superior de Justicia de Lima, Primera Sala Penal Transitoria, Cases of Barrios Altos, La Cantuta, and SIE Basements (*Alberto Fujimori Fujimori*), Judgment, Expediente AV 19-2001, 30 December 2009 (hereafter cited as *Fujimori*) (www.legal-tools.org/doc/5c51d9/) cited in Kai Ambos, "The *Fujimori* Judgment: A President's Responsibility for Crimes Against Humanity as Indirect Perpetrator by Virtue of an Organized Power Apparatus", in *Journal of International Criminal Justice*, 2011, vol. 9, no. 1, pp. 143–44.

lesser degree.[146] Latin American jurisprudence has therefore placed greater emphasis on the modes of perpetration-by-means and co-perpetration, rather than on the alternative doctrines of joint criminal enterprise and command responsibility.[147]

Furthermore, with few exceptions, Latin American courts have not extensively applied other modes, including accessorial-type modes, but have again predominantly relied on perpetration-by-means and co-perpetration as their preferred tools of attribution. This results from the common feature already mentioned, namely the fact that most of the domestic proceedings have been concerned with the criminal liability of officials at the very top of the power structures in former military regimes (for example, Argentina and Chile) or in armed groups (for instance, Colombia).

Co-perpetration has been defined as two or more persons acting with a common purpose and in concert, even if none of the co-perpetrators carries out all the material elements of the definition of the crime itself.[148] In applying this mode, the various courts of the region have generally relied on an interpretation that closely approximates the key elements established for this mode of liability in the jurisprudence of the ICC, requiring (1) the existence of a common plan or agreement, (2) a division of labor whereby the accused made an essential contribution to the occurrence of the crime(s) or to implementation of the common plan/agreement, (3) intent to commit the crime or awareness that it will occur in the ordinary course of events when implementing the plan, and (4) the accused's awareness of his essential contribution thereto.[149] With respect

---

[146] Due Process of Law Foundation, *Digest of Latin American Jurisprudence on International Crimes, Volume II*, Washington, DC, 2013, p. 33 (hereafter cited as *DPLF Digest, vol. II*).

[147] *DPLF Digest, vol. I*, 2010, p. 75, see *supra* note 143.

[148] It should be noted that this concept has been applied with differing terminology in Latin American jurisprudence, sometimes using the terms 'necessary co-operators' or 'necessary participation', though essentially with the same material elements. See, for example, Guatemala, Corte de Apelaciones de Cobán, Case of Río Negro Massacre (*Macario Alvarado Toj, et al.*), Expediente 96-2008, 24 September 2008, at II (www.legal-tools.org/doc/4a04d2/).

[149] *DPLF Digest, vol. II*, 2013, pp. 41–43, see *supra* note 146. See, for instance, Uruguay, Tribunal de Apelaciones en lo Penal de Tercer Turno, *Juan Carlos Blanco Estradé*, Appeal, IUE 17-414/2003, Sentencio no. 22, 16 February 2012 (www.legal-tools.org/doc/c0eac8/); Argentina, Cámara Federal de Apelaciones de la Plata, *Jamie Lamont Smart et al.*, Appeal, Sentencia de la expediente 5838/III, 26 May 2011 (www.legal-tools.org/doc/9eeeb7/);

to the second material element, it is notable that the various Latin American courts have accepted a relatively wide spectrum of acts as sufficient to constitute an essential contribution, ranging from providing necessary information or physical means to execute the crime, at one end of the spectrum, to defending the criminal organisation (as by supplying misleading information or making dubious claims in response to international critique or pressure), at the other end.[150]

The courts in Argentina have further developed a doctrine of "successive co-perpetration", which specifies that contributions by actors can occur at different points in time.[151]

As for the exceptions, other modes of participation that have been employed in Latin American jurisdictions include the concept of complicity. This was explored in an Argentinian case in which co-perpetration was found not to be applicable because the accused did not have joint control over the act or any direct involvement in torture. However, the accused was found to be liable because "he was aware of [the crimes], he tolerated them, and he facilitated them".[152]

Guatemala, Tribunal Primero de Sentencia Penal, Case of Dos Erres Massacre (*Roberto Aníbal Rivera Martínez, et al.*), Sentencia de primera instancia, Narcoactividad y delitos contra el ambiente, C-01076-2010-00003, Oficial 1°, 2 August 2011 (www.legal-tools.org/doc/31b80a/); Guatemala, Tribunal Tercero de Sentencia Penal, Case of Myrna Mack (*Edgar Augusto Godoy, Juan Valencia Osorio, and Juan Guillermo Oliva*), Sentencia de primera instancia, Narcoactividad y delitos contra el ambiente, C-5-99, Oficial 3ro., 3 October 2002 (www.legal-tools.org/doc/70159e/); Colombia, Corte Suprema de Justicia, Case of Pueblo Bello (*Pedro Ogazza P.*), Recurso extraordinario de casación, Radicación 14851, Aprobado por acta no. 35, MP. Carlos Augusto Galvez Argote, 8 March 2001 (www.legal-tools.org/doc/3637ba/).

150 *DPLF Digest, vol. I*, p. 43, see *supra* note 143.

151 Argentina, Tribunal Oral en lo Criminal Federal (Buenos Aires), Case of Poblete-Hlaczik (*Julio Héctor Simón*), Causas no. 1.056 and no. 1.207, 11 August 2006 (www.legal-tools.org/doc/fd1e32/). For further examples of judicial treatment of co-perpetration, see also the motion submitted by the defence of Julio Héctor Simón: Argentina, Corte Suprema de Justicia de la Nación, Simón, Julio Héctor y otros s/ privación ilegítima de la libertad, Causa no. 17.768 (Recurso de hecho), Expediente S. 1767. XXXVIII, 14 July 2005 at XII–XIII (www.legal-tools.org/doc/6321f1/). Also see Uruguay, Juez Penal 19° Turno, Case "Condor Plan" (*José Nino Gavazzo Pereira, et al.*), Sentencia 036, Ficha 98-247/2006, 26 March 2009, at VI (www.legal-tools.org/doc/dee268/).

152 Argentina, Tribunal Oral en lo Criminal Federal No. 1 de San Martín, Case of Victorio Derganz and Carlos José Fateche (*Juan Demetrio Luna*), Sentencia de primera instancia contra Juan Demetrio Luna, Causa no. 2203, 30 December 2011 (www.legal-tools.org/doc/0ea1a0/), cited in *DPLF Digest, vol. II*, 2013, pp. 57–59, see *supra* note 146. See also

---

Latin American courts have in some instances also employed doctrinal aspects that have certain commonalities with elements of the JCE doctrine and command responsibility.[153] With respect to command responsibility, the region's courts have at times made reference to this mode of participation under international law, but they have interpreted it within the framework of a domestically developed theory of failure to fulfil the role of guarantor.[154] No court, however, has relied on these doctrines for convicting a specific person.

In sum, there is a common tendency among the Latin American jurisdictions to place strong reliance on the doctrine of perpetration-by-means, while alternative modes have featured less frequently. Consequently, given the prominent role of this mode across the region, the remainder of this chapter focuses on the jurisprudential developments with respect to the liability theory of perpetration-by-means. We highlight its evolution as well as some of the challenges and controversies that have surrounded its application in the Latin American context.

9.5.2.2.   Attributing Individual Liability to High-Level Officials

The criminal codes of all the countries in the region not only include provisions stipulating individual criminal liability for those who directly carry out the objective elements of a crime, but in various ways also recognise the responsibility, as principals, of those behind-the-scenes individuals who were the masterminds of the criminal enterprise. In defining the notion of a perpetrator, the Argentinian Federal Court stated that

> the objective element of direct commission lies in having in one's hands the course of the criminal event, or the real potential, at all times, to direct the composition of the crime, [...] the perpetrator controls the act; the course of events is in his hands and he can decide the whether and the how or, put

---

Chile, Corte Suprema, Sala Penal, Case of Miguel Ángel Sandoval (*Juan Miguel Contreras Sepúlveda, et al.*), Rol no. 517-04, 17 November 2004 (www.legal-tools.org/doc/851a5a/), cited in *DPLF Digest, vol. I*, 2010, p. 121, see *supra* note 143.

[153] See, for example, Colombia, Case of Pueblo Bello (2001), where the mention of the elements of acceptance of risk, also for crimes beyond the original plan, is at least somewhat akin to the notion of extended liability of JCE I (or JCE III). Also see Peru, *Fujimori* (2009), paras. 742–43, cited in *DPLF Digest, vol. I*, 2010, p. 118, see *supra* note 143.

[154] Peru, *Fujimori* (2009), cited in *DPLF Digest, vol. I*, 2010, p. 116, see *supra* note 143.

---

more succinctly, he is able to determine the core composition
of the event.[155]

The Latin American jurisprudence regarding the notion of control or
domination over the crime has, however, undergone a gradual evolution in
response to the practical need to extend the scope of commission liability,
a process in which the doctrine of perpetration-by-means has played a key
role. To be clear, there are three forms of perpetration-by-means. First,
there is control by error, wherein the direct perpetrator is deceived about
the real circumstances of the act. Second, there is control by coercion,
which features a threat of some imminent and serious retribution against
the direct perpetrator should he decline to act. Third, there is "perpetration-by-means through domination of an organized power apparatus" (Organisationsherrschaft).[156] The prosecutors and courts in these jurisdictions
have over time become increasingly aware of how traditional modes of
participation have often proved insufficient to accurately reflect the criminal responsibility of those at the very top of a hierarchical power structure. As a result, the third version of the perpetration-by-means doctrine,
originally spelled out by the German scholar Claus Roxin and later also
adopted at the ICC,[157] has come to play an increasingly central role in Latin American trials.

In the words of the Peruvian National Criminal Court in the case
against the leaders of the Shining Path, a guerrilla organisation:

> The concept of domination over the organization has
> emerged because other criminal categories, specifically the
> rules of perpetration and participation, are inadequate to ex-
> plain and resolve cases involving those who direct and con-
> trol an organization. The search for attribution mechanisms
> that adequately and fairly address the new problems associ-
> ated with illegal organizations – particularly those involving
> the authorities, leaders, and commanders of the organiza-
> tion – aims to reinforce the deterrent effect of punishment,

---

[155] Argentina, Case of Poblete-Hlaczik (2006), cited in *DPLF Digest, vol. I,* 2010, p. 78, see
supra note 143.

[156] Peru, *Fujimori* (2009), para. 719.

[157] For the ICC jurisprudence regarding this concept, see Chapter 7, Section 7.2.2.3.

which would be profoundly undermined should the punishment target only the direct perpetrators.[158]

In line with what was noted initially, however, the application of this theory of liability has not followed a coordinated or unified pattern across the regional jurisdictions. This reflects the challenges of incorporating international concepts into the domestic context, where the distinct features of existing national legislation and judicial traditions give rise to constraints on legal practitioners. Thus, while this notion of perpetration through an organisation has become more widely accepted among Latin American jurisdictions over the years,[159] its suitability as a theory for differentiating between principals and accessories has not gone unchallenged. Especially controversial are two aspects of some of the national systems: first, a domestic legal framework based on the concept that only those who physically carry out the crime can be considered principal perpetrators, and second, a restriction of the notion of indirect perpetration to situations where the accused exercised control directly over the physical perpetrator, who himself was not criminally liable. Illustrative in this regard are two cases from Argentina and Chile.

The first of these, the Argentinian Juntas Trial, represents the first attempt to utilise the mode of indirect perpetration through an organised power structure in Latin America. In attributing liability to the high-level commanders of the military junta, the Federal Court of Appeal took a non-traditional (at that time) approach to perpetration-by-means by directly invoking Roxin's theory of domination/control of a power structure:

> We are not dealing here with the traditional domination of the will in the sense of indirect perpetration. The *instrument* which the 'man in the background' uses is the *system itself*, [...] a system which is composed of *fungible men* functioning to achieve the proposed objective. The domination, then, is not domination over a determined will, but an 'undetermined will', for whomever the executor may be, the act will

---

[158] Peru, Sala Penal Nacional, Case against Leaders of the Shining Path (*Manuel Rubén Abimael Guzmán Reynoso, et al.*), Expediente 560 03, 13 October 2006 (www.legal-tools.org/doc/6435af/), cited in *DPLF Digest, vol. I*, 2010, pp. 80–81, see *supra* note143.

[159] Ambos, 2013, p. 114, see *supra* note 11; Francisco Muñoz-Conde and Héctor Olásolo, "The Application of the Notion of Indirect Perpetration through Organized Structures of Power in Latin American and Spain", in *Journal of International Criminal Justice*, 2011, vol. 9, no. 1, p. 115.

---

be carried out regardless. The direct perpetrator loses tran-
scendence as he plays a secondary role in the execution of
the act.[160]

The Federal Court's application of this liability theory was, however,
overturned by the Chamber of Cassation of the Supreme Court, which
relied on traditional Argentinian case law, according to which only those
physically executing the *actus reus* of the crime could be considered principal perpetrators. Consequently, indirect perpetration was considered inappropriate; the majority instead convicted the accused commanders as
"necessary contributors" to the crime.[161] In more recent case law, Argentinian courts have largely moved away from this overly formalistic approach to principal liability, increasingly embracing the notion of indirect
perpetration through domination of an organised power structure in line
with the approach taken by the Federal Court of Appeal.[162]

In Chile, the controversy surrounding the introduction of the just-
mentioned liability theory has centred on what may constitute the object
of the accused's domination/control. It is important to clarify that, as indicated by the above-quoted paragraph from the Juntas trial, the doctrine of
Organisationsherrschaft is a unique form of indirect perpetration in that it
relies on control over a larger power structure rather than, as in the classic
form of indirect perpetration, direct control over an innocent agent.[163] The
difficulty faced by the Chilean judges in the case against Contreras and
Espinoza, who were convicted as indirect co-perpetrators based on their
control of the Chilean Secret Service for the murder of the foreign minister of the Allende regime and his associate, was that while the judges referred to Roxin's theory, it was not directly applicable because Article 15

---

[160] Argentina, Cámara Federal Nacional de Apelaciones en lo Criminal y Correccional de la
Capital Buenos Aires, Case of the Military Juntas, Judgment, 9 December 1985 (www.
legal-tools.org/doc/83efcc/), cited in Ambos, 2013, p. 115, emphasis in original, see *supra*
note 11.

[161] Argentina, Chamber of Cassation of the Argentinian Supreme Court, Case of the Military
Juntas, Judgment, 20 December 1986 (www.legal-tools.org/doc/149547/), cited in Muñoz-
Conde and Olásolo, 2011, pp. 117–18, see *supra* note 159.

[162] Muñoz-Conde and Olásolo, 2011, p. 118, see *supra* note 159. For the most recent Argentinian cases that have employed this liability theory, see Argentina, Tribunal Oral en lo
Criminal Federal No. 5, ESMA Mega-trial (*Garcia Tallada, Manuel Jacinto, et al.*), Sentencia de primera instancia, Causa no. 1279, 28 December 2011 (www.legal-tools.org/doc/
9aa896/); and Argentina, *Jamie Lamont Smart et al.* (2011).

[163] See Chapter 7, Section 7.2.2.3. See also Ambos, 2011, p. 145, *supra* note 145.

of the Chilean Criminal Code only provided for the classic version of indirect perpetration.[164] Despite the court's reluctance to directly apply the theory of organisational domination, the judgment faced substantial scholarly criticism for going too far in departing from existing Chilean case law, under which the notion of indirect perpetration was understood to apply only to cases in which the direct perpetrator could not be held criminally responsible; critics contended that instigation would have been the more appropriate labelling in this case.[165]

A more refined analysis of the Organisationsherrschaft doctrine in Latin American courts also reveals that it has not been uniformly applied across the various jurisdictions. The differences include not only the specific elements defined, but also their interpretation when courts seek to establish the scope of this liability theory.

The decision in Peru's most prominent case, Fujimori,[166] is among the Latin American judgments that have set out most elaborately the distinctive elements of indirect perpetration through an organised power structure.[167] The Special Chamber of the Supreme Court of Peru defined four elements pertaining to this mode of liability.[168] First, there must be established the existence of a hierarchical organisation or organised power apparatus. Upon analysing this element, the Uruguayan court in the Condor Plan case emphasised the requirement that

> [t]he 'apparatus' is imbued with sufficient objective structure
> to justify transferring the status of perpetrator to the person

---

[164] Chile, Edición Suplementaria Suprema de Justicia, Case of José Manuel Contreras and Colonel Espinoza, Judgment, 12 November 1993 (www.legal-tools.org/doc/7eceb0/), cited in Ambos, 2013, p. 116, see *supra* note 11.

[165] For a more detailed discussion of the case and the resulting criticism from Chilean scholars, see Muñoz-Conde and Olásolo, 2011, pp. 120–22, *supra* note 159.

[166] Peru, *Fujimori* (2009).

[167] The first Peruvian court to apply the notion of indirect perpetration through an organised power structure was the National Penal Chamber in the conviction of Manuel Guzmán, the founder and leader of the Maoist guerrilla organisation known as the Shining Path. Closely following Roxin's original theory, the court justified the attribution of the group's crimes to Guzmán by stating that his control over the organisation ensured automatic compliance with his orders. Peru, Case against Leaders of the Shining Path (2006), cited in Ambos, 2013, p. 117, see *supra* note 11.

[168] See Peru, *Fujimori* (2009), paras. 729–74; and Ambos, 2011, pp. 149–50, *supra* note 145. Fujimori's conviction, and the court's legal analysis on indirect co-perpetration, was confirmed in December 2009 by the First Transitory Criminal Chamber of the Supreme Court.

giving the orders, without relieving the direct perpetrator of
the crime of that same status.[169]

Second, there must be command authority or control that comes
from the perpetrator-by-means, such as "by issuing orders, whether explicit or implicit, which will be carried out due to the inherent automatici-
ty of the functional make-up of the apparatus".[170] The logic of both the
first and second elements is premised on the third element, namely that of
the interchangeability or fungibility of the direct perpetrator, which is
what effectively ensures the occurrence of virtually automatic compliance.[171] As phrased in the above-mentioned Condor Plan case, "the task is
carried out without any need for the decision-making center to know who
the specific perpetrator is; this is the fungibility of direct perpetrators".[172]
Fourth, the Fujimori judgment (alone in Latin American jurisprudence)
also held that this form of perpetration-by-means additionally requires an
organisation that deviates from legality or from the law, that is, one that
"is structured, operates, and remains outside of the national and international legal system".[173] This fourth element also serves to illustrate the
inconsistencies in the application of the doctrine across the Latin American jurisdictions, as the Argentinian jurisprudence, unlike the Peruvian,
appears not to recognise the element of deviation from the law.[174]

A particularly interesting discussion related to the delimitation of
indirect perpetration from co-perpetration, or to combinations of the two

---

[169] Uruguay, Case "Condor Plan" (2009), p. 6.

[170] Peru, *Fujimori* (2009), paras. 729–31.

[171] *Ibid.*, 737–39.

[172] Uruguay, Case "Condor Plan" (2009), p. 6.

[173] Peru, *Fujimori* (2009), paras. 733–36. Note that the court also sets out a fifth requirement,
namely the direct perpetrator's disposition to commit the act (paras. 740–41). This requirement goes beyond those traditionally considered by the Organisationsherrschaft theory, and, as pointed out by Ambos, 2011, p. 157, *supra* note 145, there is continued debate
as to whether it constitutes a required element of this doctrine.

[174] Motion submitted by the defence of Julio Héctor Simón in Argentina, Corte Suprema de
Justicia de la Nación, Simón, Julio Héctor y otros s/ privación ilegítima de la libertad,
Causa no. 17.768 (Recurso de hecho), Expediente S. 1767. XXXVIII, 14 July 2005, at XIII
(www.legal-tools.org/doc/6321f1/). Ambos 2011, p. 154, see *supra* note 145, seems to
align himself with this latter position in making reference to the ICC as having refrained
from mentioning this element in its analysis of indirect perpetration and in advocating that
this element should not be considered a necessary precondition for indirect perpetration.
See also Chapter 7, Section 7.2.2.3.

modes,[175] has flowed from the second material element set forth in the Fujimori judgment, the one pertaining to the applicability of the notion of domination/control at various levels of the hierarchical power structure. More precisely, Latin American jurisprudence has at times struggled with the question of whether the doctrine of indirect perpetration through an organised power structure, which implies absolute domination on the part of the accused, is applicable also to mid-level officials or is restricted to the leadership level alone.

On the one hand, the Supreme Court in the Fujimori judgment took a broad approach to indirect perpetration along the lines of Roxin's original concept, viewing it as also applicable to mid-level officials. This creates the possibility of a chain of indirect perpetrators spanning the hierarchy of a given power structure.[176] On the other hand, in the more recent Argentinian judgment in the case of Riveros *et al.*,[177] the court is much more restrictive in determining the scope of the doctrine: it reasoned that participants below the very top leadership level of the junta could not be labelled as indirect perpetrators because their lack of authority to interfere with the power of higher-level officials rendered them unable to possess the required total and undisturbed domination/control over the physical perpetrators. As noted by Ambos,[178] given that mid-level commanders, although exercising some level of control over their direct subordinates, primarily occupy a position within the larger power structure at the same level as other commanders, this reasoning might be (in line with the more restrictive interpretation) in favour of co-perpetration based on the functional division of labour as the more appropriate mode of participation for this level of participants.

However, the situation of mid-level commanders might be considered different in two types of factual situations: (1) when mid-level commanders are working within the power structure through meetings and other means of communication and thus are providing a necessary linkage

---

[175] See Chapter 2, Section 2.2.3.5, on the possibilities of lawful combinations and further derivation of subcategories of liability.

[176] Peru, *Fujimori* (2009), para. 731, cited in Ambos, 2011, p. 151, see *supra* note 145.

[177] Argentina, Tribunal Oral en lo Criminal Federal No. 1 de San Martín, Case of Santiago Omar Riveros *et al.*, No. 2005/2044, 12 August 2009 (www.legal-tools.org/doc/106dbc/), cited in Ambos, 2013, p. 115, see *supra* note 11.

[178] Ambos, 2011, p. 152, see *supra* note 145.

of ordering in the chain of command between the top level and the lower command structures executing the concrete crimes on the ground; and (2) when mid-level commanders (also) exercise operational command over troops at the actual crime scenes within the scope of discretion provided for by the top-level instruction. While the first scenario seems to justify the more restrictive scope of the doctrine, the second scenario may not. In the latter case, the mid-level commander takes on another role, acting also as the top-level commander of a smaller power structure operating at a specific crime scene within the larger criminal enterprise. The mid-level commander is able to control or dominate the events at that particular crime scene and thus should be considered an indirect perpetrator with respect to the particular crimes committed there.

9.5.2.3. Perpetration-by-Means

Perpetration-by-means has also been specifically distinguished from other modes of liability in Latin American courts. For example, perpetration-by-means has been described as different from co-perpetration or joint commission in that co-perpetration requires common resolve among the perpetrators, whereas in perpetration-by-means, the "man behind the scenes" and the perpetrator usually do not know one another or make joint decisions.[179] In other words, whereas co-perpetration involves functional control over the crime itself, in perpetration-by-means "the author does not actually carry out the criminal act, but retains control over the crime through a third party".[180]

Perpetration-by-means has also been distinguished from incitement or inducement. Whereas incitement or inducement do not involve control over the perpetration of the act, perpetration-by-means requires superior domination on the part of the one issuing the order, derived from his leadership.[181] Thus, in the first scenario discussed above, when mid-level commanders act primarily as a useful or even necessary linkage in the chain of command (perhaps with a certain amount of discretion to formu-

---

[179] Peru, *Fujimori* (2009), para. 719.

[180] Motion submitted by the defence of Julio Héctor Simón in Argentina, Corte Suprema de Justicia de la Nación, Simón, Julio Héctor y otros s/ privación ilegítima de la libertad, Causa no. 17.768 (Recurso de hecho), Expediente S. 1767. XXXVIII, 14 July 2005, at XIII (www.legal-tools.org/doc/6321f1/).

[181] Peru, *Fujimori* (2009), para. 719.

late more concrete instructions/orders to the next level), their ordering could instead be considered within some category of accomplice liability such as 'ordering', fully in accordance with our general theory of criminal law liability.

9.5.3. Concluding Remarks

In contrast to courts in East Timor, where those prosecuted were mainly physical perpetrators occupying low-level positions in the relevant power structures, and also in contrast to courts in Bangladesh and Ethiopia, where perpetrators ran the gamut from high-level to low-level involvement, Latin American courts have most frequently relied on forms of participation such as perpetration-by-means to prosecute high-level officials at the very top of former regimes or armed groups responsible for serious human rights violations in these countries. This distinct feature has helped shape the judicial development on modes of participation in the respective countries.

A pressing issue in many of the Latin American proceedings has been which theory of liability to apply in order to differentiate principals from accessorial participants. While Latin American courts initially were reluctant to apply the control in a power structure approach, there has been a gradual trend towards greater acknowledgment of the usefulness of, and greater reliance on, indirect perpetration through domination of an organised power structure as a means of accurately reflecting the criminal responsibility of the high-level perpetrators behind the scene. As the above analysis has demonstrated, however, the implementation of this doctrine, or mode of participation, in the domestic context has had its share of difficulties, and it has not been applied in a uniform and coordinated manner across the various Latin American jurisdictions.

9.6. Countries Emerging from the Former Yugoslavia: Selected Features

9.6.1. Common Aspects of the Balkan Trials

Turning to the European region, this subsection analyses the jurisprudence regarding modes of participation of Bosnia and Herzegovina, Croatia, and Serbia, three of the currently autonomous jurisdictions that used to be part of the former Republic of Yugoslavia.[182] All three have relied on ICL concepts in order to attribute liability to those involved in the crimes that took place during the conflict that ultimately led to the breakup of the unified republic.[183] As noted in the introduction to this chapter, these countries are of particular interest in a broader ICL context because their domestic proceedings directly complement those taking place in the corresponding international tribunal, the ICTY.

The domestic proceedings have relied, in particular in BiH, quite extensively on jurisprudence of the ICTY in defining the elements of the various modes of liability. This heavy reliance on ICTY jurisprudence, combined with the fact that, as explained in the next section, these three jurisdictions for the most part share a common legal framework for cases involving crimes committed during the Yugoslavian conflicts, means that there is substantial overlap in the way the different modes of participation have been defined and interpreted across the three jurisdictions. This does not mean, however, that some more or less important differences do not exist. In addition, the specific cases have also included different aspects of the various modes within the respective jurisdictions.

The trials, as in the other jurisdictions analysed throughout this chapter, also highlight some inconsistencies and controversies in the application of the different theories of attribution within the domestic context.

Compared to some of the other jurisdictions analysed in this chapter, the national courts in some of the countries discussed in this section have demonstrated somewhat greater concern for the rights of the accused during the course of criminal proceedings. This is evident not only at the level of fundamental principles, but also, at times, in a quite stringent application of procedural rules intended to protect the interests of the accused. An example of the former is the case of Rašević *et al.* before the Court of BiH. In assessing the accused's liability under the doctrine of JCE, the

---

[182] The Republic of Yugoslavia also included the present-day states of Macedonia, Slovenia, Montenegro, and Kosovo.

[183] This chapter's analysis of the legal framework and jurisprudence on modes of participation from these three jurisdictions is based on information and translations compiled in International Criminal Law Services, *International Criminal Law & Practice Training Materials – Module 9: Modes of Liability: Commission and Participation*, The Hague, 2011 (hereafter cited as *Module 9*).

court engaged in a comprehensive analysis of the customary status of this doctrine under international law as well as of its applicability and foreseeability under domestic law at the time the crime took place, thus ensuring that its application would not conflict either with the principle of non-retroactivity or with the general foreseeability consideration upon which the legality principle is founded.[184]

With respect to procedural rules, a further illustration is the Božić *et al.* judgment, where the court found the indictment based on JCE III was insufficiently specified and lacking in clarity with respect to the elements of this mode of liability. In the court's opinion, this was unacceptable, as it provided unsatisfactory information on the specific charges to the accused, thus undermining the right to a fair trial.[185]

9.6.2. Domestic Legal Frameworks of BiH, Croatia, and Serbia

Given that the three currently autonomous jurisdictions of BiH, Croatia, and Serbia previously formed part of the single unified jurisdiction of the former Socialist Federal Republic of Yugoslavia ('SFRY'), the legal proceedings for crimes that took place during the conflict in Yugoslavia are either directly regulated or heavily influenced by the provisions of the SFRY Criminal Code of 1976,[186] the criminal code in place at the time the crimes occurred. Let us look briefly at the modes of participation provided in that legislation.

The SFRY Criminal Code provides for dual regulation of the modes of participation.[187] First, there are the general modes of participation that pertain to all crimes, which include perpetration/co-perpetration (Article 22), incitement (Article 23), and accessorial liability/aiding and abetting

---

[184] Court of BiH, *Mitar Rašević et al.*, 1st Instance Verdict, Case X-KRZ-06/275, 28 February 2008, pp. 106–8, cited in *Module 9*, 2011, pp. 47–79 (www.legal-tools.org/doc/6a28b5/). The Trial Panel's conclusions were upheld on appeal. See Court of BiH, *Mitar Rašević et al.*, 2nd Instance Verdict, Case X-KRZ-06/275, 6 November 2008, pp. 25–26 (www.legal-tools.org/doc/d8720a/).

[185] Court of BiH, *Božić Zdravko et al.*, 2nd Instance Verdict, Case X-KRZ-06/236, 5 October 2009, in particular paras. 133–35, in *Module 9*, 2011, pp. 63–65 (www.legal-tools.org/doc/65c74d/).

[186] Socialist Federal Republic of Yugoslavia Criminal Code, adopted 28 September 1976, in force as of 1 July 1977 (www.legal-tools.org/doc/358faa/).

[187] For a more detailed overview, see *Module 9*, 2011, pp. 27–29.

(Article 24).[188] Second, Chapter XVI of the Criminal Code, which deals with universal crimes, sets out the applicable modes of liability specifically for these crimes, including perpetration/co-perpetration (all articles in this chapter), ordering,[189] instigating (Article 145(4)),[190] and organising a group for the perpetration of crimes (Article 145).[191]

These modes of participation as set out in the SFRY Criminal Code represent the main legal framework for attributing individual criminal liability for crimes emanating from the conflicts in the former Yugoslavia, although, as indicated above, there are some variations with respect to the manner in which these provisions have been implemented in each domestic context. Serbian courts either directly apply the SFRY Criminal Code or apply the FRY Criminal Code (which incorporates the SFRY provisions on modes of liability) as *tempore criminis* regulations.[192] In the Croatian jurisdiction, liability for these crimes is regulated by the criminal code known as OKZ RH,[193] which also incorporates the mode of participation from the SFRY Criminal Code.[194]

Reliance on the SFRY Criminal Code is more complex in the case of BiH. More precisely, the SFRY Criminal Code does not unequivocally apply these crimes in the BiH jurisdiction, as the applicable laws vary between various institutions: while first-level courts directly apply the provisions of the SFRY Criminal Code in prosecuting war crimes cases, the higher Court of BiH primarily uses the new BiH Criminal Code of 2003.[195] The picture is, however, further complicated by the fact that the

---

[188] *Ibid.*, p. 27.

[189] This mode is applicable to the crime of genocide (Article 141), war crimes against civilians (Article 142), war crimes against wounded and sick (Article 143), war crimes against prisoners of war (Article 144), ordering no survivors among enemy combatants (Article 146(3)), marauding (Article 147), and unjustified repatriation of POWs (Article 150(a)).

[190] Applicable to the crime of genocide (Article 141), war crimes against civilians (Article 142), war crimes against wounded and sick (Article 143), and war crimes against prisoners of war (Article 144).

[191] This is considered both a separate crime and a mode of participation; see *Module 9*, 2011, p. 27.

[192] *Ibid.*, p. 74.

[193] The OKZ RH of 1991 is the Basic Criminal Code of the Republic of Croatia (www.legal-tools.org/doc/fc3d9e/).

[194] *Module 9*, 2011, p. 67.

[195] *Ibid.*, p. 30.

Court of BiH may still apply the SFRY Criminal Code directly to specific cases if it provides a more lenient treatment of the accused.[196]

As a consequence, although the SFRY Criminal Code as a general rule does not form part of the legal framework for criminal proceedings before the Court of BiH, its provisions on modes of participation remain relevant. An example in which the Court of BiH directly considered the applicability of the SFRY Criminal Code in place of the 2003 Code is the Andrun case. Here, the court had to assess whether the provision on co-perpetration in Article 22 of the SFRY Criminal Code was more lenient for the accused than the provision regarding this mode of participation in Article 29 of the BiH Criminal Code. The Appellate Panel noted that the SFRY Criminal Code, which lacks an objective threshold with respect to the level of contribution required for a co-perpetrator, had a narrower definition of co-perpetration than the BiH Criminal Code, which requires a "decisive contribution". Therefore, the BiH Criminal Code was considered to provide the more lenient regulation in favour of the accused, rendering the SFRY Criminal Code inapplicable.[197]

Still, given that the BiH Criminal Code of 2003 provides the relevant provision in most cases, it is appropriate to also briefly sketch out its modes of participation.[198] This code mainly takes a dual approach similar to that of the SFRY Criminal Code, first setting out the modes of participation applicable to all crimes: perpetration/co-perpetration (Article 29), incitement (Article 30), and accessorial liability/aiding and abetting (Article 31). Additionally, Article 180(1) further sets out the modes of liability applicable to crimes of an international character as regulated in Chapter XVII of the BiH Criminal Code, providing for liability under the modes of perpetration/co-perpetration, planning, ordering, as well as aiding and abetting and instigation and organising a group for the purpose of committing certain universal crimes in Article 176. Lastly, Article 180(2) sets out the provisions regarding command responsibility.[199] The additional

---

[196] *Ibid.*, p. 27.

[197] Court of BiH, *Nikola Andrun*, 2nd Instance Verdict, Case X-KRŽ-05/42, 19 August 2008 (www.legal-tools.org/doc/9e90bd/). This case and the cross-jurisdictional discrepancy regarding the level of contribution required for liability as a co-perpetrator is elaborated further below.

[198] The overview here is based on that set out in *Module 9*, 2011, pp. 30 ff.

[199] *Ibid.*, pp. 31–32.

modes of participation provided under Article 180 were intended to follow international criminal law and in particular the ICTY Statute, and serve to broaden the range of modes available for prosecuting crimes of an international character.[200]

In analysing the relevant jurisprudence, the next section focuses on four modes of participation that have been most prominent in the available jurisprudence of the three countries examined here, namely co-perpetration, JCE, ordering, and aiding and abetting.

9.6.3. Application of the Modes of Liability

9.6.3.1. Introduction

Based on the available jurisprudence, the domestic courts in all three jurisdictions have relied on the modes of co-perpetration, ordering, and aiding and abetting in order to attribute criminal liability to those involved in crimes committed during the conflicts in the former Yugoslavia. In addition, courts in Bosnia and Herzegovina have also conducted rather comprehensive analysis of the doctrine of JCE.

9.6.3.2. Co-perpetration

Turning first to co-perpetration, the available jurisprudence from the three jurisdictions indicates substantial overlap in defining and interpreting the elements of this mode. However, there is also an evident discrepancy with respect to whether or not the case law has formulated an explicit *actus reus* threshold.

In all three jurisdictions, the courts have generally followed the international jurisprudence in defining the concept of co-perpetration as being based on a division of labour following a common agreement or plan to commit a criminal offence or one that will lead to its commission. As explained by the Trial Chamber in the Cantonal Court in Mostar in the Vlahovljak *et al.* case:

> In [a] case when several persons act with intent (awareness of the conduct and the will to cause the consequence) in a joint act of commission [...] and their joint activity accomplishes the consequence of this criminal act – death of one or more civilians – all those persons are, in the sense of Article

---

[200] *Ibid.*, p. 32.

22 of the adopted SFRY Criminal Code, considered co-perpetrators to the criminal act.[201]

Both Serbian and Croatian courts have underlined that this crucial element of division of labour means that it is not necessary, in order to incur liability, that each participant individually undertake all the material elements of the crime; rather, it suffices that each of them makes a partial contribution that, in combination with the other contributions, would lead to the occurrence of the crime.[202] The Court of BiH has also made clear that the accused is not required to have been physically present at the scene of the crime, as long as his prior acts made a contribution to its eventual commission in accordance with the general plan.[203] Illustrative in this regard is the Madi *et al.* case, where the accused was convicted as a co-perpetrator for having driven the other accused persons to and from the crime scene, as well as pointing out to them the house in which the victim resided. The Croatian Supreme Court rejected the argument that because Madi himself did not directly participate in the killing, he could not be convicted as a co-perpetrator. The court reasoned that because each of the co-perpetrators had made his own distinct contribution with knowledge of what was to be done by the others, each of them incurred liability for the crime as a direct perpetrator.[204]

With respect to the *mens rea*, Serbian jurisprudence has indicated that this consists of three constitutive elements. The accused must be aware of the conduct of the other co-perpetrators, and he must be aware that his own contribution forms part of the overall conduct of the group.[205]

---

[201] BiH, Cantonal Court in Mostar, *Nihad Vlahovljak et al.*, 1st Instance Verdict, Case 007-0-K-07-00 006, 8 August 2007, pp. 8–9 (www.legal-tools.org/doc/506c1b/), cited in *Module 9*, 2011, p. 39.

[202] See, for example, Croatia, County Court in Osijek, *Marguš and Dilber (Čepin)*, 1st Instance Verdict, Case K-33/06-412, 21 March 2007 (www.legal-tools.org/doc/0c41bc/); and Serbia, Belgrade District Court, *Ovčara*, 1st Instance Verdict, Case K.V. 4/2006, 12 March 2009, p. 244 (www.legal-tools.org/doc/b236a6/), cited in *Module 9*, 2011, pp. 70–72 and 78.

[203] Court of BiH, *Željko Lelek*, 2nd Instance Verdict, Case X-KRŽ-06/202, 12 January 2009, paras. 33 and 95–96, cited in *Module 9*, 2011, p. 41 (www.legal-tools.org/doc/299be4/).

[204] Supreme Court of Croatia, *Tomislav Madi et al. (Cerna)*, 2nd Instance Verdict, Case I Kz 910/08-10, 25 March 2009, p. 15, cited in *Module 9*, 2011, pp. 70–72 (www.legal-tools.org/doc/11892e/).

[205] Serbia, *Ovčara* (2009), p. 244, cited in *Module 9*, 2011, pp. 77–79.

Additionally, it must also be proven that the accused acted with intent for the criminal outcome to in fact take place.[206]

It should be noted, however, that there have been some inconsistencies within the BiH jurisprudence as to the requirement for the existence of a prior agreement on the division of labour for co-perpetration. The Supreme Court of Republika Srpska, for instance, handed down a guilty verdict under the mode of co-perpetration in the absence of evidence of such an agreement, which at least implicitly indicates that the existence of a prior agreement is not considered to form part of the material elements of co-perpetration. The Supreme Court stated:

> The Court did not accept the Prosecution claim that a prior agreement existed between the accused and the unknown uniformed persons [...]. In the end, the existence of a prior agreement [...] is not of significance for the existence of the act.[207]

By contrast, the same court in a different case explicitly made reference to a pre-existing agreement when considering whether the evidence supported a conviction of the accused as a co-perpetrator:

> [E]very accused, within the framework of that agreement, undertook actions for the realization of the act, wanting the accomplishment of the act as his own and as a joint one. Therefore, they acted with direct intent and the impugned verdict correctly decided on the awareness and the will as components of their mental relation to the act as a whole, therefore in relation to the consequence as well.[208]

Importantly, recalling the above-noted differences in the applicable law, this has had the direct consequence of inducing a crucial cross-jurisdictional discrepancy with respect to the level of contribution required as part of the *actus reus* of co-perpetration.

One the one hand, the jurisprudence emanating from both the Croatian and Serbian courts has relied on the notion of co-perpetration as de-

---

[206] Serbia, Belgrade District Court, *Anton Lekaj*, 1st Instance Verdict, Case K.V. 4/05, 18 September 2006, p. 34 (www.legal-tools.org/doc/33b891/), cited in *Module 9*, 2011, p. 78.

[207] Supreme Court of Republika Srpska, Case 118-0-KZ-K-06-000-006, 22 February 2007, p. 6 (www.legal-tools.org/doc/c89d1c/), cited in *Module 9*, 2011, p. 40.

[208] Supreme Court of Republika Srpska, Case 118-0-Kz-06-000-018, 18 April 2006, p. 5 (www.legal-tools.org/doc/4f6054/), cited in *Module 9*, 2011, p. 41.

fined in Article 22 of the SFRY Criminal Code, which is based on a strict division of labour under which any objective contribution in consonance with the common plan, irrespective of how insignificant, is sufficient to incur liability.[209] Thus, in contrast to the doctrine of co-perpetration as developed at the ICC,[210] the applicable law does not set out any qualified objective threshold, requiring neither an essential nor a substantial contribution by the accused.[211]

It should be noted, however, that there have been some sporadic indications of at least a minimum threshold being formulated by Serbian courts: for example, the War Crimes Chamber in the Lekaj case held that the accused is required to considerably contribute to the commission of the crime.[212] However, subsequent jurisprudence does suggest this to be a more or less negligible threshold, given the fact that, for instance, the Supreme Court in the Morina case accepted mere presence at the crime scene alongside fellow soldiers who carried out the crime(s) as sufficient to satisfy the "considerable contribution" requirement.[213] In the Zvornik case, although maintaining the practice of not insisting on an essential contribution, the War Crimes Chamber also made explicit use of a concept akin to the notion of control over the crime (*Tatherrschaftslehre*), concluding:

> [T]hey had *authority over [the] act*, that one accepted the conduct of the other as his own and joint ones, expressing the will to jointly commit the act.[214]

In comparison, liability under the notion of co-perpetration as set out in Article 29 of the BiH Criminal Code of 2003, which is directly built

---

[209] *Module 9*, 2011, pp. 37, 70, and 77. As explained above, the Serbian courts rely on either the SFRY or FRY code, the latter having incorporated the former's provisions on modes of participation. The Croatian courts meanwhile employ the OKZ RH, whose Article 20 reflects Article 22 of the old SFRY Criminal Code.

[210] See Chapter 7, Section 7.2.2.2.

[211] In comparison, both Article 33 of the new Serbian Criminal Code of 2006 and Article 35(3) of the Croatian Criminal Code of 1998 do specify an objective threshold, requiring the co-perpetrator to make a "substantial" or "significant" contribution, respectively.

[212] Serbia, *Lekaj* (2006), p. 34, cited in *Module 9*, 2011, p. 79.

[213] Supreme Court of Serbia, *Sinan Morina*, 2nd Instance Verdict, Case Kz. I RZ 1/08, 3 March 2009, p. 4 (www.legal-tools.org/doc/21633c/), cited in *Module 9*, 2011, p. 79.

[214] Serbia, Belgrade District Court, *Zvornik*, 1st Instance Verdict, Case K.V. 5/2005, 12 June 2008 (www.legal-tools.org/doc/9679f4/), p. 181, cited in *Module 9*, 2011, p. 79, emphasis in original.

around the notion of *Tatherrschaftslehre*, explicitly requires the co-perpetrators to have made a "decisive contribution".[215] The Court of BiH has understood this requirement to be similar to that of a coordinated essential contribution at the ICC.[216] In the words of the BiH court:

> [C]o-perpetration represents a form of perpetration that exists when several persons, who satisfy all the conditions that are required for a perpetrator, consciously and willingly commit a criminal offence based on their joint decision in the manner that *each of the co-perpetrators gives his contribution which is important and without which the criminal offence would not be committed or would not be committed in the planned way.* Therefore, along[with] the joint action of several persons in the perpetration of the criminal offence, it is necessary that they should be aware of the fact that the committed act represents a joint result of their actions.[217]

This decisive contribution, or the ability to frustrate the commission of the crime by not carrying out one's task, as phrased at the ICC,[218] is what ensures the form of joint control over the crime that underlies the control theory of co-perpetration.[219] The Court of BiH thus exhibited a more coherent interpretation of co-perpetration when based on an authority/control doctrine than that put forth by the Serbian court in the Zvornik case.

In the course of applying this theory, however, there has been some confusion in the BiH jurisprudence as to whether an omission could qualify as a "decisive contribution". Illustrative is the case of Todorović *et al.*, in which the Appellate Panel overturned the Trial Panel's conclusion that passive behaviour could constitute a decisive contribution:

> [T]he trial panel erred in law in relying on what it considered the appellants' failure to prevent the commission of the crimes to establish that the appellants decisively contributed

---

[215] *Module 9*, 2011, pp. 36–37.

[216] See Chapter 7, Section 7.2.2.2.

[217] BiH, *Andrun* (2008), p. 25 (emphasis added), cited in *Module 9*, 2011, pp. 37–38.

[218] See Chapter 7, Section 7.2.2.2.

[219] Recall that, as noted above, this objective threshold of a decisive contribution does not apply before the BiH entity-level courts, which directly apply the old SFRY Criminal Code when prosecuting war crimes emanating from the conflicts of the former Yugoslavia.

to the perpetration of the crimes of imprisonment, torture and murder.[220]

In support of this conclusion, the Appellate Panel reasoned that:

> The Trial Panel established that the Appellants participated in the commission of the criminal offenses by guarding the captured civilians before and during the perpetration of the crimes. The Trial Panel did not establish that the Appellants' omissions were culpable omissions that constituted the *actus reus* of the crimes. Accordingly, it is axiomatic that the decisiveness of the appellants' contribution to the perpetration of those crimes can only be assessed with respect to the *affirmative culpable* acts. The Trial Panel's reliance on the Appellants' omissions, their failure to prevent the crimes, as establishing the decisiveness of their contribution was therefore an error of law.[221]

Accordingly, the Appellate Panel overturned the verdict of the Trial Panel that was based on co-perpetration, instead convicting the accused as accessories to the crime.

9.6.3.3.   Aiding and Abetting

Aiding and abetting as a mode of participation has also been employed in a range of cases, and its elements have been elucidated by the various courts largely in line with the jurisprudence of the *ad hoc* tribunals. Regarding the objective elements of aiding and abetting, the War Crimes Chamber of the Serbian court in the Škorpioni case defined the *actus reus* as involving every act that supports, advances, or in any other way facilitates the commission of the crime by the direct perpetrator.[222] Relying on, among others, on the Tadić judgment of the ICTY, the Court of BiH in the Bjelić case has further made clear that the act of the aider and abettor must have had a substantial effect on the commission of the crime.[223] In

---

[220] Court of BiH, *Mirko Todorović et al.*, 2nd Instance Verdict, Case X-KRŽ-07/382, 23 January 2009, para. 155, cited in *Module 9*, 2011, p. 40 (www.legal-tools.org/doc/d83346/).

[221] *Ibid.*, para. 160, emphasis added.

[222] Serbia, Belgrade District Court, *Škorpioni*, 1st Instance Verdict, Case K.V. 6/2005, 10 April 2007, p. 101 (www.legal-tools.org/doc/d2c374/), cited in *Module 9*, 2011, p. 80. See also, for example, Court of BiH, *Abduladhim Maktouf*, 2nd Instance Verdict, Case KPZ-32/05, 4 April 2006 (www.legal-tools.org/doc/0ad159/).

[223] Court of BiH, *Veiz Bjelić*, 1st Instance Verdict, Case X-KR-07/430-1, 28 March 2008, p. 17, cited in *Module 9*, 2011, p. 43 (www.legal-tools.org/doc/eeb752/).

---

contrast to co-perpetration, however, the War Crimes Chamber in Škorpioni underlined that for accessorial liability there is no requirement to prove the existence of a prior common plan or agreement.[224]

Turning to the *mens rea* for aiding and abetting, it was set out by the Court of BiH in the Pekez *et al.* case as requiring knowledge on the part of the aider and abettor that his actions would aid the direct perpetrator in committing the crime in question.[225] However, it is not necessary that the aider and abettor know the precise crime intended by the direct perpetrator, only that he be aware of the essential elements of the crime that is about to be committed.[226] At the same time, it should be mentioned that the Serbian War Crimes Chamber in the above-mentioned Škorpioni case appears to have specified an extended twofold *mens rea*, requiring that the aider and abettor, in addition to being aware that his acts aid the direct perpetrator, also act with the intent to support, advance, or facilitate the relevant criminal outcome.[227]

As for instances of aiding and abetting by omission, Serbian jurisprudence in the Zvornik II case has established that liability can arise through passivity, provided that the accused's omission, or failure to act, had a substantial effect on the occurrence of the crime.[228] The court explicitly held that this mode of liability was established as part of customary international law, but it did not reference any specific source in support of this statement.

Importantly, in differentiating this form of liability from aiding and abetting by positive acts, the court added a material element, stating that in order for omissions to give rise to criminal liability, there must be established the existence of a duty or obligation to act on the part of the ac-

---

[224] Serbia, *Škorpioni* (2007), p. 101, cited in *Module 9*, 2011, p. 81.

[225] Court of BiH, *Mirko Pekez et al.*, 2nd Instance Verdict, Case X-KRŽ-05/96-1, 5 May 2009, para. 108, cited in *Module 9*, 2011, p. 44 44 (www.legal-tools.org/doc/d92ed4/).

[226] *Ibid.*

[227] Serbia, *Škorpioni* (2007), p. 101, cited in *Module 9*, 2011, p. 81. Note, however, that the Supreme Court returned the case to the War Crimes Chamber for a re-trial, because the reasoning on the accused's *mens rea* was considered contradictory and lacking in sufficient clarity; see Supreme Court of the Republic of Serbia, *Škorpioni*, 2nd Instance Verdict, Case Kz. I r.z. 2/07, 13 June 2008, pp. 17–18 (www.legal-tools.org/doc/c72d4e/).

[228] Serbia, Belgrade High Court, WCD, *Grujic and Popovic (Zvornik II)*, 1st Instance Verdict, Case K.Po2 28/2010, 22 November 2010, p. 299 (www.legal-tools.org/doc/874ecd/), cited in *Module 9*, 2011, pp. 81–82.

cused.[229] In further elaborating the theoretical underpinnings of this form of liability, the court held that according to both international criminal law theory and jurisprudence, such a duty/obligation arises either from legal provisions or from "previously undertaken acts of a guarantor by which he created a dangerous situation". In this specific case, and with reference to both foreign case law and the notion of "indirect subordination" in the ICRC Commentary to Additional Protocol II of the Geneva Conventions, the court considered that the accused's responsibility for the capture and internment of civilians also imposed on him a special obligation to ensure their safety while in confinement.[230] The judges further clarified that it is not necessary for the accused to have knowledge of the details of the crimes that are about to be committed. Rather, the court held, under customary international law it is sufficient to establish that the accused was aware of the "significant risk/higher probability of risk" that a crime was to be committed[231] and failed to act in response to this risk.

With respect to the question of delineating the aiding and abetting liability from co-perpetration, an illustrative case is that of Pekez *et al.* before the Appellate Panel of the Court of BiH.[232] In this case, the accused had participated in rounding up civilian villagers, but then decided to withdraw himself from the second phase, namely killing the villagers. The court reasoned that because he had withdrawn his participation before the killing started, he could not be convicted as a co-perpetrator. However, as he remained an active participant up until the villagers were brought to the execution site, he was considered liable as an aider and abettor for having aided the others in carrying out the common plan to execute the villagers.[233]

In respect to specific intent crimes, such as genocide, the Appellate Panel in the Stupar *et al.* case found that the delineation between these

---

[229] *Ibid.* This requirement of a legal duty as a fundamental rationale underlying liability for aiding and abetting by omission is in line with what is described by Jessie Ingle, "Aiding and Abetting by Omission before the International Criminal Tribunals", in *Journal of International Criminal Justice*, 2016, vol. 14, no. 4, pp. 747–69 (discussed in Chapter 6, Section 6.2.3.2).

[230] Serbia, *Zvornik II* (2010), pp. 299–300.

[231] *Ibid.*, p. 301.

[232] BiH, *Pekez et al.* (2009), cited in *Module 9*, 2011, p. 43.

[233] *Ibid.*, paras. 109–11.

---

two modes of participation would often depend on whether the accused shared the specific intent for the crime.[234] In overturning the Trial Panel's conviction of the accused as a co-perpetrator of genocide, the Appellate Panel held that

> [a]n accessory, as a form of complicity, represents the intentional support of a criminal offence committed by another person. That is, it includes actions that enable the perpetration of a criminal offence by another person. [...] If a person is only aware of the genocidal intent of the perpetrator, but the person did not share the intent, the person is an accessory to genocide.[235]

9.6.3.4. Ordering

Regarding the third mode of liability, ordering, the domestic courts in the three jurisdictions under examination have primarily followed the jurisprudence of the ICTY in developing the elements of this mode of participation, although a rather broad notion of ordering has occasionally been applied.

Referring to ICTY case law, in particular the Krstić trial judgment, the Trial Panel of the Court of BiH in the Savić case defined ordering to mean that a person in a position of authority uses his position to convince another person to commit an offence. The court also made clear that it was not necessary for the order to be issued in any particular form.[236] As for its application to the case at hand, the panel held that:

> In the present case, the accused did not personally order the residents of Dušde to go towards Višegrad, nor did he personally separate the Bosniac men from the column. [...] [However] bearing in mind that he was the Commander to the present soldiers, that it was he who was to be asked for everything, that at the particular time he was on the site, that a number of times while the column of civilians was moving

---

234 Court of BiH, *Milos Stupar et al.*, 2nd Instance Verdict, Case X-KRZ-05/24, 9 September 2009, cited in *Module 9*, 2011, p. 45 (www.legal-tools.org/doc/9404de/).

235 *Ibid.*, paras. 567 and 570. See also Court of BiH, *Petar Mitrovic*, 2nd Instance Verdict, Case X-KR-05/24-1, 7 September 2009, paras. 260–61 (www.legal-tools.org/doc/444ffa/). For the same notion at the international level, see Chapter 7, Section 7.2.3.1.

236 Court of BiH, *Momir Savić*, 1st Instance Verdict, Case X-KR-07/478, 3 July 2009, p. 106, cited in *Module 9*, 2011, pp. 34–35 (www.legal-tools.org/doc/1742d8/).

he passed by the column which was heading towards Višegrad, the Panel finds that he had the necessary authority and the active control over his soldiers, so that the Panel finds that <u>he was the only one</u> who could give orders to his soldiers to take the described actions against civilians of Bosniac ethnicity.[237]

In the case of Suva Reka before the Serbian Appellate Court, the court has further clarified that in cases where a statement does not constitute an explicit incitement to commit a crime, it may still be considered as an order for the purpose of criminal liability based on the circumstantial evidence. According to the court, this would require the prosecution to prove that (1) the circumstances of the case clearly indicate the existence of a plan to commit a crime, (2) the statement is communicated to individuals familiar with the plan, (3) those persons are aware of what the message intends to say, and (4) the message leads to the desired action.[238]

While the circumstantial evidence was considered insufficient for a conviction in that specific case, the Croatian Trial Chamber in the case of Ćurčić *et al.* employed a similar reasoning to convict the accused of ordering a range of war crimes against civilians. Despite the lack of written evidence of the alleged orders, the chamber considered that the accused's position as the police commander combined with the systematic nature of the events supported the conclusion that they could only have taken place upon the orders of the accused.[239] This reasoning appears to be based on a relatively broad notion of ordering, as the court went on to clarify that it was not important whether the accused had been the instigator of every act of violence or whether there had been a broadening of the accused's original orders; instead it was held sufficient that the accused had been in control of the implementation.[240]

---

[237] *Ibid.*, p. 107, emphasis in original.

[238] Serbia, War Crimes Department of the Appellate Court in Belgrade, *Suva Reka*, 2nd Instance Verdict, Case Kž1 Po2 4/2010, 30 June 2010, para. 2.5.1 (www.legal-tools.org/doc/b8cbb4/), cited in *Module 9*, 2011, p. 76.

[239] Croatia, County Court in Vukovar, *Ćurčić et al. (Borovo selo)*, 1st Instance Verdict, Case K-12/05, 14 December 2005, p. 36, cited in *Module 9*, 2011, p. 69 (www.legal-tools.org/doc/e702c6/).

[240] *Ibid.*

Relying on the ICTY Kvočka judgment, the Court of BiH in the above-mentioned Savić case identified the subjective element of the mode of ordering as requiring the accused to have acted with "[t]he awareness of the substantial likelihood that a criminal act or mission would occur as a consequence of his conduct".[241] The court also emphasised that this subjective element need not be explicitly expressed, but may be derived from circumstantial evidence.[242]

9.6.3.5.   Joint Criminal Enterprise

Lastly, the Court of BiH has also engaged in extensive analysis of the doctrine of JCE. This doctrine has been considered by the court to be included under Article 180(1) of the BiH Criminal Code, which the court noted was derived from and identical to Article 7(1) of the ICTY Statute.[243]

In defining the elements of JCE, the Court of BiH has also largely followed the approach set out in the jurisprudence of the ICTY. In the Rašević et al. case, while emphasising that it was not bound by the decisions of the ICTY, the court nonetheless found it appropriate to follow ICTY case law, which it considered to properly reflect customary international law on the elements of this doctrine.[244] Accordingly, the court held the elements of basic JCE I to consist of the following: (1) a plurality of persons, (2) the existence of a common plan or design that amounts to or involves the commission of a crime or crimes, (3) participation of the accused in the common plan or design, (4) a conscious participation in the crime in a manner that significantly supports or facilitates its commission, and (5) as to the mens rea, knowledge of the crime(s) or awareness that the accused's acts or omissions enabled the commission of the crime(s).[245] Concerning the element of a plurality of persons, the court emphasised that it need not take the form of any particular type of organisation, nor is the existence of an enterprise limited to members of a single organisation; rather, it may involve multiple structures.[246]

---

[241] BiH, Savić (2009), p. 106, cited in Module 9, 2011, p. 35.

[242] Ibid.

[243] BiH, Rašević et al., 1st Instance Verdict (2008), p. 103, cited in Module 9, 2011, p. 46. For the ICTY jurisprudence, see Chapter 7, Section 7.2.2.4.

[244] Ibid., pp. 111–12, cited in Module 9, 2011, p. 50.

[245] Ibid., p. 112.

[246] BiH, Rašević et al., 1st Instance Verdict (2008), p. 125, cited in Module 9, 2011, p. 52.

With respect to the systemic form (JCE II), which applies to participation within an organised system of ill-treatment, such as a concentration camp, the court held in accordance with ICTY jurisprudence that its elements are primarily differentiated from the basic form based on the *mens rea*, requiring that (1) the accused had knowledge of the organised system of ill-treatment, and (2) the accused had intent to further this system.[247] The court underlined that while it must be proven that the accused had knowledge of the type and extent of the criminal system, it is not required that the accused had knowledge of each specific crime committed within the system as whole.[248]

The Court of BiH has, however, at times displayed some confusion when incorporating the doctrine of JCE into its domestic legal framework. The confusion primarily relates to the task of differentiating the elements of the JCE doctrine under customary law, as understood to be included in Article 180(1) of the BiH Criminal Code, from those of the more classic form of co-perpetration under the code's Article 29 (as noted above).[249] More precisely, the confusion that began with the Trial Panel in the Rašević *et al.* judgment centres on the level of contribution required by each participant. The panel appears to consider JCE and co-perpetration as two overlapping doctrines within the domestic context, which again leads the panel to conflate their respective elements. In the words of the Trial Panel:

---

[247] *Ibid.*, p. 112, referring to ICTY, Appeals Chamber, *Prosecutor v. Tadić*, Judgment, IT-94-1-A, 15 July 1999, paras. 203 and 220 (www.legal-tools.org/doc/8efc3a/). Also see BiH, *Rašević et al.*, 2nd Instance Verdict (2008), p. 26, cited in *Module 9*, 2011, pp. 50 and 52.

[248] BiH, *Rašević et al.*, 1st Instance Verdict (2008), p. 138; Court of BiH, *Dušan Fuštar*, 1st Instance Verdict, Case X-KR06/2001-1, 21 April 2008, pp. 25–26, cited in *Module 9*, 2011, p. 56 (www.legal-tools.org/doc/a3f13c/). Although not relevant to the case at hand, the court also briefly defined the extended form of JCE (JCE III) as pertaining to instances where one or more members of the group committed a crime that, although not forming part of the common plan or agreement, was a natural and foreseeable consequence of the implementation of the plan; see BiH, *Rašević et al.*, 2nd Instance Verdict (2008), p. 26, cited in *Module 9*, 2011, p. 59. Extended JCE has not been charged in any other cases before the Court of BiH, with the exception of Božić *et al.*, where the indictment, as already mentioned above, was rejected on the basis of insufficient clarity with respect to which version of JCE liability was alleged.

[249] As mentioned above, Article 180 is a special provision on modes of participation exclusively applicable to the universal crimes enumerated in Chapter XVII of the code.

> [T]here is no discrepancy between customary international law for JCE and Article 29 regarding the degree of participation necessary to establish co-perpetration when the accused has participated in any way in the actus reus of the crimes. However, there is a discrepancy when the accused has taken "some other act" toward the commission of an offense. Under customary international law, all other elements of JCE having been proven, the degree of participation which that "other act" constitutes need not be "substantial or significant". However, under Article 29, it must be "decisive". As the Prosecutor has charged co-perpetration under Article 180(1) in conjunction with Article 29, and argued that the Panel should apply both, it is necessary that more than the customary international law standard be proven.[250]

The Appellate Panel rejected this interpretation, making clear that it was not necessary that the contribution of the perpetrator be qualified as decisive or substantial in order for liability under systemic JCE to apply; rather, the extent of participation simply served to inform that the accused shared the common purpose of the group.[251] Moreover, the Appellate Panel went on to say that the conceptual difference between the alternative theories of JCE and co-perpetration, as understood in the domestic context, in fact rested on liability as a co-perpetrator requiring a higher degree of contribution (decisive) than what is needed in order to attribute liability for participation in a JCE.[252]

The conceptual reasoning of the Trial Panel in Rašević et al. was also addressed in a later verdict by the Appellate Panel in the Vuković et al. case, in which the panel to some extent questioned the applicability of the JCE doctrine under the domestic legal framework. The panel considered the concepts of JCE and co-perpetration to be "mutually exclusive" and emphasised that the doctrine of JCE was not legislated or defined in the BiH Criminal Code.[253] Furthermore, the panel stated that:

> [i]t is not known whether this is a case of a particular criminal offence or a form of criminal responsibility, and if we ac-

---

[250] BiH, *Rašević et al.*, 1st Instance Verdict (2008), p. 161, cited in *Module 9*, 2011, p. 60.

[251] BiH, *Rašević et al.*, 2nd Instance Verdict (2008), p. 27, cited in *Module 9*, 2011, p. 60.

[252] *Ibid.*, cited in *Module 9*, 2011, pp. 55 and 60.

[253] Court of BiH, *Ranko Vuković et al.*, 2nd Instance Verdict, Case X-KR-06/180-2, 2 September 2008, p. 5, cited in *Module 9*, 2011, p. 60 (www.legal-tools.org/doc/e15578/).

cept the latter one, this concept is hardly in accordance with the classical concept of co-perpetration recognized by our criminal code.[254]

In moving on to directly comment on the conceptual difference between JCE and co-perpetration, the panel seems to consider the conceptual underpinnings of this mode of liability as being primarily of a subjective character, similar to what had been said by the ICC. The court held that:

> The difference is incontestable between each of the three forms of joint criminal enterprise established in the ICTY jurisprudence and the concept of co-perpetration in terms of Articles 29 and 32 of the CC BiH, particularly in the field of *mens rea*, since joint criminal enterprise implies common intent on the level of [the] subjective element, in which the first instance Verdict is also explicit, while co-perpetration implies the principle of limited responsibility, so it is impossible to equalize criminal responsibility stipulated under the cited article with the concept of joint criminal enterprise developed in the ICTY jurisprudence, as the first instance Verdict completely erroneously did.[255]

However, while being somewhat more precise as to the conceptual, subjective basis for JCE, the legal analysis of the Appellate Panel is less clear as to what is meant by its reference to a principle of "limited responsibility" with respect to the alternative doctrine of co-perpetration.

Finally, two additional aspects that have been addressed by the Court of BiH in relation to JCE are worth briefly noting. First, the Appellate Panel in the case of Božić *et al.*[256] considered the issue of whether the attribution of all the crimes that formed part of the common plan or agreement of the criminal enterprise also pertained to the low-level soldiers involved in executing the crimes, which in essence is a question of defining the outer bounds of the JCE doctrine. Having underlined the importance of adhering to the fundamental principle of personal culpability, the Appellate Panel held that common soldiers

---

[254] *Ibid.*, p. 6, cited in *Module 9*, 2011, p. 61.

[255] *Ibid.*

[256] BiH, *Božić et al.*, 2nd Instance Verdict (2009), cited in *Module 9*, 2011, p. 66.

cannot be considered criminally responsible for those crimes committed pursuant to the design of his ultimate superiors to which he did not contribute, simply on the grounds that those superiors also considered the Accused's acts as part of their design [...] the common soldiers of the VRS and the MUP [...] are responsible for the crimes they participate in, and no more. To conclude otherwise would be to assign collective responsibility to all soldiers for the crimes of their superiors.[257]

Second, the Appellate Panel in Rašević *et al.* addressed the question of assimilation of one mode of participation under another with respect to instances where the factual circumstances satisfied the elements of perpetration as a participant in a JCE and failure to punish under the mode of command responsibility. Adopting the approach of the ICTY in Krnojelac, the court reasoned that in all cases involving liability for planning, instigating, ordering, or committing a crime, any liability under the doctrine of command responsibility for failure to punish the direct perpetrator would be assimilated in any either of the former, more direct modes of participation.[258]

9.6.4. Concluding Remarks

The domestic courts of Bosnia and Herzegovina, Croatia, and Serbia have developed quite similar interpretations of modes of participation in the course of prosecuting crimes that took place during the conflicts in the former Yugoslavia. The reason for this may primarily be traced back to a common – for the most part – legal framework emanating from the former SFRY Criminal Code, as well as to extensive reliance on the jurisprudence of the *ad hoc* tribunals, primarily that of the ICTY.

As the above analysis has demonstrated, however, there are some cross-jurisdictional discrepancies. The most prominent example is the existence of an objective threshold for the mode of co-perpetration: only the Court of BiH, in applying the BiH Criminal Code of 2003, is in line with current ICC jurisprudence regarding co-perpetration in requiring a deci-

---

[257] *Ibid.*, para. 165. VRS stands for Army of Republika Srpska, while MUP is the Bosnian Ministry of the Interior.

[258] BiH, *Rašević et al.*, 2nd Instance Verdict (2008), p. 29, cited in *Module 9*, 2011, pp. 61–62. See also Court of BiH, *Željko Mejakić et al.*, 2nd Instance Verdict, Case X-KRŽ-06/200, 16 February 2009, paras. 67–68 (www.legal-tools.org/doc/c4d78a/).

sive (essential) contribution by the accused. The analysis of the three post-Yugoslavian jurisdictions, like the analysis of other countries covered in this chapter, has also highlighted some of the difficulties and controversies that seem to inevitably appear when ICL concepts are incorporated into the domestic context – the jurisprudence of the Court of BiH regarding JCE being just one example.

9.7. Conclusion

This chapter has examined the jurisprudence regarding modes of participation issued by courts in a selected, representative group of states in their efforts to attribute individual criminal liability to those involved in atrocity crimes that occurred in the territories of those states.

Several important observations have emerged from this review. The first is that taken together, these states have employed a relatively wide range of modes of participation, although there is considerable cross-jurisdictional variation. With respect to the latter, most notable is the apparent heavy reliance on commission-type liability by some of the courts, in particular those in East Timor and Latin America.[259] It is, however, important to recognise that at least part of the explanation for this can be traced to the functions occupied by the perpetrators in the respective power structures. More precisely, a reason for the strong reliance on commission-type liability before the SPSC in East Timor is that those prosecuted as part of the Serious Crimes process were primarily low-level perpetrators, namely the direct physical perpetrators. The Latin American jurisdictions, on the other hand, show a regional focus on developing an appropriate liability theory by use of the doctrine of indirect perpetration through an organised power structure to attribute liability to the highest-ranking officials, who typically operate at a remove from the actual crime scenes. The effort to hold those most responsible for the crimes liable as perpetrators – rather than as accessories, a role perceived to not accurately

---

[259] Note that this also coincides with the observations made by some ICL scholars regarding the international jurisprudence. For example, Marina Aksenova maintains that the ICC's interpretation of Article 25(3) of the Rome Statute as reflecting a hierarchy of modes of participation has induced an over-utilisation of the modes of commission under subparagraph (a) at the expense of the other forms of liability in (b) through (d) in an effort to best reflect the accused's level of responsibility. Aksenova, "The Modes of Liability at the ICC: The Labels that Don't Always Stick", in *International Criminal Law Review*, 2015, vol. 15, no. 4, pp. 629–64.

reflect their true level of responsibility – has led to the same result in terms of strong reliance on commission-type liability modes as in East Timor, although through different doctrinal approaches.

Second, there is also considerable variation in the quality of the trials and, most importantly for our purpose, in the quality of legal analysis of modes of participation and their underlying theoretical or doctrinal basis. Generally speaking, the legal analysis of personal liability in East Timor and Ethiopia has been conducted at a lower level of sophistication than in most of the Latin American and former Yugoslavian jurisdictions, as well as in the more recent cases in Bangladesh. In fact, as the review of the East Timorese jurisprudence has demonstrated, the judges of the SPSC on many occasions made little effort to define the respective elements of the various modes of participation, or to differentiate them from the separate elements of the substantive crimes. This often resulted in inaccuracies and at times outright confusion when the judges sought to apply a mode of participation to the facts of the case at hand. Similarly, the analysis with respect to personal liability in the Ethiopian Mengistu and Others trial involved a range of different modes of participation, but neither the prosecution nor the court drew a clear distinction between them, again making it difficult to precisely identify which mode of participation in fact formed the basis of the convictions of the various accused in that case.

Third, there are marked differences in the degree to which the national courts have made recourse to international jurisprudence in the course of personal liability analysis, as well as in which international court or tribunal they choose to consult. Both the Latin American and former Yugoslavian courts have relied extensively on international jurisprudence when establishing the elements of the various modes of liability. While the former Yugoslavian courts have primarily relied on the ICTY jurisprudence – perhaps not surprisingly, given the shared territorial scope – the Latin American courts have developed doctrinal liability theories more in line with the precedents developed at the ICC, a reflection in part of their civil law pedigree or preference. The reliance on the ICTY jurisprudence in the Bangladeshi courts can be explained by a shared background or interest in common law concepts. In comparison, both the SPSC in East Timor and the Ethiopian Supreme Court have relied much less on international jurisprudence during the course of their work.

That said, it is important to underline that these variations in the quality and sophistication of the legal reasoning and in the extent to which international jurisprudence was consulted do not merely represent cross-jurisdictional differences; there are also differences within some of the jurisdictions, both over time and between chambers. For instance, the examination of the jurisprudence of the SPSC and the Bangladeshi courts noted a tendency towards increased reliance on international jurisprudence over their lifetimes. In East Timor, however, such recourse was often done in a less than satisfactory manner, such as by referencing verdicts of the ICTY Trial Chambers that had already been rendered void by subsequent Appeals Chamber rulings on the legal matter at hand; while in Bangladesh, the recourse to international jurisprudence became more regular and accurate.

As has been recognised elsewhere, contributing causes of these inconsistencies in thoroughness and sophistication of the legal analysis likely include lack of sufficient resources as well as difficulties in training and recruiting experienced judges to preside over cases involving highly complex ICL concepts.[260]

Indeed, all the national jurisdictions have faced significant challenges in incorporating ICL concepts into their domestic legal frameworks. The pre-existing legal traditions and criminal provisions of a state might be more or less compatible with ICL doctrines on personal liability, as illustrated by the initial rejection and continuous critique of the adoption of the doctrine of indirect perpetration through organised power structures in several Latin American jurisdictions. In a similar vein, although the Latin American jurisdictions share a strong reliance on indirect perpetration through organised power structures, national legal peculiarities have prevented a fully coordinated and consistent development of this doctrine with respect to both the identification of its elements and their interpretation. Cross-jurisdictional inconsistencies are less pronounced among the former Yugoslavian countries, where their shared past and common legal framework have contributed, with certain noticeable exceptions, to a considerable overlap in how the modes of participation have been defined and interpreted. Considering the environment of political hostility in those countries towards many of the judgments rendered by the ICTY in similar cases, the quite unified legal approaches in the jurisprudence of the coun-

---

[260] See, for instance, Ambos, 2013, pp. 51–52, *supra* note 11.

tries, largely in compliance with the approaches of the ICTY, are quite striking.

Diversity in the application of ICL concepts and modes of criminal participation across national jurisdictions is not necessarily a major weakness in itself, as the discipline of international criminal law must be adapted to different national laws and customs. Furthermore, the general theory of criminal law liability allows for different models of implementation and modes of liability within operational criminal law subsystems, at both the international and national levels. Excessive diversity may nevertheless be a warning sign of some departures from the rule of law and the fundamental principles of criminal law liability, indicating that liability for punishable participation in universal crimes is not always fairly attributed.

10

Towards an Autonomous ICL
Matrix of Personal Liability

10.1. Purpose of the Final Chapter

In this concluding chapter we summarise the analysis and findings of the earlier chapters and then ask – and attempt to answer – the question of whether there is a theoretical as well as an empirical basis for identifying an autonomous ICL matrix of personal liability, in compliance with our proposed general theory of punishable participation in universal crimes.

The chapter starts with a summary of the empirical survey conducted in Chapters 5–9 (Section 10.2.), before briefly revisiting the general theory (10.3.). We then consider how the actual legal developments fit with the theory, taking into account the sociological context (10.4.). A substantial part of the chapter is devoted to the findings on derivative liability and modes of participation in operational ICL (10.5.), including an assessment of the range of lawful and desirable forms of attribution (10.6.). A smaller part concerns some other issues touched upon more lightly in this book, relating to concurrent participation, assimilation, and sentencing (10.7.). The chapter concludes with some final comments and broader reflections on general international law and the possible further development of an autonomous and preferably still differentiated, yet flexible, matrix of ICL personal liability (10.8.).

10.2. Summary of the Empirical Survey

Chapters 5–9 examined the concepts of forms of participation in universal crimes from a number of empirical angles. From a historical overview of these precepts as contained in international treaties having a bearing on ICL, the book went on to examine the work of the International Law Commission, the views of academic scholars in this area of law, the jurisprudence of international tribunals including the ICC, and finally the jurisprudence of national courts in a range of countries.

In providing an overview of the conclusions reached earlier in the book, we make the assumption that the present state of international criminal law in relation to forms of liability is to a large degree reflected in the case law of the international institutions. Accordingly, those findings, which were discussed in Chapter 7, will be summarised first.

Over the past quarter century, since 1993, six international judicial institutions – the ICTY, ICTR, SCSL, ECCC, EAC, and ICC – have developed what might be seen as the contours of a common jurisprudence of ICL as an autonomous legal field. Examining the jurisprudence of these six institutions, one can detect certain trends. In general, one trend has been to use all three liability classes (inchoate liability only to a limited degree, accomplice liability, and commission liability), most of the liability categories we have identified, and several derivative categories and operational modes of participation in order to capture a large number of perpetrators and accomplices. Through these legal formations, participants in different parts of large criminal enterprises closely connected to power structures in society have been held responsible for universal crimes. The participants may be linked to each other horizontally (participants positioned at the same level of a hierarchy, though in a wide variety of functions) or vertically (participants occupying lower or higher positions within the same hierarchy).

While the general trend has been towards establishing criminal responsibility for persons involved in the relevant crimes in ever-evolving and expanding circles of forms of participation, and while it appears that a number of legal concepts have now been largely settled with respect to their legal components or parameters, this does not mean that there have not been disagreements or controversies between judges or even between the different institutions since 1995, when the first modern and principled ICL judgment, a ruling by the ICTY Appeals Chamber, was issued in the famous Tadić case.

The most profound difference of opinion has emerged between the ICC on the one hand and the five tribunals on the other. This is because the tribunals, when charging persons in leadership positions, almost exclusively utilised the concept of JCE. The ICC, by contrast, has found the three (or four) forms of perpetration set out in Rome Statute Article 25(3)(a) to be more appropriate in the vast majority of cases, including a further derivative form, namely indirect co-perpetration.

However, even within the ICC there have been differences of opinion regarding almost all forms of perpetration in Article 25(3)(a). There was, at one stage, disagreement with respect to the precise nature of the meeting of the minds required for joint perpetration, that is, whether agreement or a common plan; for a time this was replaced by the requirement of a shared intent. There was also the question of whether the contribution should be at the level of an essential or direct contribution. These points have been resolved at the appeal level by requiring a common plan and an essential contribution. Consequently, the very high threshold that was about to be set for proving joint perpetration has been lowered, and the legal parameters as well do not now seem that different from those for the main forms of (derivative) JCE liability (JCE I and JCE II).

The other point of contention has been related to perpetration through another person. Here the discussion pertains to the questions of (1) whether this is possible within an organisational structure, and (2) whether the notion of indirect co-perpetration is a fourth heading of liability in Article 25(3)(a). Most judges so far have opted for the broader interpretation, which allows for perpetration via an organisation (as a derivative form of perpetration through another) as well as indirect co-perpetration as a derivative form of liability that might be applied in situations where there is a combination of horizontal co-operation between leaders of different power structures and vertical connections to the perpetrators on the ground within each structure – in effect creating a 'diagonal line' of responsibility on the part of leader A for the crimes committed under the leadership of leader B and vice versa.

In presenting a historical overview of international and transnational treaties, Chapter 5 examined the development of concepts of participation in international criminal law and transnational criminal law, along with the cross-fertilisation between these two disciplines. The IMT Charter had a number of unique features that went beyond what had been discussed with respect to participation before WWII: specifically, the preparatory acts of planning, preparation, initiation, instigation, and accomplice liability *sui generis* in the form of membership in criminal organisations. Nonetheless, the notions of conspiracy and participation in the forms of inchoate and accomplice liability had already featured in four of the pre-WWII transnational law treaties, establishing a connection between pre-WWII transnational and post-WWII ICL treaties. This connection becomes obvious when one compares the last treaty before the war with the first treaty after it. Not only the concepts but also the language regarding certain forms of participation in the pre-war Terrorism Convention and the post-war Genocide Convention are strikingly similar. Both treaties, for example, refer to attempt, conspiracy, and incitement as distinct inchoate crimes.

The ICTY Statute, which became the template for all subsequent international and internationalised tribunals, has a direct link in terms of language with the Genocide Convention regarding the definition of genocide. The wording with respect to command/superior responsibility meanwhile bears a more than passing similarity to Additional Protocol I to the Geneva Conventions. Of the other forms of participation in the ICTY Statute, namely planning, instigating, ordering, committing, and aiding and abetting, the first two duplicate forms in the IMT Charter, while aiding and abetting is a more contemporary version of the core form of accomplice liability. Ordering can also be seen as a more legally accurate, albeit likely more limited, term than the IMT references to (principal) leaders and organisers. There is no literal reference to the practically important derivative form of commission liability, JCE, in either the IMT Charter or the ICTY Statute. However, the ICTY jurisprudence used the term "committed" to derive and develop this form of participation; in other words, it gave the notion of commission a broader meaning than direct perpetration of crimes and underlying offences. In doing so, the ICTY relied to some extent on the judgment of the IMT in its (only) case concerned with the top level of the Nazi regime – the major war criminals who had been part of the most important conspiracy or had otherwise ordered, directed, or participated in large-scale crimes from within the principal leadership. But the tribunal relied even more on the case law concerning various other actors within the relevant power structures, which was developed subsequently by the military tribunals operating in occupied Germany through the military trials based on Control Council Law No. 10.

While the IMT Charter, the Genocide Convention, and the ICTY Statute show connections to earlier international law (in the case of the IMT Charter) and to each other, and thus represent incremental development in the area of ICL, the Rome Statute might at first appear to have introduced a number of new liability concepts not previously known or mentioned. But this superficial picture would be inaccurate. Some concepts, especially in Article 25(3), are new expressions of existing notions: for example, soliciting is similar to instigation, which was used in the IMT Charter and the ICTY Statute. The parameters of other concepts, such as co-perpetration and common purpose, were already discussed in the ICTY jurisprudence. In addition, some of the concepts, such as common purpose, inducing, incitement, and attempt, can also be found in TCL treaties. Even a particular form of participation not mentioned in the Rome Statute, conspiracy, which was included in the ICTY Statute and in a number of other ICL statutes, is in substance inherent in the concept of co-perpetration at the leadership level based on a common plan – and thus at least punishable when the relevant crime is completed by means of the organisation.

With respect to the work of the ILC, also discussed in Chapter 5, we found that the commission's aspiration to have its work reflect both codification and progressive development of international law has not been accomplished in the area of punishable participation in universal crimes – not in the codification aspect, and even less so in the progressive development of international law. The most egregious example of this can be seen in the ILC's efforts thus far to develop a treaty dealing with crimes against humanity. Most forms of participation in the current draft provisions are inspired by the Rome Statute, but, inexplicably, the draft includes neither joint perpetration, nor perpetration through another person, nor incitement. While the omission of the first two represents a step backwards in the evolution of ICL and thus goes contrary to the aim of codification of international law, the omission of incitement misses a golden opportunity for the progressive development of international law. This is disappointing, given the historical as well as more recent cases of socially dangerous incitement to the commission of systematic or large-scale persecution of vulnerable groups in society. As a result, the ILC's work in this area of law has been, and may continue to be, the least useful source for developing the law relating to personal criminal liability within ICL.

Chapter 6, on the work of academic commentators, found that attribution of personal criminal liability for participation in universal crimes has been a highly controversial topic. This was illustrated in the different positions of various authors with respect to several fundamental questions at both the macro and micro levels. At the macro level, there were different approaches with respect to (1) whether the question of attribution is best approached from a comparative law perspective or from an autonomous, *sui generis* understanding of ICL concepts; (2) the relative merits and suitability of a unitary versus a differentiated system of attribution in ICL; (3) the scope of discretion and boundaries of legitimacy when one combines modes of liability in order to cast a wider net of criminal liability; and (4) the uncertain applicability of the legality principle to new operational modes of liability for completed crimes, as compared to distinct inchoate crimes, where the legality principle applies with certainty. At the micro level, specific concepts of participation were examined. This included the question of whether to take a subjective or an objective approach to attribution of commission liability, as well as questions relating to different kinds of omission liability, ordering, and complicity. Chapter 6 also addressed liability for atrocity speech. It briefly discussed the recent calls for a unified liability theory of speech crimes, and what may be seen as a better approach to the complex issue of speech causation that would abandon differently formulated standards for contributing a causal factor to completed universal crimes.

Chapters 8 and 9 examined national jurisprudence, both in countries utilising territorial jurisdiction and in those using extra-territorial jurisdiction. One of the most important observations was that the notion of indirect perpetration through an organised power structure, which has been used fairly regularly by the ICC, has also been favoured in a number of countries in Latin America and in Europe as a means to attribute liability to the most high-ranking officials, who typically operate at a remove from the actual crime scenes. The same can be said for the use of co-perpetration for persons operating at a lower level of an organised structure. On the other hand, while these two forms of liability are prevalent in civil law countries, the notion of JCE, as inspired by the ICTY, has found more currency in common law countries in North America, Europe, and Asia. It was noted as well that the parameters of concepts often used at the international courts, such as co-perpetration and aiding and abetting, were remarkably consistent among jurisdictions in Latin America, Europe, and Africa, and also consistent with the general trends of application at the international courts, even when no reliance was placed on international precedents or jurisprudence.

These findings are interesting for several reasons. First, they show that reasonably consistent application of key liability concepts within all levels and subsystems of ICL is possible and within practical reach. Second, the findings as a whole show that several issues are still contested – although more so in ICL theory, it seems, probably because of different theoretical points of departures and perspectives, while in actual case law the application of similar concepts seems to be moving towards the same parameters and more consistent application. Third, these overarching findings based on empirical studies provide an interesting ground for the testing of our general theory of personal criminal liability.

10.3. Revisiting the General Theory of Personal Liability

Before drawing conclusions on the testing of the general theory against the empirical legal and sociological findings in this book, it might be useful to recall some proposed key elements of the theory set forth in Chapter 2. That chapter offered broad theoretical and analytical perspectives on universal crimes participation. In particular, it attempted to develop a comprehensive theory of personal criminal law liability. The theory may provide an overarching scientific model for assessing various issues of punishable participation, notably with a view to ICL.[1]

The general theory consists of a four-level theoretical, analytical, and normative structure, where each level forms a necessary but not in itself sufficient part. The first level of the theory consists of the *supra-principle of free choice*.[2] The second level encompasses the *fundamental principles of personal criminal law liability*. These fundamental principles include (1) the principle of legality, (2) the principle of conduct, (3) the principle of culpability, and (4) the principle of fair attribution of personal liability. All four principles are interlinked and must be applicable before acts of participation or contributions to a criminal enterprise can be considered punishable.[3]

The general theory on fair attribution of personal liability is further specified and developed through the third level of the theory, the *secondary principles of fair attribution of personal liability*.[4] There are four main secondary principles: (1) the principle of partial participation, which is especially relevant to the class of inchoate liability; (2) the principle of direct participation, relevant to the class of commission liability; (3) the principle of indirect participation, relevant to the class of accomplice liability; and (4) the cross-cutting principle of juridical entity participation,

---

[1] See Chapter 2, Section 2.1. The key components of what we have referred to as the general theory of personal criminal law liability – the proposed scientific model – were set out in Section 2.2.

[2] Chapter 2, Section 2.2.1.

[3] Chapter 2, Section 2.2.2.

[4] Chapter 2, Section 2.2.3.

relevant to liability of non-natural persons. While the three first principles have been employed throughout this book, the fourth principle makes it possible to apply criminal law liability to, for instance, corporations. Further secondary principles might also be identified, which are partly cross-cutting. The most important of them are presumably related to causation, that is, to crimes requiring a consequence (harm or the creation of danger, or a substantially increased risk of harm) and to contribution assessment for completed or attempted crimes. However, causation is not constituted as one general liability norm and must be approached with some care, as touched upon several places in this book.[5]

In Chapter 4, when discussing the international legality principle, it was held that juridical entity liability is a lawful option and thus a policy choice at the operational level of ICL.[6] This issue may serve as just one example of the claimed usefulness of a comprehensive general theory of criminal liability, because the theory may help in asking and answering important questions more clearly. In accordance with the general theory, such liability is possible both theoretically and practically. Hence the first point in the analysis under international law is that potential operational liability for non-natural persons is not generally *prohibited* by CIL or under other relevant parts of binding international law.[7] In our opinion, the burden of proof thus rests on the party who claims that juridical entity participation under specific parts of ICL would be unlawful. This does not mean that liability for non-natural persons applies *lex lata* within any particular subsystem of ICL or domestic criminal law system. To the contrary, it applies only if a specific legal basis for it has been created by means of a provision to that effect in an international court statute or domestically

---

[5] See, for example, Chapter 6, Section 6.3.2., on the discussion among authors on omission liability and causation, especially with respect to command and superior responsibility, and Section 6.3.4., on speech crimes and causation.

[6] See Chapter 4, Section 4.3.7.

[7] By 2011, more than 20 states in the Americas, Europe, Asia, and Australasia had already promulgated laws permitting corporate criminal liability, presumably applicable also to universal crimes. This militates against a CIL prohibition of such liability; see Chapter 2, Section 2.2.3.4. See also Special Tribunal for Lebanon, Appeals Chamber, *Case against New TV S.A.L. and Karma Mohamed Tahsin al Khayat*, Decision on Interlocutory Appeal concerning Personal Jurisdiction in Contempt Proceedings, 2 October 2014, paras. 33–74 (www.legal-tools.org/doc/e8fbb1/) (with a comparative analysis of 40 domestic jurisdictions in paras. 52–57).

through legislation or jurisprudence. Notably, the Rome Statute provides in Article 25(1) that the court shall have jurisdiction over "natural persons" (individuals). However, this clarification *lex lata* and confinement of competence of the ICC does not legally imply that the Rome Statute in the future could not – if considered legally desirable – be amended in order to extend the ICC's jurisdiction to allow it to prosecute corporations directly for participation in core universal crimes. Such a step would only be unlawful *per se* if corporate liability had been prohibited under international law or if such liability could not be considered in compliance with the general principles of criminal law liability in international law, which we believe is not the case. Corporate liability,[8] however, must also meet the other requirements of the general theory in order to be lawfully implemented, something that may require in particular a clarification of the principles of free choice and culpability in regard to non-natural persons.[9]

In the same section of Chapter 4 we advanced the concept of accessorial crimes to the universal crimes,[10] briefly introduced in Chapter 2.[11] Unlike the attribution of liability for punishable participation in completed main universal crimes such as genocide, crimes against humanity, war crimes, and aggression, the accessorial criminalisation of certain forms of participatory conduct relating to these main crimes is meant to apply regardless of whether or not a main crime is completed. Such criminalisation typically concerns liability for inchoate offences, but it could in principle also encompass specific forms of accomplice liability. Typical examples are conspiracy, incitement, or attempt to commit genocide, and the concept might be extended to include, for example, participation in a criminal organisation used to commit the main crime.[12] Such criminalisa-

---

[8] Corporate liability has been called "the next frontier of international criminal justice"; see Beth Van Schaack's review of *Historical Origins of International Criminal Law,* vols. 1–5, in *American Journal of International Law*, 2018, vol. 112, no. 1, p. 147.

[9] See the preliminary discussion in Chapter 2, Section 2.2.3.4. For an interesting general account of challenges relating to corporate criminal liability, see Carsten Stahn, *Liberals vs. Romantics: Challenges of an Emerging Corporate International Criminal Law* (February 21, 2018) (www.legal-tools.org/doc/230dfc/).

[10] See Chapter 4, Section 4.3.7.

[11] See Chapter 2, Section 2.1.2.

[12] The three inchoate crimes in this example are listed as distinct crime types, numbers 16–18, in the consolidated list of universal crimes in Terje Einarsen, *The Concept of Universal*

tion would be fully compatible with the general theory of criminal law liability and is thus left for policy decisions within each criminal law subsystem that respects the rule of law, fundamental principles of human rights, and the fundamental principles of criminal law liability.

Furthermore, the secondary principles at the third level of the theory also include further *derivative principles* relevant for derivative criminal law liability. These derivative principles are key to understanding how the general theory provides for establishing criminal liability not only theoretically but also practically, and in particular for understanding the source of derivative liability in the first place. The derivative principles make it possible to organise criminal law liability into classes, categories, and subcategories of liability, thus setting the scene for operational modes of liability. The third level of theory, moreover, concerns theoretical formation, combination, and assimilation of derivative liability in compliance with the general theory as such, which again may provide guidance on policy decisions and judgments at the next level.

Finally, the fourth level of theory concerns *specific provisions of the operational criminal law subsystems*. This is where the applicable modes of liability (or modes of participation) *lex lata* come into the picture; and as we know, they play a crucial role within current ICL.

It is worth recalling once more at this stage that in our conception of the general theory, accurate theoretical imposition of derivative criminal liability for participants in a criminal enterprise is dependent on the existence of *a basic type of criminal liability*. It is only from the basic type that liability logically can be further derived.[13] Furthermore, this basic type of liability, we have argued, is constituted in conjunction with a relevant crime description (the abstract crime), but the basic type of liability is not identical to either the abstract crime or the concrete crime. Thus, for reasons of plain logic, we disagree with other authors who seek to derive liability from the acts of another participant – typically a so-called principal offender, such as the physical perpetrator who completes the (underlying) crime – or from the criminal offence as such. For example, in the case of criminalised 'murder', the basic form of liability, we have argued, is

---

Crimes in International Law, Torkel Opsahl Academic EPublisher, Oslo, 2012, p. 321 (www.legal-tools.org/doc/bfda36/).

[13] See Chapter 2, Section 2.2.3.5.

'criminal law liability for murder'. This is the case whether the relevant kind of derivative criminal law liability for a particular person is some form of commission liability, accomplice liability, or inchoate liability.

One implication of this part of the general theory is that the notion of the 'principal' offender becomes superfluous for legal analysis. Consequently, there is a kind of unitary component of our liability theory,[14] in the sense of a basic type of criminal liability and a general formation of derivative personal criminal liability, *Y liability of person A for the crime of X*, where person A is not necessarily the physical perpetrator but could be any person who has actually contributed to the crime or the relevant criminal enterprise.[15] This leads to a more straightforward theory of liability attribution that is easier to understand, and probably also easier to implement fairly. As noted in Chapter 2 and implied at several other points in this book, the liability scheme of the Rome Statute is also, in our view, consistent with this conception of the general theory.

The general theory as explained may indeed justify and support the development of a strong differentiated model in current ICL.[16] In our opinion, this model is recommendable, especially within ICL, because it seems better able to capture the complex nature of universal crimes participation committed through power structures – crimes involving a number of participants in different roles with different shares of responsibility. This feature has been illuminated throughout the book, we believe. At the same time, we would like to underline that the lawful possibilities at the theoretical third level, which is concerned with derivative liability within the conception employed in this book, do not close down other options, for instance, a softer differentiated model or even a unitary model. Our general theory of criminal law liability is not conclusive with respect to how the forms of liability in practice should be legally constructed at the fourth operational level within a particular criminal law subsystem.[17] Still, it is potentially an important discovery that the general theory is at least fully compatible with a strong differentiated model, even with the possi-

---

[14] See Chapter 1, Section 1.2.5, and Chapter 6, Section 6.2.2.2, on the concept of a unitary model of liability attribution.

[15] See Chapter 2, Section 2.2.3.6.

[16] On the differentiated model or models of criminal law liability, see Chapter 1, Section 1.2.5, and Chapter 6, Section 6.2.2.2.

[17] See also the concluding remarks of this chapter, Section 10.7.

ble addition of lawful forms of liability that go beyond the current provisions and jurisprudence under the Rome Statute. The empirical data featured in Chapters 5–9 of this book furthermore seem to underpin the viability of differentiated yet fairly consistent application of various distinct forms of liability at the international and domestic levels of universal crimes prosecution and jurisprudence.

10.4. How Do Actual Legal Developments Fit with the General Theory?

10.4.1. Clarifying the Question

The general theory of personal liability as a scientific model, with a particular view to ICL, is supposed to be able to predict future observations of legal developments in statutes and judicial decisions concerned with possible criminal liability for alleged punishable participation in universal crimes.[18] The expectation is that the empirical findings today – 25 years into the most vibrant era of ICL, kick-started with the establishment of the ICTY in 1993 – would paint a picture that to a large extent should be reconcilable and in compliance with the predictions of the general theory. Otherwise the theory would not usefully help explain the developments or assist our understanding of the subject matter of criminal law liability and thus potentially aid rational and well-founded further development of the law.

The purpose of this section (10.4.) is to clarify the structure when answering the question and the more basic or overarching issues, while the next section (10.5.) deals with some other issues in more detail. The starting point is the general theory itself, as detailed in Chapter 2 and revisited in Section 10.3. above.

10.4.2. Are the Main Principles of the General Theory Reflected in Operational ICL?

With respect to the first level of the general theory, the *supra*-principle of free choice, there is no doubt that ICL is clearly premised on the notion that punishable participants in universal crimes are responsible for their acts in circumstances where they had the possibility of choosing a differ-

---

[18] On limitations of even a good legal theory for predicting judgments, see Chapter 2, Section 2.1.3.

ent way of acting, rather than committing or contributing to the crime. Conversely, a person is not considered responsible if a different choice was not in fact available to him for some specific reason, or could not be expected to be available. This principle is clearly embodied in requirements of culpability and in the possibility of concretely assessed excuses and justifications for an act that would otherwise be criminal. Hence this point need not be elaborated further below.

With respect to the second level of the general theory, the fundamental principles of personal criminal law liability, a few comments are warranted. There is no doubt that ICL has been premised on the existence of all four principles – the principles of legality, of conduct, of culpability, and of fair attribution of personal liability – generally in the law, and also assumes their applicability in concrete criminal cases. This has been demonstrated, at least implicitly, throughout this book. The question is, rather, how these principles as further specified and developed at the third level of the theory have been reflected and implemented at the operational level of ICL.

To recall once more, the four main secondary principles at the third level are (1) the principle of partial participation, which is especially relevant to the class of inchoate liability; (2) the principle of direct participation, relevant to the class of commission liability; (3) the principle of indirect participation, relevant to the class of accomplice liability; and (4) the cross-cutting principle of juridical entity participation, relevant to liability of non-natural persons. Again, there is no doubt that the first three principles and thus the *three classes of criminal law liability* have been reflected and implemented at the operational level of ICL, both internationally and domestically, in universal crimes cases, as would be expected by the prediction that all three classes are possible to implement. The picture is more complex and nuanced with respect to their further derivative forms; see Sections 10.4.4. and 10.5. below.

10.4.3. The General Theory in Sociological Context

Before we go into more detail on the derivative forms of liability, we will comment briefly on another dimension of the general theory as applied to the particular features of universal crimes. This dimension flows from the intersection of the general theory and the historical and sociological context of universal crimes committed in the real world as empirical facts. We are aware that a plain legal analysis may miss some other important aspects of universal crimes participation. For example, it could be that the general theory when applied to sociological facts might be further developed to predict liability for participants within large criminal enterprises and for actors with different roles in the power structures that are often used to commit universal crimes on a large scale. Hence, a comprehensive sociological model could be envisaged as complementary to the general theory of criminal liability. Such a model would predict in sociological terms the most relevant categories of participants in universal crimes, taking account of their different roles and professional backgrounds and their authority at different levels of the relevant power structures or power support structures typically involved in the crimes. An attempt to lay the foundation for such a model was made in Chapter 3, although mainly for the purpose of providing sociological and historical context for the legal liability analysis undertaken elsewhere in this book.

Thus, in Chapter 3 we identified 20 sociological categories of participants and grouped them into four overarching classes: (1) *high-level participants*, that is, individuals in the upper ranks of main power structures; (2) *mid-level participants*, those in the intermediate ranks of main power structures; (3) *low-level participants*, those at the lower ranks of main power structures or, in some cases, within lesser power structures; and (4) *participants in power support structures*. We also attempted to couple the sociological analysis with a survey of the different modes of liability employed in concrete cases at the international tribunals. This research provides a narrative that complements the discussion of theoretical issues. More empirical information on normative liability concepts within ICL at the international and national levels was provided in Chapters 5–9.

However, Chapter 3 already yields interesting findings, of which we shall now highlight only a few. For example, the study counted 385 persons charged in trials[19] at various international tribunals (or hybrid international/national tribunals) in the period from 1945 to 2018. Of these, 34 per cent (130 persons) were identified as high-level participants and grouped into seven sociological categories: heads of state, ministers, mili-

---

[19] The court trials may have concluded with either a conviction or an acquittal, or may have been halted for some reason; a few trials have not yet begun (this applies only to ongoing proceedings at the pre-trial stage before the ICC); see Chapter 2, Section 2.3.7.

tary leadership, leaders of other governmental power structures, leaders of political parties, leaders of financial and economic power structures, and leaders of non-state power structures. Of the same 385 persons, 30 per cent (117 persons) were mid-level participants, while 20 per cent (76 persons) were low-level participants. Perhaps surprisingly, another 16 per cent (62 persons) were participants in power support structures.

A total of 715 charges were filed in the indictments against the 385 persons, with the largest number of charges filed against participants in support structures (3.1 per person, on average). Some of the charges included multiple charges for the same crime, or multiple charges relating to different forms of personal criminal liability (that is, charges invoking several modes of liability), while others concerned different crimes committed through different acts ('real concurrence') or different crimes committed through the same act ('ideal concurrence').

It is interesting to recall from Chapter 3 that many liability concepts were counted as employed in the charges, including 14 different modes of liability with respect to high-level participants (see Table 4). Some of the concepts are overlapping in content. They cover all three liability classes identified at the third level of the general theory of criminal law liability, as well as the 12 different categories likewise identified in Chapter 2 and elaborated in parts of Chapters 5–9. Some of the modes, however, are further derivative forms of one or more (in combination) of the 12 categories, for instance joint criminal enterprise, while others are variations tied to particular crimes, such as incitement to genocide and conspiracy in war crimes. This feature explains why the number of operational modes was higher than the number of theoretical categories, but this result was also highly expected for ICL trials and fully in line with the general theory of criminal law liability.

In Chapter 2 we pointed out that the derivative principles of the general theory allow for further subcategories, in fact similar to the modes actually used at the international level since 1945 – although the popularity of certain modes may have decreased or increased over time and varied across the different international tribunals. For example, membership in a criminal organisation has not been used at the international level during the last 25 years, but it may again come into use, as evidenced by the emerging similar category of participation in a terrorist organisation: this might be viewed as a *sui generis* category employed so far only domestically and in transnational criminal law, or more plainly as a derivative form of membership in a criminal organisation. In either form, membership or participation in power structures may again emerge at the international level with respect to terrorist crimes or with respect to other universal crimes as well.

All in all, it seems safe to conclude that the sociological study does not pose any particular challenges to our liability theory, but indeed supports it. On the other hand, the theory does not, on its face, raise serious concern about the overall approach to attribution of liability at the international trials based on the empirical findings of this book. However, we need to probe a bit deeper into how the derivative principles at the third level of the general theory are reflected in more detail at the operational level of ICL.

10.4.4. Derivative Principles in Operational ICL: Points of Departure

Arguably, the most important feature of the general theory as identified and discussed in Chapter 2 remains the derivative principles of personal criminal liability. It is these principles that to a large extent link the various operational modes of liability with a comprehensive, general theory of criminal law liability.

Through the derivative principles explained in Chapter 2, three classes of liability and 12 categories of liability were identified and labelled. The first class consists of inchoate liability, divided in turn into four categories relevant to instances where the substantive crime is not completed: incitement, conspiracy, preparatory acts, and attempt. The second class is commission liability, again divided into four different forms or categories: (physical) perpetration (direct and singular); joint perpetration (direct and multiple); perpetration through another (indirect perpetration); and omission, that is, liability for a failure to act against the commission of crimes by others, with command/superior responsibility as the most prominent subcategory. The third class corresponds to accomplice liability in different forms, with four categories of ordering, instigation, complicity (including but not necessarily limited to aiding and abetting), and membership in a criminal organisation (which may include participation in a terrorist organisation). Derivative principles make it possible to derive and develop even more specific forms, such as, for example, joint criminal enterprise and further possible subcategories (for example, JCE I, II, and III).

The next section (10.5.) summarises our findings with respect to the derivative forms of liability in ICL in order to review the categories and subcategories as implemented through actual modes of participation/ liability. Before beginning that discussion, we will first explain and recall the background and limitations of our empirical findings on this topic.

In order to clarify the material and mental elements of the core operational modes, the next section considers the jurisprudence of six international criminal institutions (the ICTY, ICTR, SCSL, ECCC, EAC, and ICC) since 1993. While Chapter 3 examined their jurisprudence since World War II, the findings presented below in Section 10.5. do not consider decisions prior to 1993, for two reasons: (1) the forms of participation addressed in the post-WWII cases are with a few exceptions very similar to the ones used (albeit at times with different names) after 1993, and (2) the post-1993 jurisprudence, while it did take into account the post-WWII case law, especially near the beginning of the period in question, provides much more conceptual depth and detail. Examining the jurisprudence of the six international institutions that have developed the jurisprudence of ICL,[20] one can detect a general trend to use several derivative categories and operational modes of participation to capture a large number of perpetrators linked either horizontally or vertically. Those findings are summarised below, focusing also on the content and formulations of *actus reus* (material element) and *mens rea* (mental element) of the modes that have prevailed and have typically been applied consistently. This provides us with yet another possibility to consider whether the actual development of ICL is compatible with the fundamental principles as well as the secondary principles of the general theory.

---

[20] The national courts, while primarily relying on their countries' own criminal statutes, have generally been consistent with their international counterparts even though they have not always referred explicitly to this international jurisprudence. There has been one instance in which the national courts have deviated from the international model by taking a narrower approach; this will be mentioned in note 28 below on indirect perpetration. Deviations resulting in broader approaches will be discussed in the next subchapter.

10.5. Derivative Liability and Modes of Participation in Operational ICL

10.5.1. Forms of Inchoate Liability

10.5.1.1. Incitement

The *actus reus* of incitement is the act of directly and publicly having incited the commission of the relevant crime – that is, genocide[21] – while the *mens rea* is the intent to directly and publicly incite others to commit the crime of genocide (which presupposes specific genocidal intent).

These material and mental elements are compatible with the fundamental principles of conduct and culpability. The legality principle has been satisfied, since genocide is a crime under international law and is included in the statutes of the international institutions that have prosecuted and convicted persons for genocide, as well as in the legislation of all domestic jurisdictions that have ratified the Genocide Convention. Under the general theory, incitement as a mode of participation is not prohibited under CIL. Thus it could lawfully be extended to all universal crimes at the international level, if considered desirable by lawmakers, by means of a clear provision in the relevant court statute, such as the one on incitement to commit genocide in the Rome Statute, Article 25(3)(e). Incitement, as a distinct inchoate crime (unlike instigation), can only be criminalised in operational ICL by means of a written provision, thus complying with the legality principle and the general theory.

With respect to *lex ferenda*, in this book we have criticised the ILC's draft convention on CAH for not taking the opportunity to extend the scope of incitement to crimes against humanity; one might also ask why this type of involvement could not be extended to war crimes, and even to the crime of aggression.

10.5.1.2. Conspiracy

This form of participation can only be found in the statutes of the ICTY, ICTR, and ECCC, and then only for genocide. The *actus reus* for conspiracy to genocide is the fact of entering into an agreement to commit geno-

---

[21] This form of participation is only possible for genocide in current operational ICL.

cide, while the *mens rea* is a specific intent to destroy, in whole or in part, a national, ethnical, racial, or religious group as such.[22]

As conspiracy is a common form of inchoate crime in domestic common law jurisdictions, there should be no issue with respect to the legality of this crime, nor is there any prohibition in the general theory of criminal participation. With respect to *lex ferenda*, what was noted above with regard to incitement also applies to conspiracy insofar as there is no logical reason, under an overarching theory of personal responsibility, why this form of liability could not be extended to other universal crimes.

10.5.1.3. Preparatory Acts

This is understood as a collective category comprising different preliminary acts, such as initiation, planning, preparation, and possibly ordering, that occur at the early stages of a criminal enterprise, prior to the execution stage when the crime is completed. Planning is the only form that has been operational within some parts of ICL since 1993, but it has not been treated as a distinct inchoate crime. The *actus reus* of planning is fulfilled when one or more persons plan or design conduct constituting one or more crimes, which later are actually perpetrated (completed). To be held responsible, persons must have made a substantial contribution to the criminal enterprise, such as by actually formulating the criminal plan or endorsing a plan proposed by others. The *mens rea* of this form of participation is awareness on the part of the persons designing the plan of the substantial likelihood that a crime will be committed in the execution of the plan. Again, these material and mental elements are compatible with the fundamental principles of conduct and culpability.

However, with respect to the crime of aggression that is made operational under the Rome Statute from 17 July 2018, Article 8*bis* (1) makes punishable not only the planning of aggression, but also the preparatory acts of initiation and preparation. None of these forms is criminalised as a distinct inchoate crime. The circle of persons who might incur liability in this regard when the crime is completed or at least attempted[23] is confined to the specific leaders of a state who are in control of the political or mili-

---

[22] Genocide is a continuous crime in that the *actus reus* is also fulfilled for individuals joining the conspiracy after the original agreement, as a result of which they incur liability alongside the original conspirators.

[23] See Rome Statute, Article 25(3)*bis*, read in conjunction with Article 25(3)(f).

tary actions of the state. This new development is clearly within the boundaries of the general theory.

10.5.1.4. Attempt

There is no international jurisprudence on attempt, but a rather concise provision is contained in Article 25(3)(f) of the Rome Statute. Attempt was criminalised in the ICTY, ICTR, and ECCC Statutes, but only with respect to the crime of genocide, and no such case was prosecuted. On the other hand, provisions on attempt are one of the most common liability provisions, both in domestic legislation and in transnational criminal law treaties.

The *actus reus* is generally fulfilled when a person attempts to commit a crime by taking action that commences its execution by means of a substantial step, but the crime does not occur because of circumstances independent of the person's intentions.[24] The *mens rea* of attempt is the intent (purpose) to commit the crime or to facilitate the completion of the crime, with awareness that the conduct is unlawful or that the unlawful consequence will occur in the ordinary course of events.

Attempt, as a distinct inchoate crime, can only be criminalised in operational ICL by means of a written provision, thus complying with the legality principle and the general theory. Under the general theory, attempt is not prohibited under CIL and could lawfully be extended to all universal crimes within any subsystem of ICL or domestic law. The development that took place with the Rome Statute was thus in full compliance with the general theory.

10.5.2. Forms of Commission Liability

10.5.2.1. Singular Perpetration

Singular perpetration of universal crimes may have two different meanings: (1) a person commits the full crime and fulfils all the material and mental requirements singularly, or (2) a person commits only a relevant underlying offence singularly while being aware of the social context and gravity surrounding the offence. The latter type is the most common in ICL at the operational level, as for example when a soldier or commander

---

[24] For the exception relating to a person who completely and voluntarily gave up the criminal purpose, see Rome Statute 25(3)(f), second sentence.

chooses to kill one or more defenceless civilians by himself on his own initiative within a context of war (constituting the act as a war crime) or of a large-scale or systematic attack against a civilian population (constituting the act as a crime against humanity).

The *actus reus* of this form of participation is the physical perpetration of a criminal act or the culpable omission of an act that was mandated by a rule of criminal law, while the *mens rea* is the intent to commit the crime or the awareness of the substantial likelihood that the crime would occur as a consequence of the person's conduct.[25] These material and mental elements are fully compatible with the fundamental principles of conduct and culpability.

The legality principle as another fundamental is, furthermore, satisfied if the crime type is a crime under international law, the crime is described in the statute of an international court or in domestic law, and the accused has committed the crime.

The liability form of singular perpetration as such, however, is inherent in commission liability and does not raise any separate issue of a possible unlawful attribution of liability under the legality principle within the meaning of the general theory.[26]

10.5.2.2. Joint Perpetration

The *actus reus* for joint perpetration is twofold:

---

[25] The ICTR has also indicated that direct participation can pertain to a situation where the conduct of the accused was as much an integral part of the crimes as the crimes it enabled, in the sense that the accused approved and embraced as his own the decision to commit the crime. Examples of this approach have involved acts such as leading, supervising, or directing an attack, or directing the separation and segregation of victims before a massacre.

[26] The question may arise, however, of whether the act was sufficiently linked to a relevant universal crimes context – for example, whether the killing with genocidal intent on the part of the accused was actually capable of destroying a protected group in whole or in part and was part of a broader genocidal context in society. A more principled issue is whether the crime description of, for example, genocide can be met if a person plans and attacks a protected group with the specific intent but acts entirely on his own, an issue with similarities to the problem of 'lone wolf' terrorist attacks (consider the first and most extensive meaning of singular perpetration above). These issues may thus concern both principled interpretation and concrete application of universal crimes norms, and they must be solved within the parameters of the respective criminal law subsystem at the operational level. The concrete legal solution is this respect thus depends on the relevant legal sources, and it cannot be predicted by the general theory of personal liability.

- the existence of an agreement or common plan; this plan does not need to be explicit, nor does it need to be specifically directed at the commission of a crime, and it may include non-criminal goals, but its implementation must embody a sufficient risk that a crime will result in the ordinary course of events;

- a coordinated, essential contribution by each co-perpetrator, resulting in the commission of a crime; this requires co-perpetrators to have the ability to frustrate the commission of the crime.

The *mens rea* includes three requirements:

- the subjective element of the joint perpetrators with respect to the underlying crime;

- mutual awareness and mutual acceptance that implementation of the common plan results in the occurrence of the crime;

- awareness of the factual circumstances enabling the co-perpetrators to jointly control the crime.

Joint perpetration can be exercised in two different forms. Both forms, as discussed in Chapter 2, are fully compliant with the general theory of personal criminal law liability. However, the first form of joint perpetration, joint multiple perpetration (with several persons performing the same criminal conduct according to a common plan), has been more prevalent in domestic common law jurisdictions, while the second form, joint functional perpetration (where several persons perform different acts or roles in the agreed criminal enterprise), is seen more in domestic civil law traditions and especially in the ICC jurisprudence.[27]

10.5.2.3. Perpetration through Another

The third category of perpetration mentioned in the Rome Statute, perpetration through another, also known as indirect perpetration, refers to cases in which a person uses another person or persons as a means to commit the crime. This third person might not be liable for reasons such as young age or other shortcomings (for instance, mental incapacity) that constrain his or her ability to exercise free choice. If the choice was free but the range of choices was severely limited because of external pressures, the third person again might not be liable (mental emergency, or duress). The

---

[27] See Chapter 2, Section 2.2.3.2.

question is whether criminal law liability for the direct perpetrator discharges the indirect perpetrator from criminal law liability or changes his position to that of an inciter or accomplice in the crime. However, under the general theory of personal criminal law liability, it should not matter whether the third person was liable or not for his own conduct, because in no case should a person be discharged from his responsibility merely because another person who participated in the crime cannot or should not be held liable.

Looking beyond commission of a crime through a physical person, the ICC jurisprudence has broadened this concept by also accepting indirect perpetration through an organisation. This in fact has become the primary means of utilising this concept. In this case the *actus reus* is threefold:

- the leader must have control over the organisation;

- the organisation must consist of an organised and hierarchical apparatus of power;

- the execution of crimes must be secured by an almost automatic compliance with the orders issued by the leader.[28]

The *mens rea* is the awareness of the position the leader held within the organisation and the essential features of the organisation securing the functional automatism.

The ICC jurisprudence has also developed a new form of perpetration, called indirect co-perpetration, which combines elements of both joint perpetration and perpetration through another.[29] The *actus reus* has five elements:

- the perpetrator must be part of a common plan or an agreement with one or more persons;

---

[28] The Latin American jurisprudence with respect to indirect perpetration through an organised power structure has mostly identified the same elements, but in some cases, most notably in the Peruvian Fujimori case, national courts have required one additional element as part of the *actus*, namely that the organisation is structured, operates, and remains outside of national and international legal systems.

[29] The difference between direct co-perpetration and indirect co-perpetration is that the *actus reus* of the latter is executed by persons who are utilised by the (other) co-perpetrators for the commission of the crime, constituting a diagonal rather than a vertical relationship.

- the perpetrator and the other co-perpetrator(s) must carry out essential contributions in a coordinated manner that results in the fulfilment of the material elements of the crime;

- the perpetrator must have control over the organisation;

- the organisation must consist of an organised and hierarchical apparatus of power;

- the execution of the crimes must be secured by almost automatic compliance with the orders issued by the perpetrator.

The *mens rea* is the same as for perpetration through another person.

There has been some doubt at the international level about the expansion of indirect co-perpetration, because some ICC trial judges questioned in earlier cases whether this type of participation is regulated in the Rome Statute and therefore would violate the principle of legality. However, the ICC Appeals Chamber and subsequent Trial Chamber decisions have accepted this approach. These minor expansions do not invalidate the general theory of personal criminal law liability. To the contrary, since the expansions adhere to the fundamental principles of conduct, culpability, and personal liability, and are only applied to crimes that are completed (or attempted, in compliance with Article 25(3)(f) and the legality principle), such expansions, if needed at the operational level, fall within the predictions of the general theory and thus confirm the viability of the theory.

10.5.2.4. Joint Criminal Enterprise

The prevailing common elements for this derivative type of participation in ICL are as follows:

- a plurality of persons, who do not need to be organised in a military, political, or administrative structure;

- the existence of a common plan, design, or purpose that amounts to or involves the commission of a relevant crime; there is no necessity for this plan, design, or purpose to have been previously arranged or formulated;

- participation of the accused in the common plan or design involving the perpetration of crimes; the level of participation must be significant, meaning an act or omission that makes an enterprise efficient or effective; this participation does not need to involve the commission of a specific crime, but may take the form of assistance in, or contribution to, the execution of the common plan or purpose.

There are three forms of JCE, each of which has a different *mens rea*:

- For JCE I, all of the persons committed to the joint criminal enterprise possess the same intent to execute the common purpose, namely the crime.

- For JCE II, personal knowledge of the organised system and intent to further the criminal purpose of that system are required.

- For JCE III, the *mens rea* is twofold:
  - ➤ the accused must have the intention to participate in and contribute to the common criminal purpose;
  - ➤ in order to be held responsible for crimes that were not part of the common criminal purpose, but that were nevertheless a natural and foreseeable consequence of it, the accused must also know that such a crime might be perpetrated by a member of the group, and he must willingly take the risk that the crime might occur by joining or continuing to participate in the enterprise.

The equivalent of JCE (most likely without JCE III) is called common purpose in the Rome Statute and is contained in Article 25(3)(d). The *actus reus* includes two elements:

- a common plan, the parameters of which are the same as the common plan for perpetration;

- a level of contribution that is significant, meaning that it influences the commission of the crime with respect to its occurrence and way of commission; there is no need for a direct link between the contribution and the crime, nor for spatial proximity.

With respect to the *mens rea*, the elements are these:

- the person (1) means to engage in the relevant conduct that allegedly contributes to the crime, and (2) is at least aware that his conduct contributes to the activities of the group of persons for whose crimes he is alleged to bear responsibility;

- the person's knowledge is sufficient to incur liability for contributing to a group of persons acting with a common purpose.

At the international level, JCE as a concept (but known by a different name) was already accepted as a form of punishable participation by the tribunals operating under Control Council Law No. 10 after World War II. The ECCC has indicated that this form of responsibility was also applicable in the early 1970s, although the Cambodian tribunal has rejected the JCE III variety. ICC judges have not ruled on this matter yet, while academics have argued among other things that JCE III is difficult to reconcile with the mental element required by Article 30 and the wording of Article 25(3)(d). However, from a general overarching theory of criminal responsibility, the parameters of all three forms of JCE are not objectionable as culpable conduct and thus are possibly punishable, including JCE III. This last form is also known and applied in domestic common law jurisdictions (albeit under the name of common intention or similar). This means that JCE has been a predictable part of ICL, while the general theory leaves it to policy choices and judicial discretion at the operational level to determine to what extent the full concept should be implemented.

10.5.2.5. Command/Superior Responsibility

This form of participation is premised on the existence of a *duty to act* based upon established norms flowing from the specific position, competence, or power of a person; such a duty is different from mere moral obligations to act in a specific situation. The core elements of command/superior responsibility in ICL are as follows:

- a superior-subordinate relationship exists, meaning that the superior has effective *de jure* or *de facto* command and control over the subordinate and therefore has the material ability to prevent or punish the subordinate's criminal conduct;

- the superior knew or had reason to know that a criminal act was about to be, was being, or had been committed (this includes circumstances where information was available to the superior that would have put him on notice of such offences by subordinates);

- the superior failed to take necessary and reasonable measures to prevent or punish the conduct in question; necessary measures means appropriate action by which the superior genuinely tried to prevent the commission of acts by subordinates or punish such crimes after the fact, while reasonable measures are those reasonably falling within the material powers of the superior.

Given the fact that command/superior responsibility has been a mainstay of both IHL and ICL in cases dealing with responsibility for the commission of crimes by and within large organisations, there is little doubt that this form of hierarchical liability, as well as the concept discussed in the next section, ordering, fall within the general theory of criminal responsibility.

10.5.3. Forms of Accomplice Liability

10.5.3.1. Ordering

The *actus reus* of ordering is that a person in a position of authority uses that authority to convince another to commit an offence; that the person who received the order actually proceeds to commit the offence; and that there is a causal link between the act of ordering and the physical perpetration of a crime, in the sense that the order must have had a direct and substantial effect on the commission of the illegal act. The *mens rea* is the intent that an act constituting the relevant crime be committed or the awareness of the substantial likelihood that a crime would be committed.

10.5.3.2. Instigation

The *actus reus* of instigation is the act of encouraging or provoking with some urgency ('prompting' has been a common term in the jurisprudence) another person to commit an offence.[30] There must be a causal relationship between the instigation and the physical perpetration of the crime, in the sense that the instigation contributed substantially to the conduct of the person or persons committing the crime. The *mens rea* is the intent for a crime to be committed or prompted, with the awareness of the substantial likelihood that an act constituting a relevant crime would be committed as a result of the instigation.

The comments made above with respect to incitement[31] and the general theory of criminal responsibility apply with even more force to instigation, as the latter form applies to completed crimes, that is, crimes that have been executed. Personal criminal liability in such cases appears less controversial than in cases of inchoate crimes. It should be remem-

---

[30] Variations of this form of participation are known in Article 25(3(b) of the Rome Statute as inducing and soliciting, but there has been no jurisprudence so far.

[31] See Section 10.5.1.1.

bered nonetheless that inchoate crimes are distinct crimes and thus require a specific legal basis under the legality principle, while attribution of liability for instigation to completed crimes is possible under the general theory under the lesser requirements of compliance with rule of law and fundamental human rights. This observation on the possibility of criminal liability for instigation is strengthened by the fact that instigation is a typical form of punishable participation that is also well known at the domestic level. Because of the broad acceptance of instigation, there has been no concern about using this form of liability in connection with the well-known international crimes of genocide, war crimes, and crimes against humanity.

10.5.3.3. Complicity (Aiding and Abetting)

Complicity in the forms of aiding and abetting has been known since time immemorial as the prime means of extending responsibility in a linear fashion from the direct perpetrator to the aider and abettor; this has been the case at the domestic level as well as in the international sphere. As such there is no doubt that this form of personal liability as well as its derivative forms of aiding and abetting by omission and accessory after the fact, constitutes an important part of a general theory of criminal responsibility.

The *actus reus* of aiding and abetting consists of an act to provide practical assistance, encouragement, or moral support that has a substantial effect on the perpetration of an international crime by contributing a causal factor or by substantially increasing the risk of the kind of harm that actually happened. In this context, substantial effect/substantial contribution has often been defined by the requirement that the criminal act most probably would not have occurred in the same way had not someone acted in the role that the suspect in fact assumed.

The *mens rea* is always fulfilled if the purpose of the aider and abettor was to commit or facilitate the crime, but it can also be fulfilled if the accused had knowledge or awareness of the substantial likelihood that the practical assistance, encouragement, or moral support would assist or facilitate the commission of the offence, even though the aider and abettor did not share the intent to commit the crime. Thus, it is sufficient and necessary that the aider and abettor intended to make an actual contribution or increase the risk of harm with awareness that it would most likely assist or facilitate the criminal enterprise. While it is not necessary for the aider and abettor to have known the precise crime that was intended or how exactly it was to be committed, he must have been aware, when making his contribution, of the essential elements of the acts constituting the crime that was subsequently committed.

With respect to aiding and abetting genocide in particular, this form of commission applies if a person knowingly aided and abetted one or more persons in the commission of genocide while knowing that such person or persons were committing genocide, even though the aider and abettor himself did not have the specific intent to destroy, in whole or in part, a national, ethnical, racial, or religious group as such. Thus, to be held criminally responsible for aiding and abetting the crime of genocide, a person must have been aware of the specific intent held by the executors on the ground or by the leaders behind the crimes, for example, as expressed or understood within the organisation used to commit the crimes. This is because specific intent is an essential element of the crime of genocide.

The *actus reus* of aiding and abetting may consist of an *omission*, provided that this failure to act had a decisive effect on the commission of the crime. The critical issue here is whether it can be established that the failure to discharge a legal duty assisted, encouraged, or lent moral support to the perpetration of the crime and had a substantial effect on it. Furthermore, a person's mere presence at the scene of a crime can be an example of an omission if his presence bestowed legitimacy on or provided encouragement to the actual perpetrator.

10.5.3.4. Accessory after the Fact

The provision of assistance after completion of a universal crime can sometimes constitute a useful and important contribution to a criminal enterprise, especially when the assistance is guaranteed in advance. Accessory after the fact is a specific form of aiding and abetting, with the same *actus reus* and *mens rea*, but in addition it needs to be established that a prior agreement existed with the person who subsequently aided and abetted the criminal enterprise after the crimes were committed, in compliance with the prior agreement. In these cases, the contribution to the criminal enterprise and the subsequent crimes comprises both the agreement prior to the completed crimes and the fulfilment of the agreement after the crimes. Without a prior agreement in place, the subsequent assistance might be lawful or unlawful under domestic law, but it will not constitute liability for complicity to universal crimes. Within this framework, attribution of liability does not raise any problem under the general theory. Also, if the agreement was made but was not fulfilled because of some unforeseen circumstances independent of the person's intent to contribute, it will not *per se* be unlawful under the general theory to attribute liability for attempted accessory after the fact. At the operational level of criminal law, this might or might not be legally possible, depending on the legal rules and jurisprudence within the particular subsystem of ICL or domestic criminal law. The point is that the general theory does not require criminal law subsystems to extend liability as far as theoretically possible.

10.5.4. Concluding Remarks: Development of Punishable Participation in ICL

A number of general observations with respect to *lex lata* can be made about the legal developments regarding liability in ICL by the six institutions. The first one is that when these institutions faced a choice as to whether to utilise a narrow or broad interpretation of a form of liability, in almost all cases (with the exception of command/superior responsibility) they eventually opted in favour of a broader interpretation. This was also perhaps foreseeable from the perspective of the general theory of personal liability and the functions of ICL more specifically, as the judicial choices made by the institutions were still within the overarching theoretical parameters, while the purpose of ICL prosecutions was to seek accountability for those persons considered the most responsible for large-scale crimes.

Second, some forms of participation that at first glance do not appear close from a conceptual and labelling perspective have, in fact, turned out to have very similar key elements. The best examples are planning, instigation, ordering, aiding and abetting, and accessory after the fact, all of which require a substantial contribution to the criminal enterprise or the concrete commission of the eventual crime as part of the *actus reus*.[32] While there has been a fundamental difference between the ap-

---

[32] All forms of perpetration require a more stringent form of contribution, namely an 'essential' contribution, while JCE has a more relaxed form of contribution, namely a 'significant' contribution. This confirms the statement made in Chapter 2, Section 2.1.2., that the fundamental principle of ICL liability for participation in universal crimes is that partici-

proach of the tribunals and that of the ICC when it comes to holding persons in leadership positions responsible, the ICC has relied heavily on ICTY/ICTR jurisprudence in most areas of attribution of personal liability for participation in universal crimes, notably with respect to liability for aiding and abetting, instigation, and command/superior responsibility. Moreover, at the ICC a number of liability forms have been discussed in some detail, with some definite contours discernable in notions such as perpetration, aiding and abetting, and command responsibility.

Another observation regarding the ICC is that the responsibility for future development of personal liability concepts will – assuming that new *ad hoc* tribunals are not established – fall on this institution, as the jurisprudence of the tribunals has come to a halt. The ICTY, ICTR, and SCSL have ceased operations, and their successor mechanisms will likely have little impact on the existing jurisprudence, while activities of the ECCC and EAC will be very limited due to the small number of cases. Development of one form of liability, namely common purpose, is in its beginning stage. Here more judicial consideration is required to establish its exact parameters, especially in comparison with the co-perpetration and JCE concepts. If the past is any indication, it is quite possible that judges will continue the trend toward broad interpretation by interpreting this form of liability widely as well.

Lastly, it can be seen that all forms of liability developed so far in the international jurisprudence fall within the framework of the general theory developed in this book, while some forms of inchoate crimes not yet recognised *lex lata* at the international level could also fit within its parameters. These include the forms of incitement and conspiracy, which currently apply to genocide but could be made applicable to other universal crimes as well.

10.6. Assessing the Range of Lawful and Desirable Forms of Attribution

This section deals with forms of participation that could be considered to lie beyond the regular parameters of the contemporary jurisprudence of the international institutions discussed above. First, it concerns forms that

---

pants must have made an actual contribution to or towards the completion of the relevant crime.

have actually been applied in ICL but that are not considered to be main-stream legal concepts in current ICL. Second, it also concerns possible new forms of ICL liability and adjustment of the criteria for the traditional forms.

The outliers will be discussed from both a legal and organisational perspective. The purpose is to inquire whether the empirical sources used in Chapters 5–9 provide any examples in which courts or scholars have taken concepts beyond the parameters of jurisprudence of the international institutions but have still found sufficient legal basis to hold persons liable for the commission of universal crimes, using these broader approaches. This exercise forms an important part of testing the functioning and usefulness of the general theory of punishable participation in universal crimes, since there might be good legal and policy reasons not to limit attribution of personal criminal liability in the future to *lex lata*, but also to consider operational *lex ferenda* in compliance with the general theory in that context. To consider actual legal statements that have gone beyond the prevailing international jurisprudential norm of liability attribution might provide a considerable amount of evidence for a bridge function from a possible *lex ferenda* norm to a future new type of *lex lata* norm.

Several examples of such deviations from the more established forms have been noted in Chapters 5–9. Without assessing at this point whether these examples were the result of progressive thinking, political expediency, or a misinterpretation of legal precedents, we can say that they have come from all the sources of empirical data discussed in these five chapters. This indicates that there is a need to also discuss the less 'mainstream' liability concepts in use.

The first two examples are unusual in that these forms of participation were utilised after WWII but have fallen into disuse in modern times. One concerns the liability form of 'taking a consenting part' in crimes, provided under Control Council Law No. 10. It was applied to persons who, while not having internal responsibility in the chain of command within the relevant organisation, still had sufficiently high authority to influence others involved in the crimes, but chose to remain silent, despite their knowledge of the crimes.

The other example pertains to the concept of membership in a criminal organisation, which was contained in the statutes of the IMT and IMTFE, as well as in CC10. It was applied as a separate crime description to individuals who met certain conditions, that is, voluntary participation in an organisation deemed criminal by the IMT, with personal knowledge of the kinds of crimes regularly committed by the organisation. The concept was used to constitute a distinct accessorial crime ('B-crime') to the main crimes under international law, similar in that respect to inchoate crimes. Thus, it was not used to attribute accomplice liability for concrete crimes at particular crime scenes; rather, it was the individual's participation in the organisation and the presumed minimum responsibility of every member for the crimes committed through the organisation that justified the criminalisation. Punishment for membership alone was quite lenient, and it was possible to rebut the presumption of voluntary membership and knowledge of the crimes committed by the organisation.

The notion of 'membership' was notably applied in not a formal but a substantive sense, and was not applied to all who formed part of the criminal organisation. A certain threshold of participation had to be met, and even participants working in the organisation as officers were sometimes excused from attribution of liability under the crime of membership, either because their work and contributions were considered too removed from the criminal activities of the organisation or because the accused had expressed disapproval of the crimes.[33] In principle, such a form of personal liability for participation in an organisation deemed criminal according to a fair procedure does not seem to be in breach of the fundamental principles of conduct, culpability, and fair attribution of personal liability. This presupposes a reliable and transparent method and factual basis for labelling the organisation correctly. However, had the concept been used to attribute liability for concrete universal crimes committed at particular crime scenes, then it could hardly have been in compliance with the general theory because of problematic shortcomings with regard to personal

---

[33] See Chapter 1, Section 1.2.2., discussing the Pohl case on the accused Joseph Vogt. NMT, "The Pohl Case", in *Trials of War Criminals before the Nuernberg Military Tribunals under Control Council Law No. 10: Nuernberg, October 1946–April 1949*, vol. V, US Government Printing Office, Washington, DC, 1950 (www.legal-tools.org/doc/84ae05/). The Special Tribunal for Lebanon recently discussed the parameters of another broad concept of participation, namely the notion of criminal association in the Lebanese Criminal Code and came to the conclusion that a criminal association is committed upon the conclusion of an agreement to act collectively for the purpose of committing particular underlying offence and that it is not necessary to identify all participants in a criminal association; see STL, Appeals Chamber, *Interlocutory Decision on the Applicable Law: Criminal Association and Review of the Indictment*, STL-17-07/I/AC/R17bis, 18 October 2017, paras 37-43 (www.legal-tools.org/doc/829cbe/).

culpability and responsibility. In particular, sufficient causal links would be difficult to establish with respect to consequences of the activities of the accused within the organisation and particular crimes committed by other members of the organisation, based on the concept of causing harm or substantially increasing the risk of harm. Similarly, if used without a certain threshold for punishable participation in the organisation, taking into account individual circumstances, attribution of membership liability would conflict with the principle of fair attribution of personal liability.

More recently, it has been observed that the approach towards co-perpetration in Ethiopia comes very close in practice to a form of liability based on membership in an organisation involved in the commission of universal crimes. In addition, as pointed out earlier in this chapter, the similar liability form of participation in a terrorist organisation is gaining momentum in domestic jurisdictions in relation to the crime of terrorism, which is arguably already a crime under international law. How this form of responsibility may fit within the current framework of ICL is not clear, though, and this will need to be further explored at the operational level in the future.

Apart from these references to liability for taking a consenting part in crimes and to membership in criminal organisations in early ICL stat-utes, TCL treaties at times have also used other, typically expanded, no-tions of liability. Examples are the references to co-operation in the Apartheid Convention; to association in the 1988 Narcotics Convention; to "preparatory acts and financial operations in connexion" with drug of-fences in the 1961 and 1971 Drug Trafficking Conventions and the 1972 Drug Trafficking Protocol; and to counseling in the 2000 Palermo Con-vention on organised crime. Some other TCL treaties have included threatening as a form of participation (while it also constitutes a crime in itself); this is found in a number of conventions on terrorism, namely the 1973 Convention on Protected Persons, the 1988 Convention and Protocol regarding offences on ships and fixed platforms, the 1994 Convention re-garding United Nations personnel, the 2005 Nuclear Terrorism Conven-tion, and the 2010 Beijing Convention and Protocol. While notions such as counseling and general preparatory acts could very well fit within the general theory of criminal responsibility, others, such as threatening, are of more doubtful relevance as distinct forms of participation even though they can be seen as increasing the risk of causing harm. For example, threats to commit concrete universal crimes might be considered distinct accessorial crimes in future ICL, or, if the threatening is meant to encourage others to commit the crimes, they might rather constitute a kind of instigation when the crimes are completed.

While the above examples refer to possible additional forms of participation in ICL, innovation has also taken place at a slightly different level, namely by using an existing concept but applying it to a broader set of circumstances than has been the norm in contemporary ICL.[34] For instance, the ILC in its first Draft Code of 1954 used attribution language very similar to that of the Genocide Convention (conspiracy, incitement, complicity, and attempt), while also extending the inchoate offences of conspiracy, incitement, and attempt to all four core universal crimes, namely genocide, crimes against humanity, crimes against peace (aggression), and war crimes, rather than reserving this form of liability just for the crime of genocide. As noted above in this section, the ILC has, however, retreated since then from this line of more consistent application of liability concepts. More recently, when some judges at the ICC examined the court's version of JCE, common purpose, set out in Article 25(3)(d), they held that a lower level of contribution than 'significant' was sufficient for this type of participation, even going so far as to question whether any material contribution was necessary. A last example can be found in Chapter 6, discussing academic commentary on international jurisprudence, where some authors have proposed combining categories or modes of liability in order to cast the net of criminal liability wider than has customarily been the case. As discussed in Chapter 2, such combinations might well be compatible with our general theory of criminal law liability, but caution and a closer inspection are warranted.

At yet another, more modest level of innovation, established notions of modes of participation have also been expanded in order to establish personal liability for unusual fact situations. In this regard, the national jurisprudence has provided some interesting examples. These examples have primarily taken place in the areas of aiding and abetting and co-perpetration. For example, the Supreme Court of the Netherlands held that the *mens rea* of aiding and abetting, in addition to knowledge and intent with respect to the acts of assistance, could also include heightened forms

---

34   The opposite is true of the IMT and IMTFE Statutes, which used preparation as a general concept with a broader meaning than what became prevalent in later instruments and jurisprudence.

of *mens rea* such as *dolus directus* in either the first or second degree, namely full intent (the assistance was provided toward a shared purpose) or conditional intent (the assistance was provided with a view to some personal benefit and substantially increased the risk of harm). Insofar as these forms of *mens rea* complement and do not exclude each other, this state of law would be in compliance with the general jurisprudence at the international level and would merely provide useful specificity to the prevailing notions of complicity (aiding and abetting).

In Germany, the courts have also provided their unique perspective on aiding and abetting by stating that culpability can follow from providing moral assistance to universal crimes. They have clarified that moral assistance can be provided in the form of technical advice, that is, by imparting knowledge that results in improved prospects for a successful execution of the act. German law also recognises the possibility of psychological assistance, which influences the volition of another person, the principal actor, by reinforcing his or her decision to commit the crime. In a case highlighted in Chapter 8, the accused provided such psychological assistance by publicly declaring, in interviews, memoranda, and press releases, that he was prepared to deny or minimise the war crimes ordered by the leadership of an organised group. Also in Germany, and again for aiding and abetting, it has been assumed that a causal link between an act of assistance and the completed crime is not necessarily required. This might be an important point, for example with respect to further discussion of personal liability for certain forms of atrocity speech in ICL, predicated on the notion that not only the consequence of causing concrete harm but in addition also that causing a substantial risk of harm should be penalized.

In an Argentinian case a person was found to be liable for the commission of crimes because he was aware of the crimes, tolerated them, and facilitated them.[35] As with the German example, a further discussion about the appropriateness of this form of responsibility is necessary.

---

[35] It is interesting to note that the concept of toleration as an example of aiding and abetting has been specifically rejected by the highest courts in the United States and Canada in the context of refugee law, where there is a large amount of jurisprudence regarding the notion of exclusion from refugee status for the commission of international crimes. The cases in question are United States Supreme Court, *Fedorenko v. United States*, 499 U.S. 490, 31 January 1981 (www.legal-tools.org/doc/c7c51e/), which stated that mere acquiescence or

Regarding co-perpetration, a court in Sweden explained that two persons who were both present at an unlawful and cruel killing event, although they did not execute the beheading themselves, were to be considered joint perpetrators in accordance with the extended notion of perpetration under Swedish law because of their assistance to the executors and their active role in the criminal enterprise.

Various Latin American courts have accepted a relatively wide spectrum of acts as sufficient to constitute an essential contribution for co-perpetration. These acts range from providing necessary information or physical means to execute the crime, at one end of the spectrum, to defending the criminal organisation by supplying misleading information or making dubious claims in response to international critique or pressure, at the other. Furthermore, the courts in Argentina have also, under the same concept, developed a doctrine of successive co-perpetration, where actors can make their contributions at different points in time and still become parties to the criminal enterprise, which again could be seen as a way of penalizing acts causing unacceptable danger of serious harm.

The courts in the countries of the former Yugoslavia have also applied the notion of co-perpetration, at times in a broad fashion. In Bosnia and Herzegovina, an accused was convicted as a co-perpetrator for having driven the other accused persons to and from the crime scene, as well as pointing out to them the house in which the victim resided. The Croatian Supreme Court, furthermore, rejected an argument that a person who did not directly participate in a killing could not be convicted as a co-perpetrator. The reasoning was that as each of the co-perpetrators had made his own distinct contribution with knowledge of what was to be done by the others, each of them incurred liability for the crime as a direct perpetrator. In Serbia, the courts have held that co-perpetration requires the person to make a considerable contribution to the commission of the

---

membership in an organisation that engages in persecution is not sufficient to bar an individual from a grant of asylum, and Supreme Court of Canada, *Ezokola v. Canada*, 2013 SCC 40, 2 *Supreme Court Reports* 678 (19 July 2013) (www.legal-tools.org/doc/b8f5c7/), in which the court found that guilt by association or passive acquiescence were not culpable acts. This can be contrasted with an exclusion decision at the tribunal level in France, which held that in the context of the Rwandan genocide, toleration and encouragement of genocidal acts by persons in senior positions would lead to exclusion from refugee status; see France, Commission des Recours des Réfugiés, *Rwamucyo*, 420926, 16 December 2003 (www.legal-tools.org/doc/236489/).

crime. However, at times this appears to have set a very low threshold: indeed, one court accepted mere presence at the crime scene as amounting to co-perpetration, when the accused had merely been situated alongside fellow soldiers who carried out the actual crime. These examples of co-perpetration in five national jurisdictions are for the most part compatible with the parameters of co-perpetration as developed in the general theory of criminal responsibility in Chapter 2, although an application that allowed for presence at the criminal scene as the *actus reus* seems to have taken this approach too far.

The international jurisprudence on 'transnational' participation in universal crimes – meaning that the crimes were committed in an international armed conflict, or in a non-international armed conflict within the territory of one state through the acts of power structures or support structures originating or operating principally within another state – has so far been limited. An important transnational case, however, is the Taylor case before the Special Court for Sierra Leone. The accused in this case, Taylor, was found guilty of aiding and abetting transnational violence by assisting in the commission of war crimes and crimes against humanity in Sierra Leone from his regular base in Liberia. It is quite likely that if and when the ICC is faced with such a situation, it will not hesitate to apply the principles of punishable participation as contained in the Rome Statute, Article 25(3), regardless of the existence of any such transnational element in the factual situation to be considered.

In conclusion, while the regular international and domestic jurisprudence recalled in Section 10.4. is broadly in accordance with the general theory of criminal responsibility, more discussion and contemplation is required for some of the more esoteric forms of liability mentioned in this section. Finally, with respect to the possible reformulation of parameters of some traditional forms of liability in current ICL, it has been noted earlier in this book – and shall not be repeated in any detail here – that there may well be a need for further clarification of the approach to culpability (command and superior responsibility) and the notion of a contributing factor (notably with respect to accomplice liability such as instigation).[36]

---

[36] See Chapter 6, Sections 6.3.2. and 6.3.4.

10.7. Multiple Forms of Personal Liability, and Proportionate Sentencing

10.7.1. Clarifying the Issues and Limitations of the Analysis

There are also other issues relating to personal criminal liability, concerned with how liability is defined and applied in factual situations involving more than one form of liability and with how the different forms of personal liability may play out at the sentencing stage of universal crimes cases. These are themes that we have considered only briefly in this book. The empirical data in this respect are either sparse or difficult to extract from the jurisprudence. However, it might be useful to recall the theoretical points of departure in Chapter 2 and to point out how the data on sentencing in Chapter 3 may assist in developing a theoretical framework for the relationship between personal liability and proportionate sentencing through the lenses of gravity assessment – the key to fair infliction of penalties.

10.7.2. Combination and Assimilation of Liability, and Concurrent Liability

As discussed in Chapter 2, multiple derivations resulting in combinations of different forms of liability are possible and are not per se unlawful under the general theory of criminal liability, while at the same time there is also the complementary and inverse concept of assimilation. For example, with respect to concrete universal crimes defined by the parameters of time, location, perpetrators and other participants, and victims, commission liability for a particular person tends to assimilate inchoate liability and accomplice liability for the same person. Moreover, with respect to further derivative forms of liability there seem to be some clear rules or principles, for example that perpetration liability assimilates omission liability, while at an even further derivative level, liability for JCE or co-perpetration assimilates command and superior responsibility. In such instances, there seems to be a good correlation between the general theory and the operational level of ICL.

We have also noted that inchoate liability for incitement to genocide, which may result in a conviction for an inchoate crime when the main crime of genocide is not completed, is transformed into instigation as accomplice liability when the crime of genocide is completed. When one form of liability is thus assimilated by another, or transformed, it means that the concurrent forms of participation cannot lead to concurrent liability with respect to the same crime.

On the other hand, combinations of different liability forms may extend liability to acts that would otherwise not be punishable *lex lata*. We have seen examples of this at the derivative levels and consider it lawful under the general theory. It has also been implemented at the operational level of ICL, as illustrated by, for example, the development of JCE liability. From a theoretical perspective, JCE has been derived from commission liability and constituted by combining the distinct liability categories of conspiracy and joint perpetration/perpetration through another. Other combinations might be lawful under the general theory as well, for example complicity (aiding and abetting) in attempt and attempted complicity, although the theory does not mean that criminal law liability within a subsystem has been extended *lex lata* to all combinations that might have been lawful. The general theory concerns solutions that could be lawfully implemented, but the theory does not require all kinds of potential lawful forms of liability to be employed within a particular subsystem because the theory leaves a substantial amount of legislative and judicial discretion in this regard to the various criminal law subsystems.[37] Furthermore, assimilation of one form of concurrent participation may not always be the natural solution, for example with regard to concurrent forms of accomplice liability. For example, if a person both instigates another person to commit a war crime and assists in the execution of the crime, concurrent liability may be not only lawful under the general theory but also desirable *lex ferenda* and applicable *lex lata* in order to express the first person's full participation in the criminal enterprise.

The general point is that these quite complex issues need to be further investigated both in light of the general theory and based on more detailed empirical studies.

---

[37] However, with respect to particular subsystems the theory may also be used as a scientific model to predict more precise outcomes. For example, within ICL in general, this field of law is concerned with universal crimes, and these crimes are often committed by large criminal enterprises or by the use of power structures in society. Hence it was predictable under the general theory and in compliance with the purpose of the international tribunals that courts sought to extend liability to reach the most responsible persons, if need be through lawful derivative liability forms and the combinations of liability concepts.

10.7.3. Personal Liability and Proportionate Punishment

Gravity assessment is central to the punishment and sentencing of persons convicted of universal crimes. While proportionate punishment relative to the gravity of the unlawful acts is the key point of departure for any fair criminal justice system in compliance with fundamental human rights, several components might be important for the assessment of gravity. Due to the special character of the crimes, a model for gravity assessment within ICL was proposed in the first book of this series[38] and is reproduced here (Figure 2).

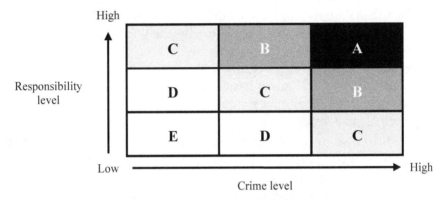

Figure 2: Gravity Function Model.

The horizontal axis shows the level of seriousness of the crimes, increasing from low to high. The vertical axis shows the responsibility level of the person/group committing the crime, likewise increasing from low to high. A diagonal arrow could be drawn to indicate ascending seriousness of the crime level and level of responsibility together, from cell E (low-low) to cell A (high-high). An underlying assumption is that for most purposes, including sentencing, both factors are of approximately equal importance. Although the present book is not mainly concerned with sentencing, it has dealt extensively with issues of classification of personal liability, and thus it has also been indirectly concerned with the vertical axis on responsibility shown in Figure 2. The question is whether the data on sentencing in Chapter 3 may assist in developing a theoretical frame-

---

[38] See Einarsen, 2012, pp. 73–82, *supra* note 12.

work for the relationship between personal liability and proportionate sentencing.

In Chapter 3, sentencing was considered in light of different classes of liability and liability concepts and in relation to the sociological classes of high-level, mid-level, and low-level participants in power structures and participants in power support structures. The picture that emerges is consistent with the assumption that persons at higher levels of power typically should be and would be punished more severely than persons at lower echelons of a hierarchy. In other respects the picture is less clear, and it is also difficult to interpret the data. For example, prosecutors at different tribunals may have used different strategies and may not have selected the accused in such a way as to allocate liability to all four main sociological classes. And if the main focus has been on the allegedly most responsible, the selection processes with respect to others might have been more accidental and might have led to sentencing of persons who are not fully representative of their group. However, there are still some interesting findings to consider.

With respect to prison terms over 30 years, persons at the highest level of their power structures represented 53 per cent of such sentences. The intermediate level represented 32 per cent and support structures approximately 15 per cent, while the low level accounted for only 1 per cent of these long sentences. The converse was also partially true, in that the majority of sentences at the low end of the sentencing range, those below 30 years, were handed either to persons at the lowest level of the power structure, at 23 per cent, or to persons within support structures, at 25 per cent, while the intermediate level of power structures contributed 34 per cent. It is also interesting that the top level contributed the remaining 18 per cent of sentences below 30 years.

Several observations can be made in regard to these findings. First, sentencing at the international institutions is far from an exact science. Second, the actual crimes committed – indicating the crime level – are missing from this account, although this factor, as noted above, may count as much as the responsibility level in any gravity analysis. Third, the specific forms and ways of participation with regard to mode of liability, and thus the more exact role and contribution of the convicted person, may have contributed significantly to the gravity assessment as well. Related to this point is a consistent trend noticed at the modern tribunals, namely that when a person at a high, intermediate, or support level has committed crimes personally in addition to the mode of participation connected to the group as a whole – for instance, by personally harming a victim while being present at the crime scene – tribunals are inclined to impose higher sentences than for similarly situated persons facing similar charges who did not choose to personally inflict suffering on their victims.

With these shortcomings and precautions in mind, one may still envisage a model for assessment of the gravity of personal liability along the vertical axis of responsibility level (see Figure 2 above) in compliance with the general theory of criminal law liability in a sociological context. Figure 3, the responsibility function model, combines the classes of liability and the sociological classes of participation, with participants in power support structures integrated at the intermediate level for this purpose. This model can be used to further specify and determine the level of responsibility, a determination that then feeds into the gravity function model in Figure 2.

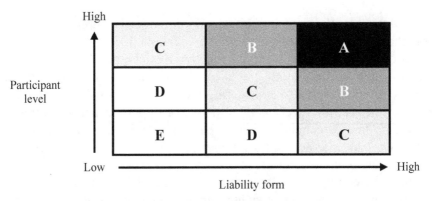

Figure 3: Responsibility Function Model.

The horizontal axis shows the level of typical seriousness of participation by liability form, increasing from low to high, where cell E concerns inchoate liability, cell D accomplice liability, and cell C commission liability. For a more detailed picture, each cell could in principle have been broken down into categories and subcategories, and into modes of liability within a particular criminal law subsystem. The vertical axis shows the participant level of the person responsible for the crime in terms of his or her location in a power structure, likewise increasing from low to high. Cell E embraces low-level participants, cell D combines mid-level participants and participants in support structures, and cell C is for high-level participants. A diagonal arrow could be drawn to indicate ascending seriousness of liability form and participant level together, from cell E (low-low) to cell A (high-high). An underlying assumption is that for most purposes, including sentencing, both factors are of approximately equal importance.

The matrix divides the set of options into nine different cells. Cell A indicates the highest level of responsibility (commission liability for high-level participants), while the two cells B also indicate a fairly high level of responsibility through either commission liability for mid-level participants or accomplice liability for high-level participants. At the other end of the spectrum, the two cells D indicate a fairly low level of responsibility through either inchoate liability for mid-level participants or accomplice liability for low-level participants. An institution like the ICC will naturally aim at persons located within cell A or cells B, but may for different strategic reasons also prosecute some persons within the three cells C.

Arguably, the responsibility function model is implicit in the general theory of punishable crimes. As mentioned, however, this model forms only one part of the gravity function model, and therefore it is only the first step in the overall gravity analysis that is key to proportionate sentencing. In addition to considering the responsibility level and the relevant crimes (crime level) as the other most important part of gravity assessment, fair sentencing within operational criminal law subsystems must also take into account a number of other factors, both aggravating and mitigating circumstances, in order to appropriately adjust the concrete punishment within a broader paradigm of rule of law and general principles of criminal law, human rights, sentencing rules and practice, and humane treatment of offenders.

10.8. An Autonomous, Differentiated, and Flexible ICL Matrix of Personal Liability

In some senses, ICL might be seen as a laboratory for experimenting with and enhancing our understanding of criminal law liability. Within this field, actors from many different legal cultures have interacted to develop both theory and practice. Operating within the complex and multi-layered legal frameworks of universal crimes, they have often enjoyed substantial discretion in applying specific legal rules relevant to punishable participation in universal crimes. These frameworks include statutes of an international court and other legal sources within particular criminal law subsystems, alleged CIL norms and general principles of criminal law, and the overarching UN paradigm of international law that requires respect for fundamental human rights and the rule of law. Some of these frameworks are applicable to any criminal law subsystem aspiring to fall within the sphere of true criminal justice. Thus their relevance is not necessarily limited to universal crimes. This means that the theoretical analysis and findings of this book, while relevant above all to the field of ICL, may also have scientific value beyond ICL – especially in the adjacent field of transnational criminal law, but also in domestic criminal law.

In this book, however, we have focused on punishable participation in universal crimes and on the general theory of personal criminal liability as it applies to this subject. At the core of this theoretical model is an analytical scheme for derivation of personal criminal liability that flows from the most abstract liability forms (basic type) to gradually more concrete forms of personal liability and finally to operational modes of liability within a concrete criminal law subsystem, such as, for instance, the Rome Statute at the international level or the criminal law system of any country at the domestic level. How specific modes are designed and developed within a particular subsystem is, however, *determined not by the theoretical model but instead by policy decisions and judicial activity within that subsystem.* What the model provides is a theoretical explanation and a basis for legal and policy evaluation of a subsystem and the attribution of criminal law liability at this operational level. The model points out the legal possibilities and requirements that have to be met under any criminal law system aspiring to be in compliance with the general theory. This would necessitate a criminal law system in general compliance with the rule of law and with fundamental human rights. It also requires internal operation in full compliance with the *supra*-principle of free choice and with the fundamental principles for conferring criminal law liability, as well as definition of personal liability in compliance with the secondary principles and additional derivative principles.

Notably, the general theory has not only been presented and discussed theoretically as a scientific model, but has also been tested by means of empirical surveys. Overall, we find that this theory seems well suited to explain why much of the legal development that has taken place was predictable and why the law as developed and applied at the operational level *lex lata* has generally been in compliance with the theoretical principles and the frameworks of international law. Hence this book ought to provide actors and academics in the field with a better understanding of the law, of the scope for lawful practices, of possible best practices, and of how the law should be further developed or reinforced at the operational levels.

At the same time, the theory itself could also be further refined and thus would surely benefit from critical academic review and debate, as well as more empirical testing. Furthermore, a more detailed analysis of one or more particular criminal law subsystems in light of the general theory, and vice versa, would further enhance our knowledge and perhaps suggest the need for revision of the theory. Such endeavours must be left, for now, to a later work or to other scholars. Before concluding this book, we will touch briefly on a few final points.

First, in our opinion the general theory in effect provides us with an *ICL matrix of personal liability*. Appendix I provides an outline of the matrix we have identified. This means that any possible form of personal liability for universal crimes – whether currently in existence or foreseeable in the future – can be described and classified theoretically and evaluated for (further) implementation. Because the ICL matrix has been especially developed with a view to universal crimes and is not limited to a particular international subsystem, the matrix has an autonomous character in the sense of not being tied to the law as it currently stands in time and space. For example, if a new international court were to be established in the future – for instance, a special tribunal to handle crimes committed in Syria since 2011 – the matrix would be immediately applicable and might even assist policymakers in designing the rules on modes of participation in the new court's statute.

Second, the general theory clearly provides for a *differentiated model* of personal liability and modes of participation through derivative principles. As noted earlier, the theory does not, however, require a particular variant of that model to be applied in practice, and it does not rule out application of a version of the unitary model instead. As long as personal liability is applied at the operational levels, in compliance with the fundamental principles of the general theory, the general theory is open to both ways of organising criminal law liability in statutes and jurisprudence. However, we believe that the general theory implicitly also provides strong arguments *lex ferenda* as to why a differentiated approach is clearly preferable at the operational levels, at least with respect to universal crimes. From a future-oriented, practical perspective, the ICL matrix is differentiated in nature and thus easily applicable to different purposes. More importantly, the ICL matrix provides for *foreseeable* criminalisation and attribution of liability. As we have shown in this book, the most important and diversified liability concepts have already been consistently applied in the international and domestic jurisprudence, and the material and mental elements of the most common modes of participation are currently quite settled with respect to their specific content. This means that *fair labelling* and *fair attribution* of liability based on differentiated forms of liability are also very much possible now, while backtracking to a new choice between a unitary and differentiated approach at the international level most likely would have led to a great deal of legal uncertainty in future universal crimes cases. As noted in our empirical studies, domestic prosecutions seem lately to have benefited from the developments at the international level towards common interpretation and application of personal liability.

Third, the general theory provides for substantial *flexibility* despite a preferably and typically differentiated approach at the operational level. This flexibility has several aspects. Criminal law subsystems are not required by the theory to make use of all possible and lawful forms of liability. With respect to the formulation and implementation of particular forms, there is also a certain amount of flexibility and scope for judicial discretion, although some formulations might now be considered better than others. The many different variants of liability concepts that have been so vigorously discussed in ICL theory and judicial practice over the last 25 years may thus basically all have been compatible with the general theory and general international law. The matter may thus in reality have been more about a choice of best practice than about unlawfulness. In part 2 of the matrix of personal criminal liability in Appendix I, we have set forth recommendable parameters (criteria) within the scope of the general theory and ICL norms. This means that the formulations may not be fully consistent with existing criteria under any particular subsystem, such as the Rome Statute of the ICC. For instance, a slight change has been made with respect to the culpability formulation for command responsibility. Instead of saying that the commander "knew or, owing to the circumstances at the time, should have known that the forces were committing or about to commit" a crime, the recommendable culpability formulation is that the commander "knew or had reason to know that the crime would be, was being, or had been committed". Arguably, the latter formulation more appropriately expresses the reasonable expectations in our time of a pro-active, well-informed, and responsible commander in control of subordinates and the operations at large.[39]

A certain amount of flexibility also applies with respect to the scope of the legality principle. Under the general theory, the principle of legality is important and must be respected, but it applies first and foremost to the requirement that the crime have a legal basis in general international law at the time when the act is committed, with a written and sufficient description of the crime in an international court statute (or in domestic criminal law if the crime is prosecuted domestically). With respect to distinct criminalisation of certain forms of liability where a written legal basis in the statutes would be required – typically inchoate crimes or certain kinds of accomplice liability made into distinct crimes such as membership or participation in an unlawful organisation – there is, however, overlap in that all the requirements of the legality principle then apply. With respect to attribution of liability for committing or contributing to completed crimes, the situation is a bit different. On attribution, a more relaxed rule of law requirement seems to apply. The relevant requirement might be described as lawfulness rather than strict legality. As long as the attribution is in compliance with the other requirements of the general theory, and reasons related to the material and mental elements are provided in the judgment, this will normally suffice. In addition, the form of liability attributed to the accused must not be prohibited under CIL, although a legal basis in CIL in accordance with the criteria for establishing new legal norms under CIL is not necessary.

However, the difference between the two sets of legality requirements might be less than it first seems. Fair attribution of liability for participation in completed crimes may well be considered part of the general principles of international law as well as the general principles of law within criminal law systems seeking to adhere to the rule of law and fundamental human rights. We are speaking here of – to borrow some language from the Rome Statute – the general principles of law derived from laws of legal systems of the world, provided that those principles are not inconsistent with international law and with internationally recognised

---

[39] See also Chapter 6, Section 6.3.2.

norms and standards. Against this backdrop, it can perhaps safely be concluded that the main principles inherent in the general theory of punishable participation in universal crimes are actually part of general international law, and are essential to aspirations of an international rule of law seeking a secure substantial basis for holding responsible persons to account.

APPENDIX I:
THE MATRIX OF PERSONAL CRIMINAL LIABILITY

This list of derivative personal liability forms indicating punishable participation in universal crimes was compiled by the authors based on the analysis and conclusions set forth in this book. The list can be read in conjunction with the list of universal crimes published in the first book in this series, which encompassed three classes of universal crimes, 10 universal crime categories, and 150 universal crime types based on the combination of one crime category and one underlying offence.[1] In the present matrix of personal criminal liability, only five universal crimes are included: the crime of aggression, genocide, crimes against humanity, war crimes, and terrorist crimes.

The first four, the so-called 'core' universal crimes, are included in the Rome Statute of the International Criminal Court ('ICC'). They are, in the authors' opinions, crimes under current international law (international crimes, or universal crimes, *lex lata*). However, we would argue that terrorist crimes should also now be recognised as a crime category under international law *lex lata*. Even if their status remains uncertain under international law, terrorist crimes are prominent examples of transnational crimes and should at least be considered universal crimes *lex ferenda*, with the potential of being recognised as crimes directly under international law within the foreseeable future. For terrorist crimes certain forms of accomplice liability have also been developed in more detail in recent years (see, for instance, Chapter 5, Section 5.2.2.2., Table 11). Under the general theory of personal criminal liability, these forms – if not prohibited under customary international law, which we believe they are not, *per se* – are in principle also applicable to the core universal crimes and may thus be employed in the future at the operational, international level of ICL as well as in domestic universal crimes cases depending on national law. In order to provide this linkage, which at least is interesting *lex ferenda*, we have included terrorist crimes in the matrix below.

---

[1] Terje Einarsen, *The Concept of Universal Crimes in International Law*, Torkel Opsahl Academic EPublisher, Oslo, 2012, Appendix 1 (www.legal-tools.org/doc/bfda36/).

The matrix is divided into two parts. Part 1 brieflysets out forms of liability in relation to the five universal crime categories, building upon the formation of three classes and 12 categories of personal criminal liability as presented in Chapter 2 (Section 2.2.3.6.). These are supplemented with additional derivative modes of liability that have been important in practice, implemented in ICL, and to some extent discussed in this book. Because the crime of aggression as a point of departure is a leadership crime and thus unique, accomplice liability here is described in more detail below.

All the classes, categories, and operational modes of liability are fundamentally derived from a basic form of liability. In its most abstract form, this can be formulated as a 'liability for crime X'. Thus, liability in this scheme is not derived from particular factual acts or omissions in the real world – for instance, the acts of those who agreed on the criminal enterprise or executed the underlying offences like murder or rape. Liability for a particular crime, for example, 'liability for crimes against humanity', is instead constituted by norms *lex lata* or *lex ferenda* in compliance with the general theory of personal criminal liability.

Personal criminal liability may in principle apply to juridical entities (juridical persons) as well as to individuals, although criminal liability as such for corporations and other juridical entities has so far not been implemented at the international level of ICL. The classes, categories, and modes included in this list are applied to the core universal crimes but also to terrorist crimes, because some forms of personal liability have been further developed and clarified with respect to terrorist crimes in treaties, by international organs such as the United Nations Security Council, and in domestic criminal law. The point is that some forms of liability that are currently being applied in terrorist cases might also be lawfully applied to the universal core crimes, or they might be lawfully applied in the foreseeable future, as indicated in the scheme below. In our view, there are no good theoretical reasons why the operational modes of liability should be more limited with respect to the core crimes or why different modes should be applicable to different core crimes. At the operational level, however, such reasons may exist within a particular criminal law subsystem.

The three classes of liability are inchoate liability, commission liability, and accomplice liability. Each has five main derivative forms, although one of these, complicity, might be further subdivided into several derivative forms, as these have already been partially applied in ICL at the international level and in laws on terrorist crimes at the domestic level in several states. The list of lawful derivative forms of personal liability includes current and potential forms of punishable participation in universal crimes, that is, personal liability for punishable participation that is being used in ICL and potential forms that may be lawfully implemented in future ICL, since the listed forms are not prohibited under customary international law.

The list does not necessarily distinguish between lawful liability based on *attribution of liability* for participation in completed main universal crimes, on the one hand, and distinctly criminalised forms of liability for acts or omissions constituting *accessorial crimes* to the main universal crimes, on the other. An example of the latter is incitement to commit genocide – an inchoate, accessorial crime. These two different ways of implementing personal liability for punishable participation could both be lawfully implemented in accordance with the general theory of personal liability, including respect for the rule of law, and with fundamental principles of human rights and criminal law, which include, for example, the legality principle applicable to all distinct crimes. It should be noted that some of the lawful forms listed may not be applicable within a particular criminal law subsystem: in particular, certain forms would not apply under the Rome Statute of the ICC unless the statute were to be amended and the additional forms included.

Part 2 of the matrix sets forth recommendable parameters (criteria) for each derivative form, in overall compliance with the general theory of personal liability and ICL norms. Due to the importance of the Rome Statute, we have marked with an asterisk (*) the forms and formulations that are clearly not applicable under the current Rome Statute. Note, however, that the formulations are generally recommendable criteria, and somewhat different formulations with different content might well be used within particular criminal law subsystems, including under the Rome Statute, still in compliance with the general theory of personal criminal liability. For example, different criminal law subsystems might have developed different thresholds for a punishable contribution to a universal crime, using terms such as 'significant', 'substantial', or 'essential' contribution. On the other hand, such expressions might also turn out to be confusing, debatable, or even misleading, since the different thresholds might be difficult to explain and justify convincingly and apply consistently. Instead we would recommend that the question to be asked, in cases of doubt about alleged punishable participation, is whether an act or omission that may have contributed to a relevant crime or criminal enterprise was sufficiently dangerous and blameworthy, from the perspectives of both social impact and foreseeability of the consequences, to justify criminal responsibility for a universal crime. For this reason, we have not used such qualifiers or yardsticks in part 2 below.

1. **The Matrix of Personal Criminal Liability, Part 1: Basic and Derivative Forms**

1.1. **Liability for the crime of aggression (basic form)**

Derivative forms:

I) **Inchoate liability, including possible distinct accessorial crimes**

   1) Direct and public incitement to commit aggression by a person in a high leadership position*

   2) Serious threats to commit aggression by a person in a high leadership position*

   3) Conspiracy to commit aggression by a person in a high leadership position*

   4) Initiation, planning, and preparation (including ordering) to commit aggression by a person in a high leadership position

   5) Attempt to commit aggression by a person in a high leadership position

II) **Commission liability, including liability for commission by omission**

   6) Perpetration of aggression by a person in a high leadership position

   7) Joint perpetration of aggression by a person in a high leadership position

   8) Perpetration of aggression by a person in a high leadership position through another person

   9) Participation in a joint criminal enterprise to commit aggression by a person in a high leadership position

10) Command and superior responsibility for aggression by a person in a high leadership position

III) Accomplice liability, including possible distinct accessorial crimes

11) Ordering execution of aggression that occurs or is attempted, by a person with authority to exercise substantial influence over decisions or acts causing aggression or a substantial risk of aggression while acting on behalf of a person in a high leadership position

12) Instigating aggression that occurs or is attempted, by a person in a high leadership position or by a person with authority to exercise substantial mental influence over decisions or acts causing aggression or a substantial risk of aggression

13) Aiding or abetting in aggression that occurs or is attempted, by a person in a high leadership position or by a person in an advanced position able to control the relevant political or military action

14) Complicity in aggression that occurs or is attempted, as possibly different from aiding or abetting, by a person in a high leadership position or by a person in an advanced position able to control the relevant political or military action

15) Membership/participation in an organisation committing aggression, by a person in a high leadership position*

1.2. Liability for genocide (basic form)

Derivative forms:

I) Inchoate liability, including possible distinct accessorial crimes

1) Direct and public incitement to commit genocide

2) Serious threats to commit genocide*

3) Conspiracy to commit genocide*

4) Initiation, planning, and preparation (including ordering) to commit genocide*

5) Attempt to commit genocide

II) Commission liability, including liability for commission by omission

    6) Perpetration of an act constituting genocide

    7) Joint perpetration of genocide

    8) Perpetration of genocide through another person

    9) Participation in a joint criminal enterprise to commit genocide

    10) Command and superior responsibility for genocide

III) Accomplice liability, including possible distinct accessorial crimes

    11) Ordering genocide that occurs or is attempted

    12) Instigating genocide that occurs or is attempted

    13) Aiding or abetting genocide that occurs or is attempted

    14) Complicity in genocide that occurs or is attempted, as possibly different from aiding or abetting

    15) Membership/participation in an organisation committing genocide*

1.3. Liability for crimes against humanity (basic form)

Derivative forms:

I) Inchoate liability, including possible distinct accessorial crimes

    1) Direct and public incitement to commit CAH*

    2) Serious threats to commit CAH*

    3) Conspiracy to commit CAH*

    4) Initiation, planning, and preparation (including ordering) to commit CAH*

    5) Attempt to commit CAH

II) Commission liability, including liability for commission by omission

    6) Perpetration of an act constituting CAH

    7) Joint perpetration of CAH

    8) Perpetration of CAH through another person

9) Participation in a joint criminal enterprise to commit CAH

10) Command and superior responsibility for CAH

III) **Accomplice liability, including possible distinct accessorial crimes**

11) Ordering CAH that occurs or is attempted

12) Instigating CAH that occurs or is attempted

13) Aiding or abetting CAH that occurs or is attempted

14) Complicity in CAH that occurs or is attempted, as possibly different from aiding or abetting

15) Membership/participation in an organisation committing CAH*

1.4. **Liability for war crimes (basic form)**

Derivative forms:

I) **Inchoate liability, including possible distinct accessorial crimes**

1) Direct and public incitement to commit war crimes*

2) Serious threats to commit war crimes*

3) Conspiracy to commit war crimes*

4) Initiation, planning, and preparation (including ordering) to commit war crimes*

5) Attempt to commit war crimes

II) **Commission liability, including liability for commission by omission**

6) Perpetration of an act constituting war crimes

7) Joint perpetration of war crimes

8) Perpetration of war crimes through another person

9) Participation in a joint criminal enterprise to commit war crimes

10) Command and superior responsibility for war crimes

III) **Accomplice liability, including possible distinct accessorial crimes**

11) Ordering war crimes that occur or are attempted

12) Instigating war crimes that occur or are attempted

13) Aiding or abetting war crimes that occur or are attempted

14) Complicity in war crimes that occur or are attempted, as possibly different from aiding or abetting

15) Membership/participation in an organisation committing war crimes*

1.5. Liability for terrorist crimes (basic form)

Derivative forms:

I) Inchoate liability, including possible distinct accessorial crimes

1) Direct and public incitement to commit terrorist crimes*

2) Serious threats to commit terrorist crimes*

3) Conspiracy to commit terrorist crimes*

4) Initiation, planning, and preparation (including ordering) to commit terrorist crimes*

5) Attempt to commit terrorist crimes*

II) Commission liability, including liability for commission by omission

6) Perpetration of an act constituting terrorist crimes*

7) Joint perpetration of terrorist crimes*

8) Perpetration of terrorist crimes through another person*

9) Participation in a joint criminal enterprise to commit terrorist crimes*

10) Command and superior responsibility for terrorist crimes*

III) Accomplice liability, including possible distinct accessorial crimes

11) Ordering terrorist crimes that occur or are attempted*

12) Instigating terrorist crimes that occur or are attempted*

13) Aiding or abetting terrorist crimes that occur or are attempted*

14) Complicity in terrorist crimes that occur or are attempted, as possibly different from aiding or abetting*

15) Membership/participation in an organisation committing terrorist crimes*

2. **The Matrix of Personal Criminal Liability, Part 2: Recommendable Parameters of the Derivative Forms of Punishable Participation in Universal Crimes**

I) **Inchoate liability, including possible distinct accessorial crimes**

1) Direct and public incitement to commit universal crimes:

A person may be found guilty of direct and public incitement to commit a relevant universal crime if the person intended to publicly provoke, encourage, or convince another person to commit the crime or to participate in a criminal enterprise that would commit the crime.

2) Serious threats to commit universal crimes:

A person may be found guilty of serious threats to commit a universal crime if the person intended to threaten another person with committing a relevant universal crime or participating in a criminal enterprise that would commit the crime.

3) Conspiracy to commit universal crimes:

A person may be found guilty of conspiracy to commit a relevant universal crime if the person entered into an agreement to commit the crime or to participate in a criminal enterprise that would commit the crime.

4) Initiation, planning, and preparation (including ordering) to commit universal crimes:

A person may be found guilty of initiation, planning, and preparation to commit a relevant universal crime if the person initiated, planned, or prepared (including by means of ordering) for the execution of a relevant universal crime.

5) Attempt to commit universal crimes:

A person may be found guilty of attempt to commit a relevant universal crime if the person undertook action or participated in a criminal enterprise that collectively undertook action that commenced execution of the crime by means of a substantial step, but the crime did not occur because of circumstances independent of the person's intentions.

II) Commission liability, including liability for commission by omission

6) Perpetration of an act constituting universal crimes:

A person may be found guilty of perpetration of a relevant universal crime if the person intended to engage in the criminal conduct, or intended to cause the criminal consequence, or was aware of the likelihood that the crime would occur in the ordinary course of events as a result of the conduct, and the crime occurs.

7) Joint perpetration of universal crimes:

A person may be found guilty of joint perpetration of a relevant universal crime if the person intended to engage in the criminal conduct, or intended to cause the criminal consequence, or was aware of the likelihood that the crime would occur in the ordinary course of events as a result of the conduct, and had a common understanding with another person or with several persons to commit the crime, and provided a coordinated contribution to the common plan or execution of the crime, and the crime occurs.

8) Perpetration of universal crimes through another person:

A person may be found guilty of perpetration through another person to commit a relevant universal crime if the person as a leader had control over another person or an organisation and used the person or the organisation as a means to commit the crime, while the person in control was aware of his control and intended to use his power or position to have the crime committed, and the crime occurs.

9) Participation in a joint criminal enterprise to commit universal crimes:

A person may be found guilty of joint criminal enterprise to commit a relevant universal crime if the person enters into a common plan and makes a further contribution to the criminal enterprise while the person intended to engage in a conduct that would contribute to the occurrence of the crime, and the crime or a foreseeable crime closely connected to the common plan occurs.

10) Command and superior responsibility for universal crimes:

A person may be found guilty of command and superior responsibility by omission when a relevant universal crime has been committed and the person had effective command or control over subordinates, while the person knew or had reason to know that the crime would be, was being, or had been committed, and the person failed to take necessary and reasonable measures to prevent the crime or punish the criminal conduct.

III) Accomplice liability, including possible distinct accessorial crimes

11) Ordering universal crimes that occur or are attempted:

A person may be found guilty of ordering a relevant universal crime if that person was in a position of authority, and with intent and knowledge of his authority used that authority to direct, convince, or threaten another person to commit the crime or to participate in a criminal enterprise that would commit the crime, and the order was a contributing factor to the crime or the criminal enterprise or caused a substantial risk of such a crime.

12) Instigating universal crimes that occur or are attempted:

A person may be found guilty of instigating a relevant universal crime if that person with intent and knowledge provoked, encouraged, or convinced another person to commit a crime or to participate in a criminal enterprise that would commit the crime, and the instigation was a contributing factor to the crime or the criminal enterprise or caused a substantial risk of such a crime.

13) Aiding or abetting universal crimes that occur or are attempted:

A person may be found guilty of aiding and abetting a relevant universal crime if that person with intent and knowledge provided practical assistance, encouragement, or moral support for the crime to be committed or for a criminal enterprise that would commit the crime, including through a relevant act of omission, and the aiding or abetting was a contributing factor to the crime or the criminal enterprise or caused a substantial risk of such a crime.

14) Complicity in universal crimes that occur or are attempted, as possibly different from aiding or abetting:

A person may be found guilty of complicity in a relevant universal crime if that person with intent and knowledge provided a contributing factor to the crime to be committed or to a criminal enterprise that would commit the crime, including through a relevant act of omission, by such acts as: silently consenting to the crime or criminal enterprise with authority different from command and superior authority over subordinates; financing the crime or criminal enterprise; recruiting another person to the crime or criminal enterprise; threatening or counselling another person for the purpose of committing the crime or being associated with or joining the criminal enterprise; preparing, organising, or facilitating other persons for the purpose of committing the crime; or, with knowledge of the completed crime, voluntarily providing practical assistance to the criminal enterprise after the fact.

15) Membership/participation in an organisation committing universal crimes:

A person may be found guilty of membership or participation in an organisation committing a relevant universal crime if that person voluntarily belonged to an organisation, had knowledge of the crime or awareness of the likelihood that the crime would occur in the ordinary course of events as a result of the purpose and operational features of the organisation, and through his membership or participation in the organisation intended to support the crime or criminal enterprise or was aware that his membership or participation in the organisation would be a contributing factor to the crime or criminal enterprise.

APPENDIX II:
LIST OF CASES

1. European Court of Human Rights ('ECHR')

ECHR, *Jorgic v. Germany*, Judgment, 74613/01, 12 July 2007 (www.legal-tools.org/doc/812753/).

ECHR, *Kononov v. Latvia*, Grand Chamber Judgment, 36376/04, 17 May 2010 (www.legal-tools.org/doc/ed0506/).

ECHR, *Ould Dah v. France*, Decision, 13113/03, 17 March 2009 (www.legal-tools.org/doc/6c588a/).

ECHR, *Sarić v. Denmark,* Decision, 31913/96, 2 February 1999 (www.legal-tools.org/doc/978814/).

ECHR, *Van Anraat v. The Netherlands*, Decision, 65389/09, 6 July 2010 (www.legal-tools.org/doc/567d90/).

2. European Court of Justice ('ECJ')

ECJ, Faraj Hassan and Chafiq Ayadi v. Council and Commission of the European Union, Judgment, C-399/06 P and C-403/06 P, 3 December 2009 (www.legal-tools.org/doc/14b236/).

ECJ, Yassin Abdullah Kadi and Al Barakaat International Foundation v. Council of the European Union and Commission of the European Communities, Judgment, C-402/05 P and C-415/05 P, 3 September 2008 (www.legal-tools.org/doc/9c3dd5/).

3. Extraordinary African Chambers ('EAC')

EAC, Trial Chamber, *Prosecutor v. Habré*, Judgment, 30 May 2016 (www.legal-tools.org/doc/98c00a/).

4. Extraordinary Chambers in the Courts of Cambodia ('ECCC')

ECCC, Pre-Trial Chamber, *Decision on Ieng Sary's Appeal against the Closing Order*, 002/19-09-2007-ECCC/OCIJ (PTC75), D427/1/30, 11 April 2011 (www.legal-tools.org/doc/d264ce/).

ECCC, Supreme Court Chamber, Case 002/01, Judgment, 002/19-09-2007-ECCC/SC, 23 November 2016 (www.legal-tools.org/doc/ e66bb3/).

ECCC, Trial Chamber, Case 002/01, Judgment, 002/19-09-2007/ECCC/TC, 7 August 2014 (www.legal-tools.org/doc/4888de/).

ECCC, Trial Chamber, *Kaing Guek Eav alias Duch*, Judgment, 001/18-07-2007/ECCC/TC, 26 July 2010 (www.legal-tools.org/doc/dbdb 62/).

5.   Inter-American Court of Human Rights ('IACHR')

IACHR, *Bayarri v. Argentina*, Judgment, 30 October 2008, Series C, no. 187 (www.legal-tools.org/doc/be621c/).

IACHR, *Miguel Castro-Castro Prison v. Peru*, Judgment, 25 November 2006, Series C, no. 160 (www.legal-tools.org/doc/7d2681/).

6.   International Court of Justice ('ICJ')

ICJ, *Anglo-Norwegian Fisheries Case* (United Kingdom v. Norway), Judgment, *I.C.J. Reports 1951*, p. 116 (www.legal-tools.org/doc/ 457811/).

ICJ, *Armed Activities on the Territory of the Congo* (Democratic Republic of Congo v. Uganda), Judgment, *I.C.J. Reports 2005*, p. 166 (www. legal-tools.org/doc/8f7fa3/).

ICJ, *Certain Expenses of the United Nations (Article 17, paragraph 2, of the Charter)*, Advisory Opinion, *I.C.J. Reports 1962*, p. 151 (www. legal-tools.org/doc/72e883/).

ICJ, *Legal Consequences of the Construction of a Wall in the Occupied Palestinian Territory*, Advisory Opinion, *I.C.J. Reports 2004*, p. 136 (www.legal-tools.org/doc/e5231b/).

ICJ, *Military and Paramilitary Activities in and against Nicaragua* (Nicaragua v. United States of America), Merits and Judgment, *I.C.J. Reports 1986*, p. 14 (www.legal-tools.org/doc/046698/).

ICJ, *North Sea Continental Shelf Cases* (Federal Republic of Germany/Denmark; Federal Republic of Germany/Netherlands), Judgment, *I.C.J. Reports 1969*, p. 3 (www.legal-tools.org/doc/38274a/).

ICJ, *Questions of Interpretation and Application of the 1971 Montreal Convention arising from the Aerial Incident at Lockerbie* (Libyan Arab Jamahiriya v. United States of America), Provisional Measures, Order, *I.C.J. Reports 1992* (www.legal-tools.org/doc/043e5b/).

7. International Criminal Court ('ICC')

ICC, Appeals Chamber, *Prosecutor v. Bemba*, Judgment, ICC-01/05-01/08 A, 8 June 2018 (www.legal-tools.org/doc/40d35b/).

ICC, Appeals Chamber, *Prosecutor v. Bemba*, Judgment, Concurring Separate Opinion of Judge Eboe-Osuji, ICC-01/05-01/08 A, 8 June 2018 (www.legal-tools.org/doc/b31f6b/).

ICC, Appeals Chamber, *Prosecutor v. Bemba*, Judgment, Dissenting Opinion of Judge Sanji Mmasenono Monageng and Judge Piotr Hofmański, ICC-01/05-01/08 A, 8 June 2018 (www.legal-tools.org/doc/dc2518/).

ICC, Appeals Chamber, *Prosecutor v. Bemba*, Judgment, Separate Opinion of Judge Van den Vyngaert and Judge Morrison, ICC-01/05-01/08 A, 8 June 2018 (www.legal-tools.org/doc/c13ef4/).

ICC, Appeals Chamber, *Prosecutor v. Lubanga*, Judgment, ICC-01/04-01/06 A5, 1 December 2014 (www.legal-tools.org/doc/585c75/).

ICC, Appeals Chamber, *Prosecutor v. Mbarushimana*, Judgment on the Appeal of the Prosecutor against the Decision of Pre-Trial Chamber I of 16 December 2011 entitled 'Decision on the Confirmation of Charges', ICC-01/04-01/10 OA 4, 30 May 2012 (www.legal-tools.org/doc/6ead30/).

ICC, Pre-Trial Chamber, *Prosecutor v. Al Mahdi*, Decision on Confirmation of Charges, ICC-01/12-01/15, 24 March 2016 (www.legal-tools.org/doc/bc8144/).

ICC, Pre-Trial Chamber, *Prosecutor v. Bemba*, Decision on Confirmation of Charges, ICC-01/05-01/08, 15 June 2009 (www.legal-tools.org/doc/07965c/).

ICC, Pre-Trial Chamber, *Prosecutor v. Blé Goudé*, Decision on Confirmation of Charges, ICC-02/11-02/11, 11 December 2014 (www.legal-tools.org/doc/0536d5/).

ICC, Pre-Trial Chamber, *Prosecutor v. Garda*, Decision on Confirmation of Charges, ICC-02/05-02/09, 8 February 2010 (www.legal-tools.org/doc/cb3614/).

ICC, Pre-Trial Chamber, *Prosecutor v. Gbagbo*, Decision on Confirmation of Charges, ICC-02/11-01/11, 12 June 2014 (www.legal-tools.org/doc/5b41bc/).

ICC, Pre-Trial Chamber, *Prosecutor v. Katanga and Chui*, Decision on Confirmation of Charges, ICC-01/04-01/07, 30 September 2008 (www.legal-tools.org/doc/67a9ec/).

ICC, Pre-Trial Chamber, *Prosecutor v. Lubanga*, Decision on Confirmation of Charges, ICC-01/04-01/06, 29 January 2007 (www.legal-tools.org/doc/b7ac4f/).

ICC, Pre-Trial Chamber, *Prosecutor v. Mbarushimana*, Decision on Confirmation of Charges, ICC-01/04-01/10, 16 December 2011 (www.legal-tools.org/doc/63028f/).

ICC, Pre-Trial Chamber, *Prosecutor v. Muthaura, Kenyatta and Ali*, Decision on Prosecutor's Application for Summons to Appear for Francis Kirimi Muthaura, Uhuru Muigai Kenyatta, and Mohammed Hussein Ali, ICC-01/09-02/11, 8 March 2011 (www.legal-tools.org/doc/df8391/).

ICC, Pre-Trial Chamber, *Prosecutor v. Nourain and Jamus*, Corrigendum of the Decision on Confirmation of Charges, ICC-02/05-03/09, 7 March 2011 (www.legal-tools.org/doc/5ac9eb/).

ICC, Pre-Trial Chamber, *Prosecutor v. Ntaganda*, Decision on Confirmation of Charges, ICC-01/04-02/06, 9 June 2014 (www.legal-tools.org/doc/5686c6/).

ICC, Pre-Trial Chamber, *Prosecutor v. Ongwen*, Decision on Confirmation of Charges, ICC-02/04-01/15, 23 March 2016 (www.legal-tools.org/doc/74fc6e/).

ICC, Pre-Trial Chamber, *Prosecutor v. Ruto, Kosgey and Sang*, Decision on Confirmation of Charges, ICC-01/09-01/11, 23 January 2012 (www.legal-tools.org/doc/96c3c2/).

ICC, Pre-Trial Chamber, *Prosecutor v. Ruto, Kosgey and Sang*, Decision on Prosecutor's Application for Summons to Appear for William Samoei Ruto, Henry Kiprono Kosgey, and Joshua Arap Sang, ICC-01/09-01/11, 8 March 2011 (www.legal-tools.org/doc/6c9fb0/).

ICC, Trial Chamber, *Prosecutor v. Al Mahdi*, Judgment, ICC-01/12-01/15, 27 September 2016 (www.legal-tools.org/doc/042397/).

ICC, Trial Chamber, *Prosecutor v. Bemba*, Judgment, ICC-01/05-01/08, 21 March 2016 (www.legal-tools.org/doc/edb0cf/).

ICC, Trial Chamber, *Prosecutor v. Bemba, Musamba, Kabongo, Wandu and Arido,* Judgment, ICC-01/05-01/13, 19 October 2016 (www.legal-tools.org/doc/fe0ce4/).

ICC, Trial Chamber. *Prosecutor v. Chui*, Judgment, ICC-01/04-02/12, 18 December 2012 (www.legal-tools.org/doc/2c2cde/).

ICC, Trial Chamber, *Prosecutor v. Chui*, Judgment, Concurring Opinion of Judge Christine Van den Wyngaert, ICC-01/04-02/12, 18 December 2012 (www.legal-tools.org/doc/7d5200/).

ICC, Trial Chamber, *Prosecutor v. Katanga*, Judgment, ICC-01/04-01/07, 7 March 2014 (www.legal-tools.org/doc/f74b4f/).

ICC, Trial Chamber, *Prosecutor v. Lubanga*, Judgment, ICC-01/04-01/06, 14 March 2012 (www.legal-tools.org/doc/677866/).

8. International Criminal Tribunal for the former Yugoslavia ('ICTY')

ICTY, Appeals Chamber, *Prosecutor v. Aleksovski*, Judgment, IT-95-14/1, 24 March 2000 (www.legal-tools.org/doc/176f05/).

ICTY, Appeals Chamber, *Prosecutor v. Blaškić*, Judgment, IT-95-14-A, 29 July 2004 (www.legal-tools.org/doc/88d8e6/).

ICTY, Appeals Chamber, *Prosecutor v. Boškoski and Tarčulovski*, Judgment, IT-04-82-A, 19 May 2010 (www.legal-tools.org/doc/54398a/).

ICTY, Appeals Chamber, *Prosecutor v. Brđanin*, Decision on Interlocutory Appeal, IT-99-36-A, 19 March 2004 (www.legal-tools.org/doc/acb003/).

ICTY, Appeals Chamber, *Prosecutor v. Brđanin*, Judgment, IT-99-36-A, 3 April 2007 (www.legal-tools.org/doc/782cef/).

ICTY, Appeals Chamber, *Prosecutor v. Đorđević*, Judgment, IT-05-87/1-A, 27 January 2014 (www.legal-tools.org/doc/e6fa92/).

ICTY, Appeals Chamber, *Prosecutor v. Erdemović*, Judgment, Separate and Dissenting Opinion of Judge Cassese, IT-96-22-A, 7 October 1997 (www.legal-tools.org/doc/a7dff6/).

ICTY, Appeals Chamber, *Prosecutor v. Gotovina and Markač*, Judgment, IT-06-90-A, 16 November 2012 (www.legal-tools.org/doc/03b685/).

ICTY, Appeals Chamber, *Prosecutor v. Hadžihasanović et al.*, Decision on Interlocutory Appeal Challenging Jurisdiction in Relation to Command Responsibility, IT-01-47-AR72, 16 July 2003 (www.legal-tools.org/doc/608f09/).

ICTY, Appeals Chamber, *Prosecutor v. Halilović*, Judgment, IT-01-48-A, 16 October 2007 (www.legal-tools.org/doc/d97ef6/).

ICTY, Appeals Chamber, *Prosecutor v. Karadžić*, Judgment (Rule 98bis), IT-95-5/18-AR98bis.1, 11 July 2013 (www.legal-tools.org/doc/ 84001b/).

ICTY, Appeals Chamber, *Prosecutor v. Kordić and Čerkez*, Judgment, IT-95-14/2-A, 17 December 2004 (www.legal-tools.org/doc/738211/).

ICTY, Appeals Chamber, *Prosecutor v. Krajišnik*, Judgment, IT-00-39-A, 17 March 2009 (www.legal-tools.org/doc/770028/).

ICTY, Appeals Chamber, *Prosecutor v. Krnojelac*, Judgment, IT-97-25-A, 17 September 2003 (www.legal-tools.org/doc/46d2e5/).

ICTY, Appeals Chamber, *Prosecutor v. Krstić*, Judgment, IT-98-33-A, 19 April 2004 (www.legal-tools.org/doc/86a108/).

ICTY, Appeals Chamber, *Prosecutor v. Kunarac et al.*, Judgment, IT-96-23/1, 12 June 2002 (www.legal-tools.org/doc/029a09/).

ICTY, Appeals Chamber, *Prosecutor v. Kvočka*, Judgment, IT-98-30/1-A, 28 February 2005 (www.legal-tools.org/doc/006011/).

ICTY, Appeals Chamber, *Prosecutor v. Limaj et al.*, Judgment, IT-03-66-A, 27 September 2007 (www.legal-tools.org/doc/6d43bf/).

ICTY, Appeals Chamber, *Prosecutor v. Lukić*, Judgment, IT-98-32/1-A, 4 December 2012 (www.legal-tools.org/doc/da785e/).

ICTY, Appeals Chamber, *Prosecutor v. Milutinović*, Decision on Drag-oljub Ojdanić's Motion Challenging Jurisdiction – Joint Criminal Enter-prise, IT-99-37-AR72, 21 May 2003 (www.legal-tools.org/doc/d6110d/).

ICTY, Appeals Chamber, *Prosecutor v. Mrkšić et al.*, Judgment, IT-95-13/1-A, 5 May 2009 (www.legal-tools.org/doc/40bc41/).

ICTY, Appeals Chamber, *Prosecutor v. Orić*, Judgment, IT-03-68-A, 3 July 2008 (www.legal-tools.org/doc/e053a4/).

ICTY, Appeals Chamber, *Prosecutor v. Perišić*, Judgment, IT-04-81-A, 28 February 2013 (www.legal-tools.org/doc/f006ba/).

ICTY, Appeals Chamber, *Prosecutor v. Popović et al.*, Judgment, IT-05-88-A, 30 January 2015 (www.legal-tools.org/doc/4c28fb/).

ICTY, Appeals Chamber, *Prosecutor v. Prlić et al.*, Judgment, IT-04-74-A, 29 November 2017 (www.legal-tools.org/doc/941285/).

ICTY, Appeals Chamber, *Prosecutor v. Šainović et al.*, Judgment, IT-05-87-A, 23 January 2014 (www.legal-tools.org/doc/81ac8c/).

ICTY, Appeals Chamber, *Prosecutor v. Stakić*, Judgment, IT-97-24-A, 22 March 2006 (www.legal-tools.org/doc/09f75f/).

ICTY, Appeals Chamber, *Prosecutor v. Stanišić and Simatović*, Judgment, IT-03-69-A, 9 December 2015 (www.legal-tools.org/doc/198c16/).

ICTY, Appeals Chamber, *Prosecutor v. Stanišić and Župljanin*, Judgment, IT-08-91-A, 30 June 2016 (www.legal-tools.org/doc/e414f6/).

ICTY, Appeals Chamber, *Prosecutor v. Tadić*, Judgment, IT-94-1-A, 15 July 1999 (www.legal-tools.org/doc/8efc3a/).

ICTY, Appeals Chamber, *Prosecutor v. Tolimir*, Judgment, IT-05-88/2-A, 8 April 2015 (www.legal-tools.org/doc/010ecb/).

ICTY, Appeals Chamber, *Prosecutor v. Vasiljević*, Judgment, IT-98-32-A, 25 February 2004 (www.legal-tools.org/doc/e35d81/).

ICTY, Trial Chamber, *Prosecutor v. Anto Furundžija*, Judgment, IT-95-17/1, 10 December 1998 (www.legal-tools.org/doc/e6081b/).

ICTY, Trial Chamber, *Prosecutor v. Blagojević & Jokić*, Judgment, IT-02-60-T, 17 January 2005 (www.legal-tools.org/doc/7483f2/).

ICTY, Trial Chamber, *Prosecutor v. Boškoski and Tarčulovski*, Judgment, IT-04-82, 10 July 2008 (www.legal-tools.org/doc/939486/).

ICTY, Trial Chamber, *Prosecutor v. Brđanin*, Judgment, IT-99-36, 1 September 2004 (www.legal-tools.org/doc/4c3228/).

ICTY, Trial Chamber, *Prosecutor v. Đorđević*, Judgment, IT-05-87/1, 23 February 2011 (www.legal-tools.org/doc/653651/).

ICTY, Trial Chamber, *Prosecutor v. Galić*, Judgment, IT-98-29-T, 5 December 2003 (www.legal-tools.org/doc/eb6006/).

ICTY, Trial Chamber, *Prosecutor v. Haradinaj et al.*, Judgment, IT-04-84bis-T, 29 November 2012 (www.legal-tools.org/doc/1bad7b/).

ICTY, Trial Chamber, *Prosecutor v. Karadžić*, Judgment, IT-95-5/18-T, 24 March 2016 (www.legal-tools.org/doc/173e23/).

ICTY, Trial Chamber, *Prosecutor v. Krajišnik*, Judgment, IT-00-39-T, 27 September 2006 (www.legal-tools.org/doc/62a710/).

ICTY, Trial Chamber, *Prosecutor v. Kunarac et al.*, Judgment, IT-96-23/IT-96-23/1, 22 February 2001 (www.legal-tools.org/doc/fd881d/).

ICTY, Trial Chamber, *Prosecutor v. Kvočka*, Judgment, IT-98-30/1, 2 November 2001 (www.legal-tools.org/doc/34428a/).

ICTY, Trial Chamber, *Prosecutor v. Milošević*, Decision on Motion for Judgment of Acquittal, IT-02-54-T, 16 June 2004 (www.legal-tools.org/doc/d7fb46/).

ICTY, Trial Chamber, *Prosecutor v. Mladić*, Judgment, IT-09-92-T, 22 November 2017 (www.legal-tools.org/doc/96f3c1/).

ICTY, Trial Chamber, *Prosecutor v. Perišić*, Judgment, IT-04-81-T, 6 September 2011 (www.legal-tools.org/doc/f3b23d/).

ICTY, Trial Chamber, *Prosecutor v. Popović et al.*, Judgment, IT-05-88-T, 10 June 2010 (www.legal-tools.org/doc/481867/).

ICTY, Trial Chamber, *Prosecutor v. Prlić et al.*, Judgment, IT-04-74, 29 May 2013 (www.legal-tools.org/doc/2daa33/).

ICTY, Trial Chamber, *Prosecutor v. Šešelj*, Judgment, IT-03-67-T, 31 March 2016 (www.legal-tools.org/doc/9a8e36/).

ICTY, Trial Chamber, *Prosecutor v. Simić*, Judgment, IT-95-9-T, 17 October 2003 (www.legal-tools.org/doc/aa9b81/).

ICTY, Trial Chamber, *Prosecutor v. Stakić*, Judgment, IT-97-24-T, 31 July 2003 (www.legal-tools.org/doc/32ecfb/).

ICTY, Trial Chamber, *Prosecutor v. Stanišić and Simatović*, Judgment, IT-03-69-T, 30 May 2013 (www.legal-tools.org/doc/066e67/).

ICTY, Trial Chamber, *Prosecutor v. Stanišić and Župljanin*, Judgment, IT-08-91-T, 27 March 2013 (www.legal-tools.org/doc/2ed57f/).

ICTY, Trial Chamber, *Prosecutor v. Tadić*, Judgment, IT-94-1-T, 7 May 1997 (www.legal-tools.org/doc/0a90ae/).

ICTY, Trial Chamber, *Prosecutor v. Tolimir*, Judgment, IT-05-88/2-T, 12 December 2012 (www.legal-tools.org/doc/445e4e/).

9.   International Criminal Tribunal for Rwanda ('ICTR')

ICTR, Appeals Chamber, *Prosecutor v. Akayesu*, Judgment, ICTR-96-4-A, 1 June 2001 (www.legal-tools.org/doc/c62d06/).

ICTR, Appeals Chamber, *Prosecutor v. Bagosora and Sengiyumva*, Judgment, ICTR-98-41-A, 14 December 2011 (www.legal-tools.org/doc/52d501/).

ICTR, Appeals Chamber, *Prosecutor v. Bizimungu*, Judgment, ICTR-00-56B-A, 30 June 2014 (www.legal-tools.org/doc/2a4ad3/).

ICTR, Appeals Chamber, *Prosecutor v. Gacumbitsi*, Judgment, ICTR-2001-64-A, 7 July 2006 (www.legal-tools.org/doc/aa51a3/).

ICTR, Appeals Chamber, *Prosecutor v. Gatete*, Judgment, ICTR-2000-61-A, 9 October 2012 (www.legal-tools.org/doc/1d0b08/).

ICTR, Appeals Chamber, *Prosecutor v. Hategekimana*, Judgment, ICTR-00-55B-A, 8 May 2012 (www.legal-tools.org/doc/885b2c/).

ICTR, Appeals Chamber, *Prosecutor v. Kalimanzira*, Judgment, ICTR-05-88-A, 20 October 2010 (www.legal-tools.org/doc/fad693/).

ICTR, Appeals Chamber, *Prosecutor v. Kamuhanda*, Judgment, ICTR-99-54A-A, 19 September 2005 (www.legal-tools.org/doc/8ff7cd/).

ICTR, Appeals Chamber, *Prosecutor v. Kanyarukiga*, Judgment, ICTR-02-78-A, 8 May 2012 (www.legal-tools.org/doc/e6e1c9/).

ICTR, Appeals Chamber, *Prosecutor v. Karemera*, Judgment, ICTR-98-44-A, 29 September 2014 (www.legal-tools.org/doc/372a64/).

ICTR, Appeals Chamber, *Prosecutor v. Kayishema and Ruzindana*, Judgment, ICTR-95-1-A, 1 June 2001 (www.legal-tools.org/doc/9ea5f4/).

ICTR, Appeals Chamber, *Prosecutor v. Munyakazi*, Judgment, ICTR-97-36A-A, 28 September 2011 (www.legal-tools.org/doc/48cbd6/).

ICTR, Appeals Chamber, *Prosecutor v. Nahimana, Barayagwiza and Ngeze* (the Media Case), Judgment, ICTR-99-52-A, 28 November 2007 (www.legal-tools.org/doc/4ad5eb/).

ICTR, Appeals Chamber, *Prosecutor v. Ndahimana*, Judgment, ICTR-01-68-A, 16 December 2013 (www.legal-tools.org/doc/7034a5/).

ICTR, Appeals Chamber, *Prosecutor v. Ndindabahizi*, Judgment, ICTR-01-71-A, 16 January 2007 (www.legal-tools.org/doc/0f3219/).

ICTR, Appeals Chamber, *Prosecutor v. Ndindiliyimana et al.*, Judgment, ICTR-00-56-A, 11 February 2014 (www.legal-tools.org/doc/4c5065/).

ICTR, Appeals Chamber, *Prosecutor v. Nizeyimana*, Judgment, ICTR-00-55C-A, 29 September 2014 (www.legal-tools.org/doc/e1fc66/).

ICTR, Appeals Chamber, *Prosecutor v. Ntabakuze*, Judgment, ICTR-98-41A-A, 8 May 2012 (www.legal-tools.org/doc/281406/).

ICTR, Appeals Chamber, *Prosecutor v. Ntakirutimana*, Judgment, ICTR-96-10-A and ICTR-96-17-A, 13 December 2004 (www.legal-tools.org/doc/af07be/).

ICTR, Appeals Chamber, *Prosecutor v. Nyiramasuhuko et al.*, Judgment, ICTR-98-42-A, 14 December 2015 (www.legal-tools.org/doc/b3584e/).

ICTR, Appeals Chamber, *Prosecutor v. Nzabonimana*, Judgment, ICTR-98-44D-A, 29 September 2014 (www.legal-tools.org/doc/a1abb4/).

ICTR, Appeals Chamber, *Prosecutor v. Rukundo*, Judgment, ICTR-2001-70-A, 20 October 2010 (www.legal-tools.org/doc/d5b969/).

ICTR, Appeals Chamber, *Prosecutor v. Rutaganda*, Judgment, ICTR-96-3-A, 26 May 2003 (www.legal-tools.org/doc/40bf4a/).

ICTR, Appeals Chamber, *Prosecutor v. Semanza*, Judgment, ICTR-97-20-A, 20 May 2005 (www.legal-tools.org/doc/a686fd/).

ICTR, Appeals Chamber, *Prosecutor v. Seromba*, Judgment, ICTR-2001-66-A, 12 March 2008 (www.legal-tools.org/doc/b4df9d/).

ICTY, Appeals Chamber, *Prosecutor v. Strugar*, Judgment, IT-01-42A, 17 July 2008 (www.legal-tools.org/doc/981b62/).

ICTR, Trial Chamber, *Prosecutor v. Akayesu*, Judgment, ICTR-96-4-T, 2 September 1998 (www.legal-tools.org/doc/b8d7bd/).

ICTR, Trial Chamber, *Prosecutor v. Bagosora, Kabiligi, Ntabakuze and Nsengiyumva*, Judgment, ICTR-98-41-T, 18 December 2008 (www.legal-tools.org/doc/6d9b0a/).

ICTR, Trial Chamber, *Prosecutor v. Bikindi*, Judgment, ICTR-01-72-T, 2 December 2008 (www.legal-tools.org/doc/a7213b/).

ICTR, Trial Chamber, *Prosecutor v. Bizimungu et al.*, Judgment, ICTR-99-50-T, 30 September 2011 (www.legal-tools.org/doc/7077fa/).

ICTR, Trial Chamber, *Prosecutor v. Gatete*, Judgment, ICTR-2000-61-T, 31 March 2011 (www.legal-tools.org/doc/f6c347/).

ICTR, Trial Chamber, *Prosecutor v. Hategekimana*, Judgment, ICTR-00-55B-T, 6 December 2010 (www.legal-tools.org/doc/6082dd/).

ICTR, Trial Chamber, *Prosecutor v. Kanyarukiga*, Judgment, ICTR-02-78, 1 November 2010 (www.legal-tools.org/doc/415384/).

ICTR, Trial Chamber, *Prosecutor v. Karemera, Ngirumpatse and Nzirorera*, Decision on Defence Motions Challenging the Pleading of a Joint Criminal Enterprise in a Count of Complicity in Genocide in the Amended Indictment, ICTR-98-44-T, 18 May 2006 (www.legal-tools.org/doc/5bc554/).

ICTR, Trial Chamber, *Prosecutor v. Karemera et al.*, Judgment, ICTR-98-44-T, 2 February 2012 (www.legal-tools.org/doc/5b9068/).

ICTR, Trial Chamber, *Prosecutor v. Kayishema and Ruzindana*, Judgment, ICTR-95-1, 21 May 1999 (www.legal-tools.org/doc/0811c9/).

ICTR, Trial Chamber, *Prosecutor v. Musema*, Judgment, ICTR-96-13-A, 27 January 2000 (www.legal-tools.org/doc/1fc6ed/).

ICTR, Trial Chamber, *Prosecutor v. Muvunyi*, Judgment, ICTR-00-55A-T, 11 February 2010 (www.legal-tools.org/doc/d2df88/).

ICTR, Trial Chamber, *Prosecutor v. Ndahimana*, Judgment, ICTR-01-68, 30 December 2011 (www.legal-tools.org/doc/d8e4f2/).

ICTR, Trial Chamber, *Prosecutor v. Ndindiliyimana et al.*, Judgment, ICTR-00-56-T, 17 May 2011 (www.legal-tools.org/doc/c71b24/).

ICTR, Trial Chamber, *Prosecutor v. Ngirabatware*, Judgment, ICTR-99-54-T, 20 December 2012 (www.legal-tools.org/doc/393335/).

ICTR, Trial Chamber, *Prosecutor v. Nizeyimana*, Judgment, ICTR-2000-55C, 19 June 2012 (www.legal-tools.org/doc/f8cdd9/).

ICTR, Trial Chamber, *Prosecutor v. Nsengimana*, Judgment, ICTR-01-69-T, 17 November 2009 (www.legal-tools.org/doc/b3866c/).

ICTR, Trial Chamber, *Prosecutor v. Nyiramasuhuko et al.*, Judgment, ICTR-98-42-T, 24 June 2011 (www.legal-tools.org/doc/e2c881/).

ICTR, Trial Chamber, *Prosecutor v. Nzabonimana*, Judgment, ICTR-98-44D-T, 31 May 2012 (www.legal-tools.org/doc/00cb8e/).

ICTR, Trial Chamber, *Prosecutor v. Rutaganda*, Judgment, ICTR-96-3, 6 December 1999 (www.legal-tools.org/doc/f0dbbb/).

ICTR, Trial Chamber, *Prosecutor v. Semanza*, Judgment, ICTR-97-20-T, 15 May 2003 (www.legal-tools.org/doc/7e668a/).

ICTR, Trial Chamber, *Prosecutor v. Seromba*, Judgment, ICTR-2001-66-I, 13 December 2006 (www.legal-tools.org/doc/091a66/).

10. International Military Tribunal ('IMT') and International Military Tribunal for the Far East ('IMTFE')

IMT, Trial of the Major War Criminals before the International Military Tribunal: Nuremberg, 14 November 1945–1 October 1946, vol. I, Nuremberg, 1947 (www.legal-tools.org/doc/f21343/).

IMT, Trial of the Major War Criminals before the International Military Tribunal: Nuremberg, 14 November 1945–1 October 1946, vol. XXII, Nuremberg, 1947 (www.legal-tools.org/doc/d1427b/).

IMTFE, Judgment, International Military Tribunal for the Far East: Tokyo, 1 November 1948, Part A, Chapter II (www.legal-tools.org/doc/3a2b6b/).

IMTFE, Judgment, International Military Tribunal for the Far East: Tokyo, 1 November 1948, Part C, Chapter X (www.legal-tools.org/doc/09f24c/).

11. Mechanism for International Criminal Tribunals ('MICT') (currently International Residual Mechanism for Criminal Tribunals)

MICT, Appeals Chamber, *Prosecutor v. Ngirabatware*, Judgment, MICT-12-29-A, 18 December 2014 (www.legal-tools.org/doc/16b4ef/).

MICT, Appeals Chamber, *Prosecutor v. Šešelj*, Judgment, MICT-16-99-A, 11 April 2018 (www.legal-tools.org/doc/96ea58/).

12. Nuernberg Military Tribunals ('NMT')

NMT, "The Justice Case", Judgment, in *Trials of War Criminals before the Nuernberg Military Tribunals under Control Council Law No. 10: Nuernberg, October 1946–April 1949*, vol. III, US Government Printing Office, Washington, DC, 1951 (www.legal-tools.org/doc/04cdaf/).

NMT, "The Medical Case", Judgment, 20 August 1947, in *Trials of War Criminals before the Nuernberg Military Tribunals under Control Council Law No. 10: Nuernberg, October 1946–April 1949*, vol. II, US Government Printing Office, Washington, DC, 1950 (www.legal-tools.org/doc/c18557/).

NMT, "The Ministries Case", Judgment, in *Trials of War Criminals before the Nuernberg Military Tribunals under Control Council Law No. 10: Nuernberg, October 1946–April 1949*, vol. XIII, US Government Printing Office, Washington, DC, 1952 (www.legal-tools.org/doc/eb20f6/).

NMT, "The Pohl Case", Judgment, 3 November 1947, in *Trials of War Criminals before the Nuernberg Military Tribunals under Control Council Law No. 10: Nuernberg, October 1946–April 1949*, vol. V, US Government Printing Office, Washington, DC, 1950 (www.legal-tools.org/doc/84ae05/).

13. Permanent Court of International Justice ('PCIJ')

PCIJ, *Case of the S.S. "Lotus"* (France v. Turkey), Judgment, Series A, No. 10, 7 September 1927 (www.legal-tools.org/doc/c54925/).

14. Special Court for Sierra Leone ('SCSL')

SCSL, Appeals Chamber, *Prosecutor v. Brima, Kamara and Kanu* (the AFRC Case), Judgment, SCSL-2004-16-A, 22 February 2008 (www.legal-tools.org/doc/4420ef/).

SCSL, Appeals Chamber, *Prosecutor v. Fofana and Kondewa* (the CDF Case), Judgment, SCSL-04-14-A, 28 May 2008 (www.legal-tools.org/doc/b31512/).

SCSL, Appeals Chamber, *Prosecutor v. Sesay, Kallon and Gbao* (the RUF Case), Judgment, SCSL-04-14-A, 26 October 2009 (www.legal-tools.org/doc/133b48/).

SCSL, Appeals Chamber, *Prosecutor v. Taylor*, Judgment, SCSL-03-01-A, 26 September 2013 (www.legal-tools.org/doc/3e7be5/).

SCSL, Trial Chamber, *Prosecutor v. Sesay, Kallon and Gbao* (the RUF Case) Judgment, SCSL-04-15-T, 2 March 2009 (www.legal-tools.org/doc/7f05b7/).

SCSL, Trial Chamber, *Prosecutor v. Taylor*, Judgment, SCSL-03-01-T, 18 May 2012 (www.legal-tools.org/doc/8075e7/).

15. Special Tribunal for Lebanon ('STL')

STL, Appeals Chamber, *Case against New TV S.A.L. and Karma Mohamed Tahsin al Khayat*, Decision on Interlocutory Appeal concerning Personal Jurisdiction in Contempt Proceedings, 2 October 2014 (www.legal-tools.org/doc/e8fbb1/).

STL, Appeals Chamber, *Interlocutory Decision on the Applicable Law: Criminal Association and Review of the Indictment*, STL-17-07/I/AC/R17bis, 18 October 2017 (www.legal-tools.org/doc/829cbe/).

STL, Appeals Chamber, *Interlocutory Decision on the Applicable Law: Terrorism, Conspiracy, Homicide, Perpetration, Cumulative Charging*, STL-11-01/I/AC/R176bis, 16 February 2011 (www.legal-tools.org/doc/ceebc3/).

16. Various National Courts

16.1. Argentina

Cámara Federal de Apelaciones de la Plata, *Jamie Lamont Smart et al.*, Appeal, Sentencia de la expediente 5838/III, 26 May 2011 (www.legal-tools.org/doc/9eeeb7/).

Cámara Federal Nacional de Apelaciones en lo Criminal y Correccional de la Capital Buenos Aires, Case of the Military Juntas, Judgment, 9 December 1985 (www.legal-tools.org/doc/83efcc/).

Chamber of Cassation of the Argentinian Supreme Court, Case of the Military Juntas, Judgment, 20 December 1986 (www.legal-tools.org/doc/149547/).

Corte Suprema de Justicia de la Nación, Simón, Julio Héctor y otros s/ privación ilegítima de la libertad, Causa no. 17.768 (Recurso de hecho), Expediente S. 1767. XXXVIII, 14 July 2005 (www.legal-tools.org/doc/6321f1/).

Tribunal Oral en lo Criminal Federal (Buenos Aires), Case of Poblete-Hlaczik (*Julio Héctor Simón*), Causas no. 1.056 and no. 1.207, 11 August 2006 (www.legal-tools.org/doc/fd1e32/).

Tribunal Oral en lo Criminal Federal No. 1 de San Martín, Case of Santiago Omar Riveros *et al.*, No. 2005/2044, 12 August 2009 (www.legal-tools.org/doc/106dbc/).

Tribunal Oral en lo Criminal Federal No. 1 de San Martín, Case of Victorio Derganz and Carlos José Fateche (*Juan Demetrio Luna*), Sentencia de primera instancia contra Juan Demetrio Luna, Causa no. 2203, 30 December 2011 (www.legal-tools.org/doc/0ea1a0/).

Tribunal Oral en lo Criminal Federal No. 5, ESMA Mega-trial (*Garcia Tallada, Manuel Jacinto, et al.*), Sentencia de primera instancia, Causa no. 1279, 28 December 2011 (www.legal-tools.org/doc/9aa896/).

16.2. Australia

High Court of Australia, Polyukhovich v. Commonwealth, 101 Australian Law Reports 545 (1991), 172 Commonwealth Law Reports 501, and 91 International Law Reports 1 (www.legal-tools.org/doc/b284c2/).

16.3. Austria

Supreme Court of Austria, Case of Cvjetković, Decision, Case 15Os99/94, 13 July 1994 (www.legal-tools.org/doc/44d3dc/).

Regional Court of Innsbruck, Judgment, 11 May 2017 (www.legal-tools.org/doc/abee9a/).

Regional Court of Linz, Judgment, 6 July 2016 (www.legal-tools.org/doc/d03778/).

16.4. Bangladesh

Bangladesh International Crimes Tribunal, *Chief Prosecutor v. Abdul Quader Molla*, ICT-BD 02 of 2012, Judgment, 5 February 2013 (www.legal-tools.org/doc/42e4c8/).

Bangladesh International Crimes Tribunal, *Chief Prosecutor v. Advocate Md. Shamsul Haque, S. M. Yusuf Ali, Md. Ashraf Hossain [absconded], Professor Sharif Ahamed alias Sharif Hossain [absconded], Md. Abdul Mannan [absconded], Md. Abdul Bari [absconded], Harun [absconded] and Md. Abul Hashem [absconded]*, ICT-BD 02 of 2015, Judgment, 18 July 2016 (www.legal-tools.org/doc/f11183/).

Bangladesh International Crimes Tribunal, *Chief Prosecutor v. Ali Ahsan Muhammad Mujahid*, ICT-BD 04 of 2012, Judgment, 17 July 2013 (www.legal-tools.org/doc/77d0d6/).

Bangladesh International Crimes Tribunal, *Chief Prosecutor v. (1) Ashrafuzzaman Khan @ Naeb Ali Khan [absconded] & Chowdhury Mueen Uddin [absconded]*, ICT-BD 01 of 2013, Judgment, 3 November 2013 (www.legal-tools.org/doc/2538dc/).

Bangladesh International Crimes Tribunal, *Chief Prosecutor v. Md. Abdul Alim @ M. A Alim*, ICT-BD 01 of 2012, Judgment, 9 October 2013 (www.legal-tools.org/doc/907c69/).

Bangladesh International Crimes Tribunal, *Chief Prosecutor v. Md. Abdul Jabbar Engineer*, ICT-BD 01 of 2014, Judgment, 24 February 2015 (www.legal-tools.org/doc/40deae/).

Bangladesh International Crimes Tribunal, *Chief Prosecutor v. Md. Forkan Mallik @ Forkan*, ICT-BD 03 of 2014, Judgment, 16 July 2015 (www.legal-tools.org/doc/55a064/).

Bangladesh International Crimes Tribunal, *Chief Prosecutor v. Md. Sakhawat Hossain, Md. Billal Hossain Biswas, Md. Lutfor Morol [died during trial], Md. Ibrahim Hossain alias Ghungur Ibrahim [absconded], Sheikh Mohammad Mujibur Rahman alias Mujibur Rahman [absconded], Md. A. Aziz Sardar son of late Ful Miah Sardar [absconded], Abdul Aziz Sardar son of late Ahmmad Sardar [absconded], Kazi Ohidul Islam alias Kazi Ohidus Salam [absconded], and Md. Abdul Khaleque Morol [absconded]*, ICT-BD 04 of 2015, Judgment, 10 August 2016 (www.legal-tools.org/doc/b1bbc7/).

Bangladesh International Crimes Tribunal, *Chief Prosecutor v. Mir Quasem Ali*, ICT-BD 03 of 2013, Judgment, 2 November 2014 (www.legal-tools.org/doc/2b3071/).

Bangladesh International Crimes Tribunal, *Chief Prosecutor v. Mohammed Kamaruzzaman*, ICT-BD 03 of 2012, Judgment, 9 May 2013 (www.legal-tools.org/doc/65ed5a/).

Bangladesh International Crimes Tribunal, *Chief Prosecutor v. Moulana Abdul Kalam Azad*, ICT-BD 05 of 2012, Judgment, 21 January 2013 (www.legal-tools.org/doc/3fdb60/).

Bangladesh International Crimes Tribunal, *Chief Prosecutor v. Moulana Abdus Sobhan*, ICT-BD 01 of 2014, Judgment, 18 February 2015 (www.legal-tools.org/doc/100a3b/).

Bangladesh International Crimes Tribunal, *Chief Prosecutor v. Professor Gholam Azam*, ICT-BD 06 of 2011, Judgment, 15 July 2013 (www.legal-tools.org/doc/436ed9/).

Bangladesh International Crimes Tribunal, *Chief Prosecutor v. Syed Md. Qaiser*, ICT-BD 04 of 2013, Judgment, 23 December 2014 (www.legal-tools.org/doc/f2e9a8/).

Bangladesh International Crimes Tribunal, *Chief Prosecutor v. Zahid Hossain Khokon @ M. A. Zahid @ Khokon Matubbar @ Khokon*, ICT-BD 04 of 2013, Judgment, 13 November 2014 (www.legal-tools.org/doc/2e7b53/).

16.5. Belgium

Cour d'Assises de l'Arrondissement Administratif de Bruxelles-Capitale, Case of Ntuyahaga, Judgment, 5 July 2007 (www.legal-tools.org/doc/cd8233/).

Cour d'Assises de l'Arrondissement Administratif de Bruxelles-Capitale, Case of Nzabonimana and Samuel Ndashyikirwa, Judgment, 29 June 2005 (www.legal-tools.org/doc/51c5bb/).

Cour d'Assises de Bruxelles, Case of Mukabutera, Mukangango, Ntezimana and Higaniro, Judgment, 8 June 2001 (www.legal-tools.org/doc/a70d94/).

Cour d'Assises de Bruxelles, Case of Nkezabera, Judgment, 1 December 2009 (www.legal-tools.org/doc/cbb892/).

16.6. Bosnia and Herzegovina

Cantonal Court in Mostar, *Nihad Vlahovljak et al.*, 1st Instance Verdict, Case 007-0-K-07-00 006, 8 August 2007 (www.legal-tools.org/doc/506c1b/).

Court of BiH, *Abduladhim Maktouf*, 2nd Instance Verdict, Case KPZ-32/05, 4 April 2006 (www.legal-tools.org/doc/0ad159/).

Court of BiH, *Božić Zdravko et al.*, 2nd Instance Verdict, Case X-KRZ-06/236, 5 October 2009 (www.legal-tools.org/doc/65c74d/).

Court of BiH, *Dušan Fuštar*, 1st Instance Verdict, Case X-KR06/2001-1, 21 April 2008 (www.legal-tools.org/doc/a3f13c/).

Court of BiH, *Milos Stupar et al.*, 2nd Instance Verdict, Case X-KRZ-05/24, 9 September 2009 (www.legal-tools.org/doc/9404de/).

Court of BiH, *Mirko Pekez et al.*, 2nd Instance Verdict, Case X-KRŽ-05/96-1, 5 May 2009 (www.legal-tools.org/doc/d92ed4/).

Court of BiH, *Mirko Todorović et al.*, 2nd Instance Verdict, Case X-KRŽ-07/382, 23 January 2009 (www.legal-tools.org/doc/d83346/).

Court of BiH, *Mitar Rašević et al.*, 1st Instance Verdict, Case X-KRZ-06/275, 28 February 2008 (www.legal-tools.org/doc/6a28b5/).

Court of BiH, *Mitar Rašević et al.*, 2nd Instance Verdict, Case X-KRZ-06/275, 6 November 2008 (www.legal-tools.org/doc/d8720a/).

Court of BiH, *Momir Savić*, 1st Instance Verdict, Case X-KR-07/478, 3 July 2009 (www.legal-tools.org/doc/1742d8/).

Court of BiH, *Nikola Andrun*, 2nd Instance Verdict, Case X-KRŽ-05/42, 19 August 2008 (www.legal-tools.org/doc/9e90bd/).

Court of BiH, *Petar Mitrovic*, 2nd Instance Verdict, Case X-KR-05/24-1, 7 September 2009 (www.legal-tools.org/doc/444ffa/).

Court of BiH, *Ranko Vuković et al.*, 2nd Instance Verdict, Case X-KR-06/180-2, 2 September 2008 (www.legal-tools.org/doc/e15578/).

Court of BiH, *Veiz Bjelić*, 1st Instance Verdict, Case X-KR-07/430-1, 28 March 2008 (www.legal-tools.org/doc/eeb752/).

Court of BiH, *Željko Lelek*, 2nd Instance Verdict, Case X-KRŽ-06/202, 12 January 2009 (www.legal-tools.org/doc/299be4/).

Court of BiH, *Željko Mejakić et al.*, 2nd Instance Verdict, Case X-KRŽ-06/200, 16 February 2009 (www.legal-tools.org/doc/c4d78a/).

Supreme Court of Republika Srpska, Case 118-0-Kz-06-000-018, 18 April 2006 (www.legal-tools.org/doc/4f6054/).

Supreme Court of Republika Srpska, Case 118-0-KZ-K-06-000-006, 22 February 2007 (www.legal-tools.org/doc/c89d1c/).

16.7. Canada

Court of Appeal of Ontario, *R. v. Ribic*, 2008 ONCA 790 (www.legal-tools.org/doc/d93112/).

Court of Appeal of Quebec, *Munyaneza v. R*, 2014 QCCA 906 (www.legal-tools.org/doc/9d2707/).

Superior Court of Ontario, Canada, *R. v. Mungwarere*, 2013 ONSC 4594 (www.legal-tools.org/doc/f68e84/).

Superior Court of Quebec, Criminal Division, *R. v. Munyaneza*, 2009 QCCS 4865 (www.legal-tools.org/doc/81e956/).

Supreme Court of Canada, *Her Majesty The Queen v. Imre Finta*, 1 *Supreme Court Reports* 701 (24 March 1994) (www.legal-tools.org/doc/f9c23e/).

Supreme Court of Canada, *Ezokola v. Canada*, 2013 SCC 40, 2 *Supreme Court Reports* 678, 19 July 2013 (www.legal-tools.org/doc/b8f5c7/).

Supreme Court of Canada, *R. v. Déry*, 2006 SCC 53, 2 *Supreme Court Reports* 669, 23 November 2006 (www.legal-tools.org/doc/96e28e/).

Superior Court of Montreal, *Her Majesty the Queen v. Munyaneza*, 500-73-002500-052, 20 November 2006 (www.legal-tools.org/doc/a15d98/).

16.8. Chile

Corte Suprema, Sala Penal, Case of Miguel Ángel Sandoval (*Juan Miguel Contreras Sepúlveda, et al.*), Rol no. 517-04, 17 November 2004 (www.legal-tools.org/doc/851a5a/).

Edición Suplementaria Suprema de Justicia, Case of José Manuel Contreras and Colonel Espinoza, Judgment, 12 November 1993 (www.legal-tools.org/doc/7eceb0/).

16.9. Colombia

Corte Suprema de Justicia, Case of Pueblo Bello (*Pedro Ogazza P.*), Recurso extraordinario de casación, Radicación 14851, Aprobado por acta no. 35, MP. Carlos Augusto Galvez Argote, 8 March 2001 (www.legal-tools.org/doc/3637ba/).

16.10. Croatia

County Court in Osijek, *Marguš and Dilber (Čepin)*, 1st Instance Verdict, Case K-33/06-412, 21 March 2007 (www.legal-tools.org/doc/0c41bc/).

County Court in Vukovar, *Ćurčić et al. (Borovo selo)*, 1st Instance Verdict, Case K-12/05, 14 December 2005 (www.legal-tools.org/doc/e702c6/).

Supreme Court of Croatia, *Tomislav Madi et al. (Cerna)*, 2nd Instance Verdict, Case I Kz 910/08-10, 25 March 2009 (www.legal-tools.org/doc/11892e/).

16.11. Denmark

Eastern Division of the Danish High Court, Case of Sarić, 25 November 1994 (www.legal-tools.org/doc/b65c87/).

Denmark, Supreme Court, Case of Sarić, 15 August 1995 (www.legal-tools.org/doc/a8de3a/)

16.12. East Timor

Court of Appeal, *Prosecutor v. dos Santos*, Judgment, Case 16/2001, 15 July 2003 (www.legal-tools.org/doc/d8d11e/).

Court of Appeal, *Prosecutor v. Soares*, Judgment, Case 11/2003, 17 February 2005 (www.legal-tools.org/doc/105fc2/).

Dili District Court, *Prosecutor v. Amati and Matos*, Decision on the Defendants' Motion on Defects in the Indictment, Case 12/2003, 11 November 2004 (www.legal-tools.org/doc/47ea51/).

Dili District Court, *Prosecutor v. de Carvalho*, Interlocutory Decision on Indictment, Case 10/2001, 27 January 2004 (www.legal-tools.org/doc/4bd0d3/).

Dili District Court, *Prosecutor v. Pedro*, Interlocutory Decision to Dismiss Amended Indictment, Case 1/2001, 22 May 2001 (www.legal-tools.org/doc/547fd0/).

Dili District Court, Trial Chamber, *Prosecutor v. Abilio Mendes Correia*, Judgment, Case 19/2001, 9 March 2004 (www.legal-tools.org/doc/6b03bf/).

Dili District Court, Trial Chamber, *Prosecutor v. Barros and Mendonca*, Judgment, Case 1/2004, 12 May 2005 (www.legal-tools.org/doc/43c772/).

Dili District Court, Trial Chamber, *Prosecutor v. Bere*, Judgment, Case 10/2000, 15 May 2001 (www.legal-tools.org/doc/7f265a/).

Dili District Court, Trial Chamber, *Prosecutor v. Cardoso*, Judgment, Case 04/2001, 5 April 2003 (www.legal-tools.org/doc/272392/).

Dili District Court, Trial Chamber, *Prosecutor v. Da Costa and Punef*, Judgment, Case 22/2003, 27 April 2005 (www.legal-tools.org/doc/8acf9a/).

Dili District Court, Trial Chamber, *Prosecutor v. da Costa Nunes*, Judgment, Case 1/2003, 10 December 2003 (www.legal-tools.org/doc/493119/).

Dili District Court, Trial Chamber, *Prosecutor v. Fernandes*, Judgment, Case 1/2000, 25 January 2000 (www.legal-tools.org/doc/e2e6d6/).

Dili District Court, Trial Chamber, *Prosecutor v. Franca Da Silva*, Judgment, Case 4a/2001, 5 December 2002 (www.legal-tools.org/doc/f1b9e9/).

Dili District Court, Trial Chamber, *Prosecutor v. Lao*, Judgment, Case 10/2003, 3 December 2004 (www.legal-tools.org/doc/17309a/).

Dili District Court, Trial Chamber, *Prosecutor v. Marques et al.*, Judgment, Case 09/2000, 11 December 2001 (www.legal-tools.org/doc/9e43e1/).

Dili District Court, Trial Chamber, *Prosecutor v. Martins and Goncalves*, Judgment, Case 11/2001, 13 November 2003 (www.legal-tools.org/doc/b77869/).

Dili District Court, Trial Chamber, *Prosecutor v. Maubere*, Judgment, Case 23/2003, 27 May 2004 (www.legal-tools.org/doc/9cf6f5/).

Dili District Court, Trial Chamber, *Prosecutor v. Pedro*, Judgment, Case 1/2001, 14 April 2005 (www.legal-tools.org/doc/99146b/).

Dili District Court, Trial Chamber, *Prosecutor v. Perreira*, Judgment, Case 34/2003, 27 April 2005 (www.legal-tools.org/doc/5ce1a8/).

Dili District Court, Trial Chamber, *Prosecutor v. Rudolfo Alves Correia*, Judgment, Case 27/2003, 25 April 2005 (www.legal-tools.org/doc/4941ef/).

Dili District Court, Trial Chamber, *Prosecutor v. Soares*, Judgment, Case 11/2003, 11 December 2003 (www.legal-tools.org/doc/96331a/).

Dili District Court, Trial Chamber, *Prosecutor v. Sufa*, Judgment, Case 4a/2003, 25 November 2004 (www.legal-tools.org/doc/48777b/).

Dili District Court, Trial Chamber, *Prosecutor v. Tacaqui*, Judgment, Case 20/2001, 12 September 2004 (www.legal-tools.org/doc/864bbe/).

Dili District Court, Trial Chamber, *Prosecutor v. Umbertus Ena and Carlos Ena*, Judgment, Case 5/2002, 23 March 2004 (www.legal-tools.org/doc/ec8173/).

16.13. Ethiopia

Ethiopian Federal High Court, *Special Prosecutor v. Debela Dinsa et al.*, File 912/89 (www.legal-tools.org/doc/5d99af/).

Ethiopian Federal High Court, *Special Prosecutor v. Kassayie Aragaw et al.*, File 923/89 (www.legal-tools.org/doc/f36eb2/).

Ethiopian Federal High Court, *Special Prosecutor v. Mengistu and Others*, File 1/87, 12 December 2006 (www.legal-tools.org/doc/671b06/).

Ethiopian Federal Supreme Court, *Special Prosecutor v. Mengistu and Others*, File 30181, 26 May 2008 (www.legal-tools.org/doc/60031b/).

16.14. Finland

District Court of Kanta-Häme, Judgment, R 16/214, 22 March 2016 (www.legal-tools.org/doc/546cd9/).

District Court of Pirkanmaa, Judgment, R 16/1304, 18 March 2016 (www.legal-tools.org/doc/96a1b2/).

District Court of Pirkanmaa, Judgment, 24 May 2017 (www.legal-tools. org/doc/b01bcf/).

District Court of Porvoos, Case of Basaramba, Judgment, Case R 09/ 404, 11 June 2010 (www.legal-tools.org/doc/f266fe/).

Supreme Court of Finland, Case of Basaramba, Judgment, 22 October 2012 (www.legal-tools.org/doc/00b95b/).

16.15. France

Commission des Recours des Réfugiés, *Rwamucyo*, 420926, 16 December 2003 (www.legal-tools.org/doc/236489/).

Cour d'Assises du Bas-Rhin, Case of Ben Saïd, Judgment, 15 December 2008 (www.legal-tools.org/doc/48acce/).

Cour d'Assises de la Meurthe et Moselle, Case of Ben Saïd, Judgment, 24 September 2010 (www.legal-tools.org/doc/682080/).

Cour d'Assises de Paris, Case of Astiz, Judgment, 16 March 1990 (www. legal-tools.org/doc/888d10/).

Cour d'Assises de Paris, Case of Ngenzi and Barahirwa, Judgment, 7 July 2016 (www.legal-tools.org/doc/b74c0f/).

Cour d'Assises de Paris, *Affaire Pascal Senyamuhara Safari alias Pascal Simbikangwa*, Judgment 13/0033, 14 March 2014 (www.legal-tools.org/ doc/c04bcc/).

Cour d'Assises de la Seine-Saint-Denis, *Affaire Pascal Senyamuhara Safari alias Pascal Simbikangwa*, Judgment, 3 December 2016 (www.legal-tools.org/doc/07161c/).

Cour de Cassation, Chambre Criminelle, Case of Ould Dah, Judgment, no. de pourvoi 02-85379 (www.legal-tools.org/doc/cb459b/).

16.16. Germany

Bundergerichthof, Case StR 57/17, 27 July 2017 (www.legal-tools.org/ doc/5d2ee7/).

Bundesgerichthof, Case of Oskar Gröning, Case 3 StR 49/16, 20 September 2016 (www.legal-tools.org/doc/4abce8/).

Bundesgerichtshof, Case of Jorgić, Case 3 StR 215/98, 30 April 1999 (www.legal-tools.org/doc/85b784/).

Bundesgerichtshof, Case of Kušljić, Case 3 StR 244/00, 21 February 2001 (www.legal-tools.org/doc/bb9913/).

Bundesgerichtshof, Case of Sokolović, Case 3 StR 372/00, 21 February 2001 (www.legal-tools.org/doc/89fb79/).

Bundesgerichtshof, Case of Rwabukombe, Case 3 StR 575/14, 21 May 2015 (www.legal-tools.org/doc/368fdd/).

Bundesverfassungsgericht, Case of Jorgić, Case 2 BvR 1290/99, 12 December 2000 (www.legal-tools.org/doc/5ef246/).

Kammergericht Berlin, Case of Rami K., 1 March 2017 (www.legal-tools.org/doc/d994aa/).

Landgericht Lüneburg, Case of Oskar Gröning, Case 27 Ks 1191 Js 98402113 (9/14), 15 July 2015 (www.legal-tools.org/doc/057092/).

Oberlandesgericht Dusseldorf, Case of Jorgić, Case 2 StE 8/96, 26 September 1997 (www.legal-tools.org/doc/853a97/).

Oberlandesgericht Frankfurt am Main, Case of Rwabukombe (no. 2), Case 4-3 StE 4/10-4-1/15, 29 December 2015 (www.legal-tools.org/doc/bd14c5/).

Oberlandesgericht Frankfurt am Main, Case of Ladjedvardi, Case 5-3 StE 2/16-4-1/16, 12 July 2016 (www.legal-tools.org/doc/f44466/).

Oberlandesgericht Frankfurt am Main, Case of Rwabukombe, Case 5-3 StE 4/10-4-3/10, 18 February 2014 (www.legal-tools.org/doc/8c79bc/).

Oberlandesgericht Frankfurt am Main, Case of Abdelkarim El B., Case 5-3 StE 4/16-4-3/16, 8 November 2016 (www.legal-tools.org/doc/57c158/).

Oberlandesgericht Stuttgart, Case of Murwanashyaka and Musoni, Case 5-3 StE 6/10, 28 September 2015 (www.legal-tools.org/doc/af8e31/).

Oberlandesgericht Stuttgart, Case of Suliman Al-S., 20 September 2017 (www.legal-tools.org/doc/c123aa/).

16.17. Guatemala

Corte de Apelaciones de Cobán, Case of Río Negro Massacre (*Macario Alvarado Toj, et al.*), Expediente 96-2008, 24 September 2008 (www.legal-tools.org/doc/4a04d2/).

Tribunal Primero de Sentencia Penal, Case of Dos Erres Massacre (*Roberto Aníbal Rivera Martínez, et al.*), Sentencia de primera instancia, Narcoactividad y delitos contra el ambiente, C-01076-2010-00003, Oficial 1°, 2 August 2011 (www.legal-tools.org/doc/31b80a/).

Tribunal Tercero de Sentencia Penal, Case of Myrna Mack (*Edgar Augusto Godoy, Juan Valencia Osorio, and Juan Guillermo Oliva*), Sentencia de primera instancia, Narcoactividad y delitos contra el ambiente, C-5-99, Oficial 3ro., 3 October 2002 (www.legal-tools.org/doc/70159e/).

16.18. Hong Kong

High Court of the Hong Kong Special Administrative Region, Court of First Instance, HCAL 132/2006, 18 February 2008 (www.legal-tools.org/doc/52a68d/).

16.19. Italy

Corte di Assise di Roma, Case of Astiz, Judgment, 14 March 2007 (www.legal-tools.org/doc/e7a51f/).

Corte di Assise di Roma, Case of Bermúdez *et al.*, Judgment, 17 January 2017 (www.legal-tools.org/doc/785768/).

Corte di Assise di Appello, Case of Astiz, Judgment, 24 April 2008 (www.legal-tools.org/doc/c4eda1/).

La Corte Supreme Di Cassazione, Case of Astiz, Judgment, no. 39.595/2008, 26 February 2009 (www.legal-tools.org/doc/e3b717/).

16.20. Netherlands

Court of Appeal, The Hague, Case ECLI:NL:GHDHA:2015:1082, 30 April 2015 (www.legal-tools.org/doc/fd647c/).

Court of Appeal, The Hague, Case ECLI:NL:GHSHE:2017:1760, 21 April 2017 (www.legal-tools.org/doc/4211df/).

Court of Appeal, The Hague, Cases LJN AZ9365 and LJN AZ9366, 29 January 2007 (www.legal-tools.org/doc/7a6292/).

Court of Appeal, The Hague, Case LJN BA6734, 9 May 2007 (www.legal-tools.org/doc/1e1b4b/).

Court of Appeal, The Hague, Case LJN BC1757, 18 December 2007 (www.legal-tools.org/doc/cec56c/).

Court of Appeal, The Hague, Case LJN BC7373, 10 March 2008 (www.legal-tools.org/doc/5990af/).

Court of Appeal, The Hague, Case LJN BJ2796, 16 July 2009 (www.legal-tools.org/doc/dc714e/).

Court of Appeal, The Hague, Case LJN BR0686, 7 July 2011 (www.legal-tools.org/doc/b7a8c9/).

District Court, The Hague, Case ECLI:NL:RBDHA:2013:8710, 1 March 2013 (www.legal-tools.org/doc/3f41c2/).

District Court, The Hague, Case ECLI:NL:RBDHA:2017:16383, 15 December 2017 (www.legal-tools.org/doc/412f02/).

District Court, The Hague, Case LJN AO7178, 7 April 2004 (www.legal-tools.org/doc/6a9117/).

District Court, The Hague, Cases LJN AU4373 and LJN AV1163, 14 October 2005 (www.legal-tools.org/doc/94c8b1/).

District Court, The Hague, Case LJN AX6406, 23 December 2005 (www.legal-tools.org/doc/35538e/).

District Court, The Hague, Case LJN AY5160, 6 June 2006 (www.legal-tools.org/doc/b13477/).

District Court, The Hague, Case LJN BA9575, 25 June 2007 (www.legal-tools.org/doc/cac017/).

District Court, The Hague, Case LJN BI2444, 23 March 2009 (www.legal-tools.org/doc/5071f2/).

District Court, The Hague, Cases LJN BU9716 and BU7200, 21 October 2011 (www.legal-tools.org/doc/255180/).

Supreme Court, Case, ECLI:NL:HR:2008:BD6568, 21 October 2008 (www.legal-tools.org/doc/cb3eae/).

Supreme Court, Cases ECLI:NL:HR:2017:574 through 2017:578, 4 April 2017 (www.legal-tools.org/doc/032ef2/).

Supreme Court, Case LJN BG1476, 8 July 2008 (www.legal-tools.org/doc/5f70ca/).

Supreme Court, Case LJN BG4822, 30 June 2009 (www.legal-tools.org/doc/ae408d/).

Supreme Court, Case LJN BK8132, 19 April 2010 (www.legal-tools.org/doc/40296a/).

Supreme Court, Case LJN BR6598, 8 November 2011 (www.legal-tools.org/doc/35f07b/).

16.21. Norway

Borgarting Court of Appeal, Case of Bugingo, Judgment, Case LB-2013-41556, 16 January 2015 (www.legal-tools.org/doc/d0cc92/).

Borgarting Court of Appeal, Case of Repak, Judgment, Case LB-2009-24039, 12 April 2010 (www.legal-tools.org/doc/6fd75f/).

Oslo Disctrict Court, Case of Bugingo, Judgment, Case 12–106377MED-OTIR/03, 15 February 2013, p. 26 (www.legal-tools.org/doc/e6c9be/)

Oslo District Court, Case of Repak, Judgment, Case 08-018985MED-OTIR/08, 2 December 2008 (www.legal-tools.org/doc/19cd6d/).

Supreme Court of Norway, Case of Repak, Judgment, Case HR-2010-2057-P, 3 December 2010 (www.legal-tools.org/doc/188d4b/).

16.22. Peru

Corte Superior de Justicia de Lima, Primera Sala Penal Transitoria, Cases of Barrios Altos, La Cantuta, and SIE Basements (*Alberto Fujimori Fujimori*), Judgment, Expediente AV 19-2001, 30 December 2009 (www.legal-tools.org/doc/5c51d9/).

Corte Superior de Justicia de Lima, Sala Penal Especial, Cases of Barrios Altos, La Cantuta, and SIE Basements (*Alberto Fujimori Fujimori*), Judgment, Expediente AV 19-2001, 7 April 2009 (www.legal-tools.org/doc/571949/).

Sala Penal Nacional, Case against Leaders of the Shining Path (*Manuel Rubén Abimael Guzmán Reynoso, et al.*), Expediente 560 03, 13 October 2006 (www.legal-tools.org/doc/6435af/).

16.23. Serbia

Belgrade District Court, *Anton Lekaj*, 1st Instance Verdict, Case K.V. 4/05, 18 September 2006 (www.legal-tools.org/doc/33b891/).

Belgrade District Court, *Ovčara*, 1st Instance Verdict, Case K.V. 4/2006, 12 March 2009 (www.legal-tools.org/doc/b236a6/).

Belgrade District Court, *Škorpioni*, 1st Instance Verdict, Case K.V. 6/2005, 10 April 2007 (www.legal-tools.org/doc/d2c374/).

Belgrade District Court, *Zvornik*, 1st Instance Verdict, Case K.V. 5/2005, 12 June 2008 (www.legal-tools.org/doc/9679f4/).

Belgrade High Court, WCD, *Grujic and Popovic (Zvornik II)*, 1st Instance Verdict, Case K.Po2 28/2010, 22 November 2010 (www.legal-tools.org/doc/874ecd/).

Supreme Court of the Republic of Serbia, *Sinan Morina*, 2nd Instance Verdict, Case Kz. I RZ 1/08, 3 March 2009 (www.legal-tools.org/doc/21633c/).

Supreme Court of the Republic of Serbia, *Škorpioni*, 2nd Instance Verdict, Case Kz. I r.z. 2/07, 13 June 2008 (www.legal-tools.org/doc/c72d4e/).

War Crimes Department of the Appellate Court in Belgrade, *Suva Reka*, 2nd Instance Verdict, Case Kž1 Po2 4/2010, 30 June 2010 (www.legal-tools.org/doc/b8cbb4/).

16.24. Spain

Audiencia Nacional, Case of Scilingo, Judgment, Case No. 16/2005, 19 April 2005 (www.legal-tools.org/doc/d042b3/).

Supreme Court of Spain, Case of Scilingo, Judgment, 3 July 2007 (www.legal-tools.org/doc/7eb774/).

16.25. Sweden

District Court of Blekinge, Case of Abdulkareem, Judgment, 6 December 2016 (www.legal-tools.org/doc/860452/).

District Court of Gothenburg, Case of al-Mandlawi and Sultan, Judgment, 14 December 2015 (www.legal-tools.org/doc/4f54c1/).

District Court of Huddinge, Case of Droubi, Judgment, 11 May 2016 (www.legal-tools.org/doc/59def0/).

District Court of Stockholm, Case of Arklöv, Judgment, 18 December 2006 (www.legal-tools.org/doc/9672e6/).

District Court of Stockholm, Case of Berinkindi, Judgment, 16 May 2016 (www.legal-tools.org/doc/baac2c/).

District Court of Stockholm, Case of Makitan, Judgment, 8 April 2011 (www.legal-tools.org/doc/e83399/).

District Court of Stockholm, Case of Martinović, Judgment, 20 January 2012 (www.legal-tools.org/doc/be8892/).

District Court of Stockholm, Case of Mbanenande, Judgment, 20 June 2013 (www.legal-tools.org/doc/51756c/).

District Court of Södertörn, Case of Abdullah, Judgment, 25 September 2017 (www.legal-tools.org/doc/6a513a/).

Scania and Blekinge Court of Appeal, B-3187-16, 11 April 2017 (www.legal-tools.org/doc/897810/).

Svea Court of Appeal, Case of Droubi, Judgment, 5 August 2016 (www.legal-tools.org/doc/a3f045/).

Svea Court of Appeal, Case of Berinkindi, Judgment, 15 February 2017 (www.legal-tools.org/doc/3936b6/).

Svea Court of Appeal, Case of Martinović, Judgment, 19 December 2012 (www.legal-tools.org/doc/be8892/).

Svea Court of Appeal, Case of Mbanenande, Judgment, Case Nr B 6659-13, 19 June 2014 (www.legal-tools.org/doc/66279c/).

Stockholm City Court, B3787-16, 16 February 2017 (www.legal-tools.org/doc/e5c4ef/).

16.26. Switzerland

Geneva Military Appeals Tribunal, Case of Niyonteze, Judgment, 26 May 2000 (www.legal-tools.org/doc/fe2edc/).

High Military Appeals Court, Case of Niyonteze, Judgment, 27 April 2001 (www.legal-tools.org/doc/ac0342/).

Lausanne Military Tribunal Division I, Case of "G", Judgment, 18 April 1997 (www.legal-tools.org/doc/d3c048/).

Lausanne Military Tribunal Division II, Case of Niyonteze, Judgment, 30 April 1999 (www.legal-tools.org/doc/bb9da0/).

Tribunal Militaire de Cassation, Case of "G", Judgment, 5 September 1997 (www.legal-tools.org/doc/08fb2f/).

16.27. United Kingdom

Central Criminal Court of England and Wales, Case of Lama, Judgment, 7 September 2016 (www.legal-tools.org/doc/03b2c8/).

Court of Appeal, Criminal Division, Case 200505339/D3, Judgment, 7 February 2007 (www.legal-tools.org/doc/e047b9/).

High Court of Justice, Queen's Bench Division, Administrative Court, *Government of Rwanda v. Nteziryayo and others*, [2017] EWHC 1912 (Admin), 28 July 2017 (www.legal-tools.org/doc/c4b49e/).

16.28. United States

United States Court of Appeals for the Eleventh Circuit, *United States of America v. Roy M. Belfast*, Case 09-10461-AA, 18 September 2009 (www.legal-tools.org/doc/221838-1/).

United States Supreme Court, *Fedorenko v. United States*, 499 U.S. 490, 31 January 1981 (www.legal-tools.org/doc/c7c51e/).

16.29. Uruguay

Juez Penal 19° Turno, Case "Condor Plan" (*José Nino Gavazzo Pereira, et al.*), Sentencia 036, Ficha 98-247/2006, 26 March 2009 (www.legal-tools.org/doc/dee268/).

Tribunal de Apelaciones en lo Penal de Tercer Turno, *Juan Carlos Blanco Estradé*, Appeal, IUE 17-414/2003, Sentencio no. 22, 16 February 2012 (www.legal-tools.org/doc/c0eac8/).

BIBLIOGRAPHY

Aegis Trust, *Suspected War Criminals and Génocidaires in the UK: Proposals to Strengthen Our Laws*, Laxton, UK, 2009.

Agbor, Avitus A., "The Substantial Contribution Requirement: The Unfortunate Outcome of an Illogical Construction and Incorrect Understanding of Article 6(1) of the Statute of the ICTR", in *International Criminal Law Review*, 2012, vol. 12, no. 2, pp. 155–92.

Aksenova, Marina, *Complicity in International Criminal Law*, Hart, Oxford, 2016.

Aksenova, Marina, "The Modes of Liability at the ICC, The Labels that Don't Always Stick", in *International Criminal Law Review*, 2015, vol. 15, no. 4, pp. 629–64.

Ambos, Kai, "Article 25", in Otto Triffterer (ed.), *Commentary on the Rome Statute of the International Criminal Court: Observers' Notes, Article by Article*, C.H. Beck, Munich, 2008.

Ambos, Kai, "The *Fujimori* Judgment: A President's Responsibility for Crimes Against Humanity as Indirect Perpetrators by Virtue of an Organized Power Apparatus", in *Journal of International Criminal Justice*, 2011, vol. 9, no. 1, pp. 137–58.

Ambos, Kai, "The German Rwabukombe Case: The Federal Court's Interpretation of Co-perpetration and the Genocidal Intent to Destroy", in *Journal of International Criminal Justice*, 2016, vol. 14, no. 5, pp. 1221–34.

Ambos, Kai, "Individual Liability for Macrocriminality: A Workshop, A Symposium and the Katanga Trial Judgment of 7 March 2014", in *Journal of International Criminal Justice*, 2014, vol. 12, no. 2, pp. 219–229.

Ambos, Kai, *Treatise on International Criminal Law, vol. 1, Foundations and General Part*, Oxford University Press, Oxford, 2013.

Amnesty International, *Germany: End Impunity through Universal Jurisdiction*, London, 2008.

Andreadis-Papadimitriou, Pavlos, "Assistance in Mass Murder under Systems of Ill-treatment: The Case of Oskar Gröning", in *Journal of International Criminal Justice*, 2017, vol. 15, no. 1, pp. 157–74.

Aneme, Girmachew Alemu, "The Anatomy of Special Prosecutor v. Colonel Mengistu Hailemariam *et al.* (1994–2008)", in *International Journal of Ethiopian Studies*, 2009, vol. 4, no. 1/2, pp. 1–53.

Arnold, Roberta, "Conclusions", in Roberta Arnold and Noëlle Quénivet (eds.), *International Humanitarian Law and Human Rights Law: Towards a New Merger in International Law*, Brill/Martinus Nijhoff, Leiden, 2008.

Ashworth, Andrew, *Principles of Criminal Law*, 2nd ed., Oxford University Press, Oxford, 1995.

Bassiouni, M. Cherif, *Introduction to International Criminal Law: Second Revised Edition*, Martinus Nijhoff, Leiden, 2012.

Bassiouni, M. Cherif, and Edward M. Wise, *Aut dedere aut judicare: The Duty to Extradite or Prosecute in International Law*, Brill, The Hague, 1995.

Boas, Gideon, James L. Bischoff, and Natalie L. Reid, *Forms of Responsibility in International Criminal Law, Volume I*, Cambridge University Press, Cambridge, 2007.

Botte-Kerrison, Auriane, "Responsibility for Bystanders in Mass Crimes: Towards a Duty to Rescue in International Criminal Justice", in *International Criminal Law Review*, 2017, vol. 17, no. 5, pp. 879–908.

Boyle, Alan, and Christine Chinkin, *The Making of International Law*, Oxford University Press, Oxford, 2007.

Brooks, Rosa Ehrenreich, "Law in the Heart of Darkness: Atrocity and Duress", in *Virginia Journal of International Law*, 2003, vol. 43, no. 3, pp. 861–88.

Brownlie, Ian, *Principles of Public International Law*, 4th ed., Clarendon Press, Oxford, 1990.

Brownlie, Ian, *The Rule of Law in International Affairs: International Law at the Fiftieth Anniversary of the United Nations*, Kluwer Law International, Alphen aan den Rijn, Netherlands, 1998.

Carcano, Andrea, "On Fragmentation and Precedents in International Criminal Law: Possible Lessons from Recent Jurisprudence on

Aiding and Abetting Liability", in *Journal of International Criminal Justice*, 2016, vol. 14, no. 4, pp. 771–92.

Cassese, Antonio, *Cassese's International Criminal Law*, 3rd ed., rev. by Antonio Cassese, Paola Gaeta, Laure Baig, Mary Fan, Christopher Gosnell, and Alex Whiting, Oxford University Press, Oxford, 2013.

CHEAH, Wui Ling and Vormbaum, Moritz, "British War Crimes Trials in Europe and Asia, 1945–1949: A Comparative Study", in *Leiden Journal of International Law*, 2018, vol. 31, no. 3, pp 669-692.

Clark, Janine, "'Specific Direction' and the Fragmentation of International Jurisprudence on Aiding and Abetting: Perišić and Beyond", in *International Criminal Law Review*, 2015, vol. 15, no. 3, pp. 411–51.

Clark, Roger S., "Crimes against Humanity at Nuremberg", in George Ginsburgs and V.N. Kudriavtsev (eds.), *The Nuremberg Trial and International Law*, Kluwer Academic, Dordrecht, Netherlands, 1990.

Clarke, Robert C., "Together Again? Customary Law and Control over the Crime", in *Criminal Law Forum*, 2015, vol. 26, no. 3, pp. 457–95.

Cohen, David, *Indifference and Accountability: The United Nations and the Politics of International Justice in East Timor*, Special Report 9, East-West Center, Honolulu, 2006.

Commission on the Responsibility of the Authors of the War and on Enforcement of Penalties: Report Presented to the Preliminary Peace Conference, in *American Journal of International Law*, 1920, vol. 14, no. 1/2.

Conot, Robert, *Justice at Nuremberg*, Basic Books, New York, 2009.

Crawford, James, "The Drafting of the Rome Statute", in Philippe Sands (ed.), *From Nuremberg to The Hague: The Future of International Criminal Justice*, Cambridge University Press, Cambridge, 2003.

Cryer, Robert, "Imputation and Complicity in Common Law States: A (Partial) View from England and Wales", in *Journal of International Criminal Justice*, 2014, vol. 12, no. 2, pp. 267–81.

Cryer, Robert, Hakan Friman, Darryl Robinson, and Elisabeth Wilmhurst, *An Introduction to International Criminal Law and Procedure*, 2nd ed., Cambridge University Press, Cambridge, 2010.

Cupido, Marjolein, "Common Purpose Liability Versus Joint Perpetration: A Practical View on the ICC's Hierarchy of Liability Theories", in *Leiden Journal of International Law*, 2016, vol. 29, no. 3, pp. 897–915.

Currie, Robert J., and Joseph Rikhof, *International & Transnational Criminal Law*, 2nd ed., Irwin Law, Toronto, 2013.

Currie, Robert J., and Ion Stancu, "*R. v. Munyaneza*: Pondering Canada's First Core Crimes Conviction", in *International Criminal Law Review*, 2010, vol. 10, no. 3, pp. 829–53.

Damgaard, Ciara, *Individual Criminal Responsibility for Core International Crimes: Selected Pertinent Issues*, Springer, Berlin-Heidelberg, 2008.

Danner, Allison M., and Jenny Martinez, "Guilty Associations: Joint Criminal Enterprise, Command Responsibility, and the Development of International Criminal Law", in *California Law Review*, 2005, vol. 93, no. 1, pp. 75–169.

Darcy, Shane, "Assistance, direction and control: Untangling international judicial opinion on individual and State responsibility for war crimes by non-State actors", International Review of the Red Cross (2014), vol. 96, no. 893, pp. 243–273.

Darcy, Shane, *Collective Responsibility and Accountability under International Law*, Transnational Publishers, Leiden, 2007.

de Minicis, Filippo, "A Unitary Theory Is Both Viable and Preferable", blog of James G. Stewart, 11 October 2017.

Den Heijer, Maarten, "Whose Rights and Which Rights? The Continuing Story of Non-Refoulement under the European Convention on Human Rights", in *European Journal of Migration and Law*, 2008, vol. 10, no. 3, pp. 277–314.

De Vos, Dieneke, "Corporate Accountability: Dutch Court Convicts Former 'Timber Baron' of War Crimes in Liberia", European University Institute, 24 April 2017.

Di Amato, Astolfo, *Criminal Law in Italy*, Kluwer International, Alphen aan den Rijn, Netherlands, 2011.

Due Process of Law Foundation, *Digest of Latin American Jurisprudence on International Crimes, Volume I*, Washington, DC, 2010.

Due Process of Law Foundation, *Digest of Latin American Jurisprudence on International Crimes, Volume II*, Washington, DC, 2013.

Einarsen, Terje, *The Concept of Universal Crimes in International Law*, Torkel Opsahl Academic EPublisher, Oslo, 2012.

Einarsen, Terje, "New Frontiers of International Criminal Law: Towards a Concept of Universal Crimes", in *Bergen Journal of Criminal Law and Criminal Justice*, 2013, vol. 1, no. 1, pp. 1–21.

Einarsen, Terje, "Prosecuting Aggression through Other Universal Core Crimes at the International Criminal Court", in Leila N. Sadat (ed.), *Seeking Accountability for the Unlawful Use of Force*, Cambridge University Press, Cambridge, 2018, pp. 337–85.

Epps, Valerie, "The Soldier's Obligation to Die When Ordered to Shoot Civilians or Face Death Himself", in *New England Law Review*, 2003, vol. 37, no. 4, pp. 987–1013.

Eser, Albin, "Individual Criminal Responsibility", in A. Cassese, P. Gaeta, and J.R.W.D. Jones (eds.), *The Rome Statute of the International Criminal Court: A Commentary*, vol. I, Oxford University Press, Oxford, 2002.

Eser, Albin, "Questions from the Unconvinced", blog of James G. Stewart, 14 October 2017.

Evans, Gareth, *The Responsibility to Protect: Ending Mass Atrocity Crimes Once and for All*, Brookings Institution Press, Washington, DC, 2008.

Finnin, Sarah, *Elements of Accessorial Modes of Liability: Article 25(3)(b) and (c) of the Rome Statute of the International Criminal Court*, Martinus Nijhoff, Leiden, 2012.

Fletcher, George P., *The Grammar of Criminal Law: American, Comparative, and International*, vol. 1, *Foundations*, Oxford University Press, Oxford, 2007.

Fletcher, George P., *Rethinking Criminal Law*, Little, Brown, Boston, 1978.

Fletcher, George P., "The Theory of Criminal Liability and International Criminal Law", in *Journal of International Criminal Justice*, 2012, vol. 10, no. 5, pp. 1029–44.

Fletcher, George P., and Jens David Ohlin, "Reclaiming Fundamental Principles of Criminal Law in the Darfur Case", in *Journal of International Criminal Justice*, 2005, vol. 3, no. 3, pp. 539–61.

Fletcher, Laurel, "From Indifference to Engagement: Bystanders and International Criminal Justice", in *Michigan Journal of International Law*, 2005, vol. 26, no. 4, pp. 1013–95.

Gallant, Kenneth S., *The Principle of Legality in International and Comparative Criminal Law*, Cambridge University Press, Cambridge, 2009.

Gil Gil, Alicia, "The Flaws of the *Scilingo* Judgment", in *Journal of International Criminal Justice*, 2005, vol. 3, no. 5, pp. 1082–91.

Gil Gil, Alicia, and Elena Maculan, "Current Trends in the Definition of 'Perpetrator' by the International Criminal Court: From the Decision on the Confirmation of Charges in the *Lubanga* Case to the *Katanga* Judgment", in *Leiden Journal of International Law*, 2015, vol. 28, no. 2, pp. 349–71.

Goldsmith, Jack L., and Eric A. Posner, *The Limits of International Law*, Oxford University Press, Oxford, 2005.

Gordon, Gregory S., *Atrocity Speech Law: Foundation, Fragmentation, Fruition*, Oxford University Press, Oxford, 2017.

Granik, Maria, "Indirect Perpetration Theory: A Defence", in *Leiden Journal of International Law*, 2015, vol. 28, no. 4, pp. 977–92.

Gray, Christine, *International Law and the Use of Force*, 3rd ed., Oxford University Press, Oxford, 2008.

Guilfoyle, Daniel, *International Criminal Law*, Oxford University Press, Oxford, 2016.

Hallevy, Gabriel, *The Matrix of Derivative Criminal Liability*, Springer, Heidelberg, 2012.

Harrendorf, Stefan, "How Can Criminology Contribute to an Explanation of International Crimes?", in *Journal of International Criminal Justice*, 2014, vol. 12, no. 2, pp. 231–52.

Hart, H.L.A., *The Concept of Law*, 2nd ed., Oxford University Press, Oxford, 1994.

Hart, H.L.A., *Punishment and Responsibility: Essays in the Philosophy of Law*, Clarendon Press, Oxford, 1968.

Hawking, Stephen, *A Brief History of Time*, Bantam Books, New York, 1988.

Heller, Kevin Jon, *The Nuremberg Military Tribunals and the Origins of International Criminal Law*, Oxford University Press, Oxford, 2012.

Heller, Kevin Jon, "'Taking a Consenting Part': The Lost Mode of Participation", in *Loyola of Los Angeles International & Comparative Law Review*, 2017, vol. 39, no. 1, pp. 247–58.

Heller, Kevin Jon, "What Is an International Crime? (A Revisionist History)", in *Harvard International Law Journal*, 2017, vol. 58, no. 2, pp. 353–420.

Hirst, Megan, and Howard Varney, *Justice Abandoned? An Assessment of the Serious Crimes Process in East Timor*, Occasional Paper Series, International Center for Transitional Justice, 2005.

Horder, Jeremy, *Ashworth's Principles of Criminal Law*, 8th ed., Oxford University Press, Oxford, 2016.

Human Rights Watch, *These Are the Crimes We Are Fleeing: Justice for Syria in Swedish and German Courts*, October 2017.

Human Rights Watch, "US: Justice Dept. Brings First Charges for Torture Abroad", 6 December 2006.

Husabø, Erling Johannes, and Ingvild Bruce, *Fighting Terrorism through Multilevel Criminal Legislation: Security Council Resolution 1373, the EU Framework Decision on Combating Terrorism and their Implementation in Nordic, Dutch and German Criminal Law*, Brill/Martinus Nijhoff, Leiden, 2009.

Ingle, Jessie, "Aiding and Abetting by Omission before the International Criminal Tribunals", in *Journal of International Criminal Justice*, 2016, vol. 14, no. 4, pp. 747–69.

International Association of Penal Law (IAPL/AIDP), "History of the International Association of Penal Law".

International Criminal Law Services, *International Criminal Law & Practice Training Materials –Module 9: Modes of Liability: Commission and Participation*, The Hague, 2011.

Jackson, Miles, "The Attribution of Responsibility and Modes of Liability in International Criminal Law", in *Leiden Journal of International Law*, 2016, vol. 29, no. 3, pp. 879–95.

Jackson, Miles, *Complicity in International Law*, Oxford University Press, Oxford, 2015.

Jackson, Robert H. (United States Representative to the International Conference on Military Trials, London, 31 July 1945), "Notes on Proposed Definition of 'Crimes'", 1945, published by the Avalon Project of Yale University Law School.

Jacobsen, Jørn, "Constitutions and Criminal Law Reform", in *Bergen Journal of Criminal Law and Criminal Justice*, 2017, vol. 5, no. 1, pp. 18–36.

Jacobsen, Jørn, "Norway: Three Codes, Three (Somewhat) Different Solutions", blog of James G. Stewart, 8 October 2017.

Jäger, Herbert, *Makrokriminalität: Studien zur Kriminologie kollektiver Gewalt*, Suhrkamp, Frankfurt am Main, 1989.

Jain, Neha, "The Control Theory in International Criminal Law", in *Chicago Journal of International Law*, 2011, vol. 12, no. 1, pp. 152–200.

Jørgensen, Nina H.B., *The Responsibility of States for International Crimes*, Oxford University Press, Oxford, 2000.

Judicial System Monitoring Programme, *Digest of the Jurisprudence of the Special Panels for Serious Crimes*, Dili, Timor Leste, April 2007.

Kahneman, Daniel, *Thinking Fast and Slow*, Farrar, Straus and Giroux, New York, 2011.

Kaleck, Wolfgang, and Patrick Kroker, "Syrian Torture Investigations in Germany and Beyond: Breathing New Life into Universal Jurisdiction in Europe?", in *Journal of International Criminal Justice*, 2018, vol. 16, no. 1, pp. 165–91.

Kamminga, Menno T., "Netherlands Judicial Decisions Involving Questions of International Law: First Conviction under the Universal Jurisdiction Provisions of the UN Convention against Torture", in *Netherlands International Law Review*, 2004, vol. 51, no. 3, pp. 439–44.

Kaye, David, "Who's Afraid of the International Criminal Court? Finding the Prosecutor Who Can Set It Straight", in *Foreign Affairs*, May/June 2011, vol. 90, no. 3.

Kelsen, Hans, *Pure Theory of Law*, translation from the second German edition by Max Knight, Lawbook Exchange, Clark, NJ, 2008.

Kirgis, Frederic L., "Custom on a Sliding Scale", in *American Journal of International Law*, 1987, vol. 81, no. 1, pp. 146–51.

Kiyani, Asad, "The Ahistoricism of Legal Pluralism in International Criminal Law", in *American Journal of Comparative Law*, 2017, vol. 65, no. 2, pp. 393–449.

Lafontaine, Fannie, "Canada's Crimes against Humanity and War Crimes Act on Trial: An Analysis of the Munyaneza Case", in *Journal of International Criminal Justice*, 2010, vol. 8, no. 1, pp. 269–88.

Lepard, Brian D., *Customary International Law: A New Theory with Practical Applications*, Cambridge University Press, Cambridge, 2010.

Linton, Suzannah, "Prosecuting Atrocities at the District Court of Dili", in *Melbourne Journal of International Law*, 2001, vol. 2, no. 2, pp. 414–58.

Lutz, Ellen L., *Prosecuting Heads of State*, Cambridge University Press, Cambridge, 2009.

Maljevic, Almin, *'Participation in a Criminal Organisation' and 'Conspiracy': Different Legal Models Against Criminal Collectives*, Duncker & Humblot, Berlin, 2011.

Manacorda, Stefano, and Chantal Meloni, "Indirect Perpetration *versus* Joint Criminal Enterprise: Concurring Approaches in the Practice of International Criminal Law?", in *Journal of International Criminal Justice*, 2011, vol. 9, no. 1, pp. 159–78.

Marchuk, Iryna, "The Unitary Form of Participation in Danish Criminal Law (and Its Potential Use in International Criminal Law)", blog of James G. Stewart, 5 October 2017.

McLeod, Saul, "The Milgram Experiment", in *Simply Psychology*, 2007, updated 2017.

Mégret, Frédéric, "Prospects for 'Constitutional' Human Rights Scrutiny of Substantive International Criminal Law by the ICC, with Special Emphasis on the General Part", paper presented at Washington University School of Law, Whitney R. Harris World Law Institute, International Legal Scholars Workshop, Roundtable in Public International Law and Theory, 4–6 February 2010.

Mégret, Frédéric, and Sienna Anstis, "The Taylor Case; Aiding and Abetting, 'Specific Direction' and the Possibility of Negligence Liability for Remote Offenders", in Charles Jalloh and Alhagi Marong (eds.), *Promoting Accountability for Gross Human Rights Violations in Africa under International Law: Essays in Honour of Prosecutor Hassan Bubacar Jallow*, Brill/Martinus Nijhoff, Leiden, 2015.

Meloni, Chantal, "Command Responsibility: Mode of Liability for the Crimes of Subordinates or Separate Offence of the Superior?", in *Journal of International Criminal Justice*, 2007, vol. 5, no. 3, pp. 619–37.

Meron, Theodor, *Human Rights and Humanitarian Norms as Customary Law*, Clarendon Press, Oxford, 1989.

Mettraux, Guénaël, "Dutch Courts' Universal Jurisdiction over Violations of Common Article 3 *qua* War Crimes", in *Journal of International Criminal Justice*, 2006, vol. 4, no. 2, pp. 362–71.

Muñoz-Conde, Francisco, and Héctor Olásolo, "The Application of the Notion of Indirect Perpetration through Organized Structures of Power in Latin America and Spain", in *Journal of International Criminal Justice*, 2011, vol. 9, no. 1, pp. 113–35.

Nersessian, David, "Comparative Approaches to Punishing Hate: The Intersection of Genocide and Crimes against Humanity", in *Stanford Journal of International Law*, vol. 43, 2007, pp. 221–64.

Nollkaemper, André, and Harmen van der Wilt, *System Criminality in International Law*, Cambridge University Press, Cambridge, 2009.

Ohlin, Jens David, "Joint Intentions to Commit International Crimes", in *Chicago Journal of International Law*, 2011, vol. 11, no. 2, pp. 693–753.

Ohlin, Jens David, "Searching for the Hinterman: In Praise of Subjective Theories of Imputation", in *Journal of International Criminal Justice*, 2014, vol. 12, no. 2, pp. 325–43.

Ohlin, Jens David, "Second-Order Linking Principles: Combining Vertical and Horizontal Modes of Liability", in *Leiden Journal of International Law*, 2012, vol. 25, no. 3, pp. 771–97.

Ohlin, Jens David, "Three Conceptual Problems with the Doctrine of Joint Criminal Enterprise", in *Journal of International Criminal Justice*, 2007, vol. 5, no. 1, pp. 69–90.

Ohlin, Jens David, Elies van Sliedregt, and Thomas Weigend, "Assessing the Control-Theory", in *Leiden Journal of International Law*, 2013, vol. 26, no. 3, pp. 725–46.

Olásolo, Héctor, *Criminal Responsibility of Political and Military Leaders for Genocide, Crimes against Humanity and War Crimes, with Special Reference to the Rome Statute and the Statute and Case Law of the Ad Hoc Tribunals*, Hart, Oxford, 2008.

Olásolo, Héctor, *The Criminal Responsibility of Senior Political and Military Leaders as Principals to International Crimes*, Hart, Oxford, 2009.

Osiel, Mark, "The Banality of Good: Aligning Incentives against Mass Atrocity", in *Columbia Law Review*, 2005, vol. 105, no. 6, pp. 1751–1862.

Osiel, Mark, *Making Sense of Mass Atrocity*, Cambridge University Press, Cambridge, 2009.

Peterson, Ines, "Open Questions Regarding Aiding and Abetting Liability in International Criminal Law: A Case Study of ICTY and ICTR Jurisprudence", in *International Criminal Law Review*, 2016, vol. 16, no. 4, pp. 565–612.

Pinzauti, Giulia, "An Instance of Reasonable Universality: The Scilingo Case", in *Journal of International Criminal Justice*, 2005, vol. 3, no. 5, pp. 1092–1105.

Powles, Steven, "Joint Criminal Enterprise: Criminal Liability by Prosecutorial Ingenuity and Judicial Creativity?" in *Journal of International Criminal Justice*, 2004, vol. 2, no. 2, pp. 606–19.

Quénivet, Noëlle, "The History of the Relationship between International Humanitarian Law and Human Rights Law", in Roberta Arnold and Noëlle Quénivet (eds.), *International Humanitarian Law and Human Rights Law: Towards a New Merger in International Law*, Brill/Martinus Nijhoff, Leiden, 2008.

Rauter, Thomas, *Judicial Practice, Customary International Criminal Law and Nullum Crimen Sine Lege*, Springer International, Cham, Switzerland, 2017.

REDRESS/FIDH, *Extraterritorial Jurisdiction in the European Union: A Study of the Laws and Practice in the 27 Member States of the European Union*, December 2010.

Reiger, Caitlin, and Marieke Wierda, *The Serious Crime Process in Timor Leste: In Retrospect*, Prosecutions Case Studies Series, International Center for Transitional Justice, 2006.

Rhea, Harry M., *The United States and International Criminal Tribunals: An Introduction*, Intersentia, Cambridge, 2012.

Rikhof, Joseph, "Analysis: A History and Typology of International Criminal Institutions", in *PKI Global Justice Journal*, 2017, vol. 1, no. 15.

Rikhof, Joseph, "Fewer Places to Hide? The Impact of Domestic War Crimes Prosecutions on International Impunity", in Morten Bergsmo (ed.), *Complementarity and the Exercise of Universal Jurisdiction for Core International Crimes*, Torkel Opsahl Academic EPublisher, Oslo, 2010.

Rikhof, Joseph, "The Istanbul and Leipzig Trials: Myth or Reality?", in Morten Bergsmo, Cheah Wui Ling, and Yi Ping (eds.), *Historical Origins of International Criminal Law, Volume 1*, Torkel Opsahl Academic EPublisher, Oslo, 2014.

Rissing-van Saan, Ruth, "The German Federal Supreme Court and the Prosecution of International Crimes Committed in the Former Yugoslavia", in *Journal of International Criminal Justice*, 2005, vol. 3, no. 2, pp. 381–99.

Robinson, Darryl, "A Justification of Command Responsibility", in *Criminal Law Forum*, 2017, vol. 28, no. 4, pp. 633-668.

Robinson, Darryl, "A Cosmopolitan Liberal Account of International Criminal Law", in *Leiden Journal of International Law*, 2013, vol. 26, no. 1, pp. 127–53.

Robinson, Darryl, "How Command Responsibility Got So Complicated: A Culpability Contradiction, Its Obfuscation, and a Simple Solution", in *Melbourne Journal of International Law*, 2012, vol. 13, no. 1, pp. 1–58.

Robinson, Darryl, "The Identity Crisis of International Criminal Law", in *Leiden Journal of International Law*, 2008, vol. 21, no. 4, pp. 925–63.

Robinson, Darryl, "International Criminal Law as Justice", in *Journal of International Criminal Justice*, 2013, vol. 11, no. 3, pp. 699–711.

Ross, Alf, *Om Ret og Rætferdighed: en indførelse i den analytiske retsfilosofi* [On Law and Justice], Nyt Nordisk Forlag, Copenhagen, 1953.

Roxin, Claus, "Crimes as Part of Organized Power Structures", *Journal of International Criminal Justice*, 2011, vol. 9, no. 1, pp. 193–205. Originally published in German in 1963; republished in 2011 in an English translation by Belinda Cooper.

Sadat, Leila Nadya, "Can the ICTY *Šainović* and *Perišić* Cases Be Reconciled?", in *American Journal of International Law*, 2014, vol. 108, no. 3, pp. 475–85.

Sadat, Leila Nadya (ed.), *Forging a Convention for Crimes against Humanity*, Cambridge University Press, Cambridge, 2011.

Sadat, Leila Nadya (ed.), *Seeking Accountability for the Unlawful Use of Force*, Cambridge University Press, Cambridge, 2018.

Sadat, Leila Nadya, and Jarrod M. Jolly, "Seven Canons of ICC Treaty Interpretation: Making Sense of Article 25's Rorschach Blot", in *Leiden Journal of International Law*, 2014, vol. 27, no. 3, pp. 755–88.

Schabas, William A., *Genocide in International Law: The Crime of Crimes*, 2nd ed., Cambridge University Press, Cambridge, 2009.

Schabas, William A., *The International Criminal Court: A Commentary on the Rome Statute*, Oxford University Press, Oxford, 2010.

Schwarzenberger, Georg, *The Inductive Approach to International Law*, Stevens, London, 1965.

Skaar, Elin, *Judicial Independence and Human Rights in Latin America: Violations, Politics, and Prosecution*, Palgrave Macmillan, New York, 2011.

Stahn, Carsten, *Liberals vs. Romantics: Challenges of an Emerging Corporate International Criminal Law*, February 21, 2018.

Stewart, James G., "Complicity", in Markus Dubber and Tatjana Hörnle (eds.), *Oxford Handbook of Criminal Law*, Oxford University Press, Oxford, 2014.

Stewart, James G., *Corporate War Crimes: Prosecuting the Pillage of Natural Resources*, Open Society Justice Initiative, New York, 2011.

Stewart, James G., "The End of 'Modes of Liability' for International Crimes", in *Leiden Journal of International Law*, 2012, vol. 25, no. 1, pp. 165–219.

Stewart, James G., "The Historical Importance of the Kouwenhoven Trial", blog of James G. Stewart, 5 May 2017.

Stewart, James G., "An Open Invitation to Further Debate (Instead of an Amicus Brief)", blog of James G. Stewart, 18 October 2017.

Stewart, James G., "The Strangely Familiar History of the Unitary Theory of Perpetration", in Bruce Ackerman *et al.* (eds.), *Visions of Justice: Essays in Honor of Professor Mirjan Damaska*, Duncker & Humblot, Berlin, 2016.

Stewart, James G., "Ten Reasons for Adopting a Universal Concept of Participation in Atrocity", in Elies van Sliedregt and Sergey Vasiliev (eds.), *Pluralism in International Criminal Law*, Oxford University Press, Oxford, 2014, pp. 320–41.

Stockholm District Court, "On the Establishment of Courts in Non-international Armed Conflict by Non-state Actors: Stockholm District Court Judgment of 16 February 2017", in *Journal of International Criminal Justice*, 2018, vol. 16, no 2, pp. 403–424.

Tiba, Firew Kebede, "Mass Trials and Modes of Criminal Responsibility for International Crimes: The Case of Ethiopia", in Kevin Jon Heller and Gerry Simpson (eds.), *The Hidden Histories of War Crimes Trials*, Oxford University Press, Oxford, 2013.

Tiba, Firew Kebede, "The *Mengistu* Genocide Trial in Ethiopia", in *Journal of International Criminal Justice*, 2007, vol. 5, no. 2, pp. 513–28.

Tiba, Firew Kebede, "The Trial of Mengistu and Other Derg Members for Genocide, Torture and Summary Executions in Ethiopia", in Chacha Murungu and Japhet Biegon (eds.), *Prosecuting International Crimes in Africa*, Pretoria University Press, Pretoria, 2011.

Tomuschat, Christian, "Issues of Universal Jurisdiction in the Scilingo Case", in *Journal of International Criminal Justice*, 2005, vol. 3, no. 5, pp. 1074–81.

Trahan, Jennifer, "From Kampala to New York: The Final Negotiations to Activate the Jurisdiction of the International Criminal Court over the Crime of Aggression", in *International Criminal Law Review*, 2018, vol. 18, no. 2, pp. 197–243.

TRIAL International, *Make Way for Justice #1: Universal Jurisdiction Annual Review 2015*, Geneva.

TRIAL International, *Make Way for Justice #2: Universal Jurisdiction Annual Review 2016*, Geneva.

TRIAL International, *Make Way for Justice #3: Universal Jurisdiction Annual Review 2017*, Geneva.

TRIAL International, *Make Way for Justice #4: Momentum Towards Accountability: Universal Jurisdiction Annual Review 2018*, Geneva.

TRIAL International, *Activity Report 2017*, Geneva.

Trouille, Helen L., "France, Universal Jurisdiction and Rwandan *génocidaires*: The *Simbikangwa* Trial", in *Journal of International Criminal Justice*, 2016, vol. 14, no. 1, pp. 202–8.

Tzanakopoulos, Antonios, *Disobeying the Security Council: Countermeasures against Wrongful Sanctions*, Oxford University Press, Oxford, 2011.

UK Parliament, Joint Committee on Human Rights, *Closing the Impunity Gap: UK Law on Genocide (and Related Crimes) and Redress for Torture Victims*, 11 August 2009.

Van den Herik, Larissa, "The Difficulties of Exercising Extraterritorial Criminal Jurisdiction: The Acquittal of a Dutch Businessman for Crimes Committed in Liberia", in *International Criminal Law Review*, 2009, vol. 9, no 1, pp. 211–26.

Van den Herik, Larissa, "A Quest for Jurisdiction and an Appropriate Definition of Crime: Mpambara before the Dutch Courts", in *Journal of International Criminal Justice*, 2009, vol. 7, no. 5, pp. 1117–31.

Van der Borght, Erwin, "Prosecution of International Crimes in the Netherlands: An Analysis of Recent Case Law", in *Criminal Law Forum*, 2007, vol. 18, no. 1, pp. 87–136.

Van der Wilt, Harmen, "Genocide, Complicity in Genocide and International v. Domestic Jurisdiction: Reflections on the *van Anraat* Case", in *Journal of International Criminal Justice*, 2006, vol. 4, no. 2, pp. 239–57.

Van Schaack, Beth, "Book Review: *Historical Origins of International Criminal Law*: Volumes 1–5", in *American Journal of International Law*, 2018, vol. 112, no. 1.

Van Sliedregt, Elies, "Article 28 of the ICC Statute: Mode of Liability and/or Separate Offence?", in *New Criminal Law Review*, 2009, vol. 12, no. 3, pp. 420–32.

Van Sliedregt, Elies, *Criminal Responsibility in International Law*, Oxford University Press, Oxford, 2012.

Van Sliedregt, Elies, "The ILC Draft Convention on Crimes Against Humanity: Criminalization Under National Law", 29 April 2018.

Van Sliedregt, Elies, *Individual Criminal Responsibility in International Law*, Oxford University Press, Oxford, 2012.

Van Sliedregt, Elies, "International Crimes before Dutch Courts: Recent Developments", in *Leiden Journal of International Law*, 2007, vol. 20, no. 4, pp. 895–908.

Van Sliedregt, Elies, and Sergey Vasiliev, "Pluralism: A New Framework for International Criminal Justice", in Elies van Sliedregt and Sergey Vasiliev (eds.), *Pluralism in International Criminal Law*, Oxford University Press, Oxford, 2014, pp. 3–38.

Van Sliedregt, Elies, and Sergey Vasiliev (eds.), *Pluralism in International Criminal Law*, Oxford University Press, Oxford, UK, 2014.

Vaughan, Sarah, "The Role of the Special Prosecutors Office", in Kjetil Tronvoll, Charles Schaefer, and Girmachew Alemu Aneme (eds.), *The Ethiopian Red Terror Trials: Transitional Justice Challenged*, James Currey, Woodbridge, UK, 2009, pp. 51–67.

Vest, Hans, "Problems of Participation: Unitarian, Differentiated Approach, or Something Else?" in *Journal of International Criminal Justice*, 2014, vol. 12, no. 2, pp. 295–309.

Wall, Illan Rua, "Duress, International Criminal Law and Literature", in *Journal of International Criminal Justice*, 2006, vol. 4, no. 4, pp. 724–44.

Weigend, Thomas, "Perpetration through an Organization: The Unexpected Career of a German Legal Concept", in *Journal of International Criminal Justice*, 2011, vol. 9, no. 1, pp. 91–111.

Weigend, Thomas, "Problems of Attribution in International Criminal Law: A German Perspective", in *Journal of International Criminal Justice*, 2014, vol. 12, no. 2, pp. 253–66.

Welsh, Jennifer M., "The Security Council and Humanitarian Intervention", in Vaughan Lowe, Adam Roberts, Jennifer Welsh, and Dominik Zaum (eds.), *The United Nations Security Council and War: The Evolution of Thought and Practice since 1945*, Oxford University Press, Oxford, 2008, pp. 535–62.

Werle, Gerhard, *Principles of International Criminal Law*, TMC Asser, The Hague, 2005.

Werle, Gerhard, *Principles of International Criminal Law*, 2nd ed., TMC Asser, The Hague, 2009.

Wharton, Sarah, "Redrawing the Line? Serious Crimes of Concern to the International Community beyond the Rome Statute", in *The Canadian Yearbook of International Law*, 2015, vol. 52, pp. 129–83.

Wheeler, Nicholas J., *Saving Strangers: Humanitarian Intervention in International Society*, Oxford University Press, Oxford, 2000.

Wilmhurst, Elisabeth, *An Introduction to International Criminal Law and Procedure*, 2nd ed., Cambridge University Press, Cambridge, 2010.

Wilson, Richard Ashby, *Incitement on Trial: Prosecuting International Speech Crimes*, Cambridge University Press, Cambridge, 2017.

Wilson, Richard Ashby, and Matthew Gillett, *The Hartford Guidelines on Speech Crimes in International Criminal Law*, Peace and Justice Initiative, The Hague, 2018.

Wirth, Steffen, "Co-Perpetration in the *Lubanga* Trial Judgment", in *Journal of International Criminal Justice*, 2012, vol. 10, no. 4, pp. 971–95.

World Justice Project, *Rule of Law Index 2016*, Washington, DC, 2016.

Yanev, Lachezar, "On Common Plans and Excess Crimes: Fragmenting the Notion of Co-Perpetration in International Criminal Law", in *Leiden Journal of International Law*, 2018, vol. 31, no. 3, pp. 693-718.

Yanev, Lachezar, "A Janus-faced Concept: Nuremberg's Law on Conspiracy *vis-à-vis* the Notion of Joint Criminal Enterprise", in *Criminal Law Forum*, 2015, vol. 26, no. 3, pp. 419–56.

Yanev, Lachezar, "Theories of Co-Perpetration in International Criminal Law", Ph.D. diss., Tilburg University, 2016. Published as *Theories of Co-Perpetration in International Criminal Law*, Brill/Martinus Nijhoff, Leiden, 2018.

Yanev, Lachezar, and Tijs Kooijmans, "Divided Minds in the Lubanga Trial Judgment: A Case against the Control Theory", in *International Criminal Law Review*, 2013, vol. 13, no. 4, pp. 789–828.

Yokohama, Kazuya, "The Failure to Control and the Failure to Prevent, Repress and Submit: The Structure of Superior Responsibility under Article 28 ICC Statute", in *International Criminal Law Review*, 2018, vol. 18, no. 2, pp. 275-303.

Zahar, Alexander, "Commentary on Trial Judgments of the East Timor Special Panels in the Case of Jose Cardoso Ferreira and Agustinho Atolan", in Andre Klip and Göran Sluiter (eds.), *Annotated Leading Cases of International Criminal Tribunals: Timor Leste: The Special Panels for Serious Crimes, 2001–2003*, Intersentia, Antwerp, 2008, pp. 762–65.

Zwanenburg, Marten, and Guido den Dekker, "Prosecutor v. *Frans* van Anraat", *American Journal of International Law*, 2010, vol. 104, no. 1, pp. 86–94.

INDEX

A

Abacunguzi Fighting Forces (Rwanda), 458, 459
Abdoullah, Mohamed, 432, 464
Abdulkareem, Raed, 463
Abu Garda, Bahar Idriss, 156
accessorial crimes, 52, 102, 247, 248, 357, 601, 626, 645–651, 654
accessorial object, 317
accomplice liability, 34, 36, 75, 76, 85, 90, 92, 107, 108, 111, 112, 114, 116, 119, 125–127, 246, 247, 333, 363, 364, 543, 568, 594–596, 599, 601, 603, 605, 608, 625, 630–632, 635, 636, 640, 643, 644
acting in concert, 133, 147, 149, 152–154, 181, 387
actus reus, 320, 342, 350, 374, 376, 382, 392, 410, 412, 416, 496, 553, 563, 573, 575, 578, 585, 609–613, 615, 617, 619–622, 630
Afghanistan, 201, 245, 430, 431, 438, 483, 502, 519
aggression, 5, 50, 51, 66, 68, 96, 98–100, 124, 137–139, 143, 146, 147, 149, 152, 160, 181, 199, 200, 218, 224, 237, 238, 245, 247, 248, 250, 258, 262, 269, 286, 288–290, 295, 334, 357, 374, 601, 610, 611, 627, 643, 644, 646, 647
planning and preparation, 286
Ahumada, Rafael, 491
aiding and abetting, iv, 15, 36, 75–76, 100, 106–107, 114, 144, 147–148, 150, 152, 154–155, 160, 167–168, 170–172, 176, 178–183, 191, 284–285, 297, 300–301, 310, 352–353, 364, 367, 369, 373, 396–397, 410, 412–413, 415–417, 421, 426, 439–441, 448–449, 451–452, 454–458, 467, 469, 475, 479–480, 483, 494–496, 499–500, 503–504, 507–510, 532–534, 541–543, 545, 572–573, 578–580, 596, 598, 608, 620–622, 627–628, 630, 632, 654

Aksenova, Marina, 87, 113, 309, 322–324, 337, 364, 365
Al-Bashir, Omar, 142, 143
Alemu, Eshetu, 435, 436, 448, 507, 511
Ali, Mir Quasem, 542, 545
Alim, Abdul, 542, 544
Altstötter, Josef, 172
Alvarez, Gregorio, 491
Ambos, Kai, 27, 28, 308, 310, 318, 327, 329–331, 335, 338, 344, 345, 348, 351, 352, 361–364, 530, 566
Ammar, Jebbar Salman, 473
Ansar Eddine, 180
Apartheid Convention, 285, 626
Araki, Sadao, 145, 147
Arce Gómez, Luis, 491
Argentina, 467, 488, 490, 491, 502, 519, 522, 556, 558, 559, 562, 629
Arklöv, Jackie, 459, 460
Armed Activities case, 252
Armed Forces Revolutionary Council (Sierra Leone), 15, 146
Army of the Republic of Bosnia and Herzegovina, 165
Assad, Bashar, 453, 462
Astiz, Alfredo, 467, 490, 492
atrocity crimes, 27, 132, 180, 519, 588
atrocity speech, 85, 360, 365, 368, 369, 409, 598, 628
attempt, 10, 17, 20, 52, 66, 68, 86, 93, 95–100, 103, 114–115, 121, 123–125, 171, 203, 247–248, 268–269, 272–285, 288–289, 293, 300, 306, 326, 334, 357, 360, 371–372, 378, 422, 436, 446, 464, 469, 474–475, 477, 479, 482, 486–487, 492, 494, 497–498, 501, 513, 529, 535–537, 540, 555, 562, 593, 596–597, 601, 606, 608, 612, 627, 632, 652
complete, 379
incomplete, 379
Australia, 111
Austria, 110, 152, 476, 498, 499, 503
Criminal Code, 477

TOAEP TEAM

Editors

Antonio Angotti, Editor
Olympia Bekou, Editor
Mats Benestad, Editor
Morten Bergsmo, Editor-in-Chief
Alf Butenschøn Skre, Senior Executive Editor
Eleni Chaitidou, Editor
CHAN Ho Shing Icarus, Editor
CHEAH Wui Ling, Editor
FAN Yuwen, Editor
Manek Minhas, Editor
Gareth Richards, Senior Editor
Nikolaus Scheffel, Editor
SIN Ngok Shek, Editor
SONG Tianying, Editor
Moritz Thörner, Editor
ZHANG Yueyao, Editor

Editorial Assistants

Pauline Brosch
Marquise Lee Houle
Genevieve Zingg

Law of the Future Series Co-Editors

Dr. Alexander (Sam) Muller
Professor Larry Cata Backer
Professor Stavros Zouridis

Nuremberg Academy Series Editor

Dr. Viviane Dittrich, Deputy Director, International Nuremberg Principles Academy

Scientific Advisers

Professor Danesh Sarooshi, Principal Scientific Adviser for International Law
Professor Andreas Zimmermann, Principal Scientific Adviser for Public International Law
Professor Kai Ambos, Principal Scientific Adviser for International Criminal Law
Dr.h.c. Asbjørn Eide, Principal Scientific Adviser for International Human Rights Law

Editorial Board

Dr. Xabier Agirre, International Criminal Court
Dr. Claudia Angermaier, Austrian judiciary
Ms. Neela Badami, Narasappa, Doraswamy and Raja
Dr. Markus Benzing, Freshfields Bruckhaus Deringer, Frankfurt

OTHER VOLUMES IN THE PUBLICATION SERIES

Morten Bergsmo, Mads Harlem and Nobuo Hayashi (editors):
Importing Core International Crimes into National Law
Torkel Opsahl Academic EPublisher
Oslo, 2010
FICHL Publication Series No. 1 (Second Edition, 2010)
ISBN: 978-82-93081-00-5

Nobuo Hayashi (editor):
National Military Manuals on the Law of Armed Conflict
Torkel Opsahl Academic EPublisher
Oslo, 2010
FICHL Publication Series No. 2 (Second Edition, 2010)
ISBN: 978-82-93081-02-9

Morten Bergsmo, Kjetil Helvig, Ilia Utmelidze and Gorana Žagovec:
The Backlog of Core International Crimes Case Files in Bosnia and Herzegovina
Torkel Opsahl Academic EPublisher
Oslo, 2010
FICHL Publication Series No. 3 (Second Edition, 2010)
ISBN: 978-82-93081-04-3

Morten Bergsmo (editor):
Criteria for Prioritizing and Selecting Core International Crimes Cases
Torkel Opsahl Academic EPublisher
Oslo, 2010
FICHL Publication Series No. 4 (Second Edition, 2010)
ISBN: 978-82-93081-06-7

Morten Bergsmo and Pablo Kalmanovitz (editors):
Law in Peace Negotiations
Torkel Opsahl Academic EPublisher
Oslo, 2010
FICHL Publication Series No. 5 (Second Edition, 2010)
ISBN: 978-82-93081-08-1

Morten Bergsmo, César Rodríguez Garavito, Pablo Kalmanovitz and Maria Paula Saffon (editors):
Distributive Justice in Transitions
Torkel Opsahl Academic EPublisher
Oslo, 2010
FICHL Publication Series No. 6 (2010)
ISBN: 978-82-93081-12-8

Morten Bergsmo, César Rodriguez-Garavito, Pablo Kalmanovitz and Maria Paula Saffon (editors):
Justicia Distributiva en Sociedades en Transición
Torkel Opsahl Academic EPublisher
Oslo, 2012
FICHL Publication Series No. 6 (2012)
ISBN: 978-82-93081-10-4

Morten Bergsmo (editor):
Complementarity and the Exercise of Universal Jurisdiction for Core International Crimes
Torkel Opsahl Academic EPublisher
Oslo, 2010
FICHL Publication Series No. 7 (2010)
ISBN: 978-82-93081-14-2

Morten Bergsmo (editor):
Active Complementarity: Legal Information Transfer
Torkel Opsahl Academic EPublisher
Oslo, 2011
FICHL Publication Series No. 8 (2011)
ISBN print: 978-82-93081-56-2
ISBN e-book: 978-82-93081-55-5

Morten Bergsmo (editor):
Abbreviated Criminal Procedures for Core International Crimes
Torkel Opsahl Academic EPublisher
Brussels, 2017
FICHL Publication Series No. 9 (2018)
ISBN print: 978-82-93081-20-3
ISBN e-book: 978-82-8348-104-4

Sam Muller, Stavros Zouridis, Morly Frishman and Laura Kistemaker (editors):
The Law of the Future and the Future of Law
Torkel Opsahl Academic EPublisher
Oslo, 2010
FICHL Publication Series No. 11 (2011)
ISBN: 978-82-93081-27-2

Morten Bergsmo, Alf Butenschøn Skre and Elisabeth J. Wood (editors):
Understanding and Proving International Sex Crimes
Torkel Opsahl Academic EPublisher
Beijing, 2012
FICHL Publication Series No. 12 (2012)
ISBN: 978-82-93081-29-6

Morten Bergsmo (editor):
Thematic Prosecution of International Sex Crimes
Torkel Opsahl Academic EPublisher
Beijing, 2012
FICHL Publication Series No. 13 (2012)
ISBN: 978-82-93081-31-9

Terje Einarsen:
The Concept of Universal Crimes in International Law
Torkel Opsahl Academic EPublisher
Oslo, 2012
FICHL Publication Series No. 14 (2012)
ISBN: 978-82-93081-33-3

莫滕·伯格斯默 凌岩(主编):
国家主权与国际刑法
Torkel Opsahl Academic EPublisher
Beijing, 2012
FICHL Publication Series No. 15 (2012)
ISBN: 978-82-93081-58-6

Morten Bergsmo and LING Yan (editors):
State Sovereignty and International Criminal Law
Torkel Opsahl Academic EPublisher
Beijing, 2012
FICHL Publication Series No. 15 (2012)
ISBN: 978-82-93081-35-7

Morten Bergsmo and CHEAH Wui Ling (editors):
Old Evidence and Core International Crimes
Torkel Opsahl Academic EPublisher
Beijing, 2012
FICHL Publication Series No. 16 (2012)
ISBN: 978-82-93081-60-9

YI Ping:
戦争と平和の間——発足期日本国際法学における「正しい戦争」の観念とその帰結
Torkel Opsahl Academic EPublisher
Beijing, 2013
FICHL Publication Series No. 17 (2013)
ISBN: 978-82-93081-66-1

Morten Bergsmo and SONG Tianying (editors):
On the Proposed Crimes Against Humanity Convention
Torkel Opsahl Academic EPublisher
Brussels, 2014
FICHL Publication Series No. 18 (2014)
ISBN: 978-82-93081-96-8

Morten Bergsmo (editor):
Quality Control in Fact-Finding
Torkel Opsahl Academic EPublisher
Florence, 2013
FICHL Publication Series No. 19 (2013)
ISBN: 978-82-93081-78-4

Morten Bergsmo, CHEAH Wui Ling and YI Ping (editors):
Historical Origins of International Criminal Law: Volume 1
Torkel Opsahl Academic EPublisher
Brussels, 2014
FICHL Publication Series No. 20 (2014)
ISBN: 978-82-93081-11-1

Morten Bergsmo, CHEAH Wui Ling and YI Ping (editors):
Historical Origins of International Criminal Law: Volume 2
Torkel Opsahl Academic EPublisher
Brussels, 2014
FICHL Publication Series No. 21 (2014)
ISBN: 978-82-93081-13-5

Morten Bergsmo, CHEAH Wui Ling, SONG Tianying and YI Ping (editors):
Historical Origins of International Criminal Law: Volume 3
Torkel Opsahl Academic EPublisher
Brussels, 2015
FICHL Publication Series No. 22 (2015)
ISBN print: 978-82-8348-015-3
ISBN e-book: 978-82-8348-014-6

Morten Bergsmo, CHEAH Wui Ling, SONG Tianying and YI Ping (editors):
Historical Origins of International Criminal Law: Volume 4
Torkel Opsahl Academic EPublisher
Brussels, 2015
FICHL Publication Series No. 23 (2015)
ISBN print: 978-82-8348-017-7
ISBN e-book: 978-82-8348-016-0

Morten Bergsmo, Klaus Rackwitz and SONG Tianying (editors):
Historical Origins of International Criminal Law: Volume 5
Torkel Opsahl Academic EPublisher
Brussels, 2017
FICHL Publication Series No. 24 (2017)
ISBN print: 978-82-8348-106-8
ISBN e-book: 978-82-8348-107-5

Morten Bergsmo and SONG Tianying (editors):
Military Self-Interest in Accountability for Core International Crimes
Torkel Opsahl Academic EPublisher
Brussels, 2015
FICHL Publication Series No. 25 (2015)
ISBN print: 978-82-93081-61-6
ISBN e-book: 978-82-93081-81-4

Wolfgang Kaleck:
Double Standards: International Criminal Law and the West
Torkel Opsahl Academic EPublisher
Brussels, 2015
FICHL Publication Series No. 26 (2015)
ISBN print: 978-82-93081-67-8
ISBN e-book: 978-82-93081-83-8

LIU Daqun and ZHANG Binxin (editors):
Historical War Crimes Trials in Asia
Torkel Opsahl Academic EPublisher
Brussels, 2016
FICHL Publication Series No. 27 (2015)
ISBN print: 978-82-8348-055-9
ISBN e-book: 978-82-8348-056-6

Mark Klamberg (editor):
Commentary on the Law of the International Criminal Court
Torkel Opsahl Academic EPublisher
Brussels, 2017
FICHL Publication Series No. 29 (2017)
ISBN print: 978-82-8348-100-6
ISBN e-book: 978-82-8348-101-3

Stian Nordengen Christensen:
Counterfactual History and Bosnia-Herzegovina
Torkel Opsahl Academic EPublisher
Brussels, 2018
Publication Series No. 30 (2018)
ISBN print: 978-82-8348-102-0
ISBN e-book: 978-82-8348-103-7

Stian Nordengen Christensen:
Possibilities and Impossibilities in a Contradictory Global Order
Torkel Opsahl Academic EPublisher
Brussels, 2018
Publication Series No. 31 (2018)
ISBN print: 978-82-8348-104-4
ISBN e-book: 978-82-8348-105-1

Morten Bergsmo and Carsten Stahn (editors):
Quality Control in Preliminary Examination: Volume 1
Torkel Opsahl Academic EPublisher
Brussels, 2018
Publication Series No. 32 (2018)
ISBN print: 978-82-8348-123-5
ISBN e-book: 978-82-8348-124-2

Morten Bergsmo and Carsten Stahn (editors):
Quality Control in Preliminary Examination: Volume 2
Torkel Opsahl Academic EPublisher
Brussels, 2018
Publication Series No. 33 (2018)
ISBN print: 978-82-8348-111-2
ISBN e-book: 978-82-8348-112-9

Morten Bergsmo and Emiliano J. Buis (editors):
Philosophical Foundations of International Criminal Law: Correlating Thinkers
Torkel Opsahl Academic EPublisher
Brussels, 2018
Publication Series No. 34 (2018)
ISBN print: 978-82-8348-117-4
ISBN e-book: 978-82-8348-118-1

All volumes are freely available online at www.toaep.org/ps/. For printed copies, see www.toaep.org/about/distribution/. For reviews of earlier books in this Series in academic journals and yearbooks, see www.toaep.org/reviews/.

CPSIA information can be obtained
at www.ICGtesting.com
Printed in the USA
LVHW080926231118
597978LV00009B/149/P

9 788283 481273